Palgrave Law Masters

Family Law

Paula Davies
Senior Lecturer in Law, BPP Law School, London

Paven Basuita
Lecturer in Law, BPP Law School, London

Ninth edition

macmillan education palgrave

This edition first published 2017 by
PALGRAVE

Palgrave in the UK is an imprint of Macmillan Publishers Limited,
registered in England, company number 785998, of 4 Crinan Street,
London, N1 9XW.

Palgrave® and Macmillan® are registered trademarks in the United States,
the United Kingdom, Europe and other countries.

ISBN 978–1–137–57551–7 paperback

This book is printed on paper suitable for recycling and made from fully managed
and sustained forest sources. Logging, pulping and manufacturing processes are
expected to conform to the environmental regulations of the country of origin.

A catalogue record for this book is available from the British Library.

A catalog record for this book is available from the Library of Congress.

Contents

Preface to the ninth edition

Two decades have passed since the publication of the first edition of *Family Law* in 1993. During that time families and family life have undergone considerable change. For instance, cohabitation has become increasingly common and families now take many different forms.

Family law has also undergone many changes, and continues to change at a pace. Proposals for reform also abound. In fact, there was a major review of the family justice system in 2011 (the 'Family Justice Review') by the Norgrove Committee which made important and wide–ranging recommendations for reform, most of which were accepted by the Government and brought into law. These recommendations included, for example, proposals to reduce delays in care and adoption cases, the creation of a new single Family Court and the introduction of a new order (a 'child arrangements order') to replace residence and contact orders.

Since the last edition of *Family Law* in 2013, Government reforms have focused on a range of different issues, for instance the introduction of same sex marriage, and of a new criminal offence of forcing someone to marry. The Law Commission, the Government's law reform body, has also looked at a range of family law issues, including, in particular, the law governing financial relief on divorce and dissolution, and has made recommendations for reform.

Family law never seems to stand still. While this makes it a fascinating subject to study, it means that keeping up to date is a challenge. However, despite the multifarious changes both to family life and family law over the years, the aim of this book remains the same as it was two decades ago, which is to provide a clear and detailed account of family law in England and Wales, including current debates and proposals for reform.

Table of cases

Table of legislation

Part I

Family law – an introduction

Chapter 1

Introduction

This chapter provides an introduction to family law in England and Wales by looking at a range of matters, such as legal and social trends and developments, the nature of judicial decision-making, the importance of agreement and the impact of human rights. It starts, however, by considering the nature of family law as a subject to be studied.

1.1 Studying family law

Family law is a fascinating but demanding area of law as it is in a constant state of flux. Keeping up to date with the changes is challenging. A wide range of legal materials also has to be absorbed. Thus, in addition to a wealth of statutory provisions and a substantial body of reported case-law, there are rules of court, detailed practice directions, guidance, Government papers and other materials which have to be digested. Furthermore, there continue to be discussions of reform on a wide range of family law issues.

Although family law is largely codified in the sense that the law is based on statute, it is also an area of law where, because of the infinite variations in family circumstances, cases are decided on their own particular facts. In other words, decisions are largely fact-specific. To do well as a family law student it is therefore necessary to have not only a sound knowledge of the relevant statutory provisions and case-law principles, but also a sense of how to apply them. A practical common-sense approach and an understanding of the human condition are therefore required. This is what family law judges have to show when exercising their various statutory powers and duties. In other words, they have to apply the statutory provisions to the facts of the case. This often requires competing considerations to be balanced, and the discretionary nature of the judicial exercise means that there may be more than one decision which is reasonable in the circumstances of the case.

A distinguishing feature of family law is that there is considerable emphasis on the parties reaching agreement, whether, for example, it is about arrangements for children on family breakdown or about property and financial matters. Agreement and settlement are actively promoted, and increasingly so. Thus, instead of taking their case to court, parties are encouraged to use non-court dispute resolution (formerly known as alternative dispute resolution), such as mediation, collaborative law or arbitration. There has also been recognition by the Supreme Court that pre-marital agreements about property and finance can, in some circumstances, be binding.

Another distinguishing feature of family law is that it involves both private and public law. Private law is the law which applies to disputes between individuals, such as spouses, civil partners or parents. A divorce dispute, for example, is a private law matter, as are a domestic violence case and a parental dispute about arrangements for children on family breakdown. Public law disputes, on the other hand, involve a public authority, such as a local authority child protection team or a housing authority. Child protection cases and housing cases are therefore public law cases.

It is important when studying family law to understand that a wide range of different people work in the family justice system. Thus, in addition to lawyers and judges, other people, such as mediators, social workers, housing officers, police officers and Cafcass officers, are often involved. In a domestic violence case, for example, the police may be involved, and, if a victim needs accommodation, a local housing officer might also be involved. This may be in addition to a solicitor. In a child protection case, not just lawyers and judges, but the police, social workers and Cafcass officers may be involved, too.

Other distinguishing features of family law are that it is an area of law where children are often involved and also where the emotions of the parties are sometimes highly charged and difficult balancing decisions have to be made. Cases therefore require sensitive handling. In addition, court decisions in family law, unlike decisions in other areas of the law, tend to be forward-looking rather than backward-looking. In other words, they look to the future rather than to the past. The court on divorce, for example, may have to consider what financial provision should be made for a party to the marriage or what future arrangements should be made for children.

Before moving on to consider some of the changes and trends in family law, it is useful to consider the functions which family law performs in order to understand the nature of the subject. Family law can be regarded as performing several functions. Thus, it can create a status, such as the status of spouse, civil partner, guardian or special guardian. It can remove a status, for example by divorce, dissolution or adoption. It can create and, where necessary, enforce the rights and obligations arising from a particular status, such as the obligation to provide financial provision to a spouse or a child. It can adjust the property and financial rights of family members, for example on family breakdown; and it can provide protection for family members, such as for victims of forced marriage, domestic violence or child abuse.

1.2   Family law – changes and trends

Family law is a dynamic area of law which is constantly changing. Thus, over the past 30 to 40 years radical changes have been made which people living in the 1970s or 1980s would not have thought possible. For example, before the 1970s, and even for some years thereafter, divorce was regarded as a social stigma; and cohabitation even more so. Divorces, whether or not defended, were heard in court with a full hearing before a judge; and cohabitation was regarded by some as 'living in sin'. Protection against domestic violence was also restricted to a much narrower group of people than it is today in that only married couples and heterosexual cohabitants could obtain injunctive protection in the family courts. With respect to arrangements for children on family breakdown, different terminology was used (namely 'custody' and 'access', and more recently 'residence' and 'contact'), and it was much more likely that mothers, rather than fathers, would be granted custody of children. Also, unlike today, all child maintenance disputes were heard in the courts. In family law cases, litigation also tended to be the norm, as mediation and other alternatives had not been widely developed.

Today's family law is therefore in many respects almost unrecognisable from what it was 30 or 40 years ago. This is due in part to the fact that a wider range of family forms exist, not just what was once considered to be the stereotypical family, namely a married heterosexual couple with children. Thus, we now have same sex marriage and civil partnership, and transsexual people can marry in their acquired sex. Many couples also now choose to cohabit. Although social changes have had, and continue to have, an impact on family law, family law may itself be partly responsible for changing social attitudes. For example, the ease with which a divorce can now be obtained may have had an impact on removing the stigma that was once attached to it. Due to increasing cohabitation, cohabitants have now been accorded more family law rights than they once had, although some commentators consider that they have not been given enough, particularly on relationship breakdown. There has also been an increasing recognition of the importance of fathers, including unmarried fathers. All of these changes in family law would probably not have been imagined possible 30 or 40 years ago.

(a)   Access to family justice – legal aid

Wide-ranging changes were made to the public funding of family law cases following the enactment of the Legal Aid, Sentencing and Punishment of Offenders Act 2012 (LASPO 2012), which came into force in April 2013. Thus, free legal advice is no longer available for most private family law cases such as divorce or disputes about finances and children unless there is evidence of domestic violence, forced marriage or child abuse, or the applicant is a child who is a party to the proceedings, or there are exceptional circumstances. Legal aid is, however, still available for mediation.

The cut-backs in legal aid mean that fewer people now have access to free legal advice than at any time since legal aid was first introduced in 1949. Many people now represent themselves as they cannot afford to consult a solicitor or to have legal representation. In other words, they are a litigant in person. The following cases demonstrate some of the difficulties which may arise when litigants are not legally represented and how the court has responded to the changes brought about by LASPO 2012.

▶ *C (A Child) & Anor v KH* **[2013] EWCA Civ 1412**

This case concerned an appeal by a father against an order prohibiting him from removing his son from the mother, or from his primary school, and which allowed him only indirect contact. The appeal was allowed on the basis of an extensive catalogue of errors and repeated breaches of the Family Procedure Rules 2010 (FPR 2010) and other statutory codes.

Ryder LJ, giving the lead judgment of the Court of Appeal, noted that at various significant points in the proceedings both parties had been litigants in person. His Lordship warned that the case presented 'a salutary lesson to us all to put in place procedures and practices which can accommodate litigants in person who do not know the rules and practice directions of the court'. He added that, since the enactment of LASPO in April 2013, the majority of parents in private law children disputes were litigants in person and the obligation upon the court to identify and implement due process should not be underestimated. He warned that this would take time and occupy a greater share of the court's limited resources.

▶ Re H [2014] EWFC B127

The father, who was legally represented, sought a child arrangements order for the children to live with him. Although it was a private law case, the local authority was involved in the case due to child protection concerns. The mother, who had speech, hearing and learning difficulties, opposed the application and was unrepresented. She had been refused legal aid as the Legal Aid Agency said that she would still have effective access to the court without it.

Although the case between the parents was resolved by agreement, HHJ Hallam gave permission for her judgment to be published in order to show the legal aid situation. She said that the mother was not able to represent herself in such a complex case and was therefore to all intents and purposes prevented from having access to the court. She said that it was difficult to see how the legal aid authorities could have come to the conclusion that the mother's rights under Article 6 (right to a fair trial) and Article 8 (right to family life) of the European Convention on Human Rights (ECHR) were not in jeopardy. Without legal aid, the mother, on her own, would have been facing two advocates pursuing a case against her. On any basis that could not be equality of arms. She was the party with the least ability and the greatest vulnerability; thus, she should have had the benefit of legal representation. It was fortunate that she had the assistance of someone acting pro bono, but it was not right that a legal professional should have had to attend a complex hearing without remuneration. If the case had proceeded to a fully contested hearing with the mother unrepresented, the court would have been put in an impossible situation.

▶ Re D (Non-Availability of Legal Aid) [2014] EWFC 39

The case concerned a father who lacked capacity and a mother with learning difficulties. The father sought to discharge a care order made in respect of their child, but legal aid was not available in respect of the applications before the court and so both were unrepresented.

Munby P adjourned the case so that the funding situation could be investigated further. He said that it was the responsibility and duty of the judges in the Family Court to ensure that proceedings before them were conducted justly and in a manner compliant with the requirements of Article 6 and Article 8 of the ECHR. In the circumstances, it would be unconscionable; it would be unjust; it would involve a breach of the parents' rights under Article 6 and Article 8 of the ECHR; and it would be a denial of justice to allow the parents to face the local authority's application without proper representation. The child would also be prejudiced as he would not have a fair trial if his parents did not. Delay in arranging for the parents' representation was also likely to prejudice the child. Munby P was also critical of the State's role in this case.

MUNBY P:

> Thus far the State has simply washed its hands of the problem, leaving the solution to the problem which the State itself has created – for the State has brought the proceedings ... – to the goodwill, the charity, of the legal profession. This is, it might be thought, both unprincipled and unconscionable. Why should the State leave it to private individuals to ensure that the State is not in breach of the State's ... obligations under the Convention?

▶ Re K [2015] EWCA Civ 543

The Lord Chancellor appealed against an order that the court service should pay for the father in the case to be legally represented. The father was seeking contact with his children in private law proceedings. An allegation had been made by the children's half-sister (Y) that he had sexually abused her and the court had ordered a hearing to establish whether this allegation was true, which would require Y to be cross-examined. As the father was unable to afford legal representation and ineligible for legal aid, the trial judge had ordered the court service to pay for a legal representative to question the witness.

The Court of Appeal allowed the Lord Chancellor's appeal. It held that the trial judge had no power to order the court service to pay for representation which lay outside the statutory legal aid scheme in LASPO 2012. The Court of Appeal did not accept that the only way in which the witness could be fairly and effectively questioned was by a legal representative and outlined other ways in which vulnerable witnesses could be cross-examined, including that the witness could be questioned by the judge or the judge's clerk, or a Children's Guardian could be appointed for the children who could conduct proceedings on their behalf. In this particular case, the trial judge should probably have questioned the witness himself.

The court did acknowledge, however, that in some cases such options might not make up for the absence of a legal representative, which might mean that the proceedings did not comply with Article 6 or Article 8 of the ECHR.

The cut-backs in legal aid have resulted in a dramatic increase in the number of litigants in person. Since April 2013, there has been a 30 per cent year-on-year increase in family court cases in which neither party had legal representation; and 80 per cent of all family court cases starting between January and March 2014 had at least one party who did not have legal representation (see National Audit Office, *Implementing Reforms to Civil Legal Aid*, HC 784, Session 2014–15, 20 November 2014). As Cobb J has pointed out, many litigants in person are some of the most disadvantaged people in society; and family breakdown, or a dispute about money or children, tends not to be their only problem ('Private law reform' [2014] Fam Law 644). For a detailed discussion of the separate but associated challenges litigants in person encounter in seeking advice in other vital areas of their lives, see the Final Report of the Low Commission (chaired by Lord Colin Low) on the future of advice and legal support (*Tackling the Advice Deficit*, January 2014). The experiences of litigants in person, and the challenges that they face, were also explored in research conducted by Trinder and Hunter for the Ministry of Justice ([2015] Fam Law 535).

(b) Legislative developments

There have been many legislative and case-law developments over the last two decades or so. During the 1990s there were many important and radical changes to family law. Of particular importance was the enactment of the Children Act 1989 (CA 1989), which came into force in October 1991 and made far-reaching changes to the law relating to children. The Child Support Act 1991 moved child maintenance from the courts into the Child Support Agency; and in the mid-1990s family law remedies for victims of domestic violence were made available to a wider class of family members by Part IV of the Family Law Act 1996 (FLA 1996). There was also an attempt in the 1990s to introduce a radically new law of divorce, although this was abandoned as the proposals were found to be unworkable in practice.

In the first few years of the new millennium there were further important legislative developments. Of particular importance was the Human Rights Act 1998 (HRA 1998), which came into force in 2000. Pension sharing on divorce was also introduced in 2000 by the Welfare Reform and Pensions Act 1999. In 2003, new provisions were introduced into the CA 1989 to allow unmarried fathers to acquire parental responsibility by birth registration. Another significant development was the introduction of civil partnerships by the Civil Partnership Act 2004; and transsexual people were given the right to enter into a valid marriage in their newly acquired sex by the Gender Recognition Act 2004. There were also changes to the law to give victims of domestic violence greater protection under new provisions introduced by the Domestic Violence, Crime and Victims Act 2004. New civil law remedies for victims of forced marriage were introduced in 2008 by Part 4A of the FLA 1996. Changes to the law governing parenthood in cases of assisted reproduction were made by the Human Fertilisation and Embryology Act 2008. Same sex marriage was introduced in 2014 by the Marriage (Same Sex Couples) Act 2013; and the Immigration Act 2014 introduced a new referral and investigation scheme to tackle sham marriages and civil partnerships in the UK. Part 10 of the Anti-social Behaviour, Crime and Policing Act 2014 introduced changes to the law in order to criminalise forced marriage; and the Inheritance and Trustees' Powers Act 2014 also reformed the law in intestacy and family provision claims on the death of a partner.

Important changes have also been made in the last decade or so to the law relating to children and parents. Radical reforms of adoption were made by the Adoption and Children Act 2002, which also introduced special guardianship and inserted new provisions into the CA 1989 to improve the facilitation and enforcement of contact on family breakdown. The Children Act 2004 (CA 2004) introduced other family law reforms, such as placing restrictions on the use of corporal punishment by parents, changing the structural framework governing the practice of child protection, and creating the office of the Children's Commissioner. Changes to the child support system were also implemented by the Child Maintenance and Other Payments Act 2008. The Children and Families Act 2014 (CFA 2014) has also introduced important and wide-ranging changes to family law, such as new time limits for public law proceedings and provisions regarding post-adoption contact. The CFA 2014 introduced a new presumption of parental involvement into the CA 1989, and replaced contact and residence orders with a new single order called a child arrangements order. It also removed the requirement for the court to consider whether to exercise its powers under the CA 1989 on divorce or dissolution. As a result, it is no longer necessary for parties to complete a Statement of Arrangements Form when filing for divorce or dissolution.

(c) Case-law developments

In addition to the many legislative developments, there have been important case-law developments. These have included decisions dealing with the approach the courts must adopt in proceedings for property and financial orders on divorce, such as the question of whether pre-marital agreements should be binding. There have been important decisions, for example, on the rights of transsexuals and also on the property rights of cohabitants on relationship breakdown as well as non-disclosure in matrimonial financial proceedings. In addition, there are an increasing number of cases involving matters with an international dimension, such as the question of whether the courts in England and Wales have jurisdiction to grant financial relief after a foreign divorce.

Important decisions have also been handed down on the law governing children, for example on the threshold conditions for making care and supervision orders, on international child abduction and on the importance of the biological bond between parent and child as a consideration in disputes about arrangements for children. Important cases on the voice of the child in family proceedings and the right of a child to refuse or consent to medical treatment have also been heard.

Due to their obligations under the HRA 1998, the family courts in England and Wales are required to exercise their powers in light of the European Convention on Human Rights (ECHR). Human rights arguments play an important part in some cases, particularly those where public authorities are involved, such as in child protection and housing cases. Human rights have also, for example, had an impact on the law regarding the right of a person to succeed to a deceased partner's tenancy and on the law governing the rights of transsexuals. In children's cases, in addition to the protection afforded by the HRA 1998 and the ECHR, the United Nations Convention on the Rights of the Child (UNCRC) gives children another set of rights.

(d)   Family law reform

A wide range of family law issues has been the subject of discussion with regard to reform. Some of these discussions have been taken no further (such as proposals to reform the law governing the property rights of cohabitants on relationship breakdown and to introduce compulsory joint birth registration), whereas other proposals may or may not be passed into law. Thus, the Law Commission has reviewed and reported on the law governing finances and property on divorce and dissolution and, at the time of writing, is awaiting a final response from the Government regarding nuptial agreements. It has also reviewed and reported on the various means by which family financial orders made under the Matrimonial Causes Act 1973, the CA 1989 and the CA 2004 are enforced. This project did not look at the basis for claims but instead considered the legal tools available to force a party to comply with an order once it has been made. The Law Commission produced a final report with its recommendations in December 2016 and is awaiting the Government's response. The Law Commission is also reviewing the law governing how and where people can marry in England and Wales. This project looks at whether the current law, which has evolved over a long period of time, provides a fair and coherent legal framework for enabling people to marry. The Law Commission produced a scoping paper setting out its findings in December 2015 and is waiting for the Government to respond to its recommendations for further work. The Family Justice Review (see below) has also recommended a wide range of reforms to the family justice system, and most of its proposals have been accepted by the Government.

With respect to children, there has been ongoing discussion about reforming the law to enable them to have a greater voice in family law proceedings and about child inclusive models of non-court dispute resolution. In June 2014 the President of the Family Division established the Vulnerable Witnesses and Children Working Group, chaired by Mr Justice Hayden and Ms Justice Russell, to look at how children can participate in family proceedings and the provision for the identification of vulnerable witnesses. In March 2015 the Working Group published its Final Report and proposed changes to the FPR 2010, including new Rules and Practice Directions to 'give prominence and emphasis to the treatment of children and parties in family proceedings; to emphasise the importance of the role of the child and the need to identify the necessary support/special measures for vulnerable witnesses and/or parties from the outset of any proceedings, or at the earliest opportunity' (para 35). In August 2015 the Family Procedure Rule Committee published draft amendment rules, many of which already exist for children in criminal proceedings following the introduction of the Youth Justice and Criminal Evidence Act 1999. The new rules, set out in a revised Part 3A, are designed to emphasise the importance of the participation of children and vulnerable people at all stages of family proceedings, in particular during early case management.

(i) The Family Justice Review

In March 2010, the then Labour Government appointed a panel, led by David Norgrove, to carry out a comprehensive independent review of the family justice system in England and Wales. The Coalition Government which took office soon afterwards supported the review. After the publication of an interim report and a consultation period during which evidence was collected, the final report of the Family Justice Review was published in November 2011 (see *Family Justice Review: Final Report*). The recommendations were comprehensive and far-reaching and applied to both private and public family law. The aim of the proposals was to make the family justice system more effective and to reduce the delays inherent in the system. Some of the key recommendations included: the introduction of a single family court; a new single 'child arrangements order' to replace residence and contact orders; and increased mediation provision.

In February 2012 the UK Government published its response to the Family Justice Review (see *The Government Response to the Family Justice Review: A system with children and families at its heart*, Cm 8273, Ministry of Justice and Department of Education). In its response, in which it accepted most of the Family Justice Review's recommendations in full, the Government announced that it would be conducting a major overhaul of the family justice system with the aim, *inter alia*, to help strengthen parenting, reduce the time it takes cases to progress through the courts and simplify the system. It proposed radical changes to both private and public family law, some of which are contained in the CFA 2014. In August 2014 the Government published an update setting out the progress that had been made since the Family Justice Review was first published in 2011 (see *A brighter future for Family Justice: A round up of what has happened since the Family Justice Review*, Ministry of Justice and Department of Education).

(ii) The Children and Families Act 2014

The CFA 2014 received Royal Assent on 13 March 2014. It is part of the Government's response to the final report of the Family Justice Review. Among other things, the Act requires parents engaged in disputes to consider mediation as an alternative means of settling the dispute rather than engaging in litigation and aims to reduce delays in care and adoption cases. It also contains provisions strengthening the powers of the English Children's Commissioner. The Act also introduces a statutory presumption in favour of parental involvement which the Government decided was needed to help ensure that children have a relationship with both parents after family separation where it is safe and in the child's best interests.

(e) Demographic and social changes

There have been important demographic and social changes which have impacted on family law. Fewer people now marry, many people cohabit and family breakdown is common. There are also increasing numbers of single-parent families and many children are born outside marriage. A particularly important change in family law has been the recognition given by legislators and the courts to different forms of family living. The 'traditional' family, a married heterosexual couple with children, is no longer the only family form. There are now same sex families and cohabitating families, for example, and also an increasing number of step-families. The recognition of these increasingly complex family forms has resulted in an increasingly complex set of statutory provisions in family law.

The driving forces behind the changes which have taken place in family life are articulated by Mr Justice Munby in the following extract.

▶ **Mr Justice Munby, 'Families old and new – the family and Article 8' [2005]** *Child and Family Law Quarterly* **487**

There have been very profound changes in family life in recent decades. They have been driven by four major developments. First, there have been enormous changes in the social and religious life of our country. The fact is that we live in a secular and pluralistic society. But we also live in a multi-cultural community of many faiths …. Secondly, there has been an increasing lack of interest in – in some instances a conscious rejection of – marriage as an institution. There is no lack of interest in family life (or at least in intimate relationships) but the figures demonstrate a striking decline in marriage. At the same time, it has never been easier for the married to be divorced. The truth is that, for all practical purposes, we permit divorce on demand. Thirdly, there has been a sea-change in society's attitudes towards same-sex unions …. Fourthly, there have been enormous advances in medical and in particular reproductive science so that reproduction is no longer confined to "natural" methods.

The following extract from the Government Green Paper *Support for All* also lists some of the changes which have had an impact on family life.

> ▶ *Support for All*, **Department for Children, Schools and Families, Cm 7787, 2010, pp. 5–6**

The very significant economic, social and demographic changes seen in recent decades have had a pronounced effect on family forms, family life and public attitudes. For example:

- ▶ in 2008 64 per cent of children were living in families with married couples, 13 per cent with cohabiting couples and 23 per cent with a lone parent;
- ▶ most children still live in a married family and marriage remains the most common form of partnership in Britain today. However, marriage rates show an overall decline since their peak in the 1970s;
- ▶ divorce rates increased considerably between the 1950s and the mid-1980s but then levelled off. In recent years they have started to fall and in 2007 the divorce rate reached its lowest level since 1981;
- ▶ the numbers of step-families are growing;
- ▶ in general, women are having fewer children and doing so later in life;
- ▶ since the Second World War the proportion of children born outside marriage has increased very significantly, right across Europe;
- ▶ about ten per cent of the adult population in England and Wales was cohabiting in 2007; cohabitation covers a wide range of relationships, including a precursor to marriage and an alternative to it;
- ▶ there is greater acceptance and recognition of same sex relationships and this is reflected in the introduction of civil partnerships; and
- ▶ people are healthier than ever and living longer which means that many more grandparents now see their grandchildren grow up.

The following extract highlights how the high incidence of family breakdown has a direct and profound impact on the private lives of many people.

> ▶ **Mr Justice Paul Coleridge, 'Lobbing a few pebbles in the pond: the funeral of a dead parrot' [2014] Fam Law 168**
>
> The incidence of family breakdown … is so terribly high now that the way in which family law is shaped and, as importantly, managed and processed, has a direct and profound impact on the private lives of huge numbers of the population …. Here are just a few of the sad and alarming facts and figures:
>
> 1. The rate of marriage is at a 100-year low: 241,000 a year at the last count. And, although the number of married couples still exceeds the unmarried, unmarried cohabitation has risen dramatically: 2.1m couples in 2001, 2.9m in 2011. On the present trajectory, by 2030, only 17 years away, it is likely to be well north of 3.7m.
> 2. The divorce rate has risen steadily since 1970 although it has now levelled off but at a very high level: 117,500 divorces in 2011. In 1983, 22 per cent of marriages ended in divorce within 15 years. By 2010 that same figure had risen to 33 per cent – a 50 per cent increase. The divorce rate is now hovering at around 42 per cent. So again, although the majority of the married still remain together for life, the rate is very high.
> 3. The real mischief is not to be found there but amongst the unmarried parents. Why? Because cohabitation, however it is defined, is far less stable. Unmarried parents are nearly three times more likely to break up before their first child's seventh birthday. And the chances of a 15-year-old still living with both his parents, if they are unmarried, is very small indeed. About 7 per cent of unmarried parents are still together by the time their children reach 15, whereas 93 per cent are married.

4. Every year 500,000 children and adults get caught up for the first time in our terribly overstretched family justice system. The total is in excess of 3m children in the system as we speak. Because, of course, the children do not come in and go out of the system like aeroplanes landing and taking off at the airport. As we know only too well, they enter and often stay there for years while their parents sort out their own and their children's lives. The financial cost is currently put at £46bn a year; more than the entire defence budget.

(For an interesting critique of Mr Justice Paul Coleridge's views see Sir Nicholas Mostyn, 'Speech to Jordan's Family Law Conference', 8 October 2014.)

1.3 Openness and transparency in family proceedings

The judiciary and the Government remain committed to ensuring that there is openness and transparency in family proceedings.

(a) Practice guidelines

In July 2013 Sir James Munby, President of the Family Division, published a set of draft practice guidelines outlining a new approach to the publication of family judgments. The guidance was intended to bring about an immediate and significant change in practice in relation to the publication of judgments in family courts. The President had previously emphasised his determination to focus on transparency within the family justice system, stating: 'I am determined to take steps to improve access to and reporting of family proceedings. I am determined that the new Family Court should not be saddled, as the family courts are at present, with the charge that we are a system of secret and unaccountable justice' ('View from the President's Chambers: the Process of Reform' [2013] Fam Law 548).

In September 2013 Munby P said that the case of *Re J (A Child)* [2013] EWHC 2694 (Fam) raised important questions about how the court should adapt its practice to the realities of the Internet, and in particular social media. He once again called for more transparency in the family courts in order to restore public confidence in the system. In this case Munby P permitted a father to post online a video of social workers removing his baby. His decision was not, however, welcomed by the social work profession.

In December 2013 in the case of *Re P (A Child)* [2013] EWHC 4048 (Fam), which concerned an application for a reporting restriction order in the case of an Italian mother whose child was delivered by Caesarean section following an order of the Court of Protection, Munby P, giving judgment, said:

> This case must surely stand as final, stark and irrefutable demonstration of the pressing need for radical changes in the way in which both the family courts and the Court of Protection approach what for shorthand I will refer to as transparency. We simply cannot go on as hitherto. Many more judgments must be published.

Subsequently, in January 2014, his Lordship issued new Practice Guidance to promote transparency in the family courts: *Transparency in the Family Courts: Publication of*

Judgments. The Guidance brought about an immediate and significant change in practice in relation to the publication of judgments in the family courts (and also in the Court of Protection). The Guidance states:

> [There] is a need for greater transparency in order to improve public understanding of the court process and confidence in the court system. At present too few judgments are made available to the public, which has a legitimate interest in being able to read what is being done by the judges in its name. The Guidance will have the effect of increasing the number of judgments available for publication (even if they will often need to be published in appropriately anonymised form).

The Guidance provides that permission to publish should always be given 'whenever the judge concludes that publication would be in the public interest' whether or not a request has been made. (For the background to these changes see Jarrett T, *Confidentiality and openness in the family courts: current rules and history of their reform*, House of Commons Library Briefing Paper, Number 07306, 23 September 2015.)

(b)   Media attendance

Changes have been made to allow the media, in certain circumstances, to attend some family proceedings. The Government's aim in allowing media attendance is to improve public confidence in the family justice system and to educate the public about the work and decisions of the family courts. In other words, the aim is to promote transparency and eliminate accusations of secrecy and bias. For the background to these changes see *Family Justice in View*, Ministry of Justice, 2008, Cm 7502.

In April 2009 the family courts were opened to accredited members of the media. Thus, media representatives can attend certain proceedings held in private subject to the court's power to exclude them from all or part of the proceedings where it is in the interests of a child, or where it is necessary to do so for the protection of a party to the proceedings or where justice will be impeded or prejudiced (r 27.11(3) Family Procedure Rules 2010 (FPR 2010)). However, the media are not permitted to attend hearings which are conducted for the purpose of, *inter alia*, judicially assisted conciliation or negotiation (r 27.11(1)(a)). There are restrictions on media access to court documents. Courts also have powers to restrict what can be reported to protect the welfare of children and families, or to relax reporting rules in individual cases.

Special restrictions apply to media attendance in children's cases. Cases in family courts involving children are heard in private and there are restrictions on publishing information about the proceedings (s 12 Administration of Justice Act 1960) and about protecting their anonymity (s 97 Children Act 1989). The court may also exclude the media from a case involving adults if such attendance may adversely affect any children involved. Thus, for example, in *Re Child X (Residence and Contact; Rights of Media Attendance; FPR Rule 10.28(4))* [2009] EWHC 1728 (Fam), the media were excluded from residence and contact proceedings involving a father who was a celebrity because of concerns about the child's welfare if the media were admitted.

As the FPR 2010 did not alter the statutory basis for media reporting, Part 2 of the Children, Schools and Families Act 2010 was enacted to give the media even greater access to family proceedings, including access to documents filed for such proceedings, and to lift some of the restrictions on publication. However, after strong opposition to this new legislation and following the recommendations of the House of Commons Justice Committee in July 2011 and the outcome of the Family Justice Review in November 2011, the Government announced that Part 2 would not be implemented. Concerns were expressed about the protection afforded to children, including their right to privacy under Article 8 of the European Convention on Human Rights; and the fact that they might be less willing to talk to experts or give evidence if they knew the media had access to what they said. For discussion of these concerns see, for example, Wall LJ [2010] Fam Law 40; Macdonald [2010] Fam Law 190; Mole [2010] Fam Law 75; and Bessant [2011] Fam Law 987. There was also a risk that cases might be misreported and sensationalised by the media. Part 2 was repealed by s 17(4) of the Crime and Courts Act 2013 (CCA 2013).

In January 2016 a pilot scheme began which allows, for the first time, the public and media to gain access to Court of Protection hearings across England and Wales. Sir James Munby, President of the Court of Protection, said:

> For the last six years accredited media have been able to attend Family Court cases and have been better informed about the work of the Family Court as a result. It is logical to look at extending this greater transparency to the Court of Protection, provided the right balance can be struck to safeguard the privacy of people who lack capacity to make their own decisions.

A new Practice Direction changes the default position to one where hearings are held in public with reporting restrictions to protect identities. In other words, this means that, when an order has been made under the pilot, both the public and media will be able to attend unless a further order has been made which excludes them. This Practice Direction applies to proceedings issued from 29 January 2016 onwards; and it also applies to proceedings issued before this date where a further hearing is necessary.

(c)   The transparency debate

There are two distinct schools of thought driving the transparency debate in the family courts: the approach put forward by Munby P (see above) and Holman J; and that put forward by Mostyn J.

Holman J, a senior High Court judge in the Family Division, is of the view that financial remedy proceedings should be held in open court with a starting point that there should be no reporting restrictions placed on the media. Thus, for example, in the case of *Luckwell v Limata* [2014] EWHC 502 (Fam) he granted full public and media access to what he described as 'an exceptionally bitter' divorce hearing with no restriction on what could be reported; and in the case of *Fields v Fields (Rev 1)* [2015] EWHC 1670 (Fam), which attracted considerable coverage in the national press, he repeated his view that there is a 'pressing need for more openness' and that 'the family courts must be more transparent'.

Mostyn J, on the other hand, made a compelling argument for privacy in financial remedy proceedings in the cases of *DL v SL* [2015] EWHC 2621 (Fam) and *Appleton & Gallagher v News Group Newspapers and PA* [2015] EWHC 2689 (Fam). He said:

> [T]here are some categories of court business, which are so personal and private that in almost every case where anonymisation is sought the right to privacy will trump the right to unfettered freedom of expression. These cases are those where the subject matter of the proceedings can rightly be categorised as 'private business'.

He concluded:

> [T]he present divergence of approach in the Family Division is very unhelpful and makes the task of advising litigants very difficult. A party may well have a very good case but is simply unprepared to have it litigated in open court. The risk of having it heard in open court may force him or her to settle on unfair terms. In my opinion the matter needs to be considered by the Court of Appeal and a common approach devised and promulgated. Obviously if the view of Holman J is upheld and adopted then the rest of us will have to follow suit.

The divergence of approach in the transparency debate in the family courts needs clarification. This may come from the Court of Appeal, as Mostyn J granted News Group Newspapers permission to appeal his decision in *Appleton & Gallagher v News Group Newspapers and PA* (see above); or it may come from the President's Consultation Paper of August 2014, *Transparency – The Next Steps: A Consultation Paper*, which seeks views on the above developments and on ways to improve transparency in the family courts. The Government's stated position is simply that it 'supports steps to increase openness whilst remaining mindful of the rights to privacy of those involved in such personal proceedings' (see Jarrett T, *Confidentiality and openness in the family courts: current rules and history of their reform*, House of Commons Library Briefing Paper, Number 07306, 23 September 2015).

1.4　The exercise of judicial discretion

A distinguishing feature of family law is that discretion plays a significant part in judicial decision-making. The outcome of cases depends to a large degree on their particular facts. Judicial discretion is essential in family matters because family life is infinitely variable – no two families are the same. The main advantage of discretion is its flexibility, in that an outcome can be decided on for each individual case and set of circumstances. The disadvantages are that it can create unpredictability and the exercise of discretion can be a time-consuming exercise which can increase the cost of litigation. There is also a risk of arbitrariness in that judges may reach different conclusions in cases which are factually similar. The alleged arbitrariness of court decisions about child maintenance was one of the reasons given by the Government for moving most of these types of cases out of the courts and into the Child Support Agency. In some areas of the law a checklist of factors is provided in the legislation to help guide judges when exercising their discretion and in reaching their decision. There are, for example, statutory checklists which must be taken into account in finance and property proceedings on divorce and dissolution, child arrangements cases and in adoption proceedings.

The discretionary nature of family law also has an impact on appeals. Thus, as there may be several possible reasonable decisions when deciding a family law dispute, the appeal courts are unwilling to overturn decisions made by the lower courts unless they are either wrong in law or plainly wrong on their facts.

1.5 The importance of reaching agreement

Most private law family matters, such as those involving divorce or dissolution and arrangements for children, are settled by the parties themselves. Thus, despite the impression given by the number of reported cases, most do not go to court. Furthermore, if family lawyers are consulted, they work within a conciliatory framework.

There is increasing emphasis on the importance of reaching agreement in family law cases. Agreement between the parties can be facilitated by the use of non-court dispute resolution techniques such as mediation, collaborative law or arbitration. In fact, there has been an increasing trend to use, and to promote the use of, non-court dispute resolution in family disputes. It has, for example, been actively promoted by Resolution (an organisation of family lawyers), whose Code of Practice requires its members to 'conduction matters in a constructive and non-confrontational way and to inform clients of the options e.g. counselling, family therapy, round-table negotiations, mediation, collaborative law and court proceedings' (see Resolution's *Guide to Good Practice*, 2014). The principles of the Code also form part of the Law Society's rules of good practice for family law solicitors (see the *Family Law Protocol*, 4th ed., 2015, Appendix 2).

(a) Mediation

Mediation is a form of non-court dispute resolution whereby a mediator helps the parties identify the issues in dispute with the aim of them reaching agreement. The mediator acts as an impartial third party. An agreement is not imposed by the mediator. It is the parties themselves who must endeavour to reach agreement. The mediator's role is merely that of facilitator. In other words, the process is non-coercive. Mediation can take place out of court or in court, and it is available from independent mediation agencies and from some law firms. In financial order proceedings on divorce, the district judge performs a mediatory role by encouraging the parties and their lawyers to reach a settlement.

The final report of the Family Justice Review (see 1.2 above) included a number of proposals to increase the use of mediation. These proposals were accepted by the Government, which wishes mediation to become the norm for parents in dispute. Thus, the Children and Families Act 2014 contained measures to increase the use of mediation, including a requirement in certain cases (such as those involving property and finance and/or children on family breakdown) that the parties must attend a mediation information and assessment meeting before going to court (s 10). The rules regarding the mediation information and assessment requirement are set out in Part 3 of the FPR 2010 and *Practice Direction 3A – Family Mediation Information and Assessment Meetings*. In addition to the mediation information and assessment requirement, the court has a general duty to encourage and facilitate the use of non-court dispute resolution (r 3.2 FPR 2010). This means that it must consider, at every stage in proceedings, whether non-court dispute resolution is appropriate (r 3.3 FPR 2010). If the court thinks that non-court dispute resolution is appropriate, it may decide to adjourn the proceedings and may require the parties to consider and/or to attempt non-court dispute resolution (r 3.4 FPR 2010).

Mediation has many advantages over going to court. For example, reaching agreement by way of mediation is more likely to result in the parties making and maintaining cooperative relationships on family breakdown. It reduces conflict and encourages continuing contact between children and parents. It also avoids the cost, trauma, uncertainty and delay of court proceedings, and helps improve communication between the parties thereby reducing conflict and bitterness. By making disputes less hostile, mediation may make things better for the parties' children. It may also empower the parties and make them better able to deal with disputes in the future. Mediation does, however, have disadvantages. For example, it may work against a party's interests if they have a lack of legal knowledge or it may fail to take sufficient account of the welfare needs of children. It may also be inappropriate if there is a history of domestic violence in the relationship or if either of the parties is particularly vulnerable.

(b) Collaborative family law

Collaborative law, like mediation, is a form of non-court dispute resolution which provides a way of resolving issues about finance and property and/or children on family breakdown. It is a relatively new practice, having first been used in England and Wales in 2003. It is used only by people who agree to use it after having received legal advice about the other options available. With collaborative law, the parties and their lawyers sign a participation agreement in which they agree to a commitment to make a transparent search for fair solutions and not go to court. The parties and their lawyers then conduct round-table negotiations in order to find the best outcome. The process is transparent and written correspondence is actively discouraged. The parties set both the pace and the scope of the negotiations, but with the assistance of their lawyers. The parties can also seek the assistance of mediation and counselling. If a settlement is not reached, and a party decides to go to court, then each party must consult a new lawyer.

Resolution has trained some of its members as collaborative lawyers, who have formed themselves into 'pods' (practice and organisational development groups). These act as support groups to enable lawyers to share experiences and to build trust with fellow lawyers with whom they work collaboratively. Research conducted by Resolution (*Collaborative Law in England and Wales: Early Findings*, 26 February 2009) found that collaborative law was increasingly and successfully being used. Disputes were settled more quickly and, in cases involving cohabitants, more generous settlements were reached than would have been possible if the law relating to cohabitants had been strictly applied. (For other research on collaborative law, see Wright [2011] CFLQ 370.)

(c) Arbitration

Arbitration is a form of non-court dispute resolution whereby disputes are resolved outside the court system by an arbitrator by whose decision the parties agree to be bound. It is beginning to be used for resolving family disputes. Thus, in February 2012 the Institute of Family Law Arbitrators launched a family law arbitration scheme to enable certain family disputes to be resolved by arbitration. The aim of the scheme is to enable financial disputes to be resolved more quickly, more cheaply and less formally than in court. It has the support of Resolution and the Family Law Bar Association. (For information on the scheme, see www.ifla.org.uk.)

In *S v S (Financial Remedies: Arbitral Award)* [2014] EWHC 7 (Fam), the President of the Family Division, Sir James Munby, affirmed and approved a financial award made by an arbitrator appointed under the Family Law Arbitration Scheme. In his judgment he said: 'There is no conceptual difference between the parties making an agreement and agreeing to give an arbitrator the power to make the decision for them.' In November 2015, following this strong endorsement of the Family Law Arbitration Scheme, the President issued new practice guidance on arbitration in the Family Court to further emphasise its importance.

More recently, the Institute of Family Law Arbitrators has developed a new Family Law Arbitration Children Scheme which allows family law disputes concerning the exercise of parental responsibility and other private law issues about the welfare of children to be resolved by arbitration. The new scheme launched in July 2016.

1.6 The single Family Court administering family law

Prior to April 2014 there were three tiers of court with jurisdiction to hear family cases: magistrates' family proceedings courts; county courts; and the Family Division of the High Court. The final report of the Family Justice Review (see 1.2 above) recommended, *inter alia*, that the three-tier court system should be replaced by a single Family Court with a single point of entry. In its *Report*, the Family Justice Review stated that there were wide variations nationally in how different cases are allocated to courts which caused confusion and uncertainty for families about where cases would be heard. This complexity was particularly difficult for litigants in person to navigate. The Family Justice Review recommended that all levels of the family judiciary (including magistrates) should sit in the Family Court and that work should be allocated according to case complexity. However, it recommended that the Family Division of the High Court should remain, and that it should have exclusive jurisdiction over cases involving the inherent jurisdiction and international issues. All other matters should be heard in the single Family Court, with High Court judges sitting in that court to hear the most complex cases and issues.

The single Family Court subsequently came into being on 22 April 2014 (under section 31A of the Matrimonial and Family Proceedings Act 1984, as amended by section 17 of Part 2 of the Crime and Courts Act 2013). The Family Court has replaced the three tiers of court which used to have jurisdiction to hear family cases with a single point of entry. It deals with all family proceedings (subject to a few limited exceptions) and there is no longer a separate jurisdiction for magistrates' courts and county courts to hear family cases. It is also a national court which sits in magistrates' and county courts in a range of geographical locations across England and Wales. The Principal Registry of the Family Division is now called the Central Family Court, but it still exists as a division of the High Court in the Royal Courts of Justice.

This change is intended to create a simpler court system, allowing cases to be allocated to a judge with the relevant level of seniority to hear the case in accordance with the Family Court (Composition and Distribution of Business) Rules 2014. The four levels of judges are: lay magistrates; district judges; circuit judges; and High Court judges. A list of the judiciary of the Family Court can be found in section 31C of the Matrimonial and Family Proceedings Act 1984 and Schedule 10 of the Crime and Courts Act 2013.

There is now also a unified system of administration, and so-called 'gatekeepers' allocate cases in accordance with, *inter alia*, the Family Court (Composition and Distribution of Business) Rules 2014 and Practice Guidance issued by the President of the Family Division. Although the Family Court has replaced the three tiers of court which used to have jurisdiction to hear family cases, the Family Division of the High Court retains its exclusive jurisdiction in cases dealing with the inherent jurisdiction and international child abduction. It is hoped that the new court system will also help to reduce delay and ensure judicial continuity.

1.7 Cafcass

Cafcass (the Children and Family Court Advisory and Support Service) was established under section 11 of the Criminal Justice and Court Services Act 2000, and is responsible for looking after the best interests of children involved in family proceedings. The principal functions of Cafcass officers (who are called 'family proceedings officers' in Wales) are: to safeguard and promote the welfare of children in family proceedings; to make provision for children to be represented; and to provide information, advice and other support for children and their families (s 12(1)).

One of Cafcass's main functions is to advise courts on issues such as arrangements for children on family breakdown and placing children in local authority care. It also performs an important reporting function in family proceedings. Cafcass performs other important tasks, including facilitating contact on family breakdown and conducting risk assessments to establish whether children are at risk of abuse or domestic violence. Cafcass provides the following officers for the family courts:

▶ *Children and Family Reporters* are usually appointed when parents cannot agree about arrangements for their children on family breakdown. The court will appoint a Children and Family Reporter who will meet and talk with the family and help and encourage parents to agree about arrangements for their children. The Children and Family Reporter may be asked to prepare a welfare report explaining what enquiries have been made and making recommendations about arrangements for the children. The Children and Family Reporter is also responsible for conveying the child's wishes and feelings to the court.

▶ *Children's Guardians* are responsible for investigating the case and safeguarding and promoting the child's welfare before the court in public law proceedings for care and supervision orders and emergency protection and child assessment orders under the Children Act 1989. They work in tandem with the lawyer who is representing the child. A Children's Guardian may also be appointed in some private law proceedings.

▶ *Reporting Officers* are responsible for ensuring that the required consents to adoption and to placements for adoption have been given.

Cafcass became a part of the Ministry of Justice on 1 April 2014. This follows the Family Justice Review's recommendation that Cafcass should become part of the Ministry of Justice in order to 'bring court social work functions closer to the court process' (see *Family Justice Review: Final Report*, November 2011).

1.8   Family law and the Human Rights Act 1998

The Human Rights Act 1998 (HRA 1998) is relevant to family law, as the family courts and public authorities must abide by its provisions. The effect of the Act is to weave the European Convention on Human Rights (ECHR) into the fabric of UK law. The Act makes Convention rights directly enforceable in the UK. Thus, the HRA 1998 gives people the right to rely on the Convention in proceedings before the domestic courts. However, people who have exhausted all their remedies before the UK courts can take their case to the European Court of Human Rights (ECtHR) in Strasbourg.

(a)   The family courts and the Human Rights Act 1998

When deciding any question which has arisen in connection with a Convention right the family courts, like other courts in the UK, must 'take into account' the judgments, decisions and opinions of the ECtHR (s 2). The courts, so far as it is possible to do so, must also read and give effect to primary and secondary legislation in a way which is compatible with Convention rights (s 3). If the High Court, the Court of Appeal or the Supreme Court determines that a UK legislative provision is not compatible with the Convention, and cannot be read to make it compatible, then it may make a 'declaration of incompatibility' to that effect (s 4).

Courts are public authorities for the purposes of the HRA 1998 and must not act in a way which is incompatible with a Convention right (s 6). Thus, in family law cases the court must ensure that it considers and upholds Convention rights; otherwise it may be in breach of the Convention.

(b)   Public authorities and the Human Rights Act 1998

It is unlawful for a public authority to act in a way which is incompatible with a Convention right, subject to some exceptions (s 6). There is no definition of 'public authority' in the HRA 1998, but the term includes Government departments, local authorities, the National Health Service, the police and any other body or person exercising a public function. Because of the obligations imposed on public authorities by the Act, the Convention is particularly important in public law family proceedings, for example in child protection and adoption cases.

(c)   Asserting a Convention right

A victim of an unlawful act or proposed act of a public authority which is a breach of a Convention right may bring free-standing court proceedings against the public authority under the HRA 1998 or rely on a Convention right in any other legal proceedings (s 7). In practice, most claims in family law are usually brought as supporting arguments in family proceedings, although human rights challenges against local authorities in child protection cases are usually brought in judicial review proceedings. If an applicant proves that a public authority has acted in breach of a Convention right, the court may grant such relief or remedy or make such order within its powers as it considers just and appropriate, including awards of damages (s 8). When assessing awards of damages the courts take into account the levels of damages set by the ECtHR, which tend to be lower than those awarded under domestic law.

(d) Convention rights

The following Convention rights are those most likely to impact on family law: the right to a fair trial (Art 6); the right to family life (Art 8); the right to marry and found a family (Art 12); the right to an effective remedy (Art 13); and the right to enjoy Convention rights without discrimination (Art 14).

The ECHR and the decisions of the ECtHR have been raised in a wide variety of different situations before the family courts in England and Wales. Thus, for example:

- Transsexuals have argued that the UK's failure to allow them to change their birth certificates and to marry in their newly acquired sex is a breach of their right to family life under Article 8 and the right to marry under Article 12.
- Children and parents have argued that corporal punishment of children by parents and teachers is inhuman and degrading treatment under Article 3.
- Unmarried fathers have argued that their lack of automatic parental responsibility is a breach of the right to family life under Article 8 and is thereby discriminatory under Article 14.
- Parents in contact cases and in relocation applications have argued that there has been a breach of their right to family life under Article 8.
- Parents have argued in child protection cases that local authorities have breached their right to family life under Article 8 and that the procedures have breached their right to a fair trial under Article 6.

(For a useful and informative account of the impact of the HRA 1998 on the family justice system in England and Wales by Moylan J, see [2010] Fam Law 810.)

(e) The right to family life (Article 8)

The right to family life in Article 8 of the ECHR is particularly relevant to family law.

Article 8 of the European Convention for the Protection of Human Rights

1. Everyone has the right to respect for his private and family life, his home and his correspondence.
2. There shall be no interference by a public authority with the exercise of this right except such as is in accordance with the law and is necessary in a democratic society in the interests of national security, public safety or the economic well-being of the country, for the prevention of disorder or crime, for the protection of heath or morals, or for the protection of the rights and freedoms of others.

The aim of Article 8 is to protect the individual against arbitrary interference by public authorities. In addition, national authorities have positive obligations to promote family life under Article 8. However, the right to family life is not an absolute right because of the exceptions laid down in Article 8(2). Thus, interference with the right is permitted, provided it is lawful, necessary and proportionate. The right to family life is also subject to the rights and freedoms of others. For example, the rights of a child might prevail over the rights of parents where that is in the child's best interests. With respect to the right to family life, States Parties enjoy a 'margin of appreciation' (see further below).

(i) What is 'family life' for the purposes of Article 8?

There is no definition of 'family life' in the ECHR. Whether or not there is family life depends on the facts and circumstances of the case. However, the ECtHR has made the following statements about 'family life' for the purposes of Article 8:

- The existence or non-existence of family life is a question of fact depending on the real existence of close personal ties (*Lebbink v The Netherlands (Application No. 45582/99) [2004] 2 FLR 463; K and T v Finland (2000) 31 EHRR 18*).
- The bond between natural parents and children is a strong indicator of the existence of family life, and that bond amounting to family life cannot be broken by subsequent events, save in exceptional circumstances (*Ahmut v The Netherlands (1997) 24 EHRR 62*).
- Family life is not just limited to relationships based on marriage or blood. The following can also have a right to family life: cohabitants (*Abdulaziz, Cabales and Balkandali v UK (1995) 7 EHRR 471*), even if they do not live together (*Kroon v The Netherlands (1995) 19 EHRR 263*); same sex couples (*Schalk and Kopf v Austria [2010] ECHR 995*); and relatives, such as a grandparent and grandchild (*Marckx v Belgium (1979) 2 EHRR 330*) or a nephew and uncle (*Boyle v UK (1995) 19 EHRR 179*). Foster-parents and foster-children can also come within the ambit of family life (*Gaskin v UK (1990) 12 EHRR 36*).
- When deciding whether a cohabitation relationship amounts to family life, the following factors are relevant: whether the couple live together; the length of their relationship; and whether they have demonstrated their commitment to each other by having children together or by any other means. Thus, for example, family life was found to exist in *X, Y and Z v UK (1997) 24 EHRR 143* where a female-to-male transsexual (X) and his female partner (Y) had a child by artificial insemination by donor. X was involved throughout the process and had acted as the child's father in every respect.
- As the ECtHR considers the Convention to be a 'living instrument' which must be interpreted in the light of societal changes (*Selmouni v France (2000) 29 EHRR 403*), courts must adapt to changing social conditions when interpreting family life. This includes, for example, the decline in marriage, the increase in cohabitation, the acceptance of same sex relationships and developments in reproductive science.
- Family life can include the potential for family life, for example the potential relationship which might have developed between an unmarried father and his child.
- For the purpose of Article 8, family life must be viewed in the context of the relevant social, religious and cultural setting.

When deciding whether family life exists, the ECtHR takes into account relevant principles of international law. It interprets Article 8 to be so far as possible in harmony with those principles, including those in the United Nations Convention on the Rights of the Child.

(ii) The European Court of Human Rights' approach to Article 8

The ECtHR has laid down the following propositions in respect of Article 8:

▶ Although the main aim of Article 8 is to protect the individual against arbitrary action by public authorities (*Kroon v The Netherlands* (1995) 19 EHRR 263), there are also positive obligations inherent in an effective 'respect' for family life.
▶ As well as a substantive right to respect for family life, there is also a procedural right inherent within Article 8.
▶ In respect of the substantive and procedural rights under Article 8, regard must be had to the fair balance that has to be struck between the competing interests of the individual and of the community as a whole; and the State enjoys a certain margin of appreciation (see *Keegan v Ireland* (1994) 18 EHRR 342).
▶ The right to family life is not an absolute right, but a qualified right. Under Article 8(2) State interference into family life is justifiable if it is: in accordance with the law; in pursuit of a legitimate aim; and necessary in a democratic society. Any intervention must be relevant and sufficient, meet a pressing social need and be proportionate to that need (*Olsson v Sweden (No. 1)* (1988) 11 EHRR 259).
▶ Under the principle of proportionality, the more serious the intervention into family life, the more compelling must be the justification (*Johansen v Norway* (1997) 23 EHRR 33).
▶ In respect of a State's obligation to take positive measures, Article 8 includes an obligation on national authorities to take measures to reunite parents with their children (*Ignaccola-Zenide v Romania* (2001) 31 EHRR 7; *Nuutinen v Finland (Application No. 32842/96)* (2000) 34 EHRR 358), unless it is contrary to the interests of those concerned, particularly the best interests of the child.
▶ When carrying out the balancing exercise under Article 8(2) between the interests of children and parents and/or the wider public, the court takes into account the paramountcy of the best interests of the child.

(f) The margin of appreciation

Claims under the ECHR have sometimes failed because the ECtHR has recognised a 'margin of appreciation' in the State's decision-making process. In other words, States Parties are accorded a reasonable amount of discretion when exercising their powers in accordance with the Convention. For example, the margin of appreciation possessed by the UK meant that for many years transsexuals failed in their claims before the ECtHR.

(g) The principle of proportionality

The principle of proportionality is an important principle in the jurisprudence of the ECtHR which must be applied by courts and public authorities in the UK. This principle requires any interference with a Convention right to be proportionate to the legitimate aim pursued. The principle of proportionality would be breached, for example, if a care order was made to protect a child from significant harm when an alternative remedy (such as a supervision order) would be adequate and appropriate.

Summary

- ▶ Family law is a fascinating but challenging subject which requires a wide range of materials to be digested. A sound knowledge of, and an ability to apply, statutory provisions is very important, as is an understanding that judges have to exercise a considerable degree of discretion when deciding cases. Distinguishing features of family law are that: there is considerable emphasis on promoting agreement and settlement; both private and public law are involved; emotions are sometimes highly charged; court decisions are often forward-looking; and a wide range of personnel are involved. The functions of family law include: conferring a status; removing a status; enforcing and adjusting rights arising from a particular status; and providing protection for family members.

- ▶ Family law is radically different today from what it was 30 or 40 years ago. There have been many legislative and case-law developments. There has also been, and continues to be, considerable discussion of reform, such as with respect to giving cohabitants rights on family breakdown, giving children a voice in family law proceedings, increasing the use of non-court dispute resolution, reforming the law governing property and finance on divorce, and changing the law governing how and where people can marry in England and Wales. In 2011 and 2012 there was an important review of the family justice system (the Family Justice Review). Most of its recommendations were taken up by the Government which proposed changes to family law, almost all of which are included in the Children and Families Act 2014. Demographic and social changes have had an impact on family law, which has changed dramatically in recent years to give 'non-traditional' family members rights, in particular same sex couples and transsexual people.

- ▶ New legal provisions have been introduced to allow the media to attend court in certain circumstances, in order to make the family justice system more open and transparent and to improve public confidence in the system. However, proposals to give the media even greater access to family proceedings, including those involving children, have met with resistance.

- ▶ Judges have considerable discretion in family law cases. The outcome of a case depends on its own facts, as no two family situations are the same. The discretionary nature of family justice also has an impact on appeals.

- ▶ The settlement of family law cases outside of court is actively encouraged. Non-court dispute resolution is being increasingly used, such as mediation, collaborative law and, more recently, arbitration. The Family Procedure Rules 2010 contain rules which promote mediation.

- ▶ Family cases are now heard in a single Family Court which deals with the vast majority of family proceedings. This has replaced the old three-tier system (magistrates' family proceedings courts, county courts and the Family Division of the High Court). All levels of judge can sit in the Family Court, from magistrates to High Court judges and above. Applications are allocated to the most appropriate level of judge by a 'gate-keeping' team based on, for example, the complexity of the case, judicial continuity, the need to minimise delay and a suitable location for hearings.

Summary cont'd

▶ Cafcass provides officers to assist the Family Court in cases involving children. In addition to its duty to provide reports (such as welfare reports), it also has other functions, such as facilitating and enforcing contact and conducting risk assessments to establish whether children are at risk of harm.

▶ The Human Rights Act 1998 is relevant to family law as it requires courts and public authorities to take account of the European Convention on Human Rights and the jurisprudence of the European Court of Human Rights. Of particular importance in family law cases is the right to family life (Article 8). However, this is not an absolute right. State Parties have a margin of appreciation, but any interference must be lawful, necessary and proportionate to the legitimate aim pursued.

Further reading and references

Bessant, 'Children, openness and the family courts' [2011] Fam Law 987.

Booth and Kennedy, 'The "traditional family" and the law' [2005] Fam Law 482.

Choudhry and Herring, *European Human Rights and Family Law*, 2010, Hart Publishing.

Cobb J, 'Private law reform' [2014] Fam Law 644.

Cobb J, 'Seen but not heard?' [2015] Fam Law 144.

Cretney, 'The family and the law – status or contract?' [2003] CFLQ 403.

Cretney, *Family Law in the Twentieth Century: A History*, 2003, Oxford University Press.

Douglas and Lowe (eds), *The Continuing Evolution of Family Law*, 2009, Family Law.

Gilmore, Herring and Probert (eds), *Landmark Cases in Family Law*, 2011, Hart Publishing.

Harris-Short, 'Family law and the Human Rights Act 1998: judicial restraint or revolution?' [2005] CFLQ 329.

Holt and Kelly, 'What has happened since the Family Justice Review: a brighter future for whom?' [2015] Fam Law 807.

Macdonald, 'Bringing rights home for children: transparency and the child's right to family life' [2010] Fam Law 190.

Maclean (ed.), *Family Law and Family Values*, 2005, Hart Publishing.

Mole, 'Media access to family courts and article 8' [2010] Fam Law 75.

Moylan J, 'What have human rights done for family justice?' [2010] Fam Law 810.

Munby J, 'Families old and new – the family and Article 8' [2005] CFLQ 487.

Munby J, 'The family justice system' [2004] Fam Law 574.

Munby LJ, 'Lost opportunities: law reform and transparency in the family courts' [2010] CFLQ 273.

Probert, '"Family law" – a modern concept?' [2004] Fam Law 901.

Roberts, *Mediation in Family Disputes*, 2008, Ashgate.

Ryder J, 'The family courts of the future' [2008] Fam Law 854.

Ryder J, 'Family justice redefined? Family justice after reform' [2014] Fam Law 590.

Smart, 'Law and family life: insights from 25 years of empirical research' [2014] CFLQ 14.

Trinder, 'The support needs and impact of litigants in person: what can research tell us?' [2014] Fam Law 664.

Trinder and Hunter, 'Access to justice? Litigants in person before and after LASPO' [2015] Fam Law 535.

Further reading and references cont'd

Wall LJ, 'Justice for children: welfare or farewell?' [2010] Fam Law 40.
Wall P, 'The President's Resolution address 2012' [2012] Fam Law 817.
Wallbank, Choudhry and Herring (eds), *Rights, Gender and Family Law*, 2009, Routledge-Cavendish.
Wright, 'The evolving role of the family lawyer: the impact of collaborative law on family law practice' [2011] CFLQ 370.

Websites

Government services

Department for Education: www.education.gov.uk (formerly the Department for Children, Schools and Families)
Department for Work and Pensions: www.dwp.gov.uk
Law Commission: www.lawcom.gov.uk
Ministry of Justice: www.justice.gov.uk
Office for National Statistics: www.ons.gov.uk
United Kingdom Parliament: www.parliament.uk

Courts, law reports and legislation

British and Irish Legal Information Institute: www.bailii.org
European Court of Human Rights: www.echr.coe.int
Her Majesty's Courts Service: www.hmcourts-service.gov.uk
Supreme Court: www.supremecourt.gov.uk
UK Legislation: www.legislation.gov.uk

Other websites

Alternative Dispute Resolution Group (ADR): www.adrgroup.co.uk
Cafcass (England): www.cafcass.gov.uk
Cafcass (Wales): www.wales.gov.uk/cafcasscymru
College of Mediators: www.collegeofmediators.co.uk
Family Mediation Council: www.familymediationcouncil.org.uk
Family Mediation Helpline: www.familymediationhelpline.co.uk
Family Mediators' Association (FMA): www.fmassoc.co.uk
The Law Society: www.lawsociety.org.uk
National Family Mediation (NFM): www.nfm.org.uk
Resolution: www.resolution.org.uk

Links to relevant websites can also be found at: www.palgravehighered.com/law/familylaw9e

Part II

Marriage, civil partnership and cohabitation

Chapter 2

Marriage and civil partnership

This chapter deals with marriage (which applies to opposite and same sex couples) and civil partnership (which applies only to same sex couples), and the legal consequences which attach to these relationships. The law and procedure which apply to civil partnerships largely replicate those which apply to marriage, although there are some important differences. This chapter also looks at the law of nullity, and then deals with the following issues: the problem of forced marriage; the changes to the law to allow transsexual people to marry in their newly acquired sex; and the recognition of an overseas marriage. Cohabitation and its legal consequences are considered in Chapter 3.

2.1 Marriage

There was a drop in the number of marriages in England and Wales in 2013, which ended the steady rise recorded between 2009 and 2012. The average ages at marriage for men and women have increased significantly and a smaller percentage of marriages are now religious. The following are figures for marriages in England and Wales in 2013.

Marriages in England and Wales in 2013

These figures were published in April 2016 by the Office for National Statistics. (www.ons.gov.uk)

▶ The number of marriages decreased by 8.6 per cent from 2012 to 2013.
▶ Over two-thirds of marriages were the first marriage for both parties.
▶ The average age at marriage was 36.7 years for men and 34.3 years for women.
▶ The number of religious ceremonies decreased by 14 per cent from 2012 to 2013.
▶ Civil ceremonies accounted for 72 per cent of all marriages.

Although marriage is a contract, it cannot be created and terminated at the will of the parties. It is an arrangement in which the State has an interest. Marriage is also a status from which legal consequences flow. Thus, as Baroness Hale in *Radmacher (Formerly Granatino) v Granatino* [2010] UKSC 42 stated:

> Marriage is, of course, a contract, in the sense that each party must agree to enter into it and once entered both are bound by its legal consequences. But it is also a status. This means two things. First, the parties are not entirely free to determine all its legal consequences for themselves. They contract into the package which the law of the land lays down. Secondly, their marriage also has legal consequences for other people and for the State. Nowadays there is considerable freedom and flexibility within the marital package but there is an irreducible minimum. This includes a couple's mutual duty to support one another and their children. We have now arrived at a position where the differing roles which either may adopt within the relationship are entitled to equal esteem.

There are legal rules governing the creation of a valid marriage (see 2.2 to 2.5 below) and its termination (see Chapter 6). The legal effect of marriage is to give the parties various rights, obligations and privileges (see 2.9 below).

(a) Marriage as a human right

Article 12 of the European Convention for the Protection of Human Rights

Men and women of marriageable age have the right to marry and to found a family according to the national laws governing the exercise of this right.

The right to marry in Article 12 of the European Convention on Human Rights (ECHR) is not an absolute right, but it is a strong right. There is no second paragraph in Article 12, as there is in Article 8 (the right to family life), permitting interferences with or limitations to the right to marry. Both the House of Lords and the European Court of Human Rights (ECtHR) have emphasised the strength and fundamental nature of the right to marry which is conferred by Article 12, as the following two cases show.

▶ *R (Baiai and Others) v Secretary of State for the Home Department* [2008] UKHL 53

Challenges were made to a provision in the Asylum and Immigration (Treatment of Claimants, etc.) Act 2004 requiring people subject to immigration control to obtain the written permission of the Home Secretary in order to marry in the UK, unless they intended to marry in the Church of England. The Certificate of Approval Scheme, which has since been abolished, was introduced to prevent people entering into marriages of convenience in the UK.

The House of Lords held that this provision breached both Article 12 and Article 14 (discrimination in respect of an ECHR right). It further held that, although the right to marry under Article 12 is not an absolute right, it is a strong right; and, whilst it can be regulated by national laws both as to procedure and as to substance, national laws cannot deprive a person (or a category of people) of full legal capacity of the right to marry or substantially interfere with their exercise of that right.

The approach in *Baiai* was upheld by the ECtHR in the following case.

▶ *O'Donoghue v UK* (Application No. 34848/07)

The case involved an application for a certificate of approval in respect of a marriage between a Nigerian national and a dual British and Irish national. The applicants argued that the Certification of Approval Scheme violated their rights under Articles 9 (the right to freedom of thought, conscience and religion), 12 and 14 of the ECHR. The applicants were successful and awarded damages and costs.

The ECtHR held, *inter alia*, that Article 12 secured the fundamental right of a man and woman to marry and found a family. Although Article 12 is subject to the national laws of Contracting States, such laws should not restrict or reduce the right in such a way as to impair its very essence. States were entitled to prevent marriages of convenience entered into solely for the purpose of securing an immigration advantage, but such laws could not otherwise deprive people of full legal capacity of the right to marry. Since the wording of Article 12 did not contain the restrictions found in, for example, Article 8, the Court had to determine only whether, having regard to the State's margin of appreciation, the impugned interference had been arbitrary or disproportionate.

Successful challenges to the ECtHR based on Article 12 brought by transsexual people led to changes being made in UK law (see 2.7 below).

2.2 Capacity to marry

To contract a valid marriage the parties must have capacity to marry *and* they must comply with the legal formalities governing the creation of a marriage (see 2.3 below), otherwise the marriage may be void. The parties have capacity to marry under section 11 of the Matrimonial Causes Act 1973 (MCA 1973) if:

- they are not within the prohibited degrees of relationship (s 11(a)(i));
- they are both over the age of 16 (s 11(a)(ii));
- they have not intermarried in disregard of certain requirements as to the formation of marriage (s 11(a)(iii)); and
- at the time of the marriage neither party is already lawfully married or a civil partner (s 11(b)).

A party to a polygamous marriage also lacks the capacity to marry if they were domiciled in England and Wales at the time of the marriage (s 11(d)).

(a) Not within the prohibited degrees of relationship (section 11(a)(i))

A marriage will be void if the parties are within the 'prohibited degrees of relationship'. Marriages between certain people related by blood or by marriage are prohibited by the Marriage Act 1949 (MA 1949).

A person cannot marry the following blood relatives: a parent; a grandparent; a child; a grandchild; a brother or sister; an uncle or aunt; or a nephew or niece. There are fewer restrictions on marrying a relative where that relationship was created by marriage. Thus, a person can marry: a step-child; a step-parent; a step-grandparent; or a parent-in-law. However, a person cannot marry a step-child unless both parties are aged 21 or over and the step-child was not at any time before the age of 18 brought up by that person as a step-child. An adopted child is in the same prohibited degrees of relationship in respect of their birth family, but fewer restrictions apply to relationships that have been created by adoption. Thus, for example, a person can marry their adopted brother or sister.

(i) 'In-law' marriages

Restrictions on certain 'in-law' marriages were removed in 2007 as a result of the following decision of the European Court of Human Rights (ECtHR).

> ▶ *B and L v UK (Application No. 36536/02)* [2006] 1 FLR 35
>
> A daughter-in-law (L) and her father-in-law (B) wished to marry. They claimed that the bar on 'in-law' marriages under the MA 1949 (as amended by the Marriage (Prohibited Degrees of Relationship) Act 1986) violated their right to marry under Article 12 of the European Convention on Human Rights (ECHR). L had been married to B's son, but their marriage had broken down and L had gone on to develop a relationship with his father. The superintendent registrar refused to give L and B permission to marry because B's son was still alive. L and B took their case to the ECtHR, which found the UK to be in breach of Article 12. The prohibition was held to be neither rational nor logical and served no useful purpose of public policy.

After the decision in *B and L*, Schedule 1 to the MA 1949 was amended by the Marriage Act 1949 (Remedial) Order 207 No. 438. This removed the restriction on a person marrying a parent of their former spouse or a former spouse of their child.

(b) Not under the age of 16 (section 11(a)(ii))

A marriage is void if either party is under the age of 16 (s 11(a)(ii)). The consent of the following people is needed if a party to the marriage is aged 16 or 17: each parent with parental responsibility for the child and each guardian (if any) of the child; a special guardian; any person with whom the child lives (or is to live) under a child arrangements order if not the parent or guardian; a local authority if the child is in care (in addition to parental and guardian consent); if a child arrangements order regulating the child's living arrangements is no longer in force but was in force immediately before the child attained the age of 16, the consent of the person(s) with whom the child lived under that order; and, if the child is a ward of court, the consent of the court (s 3 MA 1949). Consent can be dispensed with if a person whose consent is needed is absent, inaccessible or suffers from a disability. If a person refuses to give consent, the court can give consent on their behalf, but such applications are rare.

(c) Not intermarried in disregard of certain requirements as to the formation of marriage (section 11(a)(iii))

A marriage will be void if the parties have disregarded certain preliminary formalities before the marriage took place (see 2.3 below).

(d) Not already married (section 11(b))

A marriage will be void if, at the time it was contracted, either party was already married. The parties may also have committed the crime of bigamy. Where a spouse has disappeared or is thought to be dead, the other spouse can apply for a decree of presumption of death and dissolution of marriage (see 6.10). If this is granted, it prevents the second marriage being bigamous, even if the first spouse subsequently reappears.

2.3 Preliminary formalities

In addition to having capacity to marry, the parties must satisfy certain preliminary formalities before the marriage can take place as set out in the Marriage Act 1949 (MA 1949). The purpose of these rules is to establish that the required consents have been given and that there are no lawful impediments to the marriage taking place. The marriage ceremony must also comply with certain formalities (see 2.4 below), and the marriage must be registered. Two types of preliminary formalities exist depending on whether it is a non-Church of England marriage or a Church of England marriage.

(a) Preliminaries for non-Church of England marriages

Non-Church of England marriages can be solemnised only after the grant of a superintendent registrar's certificate or a Registrar General's licence.

(b) Preliminaries for Church of England marriages

Only an opposite sex couple may be married in a Church of England marriage. A Church of England marriage can be solemnised after the publication of banns or after the grant of a superintendent registrar's certificate or a Registrar General's licence.

2.4 The marriage ceremony

(a) Formalities

The marriage ceremony must also comply with certain formalities, which differ depending on whether the marriage is civil or religious.

(i) Civil marriages

After complying with the preliminary formalities (see 2.3(a) above), the marriage must be solemnised in a register office or other 'approved premises' or, in special cases, in the place where a person is housebound or detained. Under the Marriage Act 1949 (MA 1949), 'approved premises' are premises which have been approved for civil marriage by local authorities in accordance with regulations laid down by the Secretary of State (such as hotels, stately homes and historic buildings). A civil marriage is public and secular, but it may be followed by a religious ceremony in a church or chapel (s 46). However, it is the civil ceremony which is legally binding; not the religious ceremony. At the civil ceremony the parties must declare that there are no lawful impediments to the marriage and exchange vows. The ceremony must take place in the presence of at least two witnesses. Some registrars remind the parties of the solemn nature of the vows that they are making.

(ii) Church of England marriages

After complying with the preliminary formalities (see 2.3(b) above), the marriage is solemnised by a clergyman according to the rites of the Church of England in the presence of at least two witnesses.

(iii) Quaker and Jewish marriages

A Quaker or Jewish marriage can be solemnised after complying with the preliminary formalities for a civil marriage (see 2.3(a) above). Such marriages are celebrated according to their own religious requirements; and they do not need to be conducted in a register office or other approved premises, or in public, or before an authorised person. Special rules exist for the registration of Quaker and Jewish marriages.

(iv) Other religious marriages

Other religious marriages can be solemnised after complying with the preliminary formalities for a civil marriage (see 2.3(a) above). The superintendent registrar's certificate or Registrar General's licence will state where the ceremony is to be held, which will usually be in a 'registered building' in the district in which one of the parties resides. A 'registered building' is a building registered by the Registrar General as 'a place of meeting for religious worship' (s 41 MA 1949). Some Sikh and Hindu temples and Muslim mosques are registered buildings. If a marriage takes place in a building which is not registered for the purpose of marriage, the marriage may be void or there may be no marriage at all. The marriage must be attended by either a registrar or an 'authorised person', such as a religious cleric. It must take place in the presence of at least two witnesses and be open to the public. The marriage ceremony can take any form, provided that during the ceremony the required declarations are made.

(b)   Failure to comply with the formality requirements

A failure to comply with the required formalities may render a marriage void or the court may decide that there was no marriage at all (see (i) below). In certain circumstances, however, the court may hold that the marriage is valid under the common law presumption of marriage arising as a result of long cohabitation (see (ii) below).

(i) A void marriage or a non-marriage?

A failure to comply with the formality requirements may result in the court holding that the marriage is void or that there is no marriage at all (in other words, that there is a non-marriage). The distinction is important because if the court decides that there is a non-marriage then the parties are not entitled to a decree of nullity (see 2.5 below) and they have no right to apply for property and finance orders under Part II of the Matrimonial Causes Act 1973 (MCA 1973) (see Chapter 7).

In order to assist courts in determining whether there is a void marriage or a non marriage, Bodey J in *Hudson v Leigh (Status of Non-Marriage)* [2009] EWHC 1306 (Fam) provided some guidance in the form of a list of factors to be taken into account.

▶ *Hudson v Leigh (Status of Non-Marriage)* **[2009] EWHC 1306 (Fam)**

The parties went through a religious ceremony in South Africa with the intention of having a formal civil marriage on their return to England. However, the relationship broke up and the civil marriage did not take place. Bodey J held that the ceremony was void under South African law due to a failure to comply with the required formalities (they had exchanged rings but they had failed to provide identity documents and to declare whether there were any impediments to the marriage; and they had not signed the marriage register). Bodey J then had to consider whether, under English law, the marriage was a void marriage or a non-marriage. Mr Leigh argued that there was a non-marriage. Miss Hudson argued that it was a void marriage and applied for a decree of divorce (on the ground of unreasonable behaviour) or, in the alternative, a decree of nullity (on the ground of lack of appropriate formalities).

Bodey J, holding that questionable ceremonies should be addressed on a case-by-case basis, laid down the following non-exhaustive list of factors as guidance for the courts when deciding whether a marriage is a void marriage or a non-marriage:

(a) whether the ceremony or event set out or purported to be a lawful marriage;
(b) whether it bore all or enough of the hallmarks of marriage;
(c) whether the three key participants (especially the officiating official) believed, intended and understood the ceremony as giving rise to the status of lawful marriage; and
(d) the reasonable perceptions, understandings and beliefs of those in attendance.

Bodey J held that this was not a case involving a lack of consent (for the purposes of s 12(1)(c) MCA 1973), but one where the parties and the officiating minister never intended the ceremony to effect a lawful marriage. He concluded that the religious ceremony in South Africa was therefore a non-marriage under English law as, at the time that it took place, neither the parties nor the officiating minister who conducted the ceremony had intended or believed it to be legally binding. He consequently dismissed Miss Hudson's petition and made a declaration that there never was a marriage.

Bodey J's list of factors in *Hudson v Leigh* was approved by the Court of Appeal in *Leigh v Hudson* [2009] EWCA Civ 1442. Whether a marriage is a void marriage or a non-marriage depends on the facts of the case. The following cases provide examples.

▶ *Gereis v Yagoub* **[1997] 1 FLR 854**

A marriage conducted by a priest who was not authorised to perform the ceremony, and which took place in a Coptic Orthodox Church not licensed for marriages, was held to be a void marriage, and not a non-marriage. The marriage ceremony had all of the hallmarks of an ordinary Christian marriage, and the marriage had been treated as a subsisting marriage by all those who had attended.

▶ *Ghandi v Patel* **[2002] 1 FLR 603**

A Hindu ceremony of marriage conducted by a Brahmin priest in a London restaurant was held to be a non-marriage, and not a void marriage.

▶ *Alfonso-Brown v Milwood* **[2006] 2 FLR 265**

A ceremony of marriage conducted in Ghana was held to be a non-marriage, and not a void marriage. The parties lacked the necessary intent at the time of the ceremony, both having believed it was an engagement ceremony.

▶ *B v B* **[2008] 1 FLR 813**

A ceremony of marriage conducted in a hot air balloon in California was held to be a void marriage, and not a non-marriage. The parties had not obtained the necessary licence before the ceremony, but they had fulfilled the local requirements as to capacity.

▶ *El Gamal v Al Maktoum* **[2011] EWHC B27 (Fam)**

A ceremony of marriage conducted in a flat in London was held to be a non-marriage, and not a void marriage. The purported marriage ceremony had taken place in secret and with no written contract, and as such failed to comply with the formal requirements.

▶ *Dukali v Lamrani (Attorney General Intervening)* **[2012] EWHC 1748 (Fam)**

A ceremony of marriage conducted in the Moroccan Consulate in London was held to be a non-marriage, and not a void marriage. The Moroccan Consulate was not in fact registered for marriages, and as such the parties had failed to comply with the formal requirements.

▶ *Sharbatly v Shagroon* **[2012] EWCA Civ 1507**

An Islamic ceremony of marriage conducted in a hotel was held to be a non-marriage, and not a void marriage. No attempt had been made to comply with the formal requirements, or to supplement the hotel ceremony with a civil ceremony which complied with English law.

▶ *Galloway v Goldstein* **[2012] EWHC 60 (Fam)**

A ceremony of marriage conducted in a hotel in England was held to be a non-marriage, and not a void marriage. The parties had lawfully married in the USA a month earlier and must have known that the marriage ceremony in England could not confer the status of marriage.

▶ *Asaad v Kurter* **[2013] EWHC 3852 (Fam)**

A ceremony of marriage conducted in Syria was held to be a void marriage, and not a non-marriage. Although the parties had not complied with all of the formal requirements of Syrian law, it was intended by both parties to be a marriage ceremony.

(ii) The common law presumption of marriage from long cohabitation

A marriage which fails to comply with the required formalities may nonetheless be upheld under the common law presumption of marriage from long cohabitation. The following cases provide examples.

> ▶ *Chief Adjudication Officer v Bath* **[2000] 1 FLR 8**
>
> A ceremony of marriage conducted in a Sikh temple which was not registered for marriages had failed to comply with the required formalities. However, the Court of Appeal upheld the marriage under the common law presumption of marriage from long cohabitation. The couple had lived together as husband and wife for 37 years..
>
> ▶ *Pazpena de Vire v Pazpena de Vire* **[2001] 1 FLR 460**
>
> The parties had purportedly married by proxy in Uruguay, but there was no direct evidence that a marriage had taken place. The couple then moved to England where they lived as husband and wife for 35 years. The wife applied for a divorce or, in the alternative, a decree of nullity on the ground that the marriage had been defective. The High Court held that there was a valid marriage under the common law presumption of long cohabitation.

In the following two cases, however, the period of cohabitation was not long enough for the marriage to be upheld under the common law presumption of marriage from long cohabitation: *A v H (Registrar General for England and Wales and another intervening)* [2010] 1 FLR 1 (cohabitation of a year and a half); and *Al-Saedy v Musawi (Presumption of Marriage)* [2010] EWHC 3293 (cohabitation for undefined periods from time to time).

2.5 Void and voidable marriages – the law of nullity

The law of nullity (or annulment) is laid down in Part I of the Matrimonial Causes Act 1973 (MCA 1973). This is the same Act of Parliament which governs divorce and judicial separation (see Chapter 6). It is, however, important to understand the difference between divorce and nullity. Divorce terminates a valid marriage. Annulment, on the other hand, is based on a failure to comply with the capacity or formality requirements for marriage and, if an application for annulment is successful, the marriage is treated as if it never existed. Petitions for nullity are rare: only 345 nullity petitions were filed in 2011 (Ministry of Justice, *Judicial and Court Statistics*, 28 June 2012). However, one advantage of nullity is that, unlike divorce, it can be applied for in the first year of marriage. Annulment can be a useful alternative for people who have a religious or moral objection to divorce; and it has proved to be particularly useful for victims of forced marriage (see 2.6 below).

(a) Procedure for an annulment

Under the Family Procedure Rules 2010 (FPR 2010), the procedure for an undefended annulment is the same as that for an undefended divorce (see 6.6). There is no need for either party to attend court. If the annulment is defended, however, both parties will have to attend court and will usually have to give evidence on oath. To apply for an annulment, the petitioner must complete and submit a nullity petition to the court, which includes the same essential information as a petition for divorce. It will be necessary to pay a fee. Like divorce, the process of annulment involves two stages:

decree nisi followed by decree absolute. It is the decree absolute, and not the decree nisi, which annuls the marriage. On or after the grant of a decree of nullity, the court has jurisdiction under Part II of the MCA 1973 to make orders relating to property and finance in the same way as it has on divorce (see Chapter 7).

A marriage can be annulled on the ground that it is a void marriage (see (b) below) or a voidable marriage (see (c) below).

(b) A void marriage

A void marriage, unlike a voidable marriage, is void *ab initio* (right from the beginning). A decree of nullity is not technically necessary in such cases. However, it is useful because it creates certainty and it gives the court jurisdiction to make finance and property orders under Part II of the MCA 1973 (see Chapter 7). Thus, for example, a third party may bring nullity proceedings in respect of a void marriage in order to gain inheritance rights. A void marriage is not the same as a 'non-marriage' (see 2.4 above).

A marriage is void on the grounds given below.

Section 11 of the Matrimonial Causes Act 1973

A marriage celebrated after 31st July 1971 shall be void on the following grounds only, that is to say –

(a) that it is not a valid marriage under the provisions of the Marriage Acts 1949 to 1986, that is to say where –
  (i) the parties are within the prohibited degrees of relationship;
  (ii) either party is under the age of sixteen; or
  (iii) the parties have intermarried in disregard of certain requirements as to the formation of marriage;
(b) that at the time of the marriage either party was already lawfully married;
(c) repealed;
(d) in the case of a polygamous marriage entered into outside England and Wales, that either party was at the time of the marriage domiciled in England and Wales.

These grounds were considered in 2.2 above. For the purposes of section 11(a)(iii) of the MCA 1973, not every breach of the formality requirements will invalidate a marriage (see 2.4 above). There are no 'bars' (statutory defences) for void marriages as there are for voidable marriages (see 2.5(c) below).

(c) A voidable marriage

A voidable marriage is a marriage that is valid and subsisting until it is annulled by the grant of a decree of nullity (s 16 MCA 1973). A marriage is voidable on the grounds given below.

Section 12 of the Matrimonial Causes Act 1973

(1) A marriage celebrated after 31st July 1971 shall be voidable on the following grounds only, that is to say –
(a) that the marriage has not been consummated owing to the incapacity of either party to consummate it;
(b) that the marriage has not been consummated owing to the wilful refusal of the respondent to consummate it;
(c) that either party to the marriage did not validly consent to it, whether in consequence of duress, mistake, unsoundness of mind or otherwise;
(d) that at the time of the marriage either party, though capable of giving a valid consent, was suffering (whether continuously or intermittently) from mental disorder within the meaning of the Mental Health Act 1983, of such a kind or to such an extent as to be unfitted for marriage;
(e) that at the time of the marriage the respondent was suffering from venereal disease in a communicable form;
(f) that at the time of the marriage the respondent was pregnant by some person other than the petitioner;
(g) that an interim gender recognition certificate under the Gender Recognition Act 2004 has, after the time of marriage, been issued to either party to the marriage;
(h) that the respondent is a person whose gender at the time of the marriage had become the acquired gender under the Gender Recognition Act 2004.
(2) Paragraphs (a) and (b) of subsection (1) do not apply to the marriage of a same sex couple.

(i) Non-consummation (sections 12(1)(a) and (b))

Non-consummation does not apply to same sex marriages or civil partnerships. Consummation is the first act of intercourse after marriage. It must be 'ordinary and complete, not partial and imperfect' (Dr Lushington in *D-E v A-G* (1845) 1 Rob Eccl 279). Consummation takes place whether or not a condom is used (*Baxter v Baxter* [1948] AC 274), and whether or not ejaculation takes place (*R v R* [1952] 1 All ER 1194). There are two grounds for non-consummation: incapacity; and wilful refusal.

Incapacity to consummate (section 12(1)(a)) The petition can be based on the petitioner's or the respondent's incapacity to consummate. The incapacity must be permanent and incurable. It includes not just physical incapacity but also 'an invincible repugnance to the respondent due to a psychiatric or sexual aversion' (Karminski LJ in *Singh v Singh* [1971] 2 WLR 963).

Wilful refusal to consummate (section 12(1)(b)) To establish wilful refusal to consummate there must be 'a settled and definite decision come to without just excuse' and the whole history of the marriage must be looked at (Lord Jowitt LC in *Horton v Horton* [1947] 2 All ER 871). Refusal can be express or inferred. Wilful refusal has sometimes arisen in the context of certain religious marriages, for example, where a civil ceremony must be followed by a religious ceremony before the parties are deemed to be married in the eyes of their religion.

Thus, in *Kaur v Singh* [1972] 1 All ER 292, a marriage was arranged between two Sikhs and the civil ceremony took place but the husband refused to arrange the religious ceremony. Consummation was to take place after the religious ceremony.

The wife was granted a decree of nullity on the ground of her husband's wilful refusal to undergo the religious ceremony and, therefore, to consummate the marriage (see also *A v J (Nullity)* [1989] 1 FLR 110). Unlike incapacity to consummate, a petition cannot be brought on the basis of the *petitioner's* refusal to consummate the marriage. Thus, a person who is forced into marriage and refuses to consummate it must instead prove incapacity or lack of consent (see (ii) below).

Probert ([2005] Fam Law 382) has argued that non-consummation as a ground for avoiding a marriage is a legacy of ecclesiastical law and that it should be abolished in order to 'define marriage in a way that is relevant for the twenty-first century'.

(ii) Lack of consent (section 12(1)(c))

A marriage is voidable if either party did not validly consent to the marriage, whether in consequence of duress, mistake, unsoundness of mind or otherwise.

Duress   The test for establishing duress is subjective. In other words, it depends on whether the particular petitioner was under duress and not on whether a reasonable person would objectively believe so. This rule was laid down in the following case.

> ▶ *Hirani v Hirani* (1983) 4 FLR 232
>
> The petitioner, a 19-year-old Hindu woman, entered into a marriage with a man whom she had never met. She had done so because her parents had threatened to throw her out of the family home if she did not go ahead with the ceremony. The Court of Appeal held that the test for duress is subjective. The question to be asked was whether the particular petitioner, taking account of their personal qualities, had submitted to the duress. On the facts, it was held that the petitioner's will had been overborne, with the result that her consent to the marriage had been invalidated. She was therefore entitled to a decree of nullity.

The test for duress laid down in *Hirani v Hirani* is particularly relevant for protecting victims of forced marriage (see 2.6 below). In order to protect such people, very little pressure may be required (see, for example, *P v R (Forced Marriage: Annulment: Procedure)* [2003] 1 FLR 661 and *NS v MI* [2006] EWHC 1646 (Fam)).

Mistake   Two kinds of mistake can negate consent. The first is a mistake as to the other party's identity. The mistake must be in respect of the identity of the other party, and not in respect of their qualities (*Moss v Moss* [1897] P 263). Thus, for example, if one of the parties gives a false name that will be insufficient to negate consent and avoid the marriage (*Puttick v Attorney General* [1979] 3 All ER 463). The second is a mistake as to the nature of the ceremony, such as where a party mistakenly believes that it was an engagement ceremony rather than a marriage ceremony (see *Valier v Valier* (1925) 133 LT 830).

Lack of capacity to consent   Lack of capacity to consent usually arises as a result of a mental disorder or mental illness. However, it may also arise because of coercion in the context of a forced marriage. The test for capacity is whether a person can understand the nature of the marriage contract. In other words, they must be mentally capable of understanding the duties and responsibilities that normally attach to marriage (*per* Singleton LJ in *Re Estate of Park, Deceased, Park v Park* [1954] P 112 and endorsed by Munby J in *Re E (An Alleged Patient); Sheffield City Council v E and S* [2004] EWHC 2808 (Fam)).

The inherent jurisdiction of the High Court (see 8.7) can be invoked to protect a vulnerable adult who lacks the capacity to marry, as the following cases show.

▶ *M v B, A and S (By the Official Solicitor)* **[2006] 1 FLR 117**

The local authority was concerned that the parents of a 23-year-old woman, who suffered from a severe learning disability, were organising an arranged marriage for her in Pakistan. The local authority applied for declarations that the young woman lacked capacity to marry and that it was not in her best interests to leave the UK. Sumner J made the declarations sought. He held that, in appropriate circumstances, the court has jurisdiction to grant an injunction restraining those people responsible for an adult who lacks capacity from entering into a contract of marriage if such an order is required to protect that adult's best interests.

▶ *X City Council v MB, NB and Mab (By His Litigation Friend the Official Solicitor)* **[2006] 2 FLR 968**

A 25-year-old man who, as a result of autism, lacked capacity to marry was given protection by Munby J under the inherent jurisdiction of the High Court. The local authority made the application to prevent him from being taken abroad by his parents to be married in Pakistan.

▶ *Re RS (Forced Marriage Protection Order)* **[2015] EWHC 3534 (Fam)**

RS was a 25-year old man who, as a result of intellectual disability and autism, lacked capacity to marry. The local authority applied for a forced marriage protection order under Part 4A of the Family Law Act 1996 with the intention of averting an anticipated marriage, although it subsequently transpired that a marriage had already taken place in Pakistan. The proceedings were reconstituted and continued under the inherent jurisdiction of the High Court. Hayden J granted a declaration of non-recognition in relation to the marriage.

Otherwise   Section 12(1)(c) of the MCA 1973 refers to a lack of consent through factors other than duress, mistake or unsoundness of mind. This may include drunkenness (*Sullivan v Sullivan* (1812) 2 Hag Con 238), although there is no clear authority on this point. It may also include fraud and misrepresentation if that leads to a mistake as to the identity of the other party or the nature of the ceremony (see above).

(d)   Voidable marriages – statutory bars

Section 13 of the MCA 1973 lays down the following statutory bars to a petition for nullity in the case of a voidable marriage.

(iii) Statutory bars (section 13)

Approbation by the petitioner   The court cannot grant a decree of nullity on any ground in section 12 of the MCA 1973 if the respondent satisfies the court: (i) that the petitioner knew that they could have avoided the marriage but their conduct led the respondent reasonably to believe that they would not seek to do so; *and* (ii) that it would be unjust to the respondent to grant the decree (s 13(1)).

Three-year bar The court cannot grant a nullity decree on ground (c), (d), (e), (f) or (h) of section 12(1) of the MCA 1973 unless proceedings are instituted within three years of the marriage (s 13(2)). However, the court has jurisdiction to grant leave to apply after that period if: (i) it is satisfied that the petitioner has suffered from a mental disorder within the meaning of the Mental Health Act 1983 during that three-year period; and (ii) it considers that it would in all the circumstances be just to grant leave (ss 13(4), (5)). The three-year bar may be waived by the High Court in the exercise of its inherent jurisdiction, for example, in a forced marriage case (see 2.6 below).

Six-month bar A nullity decree cannot be granted on ground (g) of section 12(1) of the MCA 1973 unless proceedings were instituted within six months of the issue of an interim gender recognition certificate (s 13(2A)).

Ignorance A nullity decree cannot be granted on ground (e), (f) or (h) of section 12(1) of the MCA 1973 unless the court is satisfied that the petitioner was ignorant of those facts at the time of the marriage (s 13(3)).

2.6 Forced marriages

(a) Introduction – the problem of forced marriage

A forced marriage is one which is conducted without the valid consent of one or both of the parties and where duress is a factor. It is not the same as an arranged marriage, which is a marriage where the families of both parties take a leading role in choosing a marriage partner, but where the choice of whether or not to accept the arrangement remains with the parties. Forced marriages are sometimes used for immigration purposes. This is because, by marriage, a person can acquire British citizenship and gain entry into the UK. Forcing someone to marry involves a wide range of behaviour, such as emotional threats, imprisonment, violence, abduction and blackmail.

The courts are not opposed to arranged marriages, but they do not tolerate forced marriages. In *NS v MI* [2006] EWHC 1646 (Fam), Munby J said that, while arranged marriages were to be respected and supported, forced marriages were utterly unacceptable, and that 'the court must not hesitate to use every weapon in its protective arsenal if faced with what is, or appears to be, a case of forced marriage'. In *Re K; A Local Authority v N and Others* [2005] EWHC 2956 (Fam), Munby J described forced marriage as 'a gross abuse of human rights' and as 'a form of domestic violence that dehumanises people by denying them their right to choose how to live their lives'. It was, he said, 'an appalling practice'. In *Bedfordshire Police Constabulary v RU* [2013] EWHC 2350 (Fam), Holman J said that forced marriages 'are a scourge, which degrade the victim and can create untold human misery', and that the 'scope for psychological or other pressures in this field is obvious and enormous'.

The problem of forced marriages has come to the fore in recent years. To help deal with the problem the Forced Marriage Unit, a joint initiative of the Foreign & Commonwealth Office and the Home Office, provides trained professionals who can offer confidential advice and assistance to actual and potential victims and to other people, such as friends or relatives and also professionals working with actual or potential victims. The Forced Marriage Unit is also responsible for developing Government policy on forced marriages. The Unit dealt with 1,220 possible cases of forced marriage in 2015. However, the true number is likely to be far higher. Most cases involve young women. Some cases involve young children. Figures published by the Forced Marriage Unit in 2015 show a decrease in the number of people coming forward to seek protection, which continues the downward trend since 2009. In 80 per cent of cases the victims were female. In 27 per cent of cases the victims were aged 17 and below.

Protection for actual and potential victims of forced marriage is available in family law, tort law and criminal law.

(b) Protection in family law

The following family law 'remedies' are available for victims of forced marriage: (i) annulment; (ii) protection under the inherent jurisdiction of the High Court; and (iii) protection in wardship. In addition, since November 2008 it has been possible to apply for a forced marriage protection order in order to protect an actual or potential victim of forced marriage.

(i) Annulment

A person who enters into a forced marriage can have the marriage annulled on the ground of lack of consent to the marriage due to duress (see 2.5 above). Below is an example of the use of annulment in the case of a forced marriage.

▶ *P v R (Forced Marriage: Annulment)* [2003] 1 FLR 661

The petitioner, a 20-year-old woman, had been forced to enter into a marriage in Pakistan. Her brother threatened her with violence and she believed that, if she did not go ahead with the marriage, she would be unable to return to England. Her parents also told her that it would bring shame and disgrace on the family if she did not go ahead with the marriage, and during the ceremony her mother forced her to nod by pushing her head forward three times. She signed the marriage certificate out of fear. On her return to England, she petitioned for a decree of nullity. Coleridge J held that she had not validly consented to the marriage as her consent had been invalidated by force, both physical and emotional.

Where an applicant for nullity is reluctant to give oral evidence (if needed) as their family is present, the court will do whatever it can to afford that person protection (*per* Munby J in *NS v MI* [2006] EWHC 1646 (Fam)). A female Muslim applicant will be required to remove her veil when giving evidence, but appropriate arrangements may be made (such as screens and a female judge) to enable her to do so without breaching her religious principles (*per* Macur J in *Re S (Practice: Muslim Women Giving Evidence)* [2007] 2 FLR 461).

(ii) The inherent jurisdiction

The High Court's inherent jurisdiction (see 8.7) can be used to protect a victim of a forced marriage. The flexibility of the inherent jurisdiction is shown in the following case where it was exercised in respect of a forced marriage which had taken place overseas but where a statutory 'remedy' was not available in England and Wales.

> ▶ *B v I (Forced Marriage)* [2010] 1 FLR 1721
>
> A 16-year-old girl travelled from England to Bangladesh on what she thought was a family holiday. Whilst in Bangladesh, she was confined to a bedroom and a ceremony took place, after which her 18-year-old cousin entered the room and signed a document. She believed that the ceremony was merely a betrothal, but on her return to England she discovered that it had been one of marriage. She issued an originating summons under the inherent jurisdiction of the High Court as the three-year period within which she could petition for a decree of nullity on the basis of lack of consent had passed.
>
> Baron J held that, although section 58 of the Family Law Act 1986 prohibited the making of a declaration that the marriage was void at its inception, the court could make a declaration under its inherent jurisdiction that the ceremony in Bangladesh had not given rise to a marriage capable of recognition in England and Wales. He said it was eminently fair to provide such a declaration in the case of a forced marriage, and that the inherent jurisdiction was a flexible tool that enabled the court to provided justice for parties where statute had failed to do so.

The inherent jurisdiction of the High Court can also be invoked to protect a potential victim of a forced marriage, as the following case shows.

> ▶ *Re SA (Vulnerable Adult With Capacity: Marriage)* [2006] 1 FLR 867
>
> The local authority feared that a 17-year-old girl (who was profoundly deaf, unable to speak and had limited intellectual functioning) might be taken by her family to Pakistan for the purposes of an arranged, and potentially forced, marriage. Munby J made an order under the inherent jurisdiction of the High Court requiring that the girl be properly informed, in a manner she would understand, about any marriage prior to entering into it.

(iii) The wardship jurisdiction

This jurisdiction, which is part of the High Court's inherent jurisdiction, can be invoked in the case of a victim aged under 18. In exceptional circumstances it can even be invoked where the victim is not living in the UK, as the following two cases show.

> ▶ *Re B; RB v FB* [2008] 2 FLR 1624
>
> A 15-year-old girl who was living in Pakistan was made a ward of court on the basis that she was a British national who was in desperate need of help. The girl had approached the British High Commission in Islamabad for help after learning that it had been arranged for

her to marry an older man. Hogg J held that, in the very dire and exceptional circumstances of the case, the tentacles of the court should stretch towards Pakistan to rescue the girl from the situation she had found herself in, even though she had no connection with the UK other than the fact that her late father was British.

▶ *SB v RB* **[2008] 2 FLR 1588**

An 11-year-old girl, who had been forced to marry a 20-year-old man in Bangladesh, was made a ward of court. With the assistance of the Forced Marriage Unit, she was returned to the UK and placed with an uncle and an aunt. The marriage was subsequently declared void.

(c)   Forced marriage protection orders

Under Part 4A of the Family Law Act 1996 (FLA 1996) the court has jurisdiction to make a forced marriage protection order. These provisions were introduced with the aim of providing greater protection for actual and potential victims of forced marriage, and to send out a strong message that forced marriages are unacceptable and will not be tolerated. The provisions are modelled on the remedies available to victims of domestic violence in Part IV of the FLA 1996 (see Chapter 5). The procedural rules governing applications are laid down in Part 11 of the Family Procedure Rules 2010 (FPR 2010). *The Right to Choose: Multi-Agency Statutory Guidance* (available at www.gov.uk) sets out the responsibilities of the various agencies in England and Wales which deal with forced marriage cases; and Part 2 of the *Guidance* was issued as statutory guidance under section 63Q(1) of Part 4A of the FLA 1996.

The number of applications and orders made for forced marriage protection orders is very small. According to *Family Court Statistics Quarterly* (Ministry of Justice, March 2016), a total of 70 applications for a forced marriage protection order were made between October and December 2015.

A forced marriage protection order under Part 4A of the FLA 1996 is an order which provides legal protection to an actual or potential victim of a forced marriage or an attempted forced marriage (s 63A(1)). A forced marriage is a marriage where a person has not given full and free consent (s 63A(4)). 'Force' is defined to include not only physical coercion but also 'threats or other psychological means' (s 63A(6)).

The court has wide powers to include in a forced marriage protection order such prohibitions, restrictions or requirements or other such terms as are considered appropriate; and the terms of the order can relate to conduct outside England and Wales as well as (or instead of) conduct within England and Wales (ss 63B(1), (2)). For example, a forced marriage protection order could prohibit a parent from taking an unwilling child outside England and Wales for the purpose of marriage; or prohibit a family from contacting or molesting a victim who has taken refuge away from the family. To prevent a forced marriage occurring the court could, for example, require a passport to be handed over or order someone to reveal the whereabouts of an actual or potential victim.

(i) Orders without notice

The court can make a forced marriage protection order without notice (s 63D). In other words, it can make an order where it is just and convenient to do so even though the respondent has not been given notice of proceedings.

(ii) Undertakings

In an appropriate case, the court can accept an undertaking from a respondent instead of making a forced marriage protection order (s 63E).

(iii) Applicants

An application for a forced marriage protection order can be made by: a person who needs protection; a relevant third party (as specified by order of the Lord Chancellor); or any other person who has leave of the court (s 63C(2)). Local authorities have been designated as a relevant third party and can therefore apply without needing the court's permission. The court also has jurisdiction to make a forced marriage protection order of its own motion, in other words where no application has been made for one (s 63C(1)).

(iv) Factors governing the exercise of discretion to make the order

When deciding whether to exercise its powers to make a forced marriage protection order and, if so, in what manner, the court must consider all the circumstances of the case including the need to secure the health, safety and well-being of the victim (s 63A(2)). In ascertaining the victim's well-being the court must, in particular, have such regard to the victim's wishes and feelings (so far as they are readily ascertainable) as the court considers appropriate in the light of the victim's age and understanding (s 63A(3)). In *A Chief Constable v A* [2010] EWHC 3282 (Fam), Wall P drew attention to the pressures which may be placed upon victims, and recommended that they be seen by an appropriate expert so that a realistic assessment can to be made pursuant to section 63A(2). He also considered it desirable that victims should be separately and independently represented.

(v) Duration, discharge and variation

The duration of a forced marriage protection order can be for a specified period or until varied or discharged (s 63F). The court can vary or discharge an order (s 63G).

Breach If a respondent breaches a forced marriage protection order, it is a criminal offence (s 63CA(1)). A person must know about the order to be convicted (s 63CA(2)). A person who has breached an order can be charged under the criminal jurisdiction or dealt with by way of contempt of court, but not both (ss 63CA(3), (4)). A person found guilty of an offence under section 63CA(1) of the FLA 1996 can be fined or imprisoned for up to five years (s 63CA(5)).

(vi) Human rights and applications for a forced marriage protection order

The issue of human rights and applications for a forced marriage protection order was considered in *A Chief Constable and Another v YK and Others* [2011] 1 FLR 1493, which raised the issue of how far it is possible to achieve a fair hearing when some of the evidence cannot be safely revealed as any disclosure is likely to identify an informant and place them at risk. Wall P said that he was 'tempted to the view' that Article 6 of the European Convention on Human Rights (ECHR) (the right to a fair trial) was not engaged in an application for a forced marriage protection order, but that it was likely to be relevant to an application to set aside a forced marriage protection order.

(d)   Protection under the law of tort

Forcing someone to marry may constitute the tort of trespass to the person, false imprisonment or harassment. This gives a victim a right to obtain damages and/or injunctive relief.

(e)   Protection under the criminal law

The police take forced marriages very seriously and have policy guidelines for dealing with them. The Anti-social Behaviour, Crime and Policing Act 2014 made it an offence to force a person to marry against their will.

Section 121 of the Anti-social Behaviour, Crime and Policing Act 2014

1. A person commits an offence under the law of England and Wales if he or she –

    (a) uses violence, threats or any other form of coercion for the purpose of causing another person to enter into a marriage, and
    (b) believes, or ought reasonably to believe, that the conduct may cause the other person to enter into the marriage without free and full consent.

2. In relation to a victim who lacks capacity to consent to marriage, the offence under subsection (1) is capable of being committed by any conduct carried out for the purpose of causing the victim to enter into a marriage (whether or not the conduct amounts to violence, threats or any other form [of] coercion).

3. A person commits an offence under the law of England and Wales if he or she –

    (a) practises any form of deception with the intention of causing another person to leave the United Kingdom, and
    (b) intends the other person to be subjected to conduct outside the United Kingdom that is an offence under subsection (1) or would be an offence under that subsection if the victim were in England or Wales.

It is irrelevant whether the conduct is directed at the victim of the offence or another person (s 121(6)). A person found guilty of an offence under sections 121(1) or 121(3) of the Act can be fined or imprisoned for up to seven years (s 121(9)).

2.7   Transsexuals and marriage

Transsexualism is a medically recognised gender identity condition (gender dysphoria). People with the condition may opt to have gender reassignment, which involves hormonal treatment and, in some cases, surgery. These treatments are available on the National Health Service. With the recognition of transsexualism as a genuine medical problem and advances in medical science, the law has had to grapple with the issue of what the legal effects should be of acquiring a reassigned sex. One question that arose, before changes were made to the law, was whether a transsexual person who had undergone gender reassignment could enter into a valid marriage with a person of the transsexual's pre-reassignment sex. The starting point in the development of the law was the case of *Corbett v Corbett*.

▶ *Corbett v Corbett (Otherwise Ashley)* [1970] 2 WLR 1306

The petitioner, a man, petitioned for a decree of nullity on the ground that his marriage was void as the respondent was male. The respondent had been born male but had undergone gender reassignment surgery and hormone treatment, and had lived as a woman. Ormrod J, granting the decree of nullity, held that the marriage was void because both parties were male. He held that a person's biological sex was fixed at birth and could not be altered by a sex change operation. The respondent was male by chromosomal, gonadal and genital criteria, and it was irrelevant that the respondent considered himself philosophically, psychologically and socially to be a woman.

The test laid down in *Corbett* was applied in subsequent cases and, as a result, transsexuals began to take their cases to the European Court of Human Rights (ECtHR). They claimed that they were being discriminated against because the restricted biological approach to gender was being applied to, and was adversely affecting, other areas of their lives.

(a) Transsexuals and human rights

The biological test laid down in *Corbett* was found to be incompatible with the European Convention on Human Rights (ECHR) in *Goodwin v UK* [2002] 2 FLR 487. Subsequent to the decision in *Goodwin*, the House of Lords in *Bellinger v Bellinger* [2003] 1 FLR 1043 issued a declaration under section 4 of the Human Rights Act 1998 that section 11(c) of the Matrimonial Causes Act 1973 (MCA 1973) was incompatible with Articles 8 (the right to family life) and 12 (the right to marry) of the ECHR. After the decisions in *Goodwin* and *Bellinger*, the Government was put under pressure to reform the law in order to improve the legal position of transsexuals. As a result, the Gender Recognition Act 2004 (GRA 2004) was enacted.

(b) The Gender Recognition Act 2004

The GRA 2004 gives legal recognition in their acquired gender to transsexuals who can show that they have taken decisive steps towards living fully and permanently in their acquired gender. Under the Act, an adult transsexual person can obtain a gender recognition certificate issued by the Gender Recognition Panel (s 1). If a full gender recognition certificate is issued, that person's gender becomes for all purposes the acquired gender (s 9). The practical effect of the certificate is to provide transsexual people with legal recognition in their acquired gender. Thus, they are entitled to a new birth certificate reflecting the acquired gender; and they can lawfully enter into a valid marriage or civil partnership in their acquired gender.

Before issuing a certificate, the Gender Recognition Panel must be satisfied that the applicant: has, or has had, gender dysphoria; has lived in the acquired gender throughout the preceding two years; and intends to continue to live in the acquired gender until death (s 2). A full gender recognition certificate can be granted to an applicant who is married provided that the marriage is legally recognised in England and Wales (s 3A(3)) and their spouse consents (s 3B(8)). Only an interim gender recognition certificate can be granted to an applicant who is in a civil partnership; and the applicant will have to end their civil partnership before they can be granted a full certificate. However, if the civil partnership ends or their civil partner dies within six months of the issue of an interim certificate, the applicant can seek a full certificate (s 5A). The reason why the applicant has to end their civil partnership is because UK law does not allow civil partnerships for opposite sex couples, and so the action of one person legally acquiring a different gender would effectively convert their marriage into an unlawful opposite sex civil partnership.

(i) Parenthood

Although a full certificate results in the person's gender becoming for all purposes the acquired gender, that person retains their original status as the father or mother of a child (s 12). This provision ensures the continuity of parental rights and responsibilities.

(ii) Annulling a marriage or civil partnership to a transsexual party

A party to a marriage can petition for a decree of nullity under the MCA 1973 on the ground that it is voidable as one of the parties is seeking a certificate from the Gender Recognition Panel (see 2.5 above); or on the ground that the petitioner married a transsexual person in ignorance of that fact (s 12(1)(h)). Proceedings must be instituted within three years of the marriage, and the petitioner must have been ignorant of the facts at the time of marriage (ss 13(2), 13(3)). The same rules apply to the annulment of a civil partnership under the Civil Partnership Act 2004.

2.8 Recognition of an overseas marriage

A marriage contracted overseas (in other words, outside the jurisdiction of the UK) can be recognised as valid in England and Wales under the Family Law Act 1986 (FLA 1986) provided that: each of the parties has the capacity to marry according to their place of domicile; and the formalities required by the law of the place where the marriage was celebrated were complied with. An overseas marriage celebrated by local custom may be recognised. For example, in *McCabe v McCabe* [1994] 1 FLR 410 a marriage which took place in Ghana, involving a bottle of whisky and a sum of money, was upheld as valid. Special rules apply in certain cases, for example, where a party is serving in HM Forces.

In the following case an overseas marriage was not recognised as valid in England and Wales under the FLA 1986.

> ▶ *City of Westminster v IC (By His Litigation Friend the Official Solicitor) and KC and NNC* [2008] 2 FLR 267
>
> An arranged marriage between a severely autistic man and a woman in Bangladesh, which had taken place over the telephone, was held to be invalid even though it was agreed by all of the parties that the marriage was valid under Shariah law. The Court of Appeal refused to recognise the marriage as being valid under English law, as both parties must have capacity to enter into a marriage according to the law of their respective domiciles. The man lacked capacity, due to his disability, and he was unable to give valid consent to the marriage.

(See also *Hudson v Leigh* [2009] 2 FLR 1129, where Bodey J made a declaration that a 'marriage' conducted in South Africa did not create a valid marriage because the formal requirements for a valid marriage had not been satisfied.)

A same sex marriage contracted overseas, and which was entered into legally, can be recognised as valid by the courts in England and Wales (s 10 Marriage (Same Sex Couples) Act 2013).

2.9 The legal consequences of marriage

On marriage, the parties acquire a legal status from which various rights, obligations and privileges flow.

(a) Separate legal personalities

Each spouse has a separate legal personality. This means that each party to a marriage can own property solely (or jointly) and can bring proceedings in tort and contract separately against each other or against third parties (Law Reform (Married Women and Tortfeasors) Act 1935; s 1 Law Reform (Husband and Wife) Act 1962). They can also enter into contracts with each other. As they have separate legal personalities, they can make unilateral decisions about their own medical treatment. This includes the right of a wife to abort a child born of the marriage. Thus, in *Paton v British Pregnancy Advisory Service Trustees* [1979] QB 276, the husband failed in his application for an injunction to prohibit the defendant from carrying out an abortion on his wife.

(b) Financial obligations

Parties to a marriage have a mutual duty to maintain each other financially during the subsistence of their marriage (and in some circumstances after it has been dissolved). During a marriage, one spouse can apply for a financial provision order from the family court against the other spouse if they fail to provide reasonable maintenance. In practice, however, applications are extremely rare as a divorce is now easier to obtain and attracts little social stigma.

(i) Periodical payments and lump sum orders

Under the Domestic Proceedings and Magistrates' Courts Act 1978, the court has jurisdiction to make periodical payments and lump sum orders on the application of a spouse where the other spouse has failed to provide reasonable maintenance or has failed to provide reasonable maintenance for any child of the family; or has behaved in such a way that the applicant spouse cannot reasonably be expected to live with the respondent; or has deserted the applicant (s 1). However, these powers are rarely invoked for two reasons. One is that it is rare today for a spouse to apply for a court order *during* a marriage; and the other is that most child maintenance cases are now dealt with outside the court system (see Chapter 12). The only situation in which an application might perhaps be made is where the parties to a marriage are unable to divorce, for example, for religious reasons.

(ii) Private agreements about family finances

Married couples can enter into private agreements about their family finances, such as an agreement about maintenance for a spouse who is undertaking unpaid work in the family home. However, such an agreement cannot be conclusive as the court has the power to vary or revoke the terms of such an agreement and can insert new terms. Private maintenance agreements are not prohibited by the child support legislation, but any provision in an agreement restricting the right of a person to apply for child maintenance, or to apply to the court, is void (for pre-marital and post-marital agreements in the context of divorce, see 7.9).

(iii) Financial orders to secure payments relating to property subject to an occupation order

Under the Family Law Act 1996 (FLA 1996), the court has jurisdiction to make an order requiring the payment of rent, a mortgage and outgoings in respect of a property where an occupation order is made (see Chapter 5).

(iv) Maintenance pending suit

Under the Matrimonial Causes Act 1973 (MCA 1973), the court has jurisdiction to make an order for maintenance pending suit prior to divorce, nullity or judicial separation (see Chapter 7).

(c) Property rights

As each party to a marriage has a separate legal personality, each party may own property solely or jointly. During a marriage, the rules governing property ownership are the same as those which apply to other people, but with the exception of some special statutory provisions which apply only to spouses (see 4.2). The position is different, however, on divorce (see Chapter 7). Married people, unlike cohabitants, also enjoy statutory rights of occupation of the family home under section 30 of Part IV of the FLA 1996 (see 4.2).

(i) Property rights on death

Each spouse is free to make a will leaving their property to whomsoever they wish. On intestacy (where there is no will) the surviving spouse succeeds to the estate of the deceased spouse (see 4.12). A surviving spouse can apply under the Inheritance (Provision for Family and Dependants) Act 1975 for reasonable provision from the other party's estate without having to prove dependency or that they were being maintained by the deceased party (see 4.13). Marriage automatically revokes an existing will unless it was made in contemplation of marriage (see 4.12).

(d) Protection against domestic violence and harassment

Spouses (and former spouses) can seek remedies under Part IV of the FLA 1996 and under the Protection from Harassment Act 1997 to protect themselves and their children from violence in the home (see Chapter 5).

(e) Rights on the breakdown of a marriage

On the breakdown of a marriage, a married person can seek a decree of divorce, nullity or judicial separation under Part I of the MCA 1973 (see 2.5 above and Chapter 6). They can also apply to the court under Part II of the MCA 1973 for property and financial orders, including orders in respect of the matrimonial home and in respect of pension entitlement (see Chapter 7).

(f) Children

Parents who are married have automatic parental responsibility for their children (see 9.3) – in other words, they do not need to apply for it. They can apply for a child arrangements order and other orders under the Children Act 1989 (CA 1989) (see Chapter 10). Married people have a duty to provide maintenance for any child of the family. A party to a marriage can apply for financial provision for a child under Schedule 1 to the CA 1989, and they can also seek child support (see Chapter 12).

With respect to adoption, married couples can jointly, and in some circumstances solely, apply to adopt a child. They also have rights in respect of giving consent to, or refusing to give consent to, the adoption of their child (see Chapter 15).

2.10 Same sex marriage

(a) The debate over equal marriage

In March 2012, the UK Government announced proposals to introduce same sex marriage in England and Wales and published a consultation paper (*Equal civil marriage: a consultation*, Government Equalities Office). This was followed, in December 2012, by the publication of the Government's response to the consultation (*Equal marriage: The Government's response*, Government Equalities Office). The Government stated that it proposed to introduce legislation in England and Wales to enable same sex couples to have a *civil* marriage ceremony, and to enable certain religious organisations (except the Church of England or the Church in Wales) to conduct same sex marriage ceremonies if they wished to do so. However, the Government made it clear that no religious organisation or individual minister would be under any legal obligation to perform a same sex marriage ceremony. In addition, as the legislation would not apply to the Church of England or the Church in Wales, it would not be possible for a same sex marriage to be lawfully conducted in those churches unless there were further changes to primary legislation.

The proposals to introduce same sex marriage were not welcomed by some individuals and organisations, in particular faith groups and those who regard marriage as constituting a legal relationship between a man and a woman. However, in February 2013, MPs voted (by a majority of 225) in favour of the introduction of same sex marriage in England and Wales. This led to the Marriage (Same Sex Couples) Act 2013 (MSSCA 2013).

(b)   The Marriage (Same Sex Couples) Act 2013

Under the MSSCA 2013, same sex couples can now marry in England and Wales. The law and procedure which applies to same sex couples largely replicates that which applies to opposite sex couples, although there are some important differences. Thus, an applicant cannot rely on: the consummation grounds to have the marriage annulled (see 2.5 above); adultery as a ground for divorce if their spouse has a sexual relationship with someone else of the same sex (see 6.4); or the common law presumption that a mother's spouse is the father of the child (see 9.2). The Act does permit same sex couples to convert a civil partnership into a marriage (see 2.11 below).

2.11   Civil partnership

(a)   The background

Under the Civil Partnership Act 2004 (CPA 2004), same sex couples in the UK can register their partnership and thereby acquire rights and obligations which are virtually identical to those of married couples. Before the CPA 2004 came into force, various informal registration schemes were available in England and Wales enabling same sex couples to declare their partnership. However, these schemes created no legally recognised status and consequently had no legal effects. Because of the disadvantages and difficulties same sex couples experienced compared with married couples, there was increasing discussion about implementing new laws to permit civil partnership registration. Discussion was fuelled largely by pressure from members of the gay community, in particular the pressure group Stonewall, who argued that they were discriminated against. In fact, the House of Lords, before civil partnerships were introduced, had recognised that same sex cohabitants were discriminated against in the context of succeeding to a tenancy on their partner's death (see *Fitzpatrick v Sterling Housing Association Ltd* [2001] 1 AC 27 and *Ghaidan v Godin-Mendoza* [2004] UKHL 30).

In December 2002 the Government announced that it proposed to introduce a same sex partnership registration scheme, and in June 2003 published *Civil Partnership: A Framework for the Legal Recognition of Same-Sex Couples* in which it set out its proposals for reform.

Civil Partnerships: A Framework for the Legal Recognition of Same-Sex Couples
(Women & Equality Unit, June 2003), para 1.2

Civil partnership registration would be an important equality measure for same-sex couples in England and Wales who are unable to marry each other. It would provide for the legal recognition of same-sex partners and give legitimacy to those in, or wishing to enter into, interdependent same-sex couple relationships which are intended to be permanent. Registration would provide a framework whereby same-sex couples could acknowledge their mutual responsibilities, manage their financial arrangements and achieve recognition as each other's partner. Committed same-sex relationships would be recognised and registered partners would gain rights and responsibilities which would reflect the significance of the roles they play in each other's lives. This in turn would encourage more stable family life.

The Government was keen to emphasise, however, that civil partnership would not undermine the institution of marriage or offend religious beliefs.

Baroness Scotland QC Introducing the Second Reading of the Civil Partnership Bill

[Civil partnership] offers a secular solution to the disadvantages which same-sex couples face in the way they are treated by our laws .... This Bill does not undermine or weaken the importance of marriage and we do not propose to open civil partnership to opposite-sex couples. Civil partnership is aimed at same-sex couples who cannot marry. However, it is important for us to be clear that we continue to support marriage and recognise that it is the surest foundation for opposite-sex couples raising children.

(b) The Civil Partnership Act 2004

Civil Partnerships in England and Wales 2014

These figures were published in October 2015 by the Office for National Statistics (www.ons.gov.uk).

▶ The number of civil partnerships fell by 70 per cent from 5,646 in 2013 to 1,683 in 2014.
▶ The average age at civil partnership was 43.6 years for men and 42.3 years for women.
▶ The number of civil partnership dissolutions granted in England and Wales was 1061.

The CPA 2004 enables same sex couples to register their partnership and in so doing acquire rights, responsibilities and obligations which are virtually identical to those of married couples. If the partnership breaks down, it can be dissolved in a procedure similar to that of divorce. Separation, nullity and presumption of death decrees are also available, and the court has jurisdiction to make finance and property orders on civil partnership breakdown equivalent to those that can be made on divorce. Civil partners have rights and responsibilities in respect of children, and provision is made in respect of child arrangements orders. They also have rights on death.

Thus, the surviving civil partner can register the other partner's death, and they can claim a survivor's pension. Civil partners are entitled to bereavement benefits and compensation for fatal accidents or criminal injuries. They have rights in respect to succession of a tenancy on the death of their partner, and rights of inheritance on intestacy like those of married couples. Civil partners also have the same rights as married couples in respect of taxation.

(i) The difference between civil partnership and marriage

There are very few differences between civil partnership and marriage. As Sir Mark Potter P said in *Wilkinson v Kitzinger* [2006] EWHC 2022 (Fam), the CPA 2004 accorded to same sex couples all the advantages of civil marriage, save in name. The only differences between civil partnership and marriage are that: civil partnership is open only to same sex couples; registration is civil and non-secular; non-consummation and venereal disease are not grounds for annulment; and there is no adultery ground for dissolution.

Capacity to enter into a civil partnership   Section 3(1) of the CPA 2004 provides that in order to be able to register a civil partnership: (a) both parties must be of the same sex; (b) either party must not already be a civil partner or lawfully married; (c) each party must be aged at least 16; and (d) the parties must not be within the prohibited degrees of relationship (as determined by section 3(2) and Part I of Schedule 1 to the Act). Where a party is aged under 18, parental (or guardian) consent is required (s 4(1)).

Preliminary formalities   Local registration services are responsible for registration, a process which is similar to that for civil marriages. As with civil marriages, preliminary formalities must be satisfied.

Registration   Once the preliminaries are satisfied, registration can take place. Registration can take place in a register office or approved premises, which, since December 2010, includes religious premises which have been approved for the purpose of registration (s 6A). However, the registration itself is secular (for example, no hymns or religious readings can form part of the registration). Also, there is no obligation for religious organisations to register civil partnerships if they do not wish to do so (s 6A(3A)).

Registration is completed when each party has signed the civil registration document: at the invitation of, and in the presence of, the civil partnership registrar; and in the presence of each other and two witnesses (s 2(1)). The civil partnership document must then be signed, in the presence of the civil partners and each other, by each of the two witnesses and the civil partnership registrar (s 2(4)). There must be no religious service at the registration (s 2(5)).

Civil partnership agreements   Civil partners can enter into a civil partnership agreement (the equivalent of an engagement to marry). The same rules which apply to engagements also apply to civil partnership agreements (s 4) (see 4.3).

Legal consequences of civil partnership registration   During the civil partnership, and on its breakdown, civil partners have the same legal rights and responsibilities as married couples (see 2.9 above).

Dissolution of a civil partnership   Under sections 37–64 of the CPA 2004, the court has jurisdiction to make dissolution and nullity orders (see below) and separation and presumption of death orders. Both the law and the procedure are exactly the same as those for divorce (see 6.6), except that there is no adultery ground.

Nullity   The court has the power under sections 49–50 of the CPA 2004 to make nullity orders in respect of a void or voidable civil partnership. Both the law and the procedure are exactly the same as the law for nullity of marriage (see 2.5 above), except that non-consummation and venereal disease are not grounds for nullity in the case of a voidable civil partnership.

Application for a financial order on dissolution, nullity and separation   Under section 72 and Schedule 5 of the CPA 2004 the court has jurisdiction, on or after making a dissolution order (or a nullity or separation order), to make finance and property orders. These powers and the case-law principles which apply are exactly the same as those which apply to financial relief on divorce (see Chapter 7). Thus, for example, in *Lawrence v Gallagher* [2012] EWCA Civ 394, in addition to the statutory criteria, the concepts of fairness, needs and sharing were used in the reasoning. The court also has the power to make finance and property orders after an overseas dissolution, annulment or separation order (s 72(4) and Schedule 7), and the rules are the same as those which apply to an overseas divorce (see 6.9).

Recognition of overseas civil partnerships, dissolutions, annulments and separations   Sections 233–238 of the CPA 2004 make provision for the recognition of an overseas civil partnership, and for the recognition of an overseas dissolution, annulment or separation order. These powers are equivalent to the provisions governing the recognition of an overseas marriage (see 2.8 above) and an overseas divorce (see 6.9).

Converting a civil partnership into marriage   Under the Marriage (Same Sex Couples) Act 2013 (MSSCA 2013), same sex couples can convert a civil partnership into a marriage (s 9). When a civil partnership is converted into a marriage, the civil partnership will come to an end and the marriage will be treated as though it had existed from the date of the civil partnership (s 9(6)).

(c)   Civil partnership and human rights

Unlike marriage, civil partnership is not a human right. There is no decision of the European Court of Human Rights which suggests that, where a couple are able to enter into a legal relationship which accords full protection to all the values falling within Article 8 of the European Convention on Human Rights such as marriage, there is nonetheless State interference with the core values protected under that Article because they could not enter a different form of legal relationship which would afford them the same rights as marriage. Thus, the law does not breach the human rights of opposite sex couples who cannot obtain a civil partnership, as the following case shows.

> ▶ *Steinfeld & Anor v The Secretary of State for Education* **[2016] EWHC 128 (Admin)**
>
> The claimants, an opposite sex couple in a committed long-term relationship, wanted to formalise their relationship. They had deep-rooted and genuine ideological objections to the institution of marriage and wished instead to enter into a civil partnership, but they were prevented from doing so as they were not of the same sex. The claimants brought a human rights case against the Government on the ground that, following the enactment of the MSSCA 2013, the provisions of the CPA 2004 which preclude opposite sex couples from registering as civil partners became incompatible with Article 14 (discrimination in respect of an ECHR right) taken in conjunction with Article 8 (the right to family life) of the ECHR.
>
> Mrs Justice Andrews, sitting in the High Court, rejected the application, holding that the current law does not breach the human rights of opposite sex couples who cannot obtain a civil partnership. Her Ladyship held that the relevant provisions of the CPA 2004 have not become incompatible with Articles 8 and 14 of the ECHR just because same sex couples now have two routes to achieving legal recognition of their relationship by the State and opposite sex couples continue to have only one; and further that the difference in treatment does not infringe a personal interest close to the core of the right to family life, still less the right to family life protected by Article 8. Her Ladyship also accepted that the Government's approach to the issue ('wait and see') had been perfectly reasonable.

Summary

- ▶ Marriage is a contractual relationship which gives rise to various rights, obligations and privileges. The right to marry is guaranteed under Article 12 of the European Convention on Human Rights (ECHR), but, while it is a strong right, it is not absolute.

- ▶ To contract a valid marriage the parties must have capacity to marry and must comply with certain formalities under section 11 of the Matrimonial Causes Act 1973 (MCA 1973). Failure to comply with these requirements can render the marriage void. Parties have the capacity to marry if they are: not within the prohibited degrees of relationship; aged 16 or over; and not already married.

- ▶ Parties to a civil or religious marriage (other than a Church of England marriage) must obtain a superintendent registrar's certificate or a Registrar General's licence. Special provisions exist for housebound and detained people. A Church of England marriage can take place after the publication of banns or after the grant of a superintendent registrar's certificate or a Registrar General's licence.

- ▶ The marriage ceremony must be celebrated according to certain formalities. A civil ceremony must take place in a register office or approved premises. A religious marriage must take place in a church or other place registered for religious worship.

- ▶ A nullity decree can be sought under Part I of the MCA 1973 on the ground that a marriage is void (s 11) or voidable (s 12). There is no prohibition on seeking a decree of nullity during the first year of marriage (s 3), as there is for seeking a divorce. A decree of nullity gives the court jurisdiction to make financial orders under Part II of the MCA 1973. Breach of the formality requirements may render a marriage void, or the court may decide that the circumstances were such that there was no marriage at all. If there is no marriage at all, then a decree of nullity cannot be sought. In some circumstances, the court may decide that, despite a failure to comply with the required formalities, the marriage is valid under the common law presumption of marriage from long cohabitation.

Summary cont'd

▶ The law governing annulments is laid down in Part I of the MCA 1973. The procedure for nullity is the same as that for divorce. The grounds for a void marriage are laid down in section 11, and those for a voidable marriage are laid down in section 12. There are statutory bars to a nullity petition brought on the basis that a marriage is voidable.

▶ A victim of a forced marriage can have the marriage annulled on the ground that it is voidable due to duress under the MCA 1973 (s 12). There have also been other developments to protect actual or potential victims of forced marriage, which include the introduction of forced marriage protection orders under Part 4A of the Family Law Act 1996. Forcing a person to marry is a criminal offence under section 121 of the Anti-Social Behaviour, Crime and Policing Act 2014.

▶ Important developments in the case law of the European Court of Human Rights and the decision of the House of Lords in *Bellinger v Bellinger [2003] 1 FLR 1043* led to the enactment of the Gender Recognition Act 2004. This allows a transsexual person who acquires a full gender recognition certificate to enter into a valid marriage or civil partnership in their acquired gender.

▶ An overseas marriage may be recognised as valid in the UK under the Family Law Act 1986 provided that: each party has the capacity to marry according to their domicile; and the formalities of the place where the marriage was celebrated have been complied with. An overseas same sex marriage may be recognised in England and Wales as a valid UK marriage. An overseas civil partnership may be recognised in England and Wales as a valid UK civil partnership.

▶ On marriage, the parties acquire a legal status from which various rights, obligations and privileges flow. Married couples have separate legal personalities. They can own property separately, bring actions in tort and contract against each other, and separately or jointly against third parties. Spouses have a mutual duty to provide each other with financial support, and either party may apply for financial provision from the courts. Married couples also enjoy certain tax advantages. Married parents both have parental responsibility for their children. Married couples have rights and remedies under the criminal and civil law to protect themselves and their children against domestic violence.

▶ The Marriage (Same Sex Couples) Act 2013 permits same sex couples to enter into a marriage. The law and the procedure which applies to same sex couples largely replicate that which applies to opposite sex couples, although there are some important differences.

▶ The Civil Partnership Act 2004 permits same sex couples to enter into a registered civil partnership and thereby acquire rights, obligations and privileges which are virtually the same as those of married couples.

Further reading and references

Auchmuty, 'What's so special about marriage? The impact of *Wilkinson v Kitzinger*' [2008] CFLQ 475.

Bamforth, '"The benefits of marriage in all but name?" Same-sex couples and the Civil Partnership Act 2004' [2007] CFLQ 133.

Bamforth, 'Families but not (yet) marriages? Same-sex partners and the developing European Convention "margin of appreciation"' [2011] CFLQ 128.

Barker, 'Civil partnership: an alternative to marriage? *Ferguson and Others v UK*' [2012] Fam Law 548.

Barlow, Duncan, James and Park, *Cohabitation, Marriage and the Law: Social Change and Legal Reform in the 21st Century*, 2005, Hart Publishing.

Borkowsi, 'The presumption of marriage' [2002] CFLQ 251.

Chokowry and Skinner, 'The Forced Marriage (Civil Protection) Act 2007: two years on' [2011] Fam Law 76.

Cretney, *Same Sex Relationships: From 'Odious Crime' to 'Gay Marriage'*, 2006, Oxford University Press.

Deech, 'Cousin marriage' [2010] Fam Law 619.

Dunne, 'Ten years of gender recognition in the United Kingdom: still a "model for reform"?' [2015] Public Law 530.

Gaffney-Rhys, '*M v B, A and S (By the Official Solicitor)* – protecting vulnerable adults from being forced into marriage' [2006] CFLQ 445.

Gaffney-Rhys, '*Hudson v Leigh* – the concept of non-marriage' [2010] CFLQ 351.

Gaffney-Rhys, 'The criminalisation of forced marriage in England and Wales: one year on' [2015] Fam Law 1378.

Gilmore, '*Bellinger v Bellinger* – not quite between the ears and the legs – transsexualism and marriage in the Lords' [2003] CFLQ 295.

Haskey, 'Civil partnerships and same sex marriages in England and Wales: a social and demographic perspective' [2016] Fam Law 44.

Pearce and Gill, 'Criminalising forced marriage through stand-alone legislation: will it work?' [2012] Fam Law 534.

Probert, '*Hyde v Hyde*: defining or defending marriage?' [2007] CFLQ 322.

Proudman, 'The criminalisation of forced marriage' [2012] Fam Law 460.

Vallance-Webb, 'Forced marriage: a yielding of the lips not the mind' [2008] Fam Law 565.

Websites

Forced Marriage Unit (Foreign & Commonwealth Office): www.fco.gov.uk
Marriage Foundation: www.marriagefoundation.org.uk.

Links to relevant websites can also be found at: www.palgravehighered.com/law/familylaw9e

Chapter 3

Cohabitation

3.1 Cohabitation

(a) Introduction

One of the most striking social changes which has taken place in the last few decades is the huge increase in the number of couples who choose to cohabit. Thus, according to *Population Trends 145* (Autumn 2011, by Beaujouan and Ni Bhrolcháin), in the early 1960s fewer than one in a hundred adults under the age of 50 in Britain was estimated to have been cohabiting at any one time, compared with one in six in 2011. Cohabitation is no longer regarded as socially deviant. Many people choose to cohabit instead of marrying; and others as a precursor to marriage. Statistics are more difficult to come by than statistics on marriage and civil partnership as there are no registration and court statistics for cohabitation.

Statistical Bulletin, Families and Households 2015

These figures were published in November 2015 by the Office for National Statistics, (www.ons.gov.uk).

▶ The cohabiting couple family continues to be the fastest-growing family type in the UK in 2015, reaching 3.2 million cohabiting couple families.
▶ For opposite sex cohabiting couple families, there has been a statistically significant increase from 14 per cent of all families in 2005 to 17 per cent in 2015.
▶ Same sex cohabiting couple families also saw a statistically significant increase from 0.3 per cent of all families in 2005 to 0.5 per cent in 2015.
▶ In 2015, 41 per cent of all opposite sex cohabiting couple families had dependent children, in contrast to only 3 per cent of same sex cohabiting couple families.

A study conducted by Barlow, Burgoyne, Clery and Smithson in 2008 found that cohabitation was a popular choice of relationship in Britain, but that 53 per cent of the cohabitants surveyed mistakenly believed that 'common law marriage' gave them certain rights. Only 15 per cent of those who owned their own property had a written agreement about their share of the ownership; and only 19 per cent had sought advice about their legal position. The research found also that: few cohabitants made legal agreements; there was little support for the law to distinguish between financial remedies for married and cohabiting couples on death; and there was a widespread feeling that children of cohabitants should not be adversely affected by their parents' marital status on separation or death.

Over the past few decades there has been increasing pressure for family law to be reformed to remove the injustices which cohabitants may suffer in respect of finance and property, particularly on relationship breakdown (see Chapter 4).

(b)   The problem of defining cohabitation for legal purposes

One of the difficulties for the law, whether it is judge-made or statute, is defining the terms 'cohabitation' and 'cohabitant' for the purposes of giving cohabitants legal rights and obligations. Statutory provisions which give cohabitants rights and obligations usually define cohabitation in terms of a quasi-marital relationship, sometimes with a minimal duration and a residence requirement. Thus, in order to apply for reasonable financial provision from a deceased cohabiting partner's estate under the Inheritance (Provision for Family and Dependants) Act 1975, a cohabitant must have lived in the same household as the deceased for at least two years as if they were the husband or wife (or civil partner) of the deceased (see 4.13). For the purposes of obtaining protection against domestic violence under Part IV of the Family Law Act 1996, however, the term 'cohabitant' is defined less restrictively, as there is no minimum duration requirement (see Chapter 5). For the purposes of adoption, cohabitants are defined in the Adoption and Children Act 2002 as persons living as partners in an enduring family relationship (see 15.4). As Wong ([2012] CFLQ 60) has stated, there has been 'an increasing shift from defining cohabitation along the marriage model ... to focusing on the "couple", their commitment and interdependence as the fulcrum for extending protection'. She says this trend can be seen in recent divorce and constructive trust cases where marriage, and even cohabitation, are acknowledged as a form of partnership, and that this focus on commitment 'is to be welcomed as it moves us away from conjugality as the basis for extending recognition to cohabitants'.

In *Kimber v Kimber* [2000] 1 FLR 383, Tyrer J, while accepting that it was impossible to give a completely exhaustive definition of 'cohabitation', especially when personal relationships are so diverse, identified the following list of factors which should be taken into account by the court when determining whether couples are cohabitants: membership of the same household; stability in the relationship; shared finances; a sexual relationship; whether the parties have any children; and public acknowledgement.

How the term cohabitation is defined will be an important policy issue when discussing any future reform of the law.

(c)   The vulnerability of cohabitants

Cohabitants are often in a vulnerable position with respect to their legal rights, or lack thereof, particularly on relationship breakdown and on the death of their partner. Some cohabitants are under the mistaken belief that there is something called a 'common law marriage' which gives them quasi-marital rights. This is a myth.

Children of cohabiting couples can also be in a more vulnerable position than children whose parents are married. This is because cohabiting relationships are more prone to breakdown, and the court does not have the same powers to make arrangements for children as it has when their parents are married and divorcing (see Chapter 10). Children may also be vulnerable if a cohabiting parent loses a right to remain in the family home on relationship breakdown.

3.2 The legal consequences of cohabitation

The position of cohabitants with regard to their legal rights and obligations is, in some respects, similar to that of married couples and civil partners. In other respects, however, it is significantly different.

(a) Separate legal personalities

Like married couples, each cohabitant has a separate legal personality. This means that they can own property solely (or jointly) and can bring proceedings against each other or against third parties. They can enter into contracts with each other. They can also make unilateral decisions about their own medical treatment.

(b) Financial obligations

Cohabitants, unlike married couples, have no mutual duty during their relationship or on relationship breakdown to provide each other with financial support. Consequently, they have no right to apply to the court for orders in respect of financial provision. However, cohabiting parents do have a duty to maintain their children (see Chapter 12).

(c) Property rights

The property rights of cohabitants are for the most part determined by the law of property and the law of contract (see Chapter 4), although there is some special family law provision with respect to occupation of the family home in cases of domestic violence (see Chapter 5) and applications for financial provision and transfer of a tenancy on the death of a partner (see 4.14). With respect to property ownership on relationship breakdown, however, the family courts have no jurisdiction (like there is on divorce) to adjust the parties' rights of property ownership. Cohabitants must instead rely on equitable doctrines, such as trusts and proprietary estoppel, in order to establish interests (see 4.7 to 4.9). In addition, cohabitants, unlike married couples, have no statutory right of occupation of the family home. If they have children, however, property orders can be sought to or for the benefit of a child under Schedule 1 to the Children Act 1989 (CA 1989) (see 12.3).

The following case is often cited as the classic example of the injustices which a cohabitant can suffer on relationship breakdown, and it is often referred to in discussions of reform.

> ▶ *Burns v Burns* [1984] Ch 317
>
> The female cohabitant (she had taken her partner's name) cohabited with her partner for nearly 20 years. She brought up their children and looked after the home. On the breakdown of their relationship, she brought a claim against her former partner (the owner of the home) arguing that she had an interest in the home under a trust. Her claim was

dismissed by the Court of Appeal because there was no evidence of any intention that she was to have an interest in the home. Looking after the home and bringing up the children was held to be insufficient evidence to enable the court to infer such an intention. While expressing considerable sympathy for her, the Court of Appeal felt that any change in the law was a matter for Parliament, not the courts.

In *Hammond v Mitchell* [1991] 1 WLR 1127, on the other hand, the female cohabitant was successful in obtaining an interest in the home under a trust on facts which were similar to those in *Burns*. This was because the court accepted her evidence that she and her partner had spoken about ownership of the home, even though briefly and many years earlier; and this was held to be sufficient evidence of an inferred intention that she was to have a half-share. The different outcomes in *Burns* and *Hammond v Mitchell* demonstrate the somewhat arbitrary and unsatisfactory nature of the law in this area.

(d)   Property rights on death

On the death of a partner, the surviving cohabitant has no right to inherit from the deceased's estate on intestacy. Instead, any property goes to the deceased's children or parents. It is therefore particularly important for cohabitants to make a will. In the last few years, however, there has been discussion about whether the law should be reformed to give certain surviving cohabitants a right to inherit from a deceased partner's estate on intestacy. Thus, in October 2009, the Law Commission published a consultation paper which looked at a range of issues relating to intestacy, including whether certain surviving cohabitants should have a right to inherit from a deceased partner's estate on intestacy. In December 2011, it published its final report (*Intestacy and Family Provision Claims on Death*, LC 331) which included a draft Inheritance (Cohabitants) Bill 2012–2013 giving cohabitants the right to inherit from a deceased partner's estate on intestacy if they had lived together for five years or for two years (if they had a child together, and the child was living with them at the time when the deceased died). In March 2013, however, the Coalition Government announced that the Inheritance (Cohabitants) Bill would not be implemented (see HC Deb 21 March 2013 C WS60). In the meantime, in May 2012, the Inheritance (Cohabitants) Bill was introduced into the House of Lords (as a Private Members' Bill by Lord Lester) to make provision about the property of deceased persons who are survived by a cohabitant. The Bill did not become law. More recently, in October 2013, June 2014 and June 2015, the Cohabitation Rights Bill was introduced into the House of Lords (as a Private Members' Bill by Lord Marks). However, without the support of the Government it is unlikely to lead to a change in the law.

Notwithstanding the above, a surviving cohabitant can apply under the Inheritance (Provision for Family and Dependants) Act 1975 (see 4.13) for reasonable financial provision out of the deceased cohabitant's estate, or claim a beneficial interest in the deceased cohabitant's property under a trust or by way of proprietary estoppel (see 4.7 to 4.8). A surviving cohabitant can also succeed to a tenancy which belonged to the deceased cohabitant (see 4.14).

(e) Rights on relationship breakdown

On relationship breakdown cohabitants have a duty to maintain their children, but there is no maintenance duty between the partners themselves. Furthermore, the courts have no powers, as they have on divorce, to adjust cohabitants' property entitlements according to their needs and resources. Cohabitants can therefore be in a vulnerable position on relationship breakdown in respect of, for example, the family home, investments or pension provision.

(i) Cohabitation contracts

Cohabitants can enter into a cohabitation contract to regulate their affairs (for example to make arrangements about the allocation of property and other matters should their relationship break down). In practice, however, few do so. Cohabitation contracts were once considered to be contrary to public policy on the ground that they undermined the sanctity of marriage. This is no longer the case, but cohabitation contracts still remain open to challenge in the courts and may not be upheld, for example if there is no intention to create legal relations, or there is duress, undue influence, misrepresentation or lack of independent legal advice. Thus, for example, in *Sutton v Mishcon de Reya and Gawor & Co* [2004] 1 FLR 837 a cohabitation agreement was held not to be valid as it was an agreement about sexual services rather than about property.

(f) Protection against domestic violence and harassment

Cohabitants and former cohabitants can apply for non-molestation orders and occupation orders under Part IV of the Family Law Act 1996 to protect themselves and their children against domestic violence (see Chapter 5).

(g) Children

Cohabiting parents have the same maintenance obligations to their children as married couples (see Chapter 12). Only a cohabiting mother has automatic parental responsibility in law for her child, but a cohabitant may acquire it (see 9.4 to 9.5). A cohabiting parent can apply for section 8 orders under the CA 1989, for example a child arrangements order (see Chapter 10). With respect to adoption, cohabitants can jointly, and in some circumstances solely, apply to adopt a child, provided that their relationship is sufficiently permanent (see Chapter 15). Cohabitant parents with parental responsibility have a right to consent (or to refuse consent) to the adoption of their child (see 15.8).

3.3 Homesharers

Some people who live together are not cohabitants in the sense of being a quasi-married couple, but may instead be described as 'homesharers'. Such people do not have the same family law rights as married couples, civil partners and cohabitants, except with respect to protection against domestic violence (see Chapter 5). A 'homesharer' may be particularly vulnerable in respect of property entitlement on the death of the other homesharer, and they can suffer tax disadvantages as the following case shows.

▶ **Burden and Burden v UK (Application No 13378/05) [2008] 2 FLR 787**

Two unmarried sisters claimed that they were discriminated against in respect of inheritance tax under UK law because they did not have the same rights as same sex couples, even though they had lived together for the whole of their adult lives and owned their home in joint names. On the death of one sister, the other would have to sell their house to pay the 40 per cent inheritance tax owed on its value. After their claim failed before the English courts they took their case to the European Court of Human Rights (ECtHR), arguing that the UK inheritance tax laws discriminated against them under Article 14 taken in conjunction with Article 1 of Protocol 1 (the right to peaceful enjoyment of possessions) of the European Convention on Human Rights (ECHR). They also argued that the Civil Partnership Act 2004 was discriminatory as it gave rights to same sex, but not opposite sex, couples.

The ECtHR held by 15 votes to two that there had been no violation of the ECHR. The UK had not exceeded the wide margin of appreciation afforded to it; and the difference of treatment for the purposes of the grant of inheritance tax exceptions was reasonably and objectively justified for the purpose of Article 14. Siblings could not be equated with married couples or civil partners for the purpose of inheritance tax obligations, even though they had lived together all of their adult lives. Any workable tax system was bound to create marginal situations and individual cases of apparent hardship or injustice; and it was up to national authorities to decide how to strike the right balance between raising revenue and pursuing social policy objectives.

The Cohabitation Bill 2008–2009 (see 3.4 below) made provision for sibling homesharers. It was not, however, taken forward by the Government.

3.4 Reform of the law

This section should be read in conjunction with Chapter 4 which deals with the law governing property ownership by cohabitants.

(a) Discussion of reform

During the last 30 years or so there has been increasing dissatisfaction with the law governing the property rights of cohabitants on relationship breakdown and on the death of a cohabiting partner. There have been recommendations for reform from, for example, the Law Society, Resolution (an organisation of family lawyers), judges, lawyers, academics and the Law Commission. According to the *2008 British Social Attitudes Report*, nearly nine out of ten people were of the opinion that a cohabiting partner should have a right to financial provision on separation if the relationship was of long duration and/or included children.

As long ago as 1984 in the case of *Burns v Burns* [1984] Ch 317 (see 3.2 above), the Court of Appeal drew attention to the unfairness of the law, but said that any reform of the law was a matter for Parliament, not the courts. Since 1984, changing social and economic conditions have, arguably, made reform even more pressing.

As the law currently stands, cohabitants, unlike spouses and civil partners, are in a particularly disadvantageous position on relationship breakdown as the courts have no discretionary power to adjust their property interests. Instead, cohabitants must turn to the law of property, in particular the law of trusts. This is not only costly and time-consuming, but the law is sometimes insufficiently flexible to do justice between the parties. It is also complex and difficult to understand.

Some of the arguments for and against reform are as follows.

Arguments for reform

▶ The law should keep up to date with changing social conditions. Many couples choose to cohabit and many cohabitation relationships break down.
▶ Cohabitants can suffer unfairness and injustice in respect of property ownership, particularly on relationship breakdown.
▶ Children of cohabitants are often in a vulnerable position on relationship breakdown, particularly if the home belongs to one of the cohabiting parents.
▶ Many cohabitants mistakenly believe that there is something called a 'common law marriage' whereby cohabitants acquire the same legal rights as married couples or civil partners after a period of cohabitation.
▶ The law of trusts is doctrinally unsatisfactory, difficult to understand and not designed to deal with cohabitation breakdown. Property entitlement should therefore be determined by a family law, not a property law, regime.
▶ Many other countries (such as Scotland, Australia, New Zealand and Canada) have introduced reforms, and so England and Wales should do the same.

Arguments against reform

▶ Cohabitants can choose to marry (or enter into a civil partnership) and thereby acquire the rights that married couples and civil partners have.
▶ The social reality is that most cohabitants own their home jointly, and so very few cohabitants actually suffer any inequity and unfairness.
▶ Codification of the law would create its own set of problems.
▶ Reform of the law would be difficult.
▶ Reform would undermine the institution of marriage.
▶ Cohabitants may not want to have a quasi-divorce regime forced upon them in respect of their property interests.
▶ There is increasing emphasis on party autonomy and settlement on divorce; and so the same policy should be adopted in the context of cohabitation.

Some commentators have argued in favour of reform because cohabitants and their children can suffer serious injustice. A study by Douglas, Pearce and Woodward in 2007 found major instances of injustice caused by the current operation of the law of trusts.

▶ Douglas, Pearce and Woodward, *A Failure of Trust: Resolving Property Issues on Cohabitation Breakdown* (2007), Cardiff University Research Paper, Conclusion

Retrospective private ordering in cohabitation breakdown cases, set against a fog of uncertainty and complexity rather than the 'shadow of the law', has led to a position where trusts law may now serve to perpetuate rather than redress injustice. Even if the parties reach some sort of rough and ready compromise, ignoring or sidestepping the 'true' legal position, this comes at a cost, both actual and figurative. Whatever the fate of the Law Commission's or other similar proposals … maintenance of the status quo is unarguable. However controversial it may be, reform of the current law to meet the legitimate interests of separating cohabitants is both justified and overdue.

A former President of the Family Division, Baroness Butler-Sloss, has also drawn attention to the problems which cohabitants may suffer.

▶ **Baroness Butler-Sloss in the House of Lords debate on the Cohabitation Bill 2008 (***Hansard***, 13 March 2009)**

[There are] very real problems on the ground. Lawyers recognise them and … as a former family judge for 35 years … I have dealt with similar cases again and again. I should tell you what happens. A couple live together for, say, 17 years … and the woman subordinates her career to the man. She takes some part-time work, she brings up their children and they live as if they are married but they do not get married. At the end of 17 years the man finds a younger woman … and tells her to get out. When she says, 'But I have a share of the house,' he says, 'The house is in my name. You have not put any money into it. You are out.' … She becomes a burden on the state.

(i) Drawbacks of the law of property

In addition to the arguments set out above, the law of property is open to criticism, particularly in respect of acquiring an interest in the family home. The law is not only complex and difficult to understand, but even more difficult to apply. As Carnwarth LJ said in the Court of Appeal in *Stack v Dowden* [2006] 1 FLR 254:

> To the detached observer, the result may seem like a witch's brew, into which various esoteric ingredients have been stirred over the years, and in which different ideas bubble to the surface at different times. They include implied trust, constructive trust, resulting trust, presumption of advancement, proprietary estoppel, unjust enrichment, and so on. These ideas are likely to mean nothing to laymen, and often little more to the lawyers who use them.

Cohabitants may have to resort to the law of trusts to establish an interest in property (see Chapter 4). However, the law of trusts has the following disadvantages:

▶ The principles governing the law of trusts are based on intentions and arrangements which are often vague and may have arisen many years earlier. For this reason, it may be difficult to establish any evidence of intention; and it is possible that parties may be tempted to perjure themselves. For example, in *Hammond v Mitchell* [1991] 1 WLR 1127 (where the female cohabitant successfully claimed a half-share in the family home and a share of other property owned by the man) Waite J said that 'both parties were prone to exaggeration' and 'neither side had the monopoly of truth'. Bailey-Harris, commenting on *Rowe v Prance* [1999] 2 FLR 787 (where the female cohabitant successfully claimed a half-share in a yacht owned by the man), said that one is 'commonly left with the impression that the establishment of an interest ... turns primarily on whose account of conversations is believed by the judge' ([1999] Fam Law 623, at 624).

▶ A claimant is forced to trawl back through the relationship to find evidence of the intention needed to establish a trust, instead of being encouraged to look at future needs and resources, which is the approach adopted on divorce and on dissolution.

▶ The requirement of a direct financial contribution to establish an interest under a trust (laid down by Lord Bridge in *Lloyds Bank plc v Rosset* [1991] 1 AC 107) means that some cohabitants are unable to acquire an interest in the home even though they have spent many years contributing to its upkeep and looking after the family. The courts are unwilling to adopt a more flexible approach and accept evidence of an indirect contribution, such as looking after children or paying for household goods.

▶ There is some judicial uncertainty about whether Lord Bridge's interpretation in *Lloyds Bank plc v Rosset* of earlier authorities was correct, or whether it set the hurdle too high.

▶ Because of the vagueness of the relevant legal principles, unsatisfactory and unjust distinctions may be made. In *Hammond v Mitchell* [1991] 1 WLR 1127 the female cohabitant was granted a half-share in the family home on the basis of a conversation she had had with her partner many years earlier, but the female cohabitant in *Burns v Burns* [1984] Ch 317 failed to establish a beneficial interest in the home, despite her substantial contribution over many years to the household and family.

The drawbacks of the law were recognised by the Law Commission in its 2006 Consultation Paper:

▶ *Cohabitation: The Financial Consequences of Relationship Breakdown* **(Law Com No. 17, 2006)**

The rules contained in the general law have proved to be relatively rigid and extremely difficult to apply, and their application can lead to what many would regard as unfairness between the parties. The formulation of a claim based on these rules is time-consuming and expensive, and the nature of the inquiry before the court into the history of the relationship results in a protracted hearing for those disputes that are not compromised. The inherent uncertainty of the underlying principles makes effective bargaining difficult to achieve as parties will find it hard to predict the outcome of contested litigation.

(b) Reform – questions to be addressed

Any reform of the law governing the financial and property rights of cohabitants will have to address the following difficult questions:

▶ *Defining the term 'cohabitant'* Should there be a minimum duration requirement? Should there be evidence of financial dependency? Should there be a list of statutory factors to help define cohabitation? Should the birth of a child automatically result in a couple being deemed to be 'cohabitants'?

▶ *Remedies* Should the remedies be the same as those which are available for married couples and civil partners on relationship breakdown? Should financial provision be restricted to lump sum orders, or should cohabitants (like divorcing couples) be entitled to maintenance, and, if so, for how long? Should cohabitants be entitled to property orders and to a share of their cohabiting partner's pension?

▶ *The exercise of discretion* When deciding whether to grant a remedy, what principles should govern the exercise of the court's discretion? Should there be a statutory list of factors equivalent to those for financial orders on divorce and on dissolution?

▶ *Opting out* Should cohabitants be given the right to opt out of any new scheme, and, if so, should there be any controls on this? Thus, should certain formalities have to be completed? Should there be a requirement of independent legal advice? Should future changes of circumstance (such as the birth of a child or loss of employment) vitiate the agreement? Should there be a right to have the agreement revoked if is likely to cause manifest injustice?

▶ *A limitation period* Should there be a requirement that an application be brought within so many years of relationship breakdown and/or separation? If so, how long should this be, and should it be extended at the discretion of the court in cases where there may be injustice and/or exceptional circumstances?

▶ *Property on death* Should cohabitants on the death of a partner have the same or similar rights to those of married couples and civil partners?

(c)   Proposals for reform

Proposals for reform of the law have come from various bodies, including the Law Society, Resolution and the Law Commission (the Government's reform body). Thus, in 2002 the Law Society (see *Cohabitation: The Case for Clear Law; Proposals for Reform*) recommended reform of the law to enable cohabitants to apply for court orders similar to those available for divorcing couples. Eligibility would depend on whether the parties had lived together for at least two years in a quasi-married relationship or on whether they had children. Applications would be determined having regard to a principle of economic advantage and disadvantage suffered by either party in the interests of the other party or of the family. The proposals also included a wide range of other rights for cohabitants.

In 2000 and 2015 Resolution also published proposals for reform similar to those recommended above by the Law Society (see *Fairness for Families).* In addition, there have been attempts to introduce Bills into Parliament. Thus, at the end of 2008 Lord Lester introduced a Cohabitation Bill into Parliament, which was also promoted by Resolution. The Bill had its second reading in the House of Lords in March 2009, but met with resistance from some members of the House of Lords and went no further. A Private Member's Bill based on Lord Lester's Cohabitation Bill was presented to Parliament by Mary Creah MP and had its second reading in the House of Commons in July 2009, but it too went no further. More recently, in October 2013, June 2014 and June 2015, Lord Marks introduced a Cohabitation Rights Bill into Parliament.

It is the work of the Law Commission, however, which has been particularly important with regard to reform of the law.

(d)   Reform of the law – the work of the Law Commission

The Law Commission has spent many years addressing reform of the law to remove the injustices for cohabitants and other homesharers. As long ago as 1994 it announced that the law was unsatisfactory, arbitrary and unjust, and said that it would make proposals for reform. Its proposals were eagerly awaited, but it was not until 2002 that it published a discussion paper (*Sharing Homes: A Discussion Paper*, Law Com No. 278) in which it considered reform for homesharers generally, not just cohabitants. The Commission considered a 'contribution-based' model for reform, but concluded that this model would do nothing to improve the law for cohabitants because it was insufficiently flexible to take account of different types of relationship. The discussion paper was a considerable disappointment, particularly for those who had been in favour of reforming the law. Its downfall was that its ambit was too wide. A relationship-based, rather than a contribution-based, model was thought to offer a better solution.

In 2006, the Law Commission began another project which focused on the financial hardships which cohabitants and their children suffer on relationship breakdown and on death. It published a consultation paper (*Cohabitation: The Financial Consequences of Relationship Breakdown*, Law Com No. 179), followed in 2007 by the publication of a report (*Cohabitation: The Financial Consequences of Relationship Breakdown*, Law Com No. 307), in which it made recommendations for the introduction of a new scheme of remedies in England and Wales for cohabitants in respect of property on family breakdown and on death.

Eligibility under the proposed scheme would depend on whether the couple had cohabited for a number of years (two to five years was suggested) or on whether the parties had a child together. Cohabitants would be able to opt out of the scheme by making binding opt-out agreements, subject to safeguards. The remedies proposed were similar to those available on divorce except that no maintenance for a partner would generally be available. To obtain a remedy under the proposed scheme, a cohabitant would have to prove that the respondent had retained a benefit and that they had suffered a continuing economic disadvantage as a result of qualifying contributions made to the relationship. The Law Commission made no recommendations on the law of intestacy, but recommended that the Inheritance (Provision for Family and Dependants) Act 1975 should be amended so that cohabitants would be treated in the same way as spouses and civil partners.

The Law Commission's proposals were not taken any further by the Government. In March 2008, the Government announced that the proposals were to be shelved in order to see how similar reforms introduced in Scotland by the Family Law (Scotland) Act 2006 would work before any changes were made in England and Wales. In September 2011, after having considered the Law Commission's recommendations, together with the outcome of research on the Scottish legislation, the Government announced that there was not a sufficient basis for a change in the law and that it did not intend to take forward the Law Commission's recommendations in that Parliamentary term. In its *Report on the implementation of Law Commission proposals* (Ministry of Justice, March 2012), the Government stated that the Scottish legislation 'did not provide a sufficient basis for a change in the law and the family justice system is currently in a transitional period with major reforms on the horizon' (para 23).

In outline, the Scottish Act (see above) created new remedies for cohabitants for financial relief on separation and death, whatever the length of their relationship and regardless of whether they had children, provided the applicant had suffered an economic disadvantage. A study of the Scottish provisions by Miles, Wasoff and Mordaunt ([2011] CFLQ 302), which focused on the experiences and perspectives of Scottish family lawyers, found that respondents had given a cautious welcome to the new provisions. The Scottish provisions were considered for the first time by the Supreme Court in *Gow (FC) (Appellant) v Grant (Respondent) (Scotland)* [2012] UKSC 29, an appeal from the Scottish courts, which unanimously allowed Mrs Gow's appeal and held that she had suffered economic disadvantage in the interests of the respondent to the extent of £39,500. Baroness Hale, giving judgment, stated that there were lessons to be learned from this case in England and Wales and that there was a need for some such remedy south of the border.

(e)   Cohabitation reform – the future

At the time of writing, there are no Government proposals to reform the law governing the finance and property rights of cohabitants on relationship breakdown even though there have been reforms in Scotland and in other countries (such as in Australia, New Zealand and Canada). As such, it is vitally important that cohabitants know what rights they have and do not have. In the following extract, Baroness Deech emphasises the importance of building on the autonomy of cohabitants and of informing them of their rights.

▶ **Baroness Deech, 'Cohabitation' [2010] Fam Law 39**

What, if anything, should be done to help cohabitants sort out their legal problems? We should build on their autonomy rather than take it away. Their contracts should be recognised; they should be encouraged to make wills leaving their property to each other if that is their wish (needless to say, the proposals of automatic inheritance on intestacy for cohabitants in the recent Law Commission Consultation Paper, *Intestacy and Family Provision*, (LC 191, 2009, Part 4) suffer from the same illogicalities as those already described, albeit rather fewer because at least the relationship lasted until death); they should have explained to them that joint registration of the home in both names will mean an equal split of the equity on separation; they could nominate each other as beneficiaries in insurance and pensions. Above all there should be explained loudly and clearly that living together does not give rise to legal rights.

Summary

▶ Many couples choose to cohabit, and the number who do so has risen significantly in the last few years. However, few cohabitants make legal agreements, and some mistakenly believe that there is something called a 'common law marriage' which gives them rights. There has been increasing pressure for reform to remove the injustices which cohabitants and their children can suffer. One of the problems, particularly for reformers, is the difficulty of defining the terms 'cohabitation' and 'cohabitant'.

▶ Cohabitants are given some protection under the law (for example in respect of remedies against domestic violence). However, they are particularly vulnerable in respect of property rights on relationship breakdown and on the death of their partner. Cohabitants have no mutual duty to maintain each other, unlike spouses and civil partners. They do have a maintenance obligation to their children. Cohabitants can enter into cohabitation contracts, but these are open to challenge in the courts.

▶ Some people who live together are 'homesharers'. Homesharers are given some protection under the law (for example in respect of remedies against domestic violence), but they do not have the same rights as married couples, civil partners and cohabitants. They can be particularly vulnerable in respect of property entitlement on the death of the other homesharer, and they can suffer tax disadvantages.

▶ There has been increasing concern about the lack of adequate legal remedies in respect of property and finance on cohabitation breakdown, and about the unfairness and injustice this can cause. As a result, there have been calls for reform to remove the perceived unfairness that exists. Proposals for reform have come from the Law Society, Resolution and the Law Commission. In July 2007, the Law Commission published a report making proposals for reform, but these were taken no further by the Government, despite the fact that there have been changes to the law in Scotland. Thus, there are currently no Government proposals to change the law in England and Wales, despite the various arguments in favour of reform.

Further reading and references

Barlow, Burgoyne, Clery and Smithson, *Cohabitation and the Law: Myths, Money and the Media,* 2008, in British Social Attitudes 24th Report, Sage Publishing.

Barlow, Duncan, James and Park, *Cohabitation, Marriage and the Law: Social Change and Legal Reform in the 21st Century*, 2005, Hart Publishing.

Barlow and Smithson, 'Legal assumptions, cohabitants' talk and the rocky road to reform' [2010] CFLQ 328.

Barton, 'Cohabitants, contracts and commissioners' [2007] Fam Law 407.

Beaujouan and Ni Bhrolchán, 'Cohabitation and marriage in Britain since the 1970s', *Population Trends*, 145, Autumn 2011.

Crawford, Goodman and Joyce, 'Relationship between marital status and child outcomes in the UK using the Millennium Cohort Study' [2012] CFLQ 176.

Deech, Baroness, 'Cohabitation' [2010] Fam Law 39.

Douglas, Pearce and Woodward, *A Failure of Trust: Resolving Property Issues on Cohabitation Breakdown*, Cardiff Research Papers, No. 1 (July 2007) (available at www.law.cf.ac.uk/researchpapers/index).

Further reading and references cont'd

Douglas, Pearce and Woodward, 'Dealing with property issues on cohabitation breakdown' [2007] Fam Law 36.

Duncan, Barlow and James, 'Why don't they marry? Cohabitation, commitment and DIY marriage' [2005] CFLQ 383.

Fox, 'Reforming family property – comparisons, compromises and common dimensions' [2003] CFLQ 1.

Hess, 'The rights of cohabitants: when and how will the law be reformed?' [2009] Fam Law 405.

McCarthy, 'Cohabitation: lessons from north of the border?' [2011] CFLQ 277.

Miles, 'Property law v family law: resolving the problems of family property' (2003) *Legal Studies* 624.

Miles, Wasoff and Mordaunt, 'Cohabitation: lessons from research north of the border?' [2011] CFLQ 302.

Pawlowski, 'Constructive trusts and improvements to property' [2009] Fam Law 680.

Probert, 'The evolution of the common-law marriage myth' [2011] Fam Law 283.

Probert, 'Sutton v Mishcon De Reya and Gawor & Co – cohabitation contracts and Swedish sex slaves' [2004] CFLQ 453.

Probert, 'Trusts and the modern woman – establishing an interest in the family home' [2001] CFLQ 275.

Probert, 'Why couples still believe in common-law marriage' [2007] Fam Law 403.

Probert and Barlow, 'Displacing marriage – diversification and harmonisation within Europe' [2000] CFLQ 153.

Singer, 'What provision for unmarried couples should the law make when their relationships break down?' [2009] Fam Law 234.

Williams, Potter and Douglas, 'Cohabitation and intestacy: public opinion and law reform' [2008] CFLQ 499.

Wong, 'Shared commitment, interdependency and property relations: a socio-legal project for cohabitation' [2012] CFLQ 60.

Websites

Law Commission: www.lawcom.gov.uk
One Plus One – Married or Not: www.oneplusone.org.uk/marriedornot
The Living Together Campaign: www.advicenow.org.uk/livingtogether

Links to relevant websites can also be found at: www.palgravehighered.com/law/familylaw9e

Part III

Family property and finance

Chapter 4

Family property

4.1 Introduction

This chapter looks at the law governing the property rights of spouses, civil partners and cohabitants during their relationship, on relationship breakdown and on death. The statutory provisions and legal principles which relate to spouses and civil partners are much more extensive than those which relate to cohabitants. Thus, on the breakdown of a cohabitation relationship, the family courts have no jurisdiction to distribute the property assets of cohabitants according to their needs and resources, as they have on divorce or civil partnership dissolution. Cohabitants must rely instead on the general principles of property law, in particular the law of trusts, to determine a property dispute (such as a dispute about the family home). If they have children, they may be able to rely on the provisions of Schedule 1 of the Children Act 1989. Cohabitants may also be in a vulnerable position on the death of a cohabiting partner. Because of the unfairness that cohabitants and their children can suffer in respect of property entitlement, there have been many calls for reform. These have not, however, been taken forward.

4.2 The property rights of married couples and civil partners

During a marriage or civil partnership the general principles of property law and contract law apply to property ownership, together with the provisions of various family law statutes.

(a) Ownership of property during marriage and civil partnership

(i) Separation of property

Each spouse or civil partner can own property separately. Thus, subject to a contrary intention, any property brought into the marriage or civil partnership belongs to the party who owns it; and so does any property acquired by either party during the marriage or civil partnership. Ownership depends on the law of contract. For example, if one spouse buys some shares, then, subject to any contrary intention, that spouse owns them. On divorce or dissolution, however, the court may redistribute the couple's assets irrespective of ownership during the marriage or civil partnership (see Chapter 7).

(ii) Gifts to married couples and civil partners

There is a presumption that a spouse or civil partner owns any gift (such as a birthday present) that is given to them personally. However, if a gift is given to them as a married couple or civil partners, it is presumed to be a gift to them both. This may include a gift of financial assistance for the purpose of acquiring a home (see, for example, *Abbott v Abbott* [2007] UKPC 53). These rules are, however, subject to any contrary intention.

(iii) Improvements to property

A spouse or civil partner can acquire a share, or an enlarged share, of property (or the proceeds of sale of such property) if they have made a substantial improvement in money or money's worth to that property, subject to any contrary intention (s 37 Matrimonial Proceedings and Property Act 1970; s 65 Civil Partnership Act 2004 (CPA 2004)). These provisions also apply to couples who are engaged to be married or parties to a civil partnership agreement (see 4.3 below).

(iv) Power of the court to declare property interests

The court has jurisdiction on the application of a spouse or civil partner to make such order as it thinks fit as to the ownership or possession of any property (s 17 Married Women's Property Act 1882; s 66 CPA 2004). Under these provisions, however, the court can only declare property entitlement; it cannot create or adjust rights (*Pettitt v Pettitt* [1970] AC 777). An application can also be made in respect of money or property which has ceased to be in the other party's possession or under their control (s 7(1) Matrimonial Causes (Property and Maintenance) Act 1958; s 67 CPA 2004). Former spouses or civil partners can apply under these provisions, provided the application is made within three years of the termination of the relationship (s 39 Matrimonial Proceedings and Property Act 1970; s 68 CPA 2004). Having declared any interest, the court can order the sale of property and that the proceeds of sale be divided in accordance with the parties' interests in the property, but it cannot redistribute the proceeds of sale according to what it deems to be fair under these provisions (s 7(7) Matrimonial Causes (Property and Maintenance) Act 1958; s 66 CPA 2004).

(v) Property bought from housekeeping money provided by a husband

Any property bought using housekeeping money (an allowance for the expenses of the home) provided by a husband is presumed to belong to the husband and wife in equal shares, subject to any contrary intention (s 1 Married Women's Property Act 1964). Section 200 of the Equality Act 2010 (EA 2010) amends this provision so that it refers to housekeeping money given by either spouse to the other, not just by husbands to wives. Section 201 of the EA 2010 inserts a similar provision into the CPA 2004, extending the above provisions to civil partners (s 70A). These provisions in the EA 2010 are not yet in force.

(b) Occupation of the family home

Spouses and civil partners have a right to occupy the family home if they have a right of ownership in, or a contractual licence to occupy, the property. Spouses and civil partners who are not so entitled may nonetheless have a *statutory* right of occupation (a 'home right') under section 30(1) of Part IV of the Family Law Act 1996 (FLA 1996), as amended by Schedule 9 to the CPA 2004. If a spouse or civil partner has a 'home right' and is in occupation of the home, then they have a right not to be evicted or excluded from the home by the other spouse or civil partner, unless the court makes an order under section 33 of the FLA 1996 (s 30(2)(a)). If the spouse or civil partner has a 'home right' and they are not in occupation, then they have a right, if permission of the court is given, to enter into and occupy the home (s 30(2)(b)). A 'home right' arises only in respect of a dwelling house which is, was or was intended to be the parties' family home (s 30(7)); and it ceases on divorce, dissolution or death of either spouse or civil partner (s 30(8)), unless the court orders otherwise (s 33(5)).

A person with a 'home right' also has other rights. Thus, any payment made by a person with a 'home right' towards satisfaction of any liability of the tenant or owner in respect of rent, mortgage payments or other outgoings affecting the home must be treated by the recipient as if it was made by the tenant or owner (s 30(3)). For example, if a husband stops paying the rent on a property that was taken in his name, the wife can continue to pay the rent and the landlord will have to accept that payment as if it was made by her husband and will thereby be prevented from evicting her.

A spouse or civil partner's 'home right' is a charge on the other party's estate or interest (s 31). This charge is binding on a third party (for example a purchaser or a mortgagee) if it has been protected by a notice on the register made under the Land Registration Act 2002 or by registration of a land charge under the Land Charges Act 1972. (For more on Part IV of the FLA 1996 in respect of occupation of the family home in the context of domestic violence, see 5.5.)

4.3 The property rights of engaged couples and parties to a civil partnership agreement

The Law Reform (Miscellaneous Provisions) Act 1970 provides that an engagement to marry is not a contract giving rise to legal rights and consequently no action for breach of promise can be brought against the party who was responsible for terminating the engagement (s 1). On the termination of an engagement, any rule of law relating to the beneficial entitlement of spouses also applies to any property in which either or both parties had a beneficial interest during their engagement (s 2(1)). Also, the fact that one party was responsible for terminating the engagement does not affect any express or implied arrangement in respect of the return of any engagement gift (s 3(1)). Ownership depends on the intention of the donor. In the absence of intention, the court may infer that a gift from a relative belongs to the spouse to whom they are related (as it did in *Samson v Samson* [1982] 1 WLR 252). The same rules apply to civil partnership agreements under sections 73 and 74 of the Civil Partnership Act 2004 (CPA 2004).

An engagement ring is presumed to be an absolute gift (s 3(2)), which means that it can be kept on the termination of an engagement unless there is an express or implied condition to the contrary (for example if it is a family heirloom). There is no equivalent legislative provision for parties to a civil partnership agreement.

Engaged couples and parties to a civil partnership agreement who have contributed towards improvements to property can acquire a share in the property in the same way as married couples and civil partners (s 2 Law Reform (Miscellaneous Provisions) Act 1970; s 74 CPA 2004) (see 4.2 above). However, these provisions are not often used, and they are sometimes overlooked (see, for example, *Dibble v Pfluger* [2010] EWCA Civ 1005).

4.4 The property rights of cohabitants

(a) Ownership of property

During their relationship and on relationship breakdown, the property rights of cohabiting couples are governed by the general rules of property law. There are no special family law statutes which apply to cohabiting couples as there are for married couples, civil partners and engaged couples (see 4.2 above and Chapter 7); and there is no discretionary jurisdiction, as there is on divorce or dissolution, to adjust property rights according to their needs and resources. A cohabitant is also in a vulnerable position if their partner dies without having made a will (see 4.12 below).

A cohabitant or former cohabitant who wishes to claim a share, or an enlarged share, of property will have to turn to the law of equity (see 4.7 and 4.8 below) to bring a claim. Unlike disputes on divorce or dissolution, such claims are heard in the civil or chancery courts and are dealt with from a property law, and not a family law, perspective. Bringing a case is expensive and time-consuming, and the law of trusts is not entirely satisfactory for determining such disputes (see 3.4).

(b) Occupation of the family home

Unlike a spouse or civil partner, a cohabitant has no statutory right of occupation of the family home. Rights of occupation are instead dependent on a cohabitant having a beneficial estate or interest in, or a contractual licence to occupy, the family home. A cohabitant or former cohabitant who is a victim of domestic violence can, however, apply for an occupation order under Part IV of the Family Law Act 1996 which, if granted, will give the applicant a right of occupation of the family home, but only for the duration of the order (see 5.5).

4.5 Ownership of personal property

Personal property is property other than land such as, for example, investments and household goods. Ownership of such property depends on whether there is an interest under a contract or in equity under a trust. As a general rule, title to the property passes to the purchaser, subject to there being a valid contract and no contrary intention. In the case of gifts of personal property, ownership passes to the donee if the donor intended to transfer the gift and it was handed over.

(a) Acquiring a right of ownership

A person can claim an equitable interest in personal property under an express, resulting or constructive trust as the following cases show.

> ▶ *Paul v Constance* [1977] 1 WLR 527
>
> The claimant was held to have an interest by way of an express trust in the bank account held in her partner's sole name, as she had been authorised to draw on the account and he had told her on several occasions that the money in the account was as much hers as his.

> ▶ *Rowe v Prance* **[1999] 2 FLR 787**
>
> The claimant was held to be entitled to a half-share in a boat owned by the defendant, with whom she had been in a close relationship for 14 years. She had not contributed financially to its purchase, but her partner had referred to it as 'our boat', had spoken of 'a share of the boat together' and had said 'your security is your interest in it'. The claimant had given up rented accommodation and put furniture in storage in order to move into the boat, which they intended to use to sail around the world together. The court accepted this as sufficient evidence that the defendant was holding the boat on trust for both of them under an express trust and the claimant was entitled to an equal share.

Despite the successful outcome in the two cases above, cohabitants should be wary of taking a case to court and should instead attempt to settle any dispute outside court. Taking a case to court is costly, time-consuming and unpredictable. In *Hammond v Mitchell* [1992] 1 FLR 229, Waite J said that cohabitants on relationship breakdown should be encouraged to settle disputes about personal property outside court on the understanding that the court will usually divide such property equally.

(b) Bank accounts

If a bank account is held in one person's name then any money in the account belongs to that person, unless there is a contrary intention or another person has made a contribution to the fund. If a bank account is held in joint names then the money in the account belongs to both parties as beneficial joint tenants of the whole fund unless there is a contrary intention. With regard to the ownership of the money in a bank account, the court may hold that the money is owned in equal shares even though one of the parties put more money into the account (as it did in *Jones v Maynard* [1951] Ch 572 where the husband had put more money into the account than his wife but where the court held that they had pooled their resources). As a general rule, any property bought with funds from a bank account belongs to the purchaser. However, if the parties had a common purpose and pooled their resources, the court may decide that the property belongs to them both.

4.6 Disputes about the family home

Disputes about property are often about the family home as it is usually a couple's most valuable asset and it is needed to house the family. Disputes about the family home (and/or other property) may arise in the following situations:

- ▶ *On relationship breakdown* Spouses and civil partners who cannot agree about ownership of the family home (and/or other property) can invoke the discretionary powers of the court on divorce or dissolution to settle their property disputes (see Chapter 7). Cohabitants, on the other hand, must use the principles of property law, in particular the law of equity (see 4.7 and 4.8 below).
- ▶ *Where property interests are not defined* Where there is no mention of the parties' respective interests such as, for example, on the transfer deed, the court may have to decide what each person's interest is in the property.

▶ *Where a third party seeks possession*   Where a third party (such as a mortgagee or trustee in bankruptcy) seeks possession of the home, a spouse, civil partner, cohabitant or other family member may claim they have an interest in the home under a trust in order to defeat the claim to possession (see, for example, *Lloyds Bank plc v Rosset* [1990] 2 FLR 155 at 4.7 below).

▶ *On death*   Where there is a will, then that determines the parties' property rights. Where there is no will, then a surviving spouse or civil partner has a statutory right to succeed to the deceased's estate (see 4.12 below). Cohabitants have no such rights of succession (see 3.2), but they can bring a claim under the Inheritance (Provision for Family and Dependants) Act 1975 (see 4.13 below) or claim they have an interest in any property in equity under a trust (see 4.7 below) or on the basis of proprietary estoppel (see 4.8 below).

A claim to establish an interest in the home (other than on divorce or dissolution) is usually brought under section 14 of the Trusts of Land and Appointment of Trustees Act 1996. This is the mechanism which cohabitants use when bringing a claim to establish an interest in the home (see, for example, *Oxley v Hiscock* [2004] 2 FLR 669 at 4.7(b) below).

4.7   Acquiring a right of ownership in the family home under a trust

There are two sorts of ownership: ownership in law; and ownership in equity. A person can own property in law and equity *or* in law or equity. Thus, both cohabitants may be owners in law and equity. Alternatively, one cohabitant may be the sole legal owner of the family home but hold it on trust in equity for the other cohabitant who will have an equitable interest (sometimes referred to as a beneficial interest) in the property as a beneficiary of the trust. Having an equitable interest gives the beneficiary enforceable rights against the legal owner.

It is a requirement of section 53(1) of the Law of Property Act 1925 (LPA 1925) that interests in land and declarations of trust in land are created by writing. Thus, a cohabiting couple may enter into an express deed of trust when they acquire their home recording in writing how the property is to be shared between them. However, a person can claim a right of ownership in the family home under a trust even if there is nothing in writing to that effect, as implied, resulting and constructive trusts are exempt from the need for writing (s 53(2)). Similar rules apply in respect of contracts for the sale of land. Thus, while section 2(1) of the Law of Property (Miscellaneous Provisions) Act 1989 requires contracts for the sale of land to be in writing, section 2(5) provides that writing is not required for the creation of an implied, resulting or constructive trust of land. As section 2(5), like section 53(2) of the LPA 1925, was intended to allow a range of equitable remedies, an interest in land can also be claimed under the equitable doctrine of proprietary estoppel (*per* Beldam LJ in *Yaxley v Gotts and Gotts* [1999] 2 FLR 941, see further at 4.8 below).

An equitable interest in land, such as in the family home, can be acquired under a resulting or constructive trust. Resulting and constructive trusts are two distinct types of trust, each of which has its own body of case-law.

(a)   Acquiring an interest in the family home under a resulting trust

A resulting trust is presumed to arise where a person makes a financial contribution to the purchase of property. In the absence of a contrary intention (for example that the contribution was a gift or a loan, or that other shares were intended), a person who contributes money to the purchase of property acquires an interest under a resulting trust proportionate to their contribution. Resulting trusts were claimed in the following cases.

> ▶ *Sekhon v Alissa* [1989] 2 FLR 94
>
> The house had been bought in the name of the defendant daughter. She had contributed to the purchase price, but her mother had paid the balance. The mother claimed a share in the house under a resulting trust, arguing that, although it was bought in her daughter's name, it was purchased as a joint commercial venture and they both intended to own it in proportion to their respective financial contributions. The daughter attempted to rebut the presumption of resulting trust by arguing that her mother's financial contribution was intended as a gift or a loan. The court had to decide what the actual or presumed intention of the parties was at the time of the conveyance. The Court of Appeal held that the law presumed a resulting trust in the mother's favour, and, on the facts, the presumption was not rebutted by the daughter's allegation that the money was a gift or a loan.
>
> ▶ *Springette v Defoe* [1992] 2 FLR 388
>
> The parties, two elderly cohabitants, had bought their council house, but there was nothing in the registered transfer quantifying their respective beneficial interests. Each party had paid half the mortgage instalments, but the claimant had paid most of the balance of the purchase price. When the relationship broke down she issued an originating summons claiming that she was entitled to 75 per cent of the proceeds of sale, as this represented her contribution to the purchase. At first instance, the trial judge granted the parties an equal share of the beneficial interest, on the basis that it was their uncommunicated belief or intention that they were to share the property equally. But the Court of Appeal allowed the applicant's appeal, holding that, as there was no discussion between the parties as to their respective beneficial interests, there was no evidence to rebut the presumption that she was entitled to a 75 per cent share of the beneficial interest under a resulting trust.

Despite the fact that the resulting trust was used in the above cases, most cases are now brought on the basis of a constructive trust (see 4.7(b) below) or proprietary estoppel (see 4.8 below). The demise of the resulting trust as a mechanism for claiming a share in the family home is due, in part, to the fact that a claimant who establishes a resulting trust is limited to obtaining a share proportionate to their contribution to the purchase price. In addition, only a financial contribution to the initial purchase of property, and not a contribution made after its purchase, can give rise to an interest under a resulting trust (see *Curley v Parkes* [2004] EWCA Civ 1515). Consequently, both the House of Lords and the Supreme Court have held that the constructive trust is the appropriate tool of analysis in cases regarding ownership of the family home (see *Stack v Dowden* and *Jones v Kernott* at 4.7(c) below).

(i) The presumption of advancement

Under this presumption, a transfer of property from husband to wife and from parent to child is presumed to belong to the wife or child absolutely. It also applies to property purchased by a husband for his wife or by a parent for a child. In other words, equity presumes that the transfer or purchase is an outright gift. This presumption can be used to rebut the presumption of a resulting trust (for example by a wife arguing that her husband's contribution to the purchase of the home was an outright gift to her). However, it is regarded as a judicial instrument of last resort and one which can be easily rebutted (see, for example, *Laskar v Laskar* [2008] EWCA Civ 347). It does not apply to cohabitants (*Chapman v Jaume* [2012] EWCA Civ 476). The presumption of advancement is considered to be archaic and discriminatory as it applies only to gifts made by husbands to wives and by parents to children and therefore breaches Article 5 of Protocol 7 of the European Convention on Human Rights (equality of rights and responsibilities of spouses during marriage). It has little relevance today and is unlikely to be relied on. In fact, section 199 of the Equality Act 2010 will abolish the presumption when it comes into force.

(b) Acquiring an interest in the family home under a constructive trust

An interest in the family home can be claimed under a constructive trust or, more specifically, what is known as a 'common intention constructive trust' (to distinguish it from other types of constructive trust which are used in the commercial sphere). The court cannot find a constructive trust merely to do justice in a particular case. It must consider the evidence and ascertain what the intentions of the parties were. As Dillon LJ said in *Springette v Defoe* [1992] 2 FLR 388, the court cannot exercise a general discretion as to what the man in the street, on the general view of the case, might regard as fair. It cannot ascribe to parties intentions which they never had. Despite *obiter dicta* by Lord Walker and Baroness Hale in *Stack v Dowden* (see 4.7(c) below) that the courts should adopt a broader approach to the question of finding a common intention in constructive trusts cases involving the family home, the courts have not shown themselves willing to do so.

In a claim to a beneficial interest in the home under a constructive trust, the court conducts a two-stage exercise.

(i) The two-stage exercise

First, the court considers the evidence to establish whether or not the claimant has an interest under a constructive trust. Second, if there is such an interest, then the court considers all the evidence in order to decide the size of the claimant's interest. The leading case on constructive trusts is *Lloyds Bank plc v Rosset* (see below) in which Lord Bridge laid down the approach to be adopted by the courts. This is still the approach adopted in constructive trust cases today.

▶ *Lloyds Bank plc v Rosset* **[1990] 2 FLR 155**

The home had been purchased in Mr Rosset's sole name. Mrs Rosset had helped to renovate it, but she had made no financial contribution to its purchase or renovation. Mr Rosset charged the house to Lloyds Bank as security for a loan, which Mrs Rosset knew nothing about. When Mr Rosset went into debt, Lloyds Bank claimed possession of the home and an order for sale. Mrs Rosset, by way of defence to the bank's claim, argued that she had a beneficial interest in the house under a constructive trust and that this interest coupled with her actual occupation gave her an overriding interest under section 70(1)(g) of the Land Registration Act 1925 which would defeat the bank's claims.

The House of Lords, dismissing her appeal, held that her activities in relation to the renovation of the house were insufficient to justify the inference of a common intention that she was entitled to a beneficial interest under a constructive trust. Lord Bridge summarised and encapsulated the law as laid down in the two earlier House of Lords decisions of *Pettitt v Pettitt* [1970] AC 777 and *Gissing v Gissing* [1971] AC 886, and referred also to the Court of Appeal decision in *Grant v Edwards* [1986] Ch 638.

LORD BRIDGE: The first and fundamental question which must always be resolved is whether, independently of any inference to be drawn from the conduct of the parties in the course of sharing the house as their home and managing their joint affairs, there has at any time prior to acquisition, or exceptionally at some later date, been any agreement, arrangement or understanding reached between them that the property is to be shared beneficially. The finding of an agreement or arrangement to share in this sense can only, I think, be based on evidence of express discussions between the partners, however imperfectly remembered and however imprecise their terms may have been. Once a finding to this effect is made it will only be necessary for the partner asserting a claim to a beneficial interest against the partner entitled to the legal estate to show that he or she has acted to his or her detriment or significantly altered his or her position in reliance on the agreement in order to give rise to a constructive trust or proprietary estoppel.

In sharp contrast to this situation is the very different one where there is no evidence to support a finding of an agreement or an arrangement to share, however reasonable it might have been for the parties to reach such an agreement if they had applied their minds to the question, and where the court must rely entirely on the conduct of the parties both as the basis from which to infer a common intention to share the property beneficially and as the conduct relied on to give rise to a constructive trust. In this situation direct contributions to the purchase price by the partner who is not the legal owner, whether initially or by payment of mortgage instalments, will readily justify the inference necessary to the creation of a constructive trust. But, as I read the authorities, it is at least extremely doubtful whether anything less will do.

Lord Bridge's words in *Rosset* have formed the template of analysis in subsequent cases. Thus, in order to establish a constructive trust there must be evidence of a common intention to share the beneficial ownership of the property *and* evidence of some act(s) of detrimental reliance undertaken on the basis of that common intention. A common intention can arise where there is an express agreement, arrangement or understanding that the property is to be shared beneficially, such as a verbal agreement between the parties. However, where there is no express agreement to share, and so a common intention must be inferred from the parties' conduct, it will usually be difficult to establish a claim under a constructive trust where there has been no direct financial contribution to the purchase of the home (see the *dicta* of Lord Bridge above). A different approach is taken in joint-owner cases because it is presumed that joint legal owners own the property jointly beneficially as well as legally (see below).

In *Oxley v Hiscock* [2004] EWCA Civ 546, Chadwick LJ usefully summarised the correct approach to be adopted in cases where a claim is made to a beneficial interest under a constructive trust:

[T]he first question is whether there is evidence from which to infer a common intention, communicated by each to the other, that each shall have a beneficial share in the property. In many such cases ... there will have been some discussion between the parties at the time of the purchase which provides the answer to that question. Those are cases within the first of Lord Bridge's categories in *Lloyds Bank plc v Rosset*. In other cases – where the evidence is that the matter was not discussed at all – an affirmative answer will readily be inferred from the fact that each has made a financial contribution. These are cases within Lord Bridge's second category. And, if the answer to the first question is that there was a common intention, communicated to each other, that each should have a beneficial share in the property, then the party who does not become the legal owner will be held to have acted to his or her detriment in making a financial contribution to the purchase in reliance on the common intention.

(ii) Indirect financial contributions

In *Rosset* (see above) Lord Bridge said that, on his reading of the authorities, he doubted whether anything less than a direct financial contribution to the purchase price by the partner who is not the legal owner, whether initially or by payment of mortgage instalments, would be sufficient to establish a share in the home where there was no express agreement that the claimant should have a beneficial interest. Because of Lord Bridge's *dicta*, the courts in subsequent cases have been unwilling to accept indirect contributions (such as paying household bills or bringing up children) as evidence to establish an interest under a constructive trust. It has been suggested, however, that judges should be more willing to do so (see below).

(iii) Detrimental reliance

In addition to proving a common intention, the claimant must also prove that they suffered some detriment as a result of relying on the common intention. Detrimental reliance is usually fairly easily proved. Bringing up a family and running a home, for example, can be used as evidence of detriment. However, the act(s) of detrimental reliance must come *after* the establishment of a common intention. Thus, for example, in *Churchill v Roach* [2004] 2 FLR 989 the cohabitant's claim to property belonging to her deceased cohabitant's estate on the basis of a constructive trust failed, as the acts relied on as constituting detriment had occurred before the common intention was established.

(iv) Establishing the size of the beneficial interest

If the court finds that the claimant is entitled to a beneficial interest under a constructive trust, it must then determine the size of that interest. The approach taken at this stage of the analysis is less restrictive than that taken when establishing whether there is a common intention that the claimant should have an interest at all. In *Midland Bank plc v Cooke* [1995] 2 FLR 915 (see below), the Court of Appeal held that a 'broad-brush' approach should be adopted by the court when deciding the size of the share. Thus, the court takes account of all the circumstances of the case, including financial and non-financial circumstances and the intentions of the parties. In *Oxley v Hiscock* [2004] EWCA Civ 546, Chadwick LJ adopted a broad test based on fairness. This approach was approved by the House of Lords in *Stack v Dowden* and by the Supreme Court in *Jones v Kernott* (see 4.7(c) below).

Constructive trusts of the family home – examples from the case-law

▶ *Midland Bank plc v Cooke* **[1995] 2 FLR 915**

The husband purchased the matrimonial home for £8,450, with £6,450 from a mortgage, £1,000 of his own savings and another £1,000 which was a wedding gift from his parents. His wife made no direct contribution to the purchase, except for the £500 which represented her half-share of the wedding gift, but she made considerable financial contributions to the upkeep of the house and to the household. When the bank initiated possession proceedings she claimed a beneficial interest in the home. At first instance, the county court judge held that her beneficial interest in the house amounted to a sum equivalent to 6.47 per cent of the value of the property, representing her half-share of the wedding gift of £1,000. The wife appealed to the Court of Appeal.

The Court of Appeal allowed her appeal, holding that, as she and her husband had agreed to share everything equally, including the house, she was entitled to half the beneficial interest. In respect of establishing the share of the beneficial interest, Waite LJ said that the court was permitted to undertake a survey of the whole course of dealing between the parties in respect of their ownership and occupation of the house and their sharing of its burdens and advantages.

▶ *Oxley v Hiscock* **[2004] EWCA Civ 546**

The claimant applied under section 14 of the Trusts of Land and Appointment of Trustees Act 1996 for a declaration that the proceeds of sale were held by the defendant, her former partner, on trust for the parties in equal shares. Chadwick LJ held, in respect of calculating the share of the beneficial interest, that each party 'is entitled to that share which the court considers fair having regard to the whole course of dealing between them in relation to the property'. Applying the broad-brush approach adopted in *Midland Bank plc v Cooke* (see above), the Court of Appeal held that a fair division of the sale of the property was 60 per cent to the defendant and 40 per cent to the claimant as equal division would have given insufficient weight to the disparity in the parties' financial contributions.

▶ *Cox v Jones* **[2004] 2 FLR 1010**

The claimant had made no direct financial contribution to the purchase price of the property in dispute which was owned by her partner. She had also made no contribution to the mortgage repayments, but had spent time renovating it. Mann J found that there was an express arrangement between the parties that she was to have a share of the house, and that she had acted to her detriment by putting her practice as a barrister to one side to spend her time and energy on renovating the property that was to be their home. Mann J granted her a 25 per cent share of the beneficial interest in the property, applying the *dicta* of Chadwick LJ in *Oxley v Hiscock* (see above) that her share of the interest in the house must be 'fair having regard to the whole course of dealing between them in relation to the property'.

▶ *Walsh v Singh* **[2009] EWHC 3219 (Ch)**

The claimant had been instrumental in finding the property that her former partner had purchased in his sole name and from his own resources, and she had carried out works to make the property habitable. She had also given up her career as a lawyer at his request to concentrate on their equestrian business. After their relationship broke down, she failed to establish an interest in the home under a constructive trust (and by way of proprietary estoppel) as there was no evidence of any financial contribution. It was held, *inter alia*, by the High Court that, although she had made significant contributions to the parties' project, she had not done so pursuant to any common intention or representation that she was to have a 50 per cent interest or any other interest in the property.

▶ *Thomson v Humphrey* [2009] EWHC 3576 (Ch)

The claimant failed in her claim to a beneficial interest under a constructive trust in the former family home held in the sole name of the defendant, who was her former partner. Although she had given up her part-time job on the basis of assurances that he would look after her, and she had moved into his home with her children, Warren J dismissed her claim on the basis that the defendant's instructions to his solicitor to draft a 'living together' agreement and his attempt to get the woman to sign it made it clear that he did not intend her to have any beneficial interest in the property. Even if there had been a common intention, Warren J held that she would not have established sufficient detriment: she had given up a poorly paid job with no prospects on an assurance that she would be looked after and not on an assurance that she would have a beneficial interest in the property.

Most of the above claims to a beneficial interest under a constructive trust were brought by cohabitants. If they had been married or civil partners then the court could, in the exercise of its discretionary powers, have given them an interest in the home (see 7.7).

(v) Should the courts take a broader approach in constructive trust cases?

Should courts in constructive trust cases be more willing to infer or impute a common intention as to the existence of a beneficial interest in the home? Should judges be willing to find evidence of intention not just from direct financial contributions but also from indirect contributions (such as paying household bills, looking after the home and/or bringing up children)? Although there have been calls for the courts to adopt a broader and more flexible approach than that adopted by Lord Bridge in *Rosset* (see above) and to take indirect contributions into account, the courts themselves have been unwilling to do so because of the binding nature of *Rosset*. Nonetheless, the Law Commission in its 2002 report *Sharing Homes* (see 3.4), Lord Walker and Baroness Hale's *obiter dicta* in *Stack v Dowden* and the Supreme Court in *Jones v Kernott* (see 4.7(c) below) have recommended such an approach.

Baroness Hale, who gave the leading opinion in *Stack v Dowden*, said that imputed intentions were acceptable. Her Ladyship said that, in her view, Lord Bridge in *Rosset* might have 'set the hurdle rather too high in certain respects'. Her Ladyship was also of the opinion that the resulting trust was no longer the appropriate tool of analysis in such cases and that 'many more factors than financial contributions may be relevant to divining the parties' true intentions'. These views were subsequently endorsed by the Privy Council in *Abbott v Abbott* [2007] UKPC 53, where Lord Walker, commenting on Lord Bridge's words in *Rosset*, said: 'Whether or not Lord Bridge's observation was justified in 1990, in my opinion the law has moved on, and your Lordships should move it a little more in the same direction.' However, there is little evidence in the case-law that the courts have adopted the more flexible approach to establishing common intention recommended by Baroness Hale and Lord Walker. Thus, in *Capehorn v Harris* [2015] EWCA Civ 955, the Court of Appeal held that the trial judge had been wrong to impute an intention to the parties that the non-owning party should have an interest in the family home. An actual agreement (even if inferred from conduct) had to be found.

The following case shows the courts continuing to use the principles laid down in *Rosset*. What was distinctive about the case, however, was that the respondent owned the house *before* the appellant moved in (in other words, it was a 'post-acquisition' case). It shows that, although discussions and conduct post-acquisition of the home can be considered by the court, an inferred intention that both parties are beneficial owners is unlikely to be readily drawn from conduct alone in the absence of any evidence of express agreement.

▶ *James v Thomas* **[2007] EWCA Civ 1212**

The respondent was the sole legal owner of the property (which prior to him owning it had been owned by his family for about 20 years). Three years after he acquired the house the appellant moved in with him. She helped him with his business, but all the expenses for the house were paid from his bank account. When she moved in she gave him £5,000 to pay a tax bill, but it was unclear whether this was a gift or a loan. During the relationship various statements were made to the effect that the improvements to the property 'would benefit them both'. When their relationship ended, she claimed an interest in the property on the basis of a constructive trust or proprietary estoppel. After her claim failed at first instance, she appealed to the Court of Appeal.

The Court of Appeal dismissed her appeal. Sir John Chadwick held that a common intention to found a constructive trust can arise post-acquisition and that an intention can be inferred from the whole course of dealing between the parties. However, he held that, in the absence of an express post-acquisition agreement, the court would be slow to infer from conduct alone that the parties intended to vary the beneficial interests established at the time of acquisition. The Court of Appeal held that the evidence was insufficient to establish a constructive trust expressly or by inference; and that, in any event, she had not acted to her detriment in reliance on the assurances by the defendant.

SIR JOHN CHADWICK: Miss J's interest in the property (if any) must be determined by applying principles of law and equity which (however inadequate to meet the circumstances in which parties live together in the twenty-first century) must now be taken as well-established.

The approach in *James v Thomas* was applied in *Morris v Morris* [2008] EWCA Civ 257 (another post-acquisition case) where the Court of Appeal found no express or inferred common intention to share the property in dispute. Gibson LJ, referring to Sir John Chadwick in *James v Thomas*, held that, although a common intention could be inferred from conduct, the court would be slow to infer a subsequent common intention from conduct alone. (For a commentary on *James v Thomas* and *Morris v Morris*, see Piska [2009] CFLQ 104, who states that, while correctly decided, the fact that both claimants received nothing seems harsh.)

(c) Joint-owner cases

Cases where the parties are joint owners of the family home are treated differently from cases where the family home is put into the name of one party only. As has been seen above, in sole-owner cases the court has first to decide whether it was intended that the non-owner should have a beneficial interest in the property *at all*; and then, if so, what that beneficial interest is. In joint-owner cases it is presumed that the parties intended to share the beneficial interest. Where there is no express declaration as to the beneficial ownership, the issue the court usually needs to decide is the size of each person's share. In such cases, *Stack v Dowden* (see below) establishes that beneficial ownership of the property should follow the legal ownership, unless there is a contrary intention. It also establishes that, in determining the parties' intentions, the court may consider a wide range of factors.

Although *Stack v Dowden* was the first case to go to the House of Lords involving a dispute between cohabitants about ownership of the family home, it offers little hope for cohabitants who are non-owners of the family home. Neither does the decision of the Supreme Court in *Jones v Kernott* (see below). This is because sole-owner and joint-owner cases are treated differently. This is despite the fact that Gardner and Davidson, commenting on *Stack v Dowden* ((2011) 127 LQR 12, at 15), expressed the hope that the Supreme Court would 'make clear that constructive trusts of family homes are governed by a single regime, dispelling any impression that different rules apply to "joint names" and "single name" cases'.

▶ *Stack v Dowden* [2007] UKHL 17

The parties had cohabited for 20 years. The family home was registered in their joint names but the transfer deed contained nothing about their interests in equity, as they had failed to draw up a declaration of trust. The purchase price, other than the mortgage advance, had been provided by Ms Dowden. When the relationship broke down, Mr Stack left the house and Ms Dowden remained there with the children. Mr Stack successfully sought an order for sale of the property and was granted a 50:50 division of the proceeds of sale. The Court of Appeal allowed Ms Dowden's appeal and held that she was entitled to 65 per cent of the proceeds of sale (as she had made a greater financial contribution to the purchase of the house), applying the fairness test laid down by Chadwick LJ in *Oxley v Hiscock* (see above). Mr Stack appealed to the House of Lords.

The House of Lords unanimously dismissed his appeal (Lord Neuberger dissenting as to the reasoning) and held that, where a house is conveyed into joint names in the domestic consumer context, then *prima facie* joint and equal beneficial interests arise unless and until the contrary is proved. The burden was on the defendant to rebut the presumption by showing that equal beneficial shares were not intended. In the domestic context, factors other than financial contributions could be taken into account. Looking at the facts of the case, there were many factors to which the defendant could point to indicate that the intention of the parties was that the shares were not owned jointly in equity. For example, when the property was bought, both parties knew that the defendant had paid more than the claimant, and they had kept their financial affairs separate. The defendant had therefore made good her case for a 65 per cent share.

BARONESS HALE: The search is to ascertain the parties' shared intentions, actual, inferred or imputed, with respect to the property in the light of their whole course of conduct in relation to it.

Thus the principle recognised in *Stack v Dowden* is that, if parties purchase a family home in joint names, then it is presumed that they also intended to own the property jointly in equity. (For applications of the principle in *Stack v Dowden*, see *Fowler v Barron* [2008] EWCA Civ 377 and *Laskar v Laskar* [2008] EWCA Civ 347.)

(i) A common intention to share the beneficial interest can change over time

Stack v Dowden was considered by the Supreme Court in *Jones v Kernott* (see below) which, like *Stack v Dowden*, involved the question of the size of the respective beneficial interests in a house which the cohabitant parties had bought in joint names. At first instance, the trial judge held, on the evidence, that Ms Jones was entitled to 90 per cent of the beneficial interest in the former family home, following the fairness approach adopted in *Oxley v Hiscock* (see above). The question for the Supreme Court was whether such an approach was consistent with *Stack v Dowden*, where the House of Lords had started from the premise that a conveyance into joint names meant that the beneficial interests in the property were joint and equal. The Supreme Court answered that question in the affirmative. In other words, even though a house is bought in joint names and it is presumed that there is a common intention that the beneficial interest is held equally, the court may hold that the intention has changed over time.

> ▶ *Jones v Kernott* [2011] UKSC 53
>
> The parties, Mr Kernott and Ms Jones, were cohabitants. In 1985 they bought a house in joint names for £30,000. Ms Jones contributed £6,000, and the balance was raised by an interest-only mortgage. From this point on they shared payment of the household bills and the mortgage. In 1993, the couple separated, and Mr Kernott left the home where Ms Jones and their two children remained. Mr Kernott stopped paying his share of the bills, and contributed little or nothing towards the maintenance of the children. In 2006, Mr Kernott sought payment of his half-share of the former family home. Ms Jones responded by seeking a declaration under section 14 of the Trusts of Land and Appointment of Trustees Act 1996 that she owned the whole of the beneficial interest in the former family home.
>
> At first instance, the judge in the county court held that Ms Jones and Mr Kernott were entitled to a 90 per cent and 10 per cent share of the beneficial interest in the property respectively for, although they had bought the property in joint names, and a presumption arose that they intended to jointly share the beneficial ownership, the common intention had changed over time. Mr Kernott's appeal to the High Court was dismissed.
>
> Mr Kernott appealed successfully to the Court of Appeal which by a majority (Jacob LJ dissenting) declared that the parties owned the property as tenants in common in equal shares, applying *Stack v Dowden*. There was insufficient evidence to displace the presumption that they had intended to share the beneficial interest equally. The passage of time was insufficient to do so, even if in the meantime Mr Kernott had acquired alternative accommodation and Ms Jones had paid all the outgoings on the former family home. Mr Kernott's share in the beneficial interest was therefore quantified at 50 per cent of the value of the property.
>
> Ms Jones appealed to the Supreme Court, which unanimously allowed her appeal and reinstated the order of the county court judge. Lord Walker and Baroness Hale, who gave a joint leading opinion, held that the principle recognised in *Stack v Dowden* is that, if parties purchase a family home in joint names, then it is presumed that they also intended to own the property jointly in equity. However, this presumption may be rebutted by evidence that it was not, or it had ceased to be, the common intention of the parties to hold the property jointly. This may more readily be shown where, for example, the parties did not share their financial resources.

Although all the members of the Supreme Court were agreed on the outcome, their reasoning was different. Thus, whereas Lord Walker and Lady Hale were of the view that they were able to *infer* that the parties had intended a 90 per cent and 10 per cent share of the beneficial interest in the property, Lords Kerr and Wilson, on the other hand, considered that there was insufficient evidence to infer what the parties had intended and that it was therefore necessary to *impute* that intention. In *Barnes v Phillips* [2015] EWCA CIV 1056, the court, applying the principles in *Jones v Kernott*, held that imputation was permissible only at the quantification stage of the parties' beneficial shares, once an actual agreement to vary the beneficial ownership had been found. It can be argued that such fine linguistic distinctions (between 'inferring' and 'imputing') create unnecessary complexity and make predicting the outcome of cases more difficult and uncertain (see, for example, Pawlowski [2016] Fam Law 189).

4.8 Acquiring an interest by way of proprietary estoppel

Proprietary estoppel can be used to claim an interest in the family home (and is often used as an alternative to, or in addition to, a claim based on a constructive trust).

Although the doctrines of constructive trust and proprietary estoppel are similar in that they are both equitable doctrines providing relief against unconscionable conduct, they are legally separate and distinct. An important distinction is in respect of the remedy available. The existence of a constructive trust results in a right of ownership, whereas, if a proprietary estoppel is established, the court merely has a discretion as to the remedy to be ordered to do justice in the case.

The doctrine of proprietary estoppel was described by Balcombe LJ in *Wayling v Jones* [1995] 2 FLR 1029, at 1031, as follows:

> Where one person (A) has acted to his detriment on the faith of a belief, which was known to and encouraged by another person (B), that he either has or is going to be given a right in or over B's property, B cannot insist on his strict legal rights if to do so would be inconsistent with A's belief.

Thus, to establish a proprietary estoppel the following must be proved: the existence of a promise or assurance that the claimant would acquire a proprietary interest in specified property; reliance by the claimant on that promise or assurance; *and* some detriment to the claimant caused by such reliance. These are overlapping concepts. Once these elements are proved, then the court has to decide in the exercise of its discretion what is necessary to avoid an unconscionable result. In doing so, it has a wide discretion. Each case, however, depends on its own particular facts.

In *Gillett v Holt and Another* [2000] 2 FLR 266 the Court of Appeal stated that, as proprietary estoppel is a flexible doctrine which is based on preventing unconscionable conduct, the facts must be looked at in the round. It held that detriment is not a narrow or technical concept, but one which must be approached as part of a broad inquiry, and that reliance and detriment should not be treated as being divided into separate watertight compartments.

(a) What constitutes a promise or assurance for the purpose of establishing an estoppel?

In order to establish an estoppel there must be a clear and unambiguous promise or assurance given by the defendant and relied on by the claimant. In *Thorner v Majors and Others* [2009] UKHL 18 the House of Lords considered this requirement and held that the effect of the words or actions must be assessed in their context, and that it would be quite wrong to be unrealistically rigorous when applying the 'clear and unambiguous' test. It held that if the statement relied on to found an estoppel was ambiguous, that ambiguity should not of itself deprive a person who had reasonably relied on the assurance of all relief, although any relief should be limited to the least beneficial interpretation. Thus, in *Southwell v Blackburn* [2014] EWCA Civ 1347, although the discussions which the couple had were not specific as to ownership of the home they were moving into, the legal owner's assurances to the claimant that 'she would always have a home and be secure in this one' and the trial judge's finding that '[h]e led her to believe that she would have the sort of security that a wife would have, in terms of accommodation at the house' were clear and specific enough to give rise to a proprietary estoppel.

(b) What remedy to grant?

Once an estoppel is proved, the court must consider all the circumstances of the case and exercise its discretion to decide what remedy to grant. A claim based on estoppel may not be as advantageous as one based on a trust. This is because the claimant may not gain a right of ownership, but merely a licence to occupy the property or financial compensation.

Proprietary estoppel was claimed in the following cases.

▶ *Negus v Bahouse and Another* [2007] EWHC 2628 (Ch)

A cohabitant claimed that she had an interest by way of proprietary estoppel in a flat where she had lived with her deceased partner. Her claim failed, as the statements made by the deceased had been equivocal and were insufficient to amount to a specific agreement or understanding that she should have an interest. However, using the Inheritance (Provision for Families and Dependents) Act 1975 (see 4.13 below), the court held in the circumstances that the flat (plus a sum of £200,000) should be transferred to her.

▶ *Suggitt v Suggitt* [2011] EWHC 903 (Ch)

The claimant claimed an interest in his deceased father's estate (a large farming business) on the basis of proprietary estoppel. His claim was successful. The court held that the claimant's father had made some kind of repeated promise or assurance which had led the claimant reasonably to expect that the farmland and farmhouse would definitely be his after his father's death. With respect to reliance, the claimant had worked on the farm for no wage in the expectation and reliance that the farmland would one day be his. Thus, he had acted to his detriment or changed his position in reliance on the promises made by the deceased. Looking at matters in the round, it would be unconscionable to deprive the claimant of his expectation based on his deceased father's assurances. He was granted the farmland and farmhouse by the court.

4.9 A claim based on contract

An interest in property may be acquired under a contract, provided the legal requirements for creating a valid contract are satisfied. If a contract is for the sale or disposition of land it must be in writing (s 2(1) Law of Property (Miscellaneous

Provisions) Act 1989), but this requirement does not prevent the creation of a resulting or constructive trust, or the creation of an interest by way of proprietary estoppel. The following cases are examples where contractual claims were advanced.

▶ *Tanner v Tanner* [1975] 1 WLR 1341

The claimant purchased a house for occupation by the defendant, his female partner and their children. The claimant moved into the house, but when the relationship broke down the applicant sought possession on the basis that the defendant was only a bare licensee under a licence which he had revoked. The Court of Appeal held that there was an implied contractual licence under the terms of which the defendant was entitled to occupy the house while the children were of school age, or until some other circumstance arose which would make it unreasonable for her to remain in possession.

▶ *Layton v Martin* [1986] 2 FLR 277

The Court of Appeal held that there was no intention to create a legally enforceable contract, with the result that the claimant mistress failed in her claim against the deceased's estate even though she had accepted the man's offer that, if she were to live with him, he would give her emotional security, and also financial security on his death. Despite living with him for five years after he had made the offer, and for thirteen years in total, her claim failed.

4.10　Tenancies

(a)　Transferring a tenancy

Under section 53 and Schedule 7 of Part IV of the Family Law Act 1996, the court has jurisdiction to transfer tenancies on divorce, dissolution, and on the breakdown of cohabitation.

A tenancy is transferred by the court making a 'Part II order' which it has power to make whether a spouse, civil partner or cohabitant is solely or jointly entitled under a tenancy, provided the house was a matrimonial home in the case of a married couple, a civil partnership home in the case of civil partners, or, in the case of cohabitants, was a home in which the cohabiting couple lived together as husband and wife or as civil partners (paras 2 and 3 of Sch 7 and s 62(1)). Paragraph 1 of Schedule 7 makes it clear that 'cohabitant' includes a former cohabitant. There is no requirement that cohabitants must have lived together for a minimum period, although the court is required to take into account the length of the relationship when deciding whether or not to order a transfer.

In determining whether to make a Part II order, and, if so, in what manner, the court must consider all the circumstances of the case including: the circumstances in which the tenancy was granted, or the circumstances in which either of them became a tenant; the housing needs and housing resources of the parties and of any relevant child; their respective financial resources; the likely effect of any order (or no order) on the health, safety or well-being of the parties and of any relevant child; the conduct of the parties in relation to each other and otherwise; and the suitability of the parties as tenants (see para 5).

Where the parties are cohabitants and only one of them is entitled to occupy the house under the tenancy, the court must also consider: the nature of their relationship; the length of time they have lived together as husband and wife or as civil partners; whether there are any children who are children of both parties or for whom both parties have or have had parental responsibility; and the length of time that has elapsed since the parties ceased to live together (see para 5). Where the parties are council tenants, the housing policy of the local housing authority is another factor which the court can take into account.

(b)   Succeeding to a tenancy on the death of a tenant

See 4.14 below.

4.11   Homelessness and the family

Homelessness can arise in many different situations. A victim of domestic violence may be forced to leave the family home. A child leaving care may have no accommodation. A family relationship may break down and one of the parties may have to move out of the home.

People who are homeless can apply to their local housing authority for public sector housing. Local housing authorities are responsible for managing, regulating and controlling housing vested in them, and they have statutory duties and powers towards homeless people under Part VII of the Housing Act 1996 (HA 1996). When exercising their duties and powers, local housing authorities must comply with the *Homelessness Code of Guidance for Local Authorities* (2006) (ss 169(1) and 182(1)). They also have statutory duties to work jointly with local housing authorities, social services and other statutory, voluntary and private sector partners. Thus, for example, if homelessness persists, any children in the family could be classified as being in need and the family could seek assistance from social services who have powers and duties under the Children Act 1989 in such circumstances (see Chapter 14).

The duties and powers of local housing authorities vary depending on whether an applicant is unintentionally or intentionally homeless (s 191), and on whether or not the applicant has a priority need (s 189(1)). In some cases there is merely a duty to provide advice. In others there is a full housing duty to provide accommodation.

(a)   Housing and human rights

As local housing authorities are public authorities under section 6 of the Human Rights Act 1998, they must ensure that they exercise their powers and duties in line with the European Convention on Human Rights (ECHR). For example, in *R (Morris) v Westminster City Council* [2004] EWHC 2191 (Admin) it was held that the local housing authority had breached the applicant mother's rights under Articles 8 (the right to family life) and 14 (discrimination in respect of an ECHR right) as it had refused to treat her as having a priority need for accommodation. A decision by a local housing authority which deprives a person of accommodation must be lawful, necessary and proportionate otherwise it may breach the right to family life. Loss of a home is regarded as an extreme form of interference with that right (see *McCann v UK*

(Application No 19009/04) [2008] 2 FLR 899, where the European Court of Human Rights held that the UK was in breach of Article 8 in respect of the duties owed by local housing authorities and the courts under the housing legislation).

(b) Local housing authority duties

Under Part VII of the HA 1996 local housing authorities must provide assistance for certain eligible people who are homeless or threatened with homelessness. Local housing authorities have a range of duties depending on the circumstances of the applicant which include, for example: making inquiries to establish whether a housing duty is owed (s 184); providing advice, information and/or assistance (ss 179 and 190); providing interim accommodation (s 188); and making sure an applicant's accommodation does not cease to be available (s 195).

(c) When is a person homeless?

People are homeless if they have no accommodation available for their occupation in the UK, or elsewhere, or they have accommodation which is a movable structure and there is no place where the applicant is entitled to place it and reside in it (s 175).

A person who has accommodation is treated as being homeless if it would not be reasonable for him or her to continue to occupy that accommodation (s 175(3)). Domestic and other violence may provide a reason for not continuing to occupy accommodation (s 177).

(d) The full housing duty

The full housing duty (ss 193 and 195), which is to secure suitable accommodation or to take reasonable steps to prevent the loss of accommodation, is owed only to eligible persons who have a priority need for accommodation and who are not intentionally homeless.

(i) Priority need (section 189)

The categories of applicants who qualify as having a priority need have been extended over the years. People who have a priority need include, for example: pregnant women; people with dependent children; people who are vulnerable due to old age, mental illness, handicap or disability; people under 21 who were formerly in the care of the local authority; and people who are vulnerable due to domestic violence or threats of domestic violence.

(ii) Intentionality (sections 190–191)

A local housing authority has no duty to provide accommodation to people who are intentionally homeless, unless they are in priority need, in which case only short-term accommodation need be provided. Special rules apply in cases of domestic and other violence (see below).

A local housing authority can satisfy the full housing duty by providing accommodation from its own stock or by arranging for it to be provided by a housing association or a landlord in the private sector. However, a local housing authority must provide 'suitable' accommodation. In *R v Ealing London Borough Council ex parte Surdonja* [1999] 1 FLR 650, for example, the duty to provide accommodation was not discharged by providing accommodation for a family in separate dwellings, as families should be able to live together (s 176). In *Sharif v Camden London Borough Council* [2013] UKSC 10, however, the duty to provide accommodation was discharged by providing two separate flats on the same floor of a building for a family.

(e)   Referral to another local housing authority – the local connection

A local housing authority has a right to pass the housing duty on to another local housing authority if the applicant (or any person who might reasonably be expected to reside with the applicant) has no local connection with the local housing authority to which the application was made but has a local connection with the district of the other local housing authority. However, it cannot do so if there is a risk of domestic or other violence (s 198).

(f)   Domestic violence and other violence

Applicants who are forced to leave their home due to actual or threatened domestic or other violence are not treated as being intentionally homeless (s 177(1)). Violence is only 'domestic' if the victim and perpetrator are 'associated persons' (s 177(1A)), as defined in section 178. The definition is the same as that used for associated persons in the family law domestic violence legislation (see 5.6). Domestic violence is not defined in the HA 1996; and in the following case the Supreme Court held that it is not restricted to physical violence but can include other forms of abuse, such as psychological and emotional abuse:

▶ *Yemshaw v Hounslow London Borough Council* **[2011] UKSC 3**

Mrs Yemshaw claimed that she had been forced to leave the matrimonial home with her two young children and seek accommodation in a women's refuge because of domestic violence on the part of her husband. She applied to the defendant local housing authority for housing, claiming that, although her husband had not hit her, she was frightened that he might do. She claimed that his controlling behaviour amounted to emotional, psychological and financial abuse and that, as this was domestic violence, she was therefore homeless and eligible for priority assistance from the local housing authority. The defendant local housing authority, however, decided that she was not homeless as she had left the home voluntarily in circumstances where she had not been the victim of domestic violence.

Mrs Yemshaw's appeal to the Court of Appeal was dismissed, as it considered itself bound by the decision in *Danesh v Kensington and Chelsea Royal London Borough Council* [2006] EWCA Civ 1404 in which it had been held that 'violence' meant only physical violence.

Mrs Yemshaw appealed to the Supreme Court which unanimously allowed her appeal and held that the meaning of 'domestic violence' in section 177 of the HA 1996 was not restricted to physical contact, but included other forms of abuse, such as psychological and emotional abuse. The Supreme Court also overturned the decision in *Danesh* (see above).

Baroness Hale, who gave the leading opinion, stated that 'domestic violence' includes 'physical violence, threatening or intimidating behaviour and any other form of abuse which, directly or indirectly, may give rise to the risk of harm'.
(For a case comment on *Yemshaw*, see Knight [2012] CFLQ 95.)

The *Homelessness Code of Guidance* contains guidance on domestic violence and other forms of violence. In fact, as in *Yemshaw*, the *Guidance* adopts a wide and flexible approach to the meaning of these terms (see para 8).

Referral to another local housing authority is not permitted if there is a risk of domestic or other violence to the applicant in the area of that other housing authority (s 198). Also, a victim of domestic violence who is living in a refuge is deemed not to be intentionally homeless (see *Birmingham City Council v Ali; Moran v Manchester City Council* [2009] UKHL 36; the *Homelessness Code of Guidance*, para 16.27).

(g) Homeless families with children

(i) The duty to dependent children

If the applicant has dependent children then they will have a priority need and the local housing authority has a duty to provide accommodation for the family, provided the applicant is eligible for assistance and is not intentionally homeless (see above). The *Homelessness Code of Guidance* provides that a child need not be wholly and exclusively dependent on the applicant and/or wholly and exclusively resident with the applicant. Dependent children need not necessarily be the applicant's own children, but there must be a parent–child relationship. The child does not need to have full-time residence with the applicant. Neither does it necessarily matter that the parents are sharing care of the child in different homes (see below) because, according to the *Guidance*, local housing authorities should understand that it is usually in the best interests of children to maintain a relationship with both parents.

In discharging their duties under the HA 1996, section 11 of the Children Act 2004 (CA 2004) applies, which means that local housing authorities must ensure that account is taken of the need to safeguard and promote the welfare of the children concerned. This was confirmed in *Nzolameso v Westminster City Council* [2015] UKSC 22, where the applicant successfully appealed a decision of the local housing authority to accommodate her and her five children, who had been living in Westminster, to accommodation near Milton Keynes, some 40 miles away. The Supreme Court held that the local housing authority had not properly discharged its obligation under section 11 of the CA 2004.

(ii) Intentional homelessness

There is no duty to provide accommodation for intentionally homeless families with children, but they are entitled to advice and assistance and temporary accommodation. In addition, the children may be classified as being in need for the purposes of Part III of the Children Act 1989 (CA 1989), in which case the local authority social services department may provide accommodation for the family under section 17 or may have a duty to provide accommodation for the children under section 20 of that Act (see 14.6).

(iii) Housing applications by children are not permitted

A dependent child cannot apply for local authority housing if the child's parent has made an application and it has failed (see *R v Oldham Metropolitan Borough Council ex parte G and Related Appeals* [1993] AC 509 where the court held that the local authority owed no duty to a dependent child as the child's accommodation was provided by the parents or those looking after him).

(iv) The relationship between the housing legislation and the Children Act 1989

Local housing authorities and local authority social services departments are required to work together when dealing with cases of homelessness involving children (s 213A HA 1996). Thus, local housing authorities must have arrangements in place to ensure that social services are alerted where the applicant has children aged under 18 and the local housing authority considers that the applicant may be intentionally homeless or ineligible for assistance (s 213A HA 1996). If social services decide that the child's needs would be best met by helping the family to obtain accommodation, they can ask the local housing authority for reasonable assistance in this matter and the local housing authority must comply (s 213A HA; s 27 CA 1989).

However, there is no guarantee that a social services department will be able to find housing for families where they do not qualify for housing under the housing legislation. This is because section 17(6) of the CA 1989 gives local authorities the power, and not a duty, to provide accommodation (see 14.6). In certain circumstances, such as where section 20 of the CA 1989 applies, there will be a duty to accommodate children, but this does not extend to accommodating their families.

(v) Housing homeless teenage children

In *R (G) v Southwark London Borough Council* [2009] UKHL 26, the House of Lords held that a local authority's children's services unit could not purport to have fulfilled its duties to look after a homeless child under the CA 1989 merely by referring the child to a homeless persons' unit under Part VII of the HA 1996. Thus, social services working with children cannot 'pass the buck' by transferring their responsibilities to the local housing authority if a child or young person is a person to whom an accommodation duty is owed under section 20 of the CA 1989.

(vi) Housing and child arrangements orders regulating the child's living arrangements

The existence of a child arrangements order regulating the child's living arrangements (formerly known as a residence order) made in favour of an applicant for housing is a material consideration for a local housing authority when exercising its powers and duties under the HA 1996. However, it is not the only factor to be taken into account and will not be the determinative factor as to the allocation of housing.

(vii) Housing and child arrangements orders for shared living arrangements

Cases have sometimes arisen with respect to the duties of a local housing authority when a child arrangements order regulating the child's living arrangements has been made under the CA 1989 which provides for the child to live with more than one parent (formerly known as a shared residence order).

The following case dealt with the question of whether a parent who is the subject of a child arrangements order regulating the child's living arrangements which provides for a 50:50 division of time between the parents has a priority need under the housing legislation. The decision, which dealt with the interface between housing and family law, shows that it is ultimately the decision of the local housing authority which prevails in cases where such an order is in force.

▶ *Holmes-Moorhouse v London Borough of Richmond-upon-Thames* **[2009] UKHL 7**

Before their separation the appellant father and the mother lived with their four children in council accommodation. By consent the judge in family proceedings made a shared residence order (setting out that the three younger children should spend alternate weeks and half of each school holiday with each parent); and an order that the father should leave the family home. The father's application for housing on the basis that he had a priority need as he had dependent children who might reasonably be expected to reside with him under section 189(1)(b) of the HA 1996 was rejected by the local housing authority on the basis that he was not in priority need (as the children would merely be staying, rather than residing, with him). He challenged the decision. He failed at first instance but the Court of Appeal allowed his appeal. The local housing authority appealed to the House of Lords.

The House of Lords allowed the local housing authority's appeal and restored the decision of the county court judge, holding, *inter alia*, that:

▶ A shared residence order did not oblige a local housing authority to regard a homeless parent as being in priority need on the ground that dependent children might reasonably be expected to reside with that parent. It was for the local housing authority under Part VII of the HA 1996, not the family courts, to decide whether it was reasonable that a child who already had a home with a parent should also be able to reside with the other parent. The local housing authority could take into account the wishes of the parents and children and the court's opinion that shared residence would be in the interests of the children, but it was nonetheless entitled to decide that it was not reasonable to expect children who were not in any sense homeless to be able to live with both the mother and the father in separate accommodation.

▶ In accordance with the *Homelessness Code of Guidance for Local Authorities*, it would only be in exceptional circumstances that it would be reasonable to expect a child who had a home with one parent to be provided, under Part VII of the HA 1996, with another so that he could reside with the other parent as well.

▶ The local housing authority's reviewing officer had therefore been entitled to conclude that, in the context of the duty of the authority to make provision for the homeless, the children could not reasonably be expected to live with the father as well as the mother.

Baroness Hale was of the opinion that the shared residence order should not have been made in the first place. Her Ladyship said that orders made by the family court were meant to provide practical solutions to the practical problems faced by separating families and were not meant to be aspirational statements of what would be for the best in some ideal world which has little prospect of realisation. It was one thing to make a shared residence order when each parent had a home to offer the children, but another thing entirely when the other parent had no accommodation at all. Family courts could not conjure up resources where none existed and could not order or put pressure on public agencies to do so.

Both Lord Hoffman and Baroness Hale emphasised the different roles played by family courts and local housing authorities, and the fact that decisions made under Part VII of the HA 1996 must have regard to wider considerations than the welfare of the relevant children (for example the limited availability of public housing stock). Both Lord Hoffman and Baroness Hale were of the opinion that only in exceptional circumstances would it be reasonable to expect that, when a child has a home with one parent, the other parent would also be provided with housing under Part VII of the HA 1996.

4.12 The devolution of property on death

(a) Making a will

There is freedom of testamentary disposition in England and Wales. In other words, adults of sound mind may make a will disposing of their property to whomsoever they choose. Thus, there is no legal obligation on spouses, civil partners or cohabitants to leave their property to the other spouse, civil partner or cohabitant. Neither is there any obligation on parents to leave their property to their children. This is quite different from the law in some other jurisdictions, such as France, where it is not possible to disinherit certain family members, such as one's children. The position with respect to family members in England and Wales is, however, mitigated in that family members can, in certain circumstances, apply for reasonable financial provision out of a deceased family member's estate under the Inheritance (Provision for Family and Dependants) Act 1975 (I(PFD)A 1975) (see 4.13 below). Thus, for example, in *Ilott v Mitson & Ors* [2011] EWCA Civ 346, the Court of Appeal upheld the decision of the trial judge that an adult daughter in financial need should receive a share of her deceased mother's estate in circumstances where the mother had disinherited her daughter and instead left her estate to a range of animal charities.

A will is valid if it is made in writing and signed by the person making it in the presence of at least two witnesses, each of whom must attest and sign the will, or acknowledge the signature of the person making it (ss 7 and 9 Wills Act 1837). A will is revoked by the testator's marriage or civil partnership, unless it was made in contemplation of marriage or civil partnership to a particular person and the testator did not intend the will to be revoked (ss 18 and 18B Wills Act 1837). In the case of divorce or nullity, or dissolution or annulment of a civil partnership, then, subject to any contrary intention in the will, any legacies and gifts to a former spouse or former civil partner lapse. However, a former spouse or former civil partner may still make a claim for reasonable financial provision from the deceased's estate under the I(PFD) A 1975 (see 4.13 below).

According to research, about one-half to two-thirds of adults in England and Wales do not make a will (*Intestacy and Family Provision Claims on Death*, Law Com No. 331, para 1.3).

(b) Devolution of property on the intestacy of spouses and civil partners

The law of intestacy determines what happens to property that is not disposed of by will. If a spouse or civil partner dies intestate (without making a will), the inheritance rights of the surviving spouse or civil partner depend on the size of the estate and whether or not the deceased has children or other relatives. Following recommendations by the Law Commission (*Intestacy and Family Provision Claims on Death*, LC 331, 2011), the Government enacted the Inheritance and Trustees' Powers Act 2014 (ITPA 2014) which changed the intestacy rules to make them more favourable to surviving spouses and civil partners. In outline, the rules now provide for the estate (after the payment of debts and expenses) to be distributed or held on trust according to the following rules laid down in section 46 of the Administration of Estates Act 1925 (as amended by the ITPA 2014):

▶ *If there is a surviving spouse/civil partner and children* The spouse/civil partner inherits the personal chattels, the first £250,000 and half of what is left. The children of the deceased share the other half between them.
▶ *If there is a surviving spouse/civil partner, but no children* The surviving spouse/civil partner inherits everything.
▶ *If there are children, but no surviving spouse/civil partner* The children share everything equally.
▶ *If there is no spouse/civil partner or children* Everything passes to the next available group of relatives.
▶ *If there are no available relatives* Everything goes to the State.

(i) Rights in the family home

Where the family home was owned by the spouses or civil partners as beneficial joint tenants, it devolves to the surviving spouse or civil partner. Where it was owned by them as tenants in common, the deceased's share forms part of their estate and passes according to their will or according to the laws of intestacy. On intestacy, however, the Intestates' Estates Act 1952 allows a surviving spouse or civil partner in certain circumstances to retain the home.

(c) Cohabitants on intestacy

Where a cohabitant dies without making a will there are no provisions equivalent to those above. Thus, a surviving cohabitant has no automatic right to succeed to a deceased partner's estate whatever the length of the relationship. Instead, the estate passes to the children, or otherwise to the parent(s) of the deceased. This is with the exception of any property which was jointly owned by the parties as joint tenants (such as the home or a bank account) where ownership passes to the survivor. As cohabitants are in a vulnerable position on intestacy, it is particularly important for cohabitants to make a will.

A cohabitant can, however, make a claim for reasonable financial provision against the deceased partner's estate under the I(PFD)A 1975 (see 4.13 below). An alternative is to make a claim by way of a trust (see 4.7 above) or on the basis of proprietary estoppel (see 4.8 above). For example, in *Hyett v Stanley* [2003] EWCA Civ 942, a cohabitant was held to be entitled to an interest in her deceased partner's estate under a constructive trust arising as a result of a statement he had made during his lifetime. (See also *Negus v Bahouse and Another* [2007] EWHC 2628 (Ch), where the claimant failed to establish an interest by proprietary estoppel but succeeded in her claim under the I(PFD)A 1975.)

The Law Commission has recommended that certain cohabiting couples should have the same rights on intestacy as spouses and civil partners. However, these proposals have not been taken forward by the Government (see 3.2).

4.13 The Inheritance (Provision for Family and Dependants) Act 1975

(a) Introduction

Under the Inheritance (Provision for Family and Dependants) Act 1975 (I(PFD) A 1975) the court can make financial provision orders for certain family members and dependants out of a deceased person's estate where the deceased has failed under their will or under the laws of intestacy (or both) to make reasonable financial provision for the applicant. The Act applies if the deceased was domiciled in England and Wales at the time of death (s 1(1)). An application must be brought within six months of the date on which probate or letters of administration were taken out, or otherwise with the permission of the court (s 4).

The Act is concerned with dependency; it is not concerned with deciding how the assets should be fairly divided (*per* Goff LJ in *Re Coventry (Deceased)* [1980] Ch 461). In *Jelley v Iliffe and Others* [1981] Fam 128, Stephenson LJ said that the purpose of the Act is to remedy 'wherever reasonably possible, the injustice of one who has been put by a deceased person in a position of dependency upon him, being deprived of any financial support, either by accident or by design of the deceased, after his death'.

(i) A two-stage exercise

When considering an application, the court adopts a two-stage exercise. First (under section 3 of the Act) it has to make an objective assessment of the facts to establish whether or not the deceased made reasonable financial provision for the applicant. If the answer is no, then the court must next consider to what extent (if at all) it should exercise its powers to make financial provision for the applicant under the Act. The first part of the exercise involves a value judgment; the second a question of discretion. When conducting the two-stage exercise the court must take into account a range of factors laid down in section 3 of the Act (see below). If the court does decide to make an order, it has a wide discretion under section 2 as to the nature of the order(s) it can make.

When conducting the two-stage exercise, the court draws a distinction between spouses and civil partners and other applicants. Spouses and civil partners are treated much more favourably than other applicants under the Act.

(b) Applicants

(i) Applications by spouses and civil partners (and former spouses and civil partners)

The spouse or civil partner of the deceased can apply for reasonable financial provision (s 1(1)(a)), including someone who in good faith entered into a void marriage or void civil partnership (ss 25(4) and 25(4A)). This includes a former spouse or civil partner, provided that that person has not entered into a subsequent marriage or civil partnership (s 1(1)(b)). The court must consider the applicant's age, the duration of the marriage or civil partnership, and the applicant's contribution to the welfare of the family, including any contribution made by looking after the home or caring for the family (s 3(2)).

The divorce/dissolution comparison In addition to the above factors, the court must take into account the award the applicant spouse or civil partner might have expected to receive had the marriage or civil partnership been terminated by divorce or dissolution and not death (s 3(2)) (otherwise known as the 'divorce cross-check'). In *Fielden and Another v Cunliffe* [2006] 1 FLR 745, the Court of Appeal held that there was no reason why the principles laid down by the House of Lords in *White v White* [2000] UKHL 54 (see 7.6) should not be applied to a claim by a spouse under the I(PFD)A 1975 but that caution was necessary when considering the *White* cross-check of equality. This is because a deceased spouse is free to bequeath their estate to whomsoever they please and the only statutory obligation under the Act is to make *reasonable* financial provision for the surviving spouse, to which the concept of equality may bear little relation (*per* Wall LJ). Thus, in *Fielden and Another v Cunliffe*, the Court of Appeal allowed the executors' appeal and reduced the amount of financial provision awarded to the surviving spouse from £800,000 to £600,000, as the judge had wrongly applied the principle in *White* (having presumed a starting point of a 50:50 split of the estate).

However, each case depends on its facts; and the Court of Appeal has stated that the 'hypothetical divorce' approach in section 3(2) is only one of the factors for the court to consider, and that any decision is subject to the overriding consideration of what is reasonable in all the circumstances (*Re Krubert (Deceased)* [1997] 1 FLR 42). In *Lilleyman v Lilleyman* [2012] EWHC 821 (Ch), a 'big money' short marriage case, Briggs J confirmed that the 'hypothetical divorce' check should be treated as 'neither a floor nor a ceiling in relation to the relief available under the Inheritance Act, nor as something which requires a meticulous quasi-divorce application to be analysed side by side with the application of the separate provisions in section 3 of the Act'. Briggs J stated that the 'divorce cross-check is just that, a cross-check, no more and no less'. In recognition of this, the ITPA 2014 amended section 3(2) of the I(PFD)A 1975 to clarify that the 'divorce cross-check' exercise does not require the court to set an upper or lower limit on the level of provision which may be made. (For other cases involving a claim by a spouse see, for example, *Barron v Woodhead* [2008] EWHC 810 and *Baker v Baker* [2008] 2 FLR 1956.)

Awards are not limited to maintenance Spouses and civil partners are in a better position than cohabitants (see below), as a claim by a spouse or civil partner is not limited to maintenance (s 1(2)(a)).

Provisions relating to divorce, nullity, separation and dissolution Where a decree of divorce or nullity has been made before the death of a spouse but the other spouse has either not applied for an order under section 23 or section 24 of the Matrimonial Causes Act 1973 (MCA 1973) (see 7.3) or has applied but the proceedings have not been determined by the date of death, the court can consider their application under the I(PFD)A 1975 as if the decree of divorce or nullity had not been made absolute. However, this only applies if the decree of divorce or nullity was granted no more than 12 months prior to the application (s 14). Similar provisions apply to judicial separation (ss 14(1), (2)) and to dissolution, nullity and separation in respect of a civil partnership (s 14A).

As part of the 'clean break' policy on divorce (see 7.5), the divorce court on or after the grant of a decree nisi of divorce can, on the application of either spouse, make an order (where it is just to do so) prohibiting the other spouse from making an application under the I(PFD)A 1975 on the applicant's death (s 15). This power can also be exercised in the case of a decree of nullity, judicial separation or presumption of death. The court has the same powers in respect of a civil partnership order (s 15ZA) and after an overseas divorce, dissolution, annulment or separation (ss 15A and 15B).

A maintenance agreement between the applicant and the deceased providing for the continuation of maintenance after death can be varied or revoked by the court (s 17). Similar provisions apply where the applicant is entitled to secured periodical payments under the MCA 1973 or the Civil Partnership Act 2004 at the time of death (s 16). The court can, in certain circumstances, set aside a disposition made by the deceased within six years of their death if it was made with the intention of defeating an application under the I(PFD)A 1975 (s 10). Where a contract was made by the deceased without full valuable consideration with the intention of defeating an application for financial provision under the I(PFD)A 1975, the court can direct the personal representatives not to pass or transfer the whole or part of any money or property involved (s 11).

(ii) Applications by cohabitants

The surviving cohabitant of the deceased can apply (s 1(1)(ba)). An application is sometimes made by a cohabitant who has failed to establish an interest under a trust or by way of proprietary estoppel (see, for example, *Negus v Bahouse* [2007] EWHC 2628 (Ch) and *Webster v Webster* [2009] 1 FLR 1240).

A 'cohabitant' is defined in the Act as a person who was living in the same household as the deceased during the whole period of two years ending immediately before the date of the deceased's death, and was living as the husband or wife or civil partner of the deceased (ss 1(1A) and 1(1B)). As this definition does not include a former cohabitant, a former cohabitant will have to apply under section 1(1)(e) (see below) as a person being maintained by the deceased.

Whether the applicant and the deceased were living together in the same household is a question of fact. In *Re Watson (Deceased)* [1999] 1 FLR 878, Neuberger J held that, when considering the definition of cohabitant, the court should 'ask itself whether, in the opinion of a reasonable person with normal perceptions, it could be said that the two people in question were living together as husband and wife'.

Occasional periods of separation may be permitted (see *Gully v Dix* [2004] EWCA Civ 139, where the applicant was held to be a cohabitant even though she had separated from the deceased for the last three months of his life, due to his intolerable behaviour). But each case depends on its own facts. In the following two cases the applicants were held not to be cohabitants for the purposes of the Act: *Churchill v Roach* [2004] 2 FLR 989 (the applicant had not lived with the deceased for the full two-year period); and *Baynes v Hedger* [2008] EWHC 1587 (Ch) (the applicant had not been living in the same household as the deceased as the parties had had two separate houses and their relationship was unacknowledged and hidden).

Maintenance provision only Cohabitants are in a disadvantageous position compared with spouses and civil partners as the court is limited to making orders for their maintenance. However, 'maintenance' may be interpreted flexibly (as it was in *Webster v Webster* [2009] 1 FLR 1240 where the court ordered the home to be transferred to the applicant whose partner had died suddenly at the age of 54 without making a will).

(iii) Applications by children of the deceased and those treated as children of the deceased

Marital and non-marital children, and adopted children, can apply (s 1(1)(c)) whether born before or after the deceased's death (s 25(1)) and whether or not they are minors or adult children of the deceased.

A person who is not included under section 1(1)(c) but who was treated by the deceased as a child of the family can also apply (s 1(1)(d)). This might include, for example, a step-child or foster-child, whether or not a minor, and also covers single-parent situations (s 1(2A)).

Adult children Applicants who are adult children of the deceased can apply, but they may find it difficult to succeed in an application, particularly if they are young and able-bodied, are in employment and are capable of maintaining themselves (see, for example, *Re Jennings (Deceased)* [1994] Ch 286). However, each case depends on its own facts. In *Re Abram (Deceased)* [1996] 2 FLR 379 the adult son successfully claimed against his deceased mother's estate as he had worked for her in the family business for many years and for long hours and had received only a minimal wage. In *Garland v Morris* [2007] EWHC 2 (Ch), on the other hand, an adult daughter's claim against her deceased father's estate was dismissed as she had failed to establish that it was reasonable in all the circumstances for her father to make provision for her (she had neither spoken to nor met her father at any time in the 15 years preceding his death, and had made no real effort to do so; and she had received all of her mother's estate).

At one time the court took the view that an adult child had to prove special circumstances, or that the deceased had a moral obligation to the adult child. However, the courts no longer adopt such a restricted approach. Thus, in *Re Hancock (Deceased)* [1998] 2 FLR 346, for example, the Court of Appeal held that, although the presence of special circumstances or a moral obligation may be relevant factors, particularly where the applicant is in employment or possessed of earning capacity, their absence does not necessarily preclude a successful claim. In *Espinosa v Bourke* [1999] 1 FLR 747, the Court of Appeal allowed the 55-year-old daughter's appeal as the judge had erred in elevating moral obligation to a threshold requirement. Instead, when making its value judgment, the court should balance all the factors in section 3 of the Act (see *Ilott v Mitson & Ors* [2011] EWCA Civ 346 where the adult daughter's straitened financial circumstances and the unreasonable conduct of the deceased towards her contributed towards the judge concluding that reasonable provision had not been made).

(iv) Persons being maintained by the deceased

Any person who is not included in the categories above, but who was being maintained either wholly or partly by the deceased immediately before their death, can apply (s 1(1)(e)). Thus people such as relatives, friends and carers can apply, and so can cohabitants who do not come within the definition in section 1(1)(ba) (see above), provided that the applicant can prove that they were being maintained, wholly or partly, by the deceased. For example, in *Bouette v Rose* [2000] 1 FLR 363 a mother brought a successful claim against the estate of her deceased daughter.

Section 1(3) provides that a claimant is to be regarded as having been maintained by the deceased if the deceased was making a substantial contribution in money or money's worth towards the reasonable needs of the applicant, other than a contribution made for full valuable consideration pursuant to an arrangement of a commercial nature. An application can be struck out on the ground that there was no dependency. In order to decide whether there was dependency, the court used to balance what the deceased was contributing against what the applicant was contributing, and, if the applicant made a greater or equal contribution, the claim would be struck out (see, for example, *Jelley v Iliffe and Others* [1981] Fam 128). However, following recommendations made by the Law Commission (LC 331, 2011), section 1(3) was amended by the ITPA 2014 to remove the need for this exercise, which was described as generating uncertainty and complexity.

When considering a claim under this section the court is required to have regard to: the length of time for which, and the basis on which, the deceased maintained the applicant and the extent of the contribution made; and whether, and to what extent, the deceased assumed responsibility for maintaining the applicant (s 3(4)). This section was also amended by the ITPA 2014 after the Law Commission recommended the change to make clear that assumption of responsibility is not a pre-requisite for a successful claim under s1(1)(e), as had been suggested by some of the case-law (see, for example, *Jelley v Iliffe and Others* [1981] Fam 128). The intention of this change, together with the amendment to section 1(3) above, was to make it easier for dependants with meritorious claims to make successful applications under s1(1)(e) of the Act.

(c) 'Reasonable financial provision'

All applicants must prove that the deceased's will or the law of intestacy (or both, if there is partial intestacy) failed to make 'reasonable financial provision' for them (s 1(1)). The test is not whether reasonable provision has been made, but the more rigorous test of whether the failure to make provision was unreasonable (*per* Judge Roger Cooke in *Re Abram (Deceased)* [1996] 2 FLR 379). However, spouses and civil partners are treated more generously than other applicants, as 'reasonable financial provision' for them means 'such financial provision as it would be reasonable in all the circumstances of the case for a husband or wife or civil partner to receive, whether or not that provision is required for his or her maintenance' (ss 1(2)(a) and (aa)). With other applicants, 'reasonable financial provision' means such financial provision as it would be reasonable in all the circumstances of the case for the applicant to receive for their maintenance (s 1(2)(b)).

(i) Maintenance

With applicants other than spouses and civil partners, reasonable financial provision is limited to what it would be reasonable to provide for the applicant's maintenance. 'Maintenance' is not defined in the Act. What constitutes 'maintenance' depends therefore on the facts of the case, but it may be construed broadly (see, for example, *Rees v Newbery and the Institute of Cancer Research* [1998] 1 FLR 1041 where the provision of accommodation by the deceased for ten years at less than a market rent was held to be 'maintenance'). In *Re Coventry (Deceased)* [1980] Ch 461 Goff LJ said:

> What is proper maintenance must in all cases depend upon all the facts and circumstances of the particular case being considered at the time, but I think it is clear on the one hand that one must not put too limited a meaning on it; it does not mean just enough to enable a person to get by; on the other hand, it does not mean anything which may be regarded as reasonably desirable for his general benefit or welfare.

In *Ilott v Mitson* [2015] EWCA Civ 797 the Court of Appeal declined to define the term 'maintenance' but, when determining the appropriate level of maintenance, Arden LJ, having considered the applicant's limited income and lack of savings, said: 'The court's assessment should not be motivated by a desire to provide an improved standard of living as opposed to a desire to meet appropriate living needs. Nor on the other hand is the court bound to limit maintenance to mere subsistence level.' The Court of Appeal went on to award the applicant daughter £143,000 plus expenses to purchase a property from an estate valued at £486,000. Permission has been given to appeal the decision to the Supreme Court where the issues for the court will include the proper approach which should be taken to the quantification of awards for maintenance.

(d) Orders that can be made

The court has the power to make a wide range of orders, which include: periodical payments; a lump sum (which can be paid in instalments); a transfer of property; a settlement of property; acquisition of property and its transfer to the applicant or for the settlement of the applicant; and a variation of an ante-nuptial or post-nuptial settlement (s 2). The court can make an interim order if immediate financial assistance is needed (s 5). Periodical payments orders can be varied, discharged, suspended or revived (s 6). A periodical payments order made in favour of a former spouse or civil partner, or a spouse or civil partner subject to a decree or order of judicial separation (where separation was continuing at death), ceases to be effective on that person's remarriage or civil partnership, except in respect of any arrears due (s 19(1)).

(e) The exercise of discretion – matters to be taken into account

When deciding whether or not the deceased made reasonable financial provision for the applicant, and in what manner to exercise its powers, the court must have regard to the following matters laid down in section 3(1) of the Act.

(a) the financial resources and financial needs which the applicant has or is likely to have in the foreseeable future;
(b) the financial resources and financial needs which any other applicant ... has or is likely to have in the foreseeable future;
(c) the financial resources and financial needs which any beneficiary of the estate of the deceased has or is likely to have in the foreseeable future;
(d) any obligations and responsibilities which the deceased had towards any applicant ... or towards any beneficiary of the estate of the deceased;
(e) the size and nature of the net estate of the deceased;
(f) any physical or mental disability of any applicant ... or any beneficiary of the estate of the deceased;
(g) any other matter, including the conduct of the applicant or any other person, which in the circumstances of the case the court may consider relevant.

The weight given to each factor depends on the circumstances of each case. For example, where an application is brought by an adult child against a deceased parent, needs and resources under section 3(1)(a) and obligations and responsibilities under section 3(1)(d) are likely to be crucial (see, for example, *Espinosa v Bourke* [1999] 1 FLR 747).

In addition to the matters in section 3(1) above, the court must take into account other factors as follows.

(i) Applications by cohabitants

The court must have regard to the applicant's age, the duration of the cohabitation and the contribution which the applicant made to the welfare of the deceased's family, including any contribution made by looking after the home or caring for the family (s 3(2A)).

(ii) Applications by children or people treated like children

The court must consider the manner in which the applicant was, or might be expected to be, educated or trained (s 3(3)). Where the applicant is someone who was treated by the deceased as a child of the family, the court must also consider whether the deceased maintained the applicant (and, if so, the extent, basis and duration) and whether, and to what extent, the deceased assumed responsibility for the applicant's maintenance. The court will also consider whether, in maintaining or assuming responsibility for maintaining the applicant, the deceased did so knowing that the applicant was not his own child. Finally, the court must have regard to the liability of any other person to maintain the applicant (ss 3(3)(a)–(c)).

(iii) Applications by persons being maintained by the deceased

The court must consider the extent, basis and duration of the maintenance provided and whether, and to what extent, the deceased assumed responsibility for the applicant's maintenance (s 3(4)).

(f) Reform of the law

The Law Commission examined the operation of the I(PFD)A 1975 in its report *Intestacy and Family Provision Claims on Death*, Law Com No. 331. It recommended, *inter alia*, that a wider range of family members should be entitled to bring a claim under the Act, that the s 3 factors should be amended and that the hurdles faced by dependants of the deceased when claiming should be removed. These recommendations were adopted by the Government through the enactment of the ITPA 2014. However, the Law Commission's recommendations, which would have given cohabiting couples limited rights on intestacy, have not been taken forward (see 3.2).

4.14 Succession to a tenancy on death

Succession to a tenancy on death is governed by Schedule 1 to the Rent Act 1977 (RA 1977) (statutory tenancies) and by section 17 of the Housing Act 1988 (HA 1988) (assured tenancies). Under these Acts a spouse, civil partner or a surviving cohabitant (who had lived in a settled relationship with the deceased) can apply for a transfer of the deceased's tenancy on their death.

Under paragraph 2 of Schedule 1 to the RA 1977 a spouse, civil partner or cohabitant (living as a husband or wife, or as a civil partner of the deceased) can succeed to the deceased spouse's or cohabitant's tenancy. Under paragraph 3(1) a family member of the deceased tenant can also succeed to the tenancy. A person who succeeds to a tenancy under paragraph 2 is in a better position than a family member who succeeds under paragraph 3 because they succeed to a statutory tenancy, whereas a family member succeeds only to an assured tenancy. Statutory tenants are in a better position because they enjoy security of tenure and may register a fair rent for the property, whereas assured tenants are subject to a different form of security of tenure and may be charged a market, rather than a fair, rent.

Until amendments were made to the RA 1977 and the HA 1988, only spouses and heterosexual cohabitants could succeed to a deceased partner's tenancy under these Acts. However, the following two cases heard by the House of Lords led to a change in the law, the second of which was influenced by the European Convention on Human Rights (ECHR) as a result of the coming into force of the Human Rights Act 1998 (HRA 1998):

▶ *Fitzpatrick v Sterling Housing Association Ltd* **[2001] 1 AC 27**

The House of Lords held by a majority of three to two that a surviving same sex cohabitant could succeed to the tenancy of the deceased tenant, on the basis that they could be construed as a member of the deceased tenant's 'family' under paragraph 3(1) of Schedule 1 to the RA 1977. However, it was unanimously held that the surviving homosexual partner could not be construed as a 'spouse' of the deceased under paragraph 2(2), because they could not be regarded as 'living with the original tenant as his or her husband or wife'.

▶ *Ghaidan v Godin-Mendoza* [2004] UKHL 30

Mr Godin-Mendoza had lived in a long, close and loving homosexual relationship with his deceased partner, who was the protected tenant of a flat owned by Mr Ghaidan, the landlord. Mr Ghaidan brought possession proceedings, and Mr Godin-Mendoza claimed by way of defence that he was entitled to succeed to the tenancy under Schedule 1 to the RA 1977. At first instance, the judge held that he could only succeed to a tenancy under paragraph 3(1), applying *Fitzpatrick* (above). However, the Court of Appeal allowed his appeal, holding that there had been a breach of Article 14 of the ECHR (discrimination in respect of an ECHR right) in conjunction with Article 8 (the right to family life) and that the court had a duty under section 3 of the HRA 1998 to give effect to the RA 1977 in a way which was compliant with the ECHR. The landlord, Mr Ghaidan, appealed.

The House of Lords dismissed the appeal (Lord Millett dissenting), holding that same sex cohabitants are in the same position as married couples when it comes to security of tenure. It held that paragraph 2(2) of Schedule 1 to the RA 1977, when construed with reference to section 3 of the HRA 1998, violated the surviving partner's right under Article 14 taken together with Article 8 of the ECHR. It held that it was possible under section 3 of the IIRA 1998 (which provides that primary and subordinate legislation must be read and given effect in a way which is compatible with the ECHR) to read paragraph 2(2) in a way which was compatible with the ECHR.

Summary

▶ The statutory provisions and legal principles governing property entitlement are virtually the same for spouses and civil partners, but they are radically different for cohabitants, particularly on relationship breakdown. Thus, although the family courts have wide discretionary powers to distribute the property of married couples and civil partners on divorce and dissolution, according to their needs and resources, there is no such provision for cohabiting couples. This can leave cohabitants in a vulnerable position on the breakdown of their relationship. They can also be in a vulnerable position on the death of a cohabiting partner. For these reasons, there have been calls for reform of the law governing the property rights of cohabitants both on relationship breakdown and on the death of a partner.

▶ The property entitlements of spouses, civil partners and cohabitants during the existence of their relationship are governed by the laws of property and contract, but with the addition of some special family law statutory provisions for spouses and civil partners. Spouses and civil partners can own property solely or jointly. Spouses and civil partners with no right of ownership in the family home may have a statutory right of occupation under section 30 of the Family Law Act 1996 (FLA 1996), which includes the right to remain in occupation of the home and to enter in and occupy it, if the court so orders.

▶ Special statutory provisions apply in respect of the property rights of engaged couples and parties to a civil partnership agreement.

▶ Cohabitants have the same property law rights as spouses, civil partners and other persons during their relationship, but there are no special family law statutory provisions for cohabitants. Unlike spouses and civil partners, cohabitants have no statutory right of occupation of the family home. They have a right of occupation only if they have a right of ownership in, or a contractual licence to occupy, the family home. A cohabitant or former cohabitant who is a victim of domestic violence can apply for an occupation order under

Summary cont'd

Part IV of the FLA 1996 which, if granted, will give the applicant a right to occupy the family home, but only for the duration of the order.

▶ Ownership of personal property (which is property other than land, such as investments and household goods) is governed by the law of contract and the law of property. As a general rule, title to personal property passes to the purchaser unless it was a gift. With regard to bank accounts, the money in the account presumptively belongs to the party or parties in whose name(s) the account is held, although the presumption can be rebutted by proof of a contrary intention. A person who has no right to personal property under a contract can claim an equitable interest in that property under an express, resulting or constructive trust or on the basis of proprietary estoppel.

▶ Disputes about the family home arise in a number of situations: on relationship breakdown; where there is no mention of the parties' shares on the transfer deeds; where a third party seeks possession of the home; and on the death of a party. The courts have wide discretionary powers to adjust spouses' or civil partners' property rights on divorce or dissolution irrespective of legal ownership. Cohabitants, on the other hand, have to rely on the law of trusts or on proprietary estoppel.

▶ A person can claim an interest in the family home under a trust even if there is nothing in writing to that effect (s 53(2) Law of Property Act 1925; s 2(5) Law of Property (Miscellaneous Provisions) Act 1989). A resulting trust gives a claimant a share of the beneficial interest in the family home proportionate to their financial contribution to its purchase price, subject to any contrary intention. However, the constructive trust is the more appropriate tool of legal analysis regarding ownership of the family home. A constructive trust arises where there is an express or implied agreement, arrangement or understanding that the claimant has an interest in property and the claimant has acted to their detriment on the basis of that agreement, arrangement or understanding. Having established the existence of a beneficial interest under a constructive trust, the court must then decide what the share of that interest is. It does so by considering all the circumstances of the case. In joint-owner cases (where the parties are joint owners in law of the home, but their interests have not been defined in equity), the usual approach is that equity follows the law and they will be deemed to have equal shares unless there is any evidence of a contrary intention. However, the Supreme Court has held that an initial intention to share the beneficial interest can change over time.

▶ A person can claim an interest in the family home on the basis of proprietary estoppel. Applicants must prove that they have acted to their detriment on the basis of a belief encouraged by the other party that they are to have an interest in the property in question and that it would be inequitable for the court to deny the applicant an interest.

▶ An interest in the family home can be acquired under a contract, provided the legal requirements for the creation of a valid contract are satisfied. If a contract is for the sale or disposition of land then it must be in writing (s 2 Law of Property (Miscellaneous Provisions) Act 1989).

▶ Tenancies can be transferred between married partners, civil partners and cohabitants (including former spouses, civil partners and cohabitants) under section 53 and Schedule 7 of Part IV of the FLA 1996.

▶ Under Part VII of the Housing Act 1996 (HA 1996), local housing authorities have duties and powers with respect to persons who are homeless. The nature of these duties and powers depends largely on whether the applicant is intentionally or unintentionally homeless, and whether or not they have a priority need. Domestic violence is taken seriously by local

Summary cont'd

housing authorities; and victims of violence, or of threatened violence, are not treated as being intentionally homeless if they leave the family home.

▶ There is freedom of testamentary disposition in England and Wales. On intestacy (where there is no will), the surviving spouse or civil partner has a statutory right to succeed to the deceased's estate under the rules of intestacy laid down in the Administration of Estates Act 1925. Cohabitants, on the other hand, have no statutory rights of succession. The Law Commission has recommended that certain cohabitants should have the same rights on intestacy as spouses and civil partners. However, these proposals have not been taken forward by the Government.

▶ Under the Inheritance (Provision for Family and Dependants) Act 1975, certain family members and dependants, including spouses, civil partners, former spouses, former civil partners, cohabitants and other dependants, can apply for financial relief out of a deceased person's estate where the deceased has failed to make reasonable financial provision either under a will or under the law of intestacy (or both). Under the Act, spouses and civil partners are treated more favourably than other applicants. A deceased's tenancy can also be transferred to a surviving spouse, or civil partner, or a surviving cohabiting partner under the Rent Act 1977 or under section 17 of the HA 1988.

Further reading and references

Battersby, 'Ownership of the family home: *Stack v Dowden* in the House of Lords' [2008] CFLQ 255.

Cooke, 'Wives, widows and wicked step-mothers: a brief examination of spousal entitlement on intestacy' [2009] CFLQ 423.

Fretwell, 'The cautionary tale of *Jones v Kernott*' [2012] Fam Law 69.

Gardner and Davidson, 'The future of *Stack v Dowden*' (2011) 127 *Law Quarterly Review* 13.

Hayward, '"Family property" and the process of "familialisation" of property law' [2012] CFLQ 284.

Knight, 'Doing (linguistic) violence to prevent (domestic) violence? *Yemshaw v Hounslow LBC* in the Supreme Court' [2012] CFLQ 95.

Pawlowski, 'Imputing intention and the family home' [2016] Fam Law 189.

Piska, 'A common intention or a rare bird? Proprietary interests, personal claims and services rendered by lovers post-acquisition: *James v Thomas*: *Morris v Morris*' [2009] CFLQ 104.

(See also the reference list at the end of Chapter 3.)

Links to relevant websites can also be found at: www.palgravehighered.com/law/familylaw9e

Chapter 5

Domestic violence

5.1 Introduction

This chapter considers the law which is available to protect family members from domestic violence. In furtherance of the Government's aim to improve protection for victims, a range of legislative provisions has been enacted over the years. In addition, as part of its drive to fight domestic violence, the Government has increasingly recognised the importance of adopting multi-agency and inter-agency approaches to tackle the problem, involving not just the courts, but also the police, housing authorities and other agencies. There are various organisations which campaign for reform of the law, and which provide advice and information for victims.

(a) The scale of domestic violence

In terms of the scale of the problem, it is difficult to make accurate assessments of the number of people who are victims of domestic violence. This is due in part to a lack of standardised data and the fact that only a small percentage of victims come into contact with the statutory authorities dealing with the problem. According to recent statistics, 8.2 per cent of women and 4 per cent of men were estimated to have experienced domestic violence in the year ending March 2015, equivalent to 1.3 million female and 600,000 male victims (*Focus on Violent Crime and Sexual Offences*, Office for National Statistics, February 2016). Also, according to Women's Aid, domestic abuse-related crime is 8 per cent of total crime, one incident of domestic violence is reported to the police every 30 seconds and two women are killed by their partner or ex-partner every week.

(b) What is domestic violence?

Domestic violence can take many forms. It includes not just physical violence but also psychological and emotional abuse and harassment. It can involve, for example, pestering, nagging, making nuisance telephone calls and intimidation. The Government has adopted a wide definition of domestic violence to include not just physical violence but also other forms of abuse. The definition was extended in March 2012 to include young people aged 16 to 17 years old and controlling or coercive behaviour after a Government consultation (see *Cross-Government Definition of Domestic Violence*, Home Office, December 2011). The most recent version, at the time of writing, is as follows.

▶ *The Cross-Government Definition of Domestic Violence and Abuse*

This definition was published in March 2016 by the Home Office (www.gov.uk):

Any incident or pattern of incidents of controlling, coercive, threatening behaviour, violence or abuse between those aged 16 or over who are, or have been, intimate partners or family members regardless of gender or sexuality. The abuse can encompass, but is not limited to: psychological; physical; sexual; financial; emotional.

Controlling behaviour is a range of acts designed to make a person subordinate and/or dependent by isolating them from sources of support, exploiting their resources and capacities for personal gain, depriving them of the means needed for independence, resistance and escape and regulating their everyday behaviour.

Coercive behaviour is an act or a pattern of acts of assault, threats, humiliation and intimidation or other abuse that is used to harm, punish or frighten their victim.

According to the Government, the above definition, which is not a legal definition, includes so-called 'honour'-based violence, female genital mutilation and forced marriage. It is clear that victims of domestic violence are not confined to one gender or ethnic group.

For the purposes of providing housing assistance for victims of domestic violence, the *Homelessness Code of Guidance for Local Authorities* also adopts a wide definition, as did Baroness Hale when giving judgment in the Supreme Court in *Yemshaw v Hounslow London Borough Council* [2011] UKSC 3 (see 4.11).

(c) Housing problems

Domestic violence can create housing problems. Some victims may have to seek temporary accommodation in a refuge and/or apply to a local housing authority for public sector housing (see 4.11). Some victims may end up going through a divorce or dissolution, whereupon the court has jurisdiction to adjudicate on any dispute about ownership and occupation of the family home (see Chapter 7). In some cases, the court will provide injunctive protection, and remove the perpetrator from the home and allow the victim back in (see 5.5 below).

(d) Children and domestic violence

The civil and the criminal law both provide protection for children who witness or are victims of domestic violence. Sometimes local authority intervention may be needed under the Children Act 1989 (CA 1989) (see Chapter 14). As violence in the home can be damaging to children who witness it, the word 'harm' in the Act includes 'impairment suffered from seeing or hearing the ill-treatment of another' (s 105(1)). There is increasing recognition of the problem of domestic violence for children, particularly on family breakdown, and steps have been taken to improve protection for children in cases involving child arrangements orders where there is actual or potential violence in the home (see 11.4 and 11.5).

(e) Specialist domestic violence courts

Specialist domestic violence courts have been introduced in some parts of England and Wales with the aim of bringing more perpetrators of domestic violence to justice and ensuring that victims and their families are given support. Specialist domestic violence courts deal with criminal prosecutions and have specially trained magistrates and other staff to deal with domestic violence. Cases are fast-tracked in order to eliminate distress. Multi-agency and inter-agency approaches are adopted, bringing together the police, prosecutors, court staff, probation officers and specialist support services. Independent domestic violence advisors help keep victims and their children safe from harm from violent partners or family. They are responsible for ensuring that the safety of the victim is coordinated across the criminal justice system, and for giving advice on accessing essential services such as victim and witness agencies, housing, health, counselling and childcare.

(f) The legislation

There are various Acts of Parliament which provide protection and support for victims of domestic violence, whether they are adults or children. In family law, the important Acts of Parliament are:

▶ *Part IV of the Family Law Act 1996*   Under these provisions, the Family Court has jurisdiction to make orders giving injunctive protection to victims of domestic violence and to make provision in respect of occupation of the family home (see 5.3 to 5.6 below).
▶ *The Children Act 1989*   Children who are at risk of significant harm, which includes domestic violence, can be protected by the Family Court and by local authorities under the provisions of this Act (see Chapters 10 and 14).

In addition to the above two Acts and the various criminal laws which are available to deal with perpetrators of domestic violence (see 5.2 below), protection is also available under the Protection from Harassment Act 1997 (see 5.7 below).

(g) Further legislative developments to improve protection

The Government has taken further legislative steps to improve protection for victims. Thus, the Domestic Violence, Crime and Victims Act 2004 (DVCVA 2004) was enacted in order to, *inter alia*, make breach of a non-molestation order a criminal offence (see 5.4 below) and extend the class of people who can apply for an occupation order under Part IV of the Family Law Act 1996 (see 5.5 below). It also amended the Protection from Harassment Act 1997 to give the court the power to make a restraining order with regard to *any* criminal offence, not just harassment (see 5.7 below). In addition, the DVCVA 2004 and the Domestic Violence, Crime and Victims (Amendment) Act 2012 made changes to the criminal law to provide better protection for victims of violence in the home; and the Serious Crimes Act 2015 created a criminal offence of controlling or coercive behaviour in an intimate or family relationship (see 5.2 below).

5.2   Domestic violence – the criminal law

Domestic violence is a serious and frequently reported crime which the police are meant to treat as seriously as any other crime. Police forces are required to draw up clear policy statements about intervention in domestic violence cases and to have special domestic violence units. They are also required to support victims by, for example, finding them temporary accommodation and keeping them informed about the case. Police forces are involved in local domestic violence initiatives; and police domestic violence units work closely with solicitors, Women's Aid and other organisations. They also have powers and duties where children are suffering, or at risk of suffering, violence in the home.

The police have a wide range of powers in respect of domestic violence. Thus, for example, under the common law they can enter premises to prevent or deal with breaches of the peace, and they have a power of arrest in such circumstances. They can also enter premises under statutory law to make an arrest and/or to save life or limb or to prevent serious damage to property (s 17 Police and Criminal Evidence Act 1984). A perpetrator of violence can be prosecuted for: common assault (s 39 Criminal Justice Act 1988); assault occasioning actual bodily harm (s 47 Offences Against the Person Act 1861); rape (s 1 Sexual Offences Act 2003); sexual assault (s 3 Sexual Offences Act 2003); affray (s 3 Public Order Act 1986); criminal damage (s 1 Criminal Damage Act 1971); and harassment (s 2 Protection from Harassment Act 1997). Under section 51 of the Criminal Justice and Public Order Act 1994 it is an offence to intimidate a witness or to harm, or threaten to harm, a witness. Offences can also be committed under the Telecommunications Act 1984 (which prohibits the sending of grossly offensive, indecent, obscene or menacing communications) and under the Malicious Communications Act 1988 (which prohibits the sending of indecent or grossly offensive letters which are intended to create distress or anxiety). Victims of domestic violence may be entitled to compensation under the Criminal Injuries Compensation Scheme.

In addition to the criminal offences above, there are other criminal law provisions which relate more specifically to domestic violence. Thus, under section 5 of the Domestic Violence, Crime and Victims Act 2004 (DVCVA 2004) it is a criminal offence to cause or allow a child or a vulnerable adult to die or to suffer serious physical harm (equivalent to grievous bodily harm). Prior to 2 July 2012 the criminal offence related only to causing or allowing death, but the Domestic Violence, Crime and Victims (Amendment) Act 2012 extended this to include causing or allowing serious physical harm. Section 10(1) of the DVCVA 2004 also made common assault an arrestable offence under Schedule 1A to the Police and Criminal Evidence Act 1984, so that the police have the power to arrest a person on suspicion of assault and/or battery without an arrest warrant.

(a)   An offence of controlling or coercive behaviour

Under section 76 of the Serious Crimes Act 2015, it is a criminal offence to engage in repeated or continuous controlling or coercive behaviour in intimate or family relationships.

Section 76 of the Serious Crimes Act 2015

(1) A person (A) commits an offence if—
  (a) A repeatedly or continuously engages in behaviour towards another person (B) that is controlling or coercive,
  (b) at the time of the behaviour, A and B are personally connected,
  (c) the behaviour has a serious effect on B, and
  (d) A knows or ought to know that the behaviour will have a serious effect on B.

(2) A and B are 'personally connected' if—
  (a) A is in an intimate personal relationship with B, or
  (b) A and B live together and—
     (i) they are members of the same family, or
     (ii) they have previously been in an intimate personal relationship with each other.

(3) ...

(4) A's behaviour has a 'serious effect' on B if—
  (a) it causes B to fear, on at least two occasions, that violence will be used against B, or
  (b) it causes B serious alarm or distress which has a substantial adverse effect on B's usual day-to-day activities.

It is a defence for a person to show that, in engaging in the behaviour towards another person, they believed that they were acting in that person's best interests *and* that the behaviour was in all the circumstances reasonable (s 76(8)), unless engaging in the behaviour causes the victim to fear that violence will be used against them (s 76(10)). A person found guilty of an offence under this section can be fined or imprisoned for up to five years (s 76(11)). Prior to the introduction of this offence, case-law suggested that the law on stalking and harassment does not apply to controlling or coercive behaviour that takes place in an ongoing intimate relationship (see 5.7 below). Thus, this offence closes a gap in the law.

(b)   Domestic violence protection notices and orders

Another development to give greater protection to actual or potential victims of domestic violence is the introduction of powers under sections 24–33 of the Crime and Security Act 2010, which give senior police officers the power to issue a domestic violence protection notice. If a domestic violence protection notice has been issued, a police constable *must* apply, by way of complaint to the magistrates' courts, for a domestic violence protection order. A domestic violence protection order must contain certain specified provisions, including, *inter alia*, a provision prohibiting a person from molesting the person for whose protection it is made; and it may contain a provision regulating the occupation of the home. Breach of a domestic violence protection order is a criminal offence.

(c) Domestic Violence Disclosure Scheme

There have been further developments with a view to improving protection for victims of domestic violence. Thus, in October 2011 the Government announced a 12-week consultation on the desirability of disclosing information about an individual's history of domestic violence to a new partner, following the highly publicised death of Clare Wood who was murdered by her former partner in Greater Manchester in 2009 (see *Domestic Violence Disclosure Scheme – A Consultation*, Home Office, October 2011 and *Domestic violence Disclosure Scheme – A Consultation: Summary of Responses*, Home Office, March 2012). In March 2014, following a successful pilot scheme, the Domestic Violence Disclosure Scheme was rolled out across England and Wales. The scheme means that an individual can ask the police to check whether a new or existing partner has a violent past (the 'right to ask'). If police checks show that a person may be at risk of domestic violence from their partner, the police will consider disclosing the information (the 'right to know'). According to a Home Office assessment published in March 2016 (see *One Year On – Home Office Assessment of National Roll-Out*), the police and partner agencies were largely positive about the scheme and good practice was emerging. Practitioners, however, felt that there was some variation across the country in the number of disclosures made by police forces; and that there was some inconsistency in information given in disclosures and variation in the service provided to victims.

5.3 Family law remedies under Part IV of the Family Law Act 1996

Part IV of the Family Law Act 1996 (FLA 1996), which was enacted to consolidate the law and to provide remedies for a wider range of people, gives the Family Court jurisdiction to grant the following two remedies to protect victims of domestic violence, including children:

▶ *A non-molestation order* This is an order made under section 42 of the Act containing a provision prohibiting the respondent from molesting a person who is associated with the respondent and/or a relevant child.
▶ *An occupation order* This is an order made under section 33, 35, 36, 37 or 38 of the Act regulating, prohibiting and governing the occupation of the family home.

The procedural rules for making an application are laid down in Part 10 of the Family Procedure Rules 2010.

According to *Family Court Statistics Quarterly* (Ministry of Justice, March 2016), there was a rise in the number of applications for non-molestation orders during 2013, but there has been a drop since the end of 2014, suggesting that the trend may be stabilising. The number of applications for occupation orders showed a fairly steady trend during the same time period.

5.4 Non-molestation orders

Under Part IV of the Family Law Act 1996 (FLA 1996) the Family Court has jurisdiction to make a non-molestation order prohibiting the respondent from molesting a person who is associated with the respondent and/or from molesting a relevant child (s 42(1)). According to *Family Court Statistics Quarterly* (Ministry of Justice, March 2016), there were 18,700 applications for non-molestation orders in 2015.

(a) Applicants

A wide range of family members can apply for a non-molestation order, not just spouses and cohabitants, provided the applicant is 'associated' with the respondent and any child is a 'relevant child' (see 5.6 below for definitions). A child can apply, but, if the child is aged under 16, the court must give the child leave (permission) to apply, which it can only grant if the child has sufficient understanding to make the proposed application (s 43). The court is unlikely to grant a child leave save in the most exceptional circumstances. In fact, there are no reported decisions on applications made by children.

An application for a non-molestation order can be made where the parties are an engaged couple or a formerly engaged couple (provided the application is brought within three years of the engagement's termination) (s 42(4)). Written evidence of the engagement is required, unless the court is satisfied that the engagement is evidenced by an engagement ring or an engagement ceremony; or by a gift by one party to the agreement as a token of the agreement (s 44). Parties to a civil partnership agreement or former civil partnership agreement can also apply, and the rules are the same as those which apply to engaged couples (see s 42(4ZA); ss 44(3)–(4)).

(i) Orders can be made of the court's own motion (on its own initiative)

The court in any family proceedings can make a non-molestation order without an application having been made (s 42(2)(c)); and it can also do so in proceedings for an occupation order (s 42(4A)).

(b) What is 'molestation'?

'Molestation' is not defined in the Act, but is instead determined on a case-by-case basis by the courts. Under the law prior to the Act, the term 'molestation' was interpreted widely to include not just actual or threatened violence, but also pestering (*Vaughan v Vaughan* [1973] 3 All ER 449) and harassment (*Horner v Horner* [1982] Fam 90). The same approach is taken under the Act. In *C v C (Non-Molestation Order: Jurisdiction)* [1998] 1 FLR 554, Stephen Brown P stated that there must be some conduct which clearly harasses and affects the applicant to such a degree that the intervention of the court is called for. The order can refer to molestation in general and/or to particular acts of molestation (s 48(6)).

(c) Criteria for making a non-molestation order

When deciding whether to make a non-molestation order, and, if so, in what manner, the court must have regard to all the circumstances of the case, including the need to secure the health, safety and well-being of the applicant and of any relevant child (s 42(5)).

(d)   Orders without notice (*ex parte* orders)

As urgent action is often needed, the court, where just and convenient to do so, may make an *ex parte* non-molestation order (in other words, an order made without the respondent being given notice of the proceedings) (s 45(1)). When deciding whether to make an *ex parte* non-molestation order, the court must consider all the circumstances of the case, including: the risk of significant harm to the applicant or any relevant child by the respondent if an order is not immediately made; the likelihood of the applicant being deterred or prevented from pursuing the application if an order is not immediately made; whether there is reason to believe that the respondent is aware of the proceedings but is deliberately avoiding service; and whether the applicant or relevant child will be seriously prejudiced by a delay in effecting service of proceedings or in effecting substituted service (s 45(2)). If an *ex parte* non-molestation order is made, the court must give the respondent an opportunity to make representations relating to the order as soon as is just and convenient at a full hearing (s 45(3)).

(e)   Terms and duration of the order

A non-molestation order can refer to molestation in general and/or to particular acts of molestation (s 48(6)), and it can be made for a specified period or until further order (s 48(7)). Although the aim of a non-molestation order is to give the parties a temporary breathing space, in *Re B-J (Power of Arrest)* [2000] 2 FLR 443 the Court of Appeal held that an order can be made for an indefinite period of time in appropriate circumstances.

(f)   Undertakings

Instead of making a non-molestation order the court can accept an undertaking (a promise to the court) from any party to the proceedings (s 46(1)), unless it appears to the court that the respondent has used or threatened violence against the applicant or a relevant child and a non-molestation order is needed so that any breach can be punishable as a criminal offence under section 42A (s 46(3A)). An undertaking carries less of a stigma than a court order as the court does not make findings of fact about the respondent's behaviour and breach is not a criminal offence. Breach of an undertaking is enforceable in the same way as a court order (s 46(4)).

(g)   Variation and discharge

A non-molestation order may be varied or discharged on the application of the respondent or by the applicant for the order (s 49).

(h)   Breach of a non-molestation order

Breach of any term in a non-molestation order, without reasonable excuse, is a criminal offence (s 42A(1)). If the order was made *ex parte*, there is no criminal offence unless the person concerned was aware of the existence of the order (s 42A(2)).

A person found guilty of breaching a non-molestation order can be fined or imprisoned for up to five years (s 42A(5)).

5.5   Occupation orders

There may come a point where a victim of domestic violence can no longer tolerate living with the perpetrator and is forced to leave the family home and seek alternative accommodation. In an urgent situation a victim may need to seek accommodation in a refuge (see www.refuge.org.uk). A victim of domestic violence who is forced to leave the home, and/or who cannot seek entry to it, can apply for an occupation order which the family court has jurisdiction to make under Part IV of the Family Law Act 1996 (FLA 1996).

Occupation orders are made less frequently than non-molestation orders due to the seriousness of making an order, particularly where the respondent has a property interest in the home. But each case depends on its facts and the court may decide that the seriousness of a party having no accommodation may outweigh the seriousness of making an order, as it did, for example, in *Grubb v Grubb* [2009] EWCA Civ 976 (see below). Nevertheless, occupation orders are regarded as a short-term remedy; and, in the longer term, a victim may be forced to apply for a divorce or dissolution. According to *Family Court Statistics Quarterly* (Ministry of Justice, March 2016), there were 4,555 applications for occupation orders in 2015.

Under sections 33 and 35–38 of Part IV of the FLA 1996, the Family Court has jurisdiction to make an occupation order (s 39). It can be made by the court on an application, or of the court's own motion in any family proceedings (ss 39(1), (2)). An occupation order does not affect a person's claim to any legal or equitable interest in the home in any subsequent proceedings, including subsequent proceedings under Part IV of the Act (s 39(4)). Thus, if a person is ordered to leave the home immediately, or within a specified time, their rights of ownership in the home are not affected.

(a)   Variation and discharge

An occupation order may be varied or discharged on an application by the respondent or by the person who made the original application (s 49).

(b)   Categories of applicant

Part IV of the FLA 1996 creates two categories of applicant: 'entitled'; and 'non-entitled'. The court's powers are much wider for entitled applicants.

▶ *An 'entitled' applicant* is a person who has a right to occupy the home by virtue of a beneficial estate or interest or contract; or by virtue of any enactment giving them the right to remain in occupation; or who has 'home rights' under section 30 of the Act (see 4.2).

▶ *A 'non-entitled' applicant* is a person who has no right to occupy the home by virtue of a beneficial estate, interest, contract, or enactment, or by having 'home rights' under section 30 of the Act (see 4.2).

Different sections of the Act apply, depending on whether or not the applicant has a property entitlement and the parties' status.

(c) Applications by children

A child can apply for an occupation order, but a child under 16 needs leave of the court to do so, which can be granted only if the child has sufficient understanding to make the proposed application (s 43). Applications by children are rare, just as they are for non-molestation orders.

(d) 'Entitled' applicant and 'associated' respondent (section 33)

An entitled applicant (in other words, a person with a property interest) can apply for an occupation order if they are 'associated' with the respondent and the house is, was or was intended to be the home of both of them (s 33(1)). The term 'associated person' includes a wide range of people, not just spouses, civil partners and cohabitants, but other family members and also people living in the same household (s 62(3)). Parties to an engagement or civil partnership agreement which has been terminated no less than three years previously can apply (ss 33(2), (2A)). Proof of the engagement or civil partnership agreement may be needed in the same way as it is for an application for a non-molestation order (ss 44(3), (4)).

(i) Powers of the court

The court has wide powers to insert a range of terms in the order (s 33(3)). Thus, it may: enforce the applicant's entitlement to remain in occupation; require the respondent to allow the applicant to enter and remain in the home; regulate occupation by either or both parties; prohibit, suspend or restrict the respondent's right to occupy the home; require the respondent to leave the home or part of it; and exclude the respondent from a defined area in which the home is included. In addition, if the respondent has section 30 'home rights' in relation to the home and the applicant is the other spouse or civil partner, the court can restrict or terminate those rights.

The court has other powers under section 33 of the Act. Thus, the order may declare that the applicant is an entitled person (s 33(4)). If the applicant has section 30 'home rights', and the respondent is the applicant's spouse or civil partner, the court, where just and reasonable to do so, can, when making an order during the subsistence of a marriage or civil partnership, include a provision in the order that those rights are not to be brought to an end by the death of the other spouse or civil partner or by the termination of the marriage or civil partnership (ss 33(5) and (8)).

(ii) How the court exercises its powers

When deciding whether to exercise its powers above and, if so, in what manner, the court must first apply the so-called 'balance of harm test' in section 33(7). In other words, it must weigh in the balance the significant harm which is likely to be caused to either party and any relevant child. If it decides that the applicant or any relevant child is likely to suffer significant harm which is greater than that which the respondent or any relevant child is likely to suffer, then the court *must* make an occupation order. 'Harm', in relation to an adult, means ill-treatment (physical or non-physical) and impairment to health (physical or mental). In relation to a child, 'harm' has the same meaning, but also includes impairment to development (physical, intellectual, emotional, social or behavioural) and sexual abuse (s 63(1)). Where the question of whether the harm suffered by the child is significant turns on the child's health or development, the court must compare the child's health or development with that which could reasonably be expected of a similar child (s 63(3)). If, applying the balance of harm test, the court finds that the balance does not lie in favour of the applicant and/or any relevant child, then it must go on to conduct the discretionary exercise laid down in section 33(6) (see below).

In the following case the Court of Appeal held that the balance of harm test had been incorrectly applied in the circumstances of the case. It also held that occupation orders which overrode proprietary rights were justified only in exceptional circumstances.

▶ *Chalmers v Johns* [1998] EWCA Civ 1452

The parties were cohabitants whose relationship had always been tempestuous. There had been acts of violence by each party against the other, resulting in minor injuries. Alcohol use, particularly by the woman, had been responsible for much of this. The woman left the family home with their seven-year-old daughter and moved into temporary council accommodation. She applied for an occupation order under section 33 as she was a joint tenant of the home with the respondent. Applying the balance of harm test, the judge made an interim order on the basis that the mother and child were likely to suffer significant harm attributable to the father if the order was not made. The father appealed.

The Court of Appeal allowed his appeal, as the judge had incorrectly applied the statutory provisions. The applicant mother and the child were not likely to suffer significant harm attributable to the conduct of the respondent father if the order was not made. There was no real risk of violence or any other harm befalling the child. The Court of Appeal held that the case was one in which the court should exercise its discretion by considering all the circumstances of the case and the prescribed matters in section 33(6). It also stated that occupation orders which overrode proprietary rights were justified only in exceptional circumstances. The fact that the final hearing was to take place very shortly weighed against making such a draconian order at an interlocutory hearing, particularly as there was no evidence that any further domestic disharmony could not be managed by the imposition of injunctive orders. The trial judge had not clearly focused upon the alternative nature of the adjoining subsections of section 33(6) and 33(7), but had treated them as if they were both simultaneously applicable to the facts of the case. Had she directed herself more closely to the statutory language, she would have seen that this was a case which came nowhere near section 33(7).

But each case turns on its own facts, as the Court of Appeal emphasised in *B v B (Occupation Order)* (see below) where it allowed the husband's appeal against an occupation order as the balance of harm test had not been satisfied on the facts. The case shows the importance of taking into account *all* the relevant children in a family.

> ▶ *B v B (Occupation Order)* [1999] 1 FLR 715
>
> The wife left the matrimonial home (of which she and her husband were council tenants). She took their baby daughter with her and the husband remained in the home with his six-year-old son from a previous marriage. The Court of Appeal held that, although the husband's behaviour fully justified an occupation order being made, his position as the full-time carer of his son also had to be taken into consideration. If an occupation order was made, the husband would have to leave the matrimonial home with his son and move into unsuitable temporary council accommodation, and his son would have to change schools.

The exceptional nature of occupation orders was also emphasised by the Court of Appeal in *G v G (Occupation Order: Conduct)* [2000] 2 FLR 36, in which it was held that there was no requirement for a respondent's conduct to be intentional for the court to make an order.

(iii) The discretionary exercise under section 33(6)

If, applying the balance of harm test (see above), the balance is not in favour of making the order, then the court must still go on to conduct the discretionary exercise under section 33(6). This requires the court, when deciding whether to exercise its powers and, if so, in what manner, to have regard to all the circumstances including:

(a) the housing needs and housing resources of each of the parties and of any relevant child;

(b) the financial resources of each of the parties;

(c) the likely effect of any order, or of any decision by the court not to exercise any of the powers under s 33(3), on the health, safety or well-being of the parties and of any relevant child; and

(d) the conduct of the parties in relation to each other and otherwise.

A good example of the application of the discretionary exercise under section 33(6) can be found in the following case.

> ▶ *Grubb v Grubb* [2009] EWCA Civ 976
>
> The application for an occupation order arose in the course of divorce proceedings which the husband had initially defended. He had excluded his wife from the matrimonial home by refusing to give her the keys. The wife was granted an occupation order (her application was based on the criteria under section 33(6), so there was no need to prove significant harm based on the criteria under section 33(7)). The husband appealed against the order on the basis that, *inter alia*, the trial judge had failed to recognise the seriousness of the order.
>
> The Court of Appeal dismissed his appeal. Wilson LJ stated that an occupation order is always serious, but that it was likely to carry its greatest level of seriousness when it was made against a spouse to whom alternative accommodation was not readily available. Taking into account the circumstances of the case, immediate separation was not only 'beneficial' but 'necessary'; and the only way of achieving it was to evict the husband, to whom another property was readily available and who in any event had massive resources with which to fund his accommodation elsewhere.

The following case shows that, even though occupation orders are regarded as serious orders which should not be routinely made, physical violence is not necessarily needed. It also shows that an improper application of the statutory provisions may not necessarily invalidate the exercise of judicial discretion:

▶ *Dolan v Corby* [2011] EWCA Civ 1664

The parties were cohabitants who were joint tenants of the home in which they had been living for 30 years. The woman applied for *ex parte* non-molestation and occupation orders, alleging verbal and physical abuse by the respondent. The non-molestation order was granted, and the application for the occupation order was set down to be heard *inter partes*. Although the trial judge found no evidence of physical violence (only verbal abuse), an occupation order was made excluding the respondent from the property as the applicant, who had a history of drug abuse and suffered from psychiatric problems, was less able than the respondent to find alternative accommodation.

The respondent appealed on the basis, *inter alia*, that the trial judge had conflated the discretionary exercise under section 33(6) and the balance of harm test under section 33(7). The Court of Appeal agreed, but held that the conflation had not vitiated the exercise of discretion. Thus, it was held that the trial judge's decision was a discretionary one and could be properly construed under section 33(6) even though he had not considered the provisions separately. The respondent also argued that, following *Chalmers v Johns* and *G v G (Occupation Order: Conduct)* (see above), occupation orders are draconian orders which should be granted only in exceptional circumstances, and that, as there had been no finding of violence at first instance, he should not have been excluded from the home. However, Black LJ held that *Chalmers v Johns* and *G v G (Occupation Order: Conduct)* did not necessitate a finding of violence. The court had to have regard to 'all the circumstances' of the case and the central feature of the case was the psychiatric state of the applicant, which was capable of making the case exceptional.

(For another case where an occupation order was made excluding the husband from the jointly owned home for three months where there was no violence, but where the trial judge found that the heated arguments between the husband and wife on marriage breakdown caused their children emotional harm, see *Re L (Children)* [2012] EWCA Civ 721.)

(iv) Duration of the order

The order may be made for a specified period, or until the occurrence of a specified event, or until further order (s 33(10)). There is no time limit on the duration of the order, as there is for non-entitled applicants.

(e) Non-entitled applicants

Non-entitled applicants (people with no right to occupy the home) must apply under sections 35–38 of Part IV of the FLA 1996. Each section of the Act applies to people with a particular sort of status and relationship as follows:

(i) Non-entitled former spouse/civil partner vs entitled former spouse/civil partner (section 35)

Powers of the court These powers are similar to those in section 33(3) (see above), except that in certain circumstances there are mandatory provisions which must be included in an order. Thus, if the applicant is in occupation of the home, the order *must* contain a provision giving the applicant the right not to be evicted or excluded from the home or any part of it by the respondent for a specified period; and prohibit the respondent from evicting or excluding the applicant during that period (s 35(3)). If the applicant is *not* in occupation, the order *must* contain a provision giving the applicant the right to enter into and occupy the home for a specified period; and require the respondent to permit the exercise of that right (s 35(4)). An order *may* also (s 35(5)): regulate the occupation of the home or part of it; prohibit, suspend or restrict the respondent's right to occupy it; require the respondent to leave the home or part of it; and/or exclude the respondent from a defined area in which the home is included.

How the court exercises its powers When deciding whether to make a mandatory provision under sections 35(3) and (4) and, if so, in what manner, the court must have regard to all the circumstances including the following (s 35(6)):

(a) the housing needs and housing resources of each of the parties and of any relevant child;
(b) the financial resources of each of the parties;
(c) the likely effect of any order, or of any decision by the court not to exercise any of the powers under [subsection 35(3) and (4)], on the health, safety or well-being of the parties and of any relevant child;
(d) the conduct of the parties in relation to each other and otherwise;
(e) the length of time that has elapsed since the parties ceased to live together;
(f) the length of time that has elapsed since the marriage or civil partnership was dissolved or annulled; and
(g) the existence of any pending proceedings between the parties: – (i) for an order under s 23A or 24 of the Matrimonial Causes Act 1973 (property adjustment orders in connection with divorce proceedings etc.); (i(a)) for a property adjustment order under Part 2 of Schedule 5 to the Civil Partnership Act 2004; (ii) for an order under paragraph 1(2)(d) or (e) of Schedule 1 to the Children Act 1989 (orders for financial relief against parents); or (iii) relating to the legal or beneficial ownership of the dwelling-house.

Section 35(7) provides that, when deciding whether to include a discretionary provision in an order under section 35(5), and, if so, in what manner, the court must have regard to all the circumstances including the matters in section 35(6)(a)–(d) and consider 'the balance of harm test' laid down in section 35(8). In other words, if the court decides to make a section 35 order and it appears that if the order does not include a discretionary section 35(5) provision the applicant or any relevant child is likely to suffer significant harm attributable to the conduct of the respondent, the court *must* include a discretionary provision in the order unless it appears to the court that: (a) the respondent or any relevant child is likely to suffer significant harm if the provision is included in the order; and (b) the harm likely to be suffered by the respondent or child in that event is as great as or greater than the harm attributable to conduct of the respondent which is likely to be suffered by the applicant or child if the provision is not included (s 35(8)).

Duration of the order   The order must be limited to a specified period not exceeding six months, but can be extended on one or more occasions for a further specified period not exceeding six months (s 35(10)). While the order is in force an applicant is treated as possessing 'home rights' and sections 30(3)–(6) apply (s 35(13)). An order cannot be made after the death of either party; and an order ceases to be effective on either party's death (s 35(9)).

(ii) Non-entitled cohabitant/former cohabitant vs entitled cohabitant/former cohabitant (section 36)

Powers of the court   Where the applicant is in occupation of the home, the order *must* give the applicant the right not to be evicted or excluded from the home or any part of it by the respondent for a specified period and prohibit the respondent from evicting or excluding the applicant during that period (s 36(3)). If the applicant is not in occupation, the order *must* give the applicant the right to enter into and occupy the home for a specified period; and require the respondent to permit the exercise of that right (s 36(4)). The order *may* also contain a discretionary provision (s 36(5)): regulating the occupation of the home or part of it by either or both parties; prohibiting, suspending or restricting the respondent's right to occupy it; requiring the respondent to leave the home or part of it; or excluding the respondent from a defined area in which the home is included.

How the court exercises its powers   When deciding whether to make a mandatory order under section 36(3) or (4), and, if so, in what manner, the court must have regard to all the circumstances of the case, including (s 36(6)):

(a) the housing needs and housing resources of each of the parties and of any relevant child;
(b) the financial resources of each of the parties;
(c) the likely effect of any order, or of any decision by the court not to exercise any of the powers under section 33(3), on the health, safety or well-being of the parties and of any relevant child;
(d) the conduct of the parties in relation to each other and otherwise;
(e) the nature of the parties' relationship and in particular the level of commitment involved in it;
(f) the length of time during which they have cohabited;
(g) whether there are or have been any children who are children of both parties or for whom both parties have or have had parental responsibility;
(h) the length of time that has elapsed since the parties ceased to live together; and
(i) the existence of any pending proceedings for an order under paragraph 1(2)(d) or (e) of Schedule 1 to the Children Act 1989 (orders for financial relief against parents); or relating to the legal or beneficial interest of the dwelling-house.

When deciding whether to include one or more of the discretionary provisions under section 36(5) and, if so, in what manner, the court must have regard to all the circumstances including the matters mentioned in section 36(6)(a)–(d); and apply the 'balance of harm' test laid down in section 36(8). In other words, the court must ask whether the applicant or any relevant child is likely to suffer significant harm which is greater than that likely to be suffered by the respondent or any relevant child if a section 36(5) provision is not included in the order. However, even if the balance of harm lies in favour of the applicant and any relevant child, there is no obligation on the court to make an order as there is in an application under section 35 by an entitled applicant – the balance of harm test is merely part of the discretionary exercise.

Duration of the order   The order must be limited so as to have effect for a specified period not exceeding six months, but may be extended on one occasion for a further specified period not exceeding six months (s 36(10)). An order cannot be made after the death of either party; and an order ceases to have effect on either party's death (s 36(9)).

(iii) Neither spouse/civil partner of former spouse/former civil partner is entitled to occupy (section 37)

Either party may apply against the other for an occupation order under section 37 (ss 37(1), (2); 37(1A)). The order *may*: require the respondent to permit the applicant to enter and remain in the home or part of it; regulate the occupation of the home by either or both parties; require the respondent to leave the home or part of it; or exclude the respondent from a defined area in which the house is included (s 37(3)).

How the court exercises its powers   When deciding whether to make a discretionary order under section 37(3) and, if so, in what manner, the court must have regard to the factors in section 33(6) and the balance of harm test in section 33(7) as they apply to the exercise by the court of its powers under section 33(3) of the Act (s 37(4)).

Duration of the order   The order must be limited to six months, but may be extended on one or more occasions by a further specified period not exceeding six months (s 37(5)).

(iv) Neither cohabitant/former cohabitant entitled to occupy (section 38)

Where both cohabitants or former cohabitants occupy a house which is the home in which they cohabit or cohabited, but neither party is entitled to occupy the house, either party may apply for an occupation order (ss 38(1) and (2)).

Powers of the court   The provisions which the order may contain are the same as those for a section 37 order (s 38(3)).

How the court exercises its powers   When deciding whether to make a discretionary order under section 38(3) and, if so, in what manner, the court must have regard to all the circumstances including all of the factors in section 38(4) and the balance of harm test in section 38(5). These provisions are identical to those in section 36(6)(a)–(d) (see above), and, as in section 36(7), even if the balance of harm lies in favour of the applicant and any relevant child, there is no obligation on the court to make an order as there is in the case of an entitled applicant.

Duration of the order   The order must be limited to a specified period not exceeding six months, but can be extended on one occasion by a further specified period of up to six months (s 38(6)).

(f)   Occupation orders – other powers

(i) Undertakings, orders without notice and enforcement

The rules for undertakings, orders without notice and enforcement are the same as those for non-molestation orders (see 5.4 above), except that the restriction on accepting an undertaking (s 46(3A)) does not apply to occupation orders.

(ii) Attaching a power of arrest (section 47)

Under section 47, the court can attach a power of arrest to an occupation order. The power differs depending on whether the occupation order is made *inter partes* (with notice) or *ex parte* (without notice).

If the order is made *inter partes* and it appears to the court that the respondent has used or threatened violence against the applicant or a relevant child, it *must* attach a power of arrest to one or more provisions of the order, unless it is satisfied that the applicant or any child will otherwise be adequately protected (ss 47(1) and (2)). If the order is made *ex parte*, the court *may* attach a power of arrest to one or more provisions of the order, but only if the respondent has used or threatened violence against the applicant or a relevant child, and there is a risk that the applicant or relevant child will suffer significant harm as a result of the respondent's conduct if the power of arrest is not attached to the order immediately (s 47(3)). Although it is usually preferable for a power of arrest to have effect for the same period as the order, it can be made to have effect for a shorter period than the other provisions in the order (see s 47(4) and *Re B-J (Power of Arrest)* [2000] 2 FLR 443).

The effect of a power of arrest is to permit a constable to arrest, without warrant, a person whom he has reasonable cause to suspect is in breach of any provision in an order to which the power of arrest is attached (s 47(6)). The respondent must be brought before a judge or justice of the peace within twenty-four hours, and, if the matter is not disposed of, the respondent may be remanded in custody or on bail (s 45(7)). A power of arrest can be attached even though the respondent is a minor. Thus, for example, in *Re H (Respondent Under 18: Power of Arrest)* [2001] 1 FLR 641 the Court of Appeal upheld an occupation order which had been made with a power of arrest attached, ordering a 17-year-old boy, who had been violent and abusive to his parents, to leave the home and not to return or attempt to return.

(iii) Ancillary powers (section 40)

Where an application is made under sections 33, 35 or 36 (see above), the court has various discretionary ancillary powers under section 40 of the Act. Thus, it can impose repair and maintenance obligations, require a party to pay the rent, mortgage or other outgoings, and impose obligations in respect of the furniture or other contents of the house. It can also require a party to keep the house, furniture and any other contents secure. When deciding whether and, if so, how to exercise its powers under section 40, the court must consider all the circumstances of the case, including the parties' financial needs and resources, and their present and future financial obligations, including their financial obligations to each other and to any relevant child (s 40(2)). Ancillary orders are effective only for the duration of the occupation order (s 40(3)).

One of the problems with these ancillary powers, however, is that the courts have no power to enforce them (see *Nwogbe v Nwogbe* [2000] 2 FLR 74 where the Court of Appeal was strongly critical of this lacuna in the law).

(g)   Breach of an occupation order

Breach of an occupation order is not a criminal offence as it is for breach of a non-molestation order. Instead, civil proceedings for contempt of court will have to be brought and, if contempt is proved, the respondent will be ordered to pay a fine and/or serve a prison sentence. The courts have been increasingly willing to impose prison sentences for breach of an occupation order (see, for example, *H v O (Contempt of Court: Sentencing)* [2005] 2 FLR 329). However, as the Human Rights Act 1998 and the European Convention on Human Rights apply to committal proceedings, the Court of Appeal has held that the greatest possible care must be taken to ensure that the applicable evidential and procedural rules are properly obeyed (see *Hammerton v Hammerton* [2007] 2 FLR 1133).

5.6   Definitions for the purposes of Part IV of the Family Law Act 1996

Sections 62 and 63 of Part IV of the Family Law Act 1996 (FLA 1996) are important because they define key terms in the Act, including which people are eligible to apply for orders.

(a)   'Cohabitants' and 'former cohabitants'

The term 'cohabitants' is defined as two people who are neither married to each other nor are civil partners of each other but who are living together as if they were husband and wife or civil partners; but it does not include cohabitants who have subsequently married each other or become civil partners of each other (s 62(1)). As the court favours a purposive approach when construing the Act (in order to give victims protection), it has been held that the term 'cohabitant' can include people who maintain separate households (see, for example, *G v F (Non-Molestation Order: Jurisdiction)* [2000] 2 FLR 233).

(b)   'Relevant child'

A 'relevant child' is: any child who is living with, or who might reasonably be expected to live with, either party to the proceedings; any child in relation to whom an order under the Adoption and Children Act 2002 or the Children Act 1989 is in question in the proceedings; and any other child whose interests the court considers relevant (s 62(2)). This broad definition highlights the importance of protecting *any* child from domestic violence. Thus, the child need not be related to the applicant, nor be a child of the family.

(c) 'Associated persons'

An applicant for a non-molestation order must be 'associated' with the respondent, and so must an entitled applicant for an occupation order who is not a spouse, civil partner or cohabitant (or a former spouse, civil partner or cohabitant). 'Associated persons' are widely defined as (s 62(3)):

- spouses or former spouses;
- civil partners or former civil partners;
- cohabitants or former cohabitants;
- people who live, or have lived, in the same household, otherwise than merely by reason of one of them being the other's employee, tenant, lodger or boarder;
- relatives (see further below);
- engaged, or formerly engaged, couples;
- parties to a civil partnership agreement (whether or not that agreement has been terminated);
- people who have, or have had, an intimate personal relationship with each other which is or was of significant duration;
- in relation to any child, a person who is a parent of the child or have or have had parental responsibility for the child (s 62(4));
- parties to the same family proceedings (see definition below) other than proceedings under Part IV FLA 1996.

(d) A 'relative'

A 'relative' in relation to a person is (s 63(1)):

- the father, mother, step-father, step-mother, son, daughter, step-son, step-daughter, grandmother, grandfather, grandson or granddaughter of that person or of that person's spouse or former spouse, civil partner or former civil partner; or
- the brother, sister, uncle, aunt, niece or nephew (whether of full blood or of half blood or by marriage or civil partnership) of that person or of that person's spouse or former spouse, civil partner or former civil partner, and includes, in relation to a person who is cohabiting or has cohabited with another person, any person who would be any of the above relatives if the parties were married to each other or were civil partners of each other.

(e) Adopted children

If a child has been adopted, or an adoption agency has power to place the child for adoption by parental consent or by placement order (see Chapter 15), two persons are associated if: one of them is the natural parent of the child or a parent of such a natural parent; and the other is the child or any person who has become a parent of the child under an adoption order or has applied for an adoption order, or is any person with whom the child has at any time been placed for adoption (ss 62(5) and (7)).

(f) 'Family proceedings'

The term 'family proceedings' means any proceedings under (ss 63(1), (2)):

▶ the inherent jurisdiction of the High Court in relation to children;
▶ Part II of the Family Law Act 1996;
▶ Part IV of the Family Law Act 1996;
▶ Part 4A of the Family Law Act 1996;
▶ the Matrimonial Causes Act 1973;
▶ the Adoption Act 1976;
▶ the Domestic Proceedings and Magistrates' Courts Act 1978;
▶ Part III of the Matrimonial and Family Proceedings Act 1984;
▶ Parts I, II and IV of the Children Act 1989;
▶ Section 54 of the Human Fertilisation and Embryology Act 2008;
▶ the Adoption and Children Act 2002; and
▶ Schedules 5–7 to the Civil Partnership Act 2004.

5.7 The Protection from Harassment Act 1997

The Protection from Harassment Act 1997 (PHA 1977) was enacted primarily to provide protection from harassment and other similar conduct arising in the context of 'stalking' (the obsessive harassment of one person by another), but it is sometimes used by victims of domestic violence. The Act creates criminal offences and provides civil remedies (injunctions and damages). It has been amended by the Domestic Violence, Crime and Victims Act 2004 (DVCVA 2004) and the Serious Organised Crime and Police Act 2005.

There are important differences between applications under Part IV of the Family Law Act 1996 (FLA 1996) and the PHA 1997. Thus, under the PHA 1997: there is no requirement that the parties must be 'associated' persons; the remedies do not specifically relate to occupation of the home; damages can be awarded; and proceedings are not family proceedings.

Section 1(1) of the PHA 1997 prohibits harassment by providing that a person must not pursue a course of conduct which amounts to harassment of another, and which that person knows, or ought to know, amounts to harassment of another. There is no definition of 'harassment' in the Act, but section 7(2) provides that references to harassing a person include alarming a person or causing a person distress. The Act may therefore be used to prosecute people for acts other than stalking.

(a) Course of conduct

In order for there to be harassment, there must be a 'course of conduct'. A single incident is not enough, as there must be 'conduct on at least two occasions' (s 7(3)(a)). As 'conduct' can include speech (s 7(4)), verbal abuse can constitute harassment. In the following case, the Court of Appeal held that there must be a cogent link between the incidents involved in the 'course of conduct' in order for there to be harassment.

> ▶ *R v Hills* [2001] 1 FLR 580
>
> After the woman left the defendant he was charged with harassment under the PHA 1997. The course of conduct consisted of various assaults during a seven-month period, but centred on two separate and individual assaults which took place approximately six months apart. The defendant was convicted but appealed against his conviction.
>
> The Court of Appeal allowed his appeal, holding that a course of conduct requires proof of a cogent link between the two (or more) incidents constituting harassment. As the case centred on two separate and individual incidents, the necessary cogent link between the two assaults had not been established. The case was held to be far from the stalking type of offence for which the Act was intended. The Court of Appeal held that, where a couple were frequently coming back together and having sexual intercourse, it was unrealistic to think that the behaviour fell within the stalking category. It applied *Lau v Director of Public Prosecutions* [2000] 1 FLR 799, which concerned two incidents between a girlfriend and a boyfriend, and where it was held that, although two incidents could be enough to establish harassment, the fewer the occasions and the wider they were spread apart, the less likely it would be that a finding of harassment could reasonably be made for the purposes of the Act.

The following case shows that a number of acts of violence over a period of time may not necessarily constitute the offence of harassment, but they may constitute another offence, such as an assault.

> ▶ *R v Widdows* [2011] EWCA Crim 1500
>
> The defendant had a volatile relationship with a woman who was described as mature but emotionally vulnerable. The relationship involved a significant degree of mutual violence and volatility, with frequent arguments, separations and reconciliations. He was convicted of the section 4 offence of aggravated harassment under the PHA 1997 (see below) in respect of six incidents involving assaults over a nine-month period, culminating in two allegations of rape on the final occasion (of which he was acquitted). He appealed against his conviction.
>
> The Court of Appeal, allowing his appeal, held, *inter alia*, that, when bringing a charge under section 4, or when summing up to the jury, the concept of harassment must be borne in mind, even though the word 'harassment' is not used in section 4. Adopting Lord Nicholl's description of harassment in *Majrowski v Guy's and St Thomas's NHS Trust* [2006] UKHL 34 as implying 'stalkers, racial abusers, disruptive neighbours, bullying at work and so forth', the Court of Appeal held that the facts of the case (a number of acts of violence spread over nine months during a close and affectionate relationship) did not satisfy the course of conduct requirement or the requirement that it was conduct amounting to harassment. The Court of Appeal referred to its ruling in *R v Curtis* [2010] EWCA Crim 123, where, relying on earlier authorities (including *R v Hills* [2001] 1 FLR 580), it emphasised, on very similar facts, the need to find that the 'course of conduct' complained of 'amounts to' harassment.

(b)   Criminal offences under the Act

The PHA 1997 creates two levels of criminal offence: the section 2 offence of harassment; and the section 4 offence of aggravated harassment. A person who is found guilty of a section 2 offence is liable to a fine or imprisonment for up to six months (s 2(2)). The section 4 offence applies where a person causes another person to fear on at least two occasions that violence will be used against them (s 4(1)). This is an indictable offence and carries stricter penalties than the section 2 offence.

(i) Defences

Both offences are subject to two statutory defences: that the course of conduct was pursued for the purpose of preventing or detecting crime; or that the pursuit of the course of conduct was reasonable (ss 1(3) and 4(3)).

(ii) Restraining orders

The criminal court has the power to make restraining orders (injunctive-style orders) under section 5 of the PHA 1997. As a result of provisions inserted into the PHA 1997 by the DVCVA 2004, the criminal courts can now make restraining orders on the conviction of *any* offence, not just the offence of harassment; and they can make a restraining order where a person has been acquitted of harassment if they believe that such an order is necessary to protect a named person from harassment by the defendant in the future (s 5A). The aim of these wider powers is to give victims immediate protection and to save them having to bring a separate civil action.

With respect to duration, a restraining order may be made to have effect for a specified period or until further order (s 5(3)). Breach of an order without reasonable excuse is a criminal offence (s 5(5)) and can result in a fine or imprisonment for up to five years (s 5(6)).

(c) Civil remedies

The PHA 1997 also provides civil remedies. Section 3 creates a statutory tort of harassment by providing that a person who is, or may be, the victim of harassment, as prohibited by section 1 of the Act, can bring a claim in civil proceedings against the person responsible for the harassment (s 3(1)). Damages can be awarded, including damages for any anxiety caused by the harassment and/or any financial loss resulting from the harassment (s 3(2)). Thus, for example, in *Singh v Bhakar and Bhakar* [2007] 1 FLR 889 a young woman who suffered harassment by her mother-in-law after she joined her husband in his extended family home obtained damages under section 3 for the depression caused by the maltreatment.

Injunctive protection may also be granted. If the court grants an injunction restraining the defendant from pursuing any conduct which amounts to harassment, and the claimant considers that the defendant has done anything which is prohibited by the injunction, the claimant may apply for the issue of a warrant for the defendant's arrest (s 3(3)). Breach of an injunction restraining the defendant from pursuing any conduct which amounts to harassment is a criminal offence (s 3(6)); it is not punishable as contempt of court (s 3(7)).

In an application for a civil remedy under section 3 the standard of proof is the civil standard (on the balance of probabilities). The court must also ensure that it exercises its powers in compliance with the European Convention on Human Rights (see Tugendhat J in *Hipgrave and Hipgrave v Jones* [2005] 2 FLR 174).

5.8 Injunctions ancillary to legal proceedings

County courts and the High Court have jurisdiction (under section 38 of the County Courts Act 1984 and section 37 of the Supreme Court Act 1981 respectively) to grant injunctions ancillary to civil proceedings where it is just and convenient to do so. These powers may be useful if a victim of domestic violence is not an 'associated person' for the purposes of Part IV of the Family Law Act 1996. However, the court has jurisdiction to grant an injunction ancillary to civil proceedings only if the claimant has a legal or equitable right which is capable of being protected, such as a cause of action in tort or a proprietary interest. The House of Lords has held that it is not sufficient if another member of the family has such a right (*Hunter v Canary Wharf Ltd* [1997] 2 FLR 342).

Although these powers are rarely used by domestic violence victims because better statutory protection is available to them, they were used to protect social workers involved in a child protection case in *Tameside Metropolitan Borough Council v M (Injunctive Relief: County Courts: Jurisdiction)* [2001] Fam Law 856, where an injunction was granted ancillary to care proceedings to protect the social workers who had been threatened with violence by the children's parents. The local authority's alternative application for injunctive relief under the Protection from Harassment Act 1997 was dismissed as the local authority was not a 'person' for the purposes of that Act.

Summary

▶ Domestic violence is a serious issue and one which the Government and the judiciary are committed to fighting. The civil law and the criminal law both provide protection for victims. Multi-agency and inter-agency approaches are adopted. Domestic violence is widely defined to include not just actual or threatened physical violence but also other forms of behaviour such as emotional abuse and controlling or coercive behaviour. Housing law is sometimes relevant. The law also provides protection for children who are victims of or witness domestic violence. Specialist domestic violence courts operate in some parts of England and Wales. There are various Acts of Parliament which provide protection for victims of domestic violence, including, in particular, Part IV of the Family Law Act 1996 (FLA 1996) and the Protection from Harassment Act 1997 (PHA 1997), both of which have been amended to provide more effective protection for victims.

▶ The criminal law provides protection for victims. The police are meant to take domestic violence very seriously and have a wide range of common law and statutory law duties and powers for dealing with the problem. The police have been given greater statutory powers to protect victims in recent years.

▶ Under Part IV of the FLA 1996 the Family Court has jurisdiction to grant two injunctive-style orders to provide protection for victims of domestic violence: a non-molestation order; and an occupation order.

▶ A non-molestation order is an order made under section 42 of Part IV of the FLA 1996 which prohibits the respondent from molesting a person who is 'associated' with the respondent and/or from molesting a relevant child. 'Molestation' is not defined in the

Summary cont'd

Act, but has been widely interpreted by the courts. Where urgent action is needed, a non-molestation order can be made without notice (s 45). When deciding whether to make a non-molestation order, and, if so, in what manner, the court must take into account all the circumstances of the case, including the need to secure the health, safety and well-being of the applicant and of any relevant child (s 42(5)). A non-molestation order can be made for a specified period or until further order (s 48). Breach of a non-molestation order is a criminal offence. The court can, in certain circumstances, accept an undertaking instead of making a non-molestation order (s 46). A non-molestation order can be varied or discharged (s 49). Breach of any term in a non-molestation order without reasonable excuse is a criminal offence, and can result in a fine or imprisonment (s 42A).

▶ An occupation order, which can be made under sections 33 and 35–38 of Part IV of the FLA 1996, is an order regulating the occupation of the family home. There are two categories of applicant: entitled (persons with a proprietary right); and non-entitled (persons with no proprietary right). The court's powers are much wider for entitled applicants (s 33). An order can be made without notice (s 45). Different provisions apply to the making of an order, depending not just on whether or not the applicant is entitled, but also on their relationship status. The court has wide powers to regulate the occupation of the home. For example, it can exclude a person from the home and/or allow a person to enter into and occupy it. Occupation orders are not, however, routinely made due to the seriousness of excluding a person from their home, particularly where they have a proprietary right in the home. The criteria which govern the exercise of the court's powers are complex and, along with the outcome of the so-called 'balance of harm' test, differ depending on the type of applicant and respondent. The provisions which the court has power to include in an occupation order also differ depending on the type of applicant and respondent. The duration of the order also varies depending on which section of Part IV of the FLA 1996 the applicant falls under. The court can attach a power of arrest to an occupation order (s 47), but breach of an occupation order is not a criminal offence. Instead, civil proceedings can be brought for contempt of court. The court can accept an undertaking instead of making an occupation order (s 46). An order can be varied or discharged (s 49). A child can apply for an occupation order, but leave of the court is needed (s 43).

▶ Sections 62 and 63 of Part IV of the FLA 1996 are important because they define who can apply under the Act and other key terms.

▶ The PHA 1997 can provide protection for victims of domestic violence. It creates two criminal offences of harassment (the section 2 offence of harassment and the section 4 offence of aggravated harassment); and a civil tort of harassment for which damages are available (s 3). In order to constitute the offence of harassment, there must be a 'course of conduct', but a series of violent acts may not necessarily constitute harassment. A restraining order (to protect a named person from harassment) can be made under section 5. It can be made on the conviction of *any* offence, not just harassment; and can also be made if a defendant is acquitted of harassment (s 5A). Breach of a restraining order is a criminal offence.

▶ County courts and the High Court have jurisdiction to grant injunctions ancillary to other legal proceedings, provided it is just and convenient to do so and the applicant has a right in law or in equity which is in need of protection. Domestic violence injunctions under these powers are rare because of the statutory protection available for family members, in particular under Part IV of the FLA 1996.

Further reading and references

Burton, 'R (Rabess) v Commissioner of the Police for the Metropolis – "scream quietly or the neighbours will hear": domestic violence, "nuisance neighbours" and the public/private dichotomy revisited' [2008] CFLQ 95.

Donovan and Hester, 'Seeking help from the enemy: help-seeking strategies of those in same-sex relationships who have experienced domestic abuse' [2011] CFLQ 26.

Edwards, 'Domestic violence: not a term of art but a state of consciousness' [2011] Fam Law 1244.

Websites

End Violence Against Women: www.endviolenceagainstwomen.org.uk
ManKind Initiative: www.mankind.org.uk
Men's Advice Line: www.mensadviceline.org.uk
National Centre for Domestic Violence: www.ncdv.org.uk
Refuge: www.refuge.org.uk
Women's Aid: www.womensaid.org.uk

Links to relevant websites can also be found at: www.palgravehighered.com/law/familylaw9e

Divorce and dissolution and their consequences

Chapter 6

Divorce and dissolution

This chapter deals first with the development of divorce law, and then with the current law governing how a divorce can be obtained (which applies to both opposite and same sex married couples). The law and procedure which apply to the dissolution of civil partnerships largely replicate those of divorce law, although there are some important differences. This chapter uses the terminology of divorce, mentioning civil partnership separately where necessary to highlight substantive differences in the law. Financial and property matters on divorce and dissolution are dealt with in Chapter 7. Residence and contact with children are dealt with in Chapter 11, and financial provision for children in Chapter 12.

6.1 Development of divorce law

This section looks at the development of divorce from the end of the 19th century up to the present day. It is included in this chapter as it provides the background to the current law, which continues to be very much rooted in the 'old' origins of the law. Thus, in order to understand the current law, it is necessary to look at the earlier law and how it has developed.

(a) Grounds for divorce

Until the mid-19th century the courts had no jurisdiction to grant a decree of divorce. The ecclesiastical (church) courts could issue a decree of nullity, but they could not end a marriage. Anyone who wished to divorce had to do so by a private Act of Parliament, which was a complex, lengthy and expensive procedure. Thus, divorce was an option for only a few people. In order to remedy the inadequacies of the private Act of Parliament procedure, the Matrimonial Causes Act 1857 was passed. This gave the courts jurisdiction to grant a decree of divorce on the sole ground of adultery. In other words, divorce law was fault-based and built around the idea that one party was guilty of a matrimonial offence. Divorce was, however, more difficult for wives as they had to prove 'aggravated adultery' (adultery plus an additional factor such as incest, cruelty, bigamy, sodomy or desertion). After pressure for reform by the female emancipation movement, aggravated adultery was abolished by the Matrimonial Causes Act 1923. The Matrimonial Causes Act 1937 added three further grounds: cruelty; desertion for a continuous period of at least three years; and incurable insanity. In response to concerns that this more liberal divorce law would undermine the institution of marriage, the Act introduced an absolute bar on divorce in the first three years of marriage, unless the petitioner could prove exceptional hardship or the respondent had shown exceptional depravity.

At the end of the Second World War there was a sharp increase in the number of people who wanted to divorce and growing dissatisfaction with the law. It seemed wrong to have to prove that one spouse had committed a matrimonial offence, thereby apportioning blame, when both spouses might have been responsible for the breakdown of their marriage. It also seemed wrong for the law to prolong marriages which had completely broken down. However, it was not until the 1960s with the publication of two reports, one by the Church of England and the other by the Law Commission, that proposals for change began to be made. In 1966 a Committee appointed by the Archbishop of Canterbury produced a report (*Putting Asunder*) which recommended that divorce should be based on a sole ground – namely, irretrievable breakdown of the marriage. It also recommended that there should be a judicial inquiry in all cases to decide whether the marriage had irretrievably broken down. Shortly after the publication of *Putting Asunder*, the Law Commission published its own report (*Reform of the Grounds of Divorce: The Field of Choice*, Cmnd. 3123, 1966) in which it stated that the objectives of a good divorce law should be:

> To buttress, rather than to undermine the stability of marriage; and when, regrettably, a marriage has irretrievably broken down, to enable the empty legal shell to be destroyed with the maximum fairness, and the minimum bitterness, distress and humiliation.

The Law Commission concluded that a divorce law based on fault failed to satisfy these objectives, and agreed with the Archbishop's Committee that irretrievable breakdown should be the sole ground for divorce. However, it rejected the Committee's proposal that irretrievable breakdown should be established by holding a judicial inquiry in all cases, as this would be distressing for the parties, expensive and time-consuming. It instead proposed that irretrievable breakdown could be established on the basis of consent and/or a period of separation of a specified length. However, it recognised that a divorce law based on these requirements would not help where one party did not consent or those people who wanted to divorce more quickly. The law which emerged from these proposals therefore retained elements of the previous fault-based divorce. The new law established irretrievable breakdown as the sole ground for divorce and allowed for divorce if the petitioner could prove one of five facts. The five facts were: adultery plus intolerability; unreasonable behaviour; desertion for a period of at least two years; two years' separation with consent to the divorce; and five years' separation. The law was enacted in the Divorce Reform Act 1969 (DRA 1969) which was later re-enacted as Part I of the Matrimonial Causes Act 1973 (MCA 1973).

Since then, the most notable amendment to the divorce law contained in the MCA 1973 was the replacement of the bar on divorce in the first three years of marriage with a bar of just one year, which was introduced by the Matrimonial and Family Proceedings Act 1984. Otherwise, the reforms introduced by the DRA 1969 largely remain the law today. Despite the availability of no-fault grounds for divorce, many are still sought on the basis of adultery or unreasonable behaviour as these enable a petitioner to obtain a divorce more quickly. The Law Commission's belief that most couples would use the no-fault grounds of separation has not been realised in practice, which has led to ongoing calls for reform (see 6.2 and 6.8 below).

(b) Divorce procedure

Changes to divorce procedure have taken place over the years. Initially, because divorce was considered a serious matter, proceedings were heard only in London and by senior judges. They were also heard in open court with the petitioner giving oral evidence to prove the alleged ground. However, it was increasingly recognised that hearing divorce proceedings in open court was not only distressing for the parties, as they would have their intimate marital details exposed in public, but also unnecessarily expensive and time-consuming. Divorce was failing to achieve one of its major policy aims, namely the burial of dead marriages with the minimum of bitterness, distress and humiliation.

With the huge increase in the divorce rate, particularly after the introduction of the more liberal grounds for divorce introduced by the DRA 1969, the courts became overloaded, even though most undefended divorces were taking as little as ten minutes to be heard. Eventually a new divorce procedure, the 'special procedure', was introduced with the aim of achieving simplicity, speed and economy. It was initially introduced in 1973 for childless couples divorcing with consent, but was extended in 1975 to all childless couples, except those petitioning on the basis of unreasonable behaviour. In 1977 it was eventually extended to all undefended divorces. The introduction of the 'special procedure' was a radical change in the law, as an undefended divorce became available by what was essentially an administrative procedure; and, in most cases, neither party was required to attend court. As this procedure has now become the norm, the term 'special procedure' is no longer used.

Thus, all undefended divorces are today dealt with by what is largely a paper exercise. The judge (or, more likely now, a legal advisor) examines the papers to establish whether the fact alleged in the divorce petition is proved, whether the marriage has irretrievably broken down and whether there is any reason for not granting the divorce. A list of petitioners who satisfy the requirements is drawn up and read out in open court by the judge's clerk, after which the judge pronounces decree nisi of divorce en bloc. This judicial pronouncement is the last vestige of the public hearing of divorce. In this way, divorce procedure has evolved from a judicial to a mostly administrative process, a trend which is likely to continue.

6.2   An attempt at reform

In the late 1980s, as a result of increasing dissatisfaction with divorce law, proposals for reform were made. Although these proposals were enacted in Parts I, II and III of the Family Law Act 1996 (FLA 1996), they were never implemented because the Government concluded that they were unworkable in practice.

(a)   The background to the proposed reforms

In the 1980s, concerns about divorce law led to proposals for reform by the Law Commission (see *Facing the Future: A Discussion Paper on the Ground for Divorce*, Law Com No. 170, 1988; *Family Law: The Ground for Divorce*, Law Com No. 192, 1990; *Looking to the Future: Mediation and the Ground for Divorce*, Cm 2424, 1993; and *Looking to the Future: Mediation and the Ground for Divorce: The Government's Proposals*, Cm 2799, 1995).

The Law Commission was of the view that a major aim of the 1969 reforms – to move away from fault-based divorce – had not been achieved in practice, as most divorces were being sought on the basis of adultery and unreasonable behaviour. It concluded that divorce law was not working well for various reasons. It allowed a divorce to be obtained too quickly and easily without the parties being required to consider the consequences. It did nothing to save marriages. It could make things worse for children. It was unjust and exacerbated bitterness and hostility. Having identified the weaknesses in the law, the Law Commission made proposals for reform which, it claimed, would introduce a truly no-fault divorce law which would encourage the parties to reach agreement and consider and face up to the consequences of marital breakdown. It recommended the retention of irretrievable breakdown as the sole ground for divorce, but with divorce available at the end of a period of time. The Law Commission claimed that divorce over a period of time would encourage the parties to cooperate and consider the practical consequences of divorce, and would reinforce the idea that divorce is a process and not an event. It would also fit well with mediation.

(b) The proposed reform – 'divorce over a period of time'

'Divorce over a period of time', which was enacted as Part II of the FLA 1996, introduced a no-fault divorce law for the first time. It required couples, in most cases, to have sorted out ancillary matters relating to finance, property and children before they were able to obtain a divorce. Parties were to be given more information about divorce, and greater emphasis was to be placed on mediation.

Irretrievable breakdown was to remain the sole ground for divorce, which would be proved if: the applicant(s) had made a statement of marriage breakdown; a required period for reflection and consideration had passed; and one or both parties had declared that their marriage could not be saved. In order to obtain a divorce an applicant would first have to attend an 'information meeting' at which information about divorce would be given and, if needed, marriage counselling. At least three months later, one or both of the parties would have to send a 'statement of marital breakdown' to the court. The court would then have the power to make directions requiring the parties to attend a meeting at which mediation would be explained, and to make interim ancillary relief orders and other interim orders under the Children Act 1989. Once the statement of marital breakdown had been lodged with the court, a period for reflection and consideration (nine months in some cases, 15 in others) would have to pass. During this period the parties would be required to spend time reflecting on whether their marriage could be saved and, if not, then on making arrangements in respect of ancillary relief and the welfare of any children. At the end of that period, an application for a 'divorce order' could be made, which the court could grant if it was satisfied that: the marriage had irretrievably broken down; the information meeting requirements had been complied with; arrangements for the future had been made; there was no order preventing divorce; and the requirements in respect of the welfare of the children had been satisfied.

(c) The decision not to introduce the reforms

'Divorce over a period of time' was due to come into force on 1 January 1999, but implementation was suspended until 2000 so that the Government could consider the results of a pilot scheme to see how the information meetings would work in practice. However, the results of the pilot scheme turned out to be disappointing. Only 7 per cent of those attending information meetings were diverted into mediation, and very few couples attended the meetings together. Thus, the information meetings had failed to achieve the Government's stated objectives of saving marriages and, where they had broken down, of bringing them to an end with the minimum of distress to the parties and any children. Because the proposals had failed to fulfil the policy objectives in Part I of the Act, the reforms were never introduced.

The Government's decision not to implement the reforms was greeted with considerable relief by those who believed the proposals were inherently flawed on the grounds that they were unnecessarily complicated and unworkable in practice. One of the main criticisms was that the reforms placed impractical and impossible demands on people who were divorcing. Couples in the throes of the breakdown of their marriage would have found it difficult, and in some cases impossible, to make arrangements for the future. Cretney (1995) thought that the Government seemed 'curiously naive' about what was likely to happen during the period of reflection. He said that some couples would not spend time considering whether their marriage could be saved or making arrangements for the future, but would instead spend time conceiving children, or exploiting their emotional or financial advantage or brooding on their grievances. Freeman (1997) was critical of the length of the divorce process because he thought it would create 'more conflict, more tension, more domestic violence, unnecessary abortions and more children who [would] experience their parents' divorce while still of pre-school years'. Eekelaar (1999) criticised the need for information meetings, and considered them a form of 'social engineering'. Resolution, an organisation of family lawyers, considered the law to be cumbersome and confusing, and said it would create delay and uncertainty, which were contrary to the best interests of divorcing couples and their children.

There are no current proposals by the Government to reform the law. In Scotland, however, where divorce law is similar to that in England and Wales, a simple change to the law has been implemented. Thus, the five-year separation ground has been reduced to two, and the two-year separation with consent ground has been reduced to one. The aim of this change is to encourage the use of the non-fault separation grounds, and thereby lessen the acrimony and conflict which may be associated with fault-based divorces.

6.3 The current law of divorce – an introduction

Statistics on divorce for 2014 in England and Wales

These figures, which represent both divorces and annulments, were published in December 2016 by the Office for National Statistics (www.ons.gov.uk).

▶ There were 111,169 divorces, a decrease of 3.1 per cent compared with 2013 and a decline of 27 per cent from a peak in 2003.
▶ There were 9.3 men divorcing per thousand married males and 9.3 women divorcing per thousand married females.
▶ The average duration of marriage for divorces granted in 2014 was 11.7 years.
▶ 53 per cent of divorces granted to wives, and 38 per cent of divorces granted to husbands, were based on unreasonable behaviour.
▶ The average age at divorce was 43.1 years for women and 45.6 years for men.

The law of divorce is laid down in the Matrimonial Causes Act 1973 (MCA 1973), Part I of which deals with obtaining a divorce (or an annulment or judicial separation) and Part II with finance and property orders on divorce (or on nullity or judicial separation). The law of dissolution is laid down in the Civil Partnership Act 2004 (CPA 2004) (see 6.11 below). Procedural rules governing divorce, dissolution, nullity and judicial separation are in Part 7 of the Family Procedure Rules 2010 (FPR 2010).

An undefended divorce is obtained by means of what is essentially an administrative exercise. It can be granted in a few months without the need, in most cases, for either party or their legal representatives to attend court. Ancillary matters relating to finance, property and children can, however, take much longer if the parties cannot reach agreement. Obtaining a divorce is a two-stage process: decree nisi followed by decree absolute. A marriage is terminated only on the grant of the decree absolute. The procedure for a defended divorce is different, but divorces are rarely defended. Under the FPR 2010, the parties to a divorce are called the 'applicant' and the 'respondent'. However, the older term for 'applicant', which is 'petitioner', is still widely used and is found in the MCA 1973.

(a)   Jurisdiction

The jurisdictional rules for hearing a petition for divorce (or for nullity or judicial separation) in the courts in England and Wales are laid down in section 5(2) of the Domicile and Matrimonial Proceedings Act 1973 (DMPA 1973); and, for divorces involving Member States of the EU, in Article 3 of Council Regulation (EC) (No. 2201/2003) Concerning Jurisdiction and the Recognition and Enforcement of Judgments in Matrimonial Matters and in Matters of Parental Responsibility (Brussels II Revised). The rules are complex, but in general terms the courts in England and Wales have jurisdiction if both parties are habitually resident or domiciled in England or Wales or, in certain circumstances, where only one party is habitually resident in England or Wales. If no EU Member State has jurisdiction under Brussels II Revised, jurisdiction can be established on the basis of one party alone being domiciled in England or Wales. The rules in relation to same sex married couples are found in Schedule A1 of the DMPA 1973 and the Marriage (Same Sex Couples) (Jurisdiction and Recognition of Judgments) Regulations 2014/543, and largely replicate the rules for opposite sex married couples.

In *Mark v Mark* [2005] UKHL 42 the House of Lords held that, for the purpose of jurisdiction to entertain a petition for divorce under section 5(2) of the DMPA 1973, residence in England or Wales need not be lawful residence. Thus, a person can be habitually resident or domiciled in England or Wales even if their presence in the UK is a criminal offence under the Immigration Act 1971.

Difficulties can occur when a couple move out of the jurisdiction of the UK to another country. Thus, for example, in *Munro v Munro* [2008] 1 FLR 1613 Bennett J had to decide whether the wife should be allowed to petition for divorce in England and Wales even though she and her husband had moved to Spain shortly after marrying in England. The husband argued that, as his wife had acquired domicile in Spain, the divorce should be heard in Spain. Applying Brussels II Revised (see above), Bennett J said that cogent evidence was required to prove that, by unequivocal intentions and acts, either party had abandoned their English domicile of origin and acquired a Spanish domicile of choice; and he held on the facts that the English, not the Spanish, court had jurisdiction.

(b) Staying divorce proceedings

The DMPA 1973 gives the courts in England and Wales the power to stay divorce proceedings where they are pending in another country. Thus, for example, in *JKN v JCN* [2010] EWHC 843 (Fam) the High Court granted the husband's application for a stay of proceedings as the court in New York was the more appropriate forum for the divorce.

(c) The 'one-year bar' on divorce

Divorce proceedings cannot be commenced within the first year of marriage under the MCA 1973 (s 3(1)). This is an absolute bar – there is no discretion to waive it. However, a divorce petition can be based on matters which have happened during the first year of marriage (s 3(2)). Nullity and judicial separation proceedings, on the other hand, can be commenced within the first year of marriage.

(d) Encouraging reconciliation

As part of the policy objective of divorce law is to save marriages, certain provisions in Part I of the MCA 1973 encourage reconciliation. Thus, the court can adjourn divorce proceedings at any stage if there is a reasonable possibility of a reconciliation between the parties (s 6(2)), and certain periods of resumed cohabitation are ignored when establishing whether the marriage has irretrievably broken down. Where the applicant is legally represented, a 'reconciliation statement' must be filed with the divorce petition (see below), although in practice this is little more than a formality.

6.4 The ground for divorce and the five facts

Under Part I of the Matrimonial Causes Act 1973 (MCA 1973) there is only one ground for divorce: irretrievable breakdown of the marriage (s 1(1)). To establish irretrievable breakdown, the applicant must prove one or more of the following five 'facts' which in common parlance are referred to as the 'grounds' for divorce.

The five facts for divorce

Section 1(2) of the MCA 1973 requires the petitioner to prove to the court that:
(a) the respondent has committed adultery and the petitioner finds it intolerable to live with the respondent;
(b) the respondent has behaved in such a way that the petitioner cannot reasonably be expected to live with the respondent;
(c) the respondent has deserted the petitioner for a continuous period of at least two years immediately preceding the presentation of the petition;
(d) the parties to the marriage have lived apart for a continuous period of at least two years immediately preceding the presentation of the petition … and the respondent consents to a decree being granted; or
(e) the parties to the marriage have lived apart for a continuous period of at least five years immediately preceding the presentation of the petition.

If one of the five facts is proved, the court must grant a decree nisi of divorce unless it is satisfied that the marriage has not irretrievably broken down (s 1(4)). The court must be satisfied of *both* irretrievable breakdown *and* at least one fact. Thus, for example, in both *Richards v Richards* [1972] 1 WLR 1073 and *Buffery v Buffery* [1988] 2 FLR 365 the Court of Appeal found that irretrievable breakdown had been established, but not unreasonable behaviour.

(a)   Adultery (section 1(2)(a))

Adultery involves an act of voluntary heterosexual intercourse between two people who are not married to each other, but at least one of whom is married. This means that an applicant in a same sex marriage will *not* be able to rely on this fact if their spouse has a sexual relationship with someone else of the same sex (s 1(6)). Civil partners are also unable to rely on the fact of adultery in relation to obtaining a dissolution (see 6.11 below). This approach to adultery, and the limits it places on same sex couples, has been criticised as one of the ways in which same sex couples are still not treated equally by the law. For example, Crompton (2013) argues that the Government's fear of addressing gay sex is overriding its desire to support marriage as a sexual relationship with an expectation of fidelity. The Peter Tatchell Foundation argues that while the adultery fact may be seen by many to be antiquated, the difference in the law is an example of how the Marriage (Same Sex Couples) Act 2013 is discriminatory.

In addition to adultery, the applicant must prove that it is intolerable to live with the respondent (s 1(2)(a)). This requirement was added to buttress the stability of marriage, a policy aim of the law, so that an act of adultery would be insufficient on its own to end a marriage. Adultery and intolerability are two separate and unrelated facts (*Cleary v Cleary* [1974] 1 WLR 73). There is no need for an applicant to show that they find it intolerable to live with the respondent in consequence of the adultery; it is sufficient if the applicant genuinely finds it intolerable to do so for whatever reason (*Goodrich v Goodrich* [1971] 2 All ER 1340). As part of the policy objective of divorce law is to encourage reconciliation, a petition based on adultery cannot be heard if the parties have lived together for more than six months (in one period or aggregated periods) after the applicant discovered the adultery (s 2(1)); but a period (or aggregated periods) of living together not exceeding six months is disregarded when determining the question of intolerability (s 2(2)).

(b)   Unreasonable behaviour (section 1(2)(b))

The applicant must prove that the respondent has behaved in such a way that they cannot reasonably be expected to live with them. Although this fact is referred to as 'unreasonable behaviour', it is a misnomer; it is the effect of the respondent's behaviour on the applicant which is relevant, not whether the respondent's behaviour is unreasonable (s 1(2)(b)).

In *Livingstone-Stallard v Livingstone-Stallard* [1974] Fam 47 Dunn J adopted the following test for establishing unreasonable behaviour: 'Would any right-thinking person come to the conclusion that this husband has behaved in such a way that this wife cannot reasonably be expected to live with him, taking into account the whole of the circumstances and the characters and personalities of the parties?' This test was approved by the Court of Appeal in *O'Neill v O'Neill* [1975] 1 WLR 1118 and endorsed by the Court of Appeal in *Buffery v Buffery* [1988] 2 FLR 365.

Divorces are granted for a wide range of behaviour. However, some behaviour may be too trivial and a decree may be refused. This happened in *Buffery v Buffery* (see above) where the wife alleged that her husband was insensitive, never took her out, and that they had nothing to talk about and nothing in common after their children had grown up and left home. Her petition was dismissed, as her husband's behaviour was found to be insufficient to satisfy the behaviour ground. An accumulation of trivial incidents may, however, constitute unreasonable behaviour. This is what happened in *Livingstone-Stallard v Livingstone-Stallard* (see above), where Dunn J held that the wife 'was subjected to a constant atmosphere of criticism, disapproval and boorish behaviour on the part of her husband'. However, as each case depends on its own facts, an accumulation of various minor matters will not necessarily result in a decree being granted. In *Butterworth v Butterworth* [1997] 2 FLR 336, for example, the decree of divorce was set aside by the Court of Appeal as the petition was severely defective. The husband had denied the wife's allegations that he was a violent, possessive, sexually demanding and jealous alcoholic who had stopped her going to church. The Court of Appeal stressed that the law of divorce still gave the respondent the right to oppose a divorce and to have the allegations in the petition properly proved. The Court of Appeal held that the judge had not applied the correct test for unreasonable behaviour, or anything like it.

Sometimes the court may have to decide whether to grant a divorce where the behaviour is not the respondent's fault (for example where the respondent is physically or mentally ill). Whether or not a divorce will be granted will depend on the circumstances of the case, and, although the court will be cognisant of the fact that marriage entails a commitment which includes caring for a sick spouse, it is likely to be sympathetic to the plight of an applicant and the fact that illness can place severe strains on a marriage. A divorce may therefore be granted even though a respondent is not responsible for their own 'behaviour' (see, for example, *Katz v Katz* [1972] 1 WLR 955 where the respondent suffered from manic depression).

If the parties live together after the last instance of behaviour alleged, the court can take this into account when determining whether or not the applicant can reasonably be expected to live with the respondent. However, a period (or aggregated periods) of living together not exceeding six months must be disregarded (s 2(3)).

(c) Desertion (section 1(2)(c))

The respondent must have deserted the applicant for a continuous period of at least two years immediately preceding the petition. To prove desertion there must be: factual separation; an intention by the respondent to desert; no consent by the applicant to the desertion; and no just cause to desert. Constructive desertion is also possible (in other words, where a spouse's behaviour is so bad that the other spouse is forced to leave the home). In order to encourage reconciliation, a period of up to six months' resumed cohabitation does not prevent the desertion from being continuous (s 2(5)). Divorces based on desertion are rare.

(d) Two years' separation with consent to the divorce (section 1(2)(d))

The parties must have lived apart for a continuous period of at least two years immediately preceding the presentation of the petition, and the respondent must consent to the decree being granted. The respondent must have the capacity to consent and must be given such information as will enable them to understand the effect of a decree being granted (s 2(7)). Consent may be withdrawn at any time before decree nisi, whereupon the proceedings must be stayed. At any time before decree absolute the respondent can apply to have the decree nisi rescinded if the respondent has been misled by the applicant in respect of any matter which the respondent took into account in deciding whether to give consent (s 10(1)). The respondent can also ask for the decree absolute to be postponed in certain circumstances (see 6.5 below).

The parties must be living in separate households for separation to be established (s 2(6)). This is a question of fact. However, as 'household' does not mean 'house', separation is possible where the parties are living under the same roof. Thus, for example, in *Fuller v Fuller* [1973] 1 WLR 730 a decree nisi of divorce was granted even though the husband lived as a lodger with his wife and her new partner.

When calculating separation, no account is taken of a period of up to six months (in one period or aggregated periods) during which the parties resumed living together, but there must be an aggregated period of actual separation for at least two years (s 2(5)). If the period of resumed cohabitation is more than six months, the two-year period of separation starts again.

(e) Five years' separation (section 1(2)(e))

The parties must have lived apart for a continuous period of at least five years immediately preceding the petition. The applicant must establish factual separation, although there can still be separation even though the spouses live under the same roof. To protect the respondent, the court can refuse decree nisi or delay decree absolute (see 6.5 below).

When calculating separation, no account is taken of a period of up to six months (in one period or aggregated periods) during which the parties resumed living together, but there must be an aggregated period of actual separation for at least five years (s 2(5)). If the period of resumed cohabitation is more than six months, the five-year period of separation starts again. In practice, few spouses petition for divorce on this fact because most applicants do not wish to wait five years to obtain a divorce.

6.5 Protection for respondents

Sections 10 and 5 of the Matrimonial Causes Act 1973 (MCA 1973) provide protection for respondents who are being divorced on the basis of two or five years' separation. The aim of these provisions is to protect 'innocent' spouses who have not committed a matrimonial offence (see 6.4 above).

(a) Section 10 of the Matrimonial Causes Act 1973

Under section 10(2) a respondent to a divorce based on two or five years' separation can ask the court to consider whether their financial situation after divorce will be satisfactory. If such an application is made, the court may refuse to grant the decree absolute unless it is satisfied: that the applicant should not be required to make financial provision for the respondent; or that the provision made or to be made by the applicant is reasonable and fair, or the best that can be made in the circumstances (s 10(3)). The court may, however, grant a decree absolute in any event if it is desirable to do so without delay, and if it has obtained a satisfactory undertaking from the applicant that they will make such financial provision as the court may approve (s 10(4)).

Few applications are made under section 10, but an application may be useful as a tactical manoeuvre to put pressure on an applicant to sort out the parties' financial position, for example where there may be a problem enforcing an ancillary relief order. Thus, for example, in *Garcia v Garcia* [1992] 1 FLR 256 a section 10 application was made in order to enforce maintenance payments for a child.

(b) Section 5 of the Matrimonial Causes Act 1973

Under section 5 a respondent to a divorce based on five years' separation has a complete defence to divorce. The aim of this provision is to safeguard the position of 'innocent' spouses who do not wish to be divorced. Under section 5, the court has the power to rescind a decree nisi if the respondent proves that they will suffer grave financial or other hardship if the divorce is granted; and that it would be wrong in all the circumstances to grant the divorce. The alleged hardship must arise as a result of the dissolution of the marriage. Hardship can include the loss of the chance of acquiring a benefit which the respondent might acquire if the marriage were not dissolved (s 5(3)), such as, for instance, loss of a right to succeed under the other spouse's will or intestacy. Most of the reported cases have been in relation to pension rights (see, for example, *Archer v Archer* [1999] 1 FLR 327), but because of changes to the law on pensions on divorce this is no longer necessary (see 7.8). 'Other hardship' for the purposes of section 5 could include, for example, hardship that a respondent might suffer as a result of ostracism in the community because of social or religious attitudes to divorce.

Defences under section 5 are extremely rare and, even when they are pleaded, they rarely succeed. In most cases the court will consider it best to end the marriage.

6.6 Divorce procedure

Divorce procedure differs according to whether a divorce is undefended or defended. In practice, virtually all divorces are now undefended, because of the futility of defending a divorce.

(a) Undefended divorce

(i) Starting proceedings

To start proceedings, an applicant must complete a divorce petition and send it to court. The petition must contain the following information about the applicant and the respondent: details about the marriage; details about any other court proceedings; a statement that the marriage has irretrievably broken down on the basis of at least one of the five facts; information about either one, or both, parties' connection(s) with England and Wales; and details of their legal representatives (if any). The final part of the petition concludes with: a 'prayer' by the applicant for the marriage to be dissolved; a claim for costs (if any); and a claim for financial orders (if any) for the applicant and/or any children.

The petition must be sent with the marriage certificate. Where the applicant is legally represented, the legal representative must also file a 'reconciliation statement' with the application. In other words, a statement setting out whether the legal representative has discussed with the applicant the possibility of a reconciliation with the respondent (r 7.6 Family Procedure Rules 2010 (FPR 2010)).

(ii) The next stage

Once the petition has been filed, a copy of the petition is served on the respondent accompanied by both a 'notice of proceedings' (which explains the effect of the petition and informs the respondent of the procedure involved) and an 'acknowledgement of service'. The latter is a question-and-answer form which the respondent must complete, sign and return to the court within eight days of receiving the divorce papers, failing which a further copy of the petition may be served upon the respondent personally. The respondent must state on the form whether the petition has been received, whether the respondent intends to defend the divorce, whether consent to the divorce is given if sought on the basis of two years' separation with consent and also whether the respondent intends to apply for a financial order and/or for any other order in respect of the children.

(iii) Obtaining decree nisi

Once the respondent has returned the acknowledgement of service and it is clear that they do not wish to defend the divorce, the applicant must file an 'application for decree nisi' (asking the court to review the applicant's paperwork and decide whether to grant a decree nisi). The application must be accompanied by a written statement and questionnaire in a specified form, verified by a statement of truth signed by the applicant which provides evidence of the fact(s) that they are seeking to rely on. The court will then decide whether there is enough evidence on which to grant the divorce.

If the court is satisfied with the paperwork and that the fact is proved and the marriage has irretrievably broken down, it will issue a 'certificate of entitlement to a decree'. The certificate is sent to both parties and informs them of the date, time and place for the formal pronouncement of decree nisi. If the judge does not agree with the divorce, the parties will be sent a 'notice of refusal of judge's certificate' which will explain why it is not considered right to grant a divorce, and will, if necessary, explain whether more information and/or a formal court hearing is needed.

Pronouncement of decree nisi takes place in open court, but there is no need for the parties and/or any legal representatives to attend unless either party wishes to be heard on the question of costs. Decrees are listed together in batches and collectively read out by the judge's clerk, after which the judge pronounces decree nisi of divorce en bloc.

(iv) Obtaining decree absolute

The grant of decree nisi does not terminate the marriage. It is terminated only on the grant of the decree absolute. This is automatically granted on the application of the applicant, who can apply for it six weeks or more after decree nisi (s 1(5) Matrimonial Causes Act 1973 (MCA 1973); r 7.32(1) FPR 2010). There is no need to give the respondent notice of the application. If the applicant fails to apply for decree absolute, the respondent may apply after three months have passed from the earliest date on which the applicant could apply (s 9(2) MCA 1973). In these circumstances the court may require a court hearing before it is satisfied that a decree can be granted (r 7.33 FPR 2010). These rules are strict. If a decree absolute is obtained in breach of the rules, the divorce is void (see *Dennis v Dennis* [2000] 2 FLR 231).

Where a divorce is sought on either of the separation grounds, a decree absolute can be refused where a respondent has not been satisfactorily financially provided for by the applicant (see 6.5 above), although this is unusual.

The purpose of the gap between decree nisi and decree absolute is to enable a respondent to appeal, and for the Queen's Proctor and other people to intervene to show just cause why a decree should not be made absolute (s 8 MCA 1973). Intervention by the Queen's Proctor is, however, rare. For example, in *Bhaiji v Chauhan (Queen's Proctor Intervening)* [2003] 2 FLR 485 the Queen's Proctor opposed the grant of decrees absolute where bogus allegations of behaviour had been made to obtain divorces in respect of five marriages which had been entered into solely for the purpose of circumventing the immigration rules. In *Rapisarda v Colladon (Irregular Divorces)* [2014] EWFC 35 the Queen's Proctor opposed the grant of decrees nisi and decrees absolute where 180 petitions issued in 137 different courts had used the same address, all of which were procured by fraud; and in *Raani v Charazi* [2015] EWFC B202 the Queen's Proctor opposed the grant of a decree nisi and decree absolute where the applicant had deliberately framed the petition in a way calculated to deceive the court and committed perjury in swearing the affidavits, perverting the course of justice.

(b) Defended divorce

Defended divorce proceedings begin in the same way as an undefended divorce, but the respondent indicates an intention to defend in the acknowledgement of service. Provided various notice requirements have been satisfied (r 7.12 FPR 2010), there is an exchange of pleadings and the hearing takes place in open court with oral evidence being given and cross-examination of both parties. Defending divorce proceedings can be expensive, acrimonious and is often fruitless as there are strong policy reasons in favour of ending a marriage that is likely to have failed. According to the Family Justice Review (see 1.2), only around 2 per cent of divorces are defended. Of these, although the figures are unknown, it is likely that very few proceed to a full hearing as parties will normally reach agreement before then.

6.7 Legal effects of divorce

Once a decree absolute has been granted, the marriage is dissolved and each party is free to remarry. A decree absolute has other legal consequences. Thus, financial provision and property adjustment orders made under Part II of the Matrimonial Causes Act

1973 (MCA 1973) in favour of the parties to the marriage take effect, and orders for settlement or variation of a settlement can take effect in respect of any child of the family. All other orders for children take effect as soon as they are made. Divorce also has an effect on a will made by either party to the marriage (see 4.12). Social security and pension rights and taxation are affected, and both parties lose rights under certain matrimonial legislation, in particular rights of occupation of the home. However, as far as children are concerned, each parent retains parental responsibility, and the obligation to provide children with financial support continues (see Chapter 12). Disputes about arrangements regulating a child's living or contact arrangements can be settled by way of mediation or, in the last resort, by an application to the court (see Chapter 11).

6.8　The future of divorce

> ▶ **Stephen Cretney,** *Family Law in the Twentieth Century*, **2003, p. 391**
>
> English divorce law is in a state of confusion. The theory of the law remains that divorce is a matter in which the State has a vital interest, and that it is only allowed if the marriage can be demonstrated to have irretrievably broken down. But the practical reality is very different: divorce is readily and quickly available if both parties agree, and even if one of them is reluctant he or she will, faced with a divorce petition, almost always accept the inevitable: there is no point in denying that the marriage has broken down if one party firmly asserts it has.

Although Cretney was writing in 2003, his comments remain equally valid today as there have been virtually no changes to divorce law since the reforms made in the late 1960s. One change which has been introduced by the Children and Families Act 2014 is to remove the requirement that the court consider the proposed arrangements for any children before granting a divorce. This is in order to keep divorce and child arrangements separate.

However, this does not address the main criticisms of divorce law which continue to be voiced by judges, practitioners and academics. After the Government decided not to implement the divorce reforms in Part II of the Family Law Act 1996 (see 6.2 above), the Lord Chancellor's Family Law Advisory Board in its Fourth Annual Report in July 2001 regretted the missed opportunity to reform divorce and urged serious consideration to be given to replacing the current adversarial and partly fault-based divorce regime. It said that the serious defects in the current law identified by the Law Commission still remained. In particular, allegations of adultery and unreasonable behaviour caused unnecessary conflict between the parties, and their distress and anger impacted on children.

Senior family law judges have argued for the introduction of no-fault divorce. Thus, the Rt Hon Dame Elizabeth Butler-Sloss (a former President of the Family Division) has described obtaining a divorce on the basis of unreasonable behaviour as a 'hypocritical charade', and said that there is a need to introduce a truly no-fault divorce. The Deputy President of the Supreme Court, Baroness Hale, and the President of the Family Division, Sir James Munby, are also in favour of no-fault divorce.

Allegations of fault seem contrary to the promotion of the settlement culture which exists in respect of applications for financial remedies and child arrangements on divorce. In 2014, the *Mapping Paths to Family Justice* study found that the legal requirement that one spouse accuse the other of either adultery or unreasonable behaviour, if the parties do not want to wait two years to divorce, has the capacity to 'upset and antagonise parties and to disturb the equilibrium of the dispute resolution process'. In the same year, the *Report of the Family Mediation Task Force* found that, for some separating couples, allegations made in relation to fault-based divorce 'drive the receiving party into even greater hostility and away from mediation'.

There is also a risk that some parties may be 'steam-rollered' into divorce, because a divorce can now be obtained so quickly. As Kay (2004) states:

> Over two-thirds of divorces granted in England and Wales in 2002 were based on facts that clearly have connotations of blame and guilt, and where proceedings can be commenced in haste, without thought for the consequences of the breakdown and the legal ending of marriage. Taken as a whole, these statistics make a compelling case for reform.

Kay also points out that, although divorce law is acknowledged to be unsatisfactory, it has nevertheless been replicated in virtually the same form for civil partners under the Civil Partnership Act 2004. The possibility of introducing a purely administrative divorce has been considered from time to time. Cretney, for instance, asked ([2002] Fam Law 900):

> Should we not accept that the routine processing of marriage breakdown is no longer a judicial function and that it should accordingly be removed altogether from the courts and the judicial system, leaving them with more time to deal with the problems that do require their expertise and procedures? If we believe that respect for the law and the legal system is important, and that the 1996 reforms would have made the law even more complex and difficult to understand, should we not begin to ask whether there is not a simpler and better alternative?

Family law practitioners have supported calls for reform. For example, Resolution has campaigned for many years for no-fault divorce to be introduced. In their *Manifesto for Family Law* in 2015 they argue that divorcing couples should not have to go through 'this blame charade to bring their relationship to a dignified conclusion and move on with their lives'. They propose a new divorce procedure whereby one or both partners can give notice that the marriage has broken down irretrievably. The divorce would then proceed and, after a period of six months, if either or both partners still think they are making the right decision, the divorce would be finalised. In a submission to the Family Justice Review (see 1.2), the Law Society in 2011 expressed the opinion that the adversarial grounds for divorce should be removed and a no-fault system introduced; and that there should be no need to show why a marriage has irretrievably broken down when submitting a divorce petition. In the following extract, Sir Nicholas Wall, former President of the Family Division, has also called for reform of the law of divorce.

> ▶ **Sir Nicholas Wall, former President of the Family Division, 'The President's Resolution address 2012' [2012] Fam Law 817**
>
> My position is very simple. I am a strong believer in marriage. But I see no good arguments against no-fault divorce. At the moment, as it seems to me we have a system – so far as divorce itself is concerned – which is in fact administrative, but which masquerades as judicial. No doubt this has its roots in history. In the nineteenth century and for much of the twentieth, divorce was a matter of social status – it mattered whether you were divorced or not, and if you were, it was important to demonstrate that you were the 'innocent' party. All that, I think, has gone. Defended divorces are now effectively unheard of. The allegations in a petition under section 1(2)(b) are rarely relevant to any other aspect of the process, and if used in proceedings for ancillary relief have to be separately pleaded, and even then are only relevant if stringent criteria are attached to them. As a student, of course, I grew up with the three Cs – connivance, collusion and condonation. All those have gone. It seems to me, therefore, that the time for no-fault divorce has also come.

The Government has no plans to include divorce reform as a part of its legislative agenda.

6.9 Recognition of an overseas divorce

Part II of the Family Law Act 1986 (FLA 1986) lays down rules for the recognition in the UK of divorces (and annulments and separations) obtained overseas. The Act makes a distinction between divorces obtained in judicial or other proceedings and those otherwise obtained. Recognition is much broader for divorces obtained in judicial or other proceedings. An overseas divorce granted in judicial or other proceedings is recognised in the UK if it is effective under the law of the country where it was obtained, and at the commencement of those proceedings either party was habitually resident or domiciled in that country or was a national of that country (s 46(1)). An overseas divorce obtained otherwise than in judicial or other proceedings is recognised in the UK if it is effective in the country where it was obtained and at the date it was obtained one or both parties were domiciled there, or one party was domiciled there and the other party was domiciled in a country which recognised the divorce, and in any case neither party was habitually resident in the UK for one year immediately preceding the divorce (s 46(2)).

The English courts have a discretion to refuse recognition of an overseas divorce whether or not it was obtained in judicial or other proceedings. Thus, for example, they may under section 51(3) refuse to recognise an overseas divorce if reasonable steps have not been taken to give notice of the proceedings to a party to the marriage. For example, in *Duhur-Johnson v Duhur-Johnson (Attorney-General Intervening)* [2005] 2 FLR 1042 a Nigerian divorce was refused recognition as a valid overseas divorce because the husband had not taken reasonable steps to give notice of the divorce proceedings to his wife who he knew was in London.

An overseas divorce may not be recognised in England and Wales where recognition would be manifestly contrary to public policy (s 51(3)(c)). However, it may be difficult to argue that a divorce should not be recognised on public policy grounds. Thus, for example, in *Eroglu v Eroglu* [1994] 2 FLR 287 the wife's claim that her Turkish divorce should not be recognised in England and Wales was dismissed, despite her claim that it had been obtained by fraud. Similarly, in *H v H (The Queen's Proctor Intervening) (Validity of Japanese Divorce)* [2007] 1 FLR 1318 a Japanese divorce by agreement (a *Kyogirikon*) was recognised as a valid divorce as there was no reason to refuse recognition on the grounds of public policy.

(a) Recognition of divorces within the EU

Special rules apply to the recognition of divorces within the EU. Council Regulation (EC) (No. 2201/2003) Concerning Jurisdiction and the Recognition and Enforcement of Judgments in Matrimonial Matters and in Matters of Parental Responsibility (Brussels II Revised) applies. Thus, for example, in *D v D (Nature of Recognition of Overseas Divorce)* [2005] EWHC 3342 (Fam) a declaration was made that the Greek divorce was recognised in England and Wales under Brussels II, which had the effect of dissolving the parties' marital status.

(b) Is a talaq a valid overseas divorce?

A *talaq* is a unilateral Islamic divorce whereby a husband can divorce his wife by merely uttering the words 'I divorce you' three times without being in the presence of another person and without his wife's consent. Whether a *talaq* will be recognised in England and Wales depends on the circumstances of the case. If the *talaq* is obtained in England it will not be recognised as a valid divorce, as divorces obtained in England and Wales other than by court proceedings are not recognised. Thus, in *Sulaiman v Juffali* [2002] 1 FLR 479 a *talaq* pronounced in England, but subsequently registered in Saudi Arabia, was held not to be a valid divorce within the meaning of s 45(1) of the FLA 1986 as it was not obtained in Saudi Arabia. Even though the *talaq* had complied with all the formalities required by Sharia law in Saudi Arabia, it had clearly been obtained in England other than in a court, and thus fell foul of the FLA 1986.

Whether the court in England and Wales will recognise a *talaq* validly made outside the UK depends on the circumstances of the case, and is a matter for the discretion of the court. Thus, for example, in *El Fadl v El Fadl* [2000] 1 FLR 175 a *talaq* divorce registered with the Sharia court in Lebanon was recognised by the High Court, and, as a result, the wife's petition for an English divorce was dismissed. It was held that recognition was not contrary to public policy, even though such a divorce might offend English sensibilities. Similarly, in *H v H (Talaq Divorce)* [2007] EWHC 2945 a *talaq* divorce validly announced in Pakistan was upheld by the High Court. Sumner J said that it was important that marriages and divorces recognised in one country should be recognised in another unless there were good reasons for not doing so, especially when there were, as in this case, close links between the two countries and many people moved freely between them. There were no good reasons for refusing to recognise the *talaq* divorce in the circumstances of the case. However, each case depends on its own facts. Thus, in *A v L* [2010] EWHC 460 (Fam), where the wife petitioned for divorce in the English courts but the husband claimed they had already been divorced in Egypt by *talaq*, the High Court held that the *talaq* should not be recognised as the husband had deliberately failed to give the wife notice of the Egyptian court hearing.

6.10 Other decrees

(a) Decree of judicial separation

The court has jurisdiction to grant a decree of judicial separation under section 17 of the Matrimonial Causes Act 1973 (MCA 1973), provided the applicant can prove one of the five facts in section 1(2). However, there is no need to prove irretrievable breakdown of marriage. A decree of judicial separation does not terminate the marriage but merely removes the obligation of the applicant to continue living with the respondent (s 18(1)), although they are not obliged to separate.

On the grant of a decree, the court has jurisdiction to make financial orders under Part II of the MCA 1973 (see Chapter 7). Divorce is not precluded by a previous judicial separation, and a decree of judicial separation can be treated as proof of one or more of the five facts alleged for divorce (s 4).

Where a decree of judicial separation is in force and separation is continuing, a surviving spouse is not entitled to succeed to the deceased spouse's property on their intestacy, but judicial separation does not affect a will (s 18(2)).

Decrees of judicial separation are rarely sought, but may be useful for a spouse who does not wish to divorce or who is precluded from divorcing (for example for religious reasons) or who cannot divorce because one year of marriage has not elapsed. There were only 210 petitions filed for judicial separation in 2014, compared with 740 in 2004 (*Family Court Tables: January to March 2015*, Ministry of Justice, 2015).

(b) Decree of presumption of death

Where a spouse is missing and thought to be dead, the other spouse can petition for a decree of presumption of death under section 1 of the Presumption of Death Act 2013. If a decree is granted, the applicant can use the decree for the purposes of ending their marriage with the missing person and can contract a new valid marriage, which will remain valid even if the person presumed dead reappears. The court will grant a decree of presumption of death if it is satisfied that the missing person has died, or has not been known to be alive for a period of at least seven years (s 2).

6.11 Dissolution of civil partnership

Under sections 37–64 of the Civil Partnership Act 2004 (CPA 2004), the court has jurisdiction to make dissolution, nullity, separation and presumption of death orders. Both the law and procedure are virtually the same as those for divorce (see 6.6 above), except that there is no adultery ground. The rules in relation to jurisdiction can be found in section 221 of the CPA 2004 and the Civil Partnership (Jurisdiction and Recognition of Judgments) Regulations 2005/3334.

The terminology used by the Family Procedure Rules 2010 is different for civil partnerships. The term 'conditional order' is used in place of 'decree nisi' and 'final order' is used in place of 'decree absolute'.

Summary

▶ Until the mid-19th century the courts had no jurisdiction to grant decrees of divorce, although the ecclesiastical (church) courts could annul marriages. Anyone who wished to divorce could do so by a private Act of Parliament, but this was a complex, lengthy and expensive procedure. The Matrimonial Causes Act 1857 introduced judicial divorce, with the sole ground being adultery. The Matrimonial Causes Act 1937 extended the grounds for divorce to: adultery; cruelty; three years' desertion; and incurable insanity. It also introduced an absolute bar on divorce in the first three years of marriage. The Divorce Reform Act 1969 introduced new grounds for divorce. These provisions were later re-enacted in Part I of the Matrimonial Causes Act 1973 (MCA 1973) and remain the law today. The bar on divorce in the first three years of marriage was replaced with a one-year bar by the Matrimonial and Family Proceedings Act 1984.

▶ All divorces were once heard in open court. The 'special procedure' (an administrative form of divorce) was introduced in the 1970s for all undefended divorces and has now become the norm.

▶ In the late 1980s, as a result of increasing dissatisfaction with the law, proposals for reform were made. These proposals were enacted in Parts I, II and III of the Family Law Act 1996 (FLA 1996), but were not implemented because they were found to be unworkable in practice. Since then, there has been no new attempt to reform the law despite widespread calls for reform.

▶ The law of divorce is laid down in Parts I and II of the MCA 1973. Procedural rules are laid down in the Family Procedure Rules 2010. An undefended divorce can be granted in a few months without the need, in most cases, for either party to attend court. Disputes relating to finance, property and children can take much longer. The jurisdictional rules are complex. Special rules apply to the jurisdiction to hear a divorce in the EU (see Brussels II Revised). The Domicile and Matrimonial Proceedings Act 1973 gives the courts in England and Wales the power to stay divorce proceedings where such proceedings are pending in another country.

▶ There is only one ground for divorce under the MCA 1973: irretrievable breakdown of marriage (s 1(1)). This is established on proof of one or more of the following five facts: (a) adultery; (b) unreasonable behaviour; (c) desertion for a period of at least two years; (d) two years' separation with consent to the divorce; and/or (e) five years' separation (s 1(2)). There must be proof of irretrievable breakdown *and* at least one of the facts. There is an absolute bar on commencing divorce proceedings within the first year of marriage (s 3(1)), although an applicant can base their petition on matters which happened during the first year of marriage (s 3(2)). Respondents to two-year and five-year no-fault separation divorces are provided with some protection under the law. Undefended divorces are dealt with by what is essentially an administrative procedure and there is usually no need for the parties to attend court. Defended divorces, on the other hand, are heard in open court. Obtaining a divorce is a two-stage process: decree nisi followed by decree absolute. A marriage is terminated only on the grant of decree absolute. The rules of procedure are laid down in Part 7 of the FPR 2010.

▶ Respondents who are being divorced on the basis of two or five years' separation are afforded some protection by sections 10 and 5 of the MCA 1973. Under section 10, a

Summary cont'd

respondent can ask the court to consider whether their financial situation after divorce will be satisfactory. The court may refuse to grant the decree absolute if it is not satisfied that this is the case, unless it has obtained a satisfactory undertaking from the applicant that they will make such financial provision as the court may approve. Under section 5, a respondent can ask the court to rescind the decree nisi if the respondent can prove that they will suffer grave financial or other hardship if the divorce is granted and that it would be wrong in all the circumstances to grant the divorce.

▶ Once a decree absolute has been granted, the marriage is dissolved and each party is free to remarry. Financial provision and adjustment orders made under Part II MCA 1973 also take effect, as do orders for settlement or variation of settlement in respect of any child of the family. As far as children are concerned, each parent retains parental responsibility and the obligation to provide their children with financial support continues.

▶ There continues to be considerable criticism of the current law of divorce. Since the Government's decision not to implement the reforms in Part II of the FLA 1996, many commentators have continued to voice their concerns about the unsatisfactory state of the law. The current law of divorce is considered by many to be archaic and out of touch with social reality. There is considerable support for the introduction of no-fault divorce, although the Government has no plans to include divorce reform as part of its legislative agenda.

▶ Part II of the FLA 1986 lays down rules for the recognition in the UK of divorces obtained overseas. Overseas divorces are more likely to be recognised in the UK if they were obtained in judicial or other proceedings.

▶ Under Part I of the MCA 1973 the court has jurisdiction to grant a decree of judicial separation. A decree of judicial separation terminates the obligation of the applicant to continue living with the respondent.

▶ A decree of presumption of death can be obtained under the Presumption of Death Act 2013. This allows a spouse to dissolve their marriage where the other spouse has been missing for at least seven years and is thought dead.

▶ The law regulating the dissolution of civil partnerships is closely modelled on the law of divorce and is found in the Civil Partnership Act 2004. One of the most notable differences between divorce and dissolution is that civil partners are unable to rely on the fact of adultery to prove irretrievable breakdown.

Further reading and references

Cretney, 'Marriage, divorce and the courts' [2002] Fam Law 900.

Cretney, 'The Divorce White Paper – some reflections' [1995] Fam Law 302.

Deech, 'Divorce – a disaster?' [2009] Fam Law 1048.

Hasson, 'Setting a standard or reflecting reality? The "role" of divorce law, and the case of the Family Law Act 1996' [2003] IJLP&F 338.

Kay, 'Whose divorce is it anyway? The human rights aspect' [2004] Fam Law 892.

Shepherd, 'Ending the blame game: getting no-fault divorce back on the agenda' [2009] Fam Law 122.

Wall, President of the Family Division, 'The President's Resolution address 2012' [2012] Fam Law 817.

Websites

The Marriage Foundation: www.marriagefoundation.org.uk
The Peter Tatchell Foundation: www.petertatchellfoundation.org

Links to relevant websites can also be found at: www.palgravehighered.com/law/familylaw9e

Chapter 7

Finance and property on divorce and dissolution

This chapter deals with the law relating to financial remedies on divorce and dissolution of a civil partnership. The statutory provisions and judge-made principles herein also apply to the courts' powers to make orders on annulments and judicial separations. The law and principles governing financial remedies apply equally to divorce and dissolution, except that the provisions governing the latter are laid down in the Civil Partnership Act 2004. For this reason, the words 'marriage', 'divorce' and 'spouse' are interchangeable with 'civil partnership', 'dissolution' and 'civil partner' respectively.

7.1 Introduction

On marriage breakdown, the parties to the marriage will usually have to distribute and reallocate their property and financial assets, whether that relates to their home, a pension, investments or other assets. Obtaining a divorce (see Chapter 6) and bringing financial proceedings involve separate court proceedings; and, whereas a divorce can be obtained in a few months, a dispute about financial remedies may take much longer to resolve.

(a) A settlement culture

Despite the number of reported cases most couples do not litigate about property and finance on divorce, but instead reach agreement with or without the assistance of a lawyer, mediator or other forms of non-court dispute resolution (see 1.5). If legal advice is sought, solicitors should adopt a conciliatory approach. The rules of procedure laid down in the Family Procedure Rules 2010 also encourage and promote the use of mediation (see below). However, despite the emphasis on settlement, some couples spend vast sums of money on legal advice. In *Moore v Moore* [2007] 2 FLR 339, for example, the parties spent £1.5 million on legal fees primarily to decide whether the English or the Spanish courts should hear the case. However, judges now have the power to control proceedings in order to encourage the parties to reach agreement and thereby reduce costs.

(b) A wide range of different family situations

The courts exercise their discretion over a wide spectrum of family life. Thus, in *Dart v Dart* [1996] 2 FLR 286 Butler-Sloss LJ said that the Matrimonial Causes Act 1973 (MCA 1973) 'provides the jurisdiction for all applications for ancillary relief from the poverty-stricken to the multi-millionaire'. Where the parties are wealthy, orders in respect of vast sums of money may be made. At the opposite end of the spectrum, the court may have to consider finance and property issues in the context of State benefits and local authority housing. In low-income cases 'the assessment of the needs of the parties will lean heavily in favour of the children and the parent with whom they live' (*per* Butler-Sloss LJ in *Dart v Dart* above). Thus, for example, in *B v B (Financial Provision: Welfare of Child and Conduct)* [2001] EWCA Civ 2308 the parties' sole asset of £124,000 (which represented the proceeds of sale of the matrimonial home) was ordered to be transferred to the wife because of the need to rehouse herself and the child.

Although the same statutory provisions and legal principles apply to all cases, whether they are 'big-money' or 'small-money' cases, Sir Nicholas Wall, former President of the Family Division, in his Presidential speech to Resolution (an organisation of family lawyers) in March 2012 ([2012] Fam Law 817) expressed concern that the law is dominated by decisions made in 'big-money' cases which 'bear no resemblance to the ordinary lives of most divorcing couples and to the average case heard, day in and day out, by district judges up and down the country'. The former President also expressed concern about the disparity in representation between 'big-money' cases and 'smaller' cases. In most 'big-money' cases, the parties were represented by specialist solicitors and sometimes leading counsel. In 'smaller' cases, on the other hand, where there might be no, or inadequate, disclosure, or where there might be an impoverished wife and a better-off husband, then the difficulty was compounded if neither party received sensible advice. This problem has arguably been exacerbated by the reduction in availability of legal aid and the increase in litigants in person (see 1.2).

(c)   Judicial discretion

In England and Wales, the system governing financial remedies on divorce is based on judicial discretion. There is no community of property regime as there is in some European countries, such as France and Italy, whereby each spouse on marital breakdown is entitled to a fixed share of the matrimonial assets, subject to any agreement to the contrary. Instead, under Part II of the MCA 1973, the court has wide powers to redistribute matrimonial assets, and the outcome of each case depends on its own particular facts. The main advantage of a discretion-based system is that the court can tailor the order to fit the facts of the case. Its disadvantages, however, are that it can create uncertainty and unpredictability, and involve the court in a time-consuming and expensive exercise. It is also difficult for lawyers to advise their clients with certainty as to the likely outcome of their case.

7.2   Procedure for financial remedies

The rules of procedure governing applications for financial remedies are laid down in the Family Procedure Rules 2010 (FPR 2010) and accompanying Practice Directions. Part 9 of the FPR 2010 (Applications for a Financial Remedy) is particularly relevant, but so too are: Part 1 (Overriding Objective); Part 2 (Application and Interpretation of the Rules); and Part 3 (Non-Court Dispute Resolution). The overriding objective of the FPR 2010 is to enable the court to deal with cases justly, having regard to any welfare issues involved (r 1.1). The Law Society's *Family Law Protocol* also provides guidance on the conduct of applications, as does Resolution's *Code of Practice*.

The party who applies for financial remedies is called the 'applicant' and the other party the 'respondent'. Cases are normally heard in the Family Court, but complex or serious cases can be transferred to the High Court. With the exception of maintenance pending suit and orders to or for the benefit of a child of the family, financial orders do not take effect until the grant of decree absolute.

(a) Encouraging settlement

Part 3 of the FPR 2010 contains rules which aim to encourage and facilitate the use of non-court dispute resolution (for example mediation) in financial remedy proceedings on divorce. Under Part 3, the court has a duty to consider, at every stage of the proceedings, whether non-court dispute resolution is appropriate (r 3.3); and it can adjourn proceedings to allow non-court dispute resolution to take place (r 3.4). Before applying for financial remedies, applicants must first attend a mediation information and assessment meeting to see if the dispute can be resolved by mediation (s 10(1) Children and Families Act 2014 and Part 3 FPR 2010). However, in certain circumstances (r 3.8), an exemption can be sought (for example where there is domestic violence, the applicant is bankrupt, the case needs to be heard urgently, or if there are no mediators available within the vicinity). If mediation is unsuccessful, the parties may choose to pursue their application using the court process.

(b) The first appointment

This is the first hearing in the court process. The duties of the court at the first appointment are set out in rule 9.15 of the FPR 2010. The appointment must be conducted with the objective of defining the issues and saving costs (r 9.15(1)). Thus, the aim of the hearing is to define the issues and make directions (if needed) so that the parties can endeavour to reach agreement. The judge has various powers, such as to: direct that further documents be produced; give directions about the valuation of assets; and order that the case be adjourned for non-court dispute resolution (r 9.15).

(c) The financial dispute resolution appointment

The financial dispute resolution appointment is a 'meeting held for the purposes of discussion and negotiation' (r 9.17(1)) at which the parties must use their best endeavours to reach agreement on the matters in issue between them (r 9.17(6)). At the financial dispute resolution appointment the judge will usually provide an indication as to a suitable settlement to help the parties reach an agreement. If agreement is not possible, then the case proceeds to a final hearing.

In *Rose v Rose* [2002] 1 FLR 978 Thorpe LJ held that: although the financial dispute resolution appointment can take many forms, depending on the style and practice of the judge, it should never be superficial or ill-considered; and that, although it is an invaluable tool for dispelling unreasonable expectations, in a finely balanced case it is no substitute for a trial and should not be used to discourage either party from going to trial where the case can only be resolved in such a way. In *S v S (Ancillary Relief: Importance of FDR)* [2008] 1 FLR 944 Baron J stated, *inter alia*, that the financial dispute resolution procedure must be undertaken in an effective way in every case, because it gives the parties the opportunity to settle the litigation, to air the issues and to have neutral judicial evaluation at a time before costs have denuded assets.

(d)   The final hearing

This is the last hearing in the court process. This involves a full trial where the judge hears evidence and argument from the parties and makes a final order regarding the application(s).

(e)   Staying divorce proceedings to allow the case to be heard in another jurisdiction

In an international case, the court in England and Wales can stay (suspend) the proceedings if it considers it more appropriate for the matter to be determined in another jurisdiction. For example, in *Bentinck v Bentinck* [2007] 2 FLR 1 proceedings were stayed to allow the Swiss court to determine the issue of where the divorce and finances should be heard.

(f)   A duty of full and frank disclosure

Both parties have an absolute duty to make full, frank and clear disclosure of all their present and likely future assets, for without such disclosure the court will be unable to exercise its discretion fairly. The duty was summed up by Mostyn J in *NG v SG (Appeal: Non-Disclosure)* [2011] EWHC 3270 (Fam) who described non-disclosure as 'a bane which strikes at the very integrity of the adjudicative process' and said that without full disclosure 'the court cannot render a true certain and just verdict'.

Failure to make full and frank disclosure is therefore a serious matter and can result in an order being set aside (see 7.12 below). A costs penalty can also be imposed on a dishonest party (see, for example, *Al-Khatib v Masry* [2002] 1 FLR 1053).

(g)   Media attendance

Media representatives are permitted to attend financial remedy proceedings, unless the judge decides to exclude them or the rules provide otherwise (see r 27.11 FPR 2010 and *Practice Direction 27B*) (see 1.3).

7.3   Financial orders that can be made

Under Part II of the Matrimonial Causes Act 1973 the court has jurisdiction to make, *inter alia*, the following orders:

(a) maintenance pending suit (s 22);
(b) financial provision orders: periodic payments orders; lump sum orders (s 23);
(c) property adjustment orders: transfer of property; settlement of property; and variation of a settlement (s 24); and
(d) pension orders (ss 24B–E).

The above orders can be combined to create a workable solution. Most cases are not contested, and the orders most commonly made are property adjustment and lump sum orders.

Family Court Statistics Quarterly, October–December 2015 **(Ministry of Justice, 2016)**

▶ There were 9,062 financial remedy disposals, down 10 per cent on the equivalent quarter in 2014 and continuing a recent downward trend.
▶ 65 per cent of disposals were uncontested, 26 per cent were initially contested, and 9 per cent were contested throughout.
▶ In October to December 2015, property adjustment and lump sum orders each accounted for about a third of the total financial remedy disposal types.

(a) Maintenance pending suit (section 22)

This is a short-term interim order which exists to bridge the gap between the start of proceedings and their final determination. It terminates when the divorce suit is determined (or earlier if the court so orders). Either party can apply for maintenance pending suit. When deciding whether to make an order and, if so, in what manner, the court is required to make such order as is 'reasonable' (s 22), but in practice it performs a similar exercise to that required by section 25 (see 7.4 below). The court has a wide discretion and in an appropriate case may make a substantial order (see, for example, *M v M (Maintenance Pending Suit)* [2002] 2 FLR 123 where the wife was awarded £330,000 per annum maintenance pending suit).

Where one party cannot afford to finance the legal proceedings they may be able to obtain an order requiring the other party to pay them an amount for the purpose of obtaining legal services for the purposes of the proceedings (s 22ZA).

(b) Financial provision orders (section 23)

The following orders can be made in favour of a spouse, and to or for the benefit of any child of the family aged under 18, or a 'child' aged over 18 who is undergoing education or training or who has special circumstances (such as a disability) (ss 23(1) and 29(1), (3)).

(i) A periodical payments order (maintenance)

An order for periodical payments can be made in favour of a spouse and/or to or for the benefit of any child of the family (ss 23(1)(a) and (d)). The order can be secured or unsecured. A secured order is one where a capital asset or other property is charged as security for payment (s 23(1)(b) and (e)). Secured orders are rare in practice, but they are sometimes made where there may be difficulties enforcing an order. Periodical payments made in favour of a spouse automatically terminate if that spouse enters into another marriage after the divorce (s 28(1)), but they do not necessarily terminate if the divorced spouse enters into a cohabitation relationship. However, the fact that a party is cohabiting with a new partner after divorce can be taken into account by the court as one of the factors of the case when it is considering whether and in what form to make an order (see 7.4 below) and when it is considering whether to vary or discharge an order (see 7.12 below).

(ii) A lump sum order

This is an order for payment of a specified sum of money, which can be made in favour of a spouse and/or to or for the benefit of any child of the family (s 23(1) (c) and (f)). The court can order payment of a whole sum or order it to be paid by instalment (s 23(3)(c)), which can include the payment of interest (s 23(6)). Only one lump sum order can be made – the plural reference to 'lump sums' in section 23(1)(c) is to allow for more than one lump sum payment to be made in one order.

The advantage of a lump sum order is that it can be used to effect a 'clean break' between the parties (see 7.5 below). Sometimes a lump sum will be ordered to represent 'capitalised maintenance'; in other words, a sum which can be invested to provide an income. A *'Duxbury* calculation' is sometimes used as a guide to calculate a party's capitalised maintenance needs by taking account of certain variables, such as inflation, life expectancy, income tax, capital growth and income from investments. This calculation is not determinative, however, as it is the section 25 factors which prevail (see 7.4 below).

A lump sum order made in favour of a *spouse* is a final order which cannot be varied in variation proceedings, unless the circumstances are exceptional. A lump sum order made in favour of a *child*, on the other hand, is not a final order as the court's power to make orders for children is 'exercisable from time to time' (s 23(4)). In practice, lump sum orders in favour of children are rare, although they may sometimes be made in a 'big-money' case.

Adjourning an application where a capital sum will become available in the future   To avoid the potential injustice caused by the finality of a lump sum order, the court can in exceptional circumstances adjourn proceedings where there is a real possibility of capital from a specific source becoming available in the near future, for example an inheritance or a pension.

(c)   Property adjustment orders (section 24)

(i) A transfer of property order (section 24(1)(a))

This order directs a spouse to transfer specified property to the other spouse and/or to or for the benefit of a child of the family. Any property can be transferred, but in practice the order is usually used to transfer the matrimonial home. In such circumstances, the person transferring their share of the home may be given a charge over the property for a fixed amount or a percentage of the value which is to be realised at a later date. Alternatively, the person to whom the property is being transferred may be ordered to pay the other spouse a lump sum representing the latter's share in the home. A transfer of property is a useful way of effecting a 'clean break' (see 7.5 below). For example, a spouse could be ordered to transfer the entire matrimonial home to the other spouse with the latter agreeing to forgo any claim for maintenance as a result.

(ii) A settlement of property order (section 24(1)(b))

This order directs a spouse to settle property for the benefit of the other spouse and/or any child of the family. Under a settlement of property, property is held on trust for certain persons who have an interest in the property. Although rare in practice, such orders may be useful to give the children of the family a roof over their heads during their dependency, while also enabling the non-occupying spouse to realise a share of the property once the children become independent. This type of order is known as a '*Mesher* order' (see 7.7 below).

(iii) A variation of ante-nuptial or post-nuptial settlement order (sections 24(1)(c), (d))

The court can vary any ante-nuptial or post-nuptial settlement made by the parties. This order can be made for the benefit of the parties and/or any child of the family. Such orders are rare.

(iv) Order for the sale of property (section 24A)

Where the court has made a secured periodical payments, lump sum or property adjustment order, it can also make a further order for the sale of property in which one spouse has, or both spouses have, a beneficial interest. The power to order sale is a useful enforcement mechanism where there has been, or is likely to be, non-compliance with an order. For example, the court could order that property belonging to a spouse who has failed to pay a lump sum is to be sold and that the proceeds of sale are to be paid to the spouse who should have received the payment of a lump sum (s 24A(2)(a)). The court can defer sale until a specified event has occurred or until a specified period of time has expired (s 24A(4)). It can also order that property be offered for sale to a specified person or persons (s 24A(2)(b)). A third party with an interest in the property in dispute (such as a mortgagee) must be allowed to make representations to the court, and the third party's interest must be included as one of the circumstances of the case when the court performs its discretionary exercise (s 24A(6)).

(d) Pension orders

See 7.8 below.

7.4 How the court exercises its discretion – the section 25 factors

▶ **Lord Nicholls in *Miller v Miller; McFarlane v McFarlane* [2006] UKHL 24**

The 1973 Act gives only limited guidance on how the courts should exercise their statutory powers. Primary consideration must be given to the welfare of any children of the family. The court must consider the feasibility of a 'clean break'. Beyond this the courts are largely left to get on with it for themselves. The courts are told simply that they must have regard to all the circumstances of the case.

Of itself this direction leads nowhere. Implicitly the courts must exercise their powers so as to achieve an outcome which is fair between the parties. But an important aspect of fairness is that like cases should be treated alike. So, perforce, if there is to be an acceptable degree of consistency of decision from one case to the next, the courts must themselves articulate, if only in the broadest fashion, what are the applicable if unspoken principles guiding the court's approach.

This is not to usurp the legislative function. Rather, it is to perform a necessary judicial function in the absence of parliamentary guidance. As Lord Cooke of Thorndon said in *White v White* (1970), there is no reason to suppose that in prescribing relevant considerations the legislature had any intention of excluding the development of general judicial practice.

▶ **Baroness Hale in *Miller v Miller; McFarlane v McFarlane* [2006] UKHL 24**

'There is much to be said for the flexibility and sensitivity of the English law of ancillary relief. It avoids the straitjacket of rigid rules which can apply harshly or unfairly in an individual case. But it should not be too flexible. It must try to achieve some consistency and predictability. This is not only to secure that so far as possible like cases are treated alike but also to enable and encourage the parties to negotiate their own solutions as quickly and cheaply as possible.'

As the above extracts show, the court has wide discretionary powers when deciding whether to make an order, and, if so, in what manner. Property law principles, such as the laws of trusts, are not generally relevant and will not be investigated by the court, except where there is a genuine third-party interest in any property.

In addition to applying the section 25 factors (see below) and considering whether to effect a clean break (see 7.5 below) the courts must apply the principles laid down by the House of Lords in *White v White* [2000] UKHL 54 and *Miller v Miller; McFarlane v McFarlane* [2006] UKHL 24 (see 7.6 below), and in any other relevant case-law.

(a)   The welfare of the children and the other section 25 factors

When deciding whether to exercise its powers to make financial orders under Part II of the Matrimonial Causes Act 1973, and, if so, in what manner, the court must consider all the circumstances of the case, but with the first consideration being given to the welfare of any child of the family.

Section 25(1)

It shall be the duty of the court in deciding whether to exercise its powers … and, if so, in what manner, to have regard to all the circumstances of the case, first consideration being given to the welfare while a minor of any child of the family who has not attained the age of eighteen.

The duty in section 25(1) applies not just to the parties' own children but also to children treated by the parties as children of the family (s 52(1)). This includes, for example, step-children.

When exercising its powers in relation to a party to the marriage, the court must in particular have regard to the following list of factors laid down in section 25(2).

Section 25(2)

As regards the exercise of the powers of the court in relation to a party to the marriage, the court shall in particular have regard to the following matters –

(a) The income, earning capacity, property and other financial resources which each of the parties to the marriage has or is likely to have in the foreseeable future, including in the case of earning capacity any increase in that capacity which it would in the opinion of the court be reasonable to expect a party to the marriage to take steps to acquire.

(b) The financial needs, obligations and responsibilities which each of the parties to the marriage has or is likely to have in the foreseeable future.

(c) The standard of living enjoyed by the family before the breakdown of marriage.

(d) The age of each party to the marriage and the duration of the marriage.

(e) Any physical or mental disability of either of the parties to the marriage.

(f) The contribution which each of the parties has made or is likely in the foreseeable future to make to the welfare of the family, including any contribution by looking after the home or caring for the family.

(g) The conduct of each of the parties, if that conduct is such that it would in the opinion of the court be inequitable to disregard it.

(h) In the case of proceedings for divorce or nullity of marriage, the value to each of the parties to the marriage of any benefit which, by reason of the dissolution or annulment of the marriage, that party will lose the chance of acquiring.

The weight or importance attached to these factors depends on the facts of each case. In practice, however, financial resources and financial needs are usually particularly important.

The factors in section 25(2) are not exclusive – other factors can be taken into account, as section 25(1) refers to 'all the circumstances of the case'. Thus, for example, the terms of a pre- or post-nuptial agreement may be taken into account by the court (see 7.9 below). Cultural factors may also be taken into account, as they were in *A v T (Ancillary Relief: Cultural Factors)* [2004] 1 FLR 977 where the parties were Iranian Muslims bound by Sharia law and the High Court considered how the matter would be dealt with in Iran.

The following paragraphs consider the factors in section 25(2) in more detail.

(i) Section 25(2)(a)

The income, earning capacity, property and other financial resources which each of the parties to the marriage has or is likely to have in the foreseeable future, including in the case of earning capacity any increase in that capacity which it would in the opinion of the court be reasonable to expect a party to the marriage to take steps to acquire.

The court has the discretion to take into account any resource, such as, for example, business profits, interest on investments, insurance policies, pension rights, welfare benefits, damages for personal injury (*Mansfield v Mansfield* [2011] EWCA Civ 1056) and a windfall such as a lottery prize (*S v AG (Financial Orders: Lottery Prize)* [2011] EWHC 2637 (Fam)). However, as cases are highly fact-specific, whether various resources will be taken into account depends on the facts of the case. In some cases, the court may have the difficult task of having to decide whether a particular resource (such as an inheritance or a resource obtained before marriage) is 'matrimonial' or 'non-matrimonial' property (see 7.6(d) below).

In an appropriate case, the court may impute a notional earning capacity or infer that unidentified resources are available from a spouse's expenditure or style of living. Future earning potential is an important consideration when the court is deciding whether to effect a 'clean break' (see 7.5 below). As future financial resources must be considered, the court may decide to postpone making an order if financial resources are likely to be available in the relatively near future, for example an inheritance or assets tied up in a business which are realisable at a later date.

The impact of a new partner The court can take into account the fact that a former spouse is living with a new partner, whether a spouse or cohabitant, as this may affect the parties' financial resources and needs under section 25(2)(a). If the new partner is making, or has the potential to make, a financial contribution, then this may be taken into account. In *Grey v Grey* [2009] EWCA Civ 1424 the Court of Appeal held that the real question would generally be not what the cohabitant was contributing, but what they ought to contribute. It held, referring to the facts of the case, that the judge could not be fair to the husband without investigating whether the wife's new partner was making any financial contribution to the wife's household, and, if not, what his capacity to make a contribution was. It held that the approach in *Fleming v Fleming* [2003] EWCA Civ 184 remained sound, and was sufficiently flexible to enable the court to do justice and to reflect social and moral shifts within society. *Grey v Grey* also shows that a stable and committed relationship falling short of cohabitation may have an impact on the level of spousal maintenance, as, when the case was heard again on its facts (see *Re Grey (No 3)* [2010] EWHC 1055 (Fam)), the trial judge took account of the wife's new relationship and reduced the maintenance payable.

(ii) Section 25(2)(b)

> The financial needs, obligations and responsibilities which each of the parties to the marriage has or is likely to have in the foreseeable future.

The financial needs of the parties and any children of the family is a key factor which the court must take into account, as the decision of the House of Lords in *Miller v Miller* (see 7.6 below) recognised. Financial needs, obligations and responsibilities will vary from case to case, but they include, for example, the provision of accommodation and general living expenses. 'Need' will be a particularly important consideration in a 'small-money' case, especially where there are children of the family, but it is important even in a 'big-money case' and an award can be made which exceeds a party's reasonable needs (see *White v White* (2000) at 7.6 below). Despite the fact that the reported cases are largely 'big-money' cases, in practice most cases are still needs-based. As the meaning of 'needs' has generated uncertainty and there is confusion about the extent to which one spouse should be required to meet the other's needs on marriage breakdown, the Law Commission has conducted a project which looks, among other things, at the issue of needs (see 7.14 below).

Obligations and responsibilities to a new partner or a new family Such obligations and responsibilities can be taken into account, depending on the facts of the case and applying all the section 25 criteria. As far as the principle of equality laid down in *White v White* is concerned (see 7.6 below), different approaches have been taken in the case-law. Thus, for example, in *S v S (Financial Provision: Departing from Equality)* [2001] 2 FLR 246 it was held that obligations and responsibilities to a new family could justify a departure from equality, whereas in *H-J v H-J (Financial Provision: Equality)* [2002] 1 FLR 415 Coleridge J held that such an approach would normally be wrong in principle.

(iii) Section 25(2)(c)

The standard of living enjoyed by the family before the breakdown of marriage.

Although this factor must be taken into account, the court is under no duty to attempt to place the parties in the position they would have been in if the marriage had not broken down. In fact, in practice it is often not possible for the parties to enjoy the same standard of living after divorce as they did before it, unless there are substantial assets available for distribution.

(iv) Section 25(2)(d)

The age of each party to the marriage and the duration of the marriage.

These two factors can have an important impact on the court's decision. The needs and resources of a young (and possibly childless) couple are likely to differ significantly from those of an older couple. It may be reasonable, for example, to expect a spouse in their twenties or thirties to make their way on their own, but the court is less likely to expect a spouse in their forties or fifties to go out and find a job, particularly if they have not worked since marrying or gave up their career to look after children.

The duration of the marriage will be an important consideration when the court is considering whether assets (such as inheritance or property accrued before marriage) should be part of the pool of assets available for distribution. Thus, the longer the marriage, the less likely the court will be to categorise different types of property as 'matrimonial' or 'non-matrimonial' (see 7.6 below). In other words, the importance of the source of the assets *may* diminish over time. However, as each case depends on its facts and the application of the other factors in section 25, even in the case of a short marriage the court may make a generous award.

Pre-marital cohabitation may count towards the duration of a marriage The court may, in the exercise of its discretion, decide to take a settled and committed period of pre-marital cohabitation into account when calculating the duration of a marriage, particularly where the period of cohabitation has seamlessly and immediately preceded the marriage. In *C v C* [2009] 1 FLR 8, for example, Moylan J took into account the couple's pre-marital cohabitation of approximately four years as to do otherwise would fly in the face of the duty of the court to have regard to all the circumstances of the case.

(v) Section 25(2)(e)

Any physical or mental disability of either of the parties to the marriage.

This is significant as it may create specific needs, such as medical care, and may impact on a spouse's earning capacity and ability to be financially independent.

(vi) Section 25(2)(f)

The contribution which each of the parties has made or is likely in the foreseeable future to make to the welfare of the family, including any contribution by looking after the home or caring for the family.

Under section 25(2)(f) the court can take into account both financial and non-financial contributions to the home and to the family. The court should not favour the 'breadwinner' over the 'homemaker' as this would be contrary to the principles of fairness and non-discrimination expounded by the House of Lords in *White v White* (see 7.6 below). In *Lambert v Lambert* [2003] 1 FLR 139 Thorpe LJ held that there must be an end to the sterile suggestion that the breadwinner's contribution was more important than that of the homemaker.

(vii) Section 25(2)(g)

The conduct of each of the parties, if that conduct is such that it would in the opinion of the court be inequitable to disregard it.

The court generally takes the view that a certain amount of unpleasantness is to be expected on both sides on the breakdown of a relationship, and that such matters should not affect the outcome of an application for financial remedies. For this reason, only conduct of an extreme or exceptional kind will be taken into account, as to do otherwise would contradict one of the policy aims of divorce law, which is not to apportion blame. The section 25 exercise is regarded as a financial, not a moral, exercise. In *Miller v Miller* (2006) (see 7.6 below) the House of Lords reaffirmed the 'obvious and gross' test laid down by Lord Denning MR in *Wachtel v Wachtel* [1973] Fam 72 and held that the lower court had been wrong to take into account the husband's alleged responsibility for the marriage breakdown (he had left his wife for another woman), given that it was conduct which fell far short of 'conduct which it would be inequitable to disregard' under section 25(2)(g).

As the case-law shows, only extreme types of conduct will be taken into account, such as, for example: stabbing a spouse (*H v H (Financial Provision: Conduct)* [1994] 2 FLR 801); violently attacking the wife in the matrimonial home in front of the children (*H v H (Financial Relief: Attempted Murder as Conduct)* [2006] 1 FLR 990); and sexual assaults and other related offences by the husband on his wife's grandchildren (*K v L* [2010] EWCA Civ 125). An accumulation of serious misconduct, such as failing to make full and frank disclosure, dissipating matrimonial assets and abducting a child might constitute conduct for the purposes of section 25(2)(g), as it did in *Al-Khatib v Masry* [2002] 1 FLR 1053. However, even if the conduct is serious, the court may decide, in the exercise of its discretion, to discount that conduct and take other factors into account (see, for example, *A v A (Financial Provision: Conduct)* [1995] 1 FLR 345 where, even though the depressed and suicidal husband had assaulted his wife with a knife, other factors prevailed). Unless the violence is extremely severe it will not usually be taken into account as conduct under section 25(2)(g) (see, for example, *S v S (Non-Matrimonial Property: Conduct)* [2007] 1 FLR 1496).

If the court considers that the conduct is sufficiently serious to be taken into account, it does not necessarily mean that the 'guilty' party will receive nothing. For example, in *Clark v Clark* [1999] 2 FLR 498 the wife was granted an order even though her conduct was held to be inequitable to disregard (she had refused to consummate the marriage, had transferred her husband's property into her own name and had made him a virtual prisoner in his own home). In *H v H (Financial Provision: Conduct)* [1998] 1 FLR 971, where the husband's conduct was held to be too inequitable to ignore (he had transferred money for three years into a Swiss bank account), Singer J said that the approach to be taken was not to fix a sum as a 'penalty', but to carry out an evaluation based on all the relevant factors taken in the round.

Non-disclosure and litigation misconduct   A failure to make full and frank disclosure, or any other misconduct in respect of the process of the case, may be taken into account. In most cases it will be reflected in a costs order (see, for example, *Ezair v Ezair* [2012] EWCA Civ 893 and *Joy v Joy-Morancho* [2015] EWHC 2507 (Fam)), but in a serious case it could affect the size of the award (see *MF v SF* [2015] EWHC 1273 (Fam)).

Bigamy   Although bigamy is a criminal offence and a ground for nullity (see 2.5), a party to a bigamous marriage is not necessarily barred from applying for financial remedies on divorce, even though it is the policy of the law not to allow a person to profit from their own crime. Whether bigamy will affect an award depends on the circumstances of the case. Thus, for example, in *Whiston v Whiston* [1995] 2 FLR 268 a bigamist was barred from claiming on grounds of public policy, whereas in *Rampal v Rampal (No. 2)* [2001] 2 FLR 1179 a bigamist was allowed to pursue a claim, on the basis that he had been much less culpable than the bigamist in *Whiston*. In *Ben Hashem v Al Shayif* [2009] 1 FLR 115 Munby J awarded the wife more than £7 million as both parties were aware of the bigamy.

(viii) Section 25(2)(h)

> In the case of proceedings for divorce or nullity of marriage, the value to each of the parties to the marriage of any benefit which, by reason of the dissolution or annulment of the marriage, that party will lose the chance of acquiring.

On divorce a spouse may lose certain property rights and interests, such as the benefit of a pension, the surrender value of an insurance policy, future business profits or the right to succeed to the other spouse's estate. The court can take these and other lost benefits into account. It might, for example, decide to increase an order to compensate for the loss of future benefits, or make a deferred lump sum order, or, in an exceptional case, adjourn proceedings. Pensions on divorce are governed by special rules (see 7.8 below).

7.5 The 'clean break'

A major policy aim of the law governing financial remedies on divorce is that a divorced spouse cannot expect a 'meal ticket' for life. For this reason the court is required to determine cases in such a way as to effect, where possible, a 'clean break' between the parties. The clean break was introduced to encourage the parties to put the past behind them and begin a new life which would not be overshadowed by the relationship which had broken down (*per* Lord Scarman in *Minton v Minton* [1979] AC 593).

Baroness Hale in *Miller v Miller; McFarlane v McFarlane* [2006] UKHL 24

Section 25A is a powerful encouragement towards securing the court's objective by way of lump sum and capital adjustment (which now includes pension sharing) rather than by continuing periodical payments. This is good practical sense. Periodical payments are a continuing source of stress for both parties. They are also insecure. With the best will in the world, the paying party may fall on hard times and be unable to keep up with them. Nor is the best will in the world always evident between formerly married people. It is also the logical consequence of the retreat from the principle of the life-long obligation. Independent finances and self-sufficiency are the aims. Nevertheless, section 25A does not tell us what the outcome of the exercise required by section 25 should be. It is mainly directed at how that outcome should be put into effect.

The court encourages the parties to go their separate ways after divorce, provided it is fair in the circumstances. Thus, under section 25A(1), when exercising its powers to make finance and property orders in favour of a spouse, the court must consider 'whether it would be appropriate so to exercise those powers that the financial obligations of each party towards the other will be terminated' as soon after the divorce as the court 'considers just and reasonable'. Whether the court will effect a clean break depends on the facts of the case and also on the overarching objective of fairness laid down in *White v White* (see 7.6 below).

The court can effect a clean break between the parties in an application for periodical payments in the following ways:

▶ by dismissing the application;
▶ by dismissing the application with a direction that the applicant shall not make any further application (s 25A(3));
▶ by making a limited-term periodical payments order (s 25A(2));
▶ by making a limited-term periodical payments order with a direction that no application can be made in variation proceedings for an extension of that term (s 28(1A));
▶ by ordering a lump sum representing capitalised periodical payments as a means of discharging a party's liability to make further periodical payments (ss 31(7A) and (7B)).

The court also has a duty to consider a clean break in section 31 variation proceedings, when the court can make a limited-term order 'to enable the party in whose favour the order was made to adjust without undue hardship to the termination of those payments' (s 31(7)).

In certain circumstances, the court may decide to make a nominal periodical payments order (such as for £1 per annum), so that there is an order in place which can be varied if the circumstances change in the future.

Despite the court's duty to consider a clean break, it may be unwilling to effect one where it makes unrealistic expectations of a spouse's capacity for economic independence. In cases where there is ill-health the court may also be unwilling to effect a clean break (see *Purba v Purba* [2000] 1 FLR 444).

7.6 The discretionary exercise – *White v White* and *Miller v Miller*

Two important cases have been heard by the House of Lords on the question of how the courts should exercise their discretion in financial remedy cases on divorce: *White v White* [2000] UKHL 54; and *Miller v Miller; McFarlane v McFarlane* [2006] UKHL 24. Although both were 'big-money' cases, the principles they laid down apply to all financial remedy applications. However, if there is a pre-nuptial or post-nuptial agreement in existence, other principles may apply (see 7.9 below).

(a) *White v White* (2000)

Before the decision of the House of Lords in *White v White* [2000] UKHL 54, the Court of Appeal had adopted a 'reasonable requirements' (otherwise known as 'reasonable needs' and, in more recent cases, as 'needs (generously interpreted)') approach in 'big-money' cases, whereby an award would be made sufficient to satisfy the other spouse's needs even though it was possible to award more. This approach had resulted in wives, in particular, receiving much smaller proportions of the matrimonial assets than their husband.

In the late 1990s, however, the Court of Appeal began to wonder whether the 'reasonable requirements' approach might be causing injustice. Thus, for example, in *Dart v Dart* [1996] 2 FLR 286, where the wife was awarded £4 million of her husband's £400 million fortune, Butler-Sloss LJ questioned whether the courts might be giving too much weight to reasonable needs over the other section 25 criteria. Nonetheless the Court of Appeal in *Dart* held that any challenge to the reasonable requirements approach was a matter for Parliament, not the courts. Although the reasonable needs approach was considered unsatisfactory because it discriminated against wives and prioritised needs when there was no such hierarchy in section 25 (see 7.4 above), it was not until the following case of *White v White* that the reasonable needs approach was overturned.

> ▶ *White v White* [2000] UKHL 54
>
> After 33 years of marriage the wife obtained a divorce and sought enough capital to set herself up independently in farming, arguing that her equal contribution to the parties' farming business throughout their long marriage justified her claim to an equal share of the assets. Her husband argued that she should be given only enough to satisfy her reasonable

needs, applying the approach adopted in earlier decisions of the Court of Appeal (see above). Their overall assets were assessed at approximately £4.6 million.

At first instance, the judge adopted a reasonable needs approach and, on the basis that it was impractical for the wife to continue farming, awarded her one-fifth of their joint assets and ordered that the farming business remain with the husband.

The wife appealed to the Court of Appeal, which allowed her appeal and increased her award to £1.5 million. Butler-Sloss LJ said that cases where a wife was an equal business partner were in a wholly different category from other 'big-money' cases such as *Dart v Dart* (see above) and *Conran v Conran* [1997] 2 FLR 615 where the origin of the wealth was clearly on one side and the emphasis was rightly on contribution, not entitlement. The Court of Appeal also held that it was not the function of the judge to criticise the wife's plans to carry on farming. Both parties appealed to the House of Lords.

The House of Lords, dismissing the appeals, held that, although the judge had been mistaken in regarding reasonable requirements as the determinant factor, the award made by the Court of Appeal was within the ambit of reasonable discretion. Lord Nicholls, giving the leading opinion, laid down the following statements of principle:

▶ The objective implicit in section 25 is to achieve a fair outcome in financial arrangements on divorce, giving first consideration to the welfare of any children.
▶ Fairness requires the court to take into account all the circumstances of the case. In seeking to achieve a fair outcome, there is no place for discrimination between husband and wife in their respective roles. Fairness requires that their division of labour should not prejudice or advantage either party when considering their contributions to the welfare of the family under section 25(2)(f). If each in their different spheres contributed equally to the family, then in principle it matters not who earned the money and built up the assets. There should be no bias in favour of the money earner as against the homemaker and the child carer.
▶ Before making an order for division of assets, a judge should check his tentative views against the yardstick of equality of division. As a general rule, equality should be departed from only if, and to the extent that, there is good reason for doing so. The need to consider and articulate reasons for doing so will help the parties and the court to focus on the need to ensure the absence of discrimination.
▶ Section 25(2) does not rank the matters listed therein in any hierarchy and other matters may also be important. Financial need is only one of the several factors to be taken into account in determining a fair outcome. When considering section 25(2)(b), confusion will be avoided by courts ceasing to employ the expression 'reasonable requirements' and returning to the statutory language of 'needs', which preserves the necessary degree of flexibility.

Lord Nicholls, who laid down the propositions above, dismissed, however, the idea that there should be a presumption of equality, as this would be an impermissible judicial gloss on section 25, and because the introduction of such a presumption was a matter for Parliament, not the courts.

In *White v White* the 'reasonable needs or requirements' approach was therefore rejected and replaced by 'a yardstick of equality of division' in order to ensure fairness and abolish discrimination. *White v White* recognised that marriage is a partnership of equals and that the homemaker should not be discriminated as against the breadwinner. Discrimination was the antithesis of fairness. This was a principle of universal application which was to be applied to all cases, not just 'big-money' cases. However, in *Miller v Miller* (see above) Lord Nicholls said that the yardstick of equality was to be applied as an aid, not as a rule.

(i) Reaction to White v White

The decision in *White v White* provoked considerable comment from lawyers and academics. Duckworth and Hodson (2001) thought that the decision would increase the impetus for recognising formal agreements between spouses, especially pre-marital contracts. Although Eekelaar ([2001] Fam Law 30) thought that the equality of sharing approach might deter people from marrying, he considered that the decision in *White v White* was no great advance in the law because the House of Lords had provided no suggestions as to what sorts of reasons might justify departing from equality. Cretney ([2001] Fam Law 3) was of the opinion that the House of Lords had gone too far. He thought that the House might have been a 'trifle rash' in overturning the settled practice of the courts, particularly in a case which was highly untypical of other 'big-money' cases (both parties were in business together). He also questioned whether such a change of approach should have been taken by the House of Lords at all, but instead should have been a matter for Parliament. Cretney also stated ([2003] CFLQ 303) that the preference in *White v White* for equal division was expressed in such a muted and confused way that it would be difficult to predict how cases would be decided and that it would increase 'the expense, uncertainty and consequent destructive emotional stress of resolving the consequences of marriage breakdown'. In *Charman v Charman (No. 4)* [2007] EWCA Civ 503 (see further below) Sir Mark Potter P said that the decision in *White v White* had undoubtedly not resolved 'the problems faced by practitioners in advising clients or by clients in deciding upon what terms to compromise'.

Another criticism that might be made is that *White v White* seems riddled with contradictions. Thus, although the House of Lords emphasised the importance of applying the statute (particularly the section 25 factors), it in fact introduced an approach (a 'yardstick of equality') which had no basis in the statute. In addition, as the non-discrimination principle articulated in *White v White* is derived from section 25(2)(f), then the House of Lords appears to have elevated that factor, when it had stressed in the earlier case of *Piglowska v Piglowski* [1999] 1 WLR 1360 that there was no hierarchy in section 25. Furthermore, although the House of Lords in *White v White* said that no gloss must be put on needs in section 25 (as to whether they are reasonable or not), it nonetheless imposed fairness and equality as glosses on the section 25 factors. The relationship between section 25 and the principles enunciated in *White v White* is therefore unclear. Perhaps any 'glosses' on section 25 should have been left to Parliament, not the House of Lords. It is also rather unsatisfactory that the principles propounded by Lord Nicholls in *White v White* (equality, fairness and non-discrimination) arose in an atypical case, namely one in which both spouses were involved as partners in a family business.

(ii) The case-law after White v White *and 'special contribution'*

After *White v White* the courts began to make larger awards (at least in 'big-money' cases), as *White v White* had removed the requirement that awards should be limited to reasonable needs. As a result, husbands who felt they had been dealt with unfairly began to argue that their special business contribution justified a departure from equality. In other words, they began to argue that, as they had been responsible for the accumulation of matrimonial assets, they should be entitled to more than half of those assets on divorce. This argument was sometimes successful. Thus, for example, in *Cowan v Cowan* [2001] 2 FLR 192 the wife (after a long marriage) was awarded only a 38 per cent share of the assets (worth over £11 million) on the basis that equal division would not be fair in the circumstances, in particular because of the husband's special business talent and the great wealth which he had thereby produced. The Court of Appeal so held even though its approach seemed to contradict the non-discrimination principle laid down in *White v White*.

After *Cowan v Cowan* (see above) the courts began to take into account special contributions by husbands as a justification for departing from equality, but this began to create difficulties. Not only did it lead to detailed evidence of contribution being put forward – which increased the length and cost of litigation and was contrary to the policy objective of encouraging agreement – but the courts began to adopt different approaches to contribution. Thus, although some judges accepted special contribution as a justification for departing from equality of division, others began to express concerns about such an approach. Coleridge J, for example, in *G v G (Financial Provision: Equal Division)* [2002] 2 FLR 1143 expressed disquiet about the growing forensic practice of routinely arguing special contribution in 'big-money' cases, which, he said, invited recrimination and was not conducive to settlement.

The difficulties created by *Cowan* (of allowing arguments based on special contribution to justify a departure from equality) were eventually addressed by the Court of Appeal in *Lambert v Lambert* [2003] 1 FLR 139 where it endeavoured to confine the doctrine of exceptional or special contribution, endorsed in *Cowan*, within narrow bounds. In *Lambert*, the husband, whose business had produced more than £26 million, argued that his exceptional business contribution (which had led to the accumulation of the matrimonial assets) justified a departure from equality. His wife, on the other hand, claimed a half-share of the assets on the ground that she had been the principal homemaker and parent during the marriage and that she had played a significant role in her husband's business. At first instance, Connell J, applying *Cowan* (see above), awarded her 37.5 per cent of the assets on the basis that her contribution had been modest, in fact merely 'ornamental', whereas her husband's had been 'really special' or 'exceptional'. The wife appealed, arguing, *inter alia*, that Connell J had fallen into the trap of gender discrimination by concluding that the husband's contribution justified a departure from equality, and that there had been insufficient consideration of her needs. The Court of Appeal allowed her appeal and awarded her 50 per cent of the assets. Although Thorpe LJ said that there 'must be an end to the sterile assertion that the breadwinner's contribution weighs heavier than the homemaker's', his Lordship cautiously acknowledged that, given the infinite variety of fact and circumstance, special contribution remained a legitimate possibility in exceptional circumstances.

The courts have taken a variety of approaches to the division of matrimonial assets on the basis of special contribution. For example, in *Norris v Norris* [2003] 1 FLR 1142 Bennett J rejected the wife's claim that she was entitled to half the matrimonial assets on the basis of her exceptional domestic and financial contribution. Similarly, in *L v L (Financial Provision: Contributions)* [2002] FLR 642 Connell J rejected the wife's claim that she had played a pivotal role in the success of her husband's business, and instead awarded her only 37 per cent of the matrimonial assets because of her husband's special contribution. However, each case depends on its own facts.

(b) *Miller v Miller*; *McFarlane v McFarlane* (2006)

In *Miller v Miller* [2006] UKHL 24 (heard with *McFarlane v McFarlane*) the House of Lords had the opportunity once again to consider 'the most intractable of problems: how to achieve fairness in the division of property following a divorce' (*per* Lord Nicholls in *Miller v Miller*). But this time it had to do so in the light of the principles it had laid down in *White v White* (see above). It also had the opportunity (in *McFarlane v McFarlane*) to consider for the first time whether the principles in *White v White* should apply to the court's power to order periodical payments.

> ▶ *Miller v Miller; McFarlane v McFarlane* [2006] UKHL 24
>
> Mr and Mrs Miller had been married for less than three years, and had no children. At the time of the marriage, the husband was an exceptionally successful businessman earning about £1 million a year, whereas the wife was earning £85,000 a year. The matrimonial home was purchased by the husband for £1.8 million and he subsequently bought a second property in their joint names in the South of France. During the marriage the husband acquired shares in a new firm which subsequently proved to be extremely valuable. The wife gave up work to concentrate on furnishing their two homes. The husband left his wife for another woman, whom he subsequently married.
>
> At first instance, Singer J ordered the husband to transfer the matrimonial home to his wife and pay her a lump sum of £2.7 million. The husband appealed to the Court of Appeal, which held, dismissing his appeal, that Singer J had been entitled to take into account the husband's responsibility for the breakdown of the marriage and the wife's legitimate expectation of a higher standard of living. The husband appealed to the House of Lords.
>
> The House of Lords, dismissing the husband's appeal and applying the principles in *White v White* (see above), held, *inter alia*, that, in an application for financial relief, the redistribution of resources from one party to the other was justified on the basis of the following three principles: needs (generously interpreted) generated by the relationship between the parties; compensation for relationship-generated disadvantage; and sharing of the fruits of the matrimonial partnership. Which of these would be considered first depended on the circumstances of the case. In general it could be assumed that the marital partnership did not stay alive for the purpose of sharing future resources unless this was justified by needs and compensation. The ultimate object was to give each party an equal start on the road to independent living.
>
> The House of Lords also considered the following issues: the role of conduct and the role of special contribution in applications for financial relief; the distinction between matrimonial and non-matrimonial property; and whether periodical payment can be made to provide compensation as well as to meet financial needs (see further below).

Thus in *Miller* the House of Lords held that the following three principles must be applied by the courts when deciding how to distribute resources from one party to the other in an application for financial remedies: needs (generously interpreted); compensation; and sharing.

In the following case, the Court of Appeal considered the principles laid down by the House of Lords in *White* and *Miller*, including, in particular, special contribution and how the yardstick of equality should be applied:

▶ *Charman v Charman (No. 4)* [2007] EWCA Civ 503

The wife, who conceded that her husband had made a special contribution to the generation of matrimonial assets (worth about £131 million), sought 45 per cent of the assets but her husband offered her only £20 million. Coleridge J awarded her £48 million, representing 36.5 per cent of the assets, basing his departure from equality on both the husband's special contribution and on the greater risks inherent in the assets remaining with the husband.

The husband appealed to the Court of Appeal arguing, *inter alia*, that: insufficient allowance had been made for his special contribution; and that Coleridge J had erred by incorrectly starting with a premise of equality, instead of starting with the section 25 exercise (and then considering whether there should be a discount for his special contribution).

The Court of Appeal, led by Sir Mark Potter P, dismissed the appeal. It held, *inter alia*, that special contribution (which could include non-financial contributions) had survived *Miller v Miller; McFarlane v McFarlane* but that the bar was set very high. With respect to the *White v White* 'yardstick of equality', Sir Mark Potter P stated that, as it had developed into the 'equal sharing principle' and 'sharing entitlement', the application of the 'yardstick of equality' was no longer postponed to the end of the statutory exercise. Property should be shared equally unless there was good reason not to do so.

(i) A yardstick of equality or a principle of equal sharing?

In *White v White* the House of Lords introduced the notion of a yardstick of equality, but in *Miller v Miller* this term was referred to as 'the equal sharing principle' and to 'sharing entitlement'. In *White v White* the House of Lords held that a judge must conduct the section 25 exercise and then test their tentative view against the yardstick of equality; but in *Miller v Miller* the House of Lords appeared to adopt an approach whereby the starting point was equality of sharing rather than equality being a yardstick for testing a tentative calculation. In other words, *Miller v Miller* seemed to create a presumption of equal sharing and this was the approach adopted by Sir Mark Potter P in *Charman v Charman (No. 4)* (above). Thus, the approaches to equality in *White v White* and *Miller v Miller* appeared to be quite different; and to have the potential to produce quite different results.

In cases after *Charman (No. 4)* (above) the approach of the courts was that the *Miller v Miller* sharing principle should be determined first and the outcome checked against the parties' needs. In other words, property should be shared equally unless there was good reason to the contrary. However, in *B v B (Ancillary Relief)* [2008] 2 FLR 1627, in which Hughes and Wall LJ gave the leading judgments, and with whom Sir Mark Potter P concurred, the Court of Appeal indicated that the yardstick of equal division was *not* a sharing principle, but a tool to be used as a check at the *end* of the section 25 exercise, rather than as a principle of sharing operating within the section 25 discretionary exercise. These fine and difficult distinctions (as to whether equal sharing is a yardstick or a presumption) have muddied, rather than clarified, the law; and, as a result, they have made it more difficult for lawyers to advise their clients. Furthermore, reaction to the needs, sharing and compensation 'formula' has not been positive (see further below). As a result, there have been calls for reform of the law (see 7.14 below).

(c) How the court conducts the discretionary exercise after *White v White* and *Miller v Miller*

After the decisions of the House of Lords in *White v White* and *Miller v Miller* (see above), the court, in an application for financial remedies, must not only conduct the section 25 exercise, but must also exercise its discretion by taking into account the principle of fairness without discrimination (laid down in *White v White*) and the 'strands' of needs (generously construed), compensation and sharing (laid down in *Miller v Miller*). It must then, it seems, test its tentative conclusions against the yardstick of equality (laid down in *White v White*).

The trend in the case-law following *White v White* and *Miller v Miller* has been to emphasise the wide discretion of the court and its duty to apply the section 25 factors in order to achieve a fair result. The following propositions can be extracted from the case-law following *White v White* and *Miller v Milller*:

▶ **The section 25 factors prevail** The courts post-*Miller v Miller* have been keen to emphasise that the three 'strands' (of needs, compensation and sharing) have not supplanted the requirement that courts must apply the section 25 factors (see 7.4 above). Thus, for example, in *H v H* [2008] 2 FLR 2092 Moylan J said that the pivotal factor in every application for financial remedies is to ensure that the order is fair and for all the relevant factors in section 25 to be considered. Only afterwards would there be a consideration of needs, compensation and sharing, if these are relevant at all to the facts of the case.

▶ **Special contribution** This can be taken into account as a reason for departing from equality but only in exceptional circumstances, as otherwise the principles of fairness and non-discrimination may be jeopardised. In *Miller v Miller* the House of Lords approved the words of Thorpe LJ in *Lambert* (see above), who had acknowledged that special contribution remains a legitimate possibility but only in exceptional circumstances. In *Miller v Miller* the House of Lords stated that the question of contribution should be approached in much the same way as conduct. In other words, it should be regarded as a factor leading to a departure from equality of division only in wholly exceptional cases when it would be inequitable to disregard it (see, for example, *Cooper-Hohn v Hohn* [2014] EWHC 4122 (Fam)). In *Charman v Charman (No. 4)* (see above) Sir Mark Potter P said that special contribution includes both financial and non-financial contribution. However, the case-law suggests that financial contributions are far more likely to be regarded as a special contribution than non-financial contributions, such as, for example, contributions to the home.

▶ **The courts should adopt a flexible, not formulaic, approach** The courts have emphasised that a flexible, not formulaic, approach should be adopted in a financial remedy application in order to do what is fair in the circumstances (see, for example, *C v C* [2009] 1 FLR 8).

▶ **The three strands of needs, sharing and compensation are not to be elevated into separate 'heads of claim'** In *CR v CR* [2008] 1 FLR 323 Bodey J said that it was important that the three 'strands' should not become elevated into separate 'heads of claim' or 'loss' independent of the Matrimonial Causes Act 1973, for, if such an approach were to gain momentum, then there would be a real danger of double-counting, which the House of Lords in *Miller v Miller* had warned against. In *P v RP* [2007] 1 FLR 2105 Coleridge J warned against the introduction of an approach which separated out and quantified the element of compensation, rather than treating it as one of the strands in the overall requirement of fairness. Coleridge J's warning was endorsed by Sir Mark Potter P in *VB v JP* [2008] 1 FLR 742.

▶ *What constitutes matrimonial property and valuations of matrimonial property must be viewed broadly*   In *CR v CR* [2008] 1 FLR 323 Bodey J held that, although matrimonial property must now, post-*Miller v Miller*, be identified, the court must strive to take as broad a view as possible of what constitutes matrimonial property. In *H v H* [2008] 2 FLR 2092 Moylan J said that, in approaching valuation issues in respect of matrimonial property, the court must avoid overly artificial constructs of marital and non-marital property which could lead to an unduly formulaic approach. The valuation exercise was an art, not a science. The court was not engaged in a detailed accounting exercise, but in a broad analysis in the exercise of its jurisdiction under the Act. The purpose of valuations was to assist the court in testing the fairness of the proposed outcome, not to ensure mathematical/accounting accuracy.

▶ *Compensation may not always be a factor to be considered*   Whereas in *Miller v Miller; McFarlane v McFarlane* the House of Lords described Mrs McFarlane's case as a 'paradigm case' for an award of compensation, in many cases compensation is unlikely to be a relevant factor. In fact, it may not even be relevant in a 'big-money' case (see, for example, *McCartney v Mills McCartney* below).

▶ *Sharing yields to a consideration of need where the pool of assets is limited and there are children of the family whose welfare is the court's first consideration* (as Lord Nicholls in *White v White* made clear).

▶ *Sometimes only one of the three strands in* **Miller** *may apply*   For example in *McCartney v Mills McCartney* [2008] 1 FLR 1508 Bennett J held that needs (generously interpreted), not compensation and sharing, was the only relevant strand that applied in the circumstances of the case. Bennett J held that the compensation principle was not in any way engaged (as the wife had exaggerated her case), and neither was the sharing principle (as the marriage had been short and the husband's wealth had been accumulated before they had met).

▶ *Where the assets available for distribution exceed those required to meet the parties' needs*, a party can persuade the court to depart from ordering equal division by arguing: that a special contribution justifies a departure from equality; that the relevant property is 'non-matrimonial' property (see below) and is not therefore subject to the presumption of equal shares; and/or that a term in a marital agreement about property is binding (see 7.9 below).

(d)   Matrimonial and non-matrimonial property and short and long marriages

In exercising their discretion in an application for financial remedies, the courts may sometimes be required (usually in 'big-money' cases) to consider whether to ring-fence certain assets from the pool of assets and treat them as non-matrimonial assets. The law is complex and confusing and it is debatable whether the attempt by the courts to find principles to help in categorising property as 'matrimonial' and 'non-matrimonial' has done anything to help in practice. Depending on the facts of the case, property acquired before marriage, and inheritances and gifts received during marriage, may not be shared between the parties by the court. The length of the marriage will be an important factor when deciding whether assets have become or are matrimonial assets. In *Miller v Miller*, however, there were conflicting opinions about matrimonial and non-matrimonial property. Because of the uncertainty about how the courts should treat non-matrimonial property, this was one of the issues considered as part of the Law Commission's project on 'Matrimonial Property, Needs and Agreements' (see 7.14 below).

Whether property brought into the marriage will be treated as matrimonial or non-matrimonial for the purpose of financial remedy proceedings depends on all the circumstances of each case. In *C v C* [2009] 1 FLR 8, for example, the husband, a property developer, argued that the wife's entitlement should be limited to her needs (generously construed), on the basis that a large proportion, if not most, of his fortune had been acquired prior to their marriage (of 17 years, preceded by approximately four years' cohabitation). His wife, on the other hand, who sought half the assets (valued at £22 million), argued that the bulk of those assets had been built up during their relationship. Moylan J, who awarded the wife 40 per cent of the assets, held, *inter alia*, that the substantial wealth of the husband prior to the commencement of the parties' relationship justified a departure from equality.

In the following case, Mostyn J stated how the court should deal with the question of pre-marital property in financial proceedings on divorce.

▶ *N v F (Financial Orders: Pre-Acquired Wealth)* [2011] EWHC 586 (Fam)

The parties had been married for 16 years and had two children. At the time of the marriage the husband had assets of £21 million. As the husband had left his job as a high-earning banker and taken a job as a schoolteacher, the family had lived off capital. The total assets, at the time of the proceedings, were worth £9.7 million. Mostyn J, awarding the wife 44.7 per cent of the total assets and making orders for child maintenance, made the following statements about pre-marital property:

▶ Although the treatment of pre-marital property is highly fact-specific and very discretionary, the court's discretion must be exercised consistently and predictably.
▶ The longer the marriage, the easier it was to say, by virtue of the mingling of pre-marital property with the product of the parties' marital endeavours, that the supplier of that property had in effect agreed to share it with their spouse.
▶ If the court had decided that the existence of pre-marital property should be reflected in an order, the correct approach was to identify the scale of the non-matrimonial property to be excluded, leaving the matrimonial property alone to be divided in accordance with the equal sharing principle (see *Jones v Jones* [2011] EWCA Civ 41).
▶ However, this process was subject to the question of need, the assessment of which could be affected by factors other than the scale of available resources and the marital standard of living.

Even where the marriage is of long duration, the court must consider the source of the assets. Thus, although Baroness Hale in *Miller v Miller* had said that the 'importance of the source of the assets will diminish over time', in *Vaughan v Vaughan* [2008] 1 FLR 1108 Wilson LJ held that, despite the long marriage (of nearly 20 years), the judge in the lower court had not properly taken into account the fact that the husband had bought the matrimonial home in his sole name (free of mortgage) three years prior to the marriage.

(i) Inherited assets

There are many reported cases on how inherited wealth should be dealt with by the courts in an application for financial remedies. In *White v White* (see above), Lord Nicholls stated that inherited assets stood on a different footing from other assets acquired during marriage, and that fairness generally required that a spouse should be allowed to keep inherited property, unless the other party's financial needs could not otherwise be satisfied. However, whether inherited assets form part of the matrimonial assets to be divided on divorce depends on the circumstances of the case (as was reiterated by the Court of Appeal in *Robson v Robson* [2011] 1 FLR 751). The needs of the parties and the length of the marriage are particularly important.

In some cases, inherited property may count for little, but in others it may be of the greatest significance. For example, in *H v H (Financial Provision: Special Contribution)* [2002] 2 FLR 1021 inherited assets were quarantined from the pool of assets to be divided, but in *Norris v Norris* [2003] 1 FLR 1142 they were taken into account as being part of the pool of assets. The length of the marriage may be important as it was, for example, in *S v S* [2007] EWHC 1975 (Fam) where the wife's inherited assets were treated as part of the pool of assets as they had become amalgamated with other assets during the 20-year marriage.

Fairness may require that different types of inheritance be treated differently. For example, in *P v P (Inherited Property)* [2005] 1 FLR 576 Munby J held that the bulk of the matrimonial assets (a farm which had been in the husband's family for generations) should, in the circumstances of the case, be treated differently from a case involving a pecuniary inheritance.

The possibility of a party to the marriage receiving an inheritance in the future may be taken into account, but whether it will have a material effect on how the court exercises its distributive powers depends on the facts of the case. For example, in *J v J (Financial Orders: Wife's Long-term Needs)* [2011] EWHC 1010 (Fam) the possibility of the husband receiving an inheritance from his parents was taken into account but had no material effect on how the court exercised its distributive powers, due in part to the age of his parents and to the court's assessment of the parties' needs.

The following case, which went to the Court of Appeal, involved inherited assets, and provides a useful exposition of the law.

▶ *K v L (Non-Matrimonial Property: Special Contribution)* [2011]
EWCA Civ 550

After a 21-year relationship, the husband and wife separated. They had three children.
The wife was very wealthy, as, about 13 years before she had started cohabiting with the
husband, she had inherited shares from her grandfather which, at the date of separation,
were worth about £28 million, but which by the date of the trial (three years after the
separation) were worth £57.4 million. Neither the husband nor the wife had worked
during the marriage; and they had lived extremely modestly. The husband sought an
award of £18 million, but Bodey J awarded him £5 million, plus the matrimonial home,
on the basis that this award, plus the husband's existing capital of £300,000, would meet
his needs, generously assessed. Bodey J described the wife's inherited wealth as a factor
of 'central relevance', but indicated that it was also relevant that this wealth had always
been kept separate from their other assets.

The husband appealed to the Court of Appeal, arguing, *inter alia,* that: (i) the award
discriminated against his own contribution; and (ii) Bodey J had taken insufficient account
of Baroness Hale's proposition in *Miller v Miller; McFarlane v McFarlane* [2006] UKHL 24
that 'the importance of the source of the assets will diminish over time'.

The Court of Appeal dismissed his appeal, with Wilson LJ who gave the only judgment,
holding, *inter alia,* that:

▶ It is of the essence of the judicial function to discriminate between different sets of
   facts and thus between different claims. The discrimination outlawed by *White v
   White* [2000] UKHL 54 is discrimination in the division of labour within the family,
   in particular between the party who earns the income and the party whose work
   is in the home, unpaid. Therefore, Bodey J's finding that the wife made a financial
   contribution of great importance to the marriage did not discriminate between the
   parties in any unacceptable way; on the contrary, it correctly recognised a substantive
   difference.

▶ The *dictum* of Lord Nicholls that the importance of the source of assets *may* diminish
   over time is to be preferred to that of Baroness Hale in *Miller v Miller; McFarlane v
   McFarlane* that they *will* do so. In the circumstances of the case, there was nothing to
   justify a conclusion that, as the marriage proceeded, there was a diminution in the
   importance of the sources of the parties' entire wealth, at all times ring-fenced by share
   certificates in the wife's sole name which to a large extent were just kept safely and left
   to reproduce themselves and to grow in value.

Welstead was critical of the decision in *K v L* and of the law governing financial
remedies on divorce in general, as the following extract shows.

▶ Welstead, 'The sharing of pre-matrimonial property on divorce: *K v L*' [2012] Fam
Law 185, at 189

The law relating to ancillary relief oscillates in a schizophrenic manner as attempts
are made by the judiciary to find overriding principles, such as the tripartite ones
put forward in *Miller v McFarlane,* to guide them through the discretionary morass
of section 25 of the Matrimonial Causes Act 1925. No sooner than new principles are
articulated are they followed by decisions which erode them or expand them depending
on the viewpoint of the judiciary. *K v L* is yet one more example of such erosion. Its
restrictive approach is unlikely to lead to fairer or more certain financial awards. It has,
rather, added to the complexities of the law relating to ancillary relief.

(For other cases where the courts have had to deal with the distinction between matrimonial and non-matrimonial property, see *AR v AR (Treatment of Inherited Wealth)* [2011] EWHC 2717 (Fam) and *JL v SL* [2015] EWHC 360 (Fam)).

(e) Big-money cases and periodical payments

Although *White v White* [2000] UKHL 54 involved a lump sum, the House of Lords held in the *McFarlane* appeal in *Miller v Miller; McFarlane v McFarlane* [2006] UKHL 24 that the overriding objective of fairness laid down in *White v White* could also apply to periodical payments in an exceptional case. In *McFarlane* the facts were exceptional as there was a huge surplus of available income after the needs of the parties had been met.

> ▶ *Miller v Miller; McFarlane v McFarlane* **[2006] UKHL 24**
>
> Mr and Mrs McFarlane had been married for 16 years. They were both qualified professionals and, until shortly before the birth of their second child, earned similar sums of money. The wife gave up her highly paid career to care for the family, while the husband continued his professional career, with his annual salary increasing considerably from year to year (and which stood at £750,000 per annum by the time of the hearing). The family had insufficient capital available to achieve a clean break, but the husband earned substantially more than would be needed to meet his own and the wife's budgeted household expenditure. The district judge made a periodical payments order of £250,000 per year (on the basis that fairness required the wife to have a share of her husband's future earnings). This was reduced to £180,000 by the High Court; but the Court of Appeal allowed the wife's appeal in part, restoring the award to £250,000, but limiting the term to five years. The Court of Appeal held that in exceptional cases, and on the basis of term rather than joint lives orders, periodical payments could be used to accumulate capital. The wife appealed.
>
> The House of Lords held, upholding the £250,000 award, but removing the five-year term, that a periodical payments order could be made to afford compensation as well as to meet financial needs. However, a clean break was not to be achieved at the expense of a fair result. Thus, if a claimant was owed compensation and capital assets were not available, the social desirability of a clean break would not be sufficient reason for depriving a claimant of that compensation. There was no reason to limit periodical payments to a fixed term in the interests solely of achieving a clean break.
>
> The House held that the case was a paradigm case for an award of compensation in respect of the significant future economic disparity sustained by the wife, arising from the way the parties had conducted their marriage.
>
> **Note:** After a change of circumstances (Mr McFarlane's earnings had risen to over £1 million per annum), Mrs McFarlane obtained (in variation proceedings) a 40 per cent increase in periodical payments for herself and the three children (see *McFarlane v McFarlane* [2009] EWHC 891 (Fam)).

Cooke ([2004] Fam Law 906) was critical of the decision in *McFarlane* for extending the principles in *White v White* to income, as it perpetuated 'dependency and perhaps animosity'. In *SS v NS* [2014] EWHC 4183 (Fam), Mostyn J expressed his view that a spousal maintenance award should be made only by reference to needs, save in exceptional circumstances where the sharing or compensation principle applies.

7.7 The family home on divorce

The future of the family home on divorce is important, not just because of its financial value, but because it provides accommodation for the family. As Lord Nicholls said in *Miller v Miller; McFarlane v McFarlane* (see 7.6 above), the matrimonial home 'usually has a central place in any marriage'. The provision of accommodation is usually a primary consideration for the court when deciding how to distribute matrimonial assets. The provision of a home for any children is a particularly important consideration. As Thorpe LJ said in *M v B* [1998] 1 FLR 53: '[I]t is one of the paramount considerations, in applying the section 25 criteria, to endeavour to stretch what is available to cover the need of each for a home, particularly where there are young children involved.' Thus, the housing needs of both parties and any relevant children are taken into account, but the eventual outcome depends on the facts of the particular case.

When deciding what should happen to the home on divorce, the court has various options available. It might, for example, order one spouse to transfer the house, or their share of the house, to the other spouse with or without the other spouse making any compensating payment. It might order a transfer but make it subject to a charge in favour of the transferor, representing the value of the transferor's interest in the home which will be realised on sale at a later date. The house might be transferred for the purpose of effecting a clean break (for example by being transferred to the wife with her forbearing to claim periodical payments).

(a) A Mesher order

This is an order made under section 24(1)(b) of the Matrimonial Causes Act 1973 (MCA 1973) whereby the house is settled on trust for one or both of the spouses in certain shares, but with sale postponed until a future event (such as until the children have reached a particular age or have finished full-time education, or until the death, remarriage or cohabitation of the other spouse). *Mesher* orders were once popular with the courts, but they have become less popular because of their disadvantages. One disadvantage is that a spouse may have insufficient funds from the eventual proceeds of sale to rehouse themselves, particularly if there is a fall in house prices. Another disadvantage is that children may continue to need accommodation after the event triggering sale has occurred and even when they have reached majority. It is possible, however, for the court to take this into account, as it did in *Sawden v Sawden* [2004] EWCA Civ 339, where the Court of Appeal inserted another condition into the *Mesher* order so that the children could remain indefinitely in the home, if they wished, without their father enforcing sale and claiming his 45 per cent of the proceeds of sale. Another disadvantage of *Mesher* orders is that they are contrary to the clean break, as, until sale, the parties are tied together as joint owners, thereby restricting their chances of financial self-sufficiency.

Despite the above disadvantages, the Court of Appeal in *Clutton v Clutton* [1991] 1 WLR 359 said that a *Mesher* order might be appropriate where the family assets were sufficient to provide both parties with a roof over their heads if the matrimonial home were sold at a later date, but where the interest of the parties required the children to stay in the matrimonial home. However, Lloyd LJ stressed that, where there were any doubts about a wife's eventual ability to rehouse herself, then a *Mesher* order should not be made. The Court of Appeal held that a *Martin* order (see below) did not suffer from the same disadvantage. In *B v B (Mesher Order)* [2003] 2 FLR 285 a *Mesher* order was held not to be appropriate because of the wife's inability to generate capital at the date of the suggested *Mesher* triggering event and because it would impose a significant financial burden on her.

(b)   A Martin order

This order is similar to a *Mesher* order, except that it gives a spouse a right to occupy the house until their death, remarriage or cohabitation, after which the proceeds of sale are divided in certain shares. It therefore provides a more secure solution for the occupying spouse and any children than a *Mesher* order.

(c)   An order for sale

Under section 24A of the MCA 1973 the court can order that the matrimonial home be sold, but this power can be exercised only ancillary to the court's power to make a financial provision or property adjustment order. Thus, for example, the court could order sale of the home so that one of the parties receives a lump sum from the proceeds of sale.

   If the house is in joint names, the signatures of both parties are required for sale. However, if it is in the name of one spouse, and there is a danger that the sole owner may sell it before the divorce court has exercised its powers, the non-owner spouse should register their 'home rights' (see 4.2). If the property is sold to defeat an application for financial remedies, an application can be made under section 37 of the MCA 1973 to have the transaction set aside (see 7.11 below).

(d)   Tenancies of the home

Section 53 and Schedule 7 to Part IV of the Family Law Act 1996 make provision for the transfer of tenancies on divorce (see 4.10). A tenancy can also be transferred under section 24 of the MCA 1973.

7.8   Pensions on divorce

A pension is a valuable asset and its loss on divorce can be substantial. Although pension entitlement is something which the divorce courts have always been able to take into account as part of the section 25 discretionary exercise (see 7.4 above), amendments to the Matrimonial Causes Act 1973 (MCA 1973) have over the years improved the pension position for people who are divorcing. The following options are available in respect of pension entitlement on divorce: (a) 'off-setting'; (b) a pension attachment order; (c) a pension sharing order; and (d) pension compensation orders. The law on pensions, including pensions on divorce, is complex. Only an outline is given here.

(a) 'Off-setting'

To compensate for lost or reduced pension entitlement, the court in the exercise of its section 25 discretionary powers has the power to make compensatory adjustments in respect of the division of matrimonial assets other than the pension. In this way, rights under a pension scheme are left untouched but their value is taken into account by giving a party an appropriately enlarged share of the other party's assets. Off-setting may be useful where pension assets are inaccessible (for example where they are held outside the jurisdiction). Off-setting can be used, however, only if there are sufficient assets available to compensate for the loss of pension entitlement. If this is not the case then the other options below have to be considered. Off-setting has the advantage of creating a clean break between the parties, as there is no need for the parties to have contact with each other in the future.

(b) Pension attachment orders ('earmarking')

Pension attachment orders can be made under sections 25B–25D of the MCA 1973. Pension attachment involves a pension being 'earmarked' for the other party. If an order is made, then, once the pension becomes payable, the person responsible for the pension arrangement (the trustee or managers of the fund) must pay part of the pension income and/or a lump sum available under the pension arrangement to the other party to the marriage (s 25B(4)). Although the main advantage of a pension attachment order is that the payment is more likely to represent the actual value of the pension once it becomes payable, they have disadvantages. Thus, they undermine the policy of the clean break (as the parties remain financially tied to each other, and either party may apply for variation). It may be difficult for the court to force the pension holder to continue to make payments to the pension fund or to retire by a specified age; and it may be difficult for the court to predict the value of the pension and the needs of the parties at the point in time when the pension becomes payable. Because of these disadvantages, and others, pension sharing orders provide a better solution.

(c) Pension sharing orders

These orders were introduced in 2000 and are much more common than pension attachment orders. A pension sharing order is an order which enables pension benefits to be irrevocably split at the time of divorce, forming two separate pensions, so that one can be allocated to the other spouse to invest as they think appropriate. The pension sharing order specifies the percentage value to be transferred (s 21A(1)). An order can be made in respect of a pension which is already being paid. The provisions do not apply to the basic State retirement pension. The section 25 guidelines apply when the court is deciding whether to make a pension sharing order and, if so, in what manner.

Pension sharing has the following advantages over off-setting and pension attachment: a clean break can be effected because the pension fund is split at the time of divorce; the order allows the pension assets to be kept separate from other assets on divorce; and it avoids the problems involved in off-setting assets fairly in order to compensate for loss of a pension.

(d) Pension compensation orders

New sections were inserted into the MCA 1973 by the Pensions Act 2008 to enable Pension Protection Fund (PPF) compensation to be shared or attached in the same way as a pension can be shared or attached.

(e) The exercise of discretion in respect of a pension

The court's powers in respect of pension arrangements are governed by the section 25 factors (see 7.4 above) and the principles laid down in *White v White* and *Miller v Miller* (see 7.6 above). Section 25B(1) expressly requires the court when conducting its section 25(2) exercise to have regard to: any benefits under a pension arrangement which a party to the marriage has or is likely to have; and any benefits under a pension arrangement which, by reason of the divorce (or annulment), a party to the marriage will lose the chance of acquiring. When considering any benefits under a pension arrangement, there is no requirement that the courts take into consideration only those benefits which will be available in the foreseeable future (s 25B(1)). A pension can also be taken into account under section 25(2)(a) as a 'financial resource' which a party has or is likely to have in the future.

7.9 Agreements about property and finance

Divorcing couples are encouraged to reach agreement about legal issues arising on divorce whether they be in respect of property, finance or children. It is better to reach an amicable agreement rather than to engage in costly, unpredictable and emotionally stressful litigation. Many couples reach agreement of their own accord, but others may do so with the assistance of lawyers and/or mediators (see 1.5).

Couples can also enter into more formal written agreements about finance and property with each other; and they may do this before and during marriage, and on marriage breakdown. However, such agreements are not automatically binding, because the divorce court retains a supervisory jurisdiction in respect of such agreements.

The following agreements are considered in this section: (a) consent orders; (b) separation agreements; and (c) pre- and post-nuptial agreements. There has been discussion about reforming the law relating to nuptial agreements (see 7.14 below).

(a) Consent orders

An agreement about finance and property on divorce can be incorporated into a consent order, which the court has jurisdiction to make under section 33A of the Matrimonial Causes Act 1973 (MCA 1973). A consent order can contain only those orders which the court has power to make under Part II of the MCA 1973. In order to enable the court to exercise its discretion to make a consent order, the parties must provide the court with prescribed information. Failure to do so may result in the order being set aside (see below). Although consent orders are based on an agreement, the general principles of contract law do not determine the outcome of a case. Instead, it is the consent order itself which determines the rights and duties of the parties.

When considering whether to make a consent order, the court does not just 'rubber-stamp' the proposed agreement. It considers all the circumstances and applies the section 25 factors, the clean-break provisions and the approaches laid down in the case-law. However, the court will usually approve the agreement, as the fact that it has been drawn up and agreed to by the parties, usually with legal advice, is *prima facie* proof of its reasonableness. The terms of a consent order can be varied in variation proceedings, but only in respect of certain orders, such as orders for periodical payments (see below). Consent orders may be set aside in some circumstances, for example if there has been non-disclosure.

(b) Separation agreements

A separation agreement is an agreement made in contemplation of imminent separation, or following separation, which seeks to make financial arrangements for the period of separation and any subsequent divorce. It can be made before or after financial remedy proceedings have been commenced, and it can be made with or without legal advice. The law relating to separation agreements is distinct from that relating to pre- and post-nuptial agreements (see below). The reason for this is that, whereas pre-nuptial and post-nuptial agreements have historically been treated as immoral (as they made provision for future separation and divorce) and were therefore void, separation agreements were treated with much less suspicion because they catered for the situation where the relationship had already run its course.

Sections 34–36 of the MCA 1973 govern separation agreements. Such agreements are not automatically binding, because the divorce court retains a supervisory role with regard to such agreements. Thus, the court has power under section 35(2) to vary, revoke or insert new terms into an agreement if the terms of the agreement (or omission of terms) do not allow for a change of circumstances; or where there is no provision in the agreement for proper financial arrangements with respect to any child of the family. Any provision in an agreement restricting the right of either party to apply to the court for financial remedies is void (s 34(1)).

A separation agreement does not give rise to an enforceable legal contract (see Thorpe LJ in *Xydhias v Xydhias* [1999] 1 FLR 683), with the result that the agreement cannot exclude, or oust, the jurisdiction of the court in financial remedy proceedings; and either spouse can ask the court to ignore some, or all, of the terms in the agreement and make a different order.

Private agreements have the advantages of promoting amicable settlement and avoiding the uncertainty and cost of litigation. For these reasons, in the following case of *Edgar v Edgar (1981) 2 FLR 19* the Court of Appeal held that a formal separation agreement, entered into with competent legal advice, should generally be upheld by the court unless there are good and substantial grounds for concluding that an injustice will be done by holding the parties to the terms of their agreement.

> ▶ *Edgar v Edgar* (1981) 2 FLR 19
>
> The parties entered into a separation agreement in which the husband, a multi-millionaire, agreed to pay his wife a lump sum of £100,000 and in which she agreed to seek no further provision. The wife entered into the agreement despite her solicitor's advice that she would obtain a better settlement in divorce proceedings. Later in ancillary relief (financial remedy) proceedings on divorce she was granted a lump sum of £760,000. The husband appealed to the Court of Appeal.
>
> The Court of Appeal held, allowing his appeal and setting the order aside, that the wife was bound by the terms of the original agreement. There was no evidence that she had been exploited. She had received legal advice and there had been no adverse conduct by her husband during negotiations leading up to the agreement. A large disparity between the sum agreed and the sum that she might have been awarded in divorce proceedings was insufficient on its own for the court to ignore the agreement. The court acknowledged that it had a duty to exercise its discretionary powers under section 25, but Ormrod LJ held that it was an important general principle that 'formal agreements, properly and faithfully arrived at with competent legal advice' should not be displaced unless there are 'good and substantial grounds' for concluding that an injustice would be done by holding the parties to the terms of their agreement. Ormrod LJ said that 'good and substantial grounds' included whether there was pressure from one side, exploitation of a dominant position, inadequate knowledge, bad legal advice or an unforeseen change of circumstances. His Lordship said that 'the existence of a freely negotiated bargain entered into at the instance of one of the parties and affording him or her everything for which he or she has stipulated must be a most important element of conduct which cannot lightly be ignored'.

Baroness Hale in *MacLeod* (see further below) explicitly endorsed Ormrod LJ's analysis above, stating that, although the courts 'must be alive to the risk of unfair exploitation of superior strength', 'the fact that the agreement is not what a court would have done cannot be enough to have it set aside'.

Edgar v Edgar therefore emphasised the important policy objective of achieving finality, and the undesirability of opening up arrangements which have already been settled by the parties. The approach in *Edgar v Edgar* is still followed, with the result that a spouse will not be permitted to resile from an agreement without good reason. Thus, for example, in *G v G (Financial Provision: Separation Agreement)* [2004] 1 FLR 1011 an agreement was upheld, even though it had been drawn up without legal advice and at a time when emotional pressures were high and judgement was likely to be clouded, as both parties had had previous experience of marital breakdown and had from the outset of their marriage elected to regulate their affairs contractually.

(c) Pre- and post-nuptial agreements

A pre-nuptial agreement (sometimes referred to as an ante-nuptial agreement) is an agreement made before marriage which seeks to regulate the couple's financial affairs during their marriage or to determine the division of their property in the event of divorce or separation. A post-nuptial agreement is a similar agreement but one made during marriage. Historically, the law treated such agreements with suspicion and considered them to be immoral, as spouses had a duty to live together and marriages could not be terminated by divorce, except in restricted circumstances. Thus, the rule (laid down in *Hyman v Hyman* [1929] AC 601) was that any agreement made in contemplation of marital breakdown was contrary to public policy. For this reason, agreements which made arrangements about provision for future separation and divorce were held to be void and could not be enforced as a valid contract. Separation agreements, on the other hand, were treated differently (see above).

Although pre- and post-nuptial agreements were considered to be contrary to public policy, they could be taken into account by the divorce court as one of the circumstances of the case when it was conducting the section 25 exercise (see 7.4 above). However, until relatively recently, the courts accorded little weight to such agreements. In 1995, for example, Thorpe J stated in *F v F (Ancillary Relief: Substantial Assets)* [1995] 2 FLR 45 (where the husband had sought to rely on pre-nuptial contracts drawn up in Germany) that such agreements were of 'very limited significance' in England and Wales. As a result, Thorpe J refused to attach any significant weight to the German contracts, even though they might be strictly enforced against the wife in Germany.

However, although the courts would often refuse to recognise pre-nuptial agreements, they showed a greater willingness to accept and recognise post-nuptial agreements as they were considered to be more like separation agreements which were not contrary to public policy (see above). In fact, there were two strands of case-law depending on whether the agreement was pre-nuptial or post-nuptial, as the two types of agreement were considered to be conceptually distinct (see Baroness Hale in *MacLeod* below). However, this distinction was eroded by the majority of the Supreme Court in *Radmacher v Granatino* (see below) which held that there is no conceptual difference between pre-nuptial and post-nuptial agreements.

In recent years there has been a change of attitude and the benefits of such agreements have been increasingly recognised as an important part of the settlement culture, particularly as they are often entered into and upheld in other European jurisdictions. The Law Commission has also recommended that nuptial agreements should be enforceable, in certain circumstances (see 7.9(d) below).

The law in this area has developed rapidly in a series of cases. A key case was *MacLeod v MacLeod* [2008] UKPC 64 where the Judicial Committee of the Privy Council (with Baroness Hale giving the leading opinion) held that post-nuptial (not pre-nuptial agreements) were no longer void. However, the Privy Council (affirming *Edgar v Edgar* above) nonetheless held that it was still open to the divorce court to set aside any agreement which was unfairly entered into or which failed to make sufficient provision generally or where there had been a change of circumstances. The case involved an appeal from the Isle of Man, but, because the Manx legislation governing matrimonial law has its equivalent in the MCA 1973, the decision was also relevant to the law in England and Wales. The Privy Council, with Baroness Hale giving the leading opinion, held that the post-nuptial agreement entered into by the husband and wife was, on the facts of the case, a valid and enforceable agreement. Baroness Hale stated:

> Post-nuptial agreements ... are very different from pre-nuptial agreements. The couple are now married. They have undertaken towards one another the obligations and responsibilities of the married state .... There is nothing to stop a couple entering into contractual financial arrangements ... as this couple did as part of their 2002 agreement.

Following *MacLeod v MacLeod*, and its rejection of the *Hyman v Hyman* (see above) rule of public policy, it became more likely that *post*-marital agreements would be upheld by the courts. Thus, for example, in *S v S (Ancillary Relief)* [2009] 1 FLR 254 Eleanor King J relied on a post-marital agreement as compelling evidence that a concluded agreement had been reached between the parties and should be upheld.

However, it is the Supreme Court's decision in the landmark case of *Radmacher v Granatino* (see below) which represents the most authoritative statement of the current law on both pre-nuptial and post-nuptial agreements. The majority in *Radmacher* swept away the distinction between pre-nuptial and post-nuptial agreements established in *MacLeod v MacLeod*, holding that neither form of marital agreement was contrary to public policy *per se* and that the courts should apply the same principles to both. Thus, the rule in *Edgar v Edgar* (see above) and *MacLeod v MacLeod* (see above) on post-nuptial agreements now applies equally to pre-nuptial agreements. In *Radmacher*, Baroness Hale, who had held in *MacLeod v MacLeod* that there was a clear distinction between pre- and post-nuptial agreements, found herself dissenting with the majority in *Radmacher* which held that there was no distinction between the two types of agreement.

▶ *Radmacher (Formerly Granatino) v Granatino* [2010] **UKSC 42**

The wife (a German heiress said to be worth in excess of £100 million) and her French husband married in London in 1998 and had two children. Three months before the marriage they entered into a pre-nuptial contract which was signed in Germany in front of a notary in compliance with the legal requirements and formalities under German law, the terms of which stipulated that the effects of the marriage should be governed by German law and the matrimonial regime of a separation of property, and that in the case of the marriage ending by divorce or death neither party should have a claim against the separate property of the other. The parties divorced in England in 2007 and the husband applied for financial remedies, basing his claim on needs, not compensation and sharing. The wife argued that the pre-nuptial contract was binding.

Baron J refused to recognise and enforce the pre-nuptial contract as it 'fell foul' of a number of safeguards, including the fact that the husband had received no independent legal advice, there had been no disclosure by the wife and there was no provision for the two children of the marriage. But as the contract would have been binding in their respective home countries (Germany and France), Baron J held that it would not be right to ignore it and, in assessing the husband's needs, awarded him a lump sum of £5.56 million with a further £504,000 to provide a home for him in Germany to have contact with the children (to revert to the wife when the children completed their education) and periodical payments for the children of £70,000 per annum. The wife appealed to the Court of Appeal.

The Court of Appeal (with Thorpe LJ giving the leading judgment) allowed the wife's appeal as far as the financial provision for him as a husband was concerned, but not as a father. Thus, the Court of Appeal accepted that he needed £2.5 million to buy a home in England but held that it should revert to the wife when the father's parenting duties had ended. The court also reduced his capitalised maintenance. The court held that, although Baron J had correctly held that pre-nuptial settlements were not binding *per se*, but were a factor to be taken into account, she had not taken into account certain factors, including, *inter alia*, that: the contract was standard practice and would have been binding in the parties' home countries; and the husband had chosen not to seek independent legal advice. There was no good reason not to hold the husband to the agreement. The husband appealed to the Supreme Court.

The Supreme Court (with Lord Phillips giving the leading opinion) dismissed the husband's appeal and upheld the decision of the Court of Appeal by a majority of eight to one (with Baroness Hale dissenting). It held that:

1. The rule that it is the court, not any prior agreement between the parties that determines what will happen to the parties' financial arrangements upon divorce, still prevails. Thus, the court is not obliged to give effect to a pre- or post-nuptial agreement, but must decide how much weight to accord such an agreement, and decide whether it is fair or just to depart from it.
2. In relation to the argument that agreements providing for future separation are no longer contrary to public policy, no distinction should be drawn between pre- and post-nuptial agreements. The Privy Council was wrong in *MacLeod v MacLeod* (see above) to hold that a post-nuptial agreement is a contract but that an ante-nuptial agreement is not. Regardless of whether one or both are contracts, the court should apply the same principles when considering ante-nuptial agreements as apply to post-nuptial agreements.
3. The rebuttable presumption that courts should give effect to post-nuptial agreements (see *Edgar v Edgar and MacLeod v MacLeod*, above) now applies equally to pre-nuptial agreements. Thus, the court should give effect to any nuptial agreement that was freely entered into by each party with a full appreciation of its implications unless in the circumstances of the case it would not be fair to hold the parties to their agreement.
4. If a pre- or post-nuptial agreement is to carry full weight, both parties must enter into it of their own free will, without undue influence or pressure, and informed of its implications. The circumstances of the parties at the time of the agreement would be relevant. An important factor might be whether the marriage would have gone ahead without an agreement, or without the terms agreed.
5. The contents of a pre-nuptial agreement must be fair. The question of fairness will depend upon the facts of the particular case, but, by way of guidance, the factors to be considered include:

    ▶ A nuptial agreement cannot be allowed to prejudice the reasonable requirements of any children of the family.
    ▶ The court should accord respect to the decision of a married couple as to the manner in which their financial affairs should be regulated. It would be paternalistic and patronising to override their agreement simply on the basis that the court knows best.
    ▶ There is nothing inherently unfair in parties making express agreement as to the disposal of non-matrimonial property and there may be good objective justification for doing so (such as obligations towards existing family members).
    ▶ The longer the marriage has lasted, the more likely it is that the couple's circumstances would have changed over time in ways or to an extent that either could not be or simply was not envisaged, giving more scope for what happened over the years to make it unfair to hold them to the agreement.
    ▶ Of the three strands in *Miller v Miller* (needs, compensation and sharing), it is the first two (needs and compensation) which could most readily render it unfair to hold the parties to an agreement.

Applying the above principles to the facts, the Supreme Court held that the pre-nuptial agreement had not been tainted by the lack of independent legal advice, disclosure or negotiations. The needs of the husband were not a factor that rendered it unfair to hold him to the terms of the agreement, subject to making provision for the needs of the children of the family. There was no compensation factor in this case and the husband had agreed that he was not entitled to share in a portion of the wife's inherited wealth. Overall, it would be unfair to depart from the pre-nuptial agreement.

Baroness Hale dissented for the following reasons:

▶ Couples were not entirely free to determine for themselves all the legal consequences of marriage. Their mutual duty to support one another and their children was part of an irreducible minimum of matrimony.

▶ Although the law of marital agreements was a mess, it was the task of Parliament, with the help of the Law Commission, to review and reform the law, not a court hearing a particular case with very unusual features.

▶ Although the test to be applied to marital agreements proposed by *MacLeod* had been too strict, the test suggested by the majority in the present case was an impermissible gloss upon the courts' statutory duties, in that it introduced a presumption or starting point.

▶ The test to be applied to any and all marital agreements should be the same: 'Did each party freely enter into an agreement, intending it to have legal effect and with a full appreciation of its implications? If so, in the circumstances as they now are, would it be fair to hold them to their agreement?'

▶ The husband's appeal should have been allowed, because, although there was nothing in the circumstances in which the agreement had been made to make it unfair, the husband's role as father to the children was a relevant factor even after the children attained their majority, and would at the least have justified providing him with a home for life.

The principles that now govern both pre- and post-marital agreements were summarised in the following words of Lord Phillips who gave judgment for the majority in *Radmacher*.

LORD PHILLIPS: A court when considering the grant of ancillary relief is not obliged to give effect to nuptial agreements – whether they are ante-nuptial or post-nuptial. The parties cannot, by agreement, oust the jurisdiction of the court. The court must, however, give appropriate weight to the agreement.

... Under English law it is the court that is the arbiter of the financial arrangements between the parties when it brings a marriage to an end. A prior agreement between the parties is only one of the matters to which the court will have regard.

... The court should give effect to a nuptial agreement that is freely entered into by each party with a full appreciation of its implications unless in the circumstances prevailing it would not be fair to hold the parties to their agreement.

This approach is very similar to that taken by Ormrod LJ in *Edgar v Edgar* in 1981 (see above) with regard to separation agreements. Consequently, a pre- or post-marital agreement will be upheld by the court provided it was fairly entered into at the time it was made and subsequent circumstances have not rendered it unfair. Scherpe ([2011] CFLQ 513), commenting on *Radmacher*, explains that courts must apply a two-stage fairness test: 'a procedural fairness' stage which looks at the time when the agreement was made; and a 'substantive fairness' stage where the scrutiny is focused on the actual content of the agreement. Thus, the outcome of the Supreme Court's decision in *Radmacher* is that the courts are now more likely to recognise pre- and post-marital agreements provided they are fairly made, and where it is fair to uphold the agreement, applying the principles which apply to applications for financial remedies on divorce.

Some of the points made by Baroness Hale in her dissenting opinion seem to have considerable force, particularly as she was the sole family law expert who heard the case in the Supreme Court. Her view that the majority's approach constituted an 'impermissible gloss' on the courts' statutory duty in section 25 (see 7.4 above) has some strength in it. In other words, it is arguable that the majority in *Radmacher* engaged in 'judicial law-making' when the matter was one for the Law Commission and Parliament to address. Furthermore, according to Harris, George and Herring ([2011] Fam Law 367), 'the judgment seems to risk making agreements all but enforceable while by-passing the kinds of safeguards which any legislative scheme would almost certainly have included'. Harris *et al.* also argue that, while arguments based on respect for individual autonomy, which formed the policy basis for the decision of the majority, 'have an inherent attraction', it also needs to be recognised that marriage is a legally regulated status and that marriage and civil partnership, 'as social institutions, inevitably involve a degree of compromise between personal autonomy and state regulation'. As Baroness Hale stated in her dissenting opinion, 'the parties are not entirely free to determine all [the] legal consequences for themselves'.

The first reported case post-*Radmacher* was *Z v Z (No. 2) (Financial Remedies: Marriage Contract)* [2011] EWHC 2878 (Fam) where Moor J, referring to *Radmacher*, upheld the pre-nuptial agreement, but went on to make financial provision for the wife's needs. In *V v V (Prenuptial Agreement)* [2011] EWHC 3230 (Fam) the Court of Appeal held that the district judge had erred in according too little weight to a Swedish pre-nuptial agreement. However, in *Kremen v Agrest (No. 11) (Financial Remedy: Non-Disclosure: Post-Nuptial Agreement)* [2012] EWHC 45 (Fam) Mostyn J gave no weight whatsoever to a post-marital agreement made in Israel (which would have left the wife with approximately £1.5 million when the total assets were assessed at £20 to £30 million) as there had been a material absence of independent legal advice and disclosure. When assessing needs in the context of a pre-nuptial agreement, which is accorded weight by the court, the party seeking financial remedies may be limited to their 'real need' rather than their 'reasonable needs' (see *Hopkins v Hopkins* [2015] EWHC 812 (Fam)).

(i) A marital agreement made abroad

The fact that an agreement has been made abroad does not mean that it will necessarily be binding. However, as the Supreme Court stated in *Radmacher v Granatino* (see above), the fact that an agreement has been made abroad may be relevant to the important question of whether or not the parties *intended* the agreement to be binding (see also Charles J in *V v V* [2011] EWHC 3230 (Fam)).

(d) Reform to make marital agreements binding

As a result of the decision of the Supreme Court in *Radmacher v Granatino* (2010) (see above), the rule of public policy that rendered marital agreements void if they made financial provision for a future separation or divorce no longer applies, so that agreements can now be upheld provided they are procedurally and substantively fair. Thus, the court retains a supervisory jurisdiction to decide whether the terms of the agreement should be binding in the circumstances of the case. The question now is whether legislation should be introduced to make them binding.

Before the decision in *Radmacher* there had been discussion for many years about introducing legislation to make pre-marital contracts legally binding, subject to certain safeguards. For example, in its 1998 discussion paper *Supporting Families* (Home Office), the Government discussed this proposal, but it was taken no further. In 2004, Resolution recommended that the section 25 factors should be amended to give the court a duty to treat pre-marital agreements as legally binding, subject to the overriding safeguard of significant injustice to either party or to any minor child of the family (see *A More Certain Future – Recognition of Pre-Marital Agreements in England and Wales*). In July 2007 a Pre-Nuptial Agreement Bill to provide for the enforceability of pre-nuptial agreements was introduced into the House of Commons by Quentin Davies MP as a Private Member's Bill, but this was not taken forward.

(i) The Law Commission's recommendations

The Law Commission commenced a project in 2009 to examine the status and enforceability of nuptial agreements. In 2014 the Law Commission published its report *Matrimonial Property, Needs and Agreements*, Law Com No. 343, in which it recommended that nuptial agreements should be binding, in certain circumstances. Under their proposals a 'qualifying nuptial agreement' would be contractually binding and not subject to scrutiny by the courts. A qualifying nuptial agreement would be one which met the following criteria: the agreement must be contractually valid (and able to withstand challenge on the basis of undue influence or misrepresentation, for example); the agreement must have been made by deed and contain a statement signed by both parties that they understand that the agreement is a qualifying nuptial agreement that will partially remove the court's discretion to make financial orders; the agreement must not have been made within the 28 days immediately before the wedding or civil partnership; both parties must have received, at the time of the making of the agreement, disclosure of material information about the other party's financial situation; and both parties must have received legal advice at the time that the agreement was formed. However, qualifying nuptial agreements would not allow the parties to contract out of meeting the 'financial needs' of each other and of any children. The recommendations should therefore be considered in tandem with the Law Commission's findings as to the necessity for greater clarity on the meaning of 'financial needs' (see 7.14 below). The report included a draft Nuptial Agreements Bill which would introduce qualifying nuptial agreements in England and Wales.

(ii) Response to the recommendations

The Coalition Government stated in its interim response in September 2014 that, whilst it did not reject the recommendations, they should be left to the next Government to consider. A final response in relation to the draft bill is awaited. Resolution welcomed the recommendation to introduce legislation for qualifying nuptial agreements, but Jo Edwards (former Chair of Resolution) said that they 'would prefer to see change which would open up binding pre-nups to a wider group of people, with appropriate safeguards'. For further discussion of the Law Commission's proposals see Parker [2015] CFLQ 63 and Barton [2014] Fam Law 1124.

(iii) Should marital agreements be legally binding?

One of the reasons why the proposed reforms have not yet been taken forward, and why they are also limited in scope, is that they are likely to be controversial. There are arguments both for and against making nuptial agreements legally binding, some of which are as follows.

Arguments for making marital agreements legally binding

▶ It would remove some of the uncertainty and unpredictability created by the current discretionary system governing financial remedies on divorce, as the parties, not the courts, would be responsible for regulating their financial and property matters on divorce.
▶ It would reduce the need for costly, time-consuming and unpredictable litigation.
▶ It would respect the autonomy of the parties to choose how to regulate their own affairs.
▶ It would bring the law in England and Wales into line with Europe and other countries where marital agreements are binding.
▶ It would bring the law into line with the increasing emphasis on settlement and agreement in family matters.
▶ Provided that needs are catered for there is nothing inherently unfair in the parties agreeing not to share certain property in the event of separation.

Arguments against making marital agreements legally binding

▶ It may undermine the institutions of marriage and civil partnership.
▶ It may be unjust and unfair to make them legally binding, for example where unforeseen events happen in the marriage which are not catered for in the agreement (such as the birth of children, ill-health, loss of a job or receipt of a windfall).
▶ It may be unjust to make them legally binding where there was unfairness at the time when the agreement was made (such as non-disclosure, duress or mistake).
▶ The parties are unlikely to have equal bargaining power when they enter into the agreement and the financially weaker party may not be able to predict the consequences of contracting out of what they would otherwise be entitled to.
▶ The birth of children may cause problems because the parental obligation to support and maintain children cannot be terminated by agreement.
▶ It may be difficult to draft legislation to protect against injustice and unfairness; and any new legislation may itself lead to greater complexity and to litigation.
▶ Even if nuptial agreements did not allow parties to contract out of providing for financial needs, there is such little clarity about what 'needs' means that any reforms would still mean uncertainty for separating couples, leading to costly litigation.

7.10　Enforcing financial orders

Financial orders can be enforced in various ways (see Part 33 of the Family Procedure Rules 2010). The law on enforcement is complex and only an outline is given here. Due to the difficulties in this area, the Law Commission has considered the enforcement of financial orders on divorce (see 7.14 below).

(a)   Enforcing orders for payment of money

Procedures for enforcing orders for payment of money include:

- *A judgment summons*   The spouse who wishes to enforce payment of a financial order can apply for a judgment summons, which requires the other party to attend before a judge to be examined as to their means. At the hearing, the judge will make such order as they think fit in relation to the arrears or outstanding payment. There is a power to commit a spouse to prison for non-payment, in limited circumstances (see, for example, *Zuk v Zuk* [2012] EWCA Civ 1871).
- *A warrant of control (formerly warrant of execution) against goods*   This authorises an enforcement officer to seize and sell enough of the other spouse's goods to pay off the debt (excluding basic goods for domestic needs).
- *A third party debt order*   This order ring-fences funds in the debtor's bank account equivalent to the sum of money owed and directs that it is paid directly to the spouse. If there are insufficient funds in the debtor's bank account, the order will fail.
- *Appointment of receiver*   A court may appoint an individual to receive and protect rents, profits and other proceeds of property belonging to the defaulting spouse, or of a business carried on by that spouse, for the satisfaction of the debt. This is a very expensive remedy and is rarely used.
- *A charging order*   A court may issue a charge over one of the defaulting party's property assets (for example shares or a house) so that any debt owed is secured against that property. Once a court has issued a charging order, a spouse can apply for an order for sale of the property so that the property can be sold and the debt paid out of the proceeds of sale.
- *A writ of sequestration*   This is a process for dealing with contempt of court whereby the defaulting spouse's assets are seized until the order is complied with. It prevents the defaulting spouse from dealing with property until the default has been made good. It is a complex and expensive procedure and is rarely used in practice.
- *An attachment of earnings order*   This is of use only when the defaulting spouse is employed. A court can order that payments from the defaulter's earnings be paid by their employer to the collecting officer of the court.

(b)   Enforcing property adjustment orders

Property adjustment orders are most commonly made in respect of the family home. If a spouse fails to cooperate in completing the required formalities for a transfer of the home to the other spouse, an application can be made to the court for an order that, unless the transfer is completed within a specified time, then the document will be executed by a judge. In the case of a section 24A order for sale (see 7.3 above), if a spouse refuses to vacate the home, an application can be made to the court for an order requiring that spouse to give up possession so that the sale can proceed (r 9.24 Family Procedure Rules 2010).

7.11 Protecting matrimonial property pending an application for financial remedies

The following orders allow property to be protected pending an application for financial remedies. As these orders are considered to be severe orders, they are granted only as a last resort and only in exceptional circumstances.

(i) A freezing order

If there is a danger that a spouse may dispose, or attempt to dispose, of assets in order to defeat an application for financial remedies (for example by selling them, giving them away or sending them out of the jurisdiction), an application can be made for a 'freezing order' to preserve those assets. The application can be made under section 37 of the Matrimonial Causes Act 1973 (MCA 1973) or under the High Court's inherent jurisdiction. The applicant must prove that there is a real risk that the respondent is likely to move or dissipate assets with the intention of defeating the applicant's claim for financial remedies on divorce unless restrained from doing so by the court (see, for example, *ND v KP (Asset Freezing)* [2011] EWHC 457 (Fam)). Overseas assets can be frozen, unless there are likely to be problems enforcing the order in a foreign court. The order will not usually freeze all the defendant's assets, but only the maximum amount of property likely to be awarded in the financial remedy proceedings.

(ii) A search and seize order

This order allows a named person to enter premises to search for and seize documents which might be useful as evidence in an application for financial remedies. The aim of the order is to ensure that the respondent does not dispose of evidence which may be useful at the hearing for financial remedies. An order will be made only in exceptional circumstances, and strict rules apply to the grant of an order and to the way in which the entry and search powers can be exercised (see *Araghchinchi v Araghchinchi* [1997] 2 FLR 142).

(iii) Preventing a party leaving the jurisdiction

Where there is a risk that a party may leave the jurisdiction of the court before an application for financial remedies on divorce has been dealt with, a writ *ne exeat regno* can be sought which directs an officer of the court to arrest the respondent and bring them before a judge.

(iv) Impounding a passport

The court can make an order impounding a party's passport pending the disposal of a financial remedy claim, but, as this involves a restriction on a person's liberty, the power will be exercised with caution and for as short a period as possible. The applicant must show that the respondent is likely to leave the jurisdiction unless restrained, and that this would materially prejudice their case. If these requirements are satisfied, then an order impounding a passport will be held to represent a proportionate public policy-based restraint on freedom of movement founded on the personal conduct of the respondent. These principles were applied in *Young v Young* [2012] EWHC 138 (Fam) where Mostyn J held that impoundment of the husband's passport was lawful.

7.12   Challenging a financial order

A financial order can be challenged by: (a) applying for a rehearing; (b) applying for variation or discharge; and (c) appealing and/or applying to have the order set aside.

(a)   Applying for a rehearing

Where a party considers that there was something fundamentally wrong with the way in which the case was heard (for example there was non-disclosure or misrepresentation), an application can be made for a rehearing. Sometimes an appeal court (see below) will order a rehearing because a financial order is fundamentally flawed.

(b)   Variation or discharge

Under section 31(1) of the Matrimonial Causes Act 1973 (MCA 1973) the court has wide powers to vary or discharge an order (whether or not made by consent) or to temporarily suspend any provision in an order or revive any provision in an order so suspended. The most common applications for variation are in respect of an increase or decrease in periodical payments due to a change of circumstances. The court will list a financial dispute resolution appointment in the same way as a first application for financial remedies. If an agreement cannot be reached in the financial dispute resolution, the case will proceed to a full hearing.

The powers under section 31(1) (see above) apply only to the following orders (s 31(2)):

► maintenance pending suit or interim maintenance;
► periodical payments (secured or unsecured);
► a lump sum order payable by instalments;
► any deferred order made by virtue of section 23(1)(c) (lump sum) which includes provision made by virtue of section 25B(4), section 25C or section 25F(2) (provision in respect of pension rights);
► any order for a settlement of property under section 24(1)(b) or for a variation of settlement under section 24(1)(c) or (d), being an order made on or after the grant of a decree of judicial separation;
► an order for the sale of property under section 24A; and
► a pension sharing or pension compensation sharing order made before decree absolute.

There is no power to vary a lump sum order (except where it is payable in instalments) or to vary a property adjustment order (except in the very limited circumstances set out in section 31(4) where an order has been made on judicial separation). In other words, lump sum orders and property adjustment orders are 'once and for all' orders. The reason for the final nature of these orders is to create certainty and bring about finality in litigation, so that the parties can make plans for the future without worrying about whether an order will be overturned. Lump sum orders and property adjustment orders can, however, be appealed against or set aside (see further below).

(i) How the court exercises its powers

When exercising its powers under section 31(1), the court must consider all the circumstances of the case, but must give first consideration to the welfare of any child of the family aged under 18 and to any changes of circumstance, including any change in any of the matters to which the court was required to have regard when making the original order (s 31(7)). The court must also consider whether to effect a clean break. In other words, it must consider whether it is appropriate to bring periodical payments to an end immediately or to vary a periodical payments order so that payments will be made for a limited term sufficient to enable the payee to adjust without undue hardship to the termination of those payments (s 31(7)(a)). The court also has power to remit payment of all or part of any arrears due under any periodical payments order, including maintenance pending suit and interim maintenance (s 31(2A)). Where a periodical payments order is for a limited term, it can extend the term, unless the original order prohibited it (s 28(1A)).

For the purpose of effecting a clean break, the court can substitute periodical payments with one of the following orders: a lump sum order; a property adjustment order; a pension sharing order; or a direction that the person in whose favour the original order discharged or varied was made is not entitled to make any further application for a periodical payments order or an extension of the period to which the original order is limited by any variation made by the court (see s 31(7B)).

The court has a wide discretion in section 31 proceedings. The principles laid down by the House of Lords in *White v White* and *Miller v Miller* (see 7.6 above) apply (see, for example, *VB v JP* [2008] 1 FLR 742 where periodical payments to the wife were increased on the basis that she was entitled to an element of compensation for loss of earning capacity, applying *Miller*). In *North v North* [2008] 1 FLR 158 Thorpe LJ said that in any application under section 31 the applicant's needs were likely to be the dominant or magnetic factor, but that it did not follow that the respondent would inevitably be held responsible for any and all established needs.

(ii) Cohabitation and variation

Cohabitation after divorce may be taken into account in section 31 proceedings as one of the circumstances of the case, and may result in the reduction or termination of periodical payments. However, if the payee remarries after divorce, section 28 of the MCA 1973 provides that periodical payments automatically terminate.

Whether cohabitation will be taken into account in section 31 proceedings will depend on the facts of the case. In *K v K (Periodical Payments: Cohabitation)* [2006] 2 FLR 468 Coleridge J held that the law should keep up with changing social conditions and the court should give considerable weight to cohabitation after divorce. Here, the wife's settled cohabitation for three years had reduced her dependency on her former husband and was held to constitute a relevant circumstance under section 31(7)(b). Coleridge J stated, however, that this was 'a troubling and messy area of the law' and that the current legislation 'enacted against an utterly different social fabric [was] not adequate to deal with it'. However, in *Grey v Grey* [2009] EWCA 1424 Thorpe LJ said that, although he was sympathetically attracted by Coleridge J's philosophy in *K v K* (for a revised approach to cohabitation on the basis that it was now perceived as normal, commonplace and as acceptable as marriage), any change in the law must come from Parliament. Thorpe LJ said that, in the meantime, the approach adopted in the Court of Appeal must apply (as in *Fleming v Fleming* [2003] EWCA Civ 1841). In other words, post-divorce cohabitation is not to be equated with marriage post-divorce, but the court, in assessing the impact of cohabitation, should have regard to the overall circumstances, including the financial consequences of the case. Wall LJ in *Grey* (see above) also stated that he could find 'no warrant for equating in this context remarriage with cohabitation, a word which itself presents problems of definition'; and he did not consider that it was open to the courts to add a gloss to the existing provisions by equating cohabitation with remarriage without legislative sanction.

(c)   Appeals and applications to set aside a financial order

Appeals are allowed if there has been a procedural irregularity, or the judge has taken into account irrelevant matters or ignored relevant matters, or has otherwise reached a conclusion which is plainly wrong (*G v G* [1985] 1 WLR 647). The aim of this rule is to promote finality in litigation. It also recognises that, with discretionary judicial decision-making, such as that in financial remedy proceedings on divorce, there is a wide margin within which a decision may be reasonable even though a party may not agree with it. The mere fact that a party is not happy with the outcome of a case is not of itself sufficient ground for bringing an appeal. Permission (leave) to appeal is therefore required, except in very limited circumstances (see r 30.3 Family Procedure Rules 2010 (FPR 2010) and Practice Direction 30A). On an appeal, the court has the power, *inter alia*, to affirm the order, vary the order, set aside the order and/or order a rehearing (r 30 FPR 2010).

If the date for lodging the appeal has passed, an application for permission to appeal out of time will be required. Appeals out of time are often combined with an application to set aside the original order. An application can be made to set aside an order which has been made on an improper basis (for example because of non-disclosure, fraud, duress or misrepresentation) (see *Livesey v Jenkins* [1985] 1 AC 424 below) or where a change of circumstances has occurred which was unforeseen when the original order was made (see *Barder v Barder* [1988] AC 20 below). As the courts are unwilling to reopen litigation unless it is really necessary (because it increases costs and extends the duration of the conflict), permission to appeal out of time on the ground of new events will not be granted unless the principles laid down in the following case are satisfied.

Barder v Barder (Caluori Intervening) [1988] AC 20

A consent order was made in full and final settlement, in which the husband agreed to transfer his half-share in the matrimonial home to his wife. Four weeks after the order was made, but outside the time limit for lodging an appeal, the wife killed the children and committed suicide. The husband sought leave to appeal out of time against the order (it could not be varied under section 31 as it was a property order), arguing that the basis on which the order had been made had been fundamentally altered by the unforeseen change of circumstances – the death of his wife and children.

The House of Lords held that he should be granted leave to appeal out of time and that the order should be set aside. Lord Brandon said, however, that leave to appeal should be granted only where the following four conditions are satisfied:

▶ the new events relied on invalidate the fundamental basis or assumption on which the original order was made, so that, if leave to appeal were granted, the appeal would be certain or very likely to succeed;
▶ the new events have occurred within a relatively short time of the original order being made – probably less than a year;
▶ the application for leave to appeal has been made promptly; and
▶ the grant of leave would not prejudice third parties who acquired in good faith and for valuable consideration an interest in the property subject to the order.

Thus, not every application will result in permission to appeal being granted and an order being set aside. There must be a material change of circumstances which has undermined or invalidated the basis of the order. The *Barder* principles are strict in order to promote finality in litigation and to ensure that the courts are not swamped by meritless applications. In *Richardson v Richardson* [2011] EWCA Civ 79, where the Court of Appeal held, *inter alia*, that the wife's early death was not a '*Barder* event', Thorpe LJ stated that cases in which a '*Barder* event', as opposed to a vitiating factor, can be successfully argued are extremely rare and should be regarded as such by the specialist profession.

(i) The supervening event must be an unforeseeable event

In *Barder* (see above) it was implicit that the supervening event must be unforeseen. In *Maskell v Maskell* [2003] 1 FLR 1138, for example, the Court of Appeal held that becoming unemployed two months after an order was made was not a '*Barder* event', as it was foreseeable. However, in *Reid v Reid* [2004] 1 FLR 736, the wife's sudden death from a heart attack two months after the date of the financial order was not reasonably foreseeable.

(ii) The fundamental assumption of the order

In *Critchell v Critchell* [2015] EWCA Civ 436 the wife's application to vary a consent order succeeded when the husband received an unexpected inheritance within a month of the order. The Court of Appeal upheld the variation reducing the husband's entitlement because the fundamental assumption at the time of the consent order was that the husband needed capital from the former matrimonial home to discharge his debts. His inheritance meant that this was no longer the case.

(iii) Changes in property valuations

A change in respect of a property valuation (upward or downward) or a misrepresentation as to valuation is sometimes used as a ground for an appeal out of time, but the court will usually hold that this does not constitute a *'Barder* event' (see, for example, *B v B* [2008] 1 FLR 1279; *Walkden v Walkden* [2009] EWCA Civ 627; and *S v S (Ancillary Relief: Application to Set Aside Order)* [2009] EWHC 2377 (Fam)).

(iv) Fluctuations in the value of property such as investments

In *Cornick v Cornick* [1994] 2 FLR 530 (where the wife applied to set aside an order on the basis of a dramatic upward change in share prices) Hale J said that the case-law did not 'suggest that the natural processes of price fluctuation, whether in houses, shares or other property, and however dramatic' provided grounds for setting an order aside. Hale J said that only where there had been a misvaluation or mistake at the trial might an order be set aside. The fact that an order was unfair was an insufficient ground on its own. Hale J's *dicta* were applied by Thorpe LJ in *Myerson v Myerson (No. 2)* [2009] 2 FLR 147 where the husband (a victim of the global economic downturn) failed in his claim to appeal out of time. Had he succeeded, it would have opened the floodgates to many other claimants.

(v) Unexpected remarriage or cohabitation

In some cases unexpected marriage or cohabitation has been held to be a *'Barder* event', as it was in *Williams v Lindley* [2005] 2 FLR 710 where the wife became engaged within one month of a lump sum being ordered in her favour. However, each case depends on its facts; and in *Dixon v Marchant* [2008] 1 FLR 655 a majority of the Court of Appeal, distinguishing *Williams v Lindley*, refused to accept the husband's argument that his former wife's remarriage (seven months after a consent order had been made) was a *'Barder* event'.

(d)   Setting a financial order aside on the basis of non-disclosure

Applications to set aside a financial order are sometimes made where there was non-disclosure at the time the order was made. This occurred in the following case, which lays down the approach to be adopted by the court in such applications.

▶ *Jenkins v Livesey (Formerly Jenkins)* **[1985] 1 AC 424**

A clean-break consent order was made in which the parties agreed that the husband would transfer to his wife his half-share in the matrimonial home, on her forgoing all claims to ancillary relief. Three weeks after the house had been transferred, the wife remarried and two months later put the house up for sale. The husband appealed out of time, asking for the consent order to be set aside on the grounds of misrepresentation and non-disclosure.

The House of Lords allowed his appeal and held that parties who wished the court to exercise its discretionary powers under the MCA 1973 were under a duty in contested or consent proceedings to make full and frank disclosure of all material matters, so that the court could exercise its discretion properly. However, because of the importance of encouraging a clean break, orders should not be lightly set aside. They should be set aside only if the failure to make full and frank disclosure led the court to make an order which was substantially different from the one it would have made had there been full and frank disclosure. As the wife's engagement was a material circumstance directly relevant to the parties' agreement about ancillary relief, she was under a duty to disclose it before the agreement was put into effect by means of the consent order. Her failure to disclose the engagement invalidated the order. The order was set aside, and the case remitted for a rehearing.

The House of Lords stressed that non-disclosure of itself is not a sufficient ground for an order to be set aside. Like applications for appeals out of time, where the policy objective of finality is also upheld, the circumstances must be such that a fundamentally different order would have been made had the circumstances been known.

Thus, in *Jenkins v Livesey (formerly Jenkins)* the House of Lords held that not every breach of the duty of full and frank disclosure would necessarily result in an order being set aside. It has to be shown that the non-disclosure had led the court to make an order which was substantially different from that which would have been made had there been full disclosure.

The approach taken by the court, as established in the following case of *Sharland v Sharland* [2015] UKSC 60, will depend on whether the non-disclosure is considered fraudulent or not. Where, as in *Jenkins v Livesey (formerly Jenkins)*, the disclosure was non-fraudulent, the burden is on the party seeking to set aside the order to show that it was material. However, where the non-disclosure was fraudulent, as in the following case, the burden is on the perpetrator of the fraud to satisfy the court that the order should *not* be set aside.

▶ *Sharland v Sharland* [2015] UKSC 60

A consent order was agreed during the course of a final hearing. After the agreement had been reached the wife discovered that the husband had been making arrangements to float his company on the New York stock exchange and that his shareholding was expected to be valued at a sum far in excess of the value on which she had relied at the hearing. The wife tried to set aside the agreement, but was unsuccessful. She appealed to the Court of Appeal. The majority in the Court of Appeal, following the approach in *Livesey*, held that the critical factor, regardless of whether the non-disclosure was dishonest or not, was the effect of the non-disclosure on the court's decision embodied in its order. On the facts, the non-disclosure had not resulted in an order significantly different from that which the court would otherwise have made and so the order would not be set aside. The wife appealed to the Supreme Court.

The Supreme Court allowed the appeal and held that a consent order procured by fraud should be set aside. The only exception is where the court is satisfied that, at the time when it made the consent order, the fraud would not have influenced a reasonable person to agree to it, nor, had it known then what it knows now, would the court have made a significantly different order, whether or not the parties had agreed to it. However, the burden of satisfying the court of that lies with the perpetrator of the fraud, not the victim. On the facts, the misrepresentation and non-disclosure regarding the husband's plans for his company were highly material to the consent order. This had coloured the wife's approach to the proportionality of the balance struck between her present share in the liquid assets and her future share in the value of the husband's shareholding. The order was set aside, and the case remitted for a rehearing.

In *Gohil v Gohil* (No 2) [2015] UKSC 61, which was heard at the same time as *Sharland*, the Supreme Court took the same approach and reinstated an order setting aside a consent order agreed between the parties where the husband had been guilty of material and intentional non-disclosure.

7.13 An application for financial remedies after a foreign divorce

Under Part III of the Matrimonial and Family Proceedings Act 1984 (MFPA 1984), a person who has divorced overseas can apply for financial remedies in England and Wales provided the court in England and Wales has granted leave to apply, which it can grant only if there is a substantial ground for the making of an application (s 13(1)). Once leave has been granted, sections 17 and 18 provide that the court can exercise its powers under Part II of the Matrimonial Causes Act 1973 (MCA 1973) having regard to the section 25 factors (see 7.4 above) and applying the principles laid down in the case-law (see 7.6 above).

(a) Granting leave to apply

When deciding whether to grant leave, the court must consider whether England and Wales is the appropriate venue for the application (s 16(1)) and it must have regard to a number of specified matters (s 16(2)), such as: the connection the parties have with England and Wales, the country where they were divorced and any other country; and any financial benefit the applicant or any child of the family has received or is likely to receive by agreement or by operation of law in another country. Consideration of these matters in section 16 acts as a filter to prevent unmeritorious applications.

The following case is the leading case on applications to seek leave to apply for financial remedies in the courts in England and Wales after a foreign divorce. The Supreme Court held that hardship and injustice are factors that can be taken into account by the court, but they are not necessary preconditions for granting leave to apply for financial remedies.

▶ *Agbaje v Agbaje* [2010] UKSC 13

The parties, a Nigerian couple, had spent most of their long marriage in Nigeria, but had acquired British citizenship and spent time living in England. After their separation, the wife made her home in England. When the husband began divorce proceedings in Nigeria, the wife subsequently filed for divorce in England and also cross-petitioned for judicial separation in Nigeria. In the Nigerian proceedings she sought maintenance and property settlement orders (there was no jurisdiction to transfer property). The Nigerian court declined to stay its proceedings, and granted a divorce and awarded her a life interest in the matrimonial home (worth £83,000) and a lump sum of £21,000 as maintenance for life. The husband retained assets worth £616,000, including two London properties. The wife applied for financial remedies in the English courts under Part III of the MFPA 1984. She was granted leave on the ground that, if leave were refused, she would suffer real hardship. In the substantive application, Coleridge J, finding that the parties had a real connection with England and holding that it was appropriate for the English court to make an order, awarded her £275,000 from the sale of the English property on condition that she transferred her interest in the Nigerian property to her husband.

The Court of Appeal allowed the husband's appeal on the basis that Coleridge J had failed to address the issue of comity (respect for the law and courts of the other jurisdiction) and to explain why the case was an exceptional case which justified the wife having a 'second bite of the cherry'. It held that the parties' connection with Nigeria was more significant than with England; and Nigeria was the appropriate forum for resolving the wife's claims. Serious injustice had not been done to her by the Nigerian court. Thus, although it was plain that she would suffer real hardship in England and Wales, comity commanded respect for the overseas order. The wife appealed to the Supreme Court.

The Supreme Court, unanimously allowing her appeal and restoring the order made by Coleridge J, held, *inter alia*, that:

▶ The principal object of the filter mechanism is to prevent wholly unmeritorious claims being pursued to oppress or blackmail a former spouse.
▶ Section 16 does not require the court to consider 'whether it is appropriate for an order to be made', but whether it would be appropriate for an order to be made by a court in England and Wales.
▶ Part III contains no express reference to hardship, injustice or exceptionality. Hardship and injustice are not preconditions, although they will both be relevant factors for the court to take into consideration under both sections 16 and 18.
▶ A mere disparity between the award made by the foreign court and that which would be awarded on an English divorce will be insufficient to trigger the application of Part III. A court will not lightly characterise foreign law, or the order of a foreign court, as unjust.
▶ The amount of financial provision will depend on all the circumstances of the case and there is no rule that it should be the minimum amount required to overcome injustice (*A v S (Financial Relief after Overseas US Divorce and Financial Proceedings*) [2002] EWHC 1157 (Fam) disapproved).

On the facts, Lord Collins, delivering the judgment of the Supreme Court, concluded that 'it was not so much that there was a very large disparity between what the wife received in Nigeria and what she would have received in England, but that there was also a very large disparity between what the husband received and what the wife received such as to create real hardship and a serious injustice.'

Agbaje v Agbaje was applied in *Traversa v Freddi* [2011] EWCA Civ 81 where the husband, who was working as a waiter in England, successfully appealed against the refusal of leave to bring financial remedy proceedings in the courts in England and Wales after his wife had divorced him in Italy.

7.14 Reforming the law

(a) Criticism of the law

There has been considerable criticism of the law on financial remedies, not just the statutory provisions but also the principles laid down by the House of Lords in *White v White* and *Miller v Miller; McFarlane v McFarlane* (see 7.6 above). As a result there have been calls for reform from judges, lawyers and academics. For example, Resolution has called for reform in its *Manifesto for Family Law* (see www.resolution.

org.uk) and Mostyn QC (as he then was) has criticised the law for its continuing uncertainty ([2007] Fam Law 573).

Much of the criticism relates to the discretionary system for dealing with financial remedies, which, despite having the advantage of flexibility, creates difficulties in respect of certainty, consistency and predictability. The decisions of the higher courts have also failed to make the law clearer. In fact, Sir Mark Potter P in *Charman v Charman (No. 4)* [2007] EWCA Civ 503 was of the opinion that the decision in *White v White* had undoubtedly not resolved 'the problems faced by practitioners in advising clients, or by clients in deciding upon what terms to compromise'. According to Welstead ([2012] Fam Law 185), since 2006, 'the courts ... have been engaged in a constant struggle to understand the limitations of, and attempt to apply, the tripartite principles of fairness outlined by the House of Lords in *Miller v Miller; McFarlane v McFarlane* ... when making financial awards on divorce'. In Welstead's opinion, it is the principle of equal division which has 'caused the greatest headache for the judiciary, particularly where the only assets in existence at the end of a marriage were acquired by one of the spouses prior to the marriage'.

White v White and *Miller v Miller* have therefore been criticised for muddying rather than clarifying the law. For example, what is 'special contribution' and when is it to be taken into account? What should be regarded as 'matrimonial' or 'non-matrimonial' property? To what extent will the length of a marriage affect whether an inheritance, for example, is to be part of the matrimonial assets to be divided? What is the starting point in applications for financial remedies? Does equality apply as a yardstick to test the conclusion which has been tentatively reached by a judge after conducting the section 25 exercise, or is there a principle of equality which acts as a starting point in an application for financial remedies?

In *RP v RP* [2007] 1 FLR 2105 Coleridge J was strongly critical of the decision in *Miller v Miller*. He said that although *Miller v Miller* was a 'high profile case' which had sent 'seismic reverberations throughout the whole [family justice] system', the case had created 'very real uncertainty as to outcome' and, as a result, the 'consensual disposal of individual cases in this huge and, sadly, ever growing area of litigation' had become 'that much harder to achieve and that much more costly'. Coleridge J said that 'considerable confusion' still existed. In particular, Coleridge J said that the word 'compensation' did not appear in the statute, and that 'talk of "compensation"' in respect of the circumstances of the case in *RP* had 'added nothing except confusion and the real risk of double counting'. In *SA v PA* [2014] EWHC 392 (Fam) Mostyn J described the principle of compensation as 'extremely problematic and challenging both conceptually and legally'.

As two of the three strands laid down in *Miller v Miller* (compensation and sharing) are not mentioned in the list of statutory factors in section 25 of the Matrimonial Causes Act 1973 (MCA 1973), the House of Lords may also be criticised for introducing changes to the law by means of judicial law-making when it is Parliament's responsibility to change the law. As Cretney said (in *Family Law in the Twentieth Century*, 2003), the decision in *White v White* and *Miller v Miller; McFarlane v McFarlane* 'may come close to the imposition by the judiciary of the community of property neither Parliament nor any official advisory body had ever accepted as the basis of English matrimonial law'. One of the difficulties is that, although there have been calls for Parliament to review the law (see, for example, Deech [2015] Fam Law 105), there has been little interest on behalf of successive governments to engage in statutory reform in this area.

According to Elizabeth Cooke (the former Law Commissioner responsible for family law reform), crucial issues of principle which were left unresolved by the House of Lords in *White* and *Miller* have left the operation of section 25 of the MCA 1973 the subject of considerable uncertainty (see [2007] CFLQ 98). She said that, as divorce is common, then the principles which apply to financial remedies should be clear enough to be applied without recourse to litigation so that the parties can work matters out for themselves or with the help of a mediator or lawyer. Determining what is, or is not, matrimonial property (for the purpose of distributing property in financial proceedings on divorce) remains uncertain and unpredictable. As Cooke says, although 'the concept of non-matrimonial property is firmly embedded in law and practice ... we do not know how it is defined'. In Europe, on the other hand, community of property regimes define the term 'matrimonial property'.

Determining the question of special contribution is also difficult to predict. What sorts of contribution are 'special' and how will other factors, such as the duration of the marriage, impact on the issue? As Coleridge J said, '[f]rom the summit of the mountain, the House of Lords has pronounced some of the principles which underlie the "special contribution" issue', but '[t]hey are silent on how to apply them' (see *Charman v Charman (No. 2)* [2006] EWHC 1879 (Fam)).

In *B v S (Financial Remedy: Marital Property Regime)* [2012] EWHC 265 (Fam) Mostyn J criticised the lack of clarity in the law relating to periodical payments, saying that '[s]imple and fair guidance is needed so that the majority of cases can be settled'. He urged that awards be based on need alone, rather than on sharing or compensation, and drew attention to the difficulties facing judges deciding cases when '[t]here are not even any signposts along the road to a fair award'.

A further issue is that, even if one party obtains a financial remedy order, they may have great difficulty in enforcing it if the other party refuses to cooperate (see, for example, *Prest v Prest* [2015] EWCA Civ 714). The difficulty and complexity of enforcing financial remedy orders has been recognised by the Law Commission (see below).

The need for reform has arguably become more pressing in light of the reduction of legal aid and the increase in numbers of litigants in person (see the Law Commission's report *Matrimonial Property, Needs and Agreements* (Law Com No. 343) and Hitchings, Miles and Woodward [2013] *Assembling the jigsaw puzzle: understanding financial settlement on divorce*, available from www.nuffieldfoundation.org).

(b) Discussion of reform

As long ago as 1991 the Family Law Committee of the Law Society considered options for reform, including: making marital agreements binding; introducing a presumptive 50:50 split of matrimonial assets; and introducing a set of policy objectives to help govern the exercise of judicial discretion (see *Memorandum: Maintenance and Capital Provision on Divorce*, Law Society, 1991). At the end of the 1990s, the Government considered these options for reform in its consultation paper *Supporting Families* (Home Office, 1998). These discussions were taken further by the Lord Chancellor's

Ancillary Relief Advisory Group (chaired by the Rt Hon Lord Justice Thorpe), which concluded that there was a need for research and wide consultation, and that this should encompass both social and public policy issues (see *Report of the Lord Chancellor's Advisory Group on Ancillary Relief*, July 1998). However, the proposals for reform were not taken forward.

In July 2003, the Family Law Committee of the Law Society published a report (*Financial Provision on Divorce: Clarity and Fairness – Proposals for Reform*) in which it recommended, *inter alia*, that section 25 of the MCA 1973 should incorporate a series of guidelines for the sharing of assets. The Family Law Committee was of the view, however, that pre-marital contracts should not be given binding status but that the courts should continue to consider them as a factor to be taken into account.

In 2009, the Law Commission started to consider this area in depth (see 7.19(d) below).

(c) Options for reform

Four options for the reform of financial remedies have been discussed over the years: (i) the introduction of a 50:50 split of matrimonial assets; (ii) the introduction of a set of general principles; (iii) the introduction of a formula for calculating financial remedies; and (iv) making marital agreements binding (see 7.9(c) above).

(i) A 50:50 split of marital assets

Equal division of matrimonial assets on divorce (subject to any agreement to the contrary) is common throughout Europe and exists in some states in the USA and also in New Zealand. However, while a 50:50 split has the advantage of certainty, it may create unfairness and hardship, in particular for poorer families who might find themselves with insufficient funds to rehouse themselves. The possibility of introducing a 50:50 split in England and Wales has been discussed from time to time, but, although there have been no proposals to change the law, there has been a move towards equality of division of assets in 'big-money' cases. In fact, Cretney has claimed that 'English law now has, by virtue of judicial decision rather than legislation, a matrimonial regime of community of property' ([2003] CFLQ 403). According to Cooke ([2007] CFLQ 98), community of property was part of the thinking behind the yardstick of equality idea laid down by the House of Lords in *White v White* (see 7.6 above).

(ii) A set of general principles

Another possible reform that has been mooted is whether the MCA 1973 should be amended to include a set of general principles which would supplement the application of the section 25 factors. Although section 25 contains a list of factors which the courts must take into account, there is no express articulation of the principles and policies which govern the distribution of assets on divorce, other than that the child's welfare is the court's first consideration. There is no mention of any policy of fairness, non-discrimination between spouses or what the objective of financial orders should be (beyond the section 25A 'clean-break' principle). The Scottish legislation on financial remedies on divorce, which is similar to that in

England and Wales, includes a set of general principles which the courts must take into account when exercising their discretion. The Scottish legislation makes financial orders available for the following purposes:

(1) fair sharing of matrimonial or partnership property;
(2) taking account of economic advantages and disadvantages;
(3) fair sharing of the economic burden of looking after children;
(4) enabling a dependent partner to adjust to loss of support; and
(5) relieving serious financial hardship.

The introduction of a similar set of principles in England and Wales has been mooted from time to time. Thus, in 1998, the Government, in its discussion paper *Supporting Families* (Home Office, para 4.49), suggested the following set of general principles: seek first to promote the welfare of children by meeting their housing needs and those of their primary carer; take into account any written agreement about financial arrangements; divide any surplus so as to achieve a fair result, recognising that fairness will generally require the value of the assets to be divided equally between the parties; and try to determine financial relationships at the earliest date practicable. However, the Lord Chancellor's Advisory Group on Ancillary Relief, which reported in 1998, said that it would not be appropriate to adopt a set of principles like those in Scotland, but it was in unanimous agreement that there was a strong case for codifying in legislation the principles that are applied by the courts in England and Wales (*Report of the Lord Chancellor's Advisory Group on Ancillary Relief*, 1998). The Law Commission considered the option of introducing a set of principles (see *Matrimonial Property, Needs and Agreements*, LCCP No. 208, September 2012) but concluded that statutory reform is not necessary (see 71.9(d) below).

It is questionable whether a set of principles would improve the law. In fact, the judge-made principles enunciated by the House of Lords in *White v White* and *Miller v Miller* have done little to stem the criticism emanating from lawyers, judges and academics about the unsatisfactory nature of the law. Instead, the principles have arguably led to obfuscation, rather than clarification, of the law.

(iii) A formula for calculating financial remedies

Another possible option for reform which has been discussed is the introduction of a formula for calculating financial remedies. Thus, for example, Eekelaar has proposed a 'standard model' (in other words a formula) which could be used for calculating financial remedies on divorce (see [2010] Fam Law 359). The Law Commission in its supplementary consultation paper *Matrimonial Property, Needs and Agreements*, LCCP No. 208 discussed the possibility of introducing a formula to help determine how assets should be distributed on divorce. It looked, for example, at the American Law Institute's Principles of the Law of Family Dissolution, which sets out a formulaic approach to financial remedies, but which allows for departures where there is substantial injustice. It also looked at the Canadian formulaic approach.

Although a formulaic approach, unlike a discretionary approach, has the disadvantage of being inflexible, the availability of an intellectually coherent formula would create greater certainty and predictability and give couples some idea of what they could expect to receive, or have to pay out, with respect to financial provision on divorce. It would help couples to make informed agreements about finance and property arrangements on divorce. It would also help couples who are trying to settle their finances outside the court system and without the assistance of lawyers. In fact, most couples have no access to the discretionary approach laid down in the MCA 1973, and developed by the judges in the case-law, as they cannot afford to go to court.

(iv) Making marital agreements binding

The proposed reforms in relation to nuptial agreements are considered at 7.9(c) above.

(d) The work of the Law Commission

(i) Matrimonial Property, Needs and Agreements

Between 2009 and 2014 the Law Commission conducted a project on aspects of the law on finance and property on divorce with a view to reform of the law in England and Wales. The Law Commission's recommendations are set down in *Matrimonial Property, Needs and Agreements* (Law Com No. 343), which was published in February 2014.

Having reviewed the law relating to financial needs, the Law Commission states that '[t]he law relating to financial orders is inherently unclear. It is not possible to discern from the statute what the law requires, although the courts and family lawyers administer the law with confidence' (para 2.56). However, the Law Commission does not advocate changing the law, which is described as 'good enough' (para 2.43), although it does identify a need to address geographical inconsistency and a lack of transparency. The Law Commission states that evidence shows significant regional differences in the levels of support likely to be awarded following divorce in different courts, particularly in terms of the duration of support. Secondly, whilst lawyers may be familiar with the law and the practice at their local courts, the report notes that most people cannot afford lawyers and that, with the reduction of legal aid, people previously entitled to legal advice no longer have access to it. Whilst those people can still, in theory, access the courts, this process is more difficult without lawyers. As a result, the report notes that 'a couple seeking to negotiate a financial settlement on divorce, without the means to afford lawyers and without the inclination to go through the court process, may have great difficulty in discerning what their legal rights and responsibilities are' (para 2.55). The report therefore recommends the production of non-statutory guidance for separating couples informed by a policy objective of achieving independence following divorce.

With respect to needs (see Chapter 3), the Law Commission notes that in the vast majority of cases it is the only financial issue. In terms of adopting a principled approach to needs, the Law Commission does not, for example, support a rigid time limit on the payment of periodical payments as exists in some other jurisdictions, for example in Scotland (Principle 9(1)(d) of the Divorce (Scotland) Act 1985). However, it recommends that

> the Family Justice Council prepare guidance as to the meaning of financial needs, encouraging the courts to make orders that will enable the parties to make a transition to independence, to the extent that that is possible in the light of choices made within the marriage, the length of the marriage, the marital standard of living, the parties' expectation of a home, and their continuing shared responsibilities (para 3.88).

Such guidance is recommended to be primarily addressed at the courts, but with a 'plain English' version for litigants in person.

The Law Commission also considered and consulted on producing numerical formulae that generate guideline amounts for payment from one spouse to another. Whilst a rigid formula is rejected by the Law Commission, it does recommend that the Government support the formation of a working group to work on the possible development of a formula to generate ranges of outcomes for spousal support (para 3.159).

Chapter 8 of *Matrimonial Property, Needs and Agreements* (see above) deals with the issue of non-matrimonial property – in other words, property which is less likely to be shared on divorce, for example an inheritance, a gift or property acquired before marriage. In its supplementary consultation paper *Matrimonial Property, Needs and Agreements*, LCCP No. 208, the Law Commission made a range of provisional proposals in relation to reform regarding non-matrimonial property and asked consultees for their views. Thus, for example, it proposed that non-matrimonial property should be defined as property held in the sole name of one party to the marriage and which is received as a gift or inheritance or was acquired before the marriage; and that it should no longer be subject to the sharing principle on divorce except where it is required to meet the other party's needs. However, consultation responses raised a number of concerns such as, for example, that this approach encourages parties to focus on historical issues rather than working towards settlement. There were also divergent views regarding whether the family home could ever be regarded as non-matrimonial property. As a result, the Law Commission concluded that it would be impossible to reach a satisfactory consensus on the right direction for the development of non-matrimonial property. Also, as the issue affects only a minority of couples (namely those whose assets exceed their financial needs), it concluded that the introduction of qualifying nuptial agreements (see 7.9(d) above)) would provide adequate protection for those people.

(ii) Response to the Law Commission's recommendations

In response to the Law Commission's recommendations, the Government commissioned the Family Justice Council to produce guidance in relation to financial needs. This led to the publication, in April 2016, of a guide for litigants in person titled 'Sorting out finances on divorce'. However, the guidance addressed to the courts in relation to financial needs is still awaited. The Government also indicated its intentions to develop numerical formulae in its formal response to the Law Commission but no further developments have taken place. It is not yet known whether the Government will take steps to enact the draft Nuptial Agreements Bill which would make qualifying nuptial agreements binding (see above).

(iii) The enforcement of financial orders

In 2014, the Law Commission started a separate project on the enforcement of financial orders made under the MCA 1973 (and under the Civil Partnership Act 2004 and the Children Act 1989). The Law Commission's recommendations are set down in *Enforcement of Family Financial Orders* (Law Com No. 370), which was published in December 2016. In order to make enforcement more effective, more accessible and fairer the Law Commission recommends, *inter alia*: clearer procedural rules; greater obligations on debtors to provide financial disclosure; powers enabling the court to obtain information from third parties, such as HMRC; powers enabling the court to make orders in relation to a wider pool of assets, such as a debtor's pension; and powers enabling the court to put pressure on debtors by, for example, disqualifying them from driving or from travelling abroad. The Government's response is awaited.

(e)   Reform: the future

Despite discussions of reform, there is no consensus as to what form any reform should take, except for the fact that there is support for making marital agreements binding; and the Law Commission has made recommendations with respect to providing guidance in relation to needs and investigating the possibility of numerical formulae that generate guideline amounts for payment from one spouse to another (see above). However, the Law Commission is not advocating wholesale reform of the law, and to that extent it may be regarded as merely 'tinkering' with the law.

Some attempts at statutory reform in this area have been made. For example, Baroness Deech has sponsored a Private Member's Bill, the Divorce (Financial Provision) Bill, in successive Parliaments. The 2015–2016 version of the bill (as amended at committee stage) provides, *inter alia*, for: prenuptial agreements to be binding as long as the parties received independent legal advice, made full disclosure and entered into the agreement at least three weeks before the marriage; prevention of lump sum, property adjustment and pension sharing orders being made in relation to non-matrimonial property; and periodical payments to be limited to a term of five years, unless there is a likelihood of serious financial hardship. However, without the support of the Government, such proposals are unlikely to lead to a change in the law.

Although the discretionary system for dealing with financial remedies on divorce creates uncertainty, there is a danger that making the discretionary system more rule-based may remove the flexibility which is its great strength. According to Harris (2008), the uncertainty of the law may encourage parties to negotiate.

> [The paradox in *Miller v Miller*] is that in failing to achieve greater certainty the judges have both secured a powerful incentive for parties to negotiate rather than litigate (which incentive would be weakened if the law were more certain) and, further, have reduced the incentive for parties to incur costs and prolong cases by haggling over detailed facts.

What is clear from the discussions of reform is that it will be extremely difficult to produce a fair, just and effective system for adjusting finance and property matters on relationship breakdown which is both predictable and also flexible enough to deal with the infinite variety of family circumstances. Reforms of child support have been riddled with the same problems (see Chapter 12). In *Miller v Miller* Baroness Hale spoke of the need for flexibility but for the law not to be 'too flexible'. This is, arguably, the source of the difficulty.

Despite the difficulty of deciding on the nature of any reforms, many practitioners, judges and academics believe that reform is needed and that it ought to come from Parliament. However, so far there has been limited appetite for such reform, no doubt due to the controversial nature of this area of law, as highlighted by the Law Commission.

Summary

▶ On the breakdown of a marriage it will usually be necessary for the parties to redistribute their property and financial assets. There is an emphasis on settlement and most couples reach agreement without going to court. However, others spend vast sums of money on legal costs. If the parties cannot reach agreement, financial provision and property adjustment orders can be applied for on divorce (and on nullity or judicial separation) in an application for financial remedies under Part II of the Matrimonial Causes Act 1973 (MCA 1973). The same rules apply on civil partnership dissolution under the Civil Partnership Act 2004.

▶ The procedure for financial remedies is laid down in the Family Procedure Rules 2010 and in accompanying Practice Directions. The emphasis is on reducing delay and costs, which is done by facilitating agreement and allowing the court to have control over the conduct of proceedings. An applicant for financial remedies must attend a mediation information and assessment meeting to see if the dispute can be resolved by mediation. If mediation is unsuccessful and the claim proceeds through the court process, both parties attend a first appointment followed by a financial dispute resolution appointment at which the district judge will help the parties reach agreement. If this is not possible, then the case will proceed to a full hearing. The court can stay proceedings if it considers it more appropriate for the matter to be determined outside England and Wales. The parties are under a duty to make full, frank and clear disclosure of all their current and future assets. The media are permitted to attend financial remedy proceedings, unless the district judge or the rules of court provide otherwise.

▶ The court can make, *inter alia*, the following orders in financial remedy proceedings: maintenance pending suit (s 22); financial provision orders (s 23); property adjustment orders (s 24); orders for the sale of property (s 24A); and pension orders (ss 24B–E).

▶ When considering whether to make an order, and, if so, in what manner, the court must have regard to all the circumstances of the case, first consideration being given to the welfare of any child of the family who has not attained the age of 18 (s 25(1)). When exercising its powers in relation to the parties to the marriage the court must in particular have regard to a list of factors laid down in section 25(2), which includes, for example, the financial needs and resources of the parties, their standard of living, their ages, the length of the marriage, serious misconduct.

▶ The court must apply the clean-break provisions laid down in Part II of the MCA 1973 when making any financial order in favour of a spouse in financial remedy proceedings (s 25A) and also in variation proceedings (s 31(7)). The policy of the clean break encourages the parties to put their past behind them and go their separate ways after divorce, but the court's powers are subject to the section 25 factors (see above) and the principles laid down in the case-law, in particular, *White v White* and *Miller v Miller*.

▶ In addition to applying the section 25 factors (see above) and the clean-break provisions (see above), the court in financial remedy proceedings must apply the principles laid down by the House of Lords in *White v White* and *Miller v Miller*. Although these were 'big-money' cases, the principles they laid down apply to all applications for financial remedies. In *White v White*, the House of Lord overturned the principle laid down by the Court of Appeal in earlier cases that financial relief was limited to satisfying the parties' reasonable needs or requirements. In *White v White*, the House of Lords held that: the objective in financial relief proceedings is fairness; there must be no discrimination between husbands and wives; and, before making an order for financial relief, the court should check its tentative views against the 'yardstick' of equality'. The House of Lords in *Miller v Miller* endorsed the principles laid down in *White v White* and identified the following three guiding general principles which apply in financial

Summary cont'd

remedy proceedings: needs (generously construed); compensation; and sharing. The trend in the case-law following *White v White* and *Miller v Miller* has been to emphasise the wide discretion of the court and its duty to apply the section 25 factors in order to achieve a fair result. In some cases, it has been argued that special contribution (such as special business skills in creating the wealth) is a justification for not ordering equal, or near-equal, division of matrimonial assets. In exercising their discretion, the courts may have to consider whether or not to ring-fence certain assets (such as an inheritance) and treat them as non-matrimonial assets. The length of the marriage will be an important factor as to whether or not property is non-matrimonial or matrimonial.

▶ Various financial orders can be made in respect of the family home. Tenancies can also be transferred under section 24 of the MCA 1973 or under section 53 and Schedule 7 of the Family Law Act 1996.

▶ The court has a range of powers which it can exercise in respect of pensions on divorce, namely 'off-setting', making a pension attachment order or making a pension sharing order. The court's powers in respect of pension arrangements are governed by the section 25 criteria and the principles in *White v White* and *Miller v Miller* (see above).

▶ Married couples can make agreements about their financial arrangements should they divorce. The divorce court has jurisdiction to make consent orders (an order incorporating an agreement about matrimonial property incorporating the sorts of order which the court can make under Part II of the MCA 1973). Parties to a marriage can enter into a separation agreement (which agreements are governed by ss 34–36 of the MCA 1973). Parties to a marriage are also free to enter into a pre-nuptial (pre-marital) or post-nuptial (post-marital) agreement in which they can make arrangements about the distribution of their assets on divorce. The Supreme Court in *Radmacher v Granatino* laid down the following principles which now govern *both* pre-nuptial and post-nuptial agreements: the courts continue to have a supervisory role to play in scrutinising such agreements; and the courts can give effect to an agreement provided it was fairly entered into by each party with a full appreciation of its implications unless in the circumstances prevailing it would not be fair to hold the parties to the agreement.

▶ Financial orders can be enforced in a variety of ways. The Law Commission has looked at the law governing the enforcement of orders for financial remedies.

▶ Two orders allow matrimonial property to be protected pending an application for financial remedies: a 'freezing order' (which can be granted under section 37 of the MCA 1973 or under the High Court's inherent jurisdiction) to freeze assets; and a search and seize order to gain entry to premises to take evidence relevant to financial remedy proceedings. These orders are granted only in exceptional circumstances because of their severity. The court can lawfully impound a passport provided it is a necessary and proportionate response.

▶ A financial order can be challenged in the following ways: by asking for a rehearing; by applying to have the order varied or discharged under section 31; by appealing against the order (which may require an application for permission to appeal out of time); or by applying to have the order set aside. Appeals out of time and applications to set orders aside are granted only in exceptional circumstances because of the policy objective of achieving finality in litigation. The court will not grant permission to appeal out of time unless the *Barder* principles are satisfied. An application to set aside an order will not be granted unless the original order is fundamentally unsound (such as due to non-disclosure, misrepresentation, fraud or mistake).

Summary cont'd

▶ An application for permission to seek financial remedies in the courts in England and Wales after a foreign divorce can be sought under Part III of the Matrimonial and Family Proceedings Act 1984, but the court in England and Wales must first grant leave to apply. In *Agbaje v Agbaje* (2010) the Supreme Court laid down the rules which apply to leave applications, in particular that hardship and injustice are factors that can be taken into account by the court but which are not necessary preconditions for granting leave to apply.

▶ The law on financial remedies on divorce has been criticised for many years, largely because of its uncertainty and unpredictability; and because the decisions of the House of Lords in *White v White* and in *Miller v Miller* have not helped to resolve these problems. Reforms have been discussed, such as: a presumption in favour of a 50:50 split of matrimonial property; making marital agreements legally binding; the introduction of a set of policy guidelines to govern the exercise of judicial discretion; and a formula for calculating financial remedies.

▶ The Law Commission recommended in 2014 that legislation should be enacted to make nuptial agreements binding and that non-statutory guidance should be produced regarding financial needs. It has also made recommendations to tackle the difficulties surrounding enforcement of financial orders.

Further reading and references

Barlow and Smithson, 'Is modern marriage a bargain? Exploring perceptions of pre-nuptial agreements in England and Wales' [2012] CFLQ 304.

Barton, '*White v White* and co: the not-so-well-off and a "balance of needs"' [2012] Fam Law 963.

Barton, 'Matrimonial property, needs and agreements' [2014] Fam Law 1124.

Chandler, '"The law is now reasonably clear": the courts' approach to non-matrimonial assets' [2012] Fam Law 163.

Cooke, '*White v White* – a new yardstick for the marriage partnership' [2001] CFLQ 81.

Cooke, '*Miller/McFarlane*: law in search of discrimination' [2007] CFLQ 98.

Cooke, 'The Law Commission's consultation on marital property agreements' [2011] Fam Law 145.

Cooke, 'Pre-nups and beyond: what is the Law Commission up to now?' [2012] Fam Law 323.

Cretney, 'Community of property imposed by judicial decision' (2003) LQR 349.

Cretney, 'Private ordering and divorce – how far can we go?' [2003] Fam Law 399.

Deech, 'What is a woman worth?' [2009] Fam Law 1140.

Deech, 'Money and divorce' [2015] Fam Law 105.

Eekelaar, '*Miller v Miller*: the descent into chaos' [2005] Fam Law 870.

Eekelaar, 'Financial and property settlement: a standard deal?' [2010] Fam Law 359.

Harris, George and Herring, 'With this ring I thee wed (terms and conditions apply)' [2011] Fam Law 367.

Harris, 'Financial orders after divorce: a category error?' [2012] Fam Law 860.

Hitchings, 'The impact of recent ancillary relief jurisprudence in the "everyday" ancillary relief cases' [2010] CFLQ 93.

Further reading and references cont'd

Hitchings, Miles and Woodward [2013] *Assembling the jigsaw puzzle: understanding financial settlement on divorce*, available from www.nuffieldfoundation.org.

Miles, '*Charman v Charman (No. 4)* – making sense of need, compensation and equal sharing after *Miller/McFarlane*' [2008] CFLQ 378.

Miles and Probert (eds), *Sharing Lives, Dividing Assets*, 2009, Hart Publishing.

Mostyn, 'Charman-making straight the highway' [2007] Fam Law 573.

Parker, 'The draft Nuptial Agreements Bill and the abolition of the common law rule: "swept away" or swept under the carpet?' [2015] CFLQ 63.

Scherpe, 'Fairness, freedom and foreign elements: marital agreements in England and Wales after *Radmacher v Granatino*' [2011] CFLQ 513.

Scherpe, 'Marital agreements and matrimonial property' [2012] Fam Law 865.

Scherpe (ed.), *Marital Agreements and Private Autonomy in Comparative Perspective, 2012,* Hart Publishing.

Thompson, *Prenuptial Agreements and the Presumption of Free Choice: Issues of Power in Theory and Practice*, 2015, Hart Publishing.

Wall, President of the Family Division, 'The President's Resolution address 2012' [2012] Fam Law 817.

Welstead, 'The sharing of pre-matrimonial property on divorce: *K v L'* [2012] Fam Law 85.

Websites

Law Commission: www.lawcommission.gov.uk

Links to relevant websites can also be found at: www.palgravehighered.com/law/familylaw9e

Part V

Children and parents

Chapter 8

Children

This chapter provides a general introduction to the law relating to children. It looks in particular at children's rights, both in domestic law and under the United Nations Convention on the Rights of the Child and the European Convention on Human Rights. It considers, in particular, the child's right to make autonomous decisions and the landmark case of *Gillick v West Norfolk and Wisbech Health Authority* [1986] AC 112. The law governing the corporal punishment of children by parents and teachers is considered, and also the right of children to participate in family law proceedings. Finally, the use of the inherent jurisdiction and wardship in children's cases is considered.

8.1 Introduction

(a) Children's rights

During the 20th century there was increasing recognition and acceptance of the fact that children have rights. A major impetus for this was the children's liberationist movement in the USA in the 1960s and 1970s, which generated debate about the extent to which children should have rights. The children's liberationists took the view that children had the right to enjoy certain freedoms, in particular the right to be free to make decisions about themselves. Radical liberationists took the view that children had the right to enjoy the same freedoms as adults. However, others took a more moderate view, arguing that children have a right not to be forced into adulthood, and have rights to be protected and cared for. Also, to give children too much autonomy might undermine parental authority and have adverse repercussions for children themselves.

Some theorists have argued that it is theoretically difficult to talk about children's rights because children can have rights only if they have the necessary competence, or will, to make decisions. Some writers have preferred instead to talk about children's 'interests' (for example Eekelaar, 1986) or to view children's rights in terms of the obligations which adults owe them (for example O'Neill, in Alston *et al.*, 1992). Children therefore need adults to champion their rights.

Some writers have attempted to classify children's rights or interests. Thus, Freeman (1983), for example, proposed four categories of rights: welfare rights; protective rights; rights grounded in social justice; and rights based on autonomy. Eekelaar (1986) suggested that children have three types of interest: basic; developmental; and autonomy interests. Basic and developmental interests, he said, would prevail over autonomy interests where this was necessary to protect a child.

One of the key dilemmas in the context of children's rights is the extent to which children should have rights of self-determination or autonomy. Whereas some would argue in favour of greater autonomy for children, the law must strike a balance and recognise that, although children should have greater rights of self-determination as they near adulthood, they do also need the protection of the law.

(b)   Children's Commissioners

England and Wales each has a Children's Commissioner to act as a champion for children. The powers and duties of the English Commissioner are set out in Part I of the Children Act 2004 (CA 2004) and those of the Welsh Commissioner in the Care Standards Act 2000 (CSA 2000). The primary function of the English Commissioner is 'promoting and protecting the rights of children' (s 2(1) CA 2004); whereas the principal aim of the Welsh Commissioner is 'to safeguard and promote the rights and welfare of children' (s 72A CSA 2000).

The Children's Commissioners are responsible for promoting the United Nations Convention on the Rights of the Child (UNCRC) (see 8.2 below). From time to time, they submit reports to the United Nations Committee on the Rights of the Child whose task it is to ensure the implementation of the UNCRC in signatory states. In July 2015, the joint report of the UK Children's Commissioners identified child poverty, failures in child protection, systematic reductions in legal advice, assistance and representation, and inadequate funding for child and adolescent mental health services as some of the worst injustices suffered by children in the UK. However, their critical concern was that the imposition of austerity measures and changes to the welfare system have resulted in a failure to protect the most disadvantaged children, and those in especially vulnerable groups, from child poverty.

Provisions in the Children and Families Act 2014 have strengthened the role and remit of the English Commissioner. Thus, under the amended CA 2004, their primary function is to promote and protect children's rights (s 2(1)). The English Commissioner *must* also: have regard to the UNCRC in considering for the purposes of the primary function what constitute the rights and interests of children (s 2A); take reasonable steps to involve children in the discharge of the primary function (s 2B); and publish reports in a version which is suitable for children (s 2C). They *may* also provide advice, assistance and representation to any child who is living away from home or receiving social care (s 2D); and they have the power to enter premises, other than a private dwelling, for the purpose of interviewing a child or observing the standard of care provided to children accommodated or otherwise cared for there (s 2E). Any person exercising functions of a public nature must supply the English Commission with such information in their possession as the Commissioner may reasonably request for the purposes of the primary function or the function under section 2D (s 2F).

There have been calls to revisit the powers of the Welsh Commissioner so that they better reflect those of the English Commissioner. Thus, in December 2014, a report commissioned by the Welsh Government (see *An Independent Review of the Role and Functions of the Children's Commissioner for Wales*) recommended, *inter alia*, that the remit of the Welsh Commissioner should be extended to cover all matters, whether devolved or not, that involve the welfare of children and young people who normally reside in Wales. In March 2016, the Welsh Government published its response to the report (see *Response to the Independent Review of the Role and Functions of the Children's Commissioner for Wales*). In its response, the Welsh Government announced that it fully supports the recommendation. It said that extensive discussions have been had with the UK Government, but no resolution has yet been achieved. The Welsh Government will continue to work with its UK counterparts to find a way of moving this forward.

8.2   The United Nations Convention on the Rights of the Child 1989

The United Nations Convention on the Rights of the Child (UNCRC) was created with the aim of encouraging governments worldwide to recognise the importance of children in society and the fact that children have rights. It is the most ratified United Nations convention, with the USA being the only United Nations member that has not ratified it. It covers the social, economic and civil rights of children and young people, as well as their protection from abuse, discrimination, exploitation, abduction and armed conflict.

Although the UK has ratified the UNCRC, it does not have the same force as the European Convention on Human Rights (ECHR). This is because it has not been incorporated into all the legal systems in the UK. However, in Wales, the Rights of Children and Young Persons (Wales) Measure 2011 places a duty on Welsh Ministers to have due regard to the requirements of the UNCRC when exercising any of their functions (s 1). They must also take appropriate steps to promote knowledge and understanding of the UNCRC among the public, including children (s 5); and they have the power to make orders which will amend legislation in order to improve children's rights (s 6). Similar provisions exist in Scotland under Part I of the Children and Young People (Scotland) Act 2014.

Another drawback of the UNCRC is that there is no special court under the Convention, like the European Court of Human Rights (ECtHR), to which children and other people can go to enforce its provisions. However, despite these drawbacks, the UNCRC can be used in legal arguments before the courts, and judges also take it into account when making their decisions. The UK Government also takes it into account when considering new policies relating to children. The UNCRC has become increasingly important in the UK, due in part to the rights-based culture created in the UK by the implementation of the Human Rights Act 1998.

The following articles of the UNCRC lay down key principles, namely non-discrimination (Art 2); the best interests of the child (Art 3); and the right to life (Art 6).

United Nations Convention on the Rights of the Child 1989

Article 2(1)

States Parties shall respect and ensure the rights set forth in the present Convention to each child within their jurisdiction without discrimination of any kind, irrespective of the child's or his or her parent's or legal guardian's race, colour, sex, language, religion, political or other opinion, national, ethnic or social origin, property, disability, birth or other status.

Article 3(1)

In actions concerning children, whether undertaken by public or private social welfare institutions, courts of law, administrative authorities or legislative bodies, the best interests of the child shall be a primary consideration.

Article 6

1. States Parties recognise that every child has the inherent right to life.
2. States Parties shall ensure to the maximum extent possible the survival and development of the child.

Under the UNCRC children have rights, *inter alia*, to: freedom of expression (Art 13); freedom of association and peaceful assembly (Art 15); a private and family life (Art 16); freedom of thought, conscience and religion (Art 14); education (Art 28); minority rights (Art 30); rest and leisure (Art 31); an adequate standard of living (Art 27); protection against economic exploitation (Art 32); and social security benefits (Art 26).

Children also have a right to contact with both parents on a regular basis, except when a court decides that it is contrary to their best interests (Art 9). States Parties must also protect children from all forms of abuse, neglect, maltreatment, exploitation and sexual abuse while in the care of their parents or other persons (Art 19). Children must be protected against: drugs (Art 33); sexual exploitation (Art 34); other forms of exploitation (Art 36); abduction (Art 35); and cruel, inhuman or degrading treatment or punishment (Art 37). The UNCRC also lays down rights for refugee children (Art 22) and disabled children (Art 23), as well as rights to health care and medical provision for children (Art 24).

The UNCRC recognises the importance of the family unit and the importance of parents in the upbringing of their children. It provides that respect must be afforded to the responsibilities, rights and duties of parents, members of the extended family or community and others who are legally responsible for children (Art 5). It also recognises the importance of both parents having common responsibilities for the upbringing and development of their children, and having the primary responsibility for bringing them up (Art 18). Parents and others responsible for children must ensure that the child's living conditions are the best that can be secured in the circumstances (Art 27(2)), and States Parties must take all appropriate measures to recover maintenance for children from parents having financial responsibility (Art 27(4)).

(a) The United Nations Committee on the Rights of the Child

This Committee is responsible for monitoring the implementation of the UNCRC in Member States (Arts 43 and 44). It does so by responding to periodic reports submitted, approximately every five years, by Member States about children's rights in their State. This reporting mechanism puts pressure on Member States to change their law when the United Nations Committee's Report (which is put into the public domain) criticises them for failing to promote the rights and best interests of children. In May 2015, the UK Government submitted its Fifth Report to the United Nations Committee. After hearing evidence from non-governmental organisations, children and the UK Government, the United Nations Committee published its concluding observations in June 2016.

(b) Direct applicability of the United Nations Convention on the Rights of the Child

The question of whether the substantive rights in the UNCRC can be directly applied in UK domestic law has been the subject of a number of judgments by the Supreme Court in recent years, in particular in the context of the use of Article 3 of the UNCRC (best interests of the child) in domestic law to interpret the rights under the ECHR. In *ZH (Tanzania) v Secretary of State for the Home Department* [2011] UKSC 4, an immigration case, the Supreme Court followed the approach of the ECtHR in its use of Article 3 of the UNCRC as an interpretive tool in judicial decision-making, and accepted that it applied to any decision in respect of a child's right to family life under Article 8 of the ECHR. The Court held that the best interests of children were a primary consideration, although not the primary consideration or the paramount consideration. In *H (H) v Deputy Prosecutor of the Italian Republic, Genoa (Official Solicitor intervening); H (P) v Same (Same intervening); F-K v Polish Judicial Authority* [2012] UKSC 25 the Court made clear that the approach in *ZH (Tanzania) v Secretary of State for the Home Department* (see above) to Article 3 of the UNCRC also applies in an extradition context, even though there is a greater public interest in extraditing someone to face criminal justice abroad than in deporting an immigrant. The Court also confirmed that that there is a wider public interest and benefit to society in promoting the best interests of its children, and that as a starting point 'no factor must be given greater weight than the interests of the child'.

More recently in *R (on the application of SG) and Others v Secretary of State for Work and Pensions* [2015] UKSC 16, a case which involved an unsuccessful challenge to the Benefit Cap (Housing Benefit) Regulations 2012, the Supreme Court revisited the issue of when, and how, the substantive provisions of the UNCRC are directly enforceable in the UK. Lord Reed, delivering the leading judgment, said: 'It is not in dispute that the Convention rights protected in our domestic law by the Human Rights Act can also be interpreted in the light of international treaties, such as the UNCRC, that are applicable in the particular sphere'. A minority, Lady Hale and Lord Kerr, held that Article 3 of the UNCRC can be directly enforceable in UK domestic law; and that it creates an obligation on the UK Government to take account of children's best interests as a primary consideration in any and all decisions. However, a majority rejected this argument, stating that any breach of children's rights would have to be settled 'in the political, rather than the legal arena'. (For an interesting discussion of developments in this area see Taylor [2016] CFLQ 45).

8.3   The European Convention for the Protection of Human Rights

Although the European Convention on Human Rights (ECHR) makes no express provision for, or reference to, children, they nonetheless have rights under the Convention. The European Court of Human Rights (ECtHR) has recognised the importance of the best interests of the child. Thus, for example, in *Johansen v Norway* (1997) 23 EHRR 33 it held that 'particular weight should be attached to the best interests of the child ... which may override those of the parent'. In *Scott v UK* [2000] 1 FLR 958, which concerned the question of whether Article 8 (the right to family life) had been breached by a local authority which had applied to free a mother's child for adoption, the ECtHR stated that 'consideration of what is in the best interests of the child is always of crucial importance'.

With respect to the application of the ECHR in the courts in England and Wales, it has played a greater role in public law cases (such as in care proceedings) as a result of the Human Rights Act 1998 (HRA 1998) which gives particular protection to victims whose human rights have been breached by a public authority. In private law cases (such as in disputes about arrangements for children), on the other hand, human rights arguments are not used much, even though the courts are public authorities and have obligations under the HRA 1998 to ensure that their judgments take into account the decisions of the ECtHR. For example, as Choudhry and Herring (2010) and Fortin ([2011] Fam Law 176) point out, the reasoning of the House of Lords in *Re G (Children)* [2006] UKHL 43 (see below) would have been very different if the decision had been decided in accordance with Article 8 of the ECHR.

Despite the fact that human rights are now being used more than they used to be in children's cases, Fortin claims that they are not being used enough. Even in public law cases, where judges make 'very free use' of the ECHR, Fortin says that children's rights are 'simply spliced onto the parents' rights as if they were identical', and this precludes any analysis of the child's own rights under the Convention. She also criticises the approach of the ECtHR to children's rights, for, although it clearly recognises children's rights when dealing with applications by children (see, for example, *A v United Kingdom (Human Rights: Punishment of Child)* at 8.5 below), it has 'a record of producing an astonishingly inconsistent response to the child's individual status'. Fortin concludes: 'For lawyers working in the field of child law, the new rights framework imposed by the HRA has undoubtedly had a strong influence on the legal principles applying to children – but in a disappointingly patchy fashion.'

8.4 The autonomy of children – the *Gillick* case

As children grow older, particularly as they near adulthood, it is important that they become more autonomous in the sense that they are able to make decisions for themselves. The case of *Gillick v West Norfolk and Wisbech Health Authority* [1986] AC 112 was a landmark case in this respect as it gave greater recognition to children's right to self-determination, in particular in the context of medical treatment. The decision was also relevant to parental rights as it held that it was preferable to talk about parental responsibility, rather than parental rights.

▶ *Gillick v West Norfolk and Wisbech Health Authority* **[1986] AC 112**

A Department of Health and Social Security (DHSS) circular was sent to doctors advising them that they would not be acting unlawfully if in exceptional circumstances they prescribed contraceptives to girls under the age of 16 without first obtaining parental consent, provided they did so in good faith. Mrs Gillick, a Roman Catholic with teenage daughters, brought an action against the DHSS and her local hospital authority seeking a declaration that the circular was illegal on two grounds. First, it enabled doctors to break the criminal law by causing or encouraging unlawful sexual intercourse under the Sexual Offences Act 1956. Second, the circular was inconsistent with her parental rights. She was successful in the Court of Appeal. The defendants appealed to the House of Lords.

The House of Lords held, allowing the appeal, that:

(i) There was no rule of absolute parental authority over a child until a fixed age, but that parental authority dwindled as the child grew older and became more independent. The law recognised parental rights only in so far as they were needed for the child's protection, so that it was more appropriate to talk of duties and responsibilities than rights. Parental rights, if any, yielded to the right of the child to make his or her own decisions if of sufficient understanding and intelligence.

> Consequently a girl under the age of 16 did not merely by reason of her age lack legal capacity to consent to contraceptive treatment.
>
> (ii) Neither had any offence under the Sexual Offences Act 1956 been committed, as the *bona fide* exercise of a doctor's clinical judgement negated the necessary mental element required for that offence.
>
> **LORD SCARMAN**: The underlying principle of the law was exposed by Blackstone [in his *Commentaries on the Laws of England*] and can be seen to have been acknowledged in the case-law. It is that parental right yields to the child's right to make his own decisions when he reaches a sufficient understanding and intelligence to be capable of making up his own mind on the matter requiring decision.

Gillick was applied and upheld in the following case, despite the applicant's argument that, with the coming into force of the Human Rights Act 1998 (HRA 1998), *Gillick* could no longer be considered good law. The case focused on the question of medical confidentiality between doctors and children.

> ▶ *R (Axon) v Secretary of State for Health* [2006] EWHC 37 (Admin)
>
> The applicant, a mother of teenage daughters, applied in judicial review proceedings for the following declarations: (i) that a doctor is under no obligation to keep confidential the advice or treatment he proposes to give a young person aged under 16 in respect of contraception, sexually transmitted infections and abortion, and should therefore not provide such advice and treatment without a parent's knowledge unless to do so might prejudice the child's physical or mental health so that it was in the child's best interests not to do so; and (ii) that the Department of Health's *Best Practice Guidance for Doctors and Other Health Professionals on the Provision of Advice and Treatment to Young People Under 16 on Contraception, Sexual and Reproductive Health* (2004) was unlawful because it violated parents' rights under Article 8 of the European Convention on Human Rights (ECHR).
>
> Silber J dismissed the application, holding that the *Gillick* case was determinative of these issues. There was no different rule on waiving confidentiality when abortion advice or treatment was being discussed from when contraceptive advice or other treatment was under consideration. Silber J held that the very basis and nature of the information which a medical professional received relating to the sexual and reproductive health of any patient of whatever age deserved the highest degree of confidentiality. The proposed limitation on the young person's right to confidentiality might well be inconsistent with the current trend towards a 'keener appreciation of the autonomy of the child and the child's consequential right to participate in the decision-making-process'. The guidelines laid down in *Gillick* did not infringe parental rights under the ECHR. Not only did a young person have his or her own right to respect for family life, and a significant and compelling right to confidentiality of health information under the ECHR which would compete with, and potentially override, any right to parental authority, but also the right to parental authority dwindled as a child matured. The 2004 *Guidance* was not unlawful. *Gillick* did not establish as a matter of law that a medical professional should regard it as an exceptional practice, or unusual, to offer contraceptive advice or abortion advice or treatment to young people without first involving a parent.
>
> Silber J stated, however, that nothing in his judgment was intended to encourage young people to seek or to obtain advice or treatment on sexual matters without first informing their parents and discussing matters with them.

In *Axon* the challenge to *Gillick* on the basis that it infringed parents' rights under Article 8 of the ECHR therefore failed, and *Gillick* remains a landmark decision in the development of children's rights. It also led to the phrases '*Gillick* competency' and a '*Gillick* competent child', which means a child who is mature enough to be able to make an informed decision.

(a) The impact of *Gillick* on the Children Act 1989

The recognition in *Gillick* that children have a voice that should be heard, particularly where they are sufficiently mature, was incorporated into some of the provisions of the Children Act 1989 (CA 1989). This was due in part to the fact that *Gillick* was decided when the Law Commission was engaged in consultation and discussion about reforming and consolidating the law on children which eventually led to the enactment of the CA 1989. Thus, section 1(3)(a) of the CA 1989 provides that in section 8 order proceedings (see 10.4) and in care and supervision proceedings (see 14.7) the court must have regard to the ascertainable wishes and feelings of the child concerned, considered in the light of their age and understanding. A child can apply for section 8 orders with leave of the court (s 10(8)), which the court can grant if the child has sufficient understanding to make the application; and a child with sufficient understanding to make an informed decision can refuse to consent to a medical or psychiatric examination, or other assessment (s 38(6)).

However, although *Gillick* had an impact on the CA 1989 and the views and wishes of children of sufficient intelligence and understanding are given greater recognition, a child does not necessarily have the final say as it is always open to the court to overrule, or discount, a child's wishes. Furthermore, although there are many references to the welfare of the child in the CA 1989, nowhere is there any reference to children's 'rights'. Thus, for example, children are not usually party to court proceedings, and a child's consent is not needed to their removal from the UK or to a change of their surname.

(b) *Gillick* – its progeny

Although *Gillick* was hailed as a landmark case for children's rights, it did not give them absolute rights. In fact, the House of Lords in *Gillick* stressed that, as far as contraception was concerned, it was only in exceptional cases that there would be no parental involvement. Subsequent case-law shows that the scope of children's autonomy rights depends on the circumstances in which they are being exercised. Thus, even the wishes of a '*Gillick* competent' child can be overridden, as the child's welfare is the court's paramount consideration. Thus, whether or not the wishes of a *Gillick* competent will prevail will depend on the nature and seriousness of the decision to be taken.

(c)   Autonomy rights and medical treatment

Section 8(1) of the Family Law Reform Act 1969

Consent by persons over 16 to surgical, medical and dental treatment

8(1) The consent of a minor who has attained the age of sixteen years to any surgical, medical or dental treatment which, in the absence of consent, would constitute a trespass to his person, shall be as effective as it would be if he were of full age; and where a minor has by virtue of this section given an effective consent to any treatment it shall not be necessary to obtain any consent for it from his parent or guardian.

The issues of the autonomy rights of children and *Gillick* competency have been considered in a number of cases where young people have *refused* to consent to medical treatment. In these cases the courts have overridden their wishes and authorised the treatment, even though the children concerned were mature enough to make an informed decision, and even though section 8 of the Family Law Reform Act 1969 (FLRA 1969) above provides that 16- and 17-year-olds can consent to surgical, medical and dental treatment. The following three cases provide examples.

▶ *Re R (A Minor) (Wardship: Medical Treatment)* **[1992] Fam 11**

R, a 15-year-old girl who had a serious mental illness, had been placed in an adolescent psychiatric unit. The local authority applied in wardship (see 8.7 below) for her to be given psychiatric treatment without her consent.

   The Court of Appeal allowed the application, holding that she was not *Gillick* competent as her mental state fluctuated from day to day, but, even if she had been, the court would still have had the power to override her refusal. It held that a *Gillick* competent child could consent to medical treatment, but where such a child refused to give consent, then consent could be given by someone else with parental responsibility, including the court.

▶ *Re W (A Minor) (Medical Treatment: Court's Jurisdiction)* **[1993] 1 FLR 1**

W, a 16-year-old girl, suffered from anorexia nervosa. Her condition was rapidly deteriorating, but she refused medical treatment. The local authority applied to the court under its inherent jurisdiction (see 8.7 below) for it to authorise medical treatment for the girl, despite her refusal.

   The Court of Appeal held, authorising the medical treatment, that it has jurisdiction to override a *Gillick* competent child's refusal to consent to medical treatment, despite the provisions of section 8 of the FLRA 1969 (which allows 16- and 17-year-olds to give valid consent to surgical, medical and dental treatment), as the court under its inherent *parens patriae* jurisdiction had theoretically limitless powers extending beyond the powers of natural parents. Nolan LJ said: 'In general terms the present state of the law is that an individual who has reached the age of 18 is free to do with his life what he wishes, but it is the duty of the court to ensure so far as it can that children survive to attain that age.'

> ▶ *South Glamorgan County Council v W and B* **[1993] 1 FLR 574**
>
> An interim care order had been made in respect of a severely disturbed 15-year-old girl with a direction under section 38(6) of the CA 1989 that she receive a psychiatric examination and assessment. When she refused to consent to the examination and assessment, the court under its inherent jurisdiction overrode her wishes and gave the local authority permission to take the necessary steps for her to be treated and assessed. The court so decided, despite the fact that section 38(6) expressly states that a child of sufficient understanding to make an informed decision can refuse to submit to an examination or other assessment, and notwithstanding the fact that she was *Gillick* competent. The court had the power to override the wishes of a mature minor in respect of medical treatment, despite statutory provisions in the CA 1989 to the contrary.

In *Re M (Medical Treatment: Consent)* [1999] 2 FLR 1097 Johnson J, following *Re W* (above), authorised an urgent heart transplant operation for a 15-year-old girl, despite her refusal to give consent. In several other cases the High Court has authorised treatment where young people have refused life-saving medical treatment because of their religious beliefs (see, for example, *Re E (A Minor) (Wardship: Medical Treatment)* [1993] 1 FLR 386; and *Re P (Medical Treatment: Best Interests)* [2004] 2 FLR 1117).

The cases show that, even if children are 'Gillick competent', their wishes can be overridden. Thus, while children may have greater rights of autonomy than they used to have, they do not have absolute autonomy, particularly where they are refusing medical treatment. On reaching the age of 18, on the other hand, they are free to choose what to do with regard to their medical treatment, even though it may not be in their best interests. According to Gilmore and Herring ([2011] Fam Law 175), 'a great injustice in both [*Re R* and *Re W*] was that the children's abilities to refuse treatment were never properly ascertained'. The approach to competency described above may in future need to be considered in the light of the Mental Capacity Act 2005, which applies not only to adults but also to 16- and 17-year-olds and which covers capacity to consent and refuse medical treatment (see, for example, McFarlane [2011] Fam Law 479 and Cave [2011] CFLQ 431).

(i) What if the child is nearly an adult?

In *Re P (Medical Treatment: Best Interests)* [2004] 2 FLR 1117 Johnson J held, *obiter dicta*, that where a child is nearly an adult the court will give very careful consideration to the child's wishes about medical treatment; and that there could be cases where the refusal of a child approaching 18 would be determinative. Nonetheless, Johnson J granted the hospital leave to administer blood or blood treatments to a 17-year-old Jehovah's Witness who objected, as did his parents, to the doctors using medical treatment involving blood or blood products on the ground of his religious beliefs.

Re W (A Minor) (Medical Treatment: Court's Jurisdiction) [1993] 1 FLR 1 and *Re P (Medical Treatment: Best Interests)* (see above) were both considered in the case of *An NHS Foundation Trust Hospital v P* [2014] EWHC 1650 (Fam). Baker J, granting a declaration that it was lawful for medical practitioners entrusted with a 17-year-old patient's care to treat her for an overdose even though she refused treatment, concluded: 'The wishes and feelings of the child, in particular those of a 17-year-old young person who is almost an adult, are an important component of the analysis of her welfare. They are not, however, decisive.'

(d)   Autonomy rights and human rights

In the following two cases the court had to consider the autonomy of children in the context of their human rights, as it did in the *Axon* case. In both cases, teenage girls claimed that their human rights under the ECHR had been breached.

▶ *Re Roddy (A Child) (Identification: Restriction on Publication)* **[2004] 2 FLR 949**

Angela Roddy had given birth to a baby at the age of 12 whilst she was in the care of the local authority. Her baby was adopted despite her refusal to consent to the adoption. When she turned 16, she successfully applied to the court for the care order to be discharged, and she wanted to publish an account of her experiences in a national newspaper. The local authority applied to prevent publication, but Munby J refused the application. He held that she should be permitted to publish her story subject to conditions imposed to preserve the anonymity of the father and the baby.

Munby J, referring to *Gillick*, held that the same principles which applied in other areas of adolescent decision-making also applied to the question of whether a minor could exercise their right to freedom of expression under Article 10 of the ECHR and choose to waive their right to privacy under Article 8 of the ECHR. He held that it was the court's duty to defend the right of the child (who had sufficient understanding to make an informed decision) to make their own choice.

▶ *R (On the Application of Begum) v Headteacher and Governors of Denbigh High School* **[2006] UKHL 15**

A Muslim girl claimed that her school had breached her right to freedom of religion under Article 9 of the ECHR because she had been excluded from school for wearing a *jilbab* (a form of Muslim dress which covers the arms and legs) rather than the *shalwar kameez* (tunic and trousers) which was permitted by her school. She also claimed that the school had breached her right to education under Article 2 of Protocol 1 to the ECHR because she had been excluded from school. Her claim failed at first instance, but she was successful in the Court of Appeal. However, the House of Lords unanimously allowed the school's appeal, with the majority holding that her Article 9 right had not been breached. Lord Nicholls and Baroness Hale, on the other hand, held that her Article 9 right had been breached but that the breach was proportionate and justifiable on the facts (in particular, because the school had taken thorough steps to ensure that its school uniform policy did not offend the religious beliefs of Muslim children who attended the school, or those of their families).

8.5   The corporal punishment of children

Article 37(a) of the United Nations Convention on the Rights of the Child 1989

No child shall be subjected to torture or other cruel, inhuman or degrading treatment or punishment.

> **Article 19(1) of the United Nations Convention on the Rights of the Child 1989**
>
> States Parties shall take all appropriate legislative, administrative, social and educational measures to protect the child from all forms of physical or mental violence, injury or abuse, neglect or negligent treatment, maltreatment or exploitation, including sexual abuse, while in the care of parent(s), legal guardian(s) or any other person who has the care of the child.
>
> **Article 3 of the European Convention for the Protection of Human Rights**
>
> No one shall be subjected to torture or to inhuman or degrading treatment or punishment.

Corporal punishment of children by their parents is permitted in certain very limited circumstances, but it is outlawed in all schools.

(a)　Corporal punishment of children by their parents

The development of society's attitude to the corporal punishment of children by their parents shows how differently children are treated today. At one time it was acceptable for parents to beat their children, but today they may commit a criminal offence if they inflict corporal punishment on them.

Physical chastisement of a child can also constitute significant harm for the purposes of the Children Act 1989 (CA 1989) and result in a child being the subject of a care or supervision order (see 14.7). Each case depends on its fact and the court may decide, however, that the corporal punishment is not significant enough to constitute significant harm. Thus, for example, in *Re MA (Children) (Care Proceedings: Threshold Criteria)* [2009] EWCA Civ 853 the Court of Appeal held that the harm was insufficient to justify the intervention of the State and disturb the autonomy of the parents.

The corporal punishment of children by parents is not completely outlawed in England and Wales, as the defence of reasonable chastisement can be used in certain restricted circumstances. This defence originated in the case of *R v Hopley* (1860) 2 F&F 202. In many European countries, however, there is a total ban on parents using corporal punishment. Sweden, for example, imposed a ban in 1979, and other countries have since banned it (such as Austria, Croatia, Cyprus, Denmark, Finland, Germany, Iceland, Latvia, Norway, Romania and Ukraine). Over the years there has been increasing pressure to ban it in the UK, in particular by organisations such as the Global Initiative to End All Corporal Punishment of Children and the National Society for the Prevention of Cruelty to Children. The United Nations Committee on the Rights of the Child in its periodic reports (see 8.2 above) has been critical of the lack of an absolute ban on corporal punishment in the UK.

(i) Pressure to change the law

At the end of the 1990s the UK Government came under increasing pressure to change the law in part because of the following decision by the European Court of Human Rights (ECtHR):

▶ *A v United Kingdom (Human Rights: Punishment of Child)* [1998] ECHR 85

The applicant, a boy aged nine, was beaten with a garden cane on a number of occasions by his step-father. The step-father was charged with assault occasioning actual bodily harm (s 47 Offences Against the Persons Act 1861), but was acquitted because, although it was not disputed by the defence that the step-father had caned the boy on a number of occasions, the jury accepted his defence of 'reasonable chastisement'. The applicant claimed before the ECtHR that the UK was in breach of Article 3 (the right not to be subjected to torture or to suffer inhuman or degrading treatment or punishment) and Article 8 (the right to a private and family life) of the European Convention on Human Rights (ECHR).

The ECtHR unanimously held that the UK was in breach of Article 3, because the reasonable chastisement defence did not give a child sufficient protection. It said that the ill-treatment must attain a minimum level of severity in order to fall within Article 3. On the facts, the step-father's ill-treatment of the child had reached that level taking into account the age of the child and the severity of the treatment. It held that the following factors were particularly important when establishing whether punishment was sufficiently severe to constitute ill-treatment for the purposes of Article 3: the nature and context of the defendant's treatment; its duration; its physical and mental effects in relation to the age and personal characteristics of the victim; and the reasons given by the defendant for administering the punishment.

Having concluded that there was a breach of Article 3, it held that there was no need to consider Article 8. The applicant was awarded £10,000 by way of damages.

As a result of the decision in *A v UK*, the UK Government was obliged to consider reforming the law. However, it was not obliged to impose a complete ban on corporal punishment as the breach of Article 3 in *A v UK* related to the degree of severity of the ill-treatment and to the unsatisfactory nature of the reasonable chastisement defence. The step-father's use of corporal punishment was not of itself a breach of Article 3.

In January 2000, the Government published a consultation document (*Protecting Children, Supporting Parents: A Consultation Document on the Physical Punishment of Children*, Department of Health) in which it said that, while harmful and degrading treatment of children could never be justified, it did not consider the right way forward was to make all physical punishment by parents unlawful. It said that there was 'a common-sense distinction between the sort of mild physical rebuke which occurs in families, and which most loving parents consider acceptable, and the beating of a child' (para 1(5)). The Government said that it was considering introducing a statutory definition of the defence of 'reasonable chastisement' based on the criteria laid down in *A v UK* (nature of the treatment, its context, duration, etc.). However, with the coming into force of the Human Rights Act 1998 (HRA 1998) (see 1.8) it was no longer necessary to change the law as the courts in the UK were obliged to take account of the ruling in *A v UK* in any event due to their obligations under section 2(2) of the HRA 1998. In fact, before the HRA 1998 had come into force, the decision in *A v UK* had already been applied in *R v H (Reasonable Chastisement)* [2001] 2 FLR 431, where the Court of Appeal held that, when juries were considering the reasonableness or otherwise of reasonable chastisement, they must be instructed by the judge to consider the criteria in *A v UK*.

In November 2001, the Government published its conclusions on the responses to its consultation document (*An Analysis of Responses to Protecting Children, Supporting Parents: A Consultation Document on the Physical Punishment of Children*). It concluded that it did not believe that 'any further change to the law at this time would command widespread public support or that it would be capable of consistent enforcement' (para 76). It said that the guidance issued by the Court of Appeal in *R v H* (see above) was sufficient to provide the protection guaranteed by Article 3 of the ECHR. It did say, however, that it intended to keep the defence of reasonable chastisement under review.

The Government's refusal to change the law did not command widespread support, and further pressure was put on the Government to change the law. At the end of 2004 renewed attempts were made to prohibit parents from using corporal punishment, but proposals for an absolute ban were defeated in the House of Commons. However, a last-minute amendment to the Children Bill 2004 by Lord Lester of Herne Hill was accepted by the Government, which resulted in the enactment of section 58 of the Children Act 2004 (CA 2004).

(ii) Section 58 of the Children Act 2004

This provision does not ban all forms of corporal punishment, as it allows parents (and other persons *in loco parentis*) to raise the defence of reasonable chastisement if they are charged with the offences of common assault or battery against a child. However, section 58 has removed the availability of the reasonable chastisement defence where the accused is charged with wounding, causing grievous bodily harm, assault occasioning actual bodily harm or cruelty to a person under the age of 16.

When section 58 was going through Parliament, the Government promised to conduct a review after it had been in force for two years. The results of the review were published in October 2007 (*Review of Section 58 of the Children Act 2004*, Cm 7232, Department for Children, Schools and Families), but, on the basis of its findings, the Government concluded that it did not intend to change the law to outlaw corporal punishment completely. It considered that, through the enactment of section 58, it had met its international obligations under the United Nations Convention on the Rights of the Child (UNCRC) and the ECHR. The Government found, as part of its review, that parents were using corporal punishment less, but that 52 per cent of parents (compared with 88 per cent in 1998) still favoured retaining the right to use it. The Government accepted, however, that there appeared to be a lack of understanding about what the law did and did not allow. It said that it would do more to help with positive parenting; and that it would also ask the Crown Prosecution Service and the police to monitor the situation with regard to the use of reasonable punishment.

In early 2010, the Government commissioned Sir Roger Singleton to produce an independent report on corporal punishment. His report, which was published in March 2010, recommended, *inter alia*, that the Government should 'continue to promote positive parenting strategies and effective behaviour management techniques directed towards eliminating the use of smacking' and that 'parents who disapprove of smacking should make this clear to others who care for their children'.

(iii) Should corporal punishment by parents be outlawed completely?

Despite the restrictions imposed by section 58 of the CA 2004 on the corporal punishment of children, some people and some organisations are in favour of it being banned completely (such as the NSPCC, Save the Children, the Children's Rights Alliance and the Children's Commissioners throughout the UK). The United Nations Committee on the Rights of the Child has also recommended it be banned in the UK. Thus, in its report on the UK in October 2008, the United Nations Committee expressed concern at 'the failure of [the] State party to explicitly prohibit all corporal punishment in the home' and recommended that the UK should 'prohibit as a matter of priority all corporal punishment in the family, including through the repeal of all legal defences' (paras 40–42). In May 2014, the UK Government responded to this recommendation in its Fifth Report to the United Nations Committee on the Rights of the Child (*The Fifth Periodic Report to the UN Committee on the Rights of the Child*). In its response, it stated: 'The UK Government does not condone any violence towards children and has clear laws to deal with it. Our view is that a mild smack does not constitute violence and that parents should not be criminalised for giving a mild smack' (para 11).

There are arguments for allowing parents to administer reasonable and moderate corporal punishment, such as that: parents should have the choice; and it does not harm children. However, there are strong arguments for outlawing it completely, such as that: condoning corporal punishment creates a culture of abuse which can result in children being harmed, sometimes very seriously; the current law breaches children's human rights; and the current law is confusing. Whether corporal punishment will be banned completely remains to be seen, but, at the time of writing, there are no proposals to do so.

(b)   Corporal punishment in schools

Corporal punishment of children is banned in all schools under section 548 of the Education Act 1996 (EA 1996). Use of physical force or punishment by a teacher on a schoolchild can therefore give rise to criminal or civil liability, and there is no defence of reasonable chastisement. However, in certain circumstances teachers are permitted to use reasonable restraint on a schoolchild (s 550A).

The following case was highly influential in leading to the abolition of corporal punishment in State schools.

▶ *Campbell and Cosans v UK (1982)* **4 EHRR 293**

Two mothers from Scotland claimed that the use of corporal punishment in State schools breached their sons' rights not to suffer inhuman and degrading treatment under Article 3 of the ECHR.

The ECtHR found no breach of Article 3 – as the boys had not been punished or threatened with punishment – but held that there had been a breach of Article 2 of Protocol 1 to the ECHR, which provides that '[n]o person shall be denied the right to education', and that 'the State shall respect the right of parents to ensure such education and teaching in conformity with their own religious and philosophical convictions'. The ECtHR held that Jeffrey Cosans' right to education had been breached as he had been suspended from school for nearly a year, because his parents objected to corporal punishment. It also held that the applicants' rights had been breached, because corporal punishment was not in conformity with their philosophical convictions.

In *Costello-Roberts v UK* (1993) 19 EHRR 112 the applicant boy claimed that the corporal punishment he had suffered at his independent school breached Articles 3, 8 and 13 of the ECHR. His claim failed, but in September 1999 corporal punishment was abolished in independent schools.

In the following case, parents and teachers at certain Christian schools objected on religious grounds to the abolition of corporal punishment in schools in England and Wales:

> ▶ *R (Williamson) v Secretary of State for Education and Employment and Others* [2006] UKHL 15
>
> Head teachers, teachers and parents at certain Christian independent schools in England claimed in judicial review proceedings that the ban on corporal punishment in schools breached their rights to freedom of religion under the ECHR. They claimed that it was a tenet of their fundamental Christian belief that parents (and teachers) should be able to administer physical punishment to children. They wished teachers to be able to administer reasonable chastisement because they believed it was conducive to the moral well-being of children. They claimed that section 548 of the EA 1996 did not completely abolish the use of corporal punishment in independent schools, and that, if it did so, it was a breach of Article 9(1) (the right to freedom of religion) and Article 2 of Protocol 1 of the ECHR, which provides that '[n]o person shall be denied the right to education' and that 'the State shall respect the right of parents to ensure such education and teaching in conformity with their own religious and philosophical convictions'. Their application was rejected at first instance. Their appeal was also dismissed by the Court of Appeal, and so they appealed to the House of Lords.
>
> The House of Lords held, dismissing their appeal, that there was no breach of the ECHR. Section 548 of the EA 1996 did not breach their rights to freedom of religion under Article 9(1) because the ban complied with Article 9(2), which permits freedom of religion to be limited by law where 'necessary in a democratic society … for the protection of the rights and freedoms of others'. The statutory ban pursued a legitimate aim (to protect children from physical violence) and the means used to achieve that aim were appropriate and not disproportionate.

8.6 Children and family proceedings

> **Article 12 of the United Nations Convention on the Rights of the Child 1989**
>
> 1. States Parties should assure to the child who is capable of forming his or her own views the right to express those views freely in all matters affecting the child, the views of the child being given due weight in accordance with the age and maturity of the child.
> 2. For this purpose, the child shall in particular be provided the opportunity to be heard in any judicial and administrative proceedings affecting the child, either directly, or through a representative or an appropriate body, in a manner consistent with the procedural rules of national law.

The first paragraph of Article 12 of the United Nations Convention on the Rights of the Child (UNCRC) draws attention to the right of children, who are capable of forming their own views, to express those views in matters which affect them and for weight to be given to those views in accordance with their age and maturity. It is very similar to the notion of '*Gillick* competency' (see 8.4 above) and to section 1(3)(a) of the Children Act 1989 (CA 1989) which requires the court in most children's proceedings to take into account 'the ascertainable wishes and feelings of the child concerned (considered in the light of his age and understanding)'. It is the second paragraph in Article 12, however, which is particularly important to the question of the voice of the child in family proceedings.

The rules with respect to children in family proceedings differ depending on whether the proceedings are private or public law proceedings. Private law proceedings involve private individuals (such as parents and children), whereas public law proceedings involve a public authority (such as a local authority social services team in care or supervision proceedings).

(a)   Private law

(i) Making an application to the court

A child can apply for a section 8 order under the CA 1989 (such as a child arrangements order, see 10.4), but only with leave of the court, which the court can grant if it considers the child has sufficient understanding to make the application (s 10(8)). Although the test of sufficient understanding is that of *Gillick* competence, only older teenagers are likely to be held to have the required sufficiency of understanding (see, for example, *Re C (Residence: Child's Application for Leave)* [1995] 1 FLR 927). Children can also bring proceedings under other legislation, such as for a non-molestation order under Part IV of the Family Law Act 1996 (see 5.4). They can also bring proceedings under the inherent jurisdiction of the court (see 8.7 below). In practice, however, applications to the court in any matter are extremely rare.

(ii) Rights of representation for children

The usual way in which the voice of the child is conveyed to the court in private law proceedings is by means of a welfare report prepared by a Children and Family Reporter (an officer of Cafcass, see 1.7). Children do not have party status in family proceedings, or the legal representation that accompanies it, unless the court exercises its power under rule 16.2 of the Family Procedure Rules 2010 (FPR 2010) which provides that the court may make a child a party to proceedings if it considers it is in the best interests of the child to do so. If it does so decide, then it *must* appoint a Children's Guardian for the child unless it is satisfied that such an appointment is not necessary to safeguard the child's interests (r 16.3). The Children's Guardian will work in tandem with the lawyer acting for the child.

(iii) Separate representation of children

There has been increasing concern in the last few years that children in private family proceedings (particularly for child arrangements orders) are not being given the opportunity to instruct their own solicitor without having to do so via a Children's Guardian. Thus, although the child or the child's solicitor can ask the court for leave to remove the Children's Guardian so that the child can instruct the lawyer directly (r 16.6), in practice this rarely happens.

(iv) Practice Direction 16A – Representation of Children

This Practice Direction supplements Part 16 of the FPR 2010 which deals with 'Representation of Children and Reports in Proceedings Involving Children'. It provides, among other things, that making a child party to the proceedings is 'a step that will be taken only in cases which involve an issue of significant difficulty and consequently will occur in only a minority of cases'; and that the court should consider whether an alternative route might be preferable (para 7.1). Paragraph 7.2 of the *Practice Direction* provides guidance on the circumstances where it might be justifiable to make an order that the child should have separation representation, such as where: there is an intractable dispute about the child's living or contact arrangements; where the child has a standpoint or interest which is inconsistent with or not capable of being represented by any of the adult parties; the child's views cannot be adequately met by a report to the court; an older child is opposing a proposed course of action; or where there are complex medical, mental health or other issues which necessitate separate representation of the child. The *Practice Direction* also draws attention to the fact that granting separate representation to a child may cause delay in the resolution of proceedings (para 7.3).

The following case concerned children having the right to instruct their own lawyer in private family law proceedings:

> ▶ *Mabon v Mabon and Others* **[2005] EWCA Civ 634**
>
> Three teenage boys (aged 13, 15 and 17), who were living with their father on the breakdown of their parents' relationship, wished to be separately represented in court proceedings involving a residence dispute between their parents. The boys had three younger siblings, who were living with the mother, but the mother sought residence orders against the father in respect of all six children. A Cafcass officer filed a report and was appointed Guardian of all six children. During the trial, however, the three oldest boys contacted a solicitor. At the residence hearing the boys' solicitor applied under the Family Procedure Rules 1991 (now replaced by the FPR 2010) for them to be separately represented, but the application was refused. The boys appealed to the Court of Appeal.
>
> The Court of Appeal unanimously allowed their appeal, holding that the judge had been plainly wrong. Thorpe LJ said that it was unthinkable to exclude young men from knowledge of and participation in legal proceedings that affected them so fundamentally. He said that, in the case of articulate teenagers, courts must accept that the right to freedom of expression and participation in family life outweighed the paternalistic judgment of welfare, and that the case provided a timely opportunity to recognise the growing acknowledgement of the autonomy and consequential rights of children. Thorpe LJ said that in individual cases trial judges must equally acknowledge this shift of approach when they made a proportionate judgment of the sufficiency of the child's understanding.

Mabon v Mabon was applied in *Re C (Abduction: Separate Representation of Children)* [2008] 2 FLR 6 and *W v W (Abduction: Joinder as Party)* [2009] EWHC 3288 (Fam) where the children were granted separate representation in cases brought under the Hague Convention on Abduction (see 13.4).

In most cases, however, the court will usually consider that the child's views and best interests will be sufficiently safeguarded by asking for a welfare report under section 7 of the CA 1989. Participating in court proceedings can be a harrowing and traumatic experience for children. They may be also exposed to the risk of having to make a choice between parents or of being manipulated by a parent. The courts are therefore keen to ensure that children are protected from the potentially harmful effect of being involved in court proceedings. Allowing children to participate in family proceedings can also add to the delay and cost of the trial. In the following case a different approach was taken to that in *Mabon*.

▶ *Re N (Contact: Minor Seeking Leave to Defend and Removal of Guardian)* [2003] 1 FLR 652

Coleridge J held that an 11-year-old boy, who wished to defend the contact proceedings, did not have sufficient understanding to participate and give instructions on his own behalf without a Children's Guardian. Complex issues were involved against a background of a long and stormy contact dispute. The child would not be able to understand the issues involved. Consequently he did not have sufficient understanding to participate. Coleridge J held that the test of competence was 'not whether the child was capable of articulating instructions but whether the child was of sufficient understanding to participate as party in the proceedings, in the sense of being able to cope with all the ramifications of the proceedings and giving considered instructions of sufficient objectivity'.

Whybrow (2004), commenting on *Re N*, said that the test of competence was set high and 'would render many adults incapable of conducting their family litigation, let alone children'.

The Court of Appeal has held that there is no objection to a service, such as the National Youth Advocacy Service (www.nyas.org.uk), representing a child in private law proceedings (see *Re H (National Youth Advocacy Service)* [2007] 1 FLR 1028).

(b) Public law cases

In public law proceedings (such as for care and supervision orders) the system of representation for children operates with a Children's Guardian and a solicitor acting side by side. Thus, children involved in public law proceedings are party to the proceedings. This has been so since the mid-1970s when the practice of using guardians *ad litem* to put forward the voice of the child was introduced as a result of the recommendations made in the wake of the Maria Colwell Inquiry in 1974.

(c) The voice of the child in family proceedings

Article 12(2) of the UNCRC 1989 requires a child to be given the opportunity to be heard in legal proceedings, and section 1(3)(a) of the CA 1989 requires the court to have regard to 'the ascertainable wishes and feelings of the child concerned (considered in the light of his age and understanding)'. However, there has been concern that children are not being listened to enough in family proceedings; and that judges should be more willing to allow them to be separately represented by their own lawyer (see, for example, Macdonald [2008] Fam Law 648; [2009] Fam Law 40).

In *Mabon v Mabon* (see above), Thorpe LJ said that 'in the twenty-first century, there is a keener appreciation of the autonomy of the child and the child's consequential right to participate in decision-making processes that fundamentally affect his family life'. In *Re D (A Child) (Abduction: Rights of Custody)* [2006] UKHL 51, Baroness Hale also drew attention to the growing importance of listening to the views of children:

> [T]here is now a growing understanding of the importance of listening to children in children's cases. It is the child, more than anyone else, who will have to live with what the court decides. Those who do listen to children understand that they often have a point of view which is quite distinct from that of the person looking after them. They are quite capable of being moral actors in their own right. Just as the adults may have to do what the court decides whether they like it or not, so may the child. But that is no more reason for failing to hear what the child has to say than it is for refusing to hear the parent's views.

In the last few years, there has been a growing interest and increased debate about reforming the law governing the voice of the child in family proceedings, something which has been promoted in part by the Family Justice Council (see [2008] Fam Law 431). However, although there is considerable support for the idea that children should be more involved in family proceedings, the difficult question concerns the extent to which they should be involved. For some children it may be distressing to hear the details of their parents' case in court. As Thorpe LJ warned in *Mabon* (see above), if direct participation in proceedings 'would pose an obvious risk of harm to the child, arising out of the continuing proceedings, and, if the child is incapable of comprehending that risk, then the judge is entitled to find that sufficient understanding has not been demonstrated'. Thorpe LJ said, however, that judges also have to be 'equally alive to the risk of emotional harm that might arise from denying the child knowledge of and participation in the continuing proceedings'. There are also time and resource implications in permitting children to be separately represented. In fact, in *Re A (Contact Order)* [2010] EWCA Civ 208, where the trial judge's decision that there should be no separate representation of the child was upheld by the Court of Appeal, Thorpe LJ held that orders for the separate representation of children should in the present conditions of restricted funding for the family justice system be issued very sparingly.

There is concern not just about whether separate representation should be more widely available for children in private family proceedings, but whether children's voices are being sufficiently heard at all. Thus, a child's wishes and feelings may be overlooked by parents who are involved in a difficult conflict, and in some cases the court may decide not to commission a welfare report.

(i) A breach of human rights?

Refusing to allow a child to participate in family proceedings, with or without a Children's Guardian, may be a breach of the child's human rights under Article 12 of the UNCRC or one of the following rights guaranteed under the ECHR: Article 6 (the right to a fair trial); Article 8 (the right to family life); Article 10 (the right to freedom of expression); and Article 13 (the right to an effective remedy). In *Re A (Contact: Separate Representation)* [2001] 1 FLR 715, Butler-Sloss P recognised that there were cases where children needed to be separately represented, and cases where she suspected that the voices of children had not always been sufficiently heard. She said that the courts' attitude to separate representation needed to change as a result of Articles 6 and 8 of the ECHR. However, although the ECtHR has not ruled on the need for separate representation in children's cases, in two cases brought against Germany involving contact disputes the ECtHR was critical of the German courts' failure to hear the children's views (see *Elsholz v Germany* [2000] 2 FLR 486; and *Sahin v Germany* [2002] 1 FLR 119).

The United Nations Committee on the Rights of the Child has expressed concern about the failure of the UK courts to allow children to be represented in private law proceedings.

(ii) Separate representation of children – reform

Although section 41(6A) of the CA 1989 permits rules of court to be drawn up to allow children to have separate representation in section 8 order proceedings (such as in child arrangements proceedings, see 10.4), these rules have never been made but merely discussed. In 2006, the Government consulted on the question of allowing separate representation of children in private law proceedings but said that only a small proportion of section 8 proceedings would be suitable for separate representation (see *Consultation Paper, Separate Representation of Children*, CP 20/06, 2006). The responses to the consultation were published in July 2007 (*Separate Representation of Children: Summary of Responses to a Consultation Paper*, CP(R) 20/06), and the Government said that it proposed to extend jurisdiction for deciding whether a child should be made a party to family proceedings to all levels of court. It also proposed that children would be provided with information during proceedings to help them cope with anxieties and uncertainties; and that, subject to agreement with the judiciary, children who wished to speak to a judge or magistrate should be able to do so. Although these proposals were not introduced, there is some evidence to show that the number of children for whom the courts order separate representation has increased (see [2009] Fam Law 466).

The Family Justice Review in its *Final Report* in November 2011 (see 1.2) suggested that children and young people should be given the opportunity to have their voices heard in cases that are about them, if they so wished; and that separate representation of children was an area that needed to be kept under review. Thus, for example, in the Executive Summary to the *Report*, it was stated, with respect to the child's voice, that

> [c]hildren's interests are central to the operation of the family justice system. Decisions should take the wishes of children into account and children should know what is happening and why. People urged us to consider the need to take great care in consulting children, and for this to be handled sensitively and to take into account the child's age and understanding.

In February 2012, the Government fully endorsed these proposals, stating that the new Family Justice Board will consider how children can be best supported to make their views known and be taken into account in decisions that affect them (*The Government Response to the Family Justice Review: A System with Children and Families at Its Heart*, Cm 8273, February 2010). In its *Response* the Government stated:

> At the individual level more consistency is needed in how children are involved in the court processes which affect their lives. This needs to be done with great care and sensitivity, by practitioners who understand how to best communicate with and listen to children depending on their age and circumstances.

(iii) Judicial interviews of children

In the last few years there has been discussion about whether judges should interview children in order to discover their views. In New Zealand, for example, the courts have adopted this practice, subject to certain guidelines ([2008] Fam Law 809). Senior members of the judiciary are in favour of judicial interviews of children in appropriate cases, but, as yet, no specific measures have been introduced to make provision for this. Nonetheless, in some cases, judges have interviewed children and endorsed this practice. Thus, for example, in *Re G (Abduction: Children's Objections)* [2010] EWCA Civ 1232, a case brought under the Hague Convention on Abduction involving a 13-year-old child, Thorpe LJ endorsed the view that interviewing a child was a viable option for the judiciary and he was critical of the fact that a judicial interview with the child had not been suggested at first instance. Although he said it was 'highly unusual' to meet a child before deciding an appeal, he nevertheless endorsed the approach of the Family Justice Council which had forcefully expressed the view that judges should be meeting with children and hearing their voices.

(For a general discussion of the voice of the child in out-of-court dispute resolution in England and Wales see Ewing, Hunter, Barlow and Smithson [2015] CFLQ 43).

(d) Children giving evidence in family proceedings

In *Re W* [2010] UKSC 12 the Supreme Court held that there was no longer a presumption or even a starting point against children giving oral evidence in family proceedings. Although *Re W* was a care proceedings case, this approach also applies to other family proceeding cases. In response to *Re W*, a set of guidelines (*Guidelines in Relation to Children Giving Evidence in Family Proceedings*) were produced by the Family Justice Council Working Party on Children Giving Evidence in December 2011. The guidelines were drawn up for the benefit of the judiciary, lawyers and professionals who have to deal with applications for children to give evidence in family proceedings. The guidelines (available at www.judiciary.gov.uk.) are lengthy and detailed, but in deciding whether a child should give evidence, the court's principal objective should be to achieve a fair trial. The age and maturity of the child are, for example, considerations that the court has to take into account. Evidence by video link is possible, depending on the circumstances.

8.7 Protection for children in wardship and under the inherent jurisdiction

(a) Introduction

The inherent jurisdiction, of which wardship is a part, is an ancient jurisdiction deriving from the right and duty of the Crown as *parens patriae* (parent or protector of the realm) to take care of people who are unable to care for themselves. This includes not just children, but also incapacitated adults (for example in the context of marriage, see 2.5). Only the High Court has jurisdiction under the inherent jurisdiction and in wardship.

(i) Applications by local authorities

Before the Children Act 1989 (CA 1989) came into force, local authorities would use the inherent jurisdiction to take children into care, even though statute made provision for this. The CA 1989 changed that practice, so that a local authority could no longer use the inherent jurisdiction to: place a child in its care or under its supervision (s 100(2)(a)); accommodate a child in care (s 100(2)(b)); make a child a ward of court (s 100(2)(c)); or determine a question about any aspect of parental responsibility for a child (s 100(2)(d)).

However, a local authority is not totally precluded from invoking the inherent jurisdiction, as it can ask the High Court to give it leave to invoke it (s 100(3)). The High Court can grant such leave if it is satisfied that the result which is wanted cannot be achieved by any other order, and there is reasonable cause to believe that the child will suffer significant harm if the inherent jurisdiction is not exercised (s 100(4)). Local authorities sometimes invoke the inherent jurisdiction in cases where children need medical treatment (see 9.7). Hospitals and health authorities sometimes invoke the inherent jurisdiction in difficult medical cases in order to ask the court to authorise or terminate a child's medical treatment.

(ii) Applications by private individuals

With respect to applications by private individuals, although there is no express prohibition in the CA 1989 against them using wardship and the inherent jurisdiction, they are now rarely invoked. This is because the CA 1989 introduced two new orders (prohibited steps and specific issue orders, see 10.7 and 10.8) which allow judges to exercise similar powers to those which the High Court can exercise under its inherent jurisdiction. Thus, as in local authority cases, wardship and the inherent jurisdiction are now a residual jurisdiction which provide a safety net for children in complex and difficult cases and cases which cannot be resolved under the CA 1989, for example difficult medical cases (see 9.7), some international child abduction cases (see 13.11) and some forced marriage cases (see 2.6). However, cases which could be dealt with under the CA 1989 are sometimes dealt with by using wardship, for example, where the parents are engaged in a particularly bitter and ongoing dispute about a child as the parents were in *T v S (Wardship)* [2011] EWHC 1608 (Fam) (see below). Such uses of wardship are, however, rare as the circumstances must be exceptional before the court will intervene by way of wardship rather than making an order under the CA 1989.

(iii) Section 8 orders

As proceedings in wardship and under the inherent jurisdiction are 'family proceedings' for the purpose of the CA 1989, the High Court can make any section 8 order (see 10.4) in the proceedings, except where the child is in care, when only a child arrangement's order regulating the child's living arrangements can be made (s 9(1)). As a section 8 order cannot be made in favour of a local authority on an application by a local authority when a child is in care (ss 9(1) and (2)), a local authority wishing to resolve a question about a child in care (such as in respect of medical treatment) must apply for leave of the court to invoke the inherent jurisdiction.

(b)   Wardship

Wardship is part of the inherent jurisdiction of the High Court. The essence of wardship is that, once a child is made a ward of court, the situation is frozen and the court stands *in loco parentis* for the child. Consequently, as the court has parental responsibility for the child, any major step in the child's life requires the court's prior consent. Thus, for example, a ward cannot marry, be adopted, leave the jurisdiction or receive serious medical treatment without the consent of the court. It is this supervisory role of the court which distinguishes wardship from the inherent jurisdiction, and is sometimes the reason why it is used in children's cases. For example, in *T v S (Wardship)* [2011] EWHC 1608 (Fam) Hedley J held that wardship should be continued with respect to a four-year-old child whose parents were involved in an incessant and serious conflict about how their parental responsibility was to be exercised, as wardship would enable the court to retain care and control of the child and parental responsibility would rest with the court save insofar as it was prepared to delegate its exercise to the parents.

Wardship is also useful in urgent situations, as the High Court acquires powers in respect of the child automatically on the issue of the initial application. For this reason wardship is useful in some abduction cases (see 13.11). It has also been used in forced marriage cases (see 2.6).

The governing principle in wardship proceedings is that the welfare of the child is the court's paramount consideration. Provided the High Court has jurisdiction to make the child a ward of court, it can exercise a wide range of powers. Thus, under the CA 1989, it can: make any section 8 order; make a section 37 direction that a local authority make inquiries about a child; appoint a guardian for the child; and make orders for financial provision under Schedule 1. It also has the power to grant injunctions. Although the wardship jurisdiction is theoretically limitless, in some situations the court will refuse to exercise it (for example where it will undermine a statutory power; or in immigration and asylum cases). Inappropriate uses of wardship are therefore not permitted. The court will also refuse to exercise jurisdiction where the child has never been habitually resident or present in the UK (see, for example, *H v H (Jurisdiction to Grant Wardship)* [2011] EWCA Civ 796), although wardship has sometimes been used to protect a child who is a victim of a forced marriage but who is not currently resident in the UK (see 2.6).

(c)   The inherent jurisdiction

The High Court has a general inherent power to protect children (and incapacitated adults) which is independent of the wardship jurisdiction. The inherent jurisdiction is sometimes used to obtain the court's permission to allow or refuse medical treatment, for example: to arrange medical treatment for a 16-year-old anorexic girl in care (*Re W (A Minor) (Medical Treatment: Court's Jurisdiction)* [1993] Fam 64); to give blood transfusions to a child whose parents object to treatment on religious grounds (*Re O (A Minor) (Medical Treatment)* [1993] 2 FLR 149); and to obtain guidance on the treatment of a severely handicapped child (*Re J (A Minor) (Medical Treatment)* [1992] 2 FLR 165).

The inherent jurisdiction is also sometimes used in forced marriage cases (see 2.6) and in abduction cases (see 13.11). It has also been used in the case of vulnerable adults, in other words where a person lacks mental capacity. Thus, for example, in

A Local Authority v E [2008] 1 FLR 978 the inherent jurisdiction was used in respect of a 19-year-old woman with a severe learning difficulty who had been made the subject of a care order at the age of 15.

The inherent jurisdiction has sometimes been used to fill gaps in the law in order to protect the best interests of children, as it was in *Re D (Unborn Baby)* [2009] EWHC 446 (Fam) where Munby J made an order under the inherent jurisdiction in respect of an unborn baby, because the CA 1989 and the wardship jurisdiction could not be invoked in respect of an unborn child. In this case the local authority successfully applied for an anticipatory declaration under the inherent jurisdiction declaring that it could lawfully remove a baby at birth from her mother because there was a serious and likely risk that the mother would seriously harm the child. The inherent jurisdiction was also invoked in *Re C (Abduction: Separate Representation of Children)* [2008] 2 FLR 6 where the child concerned was too old to come within the jurisdiction of the Hague Convention on Abduction, and in *Re U (Abduction: Nigeria)* [2010] EWHC 1179 (Fam) where the children concerned were removed to a country which was not a signatory to the Hague Convention on Abduction (see 13.11).

(d)   Limits on the use of wardship and the inherent jurisdiction

In addition to the restrictions placed on local authorities (see above), the High Court may refuse to exercise the inherent jurisdiction or to make a child a ward of court even though the inherent jurisdiction and wardship are theoretically limitless. Thus, for example, in *Re F (In Utero)* [1998] Fam 122 the High Court refused to make an unborn child a ward of court, as to do so would place an unjustifiable fetter on the rights of the child's mother. In some cases, the court will refuse to make a child a ward of court because public interests prevail, such as in the context of immigration control as the following case shows.

▶ *S v S* **[2009] 1 FLR 241**

The mother of the child was resisting deportation as a failed asylum seeker. The mother's cousin began wardship proceedings in respect of the child, but Munby J dismissed the application, holding that the High Court cannot, even in the exercise of its inherent jurisdiction, make orders which in any way impinge upon or prevent the Secretary of State exercising powers lawfully conferred by statute in the context of immigration and asylum (following *R v Secretary of State for the Home Department ex parte T* [1995] 1 FLR 293; and *Re A (Care Proceedings: Asylum Seekers)* [2003] 2 FLR 921). Munby J held that, in the circumstances of the case, the wardship proceedings were not serving any useful or permissible purpose.

(e)   Protecting children from media intrusion and harmful publication

Applications to the High Court in wardship or under its inherent jurisdiction are sometimes made in order to obtain an injunction to protect a child from harmful media attention and exposure (see, for example, *Re Z (A Minor) (Freedom of Publication)*

[1996] 1 FLR 191; and *Nottingham City Council v October Films Ltd* [1999] 2 FLR 347). However, jurisdiction may be refused on the ground that freedom of speech prevails, as the following case shows.

▶ *R (Mrs) v Central Independent Television plc* [1994] Fam 192

A child was made a ward of court, on the application of her mother, in order to prevent a television programme being broadcast which discussed the child's father's conviction and imprisonment for indecency. The decision of the High Court was overturned by the Court of Appeal. Waite LJ said that no child, simply by virtue of being a child, is entitled to a right of privacy or confidentiality. As the programme had nothing to do with the care or upbringing of the child, there was nothing to put in the balance against the freedom to publish.

The Human Rights Act 1998 (HRA 1998) gives particular priority to the right to freedom of speech under Article 10 of the European Convention on Human Rights (ECHR) (see s 12(4)) and the High Court in children's cases must weigh this in the balance when considering the child's Article 8 right to a private and family life, and the child's welfare.

The following decision of the House of Lords is the leading case on preventing publication in order to protect a child.

▶ *Re S (Identification: Restriction on Publication)* [2004] UKHL 47

The guardian of an eight-year-old child obtained an injunction under the inherent jurisdiction to restrain publication of the identity of the child's mother who had been charged with the murder of the child's older brother. The judge in the High Court (on the application of the newspaper) modified the injunction so that the newspaper could, in reports of the criminal trial, publish the identity of the mother and the deceased brother and reproduce their photographs. This decision was upheld by the Court of Appeal. The child appealed to the House of Lords, arguing that his right to respect for his private and family life under Article 8 of the ECHR meant that he was entitled to protection against harmful publicity concerning his family.

The House of Lords unanimously dismissed his appeal, holding that cases decided before the HRA 1998 on the existence and scope of the High Court's inherent jurisdiction to restrain publicity no longer need to be considered. The foundation to restrain publicity now derives from rights under the ECHR. However, the case-law on the inherent jurisdiction is not wholly irrelevant, as it might remain of some interest in regard to the ultimate balancing exercise to be carried out under the provisions of the ECHR. Article 8 was engaged in the case, but the child would not be involved in the trial as a witness or otherwise. The impact of the trial on the child would be indirect. Competing rights of freedom of the press under Article 10 were also engaged but were not outweighed by the rights of the child under Article 8. Given the weight traditionally given to the importance of open reporting of criminal proceedings, it had been important for the judge, in carrying out the exercise required by the ECHR, to begin by acknowledging the force of the argument under Article 10 before considering whether the right of the child under Article 8 was sufficient to outweigh it.

The House of Lords also referred to the United Nations Convention on the Rights of the Child (UNCRC), which protects the privacy of children directly involved in criminal proceedings, but not children indirectly affected by criminal trials.

There have been other cases where the court has refused to make a child a ward of court because freedom of speech prevails. Thus, for example, it was refused in *Re X (A Minor) (Wardship: Jurisdiction)* [1975] Fam 4 where an application was made to ward a child for the purpose of prohibiting the publication of a book containing references to the salacious behaviour of her deceased father which might harm her if the book came to her knowledge. Wardship was refused on the ground that freedom of speech and freedom of publication prevailed over the child's welfare. (For another case involving wardship and restricting publication, see *Re Stedman* [2009] 2 FLR 852; and for a case involving the autonomy of the child and freedom to publish, see *Re Roddy (A Child) (Identification: Restriction on Publicity)* [2004] 2 FLR 949).

Summary

▶ It has been increasingly recognised and accepted that children have rights. Some theorists, however, have argued that it is not appropriate to talk about children's 'rights' (because children lack the necessary competence to have rights) and that it is better to talk about children's 'interests' or in terms of the obligations that adults owe them. A particularly difficult dilemma is the extent to which children should have rights of self-determination, in other words autonomy rights. The law must, however, strike a balance between allowing children greater rights of self-determination and ensuring that they are protected by the law. The Children's Commissioners throughout the UK act as champions for children, and have a statutory responsibility to promote the United Nations Convention on the Rights of the Child (UNCRC).

▶ The UNCRC has been ratified by the UK, but it does not have the same force in the UK as the European Convention on Human Rights (ECHR). This is because it has not been incorporated into all of UK law (which needs an Act of Parliament) and it does not have its own court to enforce its provisions. However, arguments based on the UNCRC can be used persuasively in court, and judges sometimes refer to it in their decisions. The Government also takes it into account when considering new policies relating to children. The United Nations Committee on the Rights of the Child is responsible for monitoring the implementation of the UNCRC and produces periodic reports on children's rights, or the lack of them, in Member States.

▶ Children have rights under the ECHR. The European Court of Human Rights (ECtHR) has recognised that a child's best interests are paramount and can sometimes prevail over parental interests. The ECHR has played a greater role for children in England and Wales since the coming into force of the Human Rights Act 1998 (HRA 1998). Human rights are used in legal argument and by judges when making decisions, but there are some concerns that they are not being used enough.

▶ *Gillick v West Norfolk and Wisbech Health Authority* (1986) was a landmark case with respect to the autonomy of children in that it gave greater recognition to the right of children to make their own decisions, not just with regard to medical treatment but in other contexts. It also gave rise to the phrases '*Gillick* competency' and the '*Gillick* competent child' (a child who is old and mature enough to make an informed decision); and it emphasised that it is better to talk about parental responsibilities rather than parental rights, a recommendation which was implemented in the Children Act 1989 (CA 1989).

▶ *Gillick* did not, however, give children absolute rights, and subsequent cases have shown that children do not always have the final say about medical treatment, or about any other matter, particularly if a proposed course of action is not in their best interests. For example, in cases where children have refused medical treatment (*Gillick* was about consent), the courts have overridden their wishes notwithstanding that the children have been '*Gillick* competent' and section 8 of the Family Law Reform Act 1969 provides that 16- and 17-year-olds can give valid consent to surgical, medical and dental treatment (see, for example, *Re R (A Minor) (Wardship: Medical Treatment)* (1992) and *Re W (A Minor) (Medical Treatment: Court's Jurisdiction)* (1993)). In *R (Axon) v Secretary of State for Health* (2006) it was held that *Gillick* was still good law after the enactment of the HRA 1998 as its guidelines about medical treatment and parental consent did not infringe parental rights to a private and family life (under Article 8 of the ECHR). *Gillick* had an impact on the content of the CA 1989 as some of its provisions require the court to listen to the wishes and feelings of a '*Gillick* competent child' (see, for example, s 1(3)(a)).

▶ Children's autonomy rights have sometimes been considered in the context of their human rights, as they were, for example, in *Re Axon* above (with respect to medical treatment), *Re Roddy (A Child) (Identification: Restriction on Publication)* (2004) (with respect to publishing a story) and *R (On the Application of Begum) v Headteacher and Governors of Denbigh High School* (2006) (with respect to wearing religious clothing in school).

▶ Parents are not prohibited from using corporal punishment on their children, but section 58 of the Children Act 2004 has outlawed the defence of reasonable punishment for all criminal charges except common assault or battery. Corporal punishment is prohibited in all State and independent schools by section 548 of the Education Act 1996 (EA 1996).

▶ The rules concerning the representation of children in public law proceedings are different from those which apply in private law proceedings. In public law proceedings (such as for care and supervision orders), a child is automatically made a party to the proceedings and is represented through a Children's Guardian. In private law proceedings (such as for a child arrangements order), a child can be made a party to those proceedings and be represented through a Children's Guardian or can instruct a solicitor without such a person, but this is at the discretion of the court (see Part 16 of the Family Procedure Rules 2010 and *Practice Direction 16A – Representation of Children*). The usual way in which the voice of the child is conveyed is through a welfare report prepared by a Cafcass officer (s 7 CA 1989).

▶ There is some concern that, despite Article 12(2) of the UNCRC and section 1(3)(a) of the CA 1989, the voice of the child is still not being sufficiently heard in private law proceedings. The Government has consulted on the question of allowing separate representation of children in private law proceedings, but no reforms have been made. There has been discussion about judges interviewing children in order to discover their views, and this is a practice which is sometimes used now, but only rarely.

▶ The presumption that children should not give oral evidence in care proceedings (and also in family law proceedings) was overturned by the Supreme Court in *Re W* (2010), and guidelines about this change in the law have been drawn up by the Family Justice Council and approved by the then President of the Family Division.

▶ The High Court has an inherent jurisdiction (which includes wardship) to protect children. This is a parental type of jurisdiction. The welfare of the child is the court's paramount consideration in such cases. The High Court's powers are not invoked as often as they once were, following changes introduced by the CA 1989. Thus, there are restrictions on local authorities using the inherent jurisdiction and wardship, although they do sometimes invoke them in difficult medical cases involving children. Wardship is useful in complex cases where urgent action is needed, such as in some international child abduction cases and forced marriage cases. It is also useful where the court wishes to retain a supervisory role with respect to a child. The High Court may refuse to exercise its inherent powers and wardship where other interests prevail over the child's welfare, for example where there is a need to uphold immigration policy or freedom of speech.

Further reading and references

Alston, Parker and Seymour (eds), *Children, Rights and the Law*, 1992, Clarendon Press.

Barton, '*A v UK* – the thirty thousand pound caning – an "English vice" in Europe' [1999] CFLQ 63.

Butler-Sloss, Baroness, 'A child's place in the big society' [2010] Fam Law 938.

Caldwell, 'Common law judges and judicial interviewing' [2011] CFLQ 41.

Cave, 'Maximisation of minors' capacity' [2011] CFLQ 431.

Cave, 'Goodbye Gillick? Identifying and resolving problems with the concept of child competence' (2014) 34 *Legal Studies* 103–122.

Choudhry and Herring, *European Human Rights and Family Law*, 2010, Hart Publishing.

Edwards, 'Imaging Islam … of meaning and metaphor symbolising the jilbab – *R (Begum) v Headteacher and Governors of Denbigh High School*' [2007] CFLQ 247.

Eekelaar, 'The emergence of children's rights' (1986) 6 OJLS 161.

Eekelaar, 'The importance of thinking that children have rights' (1992) 6 IJLF.

Eekelaar, 'The interests of the child and the child's wishes: the role of dynamic self-determinism' (1994) 8 IJLF 42.

Ewing, Hunter, Barlow and Smithson, 'Children's voices: centre-stage or sidelined in out-of-court dispute resolution in England and Wales?' [2015] CFLQ 43.

Fenwick, 'Clashing rights, the welfare of the child and the Human Rights Act' (2004) 67(6) *Modern Law Review* 889.

Fortin, *Children's Rights and the Developing Law* (3rd ed.), 2009, Cambridge University Press.

Fortin, 'A decade of the HRA and its impact on children's rights' [2011] Fam Law 176.

Gilmore, 'Children's refusal of treatment: the debate continues' [2012] Fam Law 973.

Gilmore and Herring, 'Children's refusal of medical treatment: could *Re W* be distinguished?' [2011] Fam Law 715.

Gilmore and Herring, '"No" is the hardest word: consent and children's autonomy' [2011] CFLQ 4.

Hendrick, 'When should the judge and the child meet?' [2011] Fam Law 1148.

Hunter, 'Close encounters of a judicial kind: "hearing" children's "voices" in family law proceedings' [2007] CFLQ 283.

Huxtable, '*Re M (Medical Treatment: Consent)* – time to remove the "flak jacket"' [2000] CFLQ 83.

Macdonald, 'Bringing rights home for children: arguing the UNCRC' [2009] Fam Law 1073.

Macdonald, 'The voice of the child – still a faint cry?' [2008] Fam Law 648.

Macdonald, 'The child's voice in private law: loud enough?' [2009] Fam Law 40.

McFarlane, 'Mental capacity: one standard for all ages' [2011] Fam Law 479.

Parkinson and Cashmore, *The Voice of the Child in Family Disputes*, 2008, Oxford University Press.

Taylor, 'Reversing the retreat from *Gillick? R (Axon) v Secretary of State for Health*' [2007] CFLQ 81.

Taylor, 'Putting children first? Children's interests as a primary consideration in public law' [2016] CFLQ 45.

Wall, Rt Hon Lord Justice, 'Separate representation of children' [2007] Fam Law 124.

Walsh, 'Enhancing the participation of children and young people in family proceedings: starting the debate' [2008] Fam Law 431.

Whybrow, 'Children, guardians and rule 9.5' [2004] Fam Law 504.

Websites

Association of Lawyers for Children: www.alc.org.uk

Children are Unbeatable! Alliance: www.childrenareunbeatable.org.uk

Children's Commissioner (for England): www.childrenscommissioner.gov.uk

Children's Commissioner (for Wales): www.childcom.org.uk

Children's Rights Alliance for England: www.crae.org.uk

Coram Children's Legal Centre: www.childrenslegalcentre.com

Department for Education: www.education.gov.uk

End All Corporal Punishment of Children: www.endcorporalpunishment.org

National Youth Advocacy Service: www.nyas.net

NSPCC: www.nspcc.org.uk

UN Convention on the Rights of the Child: www.unicef.org/crc

Links to relevant websites can also be found at: www.palgravehighered.com/law/familylaw9e

Chapter 9

Parents

This chapter deals with the law governing parents. It deals first with the different types of parent that exist and the importance of parents. It then considers the issue of parentage, and looks at parental responsibility and the various rights, duties and responsibilities that parents have. It concludes by looking at parenthood in the context of both assisted reproduction and surrogacy arrangements.

9.1 Introduction

(a) Who is a parent?

Most children are brought up by parents with whom they have a biological link. However, some are brought up by a person with whom they have no such link, such as a step-parent, a foster-parent, a guardian (see 9.8 below), an adoptive parent (see Chapter 15) or a special guardian (see 15.14).

The word 'parent' is not defined in the Children Act 1989 (CA 1989). In *Re G (Children) (Residence: Same-Sex Partner)* [2006] UKHL 43 (see below), Baroness Hale considered the meaning of the term 'parent'. She said that parents could be classified as 'legal' and/or 'natural' parents and that a person could be, or could become, a natural parent in one of the following three ways: by genetic parenthood (where the parent provides the egg or sperm which produces the child); by gestational parenthood (where the parent conceives and bears the child); or by social and psychological parenthood. Baroness Hale said that in the great majority of cases the child's mother would combine all three types of natural parenthood, and the father would combine two.

(i) The importance of the biological link between parent and child

The weight to be accorded to the biological link between parent and child has been a question which the courts have sometimes had to address. The courts have recognised that it is usually in a child's best interests for the child to be brought up, where possible, by their 'natural' parents; and this has generally been taken to mean their biological parents. However, although the courts regard biological parenthood as an important and significant factor in determining what is in the best interests of a child, they have been unwilling to describe it as a presumption in favour of biological parents, as the following case shows.

▶ *Re G (Children) (Residence: Same-Sex Partner)* [2006] UKHL 43

CG and CW were a same sex couple who had two daughters by artificial insemination (by an unknown donor). CG was the children's genetic and gestational mother. Their relationship broke down and CW applied for contact and shared residence. A shared

---

residence order was made with CG being granted a 70 per cent share. When CG moved to Cornwall in breach of a court order requiring the children to live in Leicester, Bracewell J made an order changing the children's primary place of residence to that of CW, as she had no confidence that CG would promote the 'essential close relationship' with CW and her family. CG's appeal to the Court of Appeal was dismissed and so she appealed to the House of Lords on the basis, *inter alia*, that it was wrong for the court to have attached no significance to the fact that she was the children's genetic and gestational mother.

The House of Lords unanimously overturned the decision of the Court of Appeal and reversed the children's living arrangements so that their primary home was once more with CG, the genetic and gestational mother. It held that it was contrary to the welfare of the children to remove them from their biological mother.

BARONESS HALE: I am driven to the conclusion that the courts below have allowed the unusual context of this case to distract them from principles which are of universal application. … [T]he fact that CG is the natural mother of these children in every sense of that term, while raising no presumption in her favour, is undoubtedly an important and significant factor in determining what will be best for them now and in the future. Yet nowhere is that factor explored in the judgment below ….

LORD NICHOLLS: [The welfare of the child] is the court's paramount consideration. In reaching its decision the court should always have in mind that in the ordinary way the rearing of a child by his or her biological parent can be expected to be in the child's best interests, both in the short term and also, importantly, in the longer term. I decry any tendency to diminish the significance of this factor. A child should not be removed from the primary care of his or her biological parents without compelling reasons. Where such a reason exists the judge should spell this out explicitly.

In the following case, which involved a residence dispute between a child's father and maternal grandmother, the Supreme Court reaffirmed the central message of *Re G*, which is that the child's welfare is the paramount consideration. It further held that the correct interpretation of *Re G* was that there should be no presumption in favour of the biological parent, as such a presumption would detract from an examination of what is in a child's best interests.

▶ *Re B (A Child) (Residence)* [2009] UKSC 5

The child, a four-year-old boy whose parents had separated before he was born, had lived from birth with his maternal grandmother. His mother had lived with them intermittently but eventually left and did not return. The father's application for a residence order was refused as the justices found no compelling reasons to disrupt the continuity of care that the grandmother had provided for him. The circuit judge and the Court of Appeal allowed the father's appeal as the justices had erred in law and had been plainly wrong in giving disproportionate weight to maintaining the status quo. Applying *Re G* (see above), in particular the observations of Lord Nicholls, it held that the court should always bear in mind that, ordinarily, the rearing of a child by their biological parent could be expected to be in their best interests. The grandmother appealed to the Supreme Court.

The Supreme Court unanimously allowed her appeal. Lord Kerr, giving the leading judgment, held that the justices had not been plainly wrong as they had recognised that the child's welfare was the paramount consideration and had carefully evaluated the evidence before them, correctly weighing up the various competing factors. The court held that:

1) The circuit judge and the Court of Appeal had misinterpreted *Re G*. In that case, when Lord Nicholls said that courts should keep in mind that the interests of a child will normally be best served by being reared by their biological parent, he was doing no more than reflecting common experience that, in general, children tend to thrive when brought up by parents to whom they have been born. All consideration of the importance of parenthood in private law disputes about residence must be firmly rooted in an examination of what is in the child's best interests. This is the paramount consideration. It is only as a contributor to the child's welfare that parenthood assumes any significance. In common with all other factors bearing on what is in the best interests of the child, it must be examined for its potential to fulfil that aim.

2) Any discussion of a child's right to be brought up by their biological parents is misplaced. The only consideration for the court is the child's welfare; and to talk of a child's rights detracts from that consideration.

3) On the facts of the case, in deciding where the child's best interests lay, the justices had been right to give significant weight to maintaining the status quo in the child's living arrangement.

Everett and Yeatman ([2010] CFLQ 290), who discussed *Re G* and *Re B*, concluded that 'the crucial factor should be the love and commitment shown by the adults in the child's life, not the source of that love, be it genetic or social'. Bainham ([2010] Fam Law 394) has questioned whether the rejection in *Re G* and *Re B*, and in other higher court decisions, of a rights-based approach in private law disputes is correct. However, in the more recent case of *E-R (Child Arrangements)* [2016] EWHC 805 (Fam), the court held that a six-year-old girl should continue to live with family friends of her mother, who had died, rather than with her father.

(ii) Step-parents

Many children are brought up by step-parents. A step-parent is not a biological parent but rather a parent created by marriage or civil partnership. Step-parents have legal obligations towards their step-children, including the duty to provide financial support. With respect to a step-child, step-parents can obtain parental responsibility (see 9.5 below) and apply for section 8 orders under the CA 1989 (see 10.4). They can also apply to be a guardian (see 9.8 below), a special guardian (see 15.14) or an adoptive parent (see Chapter 15) of their step-child.

(iii) Foster-parents

Foster-parents are people who act *in loco parentis* for a child on a fairly settled basis. In other words, they act in the place of a parent. There are two types of foster-parent: those who care for children under a private fostering arrangement; and those who look after children in local authority care. Although foster-parents do not have automatic parental responsibility in law, they nonetheless have an obligation to care for the child as they have a delegated form of parental responsibility under section 3(5) of the CA 1989. They can also acquire parental responsibility by means of a guardianship order (see 9.8 below), a child arrangements order regulating the child's living arrangements (see 10.5), a special guardianship order (see 15.14) or by adoption (see Chapter 15).

(b) The importance of parents

Governments, past and present, recognise the importance of parents and that good parenting improves the life chances of children. They also recognise that parents need support, and sometimes advice and guidance. The Government has expressed its commitment to promoting good parenting by providing advice and support. It wants parenting advice and support to be considered the norm and regards good parenting, particularly in the first five years of a child's life, as a key factor influencing social mobility (see *Opening Doors, Breaking Barriers: A Strategy for Social Mobility*, HM Government, 2011; and *Parenting Matters: Early Years and Social Mobility*, Centre Forum, 2011). However, the annual 'State of the Nation' report, published by the Social Mobility and Child Poverty Commission in December 2015, criticised the approach of the Government in this area. It states: 'The life chances of children, the poorest especially, depend on many things including good parenting, childcare, education and employment .... But it is not credible to try to improve the life chances of the poor without acknowledging the most obvious symptom of poverty, lack of money ....' (see *State of the Nation 2015: Social Mobility and Child Poverty in Great Britain*, p. 9).

The judiciary also recognise the importance of parents (as has been seen above); and so do various statutory provisions. Thus, for example, under the CA 1989 parents have an automatic right to bring proceedings for a section 8 order (see 10.9 and 10.10), whereas other people need leave (permission) of the court to apply. They also have a right to contact if their child is in care, unless this is contrary to the child's best interests (see 14.8). The adoption legislation also recognises the importance of a child's natural parents, notably in respect of their right to consent or refuse to consent to their child's adoption and placement for adoption (see 15.8).

The importance of parents is also recognised in the decisions of the European Court of Human Rights (ECtHR) which, by virtue of the Human Rights Act 1998 (HRA 1998), must be taken into account by the courts in England and Wales. For example, in *Kosmopolou v Greece (Application No. 60457/00)* [2004] 1 FLR 800, the ECtHR held that the bond between a child and their parents amounts to a right to family life under Article 8, and that this right arises from the moment of the child's birth and cannot be broken by subsequent events, other than in exceptional circumstances. It held that the mutual enjoyment of each other's company by parent and child constitutes a fundamental element of family life, even if the relationship between the parents has broken down; and that any interference must be justified under Article 8(2), applying the principles of proportionality and the best interests of the child.

Courts and public authorities in the UK must abide by the provisions of the ECHR as a result of their obligations under the HRA 1998 (see 1.8), and must therefore do their best to foster cooperation between parents in order to maintain the bond between parent and child (see *Johansen v Norway* (1997) 23 EHRR 33; and *K and T v Finland* [2001] 2 FLR 707). Thus, for example, the failure of a court in England and Wales to enforce an order for contact, or the failure of social services to allow a parent to have contact with a child in care, might breach the parent's and the child's right to family life under Article 8 of the ECHR.

The importance of parents is also recognised in the United Nations Convention on the Rights of the Child 1989 (UNCRC) (see 8.2). Thus, Article 5 provides that 'State Parties shall respect the responsibilities, rights and duties of parents'; and Article 18(1) requires States Parties to 'use their best efforts to ensure recognition of the principle that both parents have common responsibilities for the upbringing and development of the child, and that parents or guardians have the primary responsibility for the upbringing and development of the child'.

9.2 Parentage

(a) Establishing parentage

Sometimes it may be necessary to establish a child's parentage. For example, a man may need to prove that he is the father of a child so that he can seek an order under the Children Act 1989 (CA 1989) (for example a parental responsibility order or a child arrangements order). A mother may need to prove the paternity of a child so that the father can be required to pay child maintenance. Parentage may also need to be proved for the purpose of amending a birth certificate, establishing inheritance rights or for immigration reasons.

(i) Presumptions of parentage

Certain presumptions exist in respect of parentage. Under the common law presumption of legitimacy, a child born to a woman in an opposite sex marriage is presumed to be the child of the married couple. In other words, the common law presumes that the mother's husband is the child's genetic father and therefore their legal parent. This presumption applies to any child conceived or born during the marriage. However, it does not apply to same sex married couples (see the Marriage (Same Sex Couples) Act 2013, Sch 4, para 2 and Explanatory Notes, para 113) or to civil partners (see the Human Fertilisation and Embryology Act 2008, Explanatory Notes, para 175). Under section 10 of the Births and Deaths Registration Act 1953, on the presumption of birth registration, the entry of a man's name on the birth register as a child's father is *prima facie* evidence that he is the father.

These presumptions are, however, of much less relevance today as parentage can be established with virtually 100 per cent certainty by means of DNA profiling. In fact, the Court of Appeal in *Re H and A (Paternity: Blood Tests)* [2002] EWCA Civ 383 held that such presumptions should not be relied upon when scientific tests can be directed to be carried out under the relevant provisions of the Family Law Reform Act 1969 (FLRA 1969).

(ii) Directing a scientific test (sections 20–25)

Provisions governing the use of scientific tests for determining parentage in civil proceedings are laid down in sections 20–25 of the FLRA 1969. Special provisions exist under the Child Support Act 1991 in respect of determining parentage for child maintenance purposes.

Section 20(1) of the Family Law Reform Act 1969

In any civil proceedings in which the parentage of any person falls to be determined, the court may, either of its own motion or on an application by any party to the proceedings, give a direction –

(a) for the use of scientific tests to ascertain whether such tests show that a party to the proceedings is or is not the father or mother of that person; and
(b) for the taking, within a period specified in the direction, of bodily samples from all or any of the following, namely, that person, any party who is alleged to be the father or mother of that person and any other party to the proceedings;

and the court may at any time revoke or vary a direction previously given by it under this subsection.

'Bodily sample' means a sample of bodily fluid or bodily tissue taken for the purpose of scientific tests (s 25). The scientific test must be carried out by an accredited body (s 20(1A)) and the result must be reported to the court (s 20(2)). The court can draw such inferences as appear proper in the circumstances if a person fails to comply with any step required for the purpose of giving effect to a section 20 direction for scientific testing (s 23(1)) (see, for example, *Re P (Identity of Mother)* [2011] EWCA Civ 795, where a 15-year-old girl refused to participate in a DNA test in order to establish her maternity).

Consent is required (section 21)   Adults and children aged 16 or over must give their consent to a bodily sample being taken (s 21(1)). The consent of children aged 16 or 17 years old is effective as if they were an adult (s 21(2)). If the child is under 16, then the person with care and control of the child must give consent, but, if this is not forthcoming, the court can give consent, provided it is in the child's best interests to do so (s 21(3)). In *Re P (Identity of Mother)* (see above) it was felt appropriate to obtain the consent of the 15-year-old girl whose maternity was in dispute.

The approach of the courts   The approach of the courts is laid down in the following case in which Thorpe LJ stated the principles which apply to an application for a scientific test:

▶ *Re H and A (Paternity: Blood Tests)* **[2002] EWCA Civ 383**

The applicant applied for contact and parental responsibility for twins who were living with their mother and her husband. He believed that he was the twins' father, as he had had a sexual relationship with the mother. When the mother challenged his claim to paternity he applied for blood samples to be taken from the twins with the court's consent under section 21(3)(b) of the FLRA 1969. The judge refused the application because of the possible disastrous disintegrative effects upon the mother's family unit if the applicant was proved to be the father. The father appealed.

The Court of Appeal allowed his appeal and remitted the case for a retrial, as there had been fundamental flaws in the judge's assessment of the individual factors which had to be brought into the essential balancing exercise. Thorpe LJ held that the following two principles applied to cases on establishing parentage:

▶ that the interests of justice are best served by the ascertainment of the truth; and
▶ that the court should be provided with the best available science and not be confined to such unsatisfactory alternatives as presumptions and inferences.

In parentage cases, the interests of justice and the child's right to know the truth are important considerations but they are subject to the child's welfare, which is the court's paramount consideration. Thus, the general principle is that scientific tests should be ordered unless it would be contrary to the child's best interests.

The child's rights and best interests   A child has a right to be cared for by their parents and a right to know their true identity. Thus, according to the United Nations Convention on the Rights of the Child (UNCRC), a child has 'as far as possible, the right to know and be cared for by his parents' (Art 7(1)). State Parties must 'respect the right of the child to preserve his or her identity, including … family relations' (Art 8(1)); and, if a child is illegally deprived of some or all of the elements of their identity, they must 'provide assistance and protection with a view to speedily re-establishing his or her identity' (Art 8(2)). In *Re H (Paternity: Blood Tests)* [2001] 2 FLR 65, Ward LJ, referring to Article 7(1) of the UNCRC, stated that 'every child has a right to know the truth unless his welfare clearly justifies the cover-up'.

The right to family life guaranteed by Article 8 of the European Convention on Human Rights (ECHR) may also provide a justification for the truth to be known, as the following case shows.

▶ *Re T (Paternity: Ordering Blood Tests)* [2001] 2 FLR 1190

The applicant, who believed he had fathered a child during a sexual relationship with a friend's wife, wanted blood tests to be taken for DNA sampling to prove his paternity as a preliminary to applying for parental responsibility and contact. He relied on the right to family life in Article 8 of the ECHR. Bodey J ordered the tests to be taken, as it was in the child's best interests to be sure about his father's identity, and suspicions about the child's identity were already in the public domain. Bodey J balanced the rights of the adults and the child under Article 8, but held that the child's right to know his true identity carried most weight. Any interference with the mother's and her husband's rights to family life under Article 8 was proportionate to the legitimate aim of providing such knowledge to the child.

(For an interesting case where the High Court rejected an argument that the right to privacy under Article 8 of the ECHR could prevent someone from calling for the DNA of a deceased person to be tested in order to establish parentage, see *Spencer v Anderson (Paternity Testing)* [2016] EWHC 851 (Fam)).

Refusing to direct a scientific test   Although the court will usually direct a scientific test, because it is usually in the child's best interests to know the truth, it may refuse to do so where it is contrary to the child's best interests. Thus, for example, in *Re D (Paternity)* [2007] 2 FLR 26, a test was refused as it was not in the best interests of the child due to the turbulence in his life and his strong resistance to scientific testing. A test was also refused in *Re J (Paternity: Welfare of Child)* [2007] 1 FLR 1064, as the undoubted advantage of the child learning the truth was outweighed by the impact that the process would be likely to have on the child's mother and the family upon whom the child was so dependent.

Fortin has argued ([2009] CFLQ 336) that, although the idea of children having a right to know their origins appears to be reasonable, there are risks involved, and that it may not necessarily be in a child's best interests to know their parentage. She states that the child's human right to know their parentage is not an absolute right; and that when 'dealing with applications from putative fathers, it is arguable that the domestic courts are extending a child's right to know beyond its appropriate boundaries'.

Paternity fraud   Where a person fraudulently assures another person that they are the child's parent, but knows that this is not so, then that person may be liable under the common law tort of deceit to pay damages to the wronged person. Thus, for example, in *A v B (Damages: Paternity)* [2007] 2 FLR 1051 the claimant was successful in obtaining damages against the defendant mother who had repeatedly and fraudulently assured him that he was the child's biological father, with the result that he had provided maintenance for both the mother and child for several years. In *Webb v Chapman* [2009] EWCA Civ, however, the claimant was unsuccessful in obtaining damages against the defendant mother who had deceived him over the paternity of her daughter. Lord Justice Thorpe, delivering judgment, said: 'This whole case can be categorised as a misfortune to all those engaged in it. I would not wish to be the one to extend their misfortunes further.' Claims for paternity fraud are rare.

(b)   Declarations of parentage

A declaration of parentage may be required, for example, to: impose or deny a child maintenance obligation; or for the purpose of establishing citizenship, nationality or inheritance rights; or to amend a birth certificate.

Under section 55A of the Family Law Act 1986 (FLA 1986) a person domiciled in England and Wales, or habitually resident in England and Wales for at least one year, can apply for a declaration of parentage (or of non-parentage). People seeking to establish that they are a parent or that a named person is their parent have an unqualified right to apply (s 55A(4)), whereas other people must prove a sufficient personal interest in the determination of the application before the court can hear their case (s 55A(3)).

The court can refuse to hear an application if it considers that it is not in the child's best interests (s 55A(5)); and, if it does so, then it can order that no further application may be made without leave (permission) of the court (s 55A(6)).

(i) The child's involvement in proceedings

A failure to involve a child in proceedings for a declaration of parentage may breach the child's human rights, as the following case shows.

> ▶ *Re L (Family Proceedings Court) (Appeal: Jurisdiction)* [2005] 1 FLR 210
>
> A 15-year-old girl, who had learned that her parentage was in doubt, applied for permission to appeal a declaration of parentage which had been made under section 55A of the FLA 1986 for the purposes of child support. She alleged breaches of her rights under Article 6 (the right to a fair trial) and Article 8 (the right to family life) of the ECHR, as the declaration affecting her status had been made without reference to her or her mother. She had not been a party to the proceedings, had not been given notice of the proceedings and had not been given the opportunity to be heard or to make representations.
>
> Munby J held that it was not disputed that she was fully entitled to invoke what she correctly described as a basic and fundamental human right. Information about one's biological father went to the very heart of a person's identity (*per* Scott Baker J in *Rose v Secretary of State for Health and Human Fertilisation and Embryology Authority* [2002] 2 FLR 962). As her human rights had been infringed the decision could not stand. She had not been given a fair hearing under Article 6, and the declaration breached her rights under Article 8. She was therefore entitled to have the order set aside.

(ii) Adoption – declaration of parentage

A declaration of parentage may be useful in the context of adoption, as it was in the case of *M v W (Declaration of Parentage)* [2007] 2 FLR 270. In this case the petitioner, an adopted adult, applied for a declaration of parentage in respect of his natural father who had died in Australia and with whom he had never had any contact. Hogg J, granting the declaration, drew attention to the importance of adopted people knowing about their background and said that the declaration would be of assistance to the petitioner, and to his children, both emotionally and practically. Furthermore, the declaration would have no effect on the validity of the adoption order; it was 'a forever order' (*per* Hogg LJ, para 18).

(c) Declarations of legitimacy or legitimation

Under section 56 of the FLA 1986 a person may apply to the High Court or a county court for a declaration in respect of legitimacy or legitimation. An application under this provision can only be made by a child (s 56(1)). The court can make a declaration that: the applicant is the legitimate child of their parents; or that the applicant has (or has not) become a legitimated person (s 56(2)).

9.3 Parental responsibility

This section looks at parental responsibility and shows how some people have such responsibility automatically, but that other people, such as unmarried fathers, have to acquire it.

> ### Section 3(1) of the Children Act 1989
>
> In this Act 'parental responsibility' means all the rights, duties, powers, responsibilities and authority which by law a parent of a child has in relation to the child and his property.

The law governing parental responsibility is laid down in the Children Act 1989 (CA 1989) and related case-law. The term 'parental responsibility', not 'parental rights', is used in the CA 1989 to describe parental interests in children. 'Responsibility' was chosen as the preferred term to reflect the idea that children are people to whom duties are owed rather than people over whom power is wielded. As Lord Scarman said in *Gillick* (see 8.4), parental rights are derived from parental duty.

The Family Justice Review in its final report (*Family Justice Review: Final Report*, Ministry of Justice, 2011) (see 1.2) stated that the nature of parental responsibility needed to be better understood, and it recommended that the Government should find ways of strengthening the importance of a good understanding of parental responsibility in the information it gives to parents. The Government accepted the Family Justice Review's recommendations and in its response stated that it recognised that 'parents are not always aware of the concept or significance of parental responsibility, nor of the adverse impact on children of prolonged parental conflict', and that it would therefore consider 'how best to raise awareness of parental responsibility and to support parents in focusing on their child's needs, both in terms of timing and channels of communication' (*The Government Response to the Family Justice Review*, Department of Education and Ministry of Justice, 2012, para 65).

(a) Who has parental responsibility?

Some people have automatic parental responsibility, whereas other people have to acquire it. The advantage of having parental responsibility is that it allows parents (and other people who acquire it) to make important decisions about the child.

(i) Automatic parental responsibility

Over the years, the list of people who have automatic parental responsibility has increased due in part to the introduction of same sex marriage, civil partnership and changes in the law governing assisted reproduction under the Human Fertilisation and Embryology Act 2008 (HFEA 2008).

The CA 1989 provides that the following people have automatic parental responsibility for the child:

- ▶ *married parents* (s 2(1));
- ▶ *a mother and her spouse or civil partner who is a parent by virtue of section 42 of the HFEA 2008* (s 2(1A)(a));
- ▶ *a mother and her female partner who is a parent by virtue of section 43 of the HFEA 2008* (s 2(1A)(b));
- ▶ *an unmarried mother* (s 2(2)); and
- ▶ *a mother who is a parent by virtue of section 43 of the HFEA 2008* (s 2(2A).

(ii) People who can acquire parental responsibility

The CA 1989 enables the following people to acquire parental responsibility:

- ▶ *an unmarried father* (s 4);
- ▶ *a second female parent in a same sex relationship* (s 4ZA);
- ▶ *a step-parent (whether by marriage or civil partnership)* (s 4A).

Other people Parental responsibility can be acquired by other people by means of, *inter alia*, the following: a guardianship order (see 9.8 below); a child arrangements order regulating the child's living arrangements (see 10.5); a special guardianship order (see 15.14); or an adoption order (see Chapter 15). Local authorities have a limited form of parental responsibility when a child is in care (see Chapter 14); and the court has parental responsibility when a child is a ward of court (see 8.7).

More than one person can have parental responsibility for a child (s 2(5)); and parental responsibility does not terminate when another person acquires it (s 2(6)), except in the case of adoption which involves a complete legal transfer of parental responsibility (see Chapter 15). It is not lost when a child goes into local authority care; and it does not terminate on parental separation, or on divorce or dissolution. It terminates when a child reaches the age of majority or if a child is adopted. It can, in some circumstances, be terminated by a court order.

(b) The exercise of parental responsibility

People with parental responsibility can act independently of each other in meeting their responsibility except where the law requires the consent of both parents (and other people with parental responsibility), such as when: removing the child from the UK; consenting to the child's adoption; deciding on the child's education; changing the child's surname; consenting to serious or irreversible medical treatment; and consenting to the child's marriage or civil partnership if they are under the age of majority (s 2(7)).

If the parents cannot agree or consent is not forthcoming, then the court's consent can be obtained by applying for a specific issue order (see 10.7) or by invoking the wardship or inherent jurisdiction of the High Court (see 8.7). Serious medical treatment may need the consent of the court even if both parents are in agreement about the treatment (see 9.7 below).

People with parental responsibility are prohibited from exercising it in a way which is incompatible with a court order made under the CA 1989 (s 2(8)). Where people who share parental responsibility cannot agree on a particular course of action an application can be made for a section 8 order (see 10.4) or, in some cases, to the High Court under its wardship or inherent jurisdiction (see 8.7).

In certain circumstances, a person who is caring for the child (but who does not have parental responsibility for the child) may (subject to the provisions of the CA 1989) 'do what is reasonable in all the circumstances of the case for the purpose of safeguarding or promoting the child's welfare' (s 3(5)). This provision enables, for example, a doctor to act without parental or judicial consent in an emergency. As Munby J said in *R (G) v Nottingham City Council* [2008] 1 FLR 1660, doctors and midwives do not have to stand idly by waiting for a court order if a premature baby desperately needs to be put in a special unit or placed on a ventilator.

(i) Parental responsibility is not transferable

A person with parental responsibility cannot surrender or transfer any of that responsibility, although they may arrange for some or all of it to be met by one or more people acting on their behalf (s 2(9)), including another person with parental responsibility (s 2(10)). Thus, it is lawfully permissible to place the child with a person acting *in loco parentis* (for example a child-minder or babysitter) or someone else with parental responsibility. However, a person with parental responsibility cannot escape liability under the criminal or civil law by delegating that responsibility to another person (s 2(11)), and as such the onus is on parents to make proper arrangements for their children.

9.4 Unmarried fathers and parental responsibility

(a) Unmarried fathers do not have automatic parental responsibility

Unmarried fathers do not have automatic parental responsibility under the Children Act 1989 (CA 1989). In other words, an unmarried father does not have parental responsibility for his child just because he is the biological parent (s 2(2)). Thus, unless he has acquired parental responsibility (see below), his rights with respect to his child are limited. For example, he has no legal right to consent to his child's removal from the UK or adoption.

The reason why unmarried fathers were not given automatic parental responsibility by the CA 1989 was because of concerns that it might not be in the best interests of some children and their mothers. The rationale for not giving unmarried fathers automatic parental responsibility was explained by Balcombe LJ in *Re H (Illegitimate Child: Father: Parental Rights) (No. 2)* [1991] 1 FLR 214:

> The position of the natural father can be infinitely variable; at one end of the spectrum his connection with the child may be only the single act of intercourse (possibly even rape) which led to conception; at the other end of the spectrum he may have played a full part in the child's life from birth onwards, only the formality of marriage to the mother being absent. Considerable social evils might have resulted if the father at the bottom of the spectrum had been automatically granted full parental rights and duties.

A similar view was taken by the European Court of Human Rights (ECtHR) in *McMichael v UK (Application No. 16424/90)* (1995) 20 EHRR 205, where it held that, compared with married fathers, unmarried fathers inevitably vary in their commitment and interest in, or even knowledge of, their children. However, the ECtHR held that, as a general rule, unmarried fathers who had an established family life with their children should be able to claim rights of contact and custody equal to those of married fathers. Nonetheless, in the following case the ECtHR held that the lack of automatic parental responsibility for unmarried fathers in the UK did not breach their human rights.

> ▶ *B v UK* [2000] 1 FLR 1
>
> An unmarried father without parental responsibility complained that his inability to obtain a declaration that his child had been unlawfully removed from the UK (because he had no custody rights) was a breach of his right to family life under Article 8 of the European Convention on Human Rights (ECHR) and was therefore discriminatory under Article 14.
>
> The ECtHR dismissed his claim and held that unmarried fathers in the UK are not discriminated against because they do not have automatic parental responsibility. It held

that, as the relationship between unmarried fathers and their children varies from ignorance and indifference to a close stable relationship indistinguishable from the conventional family-based unit, the UK Government had an objective and reasonable justification for the difference in treatment between married and unmarried fathers with regard to the automatic acquisition of parental responsibility.

Since the implementation of the CA 1989 there has been increasing concern about unmarried fathers not having automatic parental responsibility and about the injustices it may cause. As a result, in December 2003 the law was changed to give automatic parental responsibility to unmarried fathers who are registered on their child's birth certificate with the mother (see below).

(b) The unmarried father – acquiring parental responsibility

An unmarried father can acquire parental responsibility for his child by: joint birth registration with the mother (see (i) below); making a parental responsibility agreement with the mother (see (ii) below); obtaining a parental responsibility order (see (iii) below); becoming the child's guardian on the mother's death (see 9.8 below); obtaining a child arrangements order regulating the child's living arrangements (see 10.5); obtaining a special guardianship order (see 15.14); adopting the child (see Chapter 15); or by marrying the mother (s 1 Legitimacy Act 1976). Once an unmarried father has acquired parental responsibility he has the same rights as a married father, except that his parental responsibility can be terminated by the court (unless he has acquired it by adoption or marriage). In this respect, unmarried fathers are still discriminated against.

(i) Acquiring parental responsibility by joint birth registration

Under sections 4(1)(a) and 4(1A) of the CA 1989 an unmarried father has parental responsibility for his child if he is registered with the mother on the child's birth certificate in accordance with sections 10(1)(a)–(c) and 10A(1) of the Births and Deaths Registration Act 1953. These provisions came into force in December 2003. Acquiring parental responsibility in this way is not, however, permanent, as it can be terminated by court order. There have been proposals to introduce compulsory joint birth registration by unmarried parents (see below).

(ii) Acquiring parental responsibility by agreement with the child's mother

Under section 4(1)(b) of the CA 1989 an unmarried father can enter into a parental responsibility agreement with the mother and thereby acquire parental responsibility for the child. The agreement is made on a prescribed form (available at HM Courts' Service) which must be signed by both parties, witnessed and then registered in court. There is no judicial scrutiny of the agreement, and parental responsibility acquired in this way can be revoked by court order. A local authority has no power to stop the mother of a child in care from entering into a parental responsibility agreement with the child's father (see *Re X (Parental Responsibility Agreement: Children in Care)* [2000] 1 FLR 517).

(iii) Acquiring parental responsibility by parental responsibility order

An unmarried father can apply to the court under section 4(1)(c) of the CA 1989 for an order giving him parental responsibility. When considering whether or not to grant the order, the child's welfare is the court's paramount consideration (s 1(1)). The other welfare principles apply, but not the welfare checklist (see 10.3). In *Re H (Minors) (Local Authority: Parental Rights) (No. 3)* [1991] Fam 151, Balcombe LJ held that the following three factors are important when the court is considering whether to make an order:

- ▶ the degree of commitment which the father has shown towards the child;
- ▶ the degree of attachment which exists between the father and the child; and
- ▶ the father's reasons or motivation for applying for the order.

The Court of Appeal has stated, however, that these factors are only a starting point and that other factors can be taken into account (see *Re H (Parental Responsibility)* [1998] 1 FLR 855). Even where these three factors are satisfied, the court may nonetheless decide that making a parental responsibility order is contrary to the child's best interests (as it was held to be, for example, in *Re B (Role of Biological Father)* [2008] 1 FLR 1015).

As the court recognises the important status conferred by a parental responsibility order, it will usually make the order unless it is clearly contrary to the child's welfare. Thus, parental responsibility orders have been made even where there is acrimony between the parents (*Re P (A Minor) (Parental Responsibility Order)* [1994] 1 FLR 578) and where contact with the child has been denied (*Re H (A Minor) (Parental Responsibility)* [1993] 1 FLR 484). Failure to provide child maintenance may not of itself provide a reason for refusing an order (*Re H (Parental Responsibility: Maintenance)* [1996] 1 FLR 867). In *Re S (Parental Responsibility)* [1995] 2 FLR 648 the Court of Appeal stated that, as a parental responsibility order granted an important status, it was wrong to place an undue and false emphasis on the rights, duties and powers that come with parental responsibility because any abuse of its exercise could be controlled by making a section 8 order under the CA 1989 (see 10.4).

Despite the willingness of the courts to make a parental responsibility order, as it confers an important status, an order may be refused in an exceptional case. Thus, for example, a parental responsibility order was refused in *Re H (Parental Responsibility)* [1998] 1 FLR 855 where the father had physically harmed the child; and in *Re P (Parental Responsibility)* [1998] 2 FLR 96 where the father was found to be in possession of obscene pictures of young children.

(c) Termination and revocation of parental responsibility agreements and orders

(i) Termination

Parental responsibility agreements and parental responsibility orders terminate when the child reaches 18, unless terminated earlier by court order (ss 91(7), (8)).

(ii) Revocation

A person who has acquired parental responsibility under section 4(1) of the CA 1989 (by birth registration, agreement or court order) can have it revoked by a court order made under section 4(2A) on an application made by any person with parental responsibility for the child or, with leave (permission) of the court, the child (s 4(3)). The court can grant leave to the child only if they have sufficient understanding to make the application (s 4(4)).

In revocation applications the child's welfare is the court's paramount consideration (s 1(1)). Each case depends on its own facts, but parental responsibility will be revoked only in exceptional circumstances. Thus, as parental responsibility confers an important status, there is a strong presumption in favour of its continuance. It cannot be terminated, for example, where a mother is dissatisfied with the father. Cases where it was revoked include, for example, *Re P (Terminating Parental Responsibility)* [1995] 1 FLR 1048 where the father was sent to prison for causing severe non-accidental injuries to the child and *Re F (Indirect Contact)* [2007] 1 FLR 1015 where the father had a history of serious and uncontrollable violence. Although revocation of the father's parental responsibility in these cases seemed appropriate in the circumstances, it is possible to argue that the law continues to discriminate against unmarried fathers. This is because it would not have been possible for the court to remove the parental responsibility of the fathers if they had been married. Thus, for example, in *Re M (A Minor) (Care Order: Threshold Conditions)* [1994] 2 AC 424, the married father had murdered the mother in the presence of the children, but there was no question of him losing his parental responsibility.

9.5 The second female parent in a same sex relationship, step-parents and other people – acquiring parental responsibility

(a) The second female parent in a same sex relationship

The second female parent in a same sex relationship who is not married or in a civil partnership with the child's mother does not have automatic parental responsibility. She can acquire parental responsibility in relation to the child by joint birth registration or by way of a parental responsibility agreement or parental responsibility order under section 4ZA of the Children Act 1989 (CA 1989). Parental responsibility acquired in any of these ways can be terminated by court order (s 4ZA(5)). In other words, the legal position is the same as that for unmarried fathers (see 9.4 above).

(b) Step-parents

Under section 4A of the CA 1989 a step-parent (whether by marriage or civil partnership) can acquire parental responsibility for a step-child by means of a parental responsibility agreement (see (i) below) or a parental responsibility order (see (ii) below). Other ways of acquiring parental responsibility are by means of a guardianship order (see 9.8 below), a child arrangements order regulating the child's living arrangements (see 10.5), a special guardianship order (see 15.14) or an adoption order (see Chapter 15).

(i) A parental responsibility agreement (section 4A(1)(a))

The child's parent who has parental responsibility or, if the other parent of the child also has parental responsibility for the child, both parents may enter into an agreement with the step-parent to provide for the latter to have parental responsibility for the child. This involves filling in a prescribed form (s 4A(2)). The agreement takes effect once it has been received and recorded at court.

(ii) Parental responsibility order (section 4A(1)(b))

The court may, on the application of a step-parent, order that the step-parent shall have parental responsibility for the child. The welfare of the child is the court's paramount consideration (s 1(1)). The other welfare principles apply, but not the welfare checklist (see 10.3).

(iii) Termination of parental responsibility (section 4A(3))

A step-parent's parental responsibility (whether acquired by agreement or court order) can be terminated by the court on the application of any person with parental responsibility or, with leave (permission) of the court, the child. The court can grant leave to the child if it is satisfied that the child has sufficient understanding to make the proposed application (s 4A(4)).

(c)   Other people

People other than those above can acquire parental responsibility by obtaining a guardianship order (see 9.8 below), a child arrangements order regulating the child's living arrangements (see 10.5), a special guardianship order (see 15.14) or an adoption order (see Chapter 15).

In *Re A (Joint Residence: Parental Responsibility)* [2008] 2 FLR 1593, for example, an unmarried man acquired parental responsibility by way of a joint residence order (made under section 11(4) CA 1989, now repealed, in his and the mother's favour) because he was unable to apply for a parental responsibility order. This was because, although he had been at the child's birth and had lived with the child and the mother for two years before the relationship had broken down, he was subsequently found not to be the biological father. The trial judge made a joint residence order as this was the only way in which he could obtain parental responsibility, and the decision was upheld by the Court of Appeal as a legitimate means by which parental responsibility could be acquired.

9.6   Parental responsibility and parental rights

The definition of 'parental responsibility' in section 3(1) of the Children Act 1989 (CA 1989), which defines it as 'all the rights, duties, powers, responsibilities and authority which by law a parent of a child has in relation to the child and his property', is not very helpful as it does not define its precise nature and scope. This must instead be deduced from statute and case-law.

(a)   What rights do parents have?

Despite the emphasis on parental responsibility in the CA 1989, parents do have rights. They have a right, for example, to bring proceedings under the CA 1989 and to challenge a local authority's decision to institute care and supervision proceedings. In fact, section 3(1) of the CA 1989 mentions the word 'rights' in its definition of parental responsibility, and in the *Gillick* case (see 8.4) Lord Scarman, while recognising that 'responsibility' was a more appropriate term than 'rights', nevertheless stated that parental rights clearly existed, but that the law had never treated such rights as 'sovereign or beyond review and control'.

Parents have a wide range of rights in respect of their children. They also have duties to their children, in particular a duty to provide child maintenance (see Chapter 12). Some parental rights are also duties. For example, a parent has a right and a duty to register the child's birth. Parents without parental responsibility have some, but not all, of the rights below.

(i) Parental rights are not absolute

Parents' rights are not absolute, as they are subject to the principle that the child's welfare is the court's paramount consideration. Parental wishes can therefore be overridden by the court. In *Re Z (A Minor) (Freedom of Publication)* [1996] 1 FLR 191, Sir Thomas Bingham MR said that if a parental decision 'is in accord with that of the devoted and responsible parent, well and good', but that, if not, then 'it is the duty of the court … to give effect to its own judgment'.

Thus, the court can restrain a parent from doing any act which might adversely affect the child's welfare. For example, parental consent to adoption can be dispensed with if this is in the child's best interests (see 15.8); and in applications for orders under the CA 1989 the child's welfare, not parental wishes, is paramount. In the context of medical treatment for a child, parental wishes can be overridden (see 9.7 below); and children who suffer significant harm can be taken into local authority care, whereupon parental responsibility is not removed from the child's parents, but the local authority is 'in the driving seat' (see Chapter 14).

(b) Important parental rights

The following parental rights are particularly important:

(i) A right to the physical possession of the child

The criminal and civil law relating to child abduction (see Chapter 14) and the restriction on removing a child from the UK when the child is subject to a child arrangements order regulating the child's living arrangements (s 13) show that parents have a right to physical possession of their child. This right is also evidenced by the fact that, under the CA 1989, a parent can ask a local authority to return their child if the child is not subject to a care or emergency protection order. The right to physical possession also includes the right to decide where the child lives. Thus, for example, when a child is accommodated in local authority care under a voluntary arrangement, a local authority cannot move the child from residential to foster care against the wishes of the parents (see *R v Tameside Metropolitan Borough Council ex parte J* [2000] 1 FLR 942). The right to physical possession also includes the right to decide on travel and emigration, although this right is subject to certain controls and safeguards.

(ii) A right to have contact with the child

A child arrangements order which, regulates the child's contact arrangements (see 10.5) and the presumption of reasonable contact with a child in local authority care (see 14.8) shows that parents have a right to contact with their child. However, this right is not absolute as it can be terminated by court order where it is in the child's best interests. Nonetheless, the law encourages parent–child contact, as contact is generally considered to be beneficial for the child. As contact is also considered to be a right of the child (see 11.5), then contact is not just a parental right but also a parental duty, provided that this is in the child's best interests.

(iii) A right to decide on education

Parents have a legal duty to ensure that a child of compulsory school age receives efficient full-time education (suitable to the child's age, ability and aptitude, and any special needs) either by regular attendance at school or otherwise under section 7 of the Education Act 1996 (EA 1996). The words 'or otherwise' in section 7 permit parents to lawfully educate their children at home, provided it is an efficient and suitable education (*R v Secretary of State for Education and Science, ex parte Talmud Torah Machzikei Hadass School Trust*, The Times, 12 April 1985). Children in the State education system must be educated in accordance with parental wishes so far as this is compatible with the provision of efficient instruction and training and the avoidance of unreasonable public expenditure under section 9 of the EA 1996.

(iv) A right to choose the child's religion

Parents have a right to choose the child's religion (if any), at least until the child becomes '*Gillick* competent' (see 8.4). Parents have the right to remove their child from religious instruction and school assemblies. The importance of religion is also reflected in statutory provisions relating to fostering and adoption placements, as the local authority and adoption agency must take into consideration the child's religious beliefs and background (see Chapter 15). However, parental rights with respect to their child's religious beliefs are not absolute, and in some circumstances the best interests of the child will prevail, for example in the context of corporal punishment in schools (see 8.5) and with regard to religious objections to medical treatment (see 9.7 below).

(v) A right to consent to medical treatment

See 9.7 below.

(vi) A right to consent to the child's marriage or civil partnership

Where a child is aged over 16 but under 18, the child's parents and other people with parental responsibility must give their consent to the marriage or civil partnership (see s 3 Marriage Act 1949, s 11 Marriage (Same Sex Couples) Act 2013 and s 4 Civil Partnership Act 2004). However, failure to do so is unlikely to invalidate the marriage or civil partnership.

(vii) A right to choose the child's surname and to register the child's birth

A parent can choose any surname for their child. However, if a child arrangements order regulating the child's living arrangements is in force (see 10.5), then the surname of the child who is the subject of that order cannot be changed without the *written* consent of all people with parental responsibility or with leave (permission) of the court (s 13(1)).

Parents have a statutory duty to register the child's birth under the Births and Deaths Registration Act 1953. If the mother and father are married either parent can register the child's birth. If they are not married, only the unmarried mother can register the birth, and the registrar is not permitted to enter the name of any person as the child's father in the register, unless: both parents attend together and make a joint request to register the birth; or one of them makes a request to register the child's birth and provides a statutory declaration acknowledging paternity. If both unmarried parents are registered on the birth certificate the father has parental responsibility for the child with the mother (see 9.4 above). If a child is legitimated by the parents' subsequent marriage, the parents must re-register the child's birth (s 9 Legitimacy Act 1976).

Compulsory birth registration for unmarried couples The Labour Government introduced reforms (under section 56 and Schedule 6 of the Welfare Reform Act 2009) to make joint birth registration compulsory for unmarried couples (subject to certain safeguards), but these have not been implemented. The aim of these reforms was to give unmarried fathers parental responsibility (which can be acquired by birth registration) (see 9.4 above) and to promote the involvement of both unmarried parents in the child's upbringing. For the background to these reforms, see the White Paper *Joint Birth Registration: Recording Responsibility*, Cm 7293, 2008. Wallbank ([2009] CFLQ 267) has challenged the assumption that a child's welfare is necessarily best served by having two parents with parental responsibility.

Birth registration by female couples Since 1 September 2009, as a result of amendments made to the Births and Deaths Regulations 1987 by the Human Fertilisation and Embryology Act 2008, female couples have been able to register the birth of their child conceived as a result of fertility treatment, and with both the mother and the second female parents' names being included on the birth certificate.

(viii) A right to consent to the child's adoption

Parents with parental responsibility have a right to consent to their child's adoption, but consent may be dispensed with in certain circumstances (see 15.8).

(ix) A right to discipline the child and to administer reasonable punishment

A parent has a right and a duty to discipline a child, but the use of certain forms of corporal punishment is a criminal offence (see 8.5).

(x) Other rights

Parents have other rights. Thus, they can administer the child's property and enter into contracts on the child's behalf. They have a right to appoint a guardian for the child (see 9.8 below). They also have rights to apply for court orders in respect of their children (see Chapter 10); and a right to apply for child support (see Chapter 12).

9.7 Parents and children – medical treatment

The *Gillick* case (see 8.4) did not remove the right and duty of parents to consent to their child's medical treatment. In fact, the Department of Health and Social Security circular, which was the subject of Mrs Gillick's wrath, stated that doctors should act on the presumption that parents should be consulted before contraceptives were prescribed to teenage girls.

If a child is a mature minor (in other words they are '*Gillick* competent'), then parental consent to medical treatment may not be needed. Section 8 of the Family Law Reform Act 1969 (FLRA 1969) also provides that people aged 16 or 17 years old have a statutory right to give valid consent to medical, dental or other treatment. However, despite these principles, the court has the power to override the wishes of children of whatever age and maturity, and those of parents, if it considers the medical treatment, or the withdrawal of medical treatment, is in the best interests of the child.

(a) Disputes between parents and doctors about a child's medical treatment

Although a failure to obtain parental consent can result in a medical practitioner being liable for assault under the civil and/or criminal law, parental rights in medical matters are not absolute as their wishes can be overridden by the court. Where there is a dispute between the medical profession and parents the court will be asked to intervene. The usual procedure is for the hospital or National Health Service Trust to seek a declaration from the High Court under its inherent jurisdiction (see 8.7). Another option, which is used less often, is to apply for a specific issue order under section 8 of the Children Act 1989 (CA 1989) (see 10.7), which requires leave (permission) of the court if the applicant is not the child's parent or guardian.

If doctors treat, or fail to treat, a child in defiance of parental wishes, this may be a breach of the right to family life of the parent and child under Article 8 of the European Convention on Human Rights (ECHR). Thus, for example, in *Glass v UK (Application No. 61827/00)* [2004] 1 FLR 1019 (where doctors, against the mother's wishes, stopped giving medical treatment to her child who was severely mentally and physically disabled) the European Court of Human Rights (ECtHR) held that the UK was in breach of Article 8 and awarded the mother and child damages. It held that the NHS Trust should have sought the intervention of the court before deciding to withdraw medical treatment against the mother's wishes.

(b) The governing principles in disputes between doctors and parents

The following principles are applied by the court in cases where parents are in dispute with the medical profession:

- The best interests of the child are paramount.
- The matter is to be decided by adopting an objective approach.
- Each case depends on its own particular facts.

▶ There is a very strong presumption in favour of prolonging life, but there is no obligation on the medical profession to give treatment which would be futile. In *Re J (A Minor) (Wardship: Medical Treatment)* [1991] 1 FLR 366 Lord Donaldson MR said that account had to be taken of the pain and suffering and quality of life which the child will experience if life is prolonged, and the pain and suffering involved in the proposed treatment.

Thus, the court has to conduct a balancing exercise and weigh up the advantages and disadvantages of giving, or withholding, medical treatment in order to decide what is in the child's best interests. While the courts accord great respect to parental wishes, which are usually put into the balancing exercise, such wishes hardly ever prevail over the best interests of the child (for a rare case where they seemed to do so, see *Re T (Wardship: Medical Treatment)* [1997] 1 FLR 502 below).

There are many reported cases involving disputes between parents and the medical profession about the medical treatment of children. Each case depends on its own facts, applying the principle that the child's welfare is the court's paramount consideration. The following are some examples from the case-law.

▶ *Re B (A Minor) (Wardship: Medical Treatment)* [1990] 3 All ER 927

A baby born with Down's syndrome was ordered to have a life-saving operation to remove an intestinal blockage where the parents refused to consent to the operation.

▶ *Re R (A Minor) (Blood Transfusion)* [1993] 2 FLR 757

A specific issue order was granted on the application of a local authority ordering that a child with leukaemia be given medical treatment (including blood transfusions) despite the parents' religious objections as they were Jehovah's Witnesses.

▶ *Re T (Wardship: Medical Treatment)* [1997] 1 FLR 502

The parents refused to give consent to their child having a life-saving liver transplant, as they did not wish to care for the child. The court under its inherent jurisdiction, applying the welfare principle, refused to overrule the parents' refusal. This was because, *inter alia*, the child had previously undergone unsuccessful surgery, which had caused him a lot of pain and distress, and the parents were both health care professionals who fully understood the consequences of their decision. The parents had also moved to another country, and such an order would have required them to return to the UK for the surgery.

▶ *Local Authority v SB, AB and MB* [2010] EWHC 1744 (Fam)

The parents of a six-year-old child with a rare progressive brain disease refused to consent to him having surgery as had been recommended in a medical report. Sir Nicholas Wall P, referring to *Re T* above, held that the decision was for the child's parents as they were the only people with parental responsibility. The question of whether or not the child should undergo surgery was an ongoing matter between his parents and the hospital; and, as neither the parents nor the hospital were inviting the court to decide that issue, there was no issue for the court to decide.

▶ *Re C (HIV Test)* **[1999] 2 FLR 1004**

A specific issue order was granted on the application of the local authority, so that an HIV test could be carried out on a baby, despite the mother's and father's refusal to consent.

▶ *A National Health Service Trust v D* **[2000] 2 FLR 677**

A declaration was granted that the child need not be ventilated, despite the wishes of the parents, and this was held this was held not to breach Article 2 (the right to life) or Article 3 (the right not to suffer inhuman and degrading treatment) of the ECHR.

▶ *Re A (Conjoined Twins: Medical Treatment)* **[2001] 1 FLR 1**

Conjoined twins were ordered to be separated despite their parents' wishes to the contrary, and the fact that separation would inevitably lead to the death of the weaker twin.

▶ *Portsmouth NHS Trust v Wyatt and Wyatt, Southampton NHS Trust Intervening* **[2005] 1 FLR 21**

Hedley J made declarations that aggressive treatment to prolong the life of a seriously ill one-year-old child was not in her best interests, despite her parents' wishes to the contrary (see, however, *Portsmouth NHS Trust v Wyatt and Wyatt, Southampton NHS Trust Intervening* [2005] 2 FLR 480 where the above restriction was lifted as the child showed signs of improvement).

▶ *NHS Trust v A* **[2008] 1 FLR 70**

The parents of a six-month-old child refused to consent to the child having a life-saving bone marrow transplant on religious grounds, and because they did not want her to suffer further. The doctors and the child's guardian were in favour of the treatment. The court granted the declaration sought by the NHS Trust, holding that the question of whether the court should consent to the treatment in the face of disagreement was to be decided by the application of an objective test based on the best interests of the child, considered in the widest sense.

(c) Seriously invasive medical treatment

Where the medical treatment of a child is seriously invasive the court's consent may be needed. For example, sterilisation of a child usually requires the prior sanction of the High Court under its inherent or wardship jurisdiction. However, an application by way of specific issue order was permitted in *Re HG (Specific Issue Order: Sterilisation)* [1993] 1 FLR 587.

In *Re B (A Minor) (Wardship: Sterilisation)* [1988] AC 199, the House of Lords authorised the sterilisation of a 17-year-old girl with limited intellectual development under the wardship jurisdiction. In *Re D (A Minor) (Wardship: Sterilisation)* [1976] Fam 185, on the other hand, sterilisation was refused, because the court felt that the girl might be able to give informed consent to the operation at a later date. Consent of the court may not be required where sterilisation is needed for therapeutic reasons, such as to treat cancer of the womb.

(d) Where parents cannot agree about medical treatment

The consent of the court may be needed in respect of certain types of medical treatment of a child where the child's parents cannot agree between themselves about the treatment. This is so even though section 2(7) of the CA 1989 provides that each parent with parental responsibility can act independently of the other. Medical treatment, such as circumcision and immunisation, may, for example, need the court's consent if the child's parents cannot agree about the treatment. The following cases are examples.

▶ *Re J (Specific Issue Orders: Child's Religious Upbringing and Circumcision)* [2000] 1 FLR 571

A Muslim father applied for a specific issue order under section 8 of the CA 1989 so that his five-year-old son could be circumcised, as the child's mother, a Christian, objected to it. The Court of Appeal held that a parental dispute about circumcision is one of the exceptional cases where a disagreement between those who possess parental responsibility must be determined by the courts. The father's application was refused, as the best interests of the child prevailed over the parents' religious beliefs and wishes.

(See also *Re S (Specific Issue Order: Religion: Circumcision)* [2005] 1 FLR 236 where a Muslim mother's application for a specific issue order authorising her son's circumcision, which the Hindu father had objected to, was refused, as the child might be able to make his own informed choice about circumcision when he was older.)

▶ *Re C (Welfare of Child: Immunisation)* [2003] 2 FLR 1095

Fathers who had parental responsibility and contact rights were granted specific issue orders ordering that their daughters be immunised with the MMR vaccine, despite the mothers' opposition. It was held that immunisation was in the girls' best interests, applying the welfare principle in section 1(1) of the CA 1989. It was not a breach of the mothers' right to family life under Article 8 of the ECHR, because Article 8(2) allowed a court to interfere with the rights of parents and children in order to protect the health of a child.

(e) Disputes between parents and children about medical treatment

See 8.4.

9.8 Appointing a guardian for a child

(a) Appointing a guardian for the child

The aim of guardianship is to ensure that there is a person who can exercise parental responsibility for a child on the death of the child's parents. Appointment of a guardian is governed by sections 5 and 6 of the Children Act 1989 (CA 1989). Guardianship should not be confused with special guardianship (see 15.14).

(i) Appointment by a parent, guardian or special guardian (section 5)

A parent with parental responsibility, a guardian or a special guardian can appoint a guardian for the child. Two or more people may do so jointly. The appointment must be made in writing, and it must be dated and signed by the person making the appointment. Special provisions apply if the appointer is unable to sign the document, whether made in a will or otherwise.

Revocation, disclaimer and termination of appointment (section 6) An appointment can be revoked by a subsequent appointment or by a written instrument revoking the appointment. An appointment (excluding one made in a will or codicil) can be revoked by the instrument being destroyed, provided it is the appointer's intention to revoke the appointment. An appointment made in a will or codicil is revoked if the will or codicil is revoked.

A person who is appointed as a guardian (other than by an appointment made by the court) can disclaim the appointment by an instrument in writing signed by them and made within a reasonable time of first knowing about the appointment. An appointment made by an individual (not by the court) is revoked if the person appointed is the spouse or civil partner of the appointer and the marriage or civil partnership is terminated by divorce or dissolution.

Any appointment of a guardian (by an individual or by the court) can be terminated by court order on the application of any person with parental responsibility for the child (including a local authority) or on the application of the child concerned, provided the court has given the child leave (permission) to apply. The court also has the power to terminate the appointment of its own motion in any family proceedings, in other words without any application having been made.

(ii) Appointment by the court (section 5)

The court can order that an applicant be appointed as a guardian of a child if: the child has no parent with parental responsibility; or a child arrangements order regulating the child's living arrangements was in force with respect to the child in favour of a parent, guardian or special guardian who has died; or where there is no child arrangements order regulating the child's living arrangements and the child's only surviving special guardian has died. The court can also appoint a guardian of its own motion in any family proceedings, in other words without any application for an appointment having been made. However, the court cannot appoint a guardian if a child arrangements order regulating the child's living arrangements was made in favour of a surviving parent of the child.

When exercising its powers to decide whether to appoint a guardian the child's welfare is the court's paramount consideration (s 1(1)) and the 'no delay' (s 1(2)) and 'no order' provisions (s 1(5)) apply (see 10.3). As proceedings for the appointment of a guardian are family proceedings (s 8(4)), the court can make a section 8 order under the CA 1989 (see 10.4) instead of, or in addition to, appointing a guardian.

Termination of court order (section 6) A court order appointing a guardian can be terminated by the court on the application of any person with parental responsibility for the child (including a local authority) or on the application of the child concerned, with leave (permission) of the court; or by the court of its own motion in any family proceedings.

(b) Effects of guardianship

The appointment of a guardian takes effect on the appointer's death provided no other person has parental responsibility for the child. As a guardian has parental responsibility for the child (see 9.3 above), they must ensure that the child is cared for and provided for and is educated. A guardian has a right to apply for orders under the CA 1989 (see Chapter 10) and to consent to the child's adoption (see Chapter 15). However, a guardian has no legal duty to provide financial support for the child (as this might deter people from becoming a guardian); and has no right to succeed to the child's estate on the child's intestacy.

9.9 Parenthood – assisted reproduction

Assisted reproduction is governed by the Human Fertilisation and Embryology Act 1990 (HFEA 1990) and the Human Fertilisation and Embryology Act 2008 (HFEA 2008). The HFEA 2008, which was enacted primarily in response to new technological and scientific developments, is relevant to family lawyers because Part 2 contains provisions governing the law of legal parenthood. These provisions extend the rules on legal parenthood to include second female parents, whether or not they are married or civil partners.

(a) Who is the child's legal mother?

The woman who is carrying (or has carried) a child as a result of fertility treatment (the placing in her of an embryo or of sperm and eggs), and no other woman, is treated as the child's legal mother (s 33(1)). This rules applies whether or not the woman was in the UK or elsewhere at the time of the treatment (s 33(3)).

(b) Who is the child's legal 'father' or 'second parent'?

The rules differ depending on the status of the couple's relationship.

(i) Married fathers

The husband is automatically recognised as the legal father of a child born as a result of his wife having fertility treatment, unless he did not consent to the treatment (s 35(1)). This rule applies whether or not the wife was in the UK or elsewhere at the time of the treatment (s 35(2)).

(ii) Unmarried fathers

Under sections 36–38 of the HFEA 2008, where the woman has a child as a result of insemination in a UK licensed clinic and the couple have in place (at the time of the transfer of the sperm or embryo which results in conception) current notices of the man stating that he consents to being treated as the father of any child resulting from the assisted reproduction, then he is the legal father of the child. The parties must not be within the degrees of prohibited relationship with each other (s 37(1)(e)).

(iii) Second female parents

Under sections 42–47 of the HFEA 2008, the legal position for second female parents, whether or not they are married or in a civil partnership, is the same as that for married and unmarried fathers (see above); but the term 'father' is replaced with 'second parent'.

(c) Deceased people

Sections 39 and 40 of the HFEA 2008 enable a man to be registered on the child's birth certificate as the father of a child conceived after his death using his sperm or an embryo created with his sperm before his death. It also enables a man to be registered as the father of a child conceived after his death using an embryo created using donor sperm before his death. Registration does not confer upon the child any legal status or rights as a consequence of the registration. The father must give written consent to registration of his name on the birth register.

Section 46 of the HFEA 2008 lays down similar provisions in respect of a deceased second female parent (whether or not the couple were married or in a civil partnership).

(d) Consent and assisted reproduction

Consent is an essential requirement in the law governing assisted reproduction, not just for the purpose of acquiring legal parenthood (see above), but also for the purpose of consenting to the fertility treatment itself. The issue of consent was considered in the following case in respect of section 12 of the HFEA 1990, which requires the genetic parents' consent to *in vitro* fertilisation (IVF).

▶ *Evans v Amicus Healthcare Ltd; Hadley v Midland Fertility Services Ltd* **[2004] 1 FLR 67**

In each appeal the female claimant had undergone IVF treatment with her respective partner, but after the relationship had broken down the male partner had withdrawn his consent to the treatment and to the storage of the embryos, and wished them to perish. The claimants argued that the court had the power to override the withdrawal of consent and to permit the embryos to be used. Each claimant sought an injunction to restore the man's consent. They also sought a declaration of incompatibility under the Human Rights Act 1998 arguing that the relevant provisions in the HFEA 1990 were in breach of the ECHR.

Wall J held that the court had no power to override the unconditional statutory right of either party to withdraw or vary consent to the use of embryos in connection with IVF treatment at any time before implantation in the woman. Where consent had originally been given for treatment together with a named partner it was neither effective nor valid once the parties had ceased to be together. The HFEA 1990 did not breach the claimants' right to family life under Article 8 of the ECHR. As the HFEA 1990 was enacted with sound policy reasons for requiring treatment to be consensual throughout, any interference by the State was both lawful and proportionate. There was no breach of Article 12 (the right to marry and found a family) or Article 14 (discrimination in respect of a Convention right). Nor was there a breach of Article 2 (the right to life), as an embryo is not a person in English law.

Note: Ms Evans (who had received IVF treatment prior to the surgical removal of her ovaries due to a pre-cancerous condition but whose partner subsequently refused to consent to their use when their relationship broke down) sought leave to appeal to the Court of Appeal, but leave was refused (see [2004] EWCA (Civ) 727). She subsequently applied to the ECtHR (see *Evans v UK (Application No. 6339/05)* [2007] 1 FLR 1990) claiming that the requirement of the father's consent to the continued storage and implantation of the fertilised eggs breached her rights under Articles 8 and 14 of the ECHR, and the rights of the embryos under Article 2. However, the ECtHR held by a majority of 13 to four that there had been no breach of her human rights or those of the embryos.

The same approach is taken under sections 37 and 44 of the HFEA 2008 which deal with the agreed fatherhood and female parenthood conditions respectively (see, for example, *AB v CD & Z Fertility Clinic* [2013] EWHC 1418 (Fam); *X v Y v St Bartholomew's Hospital Centre for Reproductive Medicine* [2015] EWFC 13; and *In re Human Fertilisation and Embryology Act 2008 (Cases A, B, C, D, E, F, G and H)* [2015] EWHC 2602 (Fam)).

In the following case it was held that where a man and a woman separate before a successful implantation takes place, even though it started out as a 'joint enterprise', the man may not be the legal father of the child.

▶ **Re R (IVF: Paternity of Child) [2005] 2 FLR 843**

The mother and her partner sought fertility treatment involving donor sperm. The partner signed the prescribed documents acknowledging that he intended to become the legal father of any child born as a result of the treatment. An implantation was successful, but the mother failed to inform the clinic after the pregnancy was confirmed that she had separated from her partner. Her former partner obtained a declaration of paternity but the Court of Appeal allowed the mother's appeal. Her former partner appealed to the House of Lords.

The House of Lords dismissed his appeal and held that, in conferring the relationship of parent and child on people who were related neither by blood nor marriage, the rules must be applied very strictly. If the 'joint' enterprise of fertility treatment had ended by the time the successful treatment had begun (because by that stage the couple had separated), the man was not the legal father of the resulting child.

The case above related to section 28(3) of the HFEA 1990, and the same approach is likely to be taken under sections 37(1) and 44(1) of the HFEA 2008.

9.10 Surrogacy

(a) Introduction

Some couples may resort to surrogacy to have a child. Under a surrogacy arrangement a surrogate mother acts as the birth mother for the commissioning parent(s) and she agrees to hand the child over soon after the child's birth. The practice of surrogacy is governed by the Surrogacy Arrangements Act 1985 (SAA 1985). Under the Act a surrogate mother is defined as a woman who carries a child in pursuance of an arrangement made before she began to carry the child, and with a view to any such child being handed over to, and parental responsibility being met (so far as practicable) by, another person or people (s 1(2)).

Surrogacy arrangements between private individuals are permitted in England and Wales (s 2(2)), but commercial surrogacy is prohibited. Thus, it is a criminal offence to set up a surrogacy agency commercially and to advertise and negotiate a surrogacy arrangement for money (s 2(1)). However, payment of money may in some circumstances be authorised retrospectively by the court (see further below).

Surrogacy can raise difficult legal, ethical and practical problems. For example, the surrogate mother may decide not to hand over the child (see, for example, *Re P (Surrogacy: Residence)* [2008] 1 FLR 177). Difficulties can also arise when a couple enter into a commercial surrogacy arrangement abroad and wish to apply for a parental order in the court in England and Wales. In *Re IJ (Foreign Surrogacy Agreement: Parental Order)* [2011] EWHC 921 (Fam), Hedley J drew attention to the legal difficulties which can arise, including immigration issues, and he warned of the danger of parties relying on the advice of overseas agencies who may not fully understand the legal position in England and Wales.

The following case, in which McFarlane J laid down some principles which should be borne in mind in future cases, provides a good example of the complexities that can arise in surrogacy cases. He expressed concern that surrogacy agencies, such as Childlessness Overcome Through Surrogacy (COTS), which was involved in the case, were not covered by any statutory or regulatory provision. Given that COTS was unaware of the domicile requirements to apply for a parental order (see further below) and had not realised that it was unlawful to take a child abroad for an adoption, McFarlane J said that it had to be asked whether some form of inspection or authorisation should be required in order to improve the quality of advice offered to couples who sought to have a child through surrogacy.

▶ *Re G (Surrogacy: Foreign Domicile)* [2007] EWHC 2814 (Fam)

A surrogacy arrangement was entered into whereby an English surrogate mother agreed to give birth to a surrogate child for a married couple living in Turkey. The child was conceived using the egg of the surrogate mother and the Turkish husband's sperm. The surrogate mother's estranged husband had not given written consent to the insemination due to lack of communication between the couple. The Turkish parents came to England and (as a precursor to returning to Turkey where they would apply to adopt the child) they applied for a parental order under section 30 of the HFEA 1990. However, as they had failed to satisfy the domicile requirements in section 30(3)(b) of the Act (because of the short time they had spent in the UK), McFarlane J instead made an order under section 84 of the Adoption and Children Act 2002 (ACA 2002), which confers parental responsibility on a prospective adopter.

In respect of the issue of consent to insemination by the estranged husband of the surrogate mother, McFarlane J held that, pursuant to section 28 of the HFEA 1990, the common law position applied and that the biological father was to be treated for all purposes as the child's father. The fact that there had been no written consent did not necessarily mean that the father had not consented for the purposes of section 28(2) of the

Act. The term 'consent' was not confined to the narrow meaning argued for by COTS. It was necessary for the court to look more widely than simply at whether the husband had signed the form at the clinic. McFarlane J listed the principles which should be borne in mind in trying to ensure that lessons were learned for the future:

- ▶ Non-commercial surrogacy arrangements where neither of the commissioning parents is domiciled in the UK are to be discouraged, as it is not open to them to apply for a parental order under section 30 of the HFEA 1990.
- ▶ Surrogacy agencies must ensure they are fully familiar with the basic legal requirements.
- ▶ Any application for a parental order under section 30 involving an international element should be transferred to a nominated inter-country adoption county court or the High Court.
- ▶ Any court hearing an application for a parental order under section 30 must ensure that the qualifying conditions required of the applicants are met.
- ▶ Where a surrogate mother is married, but separated from her husband, all reasonable attempts should be made before the surrogacy process begins in order to establish whether or not her husband consents to the proposed arrangement.
- ▶ The court can make orders as to costs, as costs should not be borne by the British taxpayer in such cases.

(b) Surrogacy and parenthood

The rules on parenthood in surrogacy cases are the same as those which apply in non-surrogacy cases (see 9.2 above). Thus, the birth mother (the surrogate) is the legal parent of the child. However, it is possible for legal parenthood to be transferred from the surrogate mother to the commissioning parents by means of a parental order (see below).

(c) Surrogacy and parental orders

The commissioning parents of a surrogacy arrangement can apply for a parental order which the court has jurisdiction to make under section 54 of the HFEA 2008 (which replaced section 30 of the HFEA 1990). As section 54 does not differ in substance from section 30, other than to extend the law to civil partners, the case-law on section 30 remains relevant. The law is therefore unaffected by the HFEA 2008, except that welfare is now the paramount, not the first, consideration (following the importation of section 1 of the ACA 2002 into section 54 of the HFEA 2008). Applications for a parental order must be made in the High Court.

The effect of a parental order is to provide for the child to be treated in law as the child of the applicants (s 54(1)). Where an application is made, a Children's Guardian (an officer of Cafcass) (see 1.7) will be appointed by the court to conduct a welfare inquiry. On issuing the order, the court notifies the General Register Office of Births, which re-registers the birth, and the new birth record supersedes the original one.

Section 54(1) provides that the court can make a parental order if the child has been carried by a woman who is not one of the applicants as a result of the placing in her of an embryo or sperm and eggs or her artificial insemination, the gametes of at least one of the applicants were used to bring about the creation of the embryo, and the preconditions in section 54(2) and (8) are satisfied (see below).

(i) Applicants for an order

The applicants must be: husband and wife; civil partners of each other; or a couple (opposite sex or same sex) who are living with each other as partners in an enduring family relationship and who are not within the prohibited degrees of relationship in relation to each other (s 54(2)). Following the enactment of the Marriage (Same Sex Couples) Act 2013, a same sex married couple can apply under this section (see *Re Z (A Child: Human Fertilisation and Embryology Act: Parental Order)* [2015] EWFC 73). Single people cannot apply. Thus, for example, in *Re Z* [2015] EWFC 73 the President of the Family Division, Sir James Munby, refused to grant a parental order to a sole male applicant who had entered into a surrogacy arrangement in the USA. A parental order can, however, be made if one of the couple has died after the surrogacy arrangement (see *A v P (Surrogacy: Parental Order: Death of Applicant)* [2011] EWHC 1738 (Fam)).

(ii) Preconditions to be satisfied

In addition to the above requirements, the following conditions must also be satisfied before the court can consider whether to make a parental order:

- ▶ The application must be made within six months of the child's birth (s 54(3)). Non-compliance with the six-month statutory time limit is not, however, always fatal (see, for example, *Adesina v Nursing and Midwifery Council* [2013] EWCA Civ 818 and *Re X (A Child) (Surrogacy: Time limit)* [2014] EWHC 3135 (Fam)).
- ▶ At the time of the application and of the making of the order the child's home must be with the applicants; and one or both parties must be domiciled in a part of the UK or in the Channel Islands or in the Isle of Man (s 54(4)). Thus, for example, in *Re K (Minors: Foreign Surrogacy)* [2010] EWHC 1180 (Fam), the court had no jurisdiction as the children, who had been born as a result of a commercial surrogacy arrangement in India, were still living there.
- ▶ At the time of making the order both applicants must have attained the age of 18 (s 54(5)).
- ▶ The court must be satisfied that both the woman who carried the child and any other person who is a parent of the child but is not one of the applicants (including any man who is the father by virtue of section 35 or 36 or any woman who is a parent by virtue of section 42 or 43) have freely, and with full understanding of what is involved, agreed unconditionally to the making of the order (s 54(6)). Agreement is not required if they cannot be found or are incapable of giving agreement; and the agreement of the mother who carried the child is ineffective if given less than six weeks after the child's birth (s 54(7)). Thus, for example, in *D and L (Surrogacy), Re* [2012] EWHC 2631 (Fam) a parental order was made on the application of a couple who were male civil partners even though the surrogate mother could not be found.
- ▶ The court must be satisfied that no money or other benefit (other than for expenses reasonably incurred) has been given or received by either of the applicants for or in consideration of: the making of the order; any agreement required by section 54(6) (see above); the handing over of the child to the applicants; or the making of arrangements with a view to the making of the order, unless authorised by the court (s 54(8)). On authorising payment retrospectively, see below.

(iii) The child's welfare is the court's paramount consideration

If the above preconditions are satisfied, the court will then go on to exercise its discretion to decide whether or not to make the order, applying the principle that the child's lifelong welfare is the court's paramount consideration. In *Re L (Commercial Surrogacy)* [2010] EWHC 3146 (Fam), where Hedley J retrospectively authorised payments made in excess of reasonable expenses with respect to a surrogacy arrangement made in the USA and made a parental order, it was held that the effect of the importation of the paramountcy principle into applications for a parental order was for the balance between public policy considerations and welfare to weigh decisively in favour of welfare; and that it would be only in the clearest case of an abuse of public policy that the court would be able to withhold an order if welfare considerations supported it being made.

(iv) Authorising payments

As commercial surrogacy arrangements are outlawed in the UK (see above), couples from the UK may choose to go abroad for the purpose of having a surrogate child. On their return they may decide to apply for a parental order which the court cannot consider making unless it is willing to authorise any payments which were made in excess of reasonable expenses (s 54(8)).

When considering whether payments should be retrospectively authorised, the court will ask three questions: was the sum paid disproportionate to reasonable expenses; were the applicants acting in good faith and without 'moral taint' in their dealings with the surrogate mother; and were the applicants a party to any attempt to defraud the authorities? The court will also take into account the following policy issues: that the commercial arrangement was not being used to circumvent UK childcare laws (for example, by giving people who would not have been approved as adoptive parents a right to a parental order); that payments were not simply being used to buy a child overseas; and that the sums of money were not such that they might overbear the will of a surrogate carrier.

In the following cases, payments were retrospectively authorised by the court. They show that, although the aim of section 54(8) is to prevent the commercialisation of surrogacy, the paramountcy of the child's welfare will usually result in unauthorised surrogacy payments being retrospectively authorised.

▶ *Re C (Application by Mr and Mrs X Under s.30 of the Human Fertilisation and Embryology Act 1990)* [2002] 1 FLR 909

The £12,000 paid to the surrogate mother by the commissioning parents, as they did not wish her to work during pregnancy, was authorised by Wall J as being expenses reasonably incurred.

▶ *Re X and Y (Foreign Surrogacy)* [2009] 1 FLR 733

The applicants (a married couple from the UK who had entered into a surrogacy agreement with a married woman in the Ukraine who had produced twins for them) were granted a parental order by Hedley J despite having paid the surrogate mother. Hedley J authorised the payments, applying *Re C* and finding that the three questions (see above) were satisfied and that the paramountcy of the child's lifelong welfare prevailed over the policy considerations.

▶ *Re S (Parental Order)* [2009] EWHC 2977

Hedley J granted a parental order to a married couple who had entered into a commercial surrogacy arrangement in California and who had paid $23,000 to the surrogate carrier. They had entered into the agreement in good faith without realising that it would not be recognised in England and Wales. Hedley J made clear that, without the order, the surrogate carrier would remain the legal mother and, if she were married, her husband would be the lawful father. The parental order was clearly important for the long-term well-being of the new family; and the policy issues did not militate against an order being made.

▶ *Re X and Y (Parental Order: Retrospective Authorisation of Payments)* [2011] EWHC 3147 (Fam)

The British parents entered into a surrogacy arrangement with a clinic in India to whom they paid about £27,000. Sir Nicholas Wall P authorised the payment and made a parental order, holding that: the applicants were entirely genuine; the conditions in section 54 had been met; the payments were not disproportionate; and it was plainly in the children's interests to be brought up by the applicants as their parents.

▶ *Re D and L (Surrogacy)* [2012] EWHC 2631 (Fam)

Baker J granted a parental order to the male civil partner applicants even though they had paid for the services of a surrogate mother using the services of a clinic in India (and even though the mother had not given her consent as she could not be found). Although the payment was accepted as being beyond the 'reasonable expenses' permitted by section 54(8), Baker J held that the court was under a duty to place the welfare of the children first and therefore retrospectively authorised the payments which had been made.

▶ *Re WT (A Child)* [2014] EWHC 1303 (Fam)

A parental order was granted to an unmarried opposite sex couple even though they had paid for the services of a surrogate mother using the services of a clinic in India. Theis J was entirely satisfied that the applicants had acted at all times in good faith and without moral taint. They had taken great care to select the clinic, had undertaken their own research, displayed independent judgement and complied with the directions of the court. The amounts paid to the clinic were set by the clinic and the amount paid to the surrogate mother was the amount authorised in the case of *Re D and L (Surrogacy)* (see above). There was no evidence to suggest that the surrogate mother did not freely consent to the arrangement.

(v) Section 54 proceedings are family proceedings

As section 54 proceedings for a parental order are family proceedings for the purposes of the CA 1989 (s 54(9)(a)), the court may make any section 8 order under the CA 1989 in those proceedings, either on an application or of its own motion (see 10.4).

(vi) Setting aside a parental order

There is no power to set aside a parental order under the HFEA 2008. However, in *G v G (Parental Order: Revocation)* [2012] EWHC 1979 (Fam), where an application was made by Mr G to set aside a parental order (on the ground of procedural flaws and on the basis that at the time of the order the mother had a concealed intention to separate and raise the child alone), Hedley J, refusing to set aside the order, drew parallels between the revocation of a parental order and that of an adoption order, holding that guidance could be derived from the relevant authorities (in particular, *Re M (Minors) (Adoption)* [1991] 1 FLR 458 which concerned an application for revocation on the basis of 'mistake' by one of the parties as to the factual basis of the application). Thus, the bar to set aside a parental order (like an adoption order) is set very high. Here the facts of the case were not such that the parental order should be set aside.

Summary

- Most children are brought up by parents with whom they have a biological link, but some are brought up by step-parents, foster-parents, guardians, adoptive parents or special guardians. The courts have generally recognised that it is usually in a child's best interests to be brought up, where possible, by their biological parents. This is not a legal presumption, however, as the welfare of the child is the court's paramount consideration. The importance of parents is recognised in the United Nations Convention on the Rights of the Child (UNCRC). It is also reflected in the jurisprudence of the European Court of Human Rights (ECtHR), which has held that the mutual enjoyment of each other's company by parent and child constitutes a fundamental element of family life.

- Various legal presumptions exist in respect of parentage, but they are of little relevance today as parentage can be established by DNA testing with virtually 100 per cent certainty. The courts have held that scientific tests, rather than legal presumptions, should be used to prove parentage. Provisions governing the use of scientific tests for determining parentage are laid down in the FLRA 1969. The consent of the child is needed (if aged 16 and over), or the consent of the person with the care and control of the child if the child is aged under 16. If consent is not forthcoming the court can give consent. Although the courts have held that it is normally in the best interests of the child to know their origins, and for the truth to be known, this is subject to the overriding principle that the child's welfare is the court's paramount consideration. A declaration of parentage can be made under section 55A of the Family Law Act 1986 (FLA 1986); and a declaration of legitimacy can be made under section 56 of that Act.

- The law governing parental responsibility is laid down in section 2 of the Children Act 1989 (CA 1989). The following people have automatic parental responsibility: married parents; an unmarried mother; a mother and her civil partner who is a parent by virtue of section 42 of the Human Fertilisation and Embryology Act (HFEA 2008); a mother and her female partner who is a parent by virtue of section 43 of the HFEA 2008; and a mother who is a parent by virtue of section 43 of the HFEA 2008.

- An unmarried father does not have 'automatic' parental responsibility for his children. He can acquire it by joint birth registration with the mother, making a parental responsibility agreement with the mother or by obtaining a parental responsibility order from the court under section 4 of the CA 1989. It is also possible to obtain parental responsibility through a guardianship order, a child arrangements order regulating the child's living arrangements, a special guardianship order, an adoption order or marrying the mother. When considering whether to make a parental responsibility order the court will take into account the welfare principles in section 1 of the CA 1989 (except the welfare checklist) and also: the degree of commitment which the father has shown towards the child; the degree of attachment which exists between the father and the child; and the father's reasons or motivation for applying for the order. An unmarried father who has acquired parental responsibility (and other people who do not possess it automatically) can have it revoked where such a step is in the best interests of the child (except where he has acquired parental responsibility by marriage or adoption).

▶ A second female parent in a same sex relationship which is not a marriage or civil partnership can acquire parental responsibility by joint birth registration or by way of a parental responsibility agreement or parental responsibility order under section 4ZA of the CA 1989. Parental responsibility acquired in any of these ways can be terminated by court order.

▶ Step-parents and civil partners can acquire parental responsibility by means of a parental responsibility agreement or parental responsibility order under section 4A of the CA 1989. Parental responsibility acquired in any of these ways can be terminated by court order.

▶ Other people can acquire parental responsibility by means of a child arrangements order regulating the child's living arrangements, a special guardianship order or an adoption order. Parental responsibility acquired by way of a child arrangements order regulating the child's living arrangements or a special guardianship order can be terminated by court order.

▶ Parents have rights and duties at common law and under statute, but parental rights are not absolute. These include the right to: choose where the child lives; have contact with the child; decide on the child's education; choose the child's religion; consent to the child's medical treatment; consent to the child's marriage or civil partnership; choose the child's surname and register the child's birth; consent to the child's adoption; discipline the child; administer the child's property and enter into contracts on the child's behalf; appoint a guardian for the child; and bring legal proceedings in respect of the child.

▶ Parents are responsible for consenting to their child's medical treatment except that, in some circumstances, a '*Gillick* competent' child may be able to give consent. Disputes between parents and doctors about the medical treatment of a child can be decided by means of a specific issue order under section 8 of the CA 1989, or by the High Court in the exercise of its inherent or wardship jurisdiction. The best interests of the child are paramount in these cases and, while parental wishes are respected by the courts, they do not prevail. Serious and irreversible operations on the child (such as sterilisation and circumcision) may need the consent of the court. Disputes between parents about medical treatment can be decided by means of a specific issue order, or by the High Court in the exercise of its inherent or wardship jurisdiction. A prohibited steps order under section 8 of the CA 1989 can be used to prevent the other parent making a decision about, or taking steps with respect to, the child's medical treatment.

▶ A guardian can be appointed (by a private individual or by the court) under sections 5–6 of the CA 1989. The aim is to ensure that there is a person available to exercise parental responsibility for the child should the child's parents die.

▶ The Human Fertilisation and Embryology Act 1990 (HFEA 1990) and the HFEA 2008 govern assisted reproduction. The woman who is carrying (or has carried) a child as a result of the placing in her of an embryo or of sperm and eggs, and no other woman, is treated as the

Summary cont'd

legal mother of the child. A married father is automatically recognised as the legal father of the child. An unmarried father will be recognised as the legal father of the child if, *inter alia*, he consents to being treated as such in respect of any child resulting from the assisted reproduction. The same rules apply to a second female parent, whether or not they are married or in a civil partnership.

▶ Some couples may decide to have a child by way of a surrogacy arrangement. Commercial surrogacy is unlawful in the UK and is punishable as a criminal offence under the Surrogacy Arrangements Act 1985 (SAA 1985). The commissioning parents of a surrogate arrangement can apply for a parental order under section 54 of the HFEA 2008 which has the effect of transferring legal parenthood from the surrogate mother to the commissioning parents. Only couples, not single people, can apply, namely: an opposite sex or same sex married couple; a civil partnership couple; and an opposite sex or same sex cohabiting couple who are living in an enduring family relationship and who are not within the prohibited degrees of relationship. Certain preconditions laid down in section 54 must be satisfied first, after which the court will consider whether or not to make the order, applying the principle that the child's welfare is the paramount consideration. There are many cases involving commercial surrogacy agreements entered into overseas involving payment (which is outlawed in the UK) where the court has retrospectively authorised the payment, and made the parental order, as this has been held to be in the best interests of the child.

Further reading and references

Bainham, 'Is legitimacy legitimate?' [2009] Fam Law 673.

Bainham, 'Rowing back from *Re G*? Natural parents in the Supreme Court' [2010] Fam Law 394.

Bainham, 'Is anything now left of parental rights?', Chapter 2 in Probert, Gilmore and Herring (2009), below.

Barton, 'How many sorts of domestic partnership are there?' [2015] Fam Law 393.

Blain and Worwood, 'Alternative families and changing perceptions of parenthood' [2011] Fam Law 289.

Bridge, 'Religion, culture and conviction: the medical treatment of children' [1999] CFLQ 217.

Diduck '"If only we can find the appropriate terms to use the issue will be solved": law, identity and parenthood' [2007] CFLQ 458.

Downie, '*Re C (HIV Test)* – the limits of parental autonomy' [2000] CFLQ 197.

Eekelaar, 'Are parents morally obliged to care for their children?' (1991) OJLS 340.

Eekelaar, 'Parental responsibility: state of nature or nature of the state?' (1991) JSWFL 37.

Eekelaar, 'Rethinking parental responsibility' [2001] Fam Law 428.

Everett and Yeatman, 'Are some parents more natural than others?' [2010] CFLQ 290.

Fenton-Glynn, 'The regulation and recognition of surrogacy under English law: an overview of the case-law' [2015] CFLQ 53.

Fortin, 'Accommodating children's rights in a post Human Rights Act era' (2006) *Modern Law Review* 299.

Fortin, 'Children's rights to know their origins – too far, too fast?' [2009] CFLQ 336.

Gamble and Ghevaert, 'International surrogacy: payments, public policy and media hype' [2011] Fam Law 504.

Harris and George, 'Parental responsibility and shared residence orders: parliamentary intentions and judicial interpretations' [2010] CFLQ 151.

Further reading and references cont'd

Horsey, 'Challenging presumptions: legal parenthood and surrogacy arrangements' [2010] CFLQ 499.

Issacs, Maynard, Lakin and Howells, 'Parental order time limits: policy – what policy?' [2014] Fam Law 1723.

Probert, Gilmore and Herring (eds), *Responsible Parents and Parental Responsibility,* 2009, Hart Publishing.

Smith, 'Clashing symbols? Reconciling support for fathers and fatherless families after the Human Fertilisation and Embryology Act 2008' [2010] CFLQ 42.

Wallbank, '"Bodies in the shadows": joint birth registration, parental responsibility and social class' [2009] CFLQ 267.

Welstead, 'Surrogacy update: part 1' [2015] Fam Law 931.

Welstead, 'Surrogacy update: part 2' [2015] Fam Law 1103.

Welstead, 'Biology matters: children in lesbian families update: part 1' [2016] Fam Law 356.

Welstead, 'Biology matters: part 2: disputes between lesbian birth mothers and their partners' [2016] Fam Law 477.

Websites

Advice Now: www.advicenow.org.uk
Families Need Fathers: www.fnf.org.uk
Family and Parenting Institute: www.familyandparenting.org
Human Fertilisation and Embryology Authority: www.hfea.gov.uk

Links to relevant websites can also be found at: www.palgravehighered.com/law/familylaw9e

Chapter 10

The Children Act 1989

This chapter considers the Children Act 1989. It deals first with the background to the Act and briefly sets out the main provisions therein. It then considers the important principles laid down in section 1 and the range of orders available under section 8 of the Act, before looking at the people who can apply for such orders with and without leave (permission) of the court and the power of the court to make such orders of its own motion. Finally, it concludes by looking at other orders that are available under the Act.

10.1 The Children Act 1989

The Children Act 1989 (CA 1989) contains provisions governing both the private and public law relating to parents and children. The Act came into force in 1991, but there have been many important amendments since then.

(a) Influences on the Act and its principles and policies

The CA 1989 was an important Act not only because it consolidated much of the law relating to children, but also because it introduced new principles and policies. Government reports and public inquiries relating to the management of child abuse by social workers and other agencies had a considerable influence on the Act. Of particular importance was *The Report of the Inquiry into Child Abuse in Cleveland 1987* (Cm 412, 1988), which severely criticised the over-zealous intervention of local authority social services in children's cases in Cleveland in the North-East of England (see 14.1). The *Report* had an important influence on the public law provisions of the Act, in particular in respect of emergency protection of children and the importance of promoting inter-agency cooperation.

The *Gillick* case (see 8.4), which gives children of sufficient age and understanding the right to bring proceedings and to have their views taken into account by the court, also had an impact on the Act. The Act also introduced the concept of 'parental responsibility', partly as a result of *Gillick*, in order to stress the positive ongoing nature of parental involvement in bringing up children and to remove the adversarial undertones of 'parental rights'. Another aim of the Act was to provide a flexible range of orders available in all family proceedings involving children (which can be made on an application or by the court of its own motion).

(b) Strengths and weaknesses

The CA 1989 has generally been considered to be a successful Act, and this was recognised by the inquiry which followed the tragic death of Victoria Climbié (see 14.1). However, it has been criticised by some commentators for not bringing children's interests sufficiently to the fore (see Freeman, 1998) and for failing to include any reference to children's rights (see Fortin, 2006). A major problem with proceedings under the Act is that of delay. Delays can be particularly long in child protection and adoption cases, but the Government has taken steps to reduce delay (see 14.7).

(c) Amendments to the Act

New provisions have been inserted into the CA 1989 over the years. Thus, it has been amended to allow unmarried fathers to acquire parental responsibility by birth registration (see 9.4); and to allow step-parents to acquire parental responsibility for a step-child (see 9.5). New provisions on special guardianship have been inserted into the Act (see 15.14); and also in respect of the facilitation and enforcement of contact (see 11.5). In 2009, changes were made extending the duration of child arrangements orders regulating the child's living arrangements; and new provisions were inserted governing the parental responsibility of a second female parent who has had a child by assisted reproduction (see 9.9). Amendments have also been made to the public law provisions of the Act, for example in respect of provisions concerning children leaving care (see Chapter 14).

In 2014, the Children and Families Act 2014 (CFA 2014) made significant changes to the family justice system in England and Wales, which Sir James Munby, President of the Family Division, hailed as 'a cultural revolution' and 'the largest reform of the family justice system any of us have seen or will see in our professional lifetimes' (see 11th View from the President's Chamber: The Process of Reform, 11 April 2014). The Act inserted, among other things, a new subsection into the welfare checklist in section 1 of the CA 1989, adding a presumption of parental involvement (see 10.3 below); and replaced the old 'residence order' and 'contact order' with a new single child arrangements order (see 10.5 below).

10.2 An overview of the Act

Parts I to V of the Children Act 1989 (CA 1989) are the parts most relevant to family lawyers (see below). Part XII ('Miscellaneous and General') is also important because it includes provisions about: the effect and duration of orders (s 91); privacy for children involved in certain proceedings (s 97); restrictions on the use of the wardship jurisdiction (s 100); and the interpretation section of the Act (s 105). The following schedules are also important: Schedule 1 (Financial Provision for Children); Schedule 2 (Local Authority Support for Children and Families); and Schedule 3 (Supervision Orders).

The main provisions of the CA 1989 are as follows.

Children Act 1989

Part I Introductory

The welfare principle, presumption of parental involvement and other principles applicable in proceedings under the Act (s 1). Parental responsibility (ss 2–4A). The appointment of guardians for children (ss 5–6). Welfare reports (s 7).

Part II Orders with respect to children in family proceedings

Section 8 orders (child arrangements, specific issue and prohibited steps) and the powers of the court in respect of these orders (ss 9–14), including provisions relating to the enforcement and facilitation of activity directions (ss 11A–11P). Special guardianship orders (ss 14A–14G). Orders for financial relief for children (s 15 and Schedule 1). Family assistance orders (s 16). Risk assessments (s 16A).

Part III Local authority support for children and families

Local authority services for children in need, their families and others (ss 17–19). Payments and vouchers in respect of children in need (ss 17A–B). Provision of accommodation for children in need (ss 20–21). The duties of local authorities in relation to children looked after by them (ss 22–23). Advice and assistance for children (s 24). Advice and assistance for children and young people who have left care (ss 23A–E, ss 24A–D). Secure accommodation (s 25). Independent reviewing officers (ss 25A–C). Case reviews (s 26). Co-operation between local authorities (s 27). Advocacy services for children (s 27A). Consultation with local education authorities (s 28). Recoupment of cost of providing services (s 29).

Part IV Care and supervision

Care orders, supervision orders and education supervision orders (ss 31–40). Care plans (s 31A).

Part V Protection of children

Child assessment orders (s 43). Emergency protection orders (ss 44–45). Police removal of children (s 46). Local authority duty to investigate (s 47). Power to assist in discovery of children who may be in need of emergency protection (s 48).

10.3 The welfare principles

Important principles are laid down in section 1 of the Children Act 1989 (CA 1989) which apply to most court applications involving children, whether brought by private individuals or by public authorities. These principles are as follows.

(a) The welfare principle (section 1(1))

The paramountcy of the child's welfare is the governing principle in children's cases.

Section 1(1) of the Children Act 1989

When a court determines any question with respect to—

(a) the upbringing of a child; or
(b) the administration of a child's property or the application of any income arising from it,

the child's welfare shall be the court's paramount consideration.

The child's welfare is the paramount consideration in private law proceedings (such as for a child arrangements order) and in public law proceedings (such as for care and supervision orders). The Act does not expressly require the welfare principle to be applied in applications for leave to apply for a section 8 order (see 10.4 below) or applications for financial relief for children under section 15 and Schedule 1 (see 12.3), but in practice the court will consider the child's welfare as part of its statutory obligation to consider all the circumstances of the case.

The paramountcy of the child's welfare is enshrined in Article 3(1) of the United Nations Convention on the Rights of the Child 1989 (UNCRC 1989). It is also recognised by the European Court of Human Rights (ECtHR), even though there is no express reference to children in the European Convention on Human Rights (ECHR).

(b) The presumption of parental involvement (section 1(2A))

The presumption laid down in section 1(2A) of the CA 1989 was introduced by section 11 of the Children and Families Act 2014 (CFA 2014) to send an important message to parents about the valuable role which they both play in their child's life on family breakdown. It requires the court, when deciding whether to make, vary or discharge a section 8 order or when deciding whether to award or remove parental responsibility in contested proceedings, to presume, unless the contrary is shown, that involvement of each of the relevant child's parents in their life will further the child's welfare. Thus, the presumption of parental involvement must be applied in private law proceedings.

Section 1(2A) of the Children Act 1989

A court ... is as respects each parent ... to presume, unless the contrary is shown, that involvement of that parent in the life of the child concerned will further the child's welfare.

'*Involvement*' is defined as involvement of some kind, either direct or indirect, but not any particular division of a child's time (s 1(2B)).

A '*parent*' in section 1(2A) is defined as 'a parent of the child concerned if that parent can be involved in the child's life in a way that does not put the child at risk of suffering harm' (s 1(6)(a)). A parent will be treated as such 'unless there is some evidence before the court in the particular proceedings to suggest that involvement of that parent in the child's life would put the child at risk of suffering harm whatever the form of the involvement' (s 1(6)(b)).

(c) The welfare checklist (section 1(3))

Section 1(3) contains a list of factors which creates a framework for the exercise of judicial discretion in the application of the welfare principle above. The court must have regard to the checklist when deciding whether to make, vary or discharge a section 8 order in contested proceedings (s 1(4)(a)), and when deciding whether to make, vary or discharge a special guardianship order, a care order or a supervision order (s 1(4)(b)). Thus, the checklist must be applied in private law proceedings and in public law proceedings (except in emergency protection proceedings, as to apply the checklist might hinder emergency action).

Section 1(3) of the Children Act 1989

[A] court shall have regard in particular to—

(a) the ascertainable wishes and feelings of the child concerned (considered in the light of his age and understanding);
(b) his physical, emotional and educational needs;
(c) the likely effect on him of any change in his circumstances;
(d) his age, sex, background and any characteristics of his which the court considers relevant;
(e) any harm which he has suffered or is at risk of suffering;
(f) how capable each of his parents, and any other person in relation to whom the court considers the question to be relevant, is of meeting his needs;
(g) the range of powers available to the court under this Act in the proceedings in question.

'*Harm*' in section 1(3)(e) has the same meaning as it has in section 31 of the Act (see 14.7); and this includes harm caused by seeing or hearing the ill-treatment of another person. Witnessing or hearing domestic violence can therefore constitute harm.

The list of factors in section 1(3) is not exclusive and other factors may be taken into account; and the factors are not listed in any hierarchy of importance. Furthermore, as the Act does not refer to section 1(3) as a 'checklist', a judge is not required 'to read out the seven items in s 1(3) and pronounce his conclusion on each' (*per* Staughton LJ in *H v H (Residence Order: Leave to Remove from Jurisdiction)* [1995] 1 FLR 529). In *B v B (Residence Order: Reasons for Decision)* [1997] 2 FLR 602, Holman J held that, although it is not always necessary or appropriate for a judge to go through the checklist item by item, it does represent an extremely useful and important discipline for judges to ensure that all the relevant factors and circumstances are considered and balanced. In *Re G (Children) (Residence: Same-Sex Partner)* [2006] UKHL 43, Lord Nicholls said that in a 'difficult or finely balanced case it is a great help to address each of the factors in the list, along with any others which may be relevant, so as to ensure that no particular feature of the case is given more weight than it should properly bear'.

A failure to consider one or more of the factors in the checklist may provide a successful ground for an appeal. Thus, for example, in *Re S (A Child)* [2015] EWCA Civ 689 a father successfully appealed against an order which provided for indirect contact with his daughter.

(d)   The no delay principle (section 1(2))

Section 1(2) of the Act recognises that delay is harmful for a child.

Section 1(2) of the Children Act 1989

In any proceedings in which any question with respect to the upbringing of a child arises, the court shall have regard to the general principle that any delay in determining the question is likely to prejudice the welfare of the child.

To avoid delay, the progress of cases is determined by the court, which must draw up a timetable for section 8 order proceedings (s 11) and for care and supervision proceedings (s 32). The court can give directions, and the rules of court make provision, to avoid delay. Children's issues must be determined as soon as possible so that minimum disruption is caused to the child's life and the child is not left in limbo. In November 2011, the *Final Report* of the Family Justice Review (see 1.2) criticised the unconscionable delay in the family justice system. In the Government's response to the Family Justice Review (see its *Response*, 2012), it announced radical changes to reduce the time it takes cases to progress through the courts. The CFA 2014 has subsequently introduced significant procedural reforms which include, amongst other things, removal of the 28-day time limit for interim care and supervision orders and a 26-week deadline for care and supervision proceedings (see 14.7).

(e)   The no order principle (section 1(5))

This principle laid down in section 1(5) was introduced as part of the general policy of the CA 1989 to place the primary responsibility for children on their parents.

Section 1(5) of the Children Act 1989

Where a court is considering whether or not to make one or more orders under this Act with respect to a child, it shall not make the order or any of the orders unless it considers that doing so would be better for the child than making no order at all.

The aim of section 1(5) is to discourage courts making unnecessary orders and to ensure that orders are made only if they will positively improve the child's welfare. Section 1(5) was at one time interpreted by some commentators and judges as creating a presumption in favour of making no order. However, in *Re G (Children) (Residence Order: No Order Principle)* [2006] 1 FLR 771, Ward LJ in the Court of Appeal held that this was an incorrect interpretation, as section 1(5) did not create a presumption either way. It merely required the court to ask whether making an order would be better for a child than making no order at all.

10.4   Section 8 orders

Section 8 of the Children Act 1989 (CA 1989) makes provision for the following orders which can be used in a wide range of different situations involving children:

- **a child arrangements order** (regulating with whom the child is to live, spend time or otherwise have contact, and when the child is to live, spend time or otherwise have contact with any person);
- **a prohibited steps order** (preventing an action in respect of parental responsibility being taken); and
- **a specific issue order** (determining an issue arising in respect of parental responsibility).

(a)   Applicable principles

When considering whether or not to make, vary or discharge any section 8 order, the court must apply the welfare principle (s 1(1)), the presumption of parental involvement (s 1(2A) and the welfare checklist (s 1(3)); and it must also apply the other provisions in section 1 of the Act, namely the no delay (s 1(2)) and the no order (s 1(5)) principles (see above).

(b)   Applicants

Some people have an automatic right to apply for a section 8 order, whereas other people, and children, need leave (permission) of the court to apply (see 10.10 below). Restrictions exist with regard to applications by local authorities (see below).

(c)   General provisions

The court can: make interim section 8 orders (s 11(3)); attach directions and conditions to a section 8 order (s 11(7)); and grant a section 8 order without the other party being given notice of the proceedings (if urgent action is needed).

(d)   Restrictions

Section 9 lays down the following restrictions which apply to section 8 orders:

- A court cannot make any section 8 order (other than a child arrangements order regulating a child's living arrangements) with respect to a child who is in local authority care (s 9(1)).
- A local authority cannot apply for a child arrangements order and no court shall make such an order in favour of a local authority (s 9(2)). This prohibition is to prevent local authorities using section 8 orders instead of a care or supervision order.
- A local authority foster-parent (or a person who was a foster-parent at any time during the previous six months) cannot apply for leave to apply for a section 8 order with respect to a foster-child unless: the foster-parent has the consent of the local authority; or is the relative of the child; or the foster-child has lived with the foster-parent for at least one year preceding the application (s 9(3)).
- A court cannot make a prohibited steps order or a specific issue order with a view to achieving a result which could be achieved by making a child arrangements order; or in any way which is denied to the High Court (by section 100(2)) in the exercise of its inherent jurisdiction with respect to children (s 9(5)).

- ▶ Unless the circumstances of the case are exceptional, a court cannot make a section 8 order to last after the child has reached the age of 16 (s 9(6)).
- ▶ Unless the circumstances of the case are exceptional, a court cannot make any section 8 order if the child has already reached the age of 16 (s 9(7)).

10.5 Child arrangements orders

Section 11 of the Children and Families Act 2014 (CFA 2014) inserted a new provision into section 8 of the Children Act 1989 (CA 1989), replacing the old 'residence order' and 'contact order' with a new single child arrangements order.

> **A child arrangements order** means an order 'regulating arrangements relating to with whom a child is to live, spend time or otherwise have contact, and when a child is to live, spend time or otherwise have contact with any person' (s 8(1)).

The Family Justice Review (see 1.2) in its *Final Report* stated that 'the new order would move away from loaded terms such as residence and contact which have themselves become a source of contention between parents, to bring greater focus on practical issues of the day to day care of the child' (para 112). Resolution, an organisation of family lawyers, submitted that 'changing the focus from "winners" and "losers" to the child's needs ... would be helpful as part of a wider and sustained effort to change attitudes and culture' (para 4.55); and Supreme Court Justice Lady Hale put the recommendation in further context, stating:

> The thinking behind the Children Act 1989 was that parents should be encouraged to make their own arrangements and the court would only decide what they could not decide. But their task, and the court's task, was not to allocate status or rights, so much as to settle the practical living arrangements for the child. Over the years, 'residence' and 'contact' have taken on too much of the flavour of the old 'custody' and 'access' orders. These proposals would restore the original vision underlying the 1989 Act' (para 465).

The Government agreed with the approach of the Family Justice Review. In its *Impact Assessment* it suggested that the intention of the new order was twofold: first, to remove the perception of 'winning and losing' in court which can contribute to the adversarial nature of court proceedings; and second, to remove the perception, contributed to by the wording of residence and contact orders, that the court system is biased against non-resident parents. It further stated that, '[u]ltimately, children are deemed to be the main beneficiaries of the child arrangements order', but that 'the Government anticipates that the outcome of court decisions will not be significantly different as a result of the introduction of child arrangement orders' (see the House of Commons Justice Committee Pre-Legislative Scrutiny of the Children and Families Bill Fourth Report of Session 2012–13, HC 739, December 2012, at para 124).

Any residence or contact order made before 22 April 2014 is now deemed to be a child arrangements order. The Family Proceeding Rules 2010 and accompanying *Practice Directions* have been amended to reflect these changes. In practice, however, there is little difference between a child arrangements order and the old 'residence order' and 'contact order'; and it is likely that the courts will continue to take the same approach that they did prior to the change in terminology.

(a)   A child arrangements order regulating the child's living arrangements

In addition to the general provisions and restrictions which apply to section 8 orders (see 10.4 above), the following provisions in the CA 1989 specifically apply to a child arrangements order regulating the child's living arrangements:

▶ Restrictions exist on changing the child's surname and taking the child out of the UK (ss 13(1) and (2)).
▶ If the child has two parents who have parental responsibility for them, such an order will cease to have effect if the parents live together for a continuous period of more than six months (s 11(5)).
▶ The court can impose conditions on such an order (s 11(7)).

(i) Local authorities and child arrangement orders

A child arrangements order regulating the child's living arrangements is the only section 8 order that can be made in respect of a child in local authority care (s 9(1)), as to permit otherwise would undermine a local authority's statutory powers. However, such an order cannot be applied for by, or be made in favour of, a local authority (s 9(2)), as this would allow a local authority to gain parental responsibility for a child by means other than a care order.

(ii) Child arrangement orders and parental responsibility

A child arrangements order regulating the child's living arrangements does not affect the parental responsibility of any other person who possesses such responsibility. Thus, parental responsibility is retained and continues whether or not such an order is made.

If a child arrangements order regulating the child's living arrangements is made in favour of an unmarried father without parental responsibility, the court must also make an order under section 4 giving him that responsibility (s 12(1)). The same rule applies where such an order is made in favour of a second female parent who is a parent of a child by virtue of assisted reproduction but who does not have parental responsibility; the court must then make an order under section 4ZA giving her that responsibility (s 12(1A)) (see 9.5).

Where the court makes a child arrangements order regulating the child's living arrangements in favour of any person who is not the parent or guardian of the child concerned, then that person has parental responsibility for the child while the order is in force (s 12(2)). However, that person does not have the right to agree, or refuse to agree, to the making of an adoption order; or to appoint a guardian (s 12(3)).

(b)   A child arrangements order regulating the child's contact arrangements

The welfare principles and general provisions and restrictions which apply to section 8 orders (see 10.4 above) also apply to a child arrangements order regulating the child's contact arrangements. In respect of local authorities, such an order cannot be made in respect of a child in care, and cannot be applied for by, or be made in favour of, a local authority (ss 9(1), (2)). Contact in care is governed by section 34 of the CA 1989 (see 14.8). A child arrangements order regulating the child's contact arrangements will cease to have effect if the parents live together for a continuous period of more than six months (s 11(6)).

New provisions governing the enforcement and facilitation of a child arrangements order regulating the child's contact arrangements were brought into force on 8 December 2008 (see 11.5).

10.6 Prohibited steps orders

A prohibited steps order is an order 'that no step which could be taken by a parent in meeting his parental responsibility for a child, and which is of a kind specified in the order, shall be taken by any person without the consent of the court' (s 8(1)).

A prohibited steps order is a flexible injunctive type of order which can be used in a wide range of circumstances, such as, for example, to prohibit: a parent taking a child out of the UK; or making a unilateral decision about the child's medical treatment or education; or changing the child's surname.

In addition to the general provisions and restrictions which apply to section 8 orders under the Children Act 1989 (CA 1989) (see 10.4 above), a prohibited steps order cannot be made to achieve the same result which could be achieved by making a child arrangements order, and cannot be made in any way which is denied to the High Court (by section 100(2)) in the exercise of its inherent jurisdiction with respect to children (s 9(5)).

As a prohibited steps order is an order prohibiting 'a step which could be taken by a parent in meeting his parental responsibility' for a child, it cannot be used to restrict anything other than some aspect of parental responsibility. For example, it cannot be used to restrict publicity about a child, since this is not within the scope of parental responsibility (this must be dealt with by the High Court under its inherent jurisdiction); nor to prohibit a parent from occupying the family home (see, for example, *Re D (Prohibited Steps Order)* [1996] 2 FLR 273).

10.7 Specific issue orders

A specific issue order is an order 'giving directions for the purpose of determining a specific question which has arisen, or which may arise, in connection with any aspect of parental responsibility for a child' (s 8(1)).

A specific issue order can be made to settle any dispute which has arisen, or which may arise, in respect of the exercise of parental responsibility. It is a flexible order which can be used in a wide range of different situations such as, for example: to settle a dispute arising in respect of a child's education or medical treatment; or to settle a decision to move a child abroad; or to change a child's surname. In addition to the general provisions and restrictions which apply to section 8 orders under the Children Act 1989 (CA 1989) (see 10.4 above), a specific issue order cannot be made to achieve the same result which could be achieved by making a child arrangements order, and cannot be made in any way denied to the High Court (by section 100(2)) in the exercise of its inherent jurisdiction with respect to children (s 9(5)).

With respect to local authorities, a specific issue order cannot be made in relation to a child in care (s 9(1)). A local authority will instead have to seek leave to invoke the court's inherent jurisdiction to decide the matter (ss 100(2)–(5)). A specific issue order cannot be made to deem a child to be in need for the purposes of Part III of the CA 1989 (see 14.6), as this is not an 'aspect of parental responsibility' for the purposes of the order – the appropriate remedy is judicial review (see *Re J (Specific Issue Order: Leave to Apply)* [1995] 1 FLR 669).

10.8 Power of the court to make section 8 orders of its own motion

In any family proceedings in which a question arises with respect to the welfare of any child, the court may make a section 8 order under the Children Act 1989 (CA 1989) with respect to the child if: a person is entitled to apply for a section 8 order with respect to the child; a person has been given leave of the court to make the application; or the court considers that the order should be made even though no such application has been made (s 10(1)).

'Family proceedings' are defined in sections 8(3) and (4) as any proceedings under:

- the inherent jurisdiction of the High Court in relation to children;
- Parts I, II and IV of the CA 1989;
- the Matrimonial Causes Act 1973;
- Schedule 5 to the Civil Partnership Act 2004;
- the Domestic Violence and Matrimonial Proceedings Act 1976;
- the Adoption and Children Act 2002;
- the Domestic Proceedings and Magistrates' Courts Act 1978;
- Schedule 6 to the Civil Partnership Act 2004;
- sections 1 and 9 of the Matrimonial Homes Act 1983;
- Part III of the Matrimonial and Family Proceedings Act 1984;
- the Family Law Act 1996; and
- sections 11 and 12 of the Crime and Disorder Act 1998.

Thus, section 8 orders can be made in a wide range of proceedings involving children, for example in divorce and dissolution proceedings, adoption proceedings, and proceedings for non-molestation orders and occupation orders in domestic violence cases.

10.9 Applicants for section 8 orders

In addition to having the power to make a section 8 order under the Children Act 1989 (CA 1989) of its own motion in any family proceedings (see above), the court may make an order with respect to a child on the application of a person who is entitled to apply or a person who has been granted leave by the court to do so (s 10(2)).

(a) Applicants not needing leave of the court

(i) Any section 8 order

The following people can apply for any section 8 order without needing leave of the court: a parent, guardian or special guardian of the child (s 10(4)(a)); a step-parent who has parental responsibility for the child under section 4A (s 10(4)(aa)); and any person who is named in a child arrangements order that is in force with respect to the child as a person with whom the child is to live (s 10(4)(b)).

(ii) Child arrangements order

The following people are entitled to apply for a child arrangements order without needing leave of the court: a married person or civil partner (whether or not the marriage or civil partnership is subsisting) in relation to whom the child is a child of the family (ss 10(5)(a), (aa)); any person with whom the child has lived for at least three years, which period need not be continuous but must not have begun more than five years before or have ended more than three months before applying for the order (ss 10(5)(b)); where a child arrangements order regulating the child's living arrangements is in force with respect to the child, any person who has the consent of each of the persons named in the order as a person with whom the child is to live (s 10(5)(c)(i)); any person who has the consent of the local authority when a child is in care (s 10(5)(c)(ii)); any other person who has the consent of each person (if any) who has parental responsibility for the child (s 10(5)(c)(iii)); and any person who has parental responsibility for the child who is not the parent or guardian of the child concerned but is named in a child arrangements order as a person with whom the child is to spend time or otherwise have contact, but the person is not named in the order as a person with whom the child is to live (s 10(5)(d)).

An application for a child arrangements order regulating the child's living arrangements can be made in respect of a child who is the subject of a special guardianship order, but only with leave of the court (ss 10(7A), (7B)).

(iii) A child arrangements order regulating the child's living arrangements (local authority foster-parents and relatives)

A local authority foster-parent is entitled to apply without leave of the court for such an order with respect to the child if the child has lived with them for a period of at least one year immediately preceding the application (ss 10(5A), (5C)). The same rule applies to a relative of the child (ss 10(5B), (5C)).

(b) Applicants needing leave of the court

Certain people need leave of the court to apply for a section 8 order under the CA 1989.

(i) Children

A child needs leave of the court to apply, which the court may grant only if it is satisfied that the child has sufficient understanding to make the proposed application (s 10(8)). The court can take into account the likelihood of the proposed application succeeding, and, on that basis, refuse leave even if the child has sufficiency of understanding (see Johnson J in *Re H (Residence Order: Child's Application for Leave)* [2000] 1 FLR 780). Applications for leave are heard in the High Court. There has been conflicting judicial opinion as to whether the child's welfare is paramount in leave applications; but in *Re C (Residence) (Child's Application for Leave)* [1995] 1 FLR 927, Stuart-White J considered these divergent views and concluded that the child's welfare is an important, but not a paramount, consideration. This approach was subsequently adopted by Johnson J in *Re H (Residence Order: Child's Application for Leave)* (see above).

(ii) Other people

In leave applications by people other than children the court must have particular regard to: the nature of the proposed application; the applicant's connection with the child; any risk of the proposed application disrupting the child's life to such an extent that he would be harmed by it; and (where the child is being looked after by a local authority) the local authority's plans for the child's future and the wishes and feelings of the child's parents (s 10(9)).

The welfare principle does not apply (*Re A and W (Minors) (Residence Order: Leave to Apply)* [1992] Fam 182). The application will be refused if it is frivolous or vexatious, or otherwise an abuse of the court. The case must disclose a real prospect of success, and there must be a serious issue to be tried and a good arguable case (*per* Wall J in *Re M (Minors) (Contact: Leave to Apply)* [1995] 2 FLR 98). However, although the prospects of success are relevant to an application for leave to apply, they are not necessarily decisive (*per* Black LJ in *Re B (Paternal Grandmother: Joinder as Party)* [2012] EWCA Civ 737). Leave was granted, for example, in *Re J (Leave to Issue Application for Residence Order)* [2003] 1 FLR 114 (to allow a grandmother to apply for a residence order); and in *Re H (Leave to Apply for Residence Order)* [2008] EWCA Civ 503 (to allow a married couple to apply for a residence order after they had been adjudged to be too old to apply for an adoption order in respect of a child whose half-sibling they were already legally bringing up).

Applications by donor fathers The reforms passed by the Human Fertilisation and Embryology Act 2008 (see Chapter 1) and the policy underpinning those reforms – namely, to put female same sex couples and their children in exactly the same legal position as other types of parent and children – are material considerations for the court in determining an application for leave by a 'donor' father alongside all other relevant considerations, including the factors identified in section 10(9) of the CA 1989. In some cases, the reforms, and the policy underpinning those reforms, will be decisive. Each case is, however, fact specific (*per* Baker J in *Re G; Re Z (Children: Sperm Donors: Leave to Apply for Children Act Orders)* [2013] EWHC 134 (Fam)).

Applications by grandparents There has been discussion from time to time about whether grandparents should be able to apply for a section 8 order without leave of the court. However, the Family Justice Review (see 1.2) in its *Final Report* in 2011 recommended that the leave requirement should remain in order to prevent 'hopeless or vexatious applications that are not in the interests of the child' (see para 110 of the Executive Summary). The Government agreed with this recommendation (see its *Response*, 2012) but stated that it was committed to ensuring that children have meaningful relationships with family members who are important to them following family separation, where it is in their best interests and safe. The Government said that, as a matter of good practice, supporting a child's ongoing relationships with their grandparents and wider family members should be considered when making arrangements for a child's future.

10.10 Other orders under the Children Act 1989

A range of orders other than section 8 orders can be made by the courts under the Children Act 1989 (CA 1989).

(a) Part I orders

(i) Parental responsibility orders (section 4)

The court can make an order giving the following people parental responsibility: an unmarried father (s 4); the second female parent where the mother has had a child by assisted reproduction (s 4ZA); and a step-parent (s 4A).

(ii) Order appointing a guardian of a child (section 5)

The court can appoint a person to be a guardian of a child (see 9.8).

(iii) Order for a welfare report (section 7)

When considering any question with respect to a child under the CA 1989, the court may request a report from a Cafcass officer (see 1.7) or from a local authority officer (or such other person as the authority considers appropriate) on such matters relating to the child as are required to be dealt with in the report (s 7(1)).

(b) Part II orders (orders with respect to children in family proceedings)

The following orders can be made in family proceedings under Part II of the CA 1989.

(i) Section 8 orders

See 10.4 to 10.7 above.

(ii) Activity directions and conditions etc. (sections 11A–11P)

The family courts have various powers to facilitate and enforce a child arrangements order (see 11.5).

(iii) Special guardianship orders (sections 14A–14G)

A special guardianship order is an order giving a person parental responsibility for a child which, for the duration of the order, can be exercised to the exclusion of the parental responsibility of any other person (apart from another special guardian). Special guardianship orders are sometimes used as an alternative to adoption (see 15.14).

(iv) Orders for financial relief (section 15 and Schedule 1)

The Family Courts have jurisdiction to make finance and property orders for children under Schedule 1 (see 12.3).

(v) Family assistance orders (section 16)

Under section 16 the court in family proceedings can make a family assistance order, which is an order requiring a Cafcass officer or a Welsh family proceedings officer or an officer of the local authority to assist, advise and befriend any person named in the order (s 16(1)). A family assistance order is a short-term alternative to a section 8 order, although it may also be used when a section 8 order has already been made but where additional support is required.

The following people can be named in a family assistance order: any parent, guardian or special guardian of the child; any person with whom the child is living or who is named in a child arrangements order as a person with whom the child is to live, spend time or otherwise have contact; and the child (s 16(2)). A family assistance order cannot be made without the consent of all the people who are to be named in the order (other than the child) (s 16(3)). It may direct the people named in the order to take such steps as may be so specified with a view to enabling the officer concerned to be kept informed of the address of any person named in the order and to be allowed to visit any such person (s 16(4)). The order can be made to last for up to 12 months (s 16(5)). An order cannot be made against a local authority officer unless the local authority agrees and the child concerned lives (or will live) in its area (s 16(7)).

If the court makes a family assistance order which is to be in force at the same time as a section 8 order (see above) with respect to a child, the order may direct the officer concerned to report to the court on such matters relating to the section 8 order as the court may require (including whether the section 8 order should be varied or discharged) (s 16(6)).

Section 16 has been amended to make family assistance orders useful for the purpose of facilitating contact provisions contained in a child arrangements order (see 11.5). Thus, if the court makes a family assistance order with respect to a child which is to be in force at the same time as a contact provision contained in a child arrangements order, the order may direct the officer concerned to give advice and assistance as regards establishing, improving and maintaining contact to such of the people named in the order as may be specified (s 16(4A)).

The *Practice Direction 12M – Family Assistance Orders: Consultation* provides that, before making a family assistance order, the court must obtain the opinion of a Cafcass officer or Welsh family proceedings officer as to whether it is in the best interests of the child for an order to be made; and, if so, how the order should operate and for what period. The *Practice Direction* also provides that, before making a family assistance order, the court must give any person whom it proposes to name in the order the opportunity to comment upon any opinion given by that officer.

(c) Part IV orders (care and supervision)

(i) Care and supervision orders (section 31)

Where a child is suffering, or is likely to suffer, significant harm, the court can, if certain threshold criteria are satisfied and the child's welfare requires it, make a care order placing the child in the care of a local authority or a supervision order placing the child under the supervision of a local authority officer or probation officer (see 14.7).

(ii) Order for contact with a child in care (section 34)

Where a child is in local authority care the authority must allow parents and certain other people reasonable contact with the child, and the court can make orders in respect of such contact, including the termination of contact (see 14.8).

(iii) Education supervision order (section 36)

Where a child of compulsory school age is not being properly educated, the court can, on the application of a local education authority, make an education supervision order in favour of that authority (see, for example, *Essex County Council v B* [1993] 1 FLR 866). These orders are rarely made.

(iv) Order that a local authority investigate the child's circumstances (section 37)

Where in any family proceedings a question arises in respect of the child's welfare and it may be appropriate for a care or supervision order to be made, the court may direct that a local authority undertake an investigation into the child's circumstances (s 37(1)). The Court of Appeal has held that it is for the courts, not local authorities, to determine whether the requirements for making a section 37 order are satisfied and whether directions should be made under section 37 (see *Lambeth LBC v TK and KK* [2008] 1 FLR 1229).

(d)   Part V orders (protection of children)

(i) Child assessment order (section 43)

Where there is reasonable cause to suspect that a child is suffering, or is likely to suffer, significant harm, and an assessment of the child's health and development or of the way in which the child is being treated is needed, the court can make a child assessment order (see 14.9).

(ii) Emergency protection order (section 44)

Where there is reasonable cause to believe that a child is likely to suffer significant harm, the court can in certain circumstances make an emergency protection order, which authorises the removal from, or retention of the child in, certain accommodation (see 14.9).

(e)   A section 91(14) order restricting an application to the court

Section 91(14) of the CA 1989 provides that, when disposing of any application under that Act, the court (whether or not it decides to make an order) can order that no application for an order under the Act of any specified kind may be made with respect to the child by any person named in the order without the court's permission. The aim of a section 91(14) order is to prevent unnecessary and disruptive court applications which may be detrimental to the child's best interests. It gives the court power to prevent a party from making repeated and unreasonable applications to the court. However, an order does not impose an absolute bar on applying to the court, as it can be lifted by the court where the applicant can show a need for renewed judicial investigation into the matter. Because of the human rights and natural justice implications of prohibiting access to the courts, there are strict controls on the exercise of the court's power to make a section 91(14) order (see below).

(i) The approach of the courts

The courts are very aware of the severity of making a section 91(14) order, and will do so only if there is a clear evidential basis for making it. The leading case is *Re P (Section 91(14) Guidelines) (Residence and Religious Heritage)* [1999] 2 FLR 573, where Butler-Sloss LJ in the Court of Appeal laid down the following guidelines governing the exercise of the court's discretion to make a section 91(14) order:

1. Section 91(14) should be read in conjunction with s.1(1) which makes the welfare of the child the paramount consideration.
2. The power to restrict applications to the court is discretionary and in the exercise of its discretion the court must weigh in the balance all the relevant circumstances.
3. An important consideration is that to impose a restriction is a statutory intrusion into the right of a party to bring proceedings before the court and to be heard in matters affecting his/her child.
4. The power is therefore to be used with great care and sparingly, the exception and not the rule.
5. It is generally to be seen as a useful weapon of last resort in cases of repeated and unreasonable applications.
6. In suitable circumstances (and on clear evidence), a court may impose the leave restriction in cases where the welfare of the child requires it, although there is no past history of making unreasonable applications.
7. In cases under para (6) above, the court will need to be satisfied, first, that the facts go beyond the commonly encountered need for time to settle to a regime ordered by the court and the all too common situation where there is animosity between the adults in dispute or between the local authority and the family; and, second, that there is a serious risk that, without the imposition of the restriction, the child or the primary carers will be subject to unacceptable strain.
8. A court may impose the restriction on making applications in the absence of a request from any of the parties, subject, of course, to the rules of natural justice such as an opportunity for the parties to be heard on the point.
9. A restriction may be imposed with or without limitation of time.
10. The degree of restriction should be proportionate to the harm it is intended to avoid. Therefore the court imposing the restriction should carefully consider the extent of the restriction to be imposed and specify, where appropriate, the type of application to be restrained and the duration of the order.
11. It would be undesirable in other than the most exceptional cases to make the order *ex parte*.

There are many reported cases where an appeal against the making of a section 91(14) order has been allowed by the Court of Appeal on the ground that the lower court had failed to apply the above guidelines appropriately (see, for example, *Re A (Contact: Section 91(14))* [2009] EWCA Civ 1548; and *Re G (A Child)* [2010] EWCA Civ 470).

A section 91(14) order can be made against *both* parties to the litigation (see, for example, *Re N (Section 91(14))* [2009] EWHC 3055 (Fam), where the litigation between the parents concerning the eight-year-old child had been continuous since he was two years old).

Human rights As a result of their obligations under the Human Rights Act 1998 (see 1.8) the courts must ensure that making a section 91(14) order does not infringe a person's rights under the European Convention on Human Rights (ECHR), in particular Article 6 (the right to a fair trial) and Article 8 (the right to family life). In *Re P (Section 91(14) Guidelines) (Residence and Religious Heritage)* (see above), although the Court of Appeal held that making a section 91(14) order did not breach Article 6 (as it was only a partial restriction on disallowing a claim before the court), it ruled that, because of the severity of making an order, the court should specify what type of court applications are restricted and for how long.

Summary

- The Children Act 1989 (CA 1989) contains a lot of the private and public law relating to children. It consolidated much of the law relating to children and introduced new policies and principles. Influences on the Act included *The Report of the Inquiry into Child Abuse in Cleveland 1987* (Cm 412, 1988) and the *Gillick* case. There have been many amendments to the Act.

- The following Parts of the CA 1989 are particularly important: Part I (Introductory); Part II (Orders with Respect to Children in Family Proceedings); Part III (Local Authority Support for Children and Families); Part IV (Care and Supervision); and Part V (Protection of Children). Part XII (Miscellaneous and General) is also important as it includes provisions on: the effect and duration of orders (s 91); privacy for children in certain proceedings (s 97); restrictions on the use of the inherent jurisdiction (s 100); and the interpretation of the Act (s 105). The following schedules are also important: Schedule 1 (Financial Provision for Children); Schedule 2 (Local Authority Support for Children and Families); and Schedule 3 (Supervision Orders).

- Section 1 of the Act lays down the following principles: the welfare principle (s 1(1)); the presumption of parental involvement (s 1(2A)); the welfare checklist (s 1(3)); the no delay principle (s 1(2)); and the no order principle (s 1(5)). The welfare checklist must be applied in contested section 8 order proceedings, special guardianship proceedings and in care and supervision proceedings (s 1(4)).

- The court can make the following section 8 orders: a child arrangements order; a prohibited steps order; and a specific issue order. The welfare principles (see above) apply when the court is considering whether or not to make, vary or discharge any of these orders. An order can be made on application or by the court of its own motion in any family proceedings. Some people have an automatic right to apply, but other people, including the child, need leave of the court (s 10).

- Section 11 of the Children and Families Act 2014 (CFA 2014) inserted a new provision into section 8 of the CA 1989, replacing the old 'residence order' and 'contact order' with a new child arrangements order. A child arrangements order can regulate a child's living and contact arrangements.

Summary cont'd

▶ A court can make a child arrangements order regulating the child's living arrangements. If such an order is made, there are restrictions on changing the child's surname or taking the child out of the UK (s 13(1), (2)). The court can also impose conditions on such an order (s 11(7)). Special rules apply to such an order and local authorities (ss 9(1) and (2)).

▶ A court can make a child arrangements order regulating the child's contact arrangements. The same provisions which apply to other section 8 orders apply, such as the welfare principles and the rules on applicants. Provisions governing the enforcement and facilitation of contact provisions contained in a child arrangements order are found in sections 11A–11P. Such an order cannot be made in respect of a child in local authority care (ss 9(1) and 9(2)).

▶ A prohibited steps order is an order 'that no step which could be taken by a parent in meeting his parental responsibility for a child, and which is of a kind specified in the order, shall be taken by any person without the consent of the court' (s 8(1)). The same rules which apply to other section 8 orders apply.

▶ A specific issue order is an order 'giving directions for the purpose of determining a specific question which has arisen, or which may arise, in connection with any aspect of parental responsibility for a child' (s 8(1)). The same rules which apply to other section 8 orders apply.

▶ The court in family proceedings can make a section 8 order on an application or on its own motion in any family proceedings (s 10(1) and (2)). 'Family proceedings' are defined in sections 8(3) and (4).

▶ There are two sorts of applicant for a section 8 order: people who can apply as of right (parents and guardians with or without parental responsibility); and other people who need leave of the court to apply (s 10). Children can apply with leave of the court (s 10(8)). There has been discussion about giving grandparents the right to apply without leave, but the Family Justice Review and the Government have rejected this.

▶ Under Part I of the Act, the court can make: a parental responsibility order (s 4); an order appointing a guardian of a child (s 5); and an order for a welfare report (s 7). Under Part II, in addition to section 8 orders, the court can make: a special guardianship order (ss 14A–G); orders for financial relief (s 15 and Schedule 1); and a family assistance order (s 16); and Cafcass officers and Welsh family proceedings officers have a duty to conduct risk assessments of children (s 16A). Under Part IV, the court can make a range of public law orders, including, in particular, care and supervision orders (see Chapter 14). Under Part V the court can make a child assessment order (s 43) and an emergency protection order (s 44) (see Chapter 14). Under section 91(14), the court can make an order restricting an application under the CA 1989, subject to strict requirements being satisfied.

Further reading and references

Fortin, 'Children's rights – substance or spin?' [2006] Fam Law 757.
Freeman, 'The next Children's Act' [1998] Fam Law 341.
Mitchell, *Children Act Private Law Proceedings: A Handbook* (3rd ed.), 2012, Jordans.

Websites

Legislation: www.legislation.gov.uk

Links to relevant websites can also be found at: www.palgravehighered.com/law/familylaw9e

11.1 Introduction

This chapter deals with the law governing arrangements for children when parental relationships break down. The law is laid down in the Children Act 1989 (see Chapter 10). After divorce, civil partnership dissolution or parental separation, parents continue to have parental responsibility for their children (see Chapter 9); and they also have a duty to make financial provision (see Chapter 12). Despite the legal provisions and the number of reported cases, most separating couples make their own arrangements for the care of their children without resorting to court proceedings. It is generally recognised that it is better for both parents and children if parents resolve matters themselves, rather than bringing court proceedings.

The Children and Families Act 2014 replaced contact and residence orders (including shared residence orders) with child arrangements orders. In this chapter, we continue to use the terms 'contact order', 'residence order' and 'shared residence order' when discussing those cases which pre-date the Act.

(a) The Children and Families Act 2014

The Children and Families Act 2014 (CFA 2014) was enacted to implement recommendations made by the Family Justice Review in its *Final Report*, published in November 2011 (see 1.2). In its report, the Family Justice Review identified various ways in which the processes relating to private family law on parental separation fell short.

> ▶ *Family Justice Review: Final Report* **(November 2011, Ministry of Justice), paras 105 and 106 of the Executive Summary**
>
> **105.** Our current processes fall short in many ways.
>
> - ▶ Many parents do not know where to get the information and support they need to resolve their issues without recourse to court.
> - ▶ There is limited awareness of alternatives to court, and a good deal of misunderstanding.
> - ▶ Too many cases end up in court, and court determination is a blunt instrument.
> - ▶ The court system is hard to navigate, a problem that is likely to become even more important as proposed reductions in legal aid mean more people represent themselves.
> - ▶ There is a feeling (which may or may not be right) that lawyers generally take an adversarial approach that inflames rather than reduces conflict.
> - ▶ Cases are expensive and take a long time.
>
> **106.** There are more fundamental issues that go beyond process.
>
> - ▶ Children say they do not understand what is going on and do not have enough opportunity to have their say.

- There is a lack of understanding about parental responsibility, both legally and more generally: some mistakenly think the balance of parental responsibility shifts following separation, with one parent assuming full responsibility for their child.
- This goes with the difficulty for all involved in assuring that children retain a relationship with both parents, and others, including grandparents, after separation where this is safe. Some have a perception that the system favours mothers over fathers.

The Family Justice Review made a wide range of recommendations to address the above issues in order to 'set out a clear process for separation that emphasises shared parental responsibility, provides information, manages expectations and helps people to understand the costs they face at each stage'; and with the emphasis throughout on 'enabling people to resolve their disputes safely outside court wherever possible' (para 107, Executive Summary). With respect to the law relating to children and parents on family breakdown, the Family Justice Review's recommendations included, among other things: the introduction of 'parenting agreements' in which parents would set out arrangements for their children post separation; a new 'child arrangements order' to replace residence and contact orders; a greater role for mediation; more opportunities for children to have their voice heard; and better measures for the enforcement of orders. However, the Family Justice Review argued against the introduction of a legislative presumption of shared parenting (see (h) below).

The Government accepted the Family Justice Review's recommendations, except for its recommendation that there should be no legislative presumption of shared parenting (see Part F 'Changes to private law', *The Government Response to the Family Justice Review: A system with children and families at its heart*, February 2012, Cm 8273, Ministry of Justice and Department for Education). It subsequently enacted the CFA 2014 which introduced reforms including the replacement of contact and residence orders with a single child arrangements order and the introduction of a statutory presumption in favour of parental involvement (see 10.3).

(b)   The impact of family breakdown on children

Children may suffer emotionally when their parents' relationship breaks up. They may suffer fear, anger, withdrawal, grief, depression and guilt. Research on children of divorced parents (by the Centre of Longitudinal Studies, based on the National Child Development Study, July 2008) found that divorce is not a single event in a child's life but a process which could begin years before the parents separated and which could have repercussions that reverberate through childhood and into adulthood. According to the report, children from separated families tend to do less well at school and in their subsequent careers. They are more likely to experience the break-up of their own partnerships; and more likely to have higher levels of alcohol consumption and problem-drinking in adulthood. They are also likely to have poorer levels of general health; and a small minority of young adults develop serious mental health problems associated with parental divorce. (The report is available at: www.cls.ioe.ac.uk.)

(c)   Reaching agreement and keeping cases out of the court

Because of the emotional impact that divorce and parental separation can have on parents and their children, it is better if parents make amicable arrangements for their children on family breakdown. Most parents make their own arrangements, but some fail to reach agreement and may have to apply to the court for child arrangements order. Going to court, however, can be costly, time-consuming, unpredictable and traumatic; and the judge may decide to refuse to make the order sought or make a different order. Also, having a court order does not necessarily guarantee that the other parent will comply with it.

Lawyers who deal with disputes about arrangements for children on family breakdown are meant to adopt a conciliatory, not a litigious, approach, because of the benefits of reducing hostility and bitterness where children are involved. Mediation and other forms of non-court dispute resolution are increasingly being promoted as a much better way of resolving parental disputes than going to court (see 1.5). In an effort to increase the use of non-court dispute resolution, section 10 of the CFA 2014 introduced a requirement for compulsory attendance at a mediation assessment and information meeting before parties can make an application to court in certain family proceedings. The applications to which this requirement applies are set out in Part 3 of the Family Procedure Rules 2010 (FPR 2010) and *Practice Direction* 3A and include applications for child arrangements orders, specific issue orders and prohibited steps orders. There are, however, some exceptions which are also set out in the FPR 2010.

The following words of Baroness Hale in a case on shared residence orders and housing (see 4.11) acknowledge the importance of agreement where children are concerned.

> ▶ **Baroness Hale of Richmond in *Holmes-Moorhouse v London Borough of Richmond-upon-Thames* [2009] UKHL 7**
>
> The reality is that every effort is made, both before and during any family proceedings, to encourage the parents to agree between themselves what will be best for their children. There are many good reasons for this. The parents know their own children better than anyone. They also know their own circumstances, what will suit them best, what resources are available and what they can afford. Agreed solutions tend to work much better and last much longer than solutions imposed by a court after contested proceedings. The contest is likely to entrench opposing viewpoints and inflame parental conflict. Conflict is well known to be bad for children. Not only that, the arrangements made when the couple separate are bound to have to change over time, as the children grow up and their own and their parents' circumstances change. Parents who have been able or helped, through mediation or in other ways, to agree a solution at the outset are more likely to be able to negotiate those changes for themselves, rather than to have to return to court for further orders.

Despite the fact that it is better if disputes about children on family breakdown are kept out of court, many thousands of children continue to be the subject of parental disputes on family breakdown. Thus, according to *Family Court Statistics Quarterly* (Ministry of Justice, 2016) the number of private law cases started in the period October to December 2015 was 11,180, up 8 per cent from the equivalent quarter in 2014.

(d)   Cafcass and children on family breakdown

Cafcass performs important functions with respect to children on family breakdown (see 1.7). One of its main functions is to provide officers for the court in children's cases. Of particular importance is the Children and Family Reporter who has a duty to provide a welfare report if requested by the court (see below). Cafcass officers also perform an important conciliatory role in endeavouring to help parents reach agreement about arrangements for their children. They also have to conduct risk assessments; and they have various obligations in respect of facilitating contact (see 11.5 below). A Children's Guardian, an officer of Cafcass, may be appointed by the court (under r 16.3 of the FPR 2010) to represent the interests of a child who has been made a party to family proceedings.

(e)   Welfare reports

The court has the power to order a welfare report under section 7 of the Children Act 1989 (CA 1989) by a Cafcass officer (see above). A welfare report is important as it provides an independent assessment of the case. The recommendations in the report are particularly important where a case is finely balanced; and judges must not depart from those recommendations without giving reasons. Failure to give reasons may provide grounds for an appeal (as it did in *Re M (Residence)* [2004] EWCA Civ 1574 where the Court of Appeal ordered a retrial). If the court decides to reject a clear conclusion and recommendation made in the report, it must allow the Cafcass officer to give oral evidence (see *Re R (Residence Order)* [2009] EWCA Civ 445 where the Court of Appeal held, by a majority, that the judge had erred in law in not hearing the Cafcass officer). However, where there is no clear recommendation in a report, it is not necessary for the court to adjourn proceedings to hear the officer (*Re C (Section 8 Order: Court Welfare Officer)* [1995] 1 FLR 617).

(f)   The voice of the child

Children do not have automatic party status in proceedings for a child arrangements order. However, children have been increasingly given rights of separate representation (see 8.6).

(g)   Family disputes involving matters of parental responsibility in the EU

Jurisdiction with regard to disputes between parents living in different Member States of the EU is governed by Council Regulation (EC) (No. 2201/2003) Concerning Jurisdiction and the Recognition and Enforcement of Judgments in Matrimonial Matters and in Matters of Parental Responsibility (Brussels II Revised). Article 8(1) provides that: 'The courts of a Member State shall have jurisdiction in matters of parental responsibility over a child who is habitually resident in that Member State at the time the court is seised.' The aim of Article 8(1) is to ensure that, in relation to matters of parental responsibility (including disputes regarding a child's living and contact arrangements), jurisdiction rests with the courts of the child's habitual residence; although Article 12 provides a limited opportunity for parents to elect for the jurisdiction of the court seised with the divorce proceedings if that is, *inter alia*, in the best interests of the child (see, for example, *Bush v Bush* [2008] EWCA Civ 865).

In *Re I (A Child)* [2009] UKSC 10, the Supreme Court unanimously held that Article 12 of Brussels II (Revised) can apply where a child is habitually resident outside the EU, as nothing in Article 12 limits jurisdiction to children resident in the EU. In this case the English mother wished to enforce contact with her son who was living with his paternal grandmother and aunt in Pakistan (after his father had removed him there in breach of an undertaking to return him to the UK). On the facts of the case, it was held to be in the best interests of the child for the case to be heard in the UK.

(h)   Shared parenting

There has been discussion about the possibility of introducing a statutory presumption of shared parenting. However, there has been considerable resistance in some quarters. For example, Maclean has stated (at [2011] Fam Law 669) that 'to legislate for all, rather than putting the welfare of each child in each situation first, seems at best foolhardy and at worst downright dangerous'. The Family Justice Review (see above), as part of its consideration of parental responsibility, looked at the possibility of legislative reform to introduce shared parenting. However, in the light of reforms which had taken place in Sweden and Australia, the Family Justice Review warned against introducing legislation which created a perception and expectation that there was an assumed parental right to substantially shared or equal time for both parents. In its final report (*Family Justice Review: Final Report*, Ministry of Justice, November 2011) it concluded that 'no legislation should be introduced that creates or risks creating the perception that there is a parental right to substantially shared or equal time for both parents' (para 5.76). In the Foreword to the *Final Report*, David Norgrove, Chair of the Family Justice Review, stated that the Panel believed strongly that most children benefit from a relationship with both parents post separation, but that the best way to achieve this was 'through parental education and information combined with clear, quick processes for resolution where there are disputes'. (For commentators who supported the Family Justice Review's recommendation against shared parenting, see Fehlberg [2012] Fam Law 709 and Nickols [2012] Fam Law 573.)

Alleged difficulties relating to Australian reforms introducing shared parenting was one reason why the Family Justice Review rejected the idea of introducing a shared parenting presumption in England and Wales. But Bryant CJ, an Australian judge (see [2012] *International Family Law* 269), while recognising that Australia had made some mistakes, was of the view that it might be wrong to exclude the possibility of reforms in England and Wales just because of the Australian experience. Parkinson (see [2012] Fam Law 758) claimed that none of the arguments made by the Family Justice Review about the Australian experience could be supported by the available evidence. (See also Rhoades [2012] CFLQ 158.)

The UK Government did not accept the Family Justice Review's arguments against shared parenting (see *The Government Response to the Family Justice Review: A System with Children and Families at Its Heart* Cm 8273, Ministry of Justice and Department for Education, February 2012). However, the Government said that it was mindful of the lessons which must be learnt from the Australian experience and that it would therefore consider very carefully how legislation could be framed to avoid the pitfalls of the Australian experience. Between June and September 2012, the Government conducted a consultation on shared parenting to consider four options for amending section 1 of the CA 1989 in order to enshrine shared parenting in the law (see *Cooperative Parenting Following Family Separation: Proposed Legislation on the Involvement of Both Parents in a Child's Life*, Department for Education, 13 June 2012). The Government's preferred option was the introduction of a legislative provision which 'requires the court to work on the presumption that a child's welfare is likely to be furthered through safe involvement with both parents – unless the evidence shows this not to be safe or in the child's best interests'. This led to the insertion into the CA 1989 of a new section 1(2A) which contains a presumption that, unless the contrary is shown, the involvement of both parents in the life of the child concerned will further the child's welfare (see 10.3). Section 1(2B) explains that '"involvement" means 'involvement of some kind, either direct or indirect, but not any particular division of a child's time'. Therefore, the statutory presumption does not mean a presumption in favour of a 50:50 shared care arrangement.

11.2 Human rights and family breakdown

The Human Rights Act 1998 (HRA 1998) requires courts to comply with the European Convention on Human Rights (ECHR) and to take into account the decisions of the European Court of Human Rights (ECtHR) (see 1.8). In *Hoppe v Germany (Application No. 28422/95)* [2003] 1 FLR 384 the ECtHR identified the following general principles which courts must take into account when exercising their powers in the context of children on family breakdown:

- ▶ The mutual enjoyment by parent and child of each other's company constitutes a fundamental element of family life, even if the parents' relationship has broken down; and any measures which hinder such enjoyment amount to an interference with Article 8 (the right to family life).
- ▶ The task of the ECtHR is not to substitute itself for the domestic authorities in the exercise of their responsibilities regarding custody and access, but to review, in the light of the ECHR, their decisions in the exercise of their margin of appreciation.
- ▶ In determining whether the interference into family life is necessary in a democratic society for the purposes of Article 8(2) (see 1.8), consideration of what lies in the best interests of the child is of crucial importance. A fair balance must be struck between the child's interests and those of the parent, and, in striking such a balance, particular importance must be attached to the best interests of the child, which, depending on their nature and seriousness, may override those of the parent.
- ▶ In cases concerning a person's relationship with his or her child there is a duty to exercise exceptional diligence in view of the risk that the passage of time may result in a *de facto* determination of the matter.
- ▶ The manner in which Article 6 (the right to a fair and public hearing) applies to proceedings before courts of appeal depends on the special features of the proceedings viewed as a whole.

▶ It is not a breach of Article 6 if proceedings involving children are heard in private.

▶ The court must avoid delay in reaching a final decision.

In *Sahin v Germany; Sommerfeld v Germany(Application Nos. 30943/96 and 31871/96)* [2003] 2 FLR 671 the ECtHR held that, although national authorities enjoy a wide margin of appreciation when deciding on custody matters, stricter scrutiny is called for regarding any further limitations, such as restrictions placed on parental rights of access. As regards hearing a child in court on the issue of access, the ECtHR held that domestic courts are not always required to hear the child. It depends on the facts of each case, having regard to the age and maturity of the child concerned.

11.3 Disputes over a child's living arrangements

An unresolvable dispute about the living arrangements for a child on family breakdown can be decided by making an application for a child arrangements order regulating the child's living arrangements under section 8 of the Children Act 1989 (CA 1989) (see 10.5). Such disputes often go hand in hand with disputes about the contact arrangements for a child on family breakdown, as the non-resident parent may wish to have contact with the child (see 11.5 below). Other parental disputes (for example about education, medical treatment, taking a child out of the UK and changing the child's name) can be decided by making an application for a prohibited steps or specific issue order (see 10.6 and 10.7). Parents who are in dispute regarding financial provision for their children on separation may need to turn to the Government's child maintenance scheme or bring proceedings under Schedule 1 of the CA 1989, the Matrimonial Causes Act 1973 or the Civil Partnership Act 2004 (see Chapter 12).

Child arrangements orders made in England and Wales can be enforced in other parts of the UK under section 25 of the Family Law Act 1986.

(a) Child arrangements orders regulating the child's living arrangements

Before the CA 1989 came into force, unresolvable parental disputes about children on family breakdown were decided by way of custody proceedings. However, in discussions leading up to the CA 1989 the Law Commission was critical of the term 'custody' because it created a parental claim right and therefore had the potential to increase hostility and bitterness between parents, which was detrimental for children. The CA 1989 therefore introduced residence orders to replace custody orders, with the aim of placing the emphasis on a child's living arrangements, not on which of the parents had a greater claim to the child. The idea was to encourage the view that parents have responsibilities for their children, not claims to them, an idea that was partly influenced by Lord Scarman's preference (in the *Gillick* case – see 8.4) for the term 'responsibility' rather than 'rights'.

However, in 2011 the Family Justice Review (see 11.1 above) recommended a further change, namely, the replacement of residence and contact orders with a single 'child arrangements order.' The Government, in response, said that it saw 'value in changing the emphasis of court orders to focus on the practical arrangements for caring for the child, and [to] remove the current emphasis on the labels "contact" and "residence"' (*The Government Response to the Family Justice Review*, Ministry of Justice and Department of Education, February 2012). This recommendation was implemented by the Children and Families Act 2014 (CFA 2014).

The significance of the changes introduced by the CFA 2014 was explained by Ryder J in the following case.

▶ **Mr Justice Ryder in *K (Children)* [2014] EWCA Civ 1195**

The recent legislative changes have removed the labels of residence and contact so as to help emphasise that in a case where there is no distinguishing welfare element such as the risk of harm from a parent, that relationship is meant to be of equivalent importance i.e. it derives from the equivalence of the parental responsibility which each parent holds ....
There is no priority of one parent over another and where a child lives (formerly known as residence) is simply that, albeit that there are often very good reasons for ensuring stability of care supported by a practicable routine. The oft cited security, stability and permanence of care that every child needs are features of the parental relationship that they experience from both parents (where there are two parents who are available to exercise and share their parental responsibilities), not simply a consequence of the place where they live or exclusively from the parent with whom they live.

However, despite the replacement of residence and contact orders with a single child arrangements order, there remain important legal differences between a child arrangements order regulating the child's living arrangements and one which regulates the child's contact arrangements (such as the requirements relating to consent for removal from the jurisdiction – see 11.7 below).

(i) Applicants

The child's parents (married or unmarried, and whether or not the father has parental responsibility) can apply. Other people, including the child, can apply, but only with leave (permission) of the court (see Chapter 10).

(ii) Applicable principles

See 11.3(b) below.

(iii) Other powers

The court can: attach a condition to a child arrangements order regulating the child's living arrangements (s 11(7)); order a welfare report (s 7); and direct that a local authority investigate the child's circumstances (s 37). It can also make a child arrangements order providing for the child to live with more than one person. Such orders used to be known as shared residence orders (see 11.3(c) below).

(iv) Duration

The order can be made to last until the child reaches the age of 18 (s 91(11)).

(b) How the court exercises its powers

When exercising its powers to decide whether or not to make a child arrangements order regulating the child's living arrangements, the court must apply the principles in section 1 of the CA 1989 (see 10.3). Thus, it must apply the welfare principle (s 1(1)), the no delay principle (s 1(2)) and the no order principle (s 1(5)). In contested proceedings it must also apply the section 1(3) 'welfare checklist' and the presumption of parental involvement (s 1(2A).

(i) The welfare checklist (section 1(3))

In addition to considering the paramountcy of the child's welfare (s 1(1)), the court in contested proceedings for a child arrangements order must apply the factors listed in section 1(3) of the CA 1989. The list is not exhaustive – other factors can be taken into account – and the factors are not in any hierarchy of importance. Under section 1(3) the court must take into account the following factors.

Section 1(3)(a) The child's wishes in the light of the child's age and understanding If the child is sufficiently mature and intelligent enough (in other words he or she is '*Gillick* competent' – see 8.4), then the child's wishes may determine the matter, all other things being equal. The child's wishes are ascertained by a Cafcass Children and Family Reporter or a Welsh family proceedings officer, who has a duty to report to the court and to consider the best interests of the child; and who may be cross-examined on the report. The court also has the power to appoint a Children's Guardian to represent the child, and to permit the child to be represented by his or her own solicitor without a Children's Guardian (see 8.6). A failure to give any real effect to a child's wishes may provide grounds for an appeal, as it did, for example, in *Re R (Residence Order)* [2009] EWCA Civ 445 where the Court of Appeal held by a majority that the judge had erred in not giving any real effect to the wishes of the child, aged nine. However, this does not prevent the court from going against the wishes of a child, even in the case of an older child who is expressing a wish to live with a particular parent (see, for example, *S-K (A Child)* [2013] EWCA Civ 1247 where the Court of Appeal refused a father permission to appeal against an order refusing him residence of the children and held that the trial judge had been entitled to go against the views of the older children, aged 11 and 14, who said that they wanted to live with their father rather than with their mother).

Section 1(3)(b) The child's physical and emotional needs The child's physical and emotional needs might include, for example, the emotional and psychological attachment a child has to a particular parent, and also a child's housing needs. In earlier case-law the courts took the view that it was usually better for young children, particularly babies, to be brought up by their mother (an approach which was endorsed by the House of Lords in *Brixey v Lynas* [1996] 2 FLR 499). Over the years, however, as the courts have given increasing recognition to the importance of fathers, they are likely to consider the child's emotional and psychological attachment to *both* parents, not just the mother. In respect of the child's needs, the fact that one parent is wealthier than the other is likely to count for little.

Section 1(3)(c) The likely effect on the child of a change of circumstances This is similar to the 'continuity of care' or 'status quo' factor which was an important consideration in the case-law prior to the CA 1989 when there was no welfare checklist in the relevant legislation. However, in *Re F (Shared Residence Order)* [2009] EWCA Civ 313 the

Court of Appeal held that it was better, since the enactment of the CA 1989, to address the factors in the welfare checklist rather than to rely on any presumption of fact that might arise from status quo arguments. (For cases where the status quo prevailed, see, for example, *Re B (Residence Order: Status Quo)* [1998] 1 FLR 368 (as the father had cared for the eight-year-old child since the age of two); and *Re C (Residence)* [2008] 1 FLR 826 (as the child had spent all his life in his mother's care and had a strong and beneficial bond with her).)

Under section (1)(3)(c) the court may be unwilling to disrupt existing living arrangements if to do so would split up brothers and sisters, disrupt schooling arrangements or result in the child losing contact with relatives and friends.

Section 1(3)(d) The age, sex, background and any of the child's characteristics which the court considers relevant   The child's religious preferences, racial and cultural background, health and disabilities, for example, can be considered under section 1(3)(d).

Section 1(3)(e) Any harm the child has suffered or is at risk of suffering   'Harm' has the same meaning as it has in section 31 of the CA 1989 and includes harm caused by 'hearing or seeing the ill treatment of another'. Thus, witnessing domestic violence can constitute harm.

Religious beliefs   Making an order in favour of a parent with extreme religious beliefs will not necessarily constitute harm. In *Re R (A Minor) (Residence: Religion)* [1993] 2 FLR 163, for example, a residence order was made in favour of the father, as the mother had died, even though he was a member of the Exclusive Brethren, an extreme religious sect in which members are not allowed to mix socially with anyone outside the fellowship (the court also made a supervision order in favour of the local authority to ensure the child's safety). In *M v H (Education: Welfare)* [2008] EWHC 324 (Fam) Charles J held, *inter alia*, that the fact that one parent was a Catholic and the other a Jehovah's Witness was not of itself relevant in the circumstances of the case. However, if the religion is deemed to be harmful, the court will take it into account, as it did in *Re B and G (Minors) (Custody)* [1985] FLR 493 where the court described the views held by members of the Church of Scientology as 'immoral and obnoxious' and denied the father and step-mother the care of the children in preference to the mother and step-father who had left the church.

A refusal to make a child arrangements order providing for a child to live with a particular parent on the basis of their religious beliefs may constitute a breach of the European Convention on Human Rights (ECHR). But each case depends on its own facts. In *Palau-Martinez v France (Application No. 64927/01)* [2004] 2 FLR 810, for example, the European Court of Human Rights (ECtHR) held that an order granting residence to the child's father, not the mother, because of her religious convictions (she was a Jehovah's Witness), breached the mother's right to a private and family life under Article 8 and was discriminatory under Article 14. On the other hand, in *Ismailova v Russia (Application No. 37614/02)* [2008] 1 FLR 533 the ECtHR upheld the decision of the Russian courts to deprive the mother of custody because of the effect of her religion on the children.

Steps the court can take when there is a risk of harm   If the court is concerned about making a child arrangements order because of a risk of harm, it can make an interim order or back up the child arrangements order with another order, such as a specific issue order, a prohibited steps order, a family assistance order or a section 37 direction that the local authority investigate the case (see Chapter 10). Cafcass has a duty under section 16A of the CA 1989 to make risk assessments where it believes that a child might be at risk of significant harm (see 11.4 below).

Section 1(3)(f) How capable each parent is of meeting the child's needs The court might consider, for example, whether a parent can provide accommodation, love, emotional security, intellectual stimulation and care during working hours.

Section 1(3)(g) The range of powers available to the court under the Children Act 1989 As proceedings for a child arrangements order are family proceedings under the CA 1989 (s 8(3)), the court can make other orders on an application or of its own motion. Thus, for example, it can make: any other section 8 order; a family assessment order; an order appointing a guardian; or a section 37 direction that a local authority investigate the child's circumstances (see Chapter 10).

(c) Shared living arrangements

Prior to the changes brought about by the CFA 2014, the CA 1989 specifically provided for what was known then as a 'shared' residence order. This was a residence order 'made in favour of two or more persons who do not themselves all live together', specifying 'the periods during which the child is to live in the different households concerned' under section 11(4). However, this provision was repealed by the CFA 2014. It is no longer necessary because a child arrangements order is flexible enough to accommodate shared living arrangements by providing when a child is to live with each of the different people named in the order. Orders which provide for shared living arrangements do not require, or imply, an equal division of the child's time between the two homes (see *A v A (Shared Residence and Contact)* [2004] EWHC 142 (Fam)).

The issue of whether, and in what circumstances, the court should order shared living arrangements has generated much case-law, an overview of which is provided below. The general trend has been that the courts have become more willing to order shared living arrangements since the CA 1989 was enacted and such orders are no longer unusual. However, it is less common for the courts to order a genuine 50:50 division of the child's time between two homes, partly due to the inherent practical difficulties with such arrangements. In *Re M* [2014] EWCA Civ 1755 McFarlane LJ expressed his view that 'a division of time 50/50 will remain, in my view, a rare order and only to be contemplated where there is some confidence that it will not work to the disadvantage of the child, albeit that the aim is to give good quality and substantial time with each parent'. For an example of where broadly equal time was ordered see *Re N (A Child: Religion: Jehovah's Witness)* [2011] EWHC 3737 (Fam), where it was held that the child's welfare required that the child spend broadly equal time with each parent in order to try to guard against the risk that the different religious perspectives of the parents would predominate.

(i) The development of the law

In cases decided shortly after the CA 1989 came into force, judges were reluctant to make shared residence orders (as they were then known) because they were of the view that they might create uncertainty and insecurity for children (see, for example, *Re H (A Minor) (Shared Residence)* [1994] 1 FLR 717, where the Court of Appeal held that shared residence orders should be made only in exceptional circumstances). Over the years, however, judges became more willing to make them, as demonstrated in *D v D (Shared Residence Order)* [2001] 1 FLR 495 below, which established that there was no need for the circumstances to be exceptional to justify a shared residence order being made.

▶ *D v D (Shared Residence Order)* [2001] 1 FLR 495

A pattern had been established on marriage breakdown whereby the three children spent substantial periods of time with each parent, but where the arrangements were subject to a high degree of animosity between the parents, and frequent legal proceedings had been brought to sort out the details. The father applied for a shared residence order, which was granted at first instance. The mother appealed. The Court of Appeal dismissed her appeal, and held that, contrary to earlier case-law, it was not necessary to show that exceptional circumstances existed before shared residence could be granted; and neither was it probably necessary to show a positive benefit to the child. What must be shown is that the order is in the child's best interests in accordance with the welfare principle in section 1 of the CA 1989. Here, on the facts, it was necessary to make a shared residence order to lessen the animosity between the parties.

In *Re A (Joint Residence: Parental Responsibility)* [2008] EWCA Civ 867, Sir Mark Potter P, who gave the leading judgment, stated:

> It is now recognised by the court that a shared residence order may be regarded as appropriate where it provides legal confirmation of the factual reality of a child's life or where, in a case where one has the primary care of a child, it may be psychologically beneficial to the parents in emphasising the equality of their position and responsibilities.

In *Re AR (A Child: Relocation)* [2010] EWHC 1346, Mostyn J went so far as to say that a shared residence order 'is nowadays the rule rather than the exception, even where the quantum of care undertaken by each parent is decidedly unequal'. However, in *T v T* [2010] EWCA Civ 1366, Black LJ was of the view that Mostyn J's approach in *Re AR* went too far, and that whether or not a shared residence order should be granted depended on a determination of what was in the child's best interests in the light of all the factors in the case.

Concern has been expressed about the trend towards making orders for shared living arrangements for the purpose of encouraging cooperative parenting (see, for example, Bevan [2012] Fam Law 862 who refers to evidence from Sweden given by Newnham [2011] CFLQ 251).

(ii) How the court exercises its powers

When deciding whether or not to make a child arrangements order for shared living arrangements, the court must apply the welfare principles in section 1(1) of the CA 1989 (see 10.3). There is no presumption in favour of shared living arrangements. Although the outcome of each case depends on its own facts, the following propositions can be extracted from the case-law:

▶ It is not necessary to show exceptional or unusual circumstances before an order for shared living arrangements can be granted (*D v D (Shared Residence Order*, above).

▶ There is no requirement that a child should be spending time evenly, or more or less evenly, in the two homes before an order for shared living arrangements can be made (*Re F (Shared Residence Order)* [2003] EWCA Civ 592; endorsed in *Re W (Shared Residence Order)* [2009] EWCA Civ 370).

▶ The court will be alert to discern any malign intent on the part of a parent to use an application for shared living arrangements for the purpose of disrupting or interfering with the other parent's role in the management of the child's life (*Re K (Shared Residence Order)* [2008] EWCA Civ 526).

▶ Although it may be appropriate to make an order for shared living arrangements in a case where there is likely to be a problem facilitating or enforcing contact, the court is unlikely to make such an order where there is little contact between the parties (*A v A (Shared Residence)* [2004] EWHC 142 (Fam)).

▶ An order for shared living arrangements can be made even though there is a substantial geographical distance between the parents (see, for example, *Re F (Shared Residence Order)* [2003] EWCA Civ 592, where one parent lived in England and the other in Scotland and *Re C* [2015] EWCA Civ 1305).

▶ A lack of cooperation and goodwill between the parties is not necessarily a bar to making an order for shared living arrangements (see, for example, *Re R (Residence: Shared Care: Children's Views)* [2005] EWCA Civ 542).

▶ Although the inability of the parents to work in harmony is not by itself a reason for making an order for shared living arrangements, a possible consequence of the parents' inability to work in harmony (namely a deliberate and sustained marginalisation of one parent by the other) may sometimes be so (*Re W (Shared Residence Order)* [2009] EWCA Civ 370).

(iii) Examples from the law reports

There are many cases in the law reports where orders for shared living arrangements have been made.

▶ *A v A (Shared Residence)* **[2004] EWHC 142 (Fam)**

A shared residence order was made (even though the parents were not able to cooperate), as the children had been spending 50 per cent of their time with each parent. Wall J made the order partly to reflect the fact that the parents are equal in the eyes of the law, and have equal duties and responsibilities towards their children.

▶ *Re C (A Child)* **[2006] EWCA Civ 235**

The Court of Appeal described the case as 'a paradigm' case where a shared residence order should be granted. The child had a strong attachment to both parents and was happy and confident in both homes, which were proximate to each other and close to the child's school. The child had a real familiarity with both homes and a sense of belonging in each, and he had a clear perception that he had two homes. There was a post-separation history of the child's care being shared.

(iv) Shared living arrangements or defined contact arrangements?

The court may, depending on the circumstances, decide that it is sufficient to make a child arrangements order defining the child's contact arrangements rather than an order for shared living arrangements. This was considered in *Re K (Shared Residence Order)* [2008] EWCA Civ 526 where the father applied to have increased contact with the child (from 40 per cent to 50 per cent) and also applied for a shared residence order. The Court of Appeal held that the court should decide on the division of time the child is to spend with each parent and then determine whether that time should be effected by a shared residence order or a contact order. The Court of Appeal held that a shared residence order was more appropriate in the circumstances of the case. The court must make either a shared residence order *or* a defined contact order – not both – as the Court of Appeal has held that it is a contradiction in terms to grant a contact order to a person who already has a shared residence order (*Re W (Shared Residence Order)* [2009] EWCA Civ 370).

(v) Making an order for shared living arrangements as a means of acquiring parental responsibility

An order for shared living arrangements can be made for the purpose of conferring parental responsibility on a person who does not possess it and who is not otherwise able to apply for it. Thus, for example, in *Re A (Shared Residence: Parental Responsibility)* [2008] EWCA Civ 867 a shared residence order was made to confer parental responsibility on a man who was not the child's biological father but who had, with the mother, brought the child up on the assumption that he was.

(vi) Orders for shared living arrangements and housing

The House of Lords in *Holmes-Moorhouse v London Borough of Richmond-upon-Thames* [2009] UKHL 7 (see 4.11) held that, when deciding whether to make a shared residence order, the court must take into account any housing needs of the parties and the fact that there is a shortage of local authority housing and that housing authorities have limited resources. The House of Lords held that a family court should not make a shared residence order unless it appeared reasonably likely that both parents would have accommodation in which the child could reside. Baroness Hale said that the family court 'should not use a residence order as a means of putting pressure upon a local housing authority to allocate their resources in a particular way'.

(d) Attaching a direction or condition to a child arrangements order regulating the child's living arrangements and restricting residence

The court can attach a direction or condition to a child arrangements order regulating the child's living arrangements (s 11(7)). Placing a condition on such an order which requires a person to live in a particular place is unusual, as such a restriction is considered to be 'an unwarranted imposition upon the right of a parent to choose where he/she will live within the UK' (per Baroness Hale in *Re G (Children)* [2006] UKHL 43). But each case depends on its own facts; and in *B v B (Residence: Condition Limiting Geographic Area)* [2004] 2 FLR 979 a condition was imposed that the mother and child live within a specified geographic area, as the mother had made two applications to remove the child to Australia and her prime motive in moving the child's residence from the South to the North of England was to escape from the child's father. In *Re C (Internal Relocation)* [2015] EWCA Civ 1305 (see further at 11.7(e) below), the Court of Appeal held that there is no rule that moving a child within the UK could be prevented only in exceptional cases.

(e) Enforcing and facilitating child arrangements orders regulating the child's living arrangements

Sections 11A–11P of the CA 1989 give the court specific powers to impose activity and contact directions and conditions on child arrangements orders and to make enforcement orders. Enforcement orders can be made in relation to non-compliance with a child arrangements order regulating the child's living arrangements. While previously such orders could be made only in relation to a failure to comply with contact arrangements ordered by the court, they can now be made in relation to child arrangements orders regulating living arrangements (see 11.5 below for further detail on these provisions).

11.4 Disputes over a child's contact arrangements

> **Article 9(3) of the UN Convention on the Rights of the Child 1989**
>
> States Parties shall respect the right of the child ... to maintain personal relations and direct contact with both parents on a regular basis, except if it is contrary to the child's best interests.

(a) Introduction

Contact arrangements are best settled by the parents themselves, but if they cannot reach agreement, and mediation or collaborative law fail, then an application can be made to the court for a child arrangements order regulating the child's contact arrangements under section 8 of the Children Act 1989 (CA 1989). Such orders replace what were previously known as 'contact orders'. Despite the possibility of seeking a court order, most parents in fact make their own contact arrangements. Research by Hunt and Macleod of the Oxford Centre for Family Law and Policy found that less than one in ten parents applied to the court for contact arrangements to be settled (*Outcomes of Applications to Court for Contact Orders After Parental Separation or Divorce*, 2008, available at www.gov.uk). Their research also found that, even if cases did go to court, most parties reached agreement and it was rare for the court to have to make a final ruling. Also, most cases ended with face-to-face contact; and contact typically involved overnight stays, at least fortnightly.

It is better if parents reach agreement about contact, because research has shown that parents who turn to the law to settle serious contact disputes risk making matters worse (see Trinder *et al.*, *Making Contact: How Parents and Children Negotiate and Experience Contact After Divorce*, Joseph Rowntree Foundation, [2002] Fam Law 872).

Research conducted by Goisis *et al.* found that the frequency and quality of contact between the child and the non-resident parent was higher among families who did not report court involvement (for contact or financial arrangements) during the separation process (see *Child Outcomes After Parental Separation: Variations by Contact and Court Involvement*, 2016, Ministry of Justice). It has been recognised by the judiciary and by the Government that contact cases are best dealt with outside the courts. Wall J, speaking at a conference on contact, said (see [2003] Fam Law 275):

> The law, which of necessity, operates within the discipline of defined orders is, in my judgment, ill-suited to deal with the complex family dynamics inherent in disputed contact applications. Arrangements for contact stand more prospect of enduring if they are consensual. Wherever possible, contact disputes should be dealt with outside the courtroom.

(i) Human rights and contact

The European Court of Human Rights (ECtHR) recognises the importance of contact between parents and children as part of the right to family life under Article 8 of the European Convention on Human Rights (ECHR) (see, for example, *Johansen v Norway* (1997) 23 EHRR 33). In *Kosmopolou v Greece (Application No. 60457/00)* [2004] 1 FLR 800, the ECtHR held that

> the mutual enjoyment by parent and child of each other's company constitutes a fundamental element of family life, even if the relationship between the parents has broken down, and domestic measures hindering such enjoyment amount to an interference with the right protected by Art. 8 of the Convention.

Thus, the ECtHR takes the view that, unless the circumstances of the case are exceptional, the mutual enjoyment by parent and child of each other's company constitutes a right to family life under Article 8. In *Hansen v Turkey (Application No. 36141/97)* [2004] 1 FLR 142, for example, the ECtHR held that the failure of the Turkish authorities to take realistic coercive measures against the father (who had custody) to allow the mother to have access to the child was a breach of her right to family life under Article 8. As the Human Rights Act 1998 requires courts in the UK to take account of the decisions of the ECtHR, they must ensure that they order contact and enforce it, unless it is contrary to the child's best interests. The ECtHR has held, however, that the duty on national authorities to enforce and facilitate contact is not absolute. The question to be asked is whether the national authorities concerned have taken all the necessary steps to enforce and facilitate contact that could reasonably be demanded in the circumstances of the case (see, for example, *Zadwadka v Poland (Application No. 48542/99)* [2005] 2 FLR 897; and *Kaleta v Poland (Case No. 11375/02)*, [2009] 1 FLR 927). Each case therefore depends on its facts. Thus, for example, in *Glaser v UK* (2001) 33 EHRR 1 the ECtHR rejected a complaint that the UK authorities were in breach of the ECHR by failing to take adequate steps to enforce contact against a mother.

Delay in the court process in respect of enforcing contact may constitute a breach of Article 6 (the right to a fair trial) as it did in *Adam v Germany (No. 44036/02)* [2009] 1 FLR 560 where the ECtHR held that the rights of the child's father and paternal grandparents had been breached under Article 6 due to the avoidable delays and protracted nature of the proceedings to enforce contact with the child (which had been going on for more than four years).

(ii) Contact – difficult areas

Contact disputes are 'among the most difficult and sensitive cases' which the courts have to deal with (*per* Wall LJ [2005] Fam Law 26). Contact disputes are often lengthy and intractable. Cases sometimes drag on for years, which not only takes up court time but is contrary to the best interests of children (see, for example, *Re A-H (Contact Order)* [2008] EWCA Civ 630 where, after five years, the contact question had not been resolved). There have also been problems with contact in the context of domestic violence (see 11.4(f) below), and in respect of the enforcement and facilitation of contact (see 11.5 below). There has also been increasing pressure by proponents of children's rights, including the United Nations Committee on the Rights of the Child, for children's views to be heard more in contact cases and for children to have separate representation (but see *Re S (Contact: Children's Views)* [2002] EWHC 540 (Fam) where a contact order was refused because of the views of the two children who were aged 14 and 16). Although an intractable parental contact case may be a suitable case for separate representation of the child involved, in practice separate representation is rarely exercised.

(iii) Contact and child maintenance

Some parents may make a link between contact and child maintenance. For example, one parent may decide that, as the other parent is not paying maintenance for the child, then they should have no or limited contact; or a parent may think that, because they are paying maintenance, then they have a right to contact. The Family Justice Review (see 1.2) has stated, however, that there should be no link of any kind between contact and maintenance. A similar view was put forward by Wilson LJ, in *Re B (Contact: Child Support)* [2006] EWCA Civ 1574, who stated that it would be 'positively unlawful' to consider the consequences of statutory provisions regarding payment of child maintenance when making orders for contact or residence, 'because it would be to introduce a consideration unrelated to the child's welfare'. However, while the court may not treat the two issues as related, for those parents who reach an agreement outside court, and without having received independent legal advice, there is a danger that they may make a link between contact and child maintenance, which may be detrimental to children. (For a discussion of whether there should be some sort of legal linkage between contact and the payment of child maintenance, see Douglas ([2011] Fam Law 491.)

(b) Child arrangements orders regulating the child's contact arrangements

Where a contact dispute cannot be settled by agreement, an application can be made for a child arrangements order regulating the child's contact arrangements under section 8 of the CA 1989 (see 10.5). Such an order may regulate with whom a child is to spend time or otherwise have contact and when they are to spend time or otherwise have contact with that person (s 8(1)). The term 'contact' was introduced by the Children Act to replace 'access', because 'contact' was considered to be a more child-centred term as it allows for a child to have contact rather than giving a parent a right to have access.

(i) Applicants

The child's parents (married or unmarried, and whether or not they have parental responsibility) can apply. Other people, including the child, can apply, but only with leave of the court (see 10.5).

(ii) Other powers

The court can order a welfare report on the child (s 7); and direct that a local authority investigate the child's circumstances (s 37). The court can also attach a condition to a child arrangements order regulating the child's contact arrangements (s 11(7)), but its power to do so is not unlimited. For example, a condition cannot be attached to such an order for the purposes of ousting a person from the family home (see *Re K (Contact: Condition Ousting Parent from Family Home)* [2011] EWCA Civ 1075).

(iii) Duration

A child arrangements order regulating the child's contact arrangements cannot be made to last beyond the child's 16th birthday, unless there are exceptional circumstances (s 9(6)).

(iv) A welfare report

The court may order that a Cafcass officer prepare a welfare report for the purposes of the contact proceedings (s 7). The recommendations in the report are an important consideration for the court when reaching its decision.

(c)   How the court exercises its discretion in contact cases

When considering whether to make a child arrangements order regulating the child's contact arrangements and, if so, in what manner, the court must apply the welfare principle (s 1(1)), the no order principle (s 1(5)), the no delay principle (s 1(2)) and, in a contested application, the section 1(3) welfare checklist and the presumption of parental involvement (s 1(2A)) (see 10.3). (For an analysis of reported contact cases from 1994 to 2010, see Kaganas [2011] CFLQ 63.)

(i) Contact as a right of the child

Like the United Nations Convention on the Rights of the Child and the ECtHR (see 11.4(a) above), the courts in England and Wales have also referred to contact as a right of the child. As Sir Stephen Brown P said in *Re W (A Minor) (Contact)* [1994] 2 FLR 441, it is 'quite clear that contact with a parent is a fundamental right of a child, save in wholly exceptional circumstances'. Cogent reasons will therefore be needed to deprive a child of contact (see *Re H (Contact Principles)* [1994] 2 FLR 969). In *Re R (A Minor) (Contact)* [1993] 2 FLR 762 Butler-Sloss LJ stated that it 'is a right of a child to have a continuing relationship with both parents wherever possible' and that in general the parent with whom the child does not live has a continuing role to play, which is endorsed in the CA 1989.

In most cases the court will usually decide that it is in the child's best interests for the non-resident parent to have contact. Due to the importance attached to a child knowing their natural parent, the court may decide to order contact even where the other parent is absent, for example, because they are in prison (*A v L (Contact)* [1998] 1 FLR 361). Because of the importance of contact for children, the Court of Appeal has emphasised that the court should explore all options before contact is terminated (*Re W (Contact)* [2007] EWCA Civ 753). In *Re C (Suspension of Contact)* [2011] EWCA Civ 521 Munby LJ explained that the law imposed

> a positive obligation on the State, and therefore on the judge … to maintain or restore contact …. The judge must grapple with all the available alternatives before abandoning hope of achieving some contact …. [C]ontact is to be stopped only as a last resort and only once it has become clear that the child will not benefit from continuing the attempt.

Gilmore ([2008] Fam Law 1226) has argued, however, that it is not contact *per se* that is beneficial for the child but the nature and quality of the contact. Similarly, research conducted by Fortin, Hunt and Scanlan into young people's experiences of parental separation led them to conclude that 'the courts' current approach that contact is almost always in the interests of children is not sufficiently nuanced but should take account of the child's need for good contact rather than simply any contact' (see *Taking a Longer View of Contact: The Perspectives of Young Adults Who Experienced Parental Separation in Their Youth*, 2012, Sussex Law School).

(ii) A presumption or assumption in favour of contact?

Although contact is considered to be a right of the child (see above), and is considered to be beneficial to a child, Thorpe LJ in *Re L, V, M and H* [2000] 2 FLR 334 (which involved contact and domestic violence – see 11.4(f) below) said that, although there was a 'universal judicial recognition of the importance of contact to a child's development', he was wary of talking of presumptions in the context of contact because it might 'inhibit or distort the rigorous search for the welfare solution'. For this reason, he preferred to talk about an 'assumption' in favour of contact or an assumption that contact is beneficial. Thorpe LJ was in no doubt, however, 'of the secure foundation for the assumption that contact benefits children'. (For an example of when contact was terminated by the court see *Re W (Contact Dispute) (No. 2)* [2014] EWCA Civ 401 where the children were vehemently opposed to contact with their father and lengthy attempts to restore contact with the assistance of professionals had failed.)

(d) Types of contact

Different types of contact may be ordered depending on the circumstances. Direct contact (visiting or staying contact) will usually be ordered, unless there are cogent reasons to the contrary affecting the child's welfare (such as where there has been violence). Instead of ordering direct contact, especially where it is of significant duration, the court may instead make a child arrangements order for shared living arrangements (see 11.3(c) above).

Sometimes the court will order indirect or supervised contact (the word 'otherwise' in section 8(1) allows this). The court may decide to add a condition to a contact order (under section 11(7)) to specify what arrangements are to take place (for example indirect contact by letter, email, birthday cards, Christmas cards, or telephone conversations or Skype). Indirect contact was ordered, for example, in: *Re P (Contact: Indirect Contact)* [1999] 2 FLR 893 (the father was a former drug addict who had just been released from prison); *Re L (Contact: Genuine Fear)* [2002] 1 FLR 621 (the mother was genuinely and intensely frightened of the father, so that direct contact would cause the child emotional harm); and in *Re F (Indirect Contact)* [2006] EWCA Civ 1426 (the father had a history of serious and uncontrollable violence). Indirect contact may be used as a precursor to direct contact, particularly if, for example, the child has never known the parent seeking contact or there has been a long gap since contact last took place.

Where there is a risk that contact may be harmful for the child, supervised contact can be ordered whereby contact takes place in the presence of a third party. Sometimes it takes place in a contact centre run under the auspices of the National Association of Child Contact Centres, where children can enjoy contact with one or both parents (and other family members) in a comfortable and safe environment. Although a judge has a positive duty to promote contact and must look at any alternative options available before refusing contact, in some cases even supervised contact may not be appropriate and an order of no contact may be made (as in *Re K (Children: Refusal of Direct Contact)* [2011] EWCA Civ 1064 where the father had committed sexual offences against children; and in *Re J (Refusal of Contact)* [2012] EWCA Civ 720 where there were findings against the father of physical and emotional abuse to the mother and her extended family, including threats of rape of the mother's sisters and a threat to abduct the child). In an exceptional case, the court may not only decide to order that there be no contact, but it may also make an order under section 91(14) of the CA 1989 (see 10.1) that no further application can be made to the court without leave of the court (as it did, for example, in *Re T (A Child: One Parent Killed by Other Parent)* [2012] 1 FLR 472 where the father, a paranoid schizophrenic, had stabbed and killed the child's mother).

(e) Parental hostility to contact

As contact is considered to be a right of a child and beneficial for a child, the courts are reluctant to allow contact to be thwarted because of parental hostility to it. In *Re H (A Minor) (Contact)* [1994] 2 FLR 776 Butler-Sloss LJ said that it was important that there should not be 'a selfish parents' charter' whereby a parent could make such a fuss about contact that it could prevent the court ordering it. Only in highly exceptional cases would contact be refused because of a parent's strong opposition and hostility to contact (see, for example, *Re J (A Minor) (Contact)* [1994] 1 FLR 729 where the mother's hostility to contact with the father caused the child stress).

Over the years the courts began increasingly to realise, however, that some parents had genuinely held reasons for being intractably hostile to contact, for example because of fear that the child might suffer violence (see *Re H (Contact: Domestic Violence)* [1998] 2 FLR 42). Courts began to take allegations of domestic violence and hostility to contact more seriously. However, in cases where there is hostility to contact, but contact is deemed to be in the best interests of the child, the court now has stronger enforcement powers if one parent refuses to facilitate contact (see 11.5 below).

(f) Contact and domestic violence

For many years allegations of domestic violence were not taken as seriously as they might have been in contact cases. There were various reasons for this, such as that research on domestic violence had tended to concentrate on adult victims rather than children; and the courts were of the view that, as children had a right to contact and contact was beneficial to them, then contact should usually be ordered. The courts were also distrustful of mothers who made allegations of violence by fathers, and considered that they were merely being hostile to contact; and they were keen to ensure that children were brought up having a positive image of a father, even where there were allegations of violence. Furthermore, there was nothing expressly about domestic violence in the CA 1989.

Increasing concern began to be voiced, however, that the courts had perhaps created too high a threshold for a denial of contact, and that contact was being ordered in cases even though there was a risk of violence. An important impetus for a change of approach was psychiatric research which showed that domestic violence could have a harmful emotional impact on children. Another impetus for change was the publication of a report by Radford (*Unreasonable Fears? Child Contact in the Context of Domestic Violence: A Survey of Mothers' Perception of Harm*, 1999, Women's Aid), which provided evidence of children being physically and sexually abused as a result of contact being ordered; and which recommended the introduction of a rebuttable presumption against residence and direct or unsupervised contact in cases where there was a risk of violence.

In June 1999 a consultation paper by the Children Act Sub-Committee of the Advisory Board on Family Law (*Contact Between Children and Violent Parents: The Question of Parental Contact in Cases where there is Domestic Violence*) was published, proposing guidelines for good practice in contact cases where there were allegations of domestic violence. But the consultation paper was not in favour of introducing a legislative presumption against contact in domestic violence cases, which existed in some countries. The Government began to acknowledge that domestic violence had not been fully or appropriately handled by the courts in contact cases, and that something needed to be done. In a report to the Lord Chancellor (*The Question of Parental Contact in Cases Where There Is Domestic Violence*, 2002) it was recommended that: guidelines for good practice should be drawn up; professionals involved should be better informed and better trained; and there should be more research into contact and domestic violence.

As a result of the concerns voiced about contact and domestic violence, the courts began to take domestic violence more seriously in contact cases and would order indirect or supervised contact, or refuse contact, where there was violence (see, for example, *Re M (Contact: Violent Parent)* [1999] 2 FLR 321; and *Re K (Contact: Mother's Anxiety)* [1999] 2 FLR 703). The courts began to take the view that, where there was evidence of domestic violence, a perpetrator would have to show a future track record of proper behaviour, including taking up the offer of indirect contact, before successfully gaining direct contact (see the *dicta* of Wall J in *Re O (Contact: Imposition of Conditions)* [1995] 2 FLR 124, approved by Cazalet J in *Re S (Violent Parent: Indirect Contact)* [2000] 1 FLR 481).

It was the following case, however, which was particularly important in the development of the law in contact cases where there were allegations of domestic violence. In this case the Court of Appeal considered the report by the Children Act Sub-Committee (see above) and a joint report by two child psychiatrists, Dr Sturge and Dr Glaser, which stated that domestic violence involved a significant failure in parenting and that, where it was proved, the balance should tip against contact with the abusive parent unless that parent: fully acknowledged the inappropriateness of the violence; recognised its likely ill-effects on the child; had a genuine interest in the child's welfare; and was fully committed to making reparation to the child.

> ▶ *Re L (Contact: Domestic Violence); Re V (Contact: Domestic Violence); Re M (Contact: Domestic Violence); Re H (Contact: Domestic Violence)* [2000] 2 FLR 334
>
> The fathers in the four conjoined appeals appealed against the judge's refusal to allow them direct contact with their children against a background of domestic violence. The violence or threats of violence had been proved, the fears of the resident parents were reasonable and serious issues arose as to the risk of emotional harm to the children.
>
> The Court of Appeal, dismissing all four appeals, laid down the following principles which were to be applied in contact cases where there were allegations of domestic violence:
>
> ▶ Judges and magistrates need to have a heightened awareness of the existence, and consequences for children, of exposure to domestic violence.
> ▶ Allegations of domestic violence which might affect the outcome of a contact application must be adjudicated upon and found proved or not proved.
> ▶ Where domestic violence is proved, there is not, nor should there be, a presumption of no contact. As a matter of principle, domestic violence cannot of itself constitute a bar to contact.
> ▶ Domestic violence is a highly relevant and important factor, among others, which must be taken into account by the judge when carrying out the difficult and delicate balancing exercise of discretion, applying the welfare principle in section 1(1) of the CA 1989, and the welfare checklist in section 1(3).
> ▶ Where domestic violence is proved, the court should weigh in the balance the seriousness of the violence, the risks involved and the impact on the child against the positive factors, if any, of contact between the parent found to have been violent and the child.
> ▶ Where domestic violence is proved, the following factors, among others, are of particular significance: the extent of the violence; its effect upon the primary carer; its effect upon the child; and, in particular, the ability of the offender to recognise their past behaviour, to be aware of the need for change and to make genuine attempts to change it.
> ▶ In respect of Article 8 (the right to family life) of the ECHR, where there is a conflict between the rights and interests of a child and those of a parent, the child's interests must prevail under Article 8(2).
> ▶ On an application for interim contact, when allegations of domestic violence have not been adjudicated upon, the court should give particular consideration to the likely risk of harm (physical or emotional) to the child if contact is granted or refused. The court should ensure, as far as it can, that any risk of harm to the child is minimised, and that the safety of the child and the residential parent is secured before, during and after any such contact.

The message which came out of *Re LVMH* was that courts and lawyers needed to be more aware of domestic violence and its effect on children. After *Re LVMH*, courts began to take allegations of violence in contact cases seriously, and, where violence was proved, they would consider ordering indirect or supervised contact, or, in an extreme case, no contact. According to Kaganas ([2000] CFLQ 311, at 311), what *Re LVMH* did was 'to rein back, in domestic violence cases, what was a very strong trend to prioritise contact between children and non-resident parents and to downgrade the risks to which such contact might expose mothers and children'.

(i) Other developments

In response to concerns about children and domestic violence, the definition of 'harm' in the welfare checklist in section 1(3) of the Children Act 1998 (see 10.3) was redefined to include 'impairment suffered from seeing or hearing the ill-treatment of another'. Cafcass was also given an increased role to monitor domestic violence and conduct risk assessments (see below). Another development was the introduction of a new form (C1A) which must be completed in proceedings for a section 8 order if the child may have experienced, or be at risk of experiencing, harm. This is to ensure that safety issues are prioritised throughout the proceedings and brought to the attention of the court and Cafcass.

A Practice Direction was also issued (see *Practice Direction 12J – Child Arrangements and Contact Order: Domestic Violence and Harm* which supplements the Family Procedure Rules 2010) laying down rules of practice to be adopted in any family proceedings where there is an application for a child arrangements order and there is an allegation, or other reason to suppose, that a child or party has experienced domestic violence perpetrated by another party or that there is a risk of domestic violence. A failure to follow the fact-finding requirements of the *Practice Direction* may provide grounds for a successful appeal, as it did in *Re Z (Unsupervised Contact: Allegations of Domestic Violence)* [2009] EWCA Civ 430 where, although the Cafcass officer had reported risks of violence, the judge decided that a fact-finding hearing should not go ahead. (See also *Re W (Children: Domestic Violence)* [2012] EWCA Civ 528 where the Court of Appeal allowed the father's appeal because the judge had not discharged his obligation, either explicitly or implicitly, to examine the factors set out in the *Practice Direction*.)

However, despite the increased awareness of domestic violence and its impact on children, some academics, lawyers and charities remain concerned about the approach of the courts. For example, Polly Neate, Chief Executive of Women's Aid, argues that 'the desire by the family courts to treat parents in exactly the same way, and get cases over with quickly, blinds them to the consequences of unsafe child contact' (see press release for Women's Aid's report *Nineteen Child Homicides*, 2016). Barnett ([2014] CFLQ 439) notes that, despite the prevalence of domestic violence in private law proceedings, the courts rarely refuse to make contact orders. She suggests that this is in part due to the perceptions of professionals involved and says that victims of domestic violence are likely to be encouraged or pressurised into agreeing to direct contact by the court and their own representatives, except in very extreme circumstances. (For a contrasting view written by Wall LJ, which questions some of the claims made by Women's Aid in an earlier report, see *A Report to the President of the Family Division on the Publication of the Women's Aid Federation of England entitled Twenty-Nine Child Homicides*, 2006, available from www.judiciary.gov.uk.)

(ii) Risk assessments (section 16A of the Children Act 1989)

Cafcass officers (see 1.7), when exercising any of their functions in respect of any of the orders that can be made under Part II of the CA 1989 (see 10.2), and who suspect that the child concerned is at risk of harm, must make a risk assessment in relation to the child and make that assessment available for the court (ss 16A(1), (2)). The assessment must be presented to the court even if the officer concludes that there is no risk of harm to the child; as the fact that a risk assessment has been carried out is a material fact which should be placed before the court (see *Practice Direction 12L – Children Act 1989: Risk Assessments Under Section 16A*, which supplements the Family Procedure Rules 2010).

11.5 Enforcing and facilitating contact

Baroness Hale in *Re G (Children) (Residence: Same-Sex Partner)* [2006] UKHL 43

Making contact happen and, even more importantly, making contact work is one of the most difficult and contentious challenges in the whole of family law. It has recently received a great deal of public attention. Courts understandably regard the conventional methods of enforcing court orders as a last resort: fining the primary carer will only mean that she has even less to spend on the children; sending her to prison will deprive them of their primary carer and give them a reason to resent the other parent who invited this. Nor does punishment address the real sources of the problem, which may range from a simple failure to understand what the children need, to more complex fears resulting from the parents' own relationships.

The courts in England and Wales must take effective steps to enforce contact, otherwise they risk being in breach of the European Convention for the Protection of Human Rights (ECHR) and the United Nations Convention on the Rights of the Child (UNCRC). Enforcement remains difficult in some cases, however, even though the court now has wider powers to enforce and facilitate contact.

(a) Enforcing and facilitating contact

In order to improve matters, sections 11A–11P were inserted into the Children Act 1989 (CA 1989) to give the courts new and wider powers to enforce and facilitate contact and resolve child contact disputes. The provisions have since been extended to cover child arrangements orders regulating living arrangements.

(i) The background to the provisions

In 2002 the Children Act Sub-Committee of the Lord Chancellor's Advisory Board on Family Law, chaired by Wall J, published *Making Contact Work: A Report to the Lord Chancellor on the Facilitation of Arrangements for Contact Between Children and Their Non-Residential Parents and the Enforcement of Court Orders for Contact*. The report made various recommendations, including: providing more information about contact; giving contact centres extra funding to facilitate contact; promoting mediation, conciliation and negotiation; amending the provisions governing family assistance orders; giving courts the power to refer a parent to a psychiatrist or psychologist, or to an education programme; imposing community service orders for breach of contact orders; and awarding financial compensation to parents who suffered financial loss as a result of loss of contact. Many of these recommendations were incorporated in the new law.

Two years later, in 2004, the Government published a consultation paper, *Parental Separation: Children's Needs and Parents' Responsibilities* (Cm 6273), in which it acknowledged that the current system for enforcing and facilitating contact was not working well. The consultation paper was followed, in 2005, by the White Paper *Parental Separation: Children's Needs and Parents' Responsibilities, Next Steps* (Cm 6452), which recommended various reforms to improve the enforcement and facilitation of contact, including, for example: a wider range of services to support contact; a greater role for Cafcass in the promotion and enforcement of contact; additional powers for the court before making contact orders; changes to family assistance orders to make them better suited to being used in difficult contact cases; and a greater role for mediation.

(ii) The provisions

Many of the above recommendations were enacted in Part 1 of the Children and Adoption Act 2006, which inserted sections 11A–11P into the CA 1989. In addition to giving the courts additional powers when dealing with applications for contact orders, the provisions placed a number of new duties on Cafcass officers (including monitoring compliance with contact orders, contact activities and enforcement, and reporting back to the court). The provisions also give the courts more flexibility in dealing with breaches of contact orders.

Under sections 11A–11P the following steps can be taken:

Activity directions and conditions The court at the interim stage of a child arrangements dispute can make an 'activity direction' (under section 11A) directing a party to the proceedings to take part in a specified activity which helps to establish, maintain or improve the involvement of that person, or another party's involvement, in the child's life. Activities can include, *inter alia*, the following: classes; counselling; guidance; information and advice about contact; and information about mediation.

An activity which a judge may decide to order a parent to participate in is a separated parents information programme, which is designed to help parents focus on their children's needs and improve relationships with their former partner in order to come to amicable child arrangements. When considering whether to make an activity direction, the child's welfare is the court's paramount consideration.

When making or varying a child arrangements order for shared living arrangements or regulating contact, the court can include an 'activity condition' (under section 11C) in the order. This can require the person with whom the child lives (or is to live) and/or a person whose contact with the child is being regulated and/or a person subject to a condition attached to the order to take part in an activity that helps to establish, maintain or improve the involvement of that person, or another party's involvement, in the child's life.

Before making an activity direction or condition, the court must be satisfied (under section 11E) that: the activity is appropriate; the activity provider is suitable to provide the activity; and the proposed activity is in a place to which the person subject to the direction or condition can reasonably be expected to travel. The court must also obtain and consider information about the person who is to be subject to the direction or condition; and consider the likely effect of the direction or condition on that person. This may include information about any conflict with the person's religious beliefs and any interference with that person's work or education.

Monitoring contact and shared living arrangements (section 11H) The court can ask a Cafcass officer to monitor compliance with a child arrangements order regulating the child's contact arrangements or a child arrangements order providing for shared living arrangements and report to the court on such matters relating to compliance as the court may specify. This monitoring role can only last for up to 12 months.

Warning notices (section 11I) When a court makes, or varies, a child arrangements order it must attach a warning notice to the order providing information about the consequences of failing to comply with the order.

Enforcement orders (sections 11J–11N) If the court is satisfied beyond reasonable doubt that a child arrangements order has been breached without reasonable excuse, it can make an 'enforcement order' imposing an unpaid work requirement (community service) on the person in breach (see s 11J), unless that person proves on the balance of probabilities that he or she has a reasonable excuse for failing to comply with the contact order.

The following people can apply for an enforcement order: the person who for the purpose of the child arrangements order is the person with whom the child lives (or is to live); the person whose contact with the child is provided for in the child arrangements order; any person subject to a condition under section 11(7)(b)) or to an activity condition imposed by the child arrangements order; or the child concerned (but only with leave of the court, which it can grant if the child has sufficient understanding to make the application). Schedule A1 to the CA 1989 makes further provision in respect of enforcement orders.

Before making an enforcement order the court must be satisfied (under section 11L) that: the order is necessary to secure compliance with the child arrangements order; and that the likely effect of the order on the person in breach is proportionate to the seriousness of the breach. It must also be satisfied that the provision for the person to work under an unpaid work requirement can be made in the local area in which the person in breach resides, or will reside. The court must obtain and consider information about the person and the likely effect of the order on that person before making the order. When making the order, the court must take into account the welfare of the child who is the subject of the child arrangements order.

Compensation for financial loss (section 11O) A person who breaches a child arrangements order can be ordered to pay compensation for financial loss resulting from the breach (such as the cost of a holiday for the child). The following people can apply for compensation: the person who, for the purposes of the child arrangements order, is the person with whom the child lives (or is to live); the person for whom contact is provided in the child arrangements order, or a person subject to a section 11(7) (b) condition or an activity condition; or the child concerned (but only with leave of the court, which it can grant if the child has sufficient understanding to make the application). The court cannot make an order if it is satisfied that the person in breach had a reasonable excuse for failing to comply with the child arrangements order, it cannot order compensation in excess of the applicant's loss and it must take into account the financial circumstances of the person in breach. In exercising its powers, the court must take into account the child's welfare.

Despite the existence of these powers, the number of applications made to enforce contact arrangements is small; and punitive sanctions, such as the unpaid work requirement, are rarely used. Research conducted by Trinder *et al.* [2013] found that fewer than 1,400 applications for enforcement orders were made between 2011 and 2012 and only a minority of those resulted in an enforcement order being made (see *Enforcing Contact Orders: Problem-Solving or Punishment?*, University of Exeter and Nuffield Foundation, 2013).

(b) Other measures with respect to enforcing and facilitating contact

The following powers are also available for the purpose of enforcement and facilitation of contact, but, with the introduction of the provisions above, they are less likely to be used.

(i) Family assistance order (section 16)

A family assistance order (see 10.10) can be made under section 16 of the CA 1989 for the purpose of facilitating contact in a difficult case. Thus, a family assistance order can be made (when a contact provision in a child arrangements order is in force) directing a Cafcass officer or a local authority officer to give advice and assistance with regard to establishing, improving and maintaining contact to those specified in the family assistance order (s 16(4A)).

(ii) Contempt of court

Breach of a child arrangements order is contempt of court, punishable by fine or imprisonment, although, with the introduction of the enforcement measures above, contempt of court is now less likely. Although imposing a fine or a prison term is a rather unsatisfactory measure in family cases (as fining a parent reduces the amount of money available for the child, and sending a parent to prison may be emotionally damaging for the child), the courts have sometimes imposed fines and prison sentences for breaches of contact orders (see, for example, *Re S (Contact Dispute: Committal)* [2004] EWCA Civ 1790). The Court of Appeal has warned, however, that a custodial sentence should not be imposed where a fine is appropriate (see *Re M (Contact Order)* [2005] EWCA Civ 615). In *Re L-W (Enforcement and Committal: Contact); CPL v CH-W and Others* [2010] EWCA Civ 1253, where a committal order against the father was set aside in the circumstances of the case, Munby LJ held that committal should not be used unless it is a proportionate response to the problem nor if some less drastic remedy will provide an adequate solution.

Contempt proceedings must comply with Article 6 (the right to a fair trial) and Article 8 (the right to family life) of the ECHR. Thus, for example, in *Re K (Contact: Committal Order)* [2002] EWCA Civ 1559 a mother successfully appealed against her committal to prison for 42 days for breach of a contact order as there had been a breach of Article 6 (as she had had no legal representation) and Article 8 (as the court had failed to consider the fact that committal would separate her from her children).

(iii) Transfer of living arrangements to the other parent

Where there are protracted difficulties in enforcing contact the court may in exceptional circumstances decide that the child's residence should be transferred from the resident-parent to the non-resident parent (as it did, for example, in *V v V (Contact: Implacable Hostility)* [2004] EWHC 1215 (Fam) where Bracewell J transferred residence to the father because the mother's behaviour constituted emotional abuse of the children). However, a transfer of living arrangements will be ordered only in the last resort and where it is not contrary to the child's best interests. In *Re A (Residence Order)* [2009] EWCA Civ 1141, for example, the transfer of residence from the mother to the father was held to be premature and too risky for the children concerned. On the other hand, in *Re W (Residence: Leave to Appeal)* [2010] EWCA Civ 1280 the Court of Appeal refused to grant the mother leave to appeal against the trial judge's decision to transfer residence of her three-year-old child to the paternal grandmother as she had continually flouted court orders for her to comply with a contact order in favour of the father.

11.6 Changing a child's name on family breakdown

On family breakdown the parent with whom the child lives may wish to change the child's surname (perhaps because of a desire to sever ties with the other parent or for the child to acquire a new partner's surname). There are restrictions on changing a child's surname, but not their first name (see *Re H (Child's Name: First Name)* [2002] EWCA Civ 190). A child's surname can be changed by a person with parental responsibility for the child provided every other person with parental responsibility gives consent. However, if there is a child arrangements order regulating the child's living arrangements in force with respect to the child, then *written* consent is required under the Children Act 1989 (CA 1989) (s 13(1)(b)). Written consent to a change of surname is also required if a child is in local authority care (s 33(7)). If consent is not forthcoming, then the court's consent will be needed.

A dispute about a child's surname can be settled by making an application for a specific issue order (see 10.7), or, if a child arrangements order regulating the child's living arrangements is in force, by making an application under section 13. Where a change of name appears imminent, then a prohibited steps order (see 10.6) may be necessary to prevent the change of surname. When considering an application for a change of surname, the child's welfare is the court's paramount consideration (s 1(1)), and the section 1(3) welfare checklist and presumption of parental involvement (s 1(2A) apply if the application is by way of a specific issue or prohibited steps order (see s 1(4)). Although the CA 1989 does not require the court to consider the welfare checklist in an application for a change of surname under section 13, the court is likely to perform the same sort of exercise.

The courts take the view that changing a child's surname is a serious matter (*Dawson v Wearmouth* [1999] AC 308); and that the child's wishes, not those of the parent, may prevail. In *Re C (Change of Surname)* [1998] 2 FLR 656 the Court of Appeal held that good reasons have to be shown before a judge will allow a change of name. In *Re W; Re A; Re B (Change of Name)* [1999] 2 FLR 930 Butler-Sloss LJ said that a desire to change a child's name because the applicant parent does not have the same name as the child will generally not carry much weight.

The court will take into account cultural and religious circumstances when deciding whether to permit a change of surname, but even then it may be unwilling to permit a change (see, for example, *Re S (Change of Names: Cultural Factors)* [2001] 2 FLR 1005 where Wilson J refused to give the mother permission to change the child's Sikh names to Muslim names after she had moved back into a Muslim community on family breakdown). A change of surname may, however, be permitted where the child's welfare requires it, for example, where there is a need to protect a child against the risk of domestic violence or abduction (see, for example, *Re F (Contact)* [2007] EWHC 2543 (Fam) where the father had made repeated threats to abduct the children).

In *Re R (Surname: Using Both Parents')* [2001] EWCA Civ 1344 it was suggested that parents should be encouraged to use the Spanish custom of combining the paternal and maternal surnames as a way of avoiding surname disputes.

11.7 Relocation on family breakdown

(a) Removing a child lawfully from the UK

On family breakdown, a parent may wish to take the child temporarily or permanently out of the UK. A parent can do this, provided he or she is not in breach of any statutory provision or court order and has obtained the necessary consents.

(i) Obtaining the necessary consents

A parent who wishes to take a child out of the UK must obtain the consent of everyone with parental responsibility for the child, otherwise he or she may commit the criminal offence of child abduction or kidnapping (see 13.3) or be in contempt of court (if there is a court order prohibiting the child's removal). Oral consent to take the child abroad is usually sufficient, unless there is a court order to the contrary or there is a child arrangements order regulating the child's living arrangements in force under section 8 of the Children Act 1989 (CA 1989), in which case *written* consent is needed. There is an exception to this requirement for consent if a person named in the child arrangements order as someone with whom the child should live wishes to go abroad for less than one month (s 13(1)(b)). If consent is not forthcoming then the court's permission to leave the UK will have to be obtained. Applications to relocate permanently to another country are normally known as 'relocation applications'.

(b) International relocation applications

After family breakdown, a parent may wish to take the child out of the UK, perhaps to start a new relationship, or to take up a new job, or to move back to their country of origin. The other parent may refuse to agree to this, perhaps because of the difficulty of maintaining contact or because of a fear that the child will not be returned. Where the necessary consents to taking the child out of the UK are not forthcoming (see above), the court's permission must be sought in order to avoid committing a criminal offence or being in contempt of court.

Permission to leave the UK (to relocate) with a child can be sought by applying for a specific issue order (see 10.7), or, if a child arrangements order regulating the child's living arrangements is in force, by applying under section 13(1) of the CA 1989. The court must apply the welfare principle in section 1(1) and the other welfare principles in section 1 of the CA 1989 (see 10.3). The court will usually ask a Cafcass officer to prepare a report, but they are not invariably ordered and a failure to do so will not necessarily be a sufficient ground for an appeal (see *Re R (Leave to Remove: Contact)* [2010] EWCA Civ 1137).

(i) The voice of the child

The child's views can be taken into account in a relocation application. The usual way in which the child's voice is put before the court is by way of a Cafcass report. Separate representation of the child is permitted but is rarely exercised in practice. The child's wishes may be an important consideration in tilting the balance one way or the other if the child is mature enough to understand the situation. Thus, for example, in *Re W (Leave to Remove)* [2008] EWCA Civ 538 the Court of Appeal allowed the mother's appeal, and granted her permission to take the children to Sweden, on the ground, *inter alia*, that the judge had failed to sufficiently consider the wishes of the three children (aged 11, 13 and 15), who were particularly intelligent, mature and sophisticated for their ages, and who supported the proposed move to Sweden.

(ii) The approach of the courts in relocation applications

The approach laid down by the Court of Appeal in *Poel v Poel* [1970] WLR 1469 was to allow a reasonable and properly thought-out application, unless this was clearly incompatible with the child's welfare. This approach was upheld by the courts in subsequent cases, notably in *Payne v Payne* [2001] EWCA Civ 1166 (see below). This approach has led to much criticism from parents (often fathers), lawyers and academics (see further below) as it seems to place the burden on the parent trying to prevent the move to show why it is not in the child's best interests. Although both *Poel* and *Payne* remain good law, the Court of Appeal has warned against excessive reliance on the guidance contained in these cases and has emphasised that there is no presumption in favour of a parent wishing to move (see *K v K (Relocation: Shared Care Arrangement)* [2011] EWCA Civ 793, *Re F (International Relocation Cases)* [2015] EWCA Civ 882 and *Re C (Internal Relocation)* [2015] EWCA Civ 1305 below).

(iii) The development of the court's approach since Poel

With the coming into force of the Human Rights Act 1998 (HRA 1998), parents began to argue that the approach in *Poel* breached their human rights and those of the child. They also argued that the approach was contrary to the welfare principle in section 1(1) of the CA 1989 because it failed to treat the child's welfare as the court's paramount consideration. Thus, for example, in *Re A (Permission to Remove Child from Jurisdiction: Human Rights)* [2000] 2 FLR 225 the father argued that, if permission was given to allow the mother to take their child to New York, it would breach his right to family life under Article 8 of the European Convention on Human Rights (ECHR). However, the Court of Appeal, dismissing his appeal, held that Article 8(2) required the court to balance such rights where they were in conflict. It held that the test laid down in *Poel* was not in conflict with the ECHR. In fact, Buxton LJ doubted whether difficult balancing questions of this nature fell within the purview of the ECHR at all.

(iv) The leading case of Payne v Payne

In *Payne*, which is the leading case in relocation applications, the Court of Appeal reviewed the long line of authority on relocation applications in the light of the new obligations imposed on the courts by the HRA 1998.

▶ *Payne v Payne* [2001] EWCA Civ 1166

The mother (the primary carer) applied for permission to remove her four-year-old daughter permanently from the UK to live with her in New Zealand. The father opposed the application and applied for a residence order. The father and paternal grandmother had regular and exceptionally good staying contact with the child. The mother's application was granted at first instance, applying the principle in *Poel* (namely, to allow a reasonable and properly thought-out application unless it is clearly incompatible with the child's welfare). The father appealed arguing that: contact between children and non-residential parents had increased in importance since the decision in *Poel*; the principles in relocation applications were inconsistent with the CA 1989, as they created a presumption in favour of the applicant; and the court's approach was inconsistent with the HRA 1998.

The Court of Appeal dismissed his appeal, holding that there was no conflict between the case-law governing relocation applications and the ECHR, and the CA 1989. It held that the proposition in *Poel* (that a reasonable application would be allowed) did not amount to a presumption in favour of the primary carer. The child's welfare is always the court's paramount consideration, and the welfare checklist in section 1(3) CA 1989 (see 10.3) should be used by a judge when carrying out the welfare test.

Butler-Sloss P said that, although the reasonable proposals of the residential parent wishing to live abroad carried great weight, they had to be scrutinised carefully so that the court could be satisfied that there was a genuine motivation for the move and not an intention to terminate contact between the child and the other parent. Her Ladyship said that the effect on the child of a denial of contact with the non-resident parent and his family was an important consideration, and that the opportunity for continuing contact between the child and the parent left behind in the UK might be a very significant factor.

Thorpe LJ agreed with Ward LJ in *Re A (Permission to Remove Child from Jurisdiction: Human Rights)* (see above) that the advent of the ECHR in domestic law by the HRA 1998 did not necessitate a revision of the fundamental approach to relocation applications formulated by the Court of Appeal and consistently applied over so many years. Thorpe LJ said that 'in a united family the right to family life is a shared right', but that 'once a family unit disintegrates the separating members' separate rights can only be to a fragmented family life'. In the present case the mother's right to mobility under Article 2 of Protocol 4 of the ECHR was another relevant right to be considered. Thorpe LJ said that he did not consider that a reasonable request by the primary carer created a legal presumption of permission to relocate. He also proposed a 'discipline' which the courts should use in relocation cases (see below).

(v) The 'discipline' which courts should use

Thorpe LJ in *Payne* suggested that the following framework or 'discipline' should be used by the courts when deciding relocation applications:

(a) Pose the question: is the mother's application genuine in the sense that it is not motivated by some selfish desire to exclude the father from the child's life? Then ask is the mother's application realistic, by which I mean founded on practical proposals both well researched and investigated? If the application fails either of these tests refusal will inevitably follow.

(b) If however the application passes these tests then there must be a careful appraisal of the father's opposition: is it motivated by genuine concern for the future of the child's welfare or is it driven by some ulterior motive? What would be the extent of the detriment to him and his future relationship with the child were the application granted? To what extent would that be offset by extension of the child's relationships with the maternal family and homeland?

(c) What would be the impact on the mother, either as the single parent or as a new wife, of a refusal of her realistic proposal?

(d) The outcome of the second and third appraisals must then be brought into an overriding review of the child's welfare as the paramount consideration, directed by the statutory checklist in so far as appropriate.

The principles laid down in *Payne* were endorsed by the Court of Appeal in *Re G (Leave to Remove)* [2007] EWCA Civ 1497 where the father sought leave to appeal against the trial judge's decision to grant the mother leave to relocate to Germany, on the basis that judges were misapplying *Payne* in that they were inappropriately prioritising the impact of refusal on the primary carer, and were disregarding modern views on the importance of co-parenting. The Court of Appeal refused permission to appeal. Thorpe LJ, giving judgment, held that it was not possible to argue that the principles in *Payne* were being widely misunderstood or misapplied by judges; but he said that he did recognise that relocation cases were very difficult for judges and that often the balance between grant and refusal was a very fine one.

(vi) Practical matters

While each relocation application turns on its own facts, practical matters (such as housing, education, contact arrangements and potential cultural difficulties for the child) will be important (see, for example, *Re F (Leave to Remove)* [2005] EWHC 2705 (Fam) where the mother's application to remove the child to Jamaica was refused on the basis, *inter alia*, of her failure to make adequate plans in respect of supporting herself and the child and in respect of the child's schooling; and because there were insufficient funds available to pay for regular airfares for contact visits to the father).

However, where the primary carer is returning to a completely familiar home life after a brief absence, the Court of Appeal has held that the bar in respect of practical matters is set relatively low (see *Re F and H (Children: Relocation)* [2007] EWCA Civ 692 where the mother was granted permission to return to Texas with the children after a relatively brief absence from her home city, her family and all that was familiar). But, even if the caring parent is returning to their homeland, the application will not necessarily be allowed, as each case depends on its own facts (see *Re H (Removal from Jurisdiction)* [2007] EWCA Civ 222 where the American mother's application to move back to the USA with her five-year-old child and her new husband failed, as, although it was clear that if leave was refused the mother would be distressed and unhappy in the short term, there was no risk of her compromising the care of the child).

(vii) The psychological impact of relocation

In *Re B (Leave to Remove: Impact of Refusal)* [2004] EWCA Civ 956 Thorpe LJ, with whom May and Scott Baker LJJ agreed, said that it was important to give great weight to the emotional and psychological well-being of the primary carer, and not merely take note of the impact on the primary carer of refusing the application to relocate.

However, in respect of possible mental harm to the applicant, it was held in *Re G (Removal from Jurisdiction)* [2005] EWCA Civ 170 that an applicant is not required to prove that they will suffer psychological damage if permission to relocate is refused – all that is required is that a refusal will have an impact on the applicant's sense of well-being and that this will be transmitted to the children.

The psychological impact of relocation on the children will be an important consideration under the welfare test. Thus, for example, in *Re B (Leave to Remove)* [2008] EWCA Civ 1034 the mother's application to remove the children of the marriage to Germany was refused as there was strong evidence from a psychologist that relocation to Germany would have a very negative effect on the children and severely damage their relationship with their father.

The impact on the 'left-behind' parent will also be considered by the court. However, the courts have emphasised that the impact on either parent is relevant only insofar as it impacts on the child (see, for example, Hedley J in *S v T (Permission to Relocate to Russia)* [2012] EWHC 4023).

(viii) Cultural and religious objections to relocation

Cultural and religious objections to a parent relocating outside the UK will not usually be allowed to prevail over the primary consideration of the child's welfare. Thus, in *Re A (Leave to Remove: Cultural and Religious Considerations)* [2006] EWHC 421 (Fam) Hedley J allowed the child's mother to relocate with her nine-year-old son to the Netherlands where she lived with her new husband, despite the father's arguments that his son should remain in England for religious and cultural reasons (in particular, so that he could succeed to the mantle of head of the family group).

(ix) Shared care and a reassessment of Payne

The following decision of the Court of Appeal is an important case for its discussion of *Payne v Payne*. It shows how the courts approached a case where, unlike in *Payne*, there was no primary carer as both parents shared care of the child. The case also highlighted the need for courts to focus on the welfare of the child and the proper application of the welfare checklist to the particular circumstances of the case, rather than rigidly applying the *Payne* discipline.

▶ *K v K (Relocation: Shared Care Arrangement)* [2011] EWCA Civ 793

The care of two young children was shared as both parents were working part-time. The children spent six consecutive days with the father and eight with the mother each fortnight (though some of these days also involved time with a nanny).

The mother sought leave to relocate with the children to Canada on marriage breakdown as she was unhappy and isolated in London, was not getting on well with the father's family and wanted additional support from her own family. The Cafcass report, while describing the case as finely balanced, recommended that there be no relocation in the immediate future, but that it might be best for the children in three to four years. The trial judge granted leave to relocate, and the father appealed arguing that: the judge had failed to give reasons for departing from the Cafcass recommendations; the judge had directed herself by reference to *Payne* (a primary carer case) when she should have been guided by the decision of Hedley J in *Re Y (Leave to Remove from Jurisdiction)* (a shared care case); and the judge's analysis had been one-sided, in that she had looked only at the mother's case and not adequately addressed his case.

The Court of Appeal allowed the appeal, and remitted the case for a retrial before a different judge. All three judges concluded that the only principle to be extracted from *Payne v Payne* was the paramountcy principle. Black LJ described the welfare principle as being the only 'authentic principle' found in *Payne* and as 'the only truly inescapable principle in the relocation jurisprudence'. Her Ladyship stated that judges were not at liberty to ignore the 'valuable guidance' contained in *Payne*, but that it must be taken into account as guidance, not as a rigid principle. Black LJ also said that an important point which must always be borne in mind is how highly fact specific relocation applications are. Moore-Bick LJ said that the controversy which surrounds *Payne* is the result of a failure to distinguish between legal principle and guidance. His Lordship warned against an unduly mechanistic application of the guidance and reminded the court that, while the decision in *Payne* is binding, the only principle of law enunciated in *Payne* is that the welfare of the child is paramount, and all the rest is merely guidance.

Thorpe LJ, while agreeing that the child's welfare was the paramount consideration, took a different approach to Black LJ (who said that the *Payne* guidance could also be relevant to shared care cases) and said that the guidance in *Payne* was posited on the premise that the applicant is the primary carer of the child. Therefore, where each parent is providing a broadly equal proportion of care and one seeks to relocate externally, he said that the *Payne* 'discipline' should not be utilised.

The case of *K v K* led to some argument about whether or not the *Payne* guidance should apply in a case involving shared care, particularly in light of Thorpe LJ's judgment. However, in *Re F (Relocation)* [2012] EWCA Civ 1364, Munby LJ approved the approach taken by the majority, Black LJ and Moore-Bick LJ, that the guidance given in *Payne* was not confined to cases where the applicant was the primary carer. The *Payne* guidance could be utilised in other kinds of relocation case if the judge considered it helpful and appropriate.

George, commenting on *K v K* (see [2012] CFLQ 108), wondered why the Court of Appeal felt it necessary to emphasise the welfare principle so much when that principle is clearly encapsulated in statute. Eaton, commenting on *K v K* ([2011] Fam Law 1093), stated that, 'though without explicitly doing away with *Payne* (as of course it could not do so), the Court of Appeal has made [a review to the Supreme Court] unnecessary', and that '[t]he golden thread running through all the judgments is that the *Payne* guidance is subordinate to a welfare assessment – in every case'.

The Court of Appeal provided further guidance as to the status of *Payne* and the proper approach to be taken in relocation cases in the following case, where the trial judge was held to have erred in law by relying too heavily on the *Payne* guidance.

▶ *Re F (International Relocation Cases)* [2015] EWCA Civ 882

The father appealed against a decision granting the mother, who was German, permission to relocate from England to Germany with their 12-year-old daughter. The father had contact with the child, including overnight stays. The issue for the Court of Appeal was whether the judge had applied the correct approach to the relocation application and, in particular, whether the trial judge had allowed herself to be constrained by the guidance in *Payne* when carrying out the welfare analysis.

The Court of Appeal allowed the father's appeal and ordered a rehearing. Ryder LJ, who gave the leading judgment, said that the law to be applied in an international child relocation case was that contained in *K v K* [2011] EWCA Civ 793 and *Re F* [2012] EWCA Civ 1364, and that *Payne* was to be read in the context of those authorities and not in substitution for, or in priority over, them. The only principle to be applied when determining an application to remove a child permanently from the jurisdiction was that the welfare of the child was paramount. Selective or partial citation from *Payne* without any wider legal analysis was likely to be regarded as an error of law. The appropriate approach in a relocation case was a holistic evaluative analysis, and such applications might also require a proportionality evaluation because of the likelihood of severing the relationship between the child and one of her parents.

On the facts of the case, the trial judge had attached too great an importance to the discipline in *Payne*, and there was no clear identification of any overall welfare analysis. She had taken no account of the erosion in the quality of the daughter's relationship with the father if she was to move to Germany. High on the list of important questions should have been an evaluation of the harm to the daughter of leave being refused, as against the harm that would result from separation from her father. There had been no proportionality cross-check.

MCFARLANE LJ: [A] 'global, holistic evaluation' is no more than shorthand for the overall, comprehensive analysis of a child's welfare seen as a whole, having regard in particular to the circumstances set out in the relevant welfare checklist.

George [2015] CFLQ 377 argues that *Re F* [2015] represents a further shift in the approach of the courts following *K v K* and 'reduces the significance of *Payne*'. (For a detailed analysis of *Re F* [2015] see Devereux and George [2015] Fam Law 1232).

(c)   Is the approach in relocation cases the correct one?

The approach to international relocation as laid down by the Court of Appeal in *Poel v Poel* and endorsed in *Payne v Payne* (see above) has been the subject of considerable debate and criticism. It is felt that resident parents (often mothers) are favoured too much over the other parent and that the resident parent's welfare, not that of the child, seems to be the primary consideration. In other words, the courts place too much emphasis on the wishes and proposals of the parent who wishes to relocate rather than looking at the best interests of the child from the point of view of having the benefit of maintaining a relationship with both parents. There is also concern that courts are denying children their right to contact with both parents. In addition, *Poel v Poel* was decided in the 1970s when different conceptions of parenthood prevailed in that mothers were usually responsible for the day-to-day care of children and were granted custody, whereas today both parents are often engaged in parenting.

Hayes (2006) argues that trial judges are being prevented by strong rulings from the Court of Appeal from exercising their discretion in relocation cases in a broad and principled manner. She claims that the 'discipline' recommended in *Payne*, and entrenched in subsequent Court of Appeal judgments, is misguided as it places a gloss on the welfare principle, narrows the proper application of that principle and is biased in favour of the residential parent (who is almost invariably the mother). Herring and Taylor (2006) claim that principles adopted in relocation cases fail to take adequate account of the impact of human rights reasoning. Geekie (2008) argues that the approach in relocation cases seems to be at odds with the approach adopted in shared residence cases where the approach has been to shake off 'the shackles of a dated approach to shared parenting'. Pressdee (2008) argues that Thorpe LJ's approach in *Payne* needs to be applied with greater flexibility. Thomas ([2010] Fam Law 982) has argued for 'greater weight to be placed on the best interests of the child being found in the stability and continuity of home, education, community, culture and wider family rather than the relationship abroad with one parent'.

In *Re F (International Relocation Cases)* (see above) Ryder LJ expressed his concerns regarding *Payne* saying:

> [I]n the decade or more since *Payne* it would seem odd indeed for this court to use guidance which out of the context which was intended is redolent with gender based assumptions as to the role and relationships of parents with a child. Likewise, the absence of any emphasis on the child's wishes and feelings or to take the question one step back, the child's participation in the decision making process, is stark.

Some countries take a different view to relocation. For example, the New Zealand Court of Appeal in *D v S* [2002] NZFLR 116 has rejected *Payne v Payne* as the leading precedent in relocation cases on the basis that it puts the mother's needs above those of the child. (For a comparative study of relocation in England and New Zealand, see George [2011] CFLQ 178.) The debate on relocation in England and Wales has also focused on the Washington Declaration on International Family Relocation 2010, which includes a non-exhaustive list of 13 factors for the court to consider when deciding on a child's best interests in a relocation dispute. Mostyn J in *Re AR (A Child: Relocation)* [2010] EWHC 1346 was of the view that the Washington Declaration provided 'a more balanced and neutral approach to a relocation application'. His Lordship was also of the opinion that a review of the ideology of *Poel/Payne* by the Supreme Court is urgently needed. However, in *Re H (Leave to Remove)* [2010] EWCA Civ 915, where the father argued, *inter alia*, that the Washington Declaration should replace the guidance in *Payne*, the Court of Appeal held that, while the Washington Declaration might prove a valuable means of harmonising the approaches to relocation applications in different jurisdictions, it could not replace the guidance in *Payne*.

Despite widespread concern and criticism of the approach to relocation applications, and in the absence of Supreme Court consideration of the law of relocation, *Payne* remains good law. However, the case of *Re F (International Relocation Cases)* (see above) demonstrates the dangers of judges relying too heavily, or exclusively, on the *Payne* guidance.

(d) Temporary removals from the UK

Sometimes a parent may wish to take the child temporarily out of the UK (for example for a holiday). As with permanent relocations, this requires the consent of every person with parental responsibility. If a child arrangements order regulating the child's living arrangements is in force and a person named in such order as someone with whom the child is to live wishes to take the child out of the UK temporarily for more than one month, then the *written* consent of all those with parental responsibility is needed, or otherwise the consent of the court under section 13(1)(b) of the CA 1989. In the following case, the Court of Appeal considered how the courts should deal with applications for temporary removal.

> ▶ *Re A (Temporary Removal from Jurisdiction)* [2004] EWCA Civ 1587
>
> The four-year-old child spent five nights a week with the mother and two nights with the father under the terms of a shared residence order. The mother applied for permission to take the child to South Africa for two years to carry out research for her doctorate. The judge, applying the principles in *Payne v Payne* (see above), refused the application. The Court of Appeal allowed the mother's appeal, as the judge had erred in holding that the considerations which govern decisions about applications for permanent removal of the child should also apply, without modification, to applications for temporary removal. The considerations relevant to an application for permission to relocate permanently were not automatically applicable to applications for temporary removal. Thorpe LJ said: 'The more temporary the removal, the less regard should be paid to the principles stated in *Payne v Payne*.'

Thus, the approach in *Payne* is unlikely to apply, particularly where the temporary removal is for a short duration.

(i) Removal to a non-Hague Convention country

Where one parent wishes to take the child to a country which is not a signatory to the Hague Convention on the Civil Aspects of International Child Abduction 1980 then, if that parent does not return the child, the consequences can be particularly severe (see 13.11). The approach that the court will take was summarised in *Re R* [2013] EWCA Civ 1115 where the Court of Appeal, summarising earlier case-law, said that, in an application for temporary removal to a non-Hague Convention country, the overriding consideration was the best interests of the child and that such cases would involve consideration of the following elements:

a) the magnitude of the risk of the order being breached, if permission is given;
b) the magnitude of the consequences of such a breach; and
c) the level of security that may be achieved by building into the arrangements all of the available safeguards.

(ii) Practical safeguards to ensure the child's return

If there is a risk that a parent will not return after a temporary stay outside the UK, the court in England and Wales can impose certain safeguards. Thus, it may: impose a condition on a court order; require an undertaking to be given to the court; require the parties to enter into a notarised agreement containing provisions about returning the child; require 'mirror' orders (orders equivalent to English orders) to be applied for in the foreign court; order a parent to swear on the Holy Qur'an before a Shariah Court that the child will be returned; and/or order a parent to provide a sum of money as surety for the child's return (see, for example, *Re L (Removal from Jurisdiction: Holiday)* [2001] 1 FLR 241).

The following case provides an example of the court imposing a range of practical safeguards to ensure the children's return.

▶ *Re S (Leave to Remove from Jurisdiction: Securing Return from Holiday)* [2001] 2 FLR 507

The court wished to ensure that the mother would return the children after taking them to India on holiday. She was ordered: to return them by a certain date and not to return them to India without the father's written permission; to deposit the children's passports with her solicitors in India; to provide the father with copies of the airline tickets and the children's visas from the Indian High Commission; to seek only short tourist visas (that order to be served on the Indian High Commission); and not to seek Indian passports or Indian citizenship for the children while in India. The children were made wards of court, and the court made declarations that their habitual residence was England and Wales and that they were British citizens.

The approach in *Re S* above was followed in *Re DS (Removal from Jurisdiction)* [2009] EWHC 1594 (Fam) where a mother wished to take the child to India for a family wedding, but where the child was at risk because the mother had on a previous occasion been a month late in returning from India to the UK. She was granted leave to make the trip on the basis of a range of undertakings and a declaration as to the child's citizenship and habitual residence. (For an example of where permission was refused see *C v K (Children: Application for Temporary Removal to Algeria)* [2014] EWHC 4125 (Fam) where there was a lack of safeguards sufficient to mitigate the clear and identifiable risk that the mother would not return the children from a proposed holiday to Algeria.)

(e) Relocation within the UK

Moving a child from England and Wales to another part of the UK (Scotland or Northern Ireland), unlike moving a child *from* the UK, does not require the oral or written consent of the other parent or anyone else with parental responsibility whether or not a child arrangements order regulating the child's living arrangements is in force. Neither is it a criminal offence under the Child Abduction Act 1984 (see 13.3), although it could constitute the offence of kidnapping.

(i) Steps to prevent removal

A parent (or other person with parental responsibility) who wishes to prevent the other parent (or person with parental responsibility) from moving the child from England and Wales to another part of the UK can apply under the CA 1989 for a prohibited steps order or a child arrangements order regulating the child's living arrangements, with a condition attached under section 11(7), or apply to make the child a ward of court (see 8.7).

(ii) Resolving a dispute about removal

An unresolvable dispute between parents (and other people with parental responsibility for a child) about a child's removal to another part of the UK can be determined by applying for a child arrangements order regulating the child's living arrangements or specific issue order under the CA 1989 (see 10.5 and 10.7). In such a case the court must apply the welfare principle, the welfare checklist and the other principles in section 1 of the CA 1989 (see 10.3). The Court of Appeal has held that a dispute about relocation within the UK must be decided by adopting the same approach as that set out in *Payne v Payne* (see *Re C (Internal Relocation)* [2015] EWCA Civ 1305 below). However, different factors will be relevant because in an internal relocation it is likely, for example, that the distances involved will be less and the amount of change which the child will have to adapt to will be less than that involved with an international relocation. It may therefore be easier for an applicant to succeed in an internal relocation case than in an international case.

(iii) Restricting living arrangements

The Court of Appeal has held that an order, or a condition in an order (which can be made under section 11(7) of the CA 1989), restricting a primary carer's right to choose where they live should be made only in exceptional circumstances (see, for example, *Re E (Residence: Imposition of Conditions)* [1997] 2 FLR 638; and *Re B (Prohibited Steps Order)* [2007] EWCA Civ 1055, where the Court of Appeal allowed the mother's appeal against a prohibited steps order which had prohibited her from changing the child's residence from England and Wales to Northern Ireland).

However, the Court of Appeal has since rejected the notion of an exceptionality principle, as demonstrated in the following case, which clarified the approach to be taken in internal relocation cases:

▶ **Re C (Internal Relocation) [2015] EWCA Civ 1305**

The father appealed against a decision allowing the mother to relocate from London to Cumbria with their ten-year-old daughter. The child spent two nights a week and alternate weekends with the father and they had a good relationship. The judge at first instance permitted the mother to move, because, *inter alia*, of the detrimental impact on the mother if the move was refused and her genuine motivations for relocating, and because the child supported the move. This decision was reached despite a Cafcass report which said that the move would not be in the child's best interests. The father appealed to the Court of Appeal arguing that the trial judge had erred in his overall approach to the case.

The Court of Appeal unanimously dismissed the father's appeal and held that the approach taken by the judge had been correct. Black LJ, who gave the leading judgment, and with whom the other judges agreed, clarified the principles to be applied:

▶ Historically the courts had appeared to adopt a different approach in internal and external relocation cases whereby the freedom of a parent to move appeared to have been accorded greater weight in internal relocation cases than in external relocation cases. However, there was no justification for applying a different approach. In both internal and external relocation cases, the governing principle is the welfare principle.

> ▶ There was no rule that moving a child within the UK could only be prevented in exceptional cases and this had never become a binding, legal principle. Although the courts would be resistant to preventing parents from exercising their choice as to where to live in the UK unless the child's welfare required it, that was not because of a rule that such a move could be prevented only in exceptional cases, but because the welfare analysis led to that conclusion.
> ▶ Guidance as to the factors to be weighed in determining what was in the child's best interests, such as that in *Payne,* was valuable in helping judges to identify the likely important factors, but was not to be applied rigidly.

(For a critique of *Re C* see Bainham [2016] Fam Law 458.)

(iv) Relocation and shared living arrangements

In *Re L (Shared Residence: Relocation)* [2009] EWCA Civ 20 (where there was a shared residence order and the mother wished to move from London to Somerset), the Court of Appeal held, dismissing her appeal, that a shared residence order is not an automatic bar to relocation, as it may well be in the child's best interests to relocate notwithstanding the existence of such an order. It held that the correct approach to relocation in the context of shared residence is for the court to look at the underlying factual substratum in welfare terms bearing in mind the tension which may well exist between a parent's freedom to relocate and the welfare of the child which may militate against relocation. (See also *Re F (Internal Relocation)* [2010] EWCA Civ 1428, where the mother's application by means of a specific issue order to move the four children (who were subject to a shared caring arrangement) to the Orkney Islands in Scotland (as she had strong Scottish connections) was refused at first instance and on appeal on the basis of the circumstances of the case which militated against her being granted permission.)

Summary

▶ The law governing arrangements for children on family breakdown is laid down in the Children Act 1989 (CA 1989). Parents retain parental responsibility for their children on family breakdown (see Chapter 9). For finance and property arrangements for children on parental separation, see Chapter 12.

▶ The Family Justice Review made various recommendations to improve the law governing children and families on family breakdown (such as the introduction of 'parenting agreements' and a new child arrangements order). These recommendations were accepted by the Government, except for the recommendation that there should be no change to the law regarding shared parenting, and led to the enactment of the Children and Families Act 2014.

▶ Many children experience parental relationship breakdown; and this may have an adverse effect on some of them. It is therefore better for children (and parents) if the parties reach agreement about arrangements for their children on family breakdown. Going to court is regarded as the last resort, and other forms of dispute resolution are being increasingly promoted.

▶ Cafcass performs various important functions on family breakdown, namely: making reports for the court if needed; helping parents to reach agreement about contact; and conducting risk assessments. Welfare reports have an important role to play in children's cases.

▶ Jurisdiction in family disputes involving matters of parental responsibility in the EU is governed by Council Regulation (EC) (No. 2201/2003) Concerning Jurisdiction and the Recognition and Enforcement of Judgments in Matrimonial Matters and in Matters of Parental Responsibility (Brussels II Revised).

▶ There has been discussion about introducing a presumption of shared parenting. Although the Family Justice Review was opposed to this, the Government introduced a presumption of parental involvement into the CA 1989, although this does not imply any particular division of the child's time.

▶ In cases dealing with children's disputes on family breakdown (for example in respect of living and contact arrangements), the family courts must ensure that they comply with the European Convention on Human Rights and the jurisprudence of the European Court of Human Rights as a result of their obligations under the Human Rights Act 1998.

▶ An unresolvable dispute about which parent a child should live with on family breakdown can be settled by making an application for a child arrangements order regulating the child's living arrangements under the CA 1989 (see Chapter 10). The welfare of the child is the court's paramount consideration (s 1(1)) and the other welfare principles in section 1 apply. An order for shared living arrangements can be made. Once a child arrangements order regulating the child's living arrangements is made, no person can change the child's surname or remove the child from the UK (except for up to one month) without the *written* consent of all those with parental responsibility, or otherwise with permission of the court (ss 13(1), (2)).

▶ An unresolvable dispute about contact can be determined by an application for a child's arrangements order regulating the child's contact arrangements under section 8 of the CA 1989. The court must apply the welfare principles in section 1 of the Act. Direct contact, indirect contact, supervised contact and an order of no contact are possible options for the court. Hostility to contact by residential parents has caused difficulties for the court. Domestic violence is a serious factor to be considered by the court, and various steps have been put in place to improve protection for children who may experience domestic violence in the context of contact. The European Court of Human Rights recognises the importance of contact between parents and children as part of the right to family life under Article 8 of the European Convention on Human Rights.

▶ Sections 11A–11P of the CA 1989 were enacted to improve and resolve contact difficulties on family breakdown, and include: activity directions and conditions; monitoring contact orders; warning notices; enforcement orders; and compensation orders. These provisions have been extended so that they also apply to orders regulating living arrangements. Other measures for promoting the enforcement and facilitation of contact include: a family assistance order; proceedings for contempt of court; and transferring the living arrangements of the child.

▶ A dispute about a child's surname can be decided by making an application for a specific issue order, or, if a child arrangements order regulating living arrangements is in force, by making an application under section 13 of the CA 1989. The child's welfare, not the parents' wishes, prevails in such proceedings.

Summary cont'd

▶ Where a parent who wishes to take a child out of the UK cannot obtain the consent of the other parent and/or other people with parental responsibility, then they will have to make a relocation application in order to avoid committing a criminal offence or being in contempt of court. The parent who wishes to relocate can apply for a specific issue order, or, if a child arrangements order regulating living arrangements is in force, by making an application under section 13 of the CA 1989. The child's welfare is the court's paramount consideration.

▶ The 'discipline' for deciding relocation applications was laid down by the Court of Appeal in *Payne v Payne* (2001) and this is still the leading case. However, the Court of Appeal has recently emphasised that the primary consideration is the *welfare* of the child and that the *Payne* 'discipline' is merely guidance.

▶ *Payne* is unlikely to apply to an application to take a child temporarily out of the UK (for example for a holiday), unless it is for a considerable period of time. A range of practical safeguards are available for ensuring that a child is returned after a temporary removal.

▶ Moving a child from England and Wales to another part of the UK does not require the oral or written consent of the other parent or anyone else with parental responsibility. Neither is it a criminal offence under the Child Abduction Act 1984, although it could constitute the offence of kidnapping. A person who wishes to prevent a child moving to another part of the UK can apply for a prohibited steps order or a child arrangements order (with a condition attached) or apply to make the child a ward of court.

▶ An unresolvable dispute between parents (and other people with parental responsibility for a child) about a child's removal to another part of the UK can be determined by applying for a child arrangements order regulating the child's living arrangements or a specific issue order under section 8 of the CA 1989. The welfare principles in section 1 of the CA 1989 apply. The court will adopt the same approach to that adopted in *Payne v Payne*.

Further reading and references

Bainham, 'Camberley to Carlisle: where are we now on internal relocation?' [2016] Fam Law 458.

Barnett, 'Contact at all costs? Domestic violence and children's welfare' [2014] CFLQ 439.

Bevan, 'What's in a name? A practitioner's view on reform of residence orders' [2012] Fam Law 862.

Brasse, District Judge, 'The *Payne* threshold: leaving the jurisdiction' [2005] Fam Law 780.

Braver *et al.*, 'Relocation of children after divorce and children's best interests: new evidence and legal considerations' (2003) 17(2) *Journal of Family Psychology* 206.

Bryan, Chief Justice of the Family Court of Australia, 'An Australian perspective on the Family Justice Review' [2012] *International Family Law Journal* 269.

Butler *et al.*, *Divorcing Children: Children's Experience of Their Parents' Divorce*, 2003, Jessica Kingsley.

Devereux and George, '"Alas poor Payne, I knew him ..."': an interpretation of the Court of Appeal's decision in Re F (International Relocation Cases)' [2015] Fam Law 1232.

Douglas, 'Contact is not a commodity to be bartered for money' [2011] Fam Law 491.

Douglas and Ferguson, 'The role of grandparents in divorced families' (2003) *International Journal of Law, Policy and the Family* 41.

Further reading and references cont'd

Eaton, 'Relocation after *K* v *K'* [2011] Fam Law 1093.

Fehlberg, 'Legislating for shared parenting: how the Family Justice Review got it right' [2012] Fam Law 709.

Fortin, Richie and Buchanan, 'Young adults' perceptions of court-ordered contact' [2007] CFLQ 211.

Freeman, 'Relocation and the child's best interests' [2010] *International Family Law* 248.

Geekie, 'Relocation and shared residence: one route or two?' [2008] Fam Law 446.

George, 'Practitioners' views on children's welfare in relocation disputes: comparing approaches in England and New Zealand' [2011] CFLQ 178.

George, 'Reviewing relocation? *Re W (Relocation: Removal Outside Jurisdiction)* [2011] EWCA Civ 345 and *K* v *K (Relocation: Shared Care Arrangement)* [2011] EWCA Civ 793' [2012] CFLQ 108.

Gilmore, 'The *Payne* saga: precedent and family law cases' [2011] Fam Law 970.

Gilmore, 'Contact/shared residence and child well-being: research evidence and its implications for legal decision-making' [2006] *International Journal of Law, Policy and the Family* 344.

Gilmore, 'Court decision-making in shared residence order cases: a critical examination' [2006] CFLQ 478.

Gilmore, 'Disputing contact: challenging some assumptions' [2008] CFLQ 285.

Gilmore, 'The assumption that contact is beneficial: challenging the "secure foundation"' [2008] Fam Law 1226.

Harris and George, 'Parental responsibility and shared residence orders: parliamentary intentions and judicial interpretations' [2010] CFLQ 151.

Hayes, 'Relocation cases: is the Court of Appeal applying the correct principles?' [2006] CFLQ 351.

Henaghan, 'Relocation cases: the rhetoric and the reality of a child's best interests: a view from the bottom of the world' [2011] CFLQ 226.

Herring and Taylor, 'Relocating relocation' [2006] CFLQ 517.

Humphreys and Harrison, 'Focusing on safety – domestic violence and the role of child contact centres' [2003] CFLQ 237.

Hunt, Masson and Trinder, 'Shared parenting: the law, the evidence and guidance from Families Need Fathers' [2009] Fam Law 831.

Johnson, 'Shared residence orders: for and against' [2009] Fam Law 131.

Kaganas, 'Regulating emotion: judging contact disputes' [2011] CFLQ 63.

Kaganas, '*Re L (Contact: Domestic Violence); Re V (Contact: Domestic Violence); Re M (Contact: Domestic Violence); Re H (Contact: Domestic Violence)*: contact and domestic violence' [2000] CFLQ 311.

Murch with Keehan, *The Voice of the Child in Private Family Law Proceedings*, 2003, Family Law.

Newnham, 'Shared residence: lessons from Sweden' [2011] CFLQ 251.

Nickols, 'A presumption of shared parenting: long awaited or misguided?' [2012] Fam Law 573.

Perry, '*Payne v Payne* – leave to remove from the jurisdiction' [2001] CFLQ 455.

Pressdee, 'Relocation, relocation, relocation: rigorous scrutiny revisited' [2008] Fam Law 220.

Reece, 'UK women's groups' child contact campaign: "so long as it is safe"' [2006] CFLQ 538.

Further reading and references cont'd

Relocation and Leave to Remove, A Report by Custody Minefield (www.thecustodyminefield.com), December 2009.

Rhoades, 'Legislating to promote children's welfare and the quest for certainty' [2012] CLQ 158.

Spon-Smith, 'Relocation revisited' [2004] Fam Law 191.

Thomas, 'Gain a new country but lose a child' [2010] Fam Law 982.

Thomas LJ, 'Relocation development' [2010] Fam Law 565.

Thorpe LJ, 'Relocation: the search for common principles' [2010] *International Family Law* 242.

Trinder, 'Shared residence: a review of recent research evidence' [2010] Fam Law 1192.

Wall J, 'Making contact' [2003] Fam Law 275.

Wall LJ, 'Making contact work in 2009' [2009] Fam Law 590.

Worwood, 'International relocation – the debate' [2005] Fam Law 621.

Websites

Association for Shared Parenting: www.sharedparenting.org.uk

Cafcass: www.cafcass.gov.uk

Families Need Fathers: www.fnf.org.uk

Family and Parenting Institute: www.familyandparenting.org

National Association of Child Contact Centres: www.naccc.org.uk

Links to relevant websites can also be found at: www.palgravehighered.com/law/familylaw9e

Chapter 12

Financial provision for children

All parents have a duty to provide financial support for their children, and this obligation continues when parental relationships break down. Financial provision for children is usually made in the form of periodical payments (child maintenance), although the family courts also have powers to make lump sum and property orders to or for the benefit of a child.

12.1 Child maintenance

Child maintenance is regular financial support towards a child's everyday living costs whereby the parent who does not have the main day-to-day care of the child pays specified sums of money to the parent or person who has the main day-to-day care of that child. Most parents reach their own agreements about how much the parent without day-to-day care of the child should pay by way of maintenance. However, if separated parents are unable to agree, they may need to rely on the statutory child maintenance scheme which is contained in the Child Support Act 1991 (CSA 1991) and is administered by the Government's Child Maintenance Service (formerly known as the Child Support Agency). In certain, limited situations it may be possible to seek child maintenance through the family courts.

(a) The development of the law

Until April 1993, child maintenance disputes were heard by the courts, which had discretionary powers to make maintenance orders for children according to the circumstances of each case. However, in 1990, as a result of dissatisfaction with the court-based system, radical new proposals were made to move most child maintenance disputes from the courts to a Government agency, the Child Support Agency (see the White Paper *Children Come First*, Cm 1264). The case for reform was based on various arguments, for example that the discretion-based court system was resulting in arbitrary and unpredictable awards and that it was 'unnecessarily fragmented, uncertain in its results, slow and ineffective' (para 2). Also, the fact that many fathers were failing to fulfil their child maintenance obligations meant that the cost was being thrown onto the State, and consequently onto the taxpayer. Thus, the welfare needs of children were not being sufficiently protected.

The proposed changes were passed into law by the CSA 1991 which: transferred the task of assessing, reviewing, collecting and enforcing child maintenance from the courts to the Child Support Agency; prohibited the courts from making maintenance orders for children where the Child Support Agency had jurisdiction to make a maintenance assessment; and introduced a formula for calculating child maintenance. Right from the beginning, and up till the present day, the scheme has been riddled with problems, in particular, in respect of enforcement of payments, delays in assessments and errors in calculation. By July 2006, £3 billion was owed in unpaid child maintenance and the Child Support Agency had a backlog of 300,000 cases.

In February 2006 the Government commissioned Sir David Henshaw to investigate the scheme and make suggestions for reform. In his report (*Recovering Child Support: Routes to Responsibility*, Cm 6894, DWP, 2006) he identified major failings in the system and recommended it be replaced with a completely new system where the emphasis would be on parents making private child maintenance agreements and where difficult cases would be dealt with by a new body with tougher enforcement powers. In July 2006, the Government's response to the Henshaw Report was presented to Parliament (*A Fresh Start: Child Support Redesign*, Cm 6895, DWP). This was followed in December 2006 by a White Paper (*A New System of Child Maintenance*, Cm 6979, DWP) which set out a new child maintenance system that would empower parents to take responsibility for making their own child maintenance agreements and radically strengthen enforcement powers in cases of non-compliance.

As a result of the above discussions and recommendations, changes to the child maintenance system were made by the Child Maintenance and Other Payments Act 2008 (CMOPA 2008) in order to encourage parents to make their own agreements, to strengthen collection and enforcement procedures, and to improve the assessment process. The CMOPA 2008 created a new body, the Child Maintenance and Enforcement Commission, with responsibility for the work of the Child Support Agency and for 'Child Maintenance Options', a new information and support service. However, the Child Maintenance and Enforcement Commission was abolished on 1 August 2012 and its work was transferred to the Department for Work and Pensions, which now manages the child maintenance system. It funds information and support for separating parents, including the Child Maintenance Options service; and it is responsible for running the statutory child maintenance scheme which has been transferred from the Child Support Agency to the Child Maintenance Service.

Discussions of reform have continued. Thus, in January 2011, the Coalition Government published a Green Paper on the future of the child maintenance system (*Strengthening Families, Promoting Parental Responsibility: The Future of Child Maintenance*, Cm 7990, DWP). This was followed, in July 2012, by the publication of a consultation paper (*Public Consultation: Supporting Separated Families; Securing Children's Futures*, Cm 8399, DWP), setting out the Government's vision for transforming the child maintenance system so that the emphasis is placed on supporting families to make their own arrangements.

There have, however, been some concerns about the reduction in State intervention. Thus, for example, research funded by the Nuffield Foundation found that private arrangements for paying child maintenance were difficult to sustain over time (see Bryson *et al.*, *Kids Aren't Free: The Child Maintenance Arrangements of Single Parents on Benefit*, 2012).

Changes brought in by the CMOPA 2008 have come into force gradually. Thus, a new formula for calculating child maintenance has been rolled out which is based on the payer's gross income, rather than their net income. This applies to all applications made after 23 November 2013. Charges have also been introduced for parents wishing to use the statutory child maintenance scheme. In an attempt to tackle the problem of non-payment, tougher enforcement powers have also been introduced (see 12.1(b)(iv) below).

(b)   Maintenance options

Separated parents have several options with respect to making child maintenance arrangements. If they are in agreement then they can make a private 'family-based arrangement' between themselves (see below). They can also apply to the court for a consent order containing an agreement about child maintenance (see 7.9 and 12.2(b) below). If they cannot agree on child maintenance, either party can apply to the Child Maintenance Service for a maintenance calculation (see 12(b)(ii) below). In certain circumstances, the court has jurisdiction to make financial provision for a child (see 12.1(d) and 12.2 below). Thus, in certain circumstances parents can apply for child maintenance from the court, for example for school fees or provision for disabled children (ss 8(7), and 8(8)). Parents can also make applications to the court for lump sum and property orders to or for the benefit of a child, as capital provision for children is not dealt with by the CSA 1991.

(i) A private 'family-based' agreement

Parents can make their own private agreements about child maintenance. The problem with this option is that, as the agreement is not legally binding, enforcement can be a problem as can varying the agreement when circumstances change. The amount of child maintenance agreed upon may also be inadequate. If the agreement breaks down or is considered to be unsatisfactory, either parent can apply to the Child Maintenance Service.

(c)   The Government's child maintenance scheme

The Department for Work and Pensions is responsible for the child maintenance scheme. It funds information and support for separating parents and runs the statutory scheme which is operated through the Child Maintenance Service. The powers and duties of the Child Maintenance Service are set out in the CSA 1991.

(i) The welfare of the child

Unlike court applications, the welfare of the child plays a limited role in applications for child maintenance under the CSA 1991. Thus, a duty to consider the welfare of any child arises only in respect of any discretionary decisions made by the Child Maintenance Service (s 2). However, as section 2 applies to *any* child affected by a decision, the duty is not limited to children for whose benefit the child maintenance is being sought but can include, for example, children in the payer's own household and the payer's own children from a new relationship (see *Brookes v Secretary of State for Work and Pensions* [2010] EWCA Civ 420).

(ii) Applicants and 'qualifying' children

An application to the Child Maintenance Service can be made by the person with care of the child (a parent or other person who is responsible for the main day-to-day care of the child, such as a grandparent) or by the parent without care of the child, provided:

- the person with care of the child lives in the UK (s 44);
- the parent without care of the child lives in the UK (s 44(1)) or, if they are not habitually resident in the UK, works in the civil service, the armed forces or for a UK-based company (s 44(2A)); and
- the child is under 16 or the child is under 20 and either in full-time education (not including higher education) or the person with care of the child is registered for Child Benefit (s 55).

An application to the Child Maintenance Service *cannot* be made if: there is a court order in place regarding child maintenance which was made before 3 March 2003; or if a court order was made after 3 March 2003 and that order has been in place for less than 12 months (s 4).

(iii) How is statutory child maintenance calculated?

The Child Maintenance Service calculates the amount of child maintenance using different rates, depending on the paying parent's gross weekly income. The rules are complex and what follows is an overview only. When the Child Maintenance Service is working out the paying parent's gross weekly income they will disregard certain payments, such as pension contributions and tax credits. Adjustments are also made for 'relevant other children' which include children of the payer for which they or their partner get child benefit and/or where there is a shared care arrangement (see further below). In summary, the rates applied at the time of writing include the following:

- *The Basic Plus Rate* This applies if the payer's gross weekly income is between £800 and £3,000. They will pay the following percentage in child maintenance on their income above the basic rate (see below): 9 per cent for one qualifying child; 12 per cent for two qualifying children; and 15 per cent for three or more qualifying children.
- *The Basic Rate* This applies if the paying parent's gross weekly income is between £200 and £800. They will pay the following percentage of their gross weekly income as child maintenance: 12 per cent for one qualifying child; 16 per cent for two qualifying children; and 19 per cent for three or more qualifying children.
- *The Reduced Rate* This applies if the paying parent's gross weekly income is between £100 and £200. They will pay a flat rate of £7 on the first £100 and the following percentage of their gross weekly income over £100 as child maintenance: 17 per cent for one qualifying child; 25 per cent for two qualifying children; and 31 per cent for three or more qualifying children.
- *The Flat Rate* This applies if the payer's gross weekly income is between £5 and £100 and they do not qualify for the Nil Rate. It also applies if the paying parent or their partner gets certain benefits such as income support. They will pay £7 as child maintenance no matter how many qualifying or relevant other children are involved.
- *The Nil Rate* This applies in certain situations, for example where the paying parent's gross weekly income is below £7. They will not pay child maintenance.

Special rules apply in the following situations:

▶ If the care of a child is shared by both parents for 52 or more nights a year, a discount is made when calculating the amount of child maintenance payable. If, however, there is equal shared care then no child maintenance is payable.

▶ Where the payer's gross weekly income exceeds the maximum that can be taken into account when making a calculation (currently £3,000), then the parent with care can apply to the court for 'top-up' child maintenance (s 8(6)) (see 12.1(d), 12.2 and 12.3 below).

▶ Variations from the formula (upward or downward) are permitted in certain circumstances (see Schedule 4B, Part 1, CSA 1991 and Part 5 of the Child Support Maintenance Calculation Regulations 2012/2677). An upward variation can be made for special expenses incurred by the payer, for example contact costs, looking after a disabled child, boarding school fees and some prior debts; and it may also be permitted if the payer has additional income or has diverted their income.

(iv) How is statutory child maintenance paid?

The payer can pay child maintenance directly to the other parent or use the Child Maintenance Service's collection service.

(v) How are statutory child maintenance payments enforced?

Enforcement has proved to be one of the major difficulties of the child maintenance system. The following enforcement measures are currently available when a payer defaults with respect to a maintenance calculation made by the Child Maintenance Service:

▶ *A deduction from earnings order (section 31)* This order, which is made by the Child Maintenance Service and is usually the first step it takes, instructs the payer's employer to make deductions of child maintenance from the payer's earnings or pension and send them to the Child Maintenance Service which then passes the payments onto the person with care of the child. An employer who fails to comply with the order, without good reason, can be taken to court and fined.

▶ *A deduction order (sections 32A–32F)* A regular deduction order (s 32A) is an order made by the Child Maintenance Service which orders the deduction of regular payments of child maintenance from a deposit or other account held by the defaulter (for example a bank or a building society account). A lump sum deduction order (ss 32E and 32F) requires a deposit-taker of a deposit or savings account held by the defaulter to pay the Child Maintenance Service any outstanding arrears of child maintenance.

▶ *A liability order (section 33)* If it is not appropriate to make the above orders, or such an order is ineffective, the Child Maintenance Service can apply to the magistrates' court for a liability order. Once the order is made, the Child Maintenance Service can then take various steps to ensure payment, for example by: arranging for sale and seizure of the defaulter's goods by a bailiff; obtaining a third-party debt order in the county court freezing funds in the defaulter's bank or building society; or charging and selling the defaulter's property to make payment. As the Child Maintenance Service can enter a liability order on the Register of Judgments, Orders and Fines, the order can affect the defaulter's credit rating. It has been held that the court has no power to challenge the actual assessment (s 33(4)) (see *Farley v Secretary of State for Work and Pensions* [2006] UKHL 31; and *Child Support Agency v Learad; Child Support Agency v Buddles* [2008] EWHC 2193 (Admin)). In *R (Joplin) v Child Maintenance and Enforcement Commission* [2010] EWHC 1623 (Admin) it was held that considerations of the welfare of any children should ideally be taken into account before an application is made for a liability order, and any such consideration should be properly minuted and taken in a robust and transparent way.

▶ *An avoidance of disposition order (section 32L)* The Child Maintenance Service can apply for an order restraining or setting aside the disposal or transfer of assets made with the intention of avoiding payment of child maintenance. The Child Maintenance Service must prove that a person: has failed to pay an amount of child maintenance; and, with the intention of avoiding payment, is about to make a disposition or to transfer out of the jurisdiction or otherwise deal with any property.

▶ *Other measures: removal of a driving licence and imprisonment* If the above enforcement measures fail, more severe measures can be imposed. Thus, the Child Maintenance Service can apply to the magistrates' court for an order removing a defaulter's driving licence for up to two years (or preventing the defaulter from obtaining one) if there is wilful refusal or culpable neglect in respect of paying child maintenance (ss 39A and 40B). In the last resort, a defaulter may be committed to prison, on proof of wilful refusal or culpable neglect to make payment (s 40).

(vi) Human rights and enforcement measures

All of the enforcement measures above must be human rights compliant. In *Karoonian v CMEC; Gibbons v CMEC* [2012] EWCA Civ 1379 the Court of Appeal condemned the Child Maintenance and Enforcement Commission (the precursor to the Child Maintenance Service) for giving two fathers suspended jail sentences without attempting other, less serious enforcement measures first. Ward LJ said that the procedures adopted by the Child Maintenance and Enforcement Commission did not comply with the right to a fair trial under Article 6 of the European Convention for the Protection of Human Rights (ECHR) as they obliged the defendants to incriminate themselves. His Lordship also criticised the Child Maintenance and Enforcement Commission's practices as they sought to shift the burden of proof for establishing the defendants' liability from themselves to the defendants.

(vii) A parent cannot institute court proceedings to enforce statutory child maintenance payments

Legal actions have been brought in the courts by parents wanting to challenge the Child Maintenance Service's failure to enforce the payment of arrears of child maintenance. However, their claims have been dismissed for policy reasons; and on the basis that the CSA 1991 provides a complete code for child maintenance, including its enforcement. The following cases provide examples.

> ▶ *R (On the Application of Kehoe) v Secretary of State for Work and Pensions* [2005]
> **UKHL 48**
>
> After various enforcement measures taken by the Child Support Agency had failed, the
> mother brought judicial review proceedings seeking a declaration of incompatibility under
> section 4(2) of the Human Rights Act 1998 (HRA 1998) on the basis that the enforcement
> provisions of the CSA 1991 were incompatible with her right to a fair trial under Article 6 of
> the ECHR, as they precluded a parent from bringing enforcement proceedings in the court
> in her own name or on behalf of her children. She also sought a declaration that the delay
> by the Child Support Agency constituted a breach of her Article 6 rights; and she claimed
> damages under section 7 of the HRA 1998. After her claim failed at first instance and on
> appeal to the Court of Appeal, she appealed to the House of Lords.
>
> The House of Lords by a majority dismissed her appeal, holding that the claimant had
> no substantive right in domestic law which was capable of engaging in Convention law of engaging
> the guarantees that were afforded with regard to 'civil rights and obligations' by Article
> 6(1). Enforcement was, by virtue of section 4 of the CSA 1991, exclusively a matter for the
> Secretary of State. As Article 6(1) was not engaged, the Child Support Agency could not
> be said to have acted unlawfully within the meaning of section 7 of the HRA 1998; and
> accordingly the claimant had no remedy under that Act.
>
> Baroness Hale, however, dissented, on the basis that the case involved the civil rights of
> children:
>
> > [I]f I am right that the children's civil rights to be properly maintained by their parents are
> > engaged, it follows that the public authority which is charged by Parliament with securing
> > the determination and enforcement of their rights is under a duty to act compatibly
> > with their Article 6 right to the speedy determination and effective enforcement of
> > those rights .... Just as the courts, as public authorities, have to act compliantly with the
> > Convention rights, so does the Agency.

The mother took her case to the European Court of Human Rights (see *Kehoe v UK
(Application No. 2010/06)* [2008] ECHR 528) but her claim was unanimously dismissed
as there had been no breach of Article 6 of the ECHR.

In the following case the High Court adopted a similar approach to that taken by
the House of Lords in *Kehoe*.

> ▶ *Treharne v Secretary of State for Work and Pensions* [2008] EWHC 3222 (QB)
>
> The applicants were adults who had been denied child maintenance owed to them during
> their minority, because of failures on the part of the Child Support Agency to take steps
> to enforce payment. They argued that the Child Support Agency's maladministration had
> violated their right to family life under Article 8 of the ECHR, and they sought damages.
> Their claim failed. Cranston J, dismissing their appeal, held that the failure of the Child
> Support Agency to function effectively and to enforce the maintenance assessments could
> not found a claim for damages, as Article 8 of the ECHR did not include an economic right
> to reasonably regular maintenance from the State.

In the following case a claim in negligence was made against the Child Support
Agency for failing to enforce arrears of child maintenance, but, like the cases above,
the claim failed.

> ▶ *R (Rowley) v Secretary of State for Work and Pensions* [2007] EWCA Civ 598
>
> The mother and her three children sued the Child Support Agency in negligence for failure to enforce the child maintenance due. Their claim failed. The Court of Appeal held that there was no assumption of responsibility on the part of the Secretary of State; and to impose a duty of care in negligence would not be an incremental development of the law but a massive extension of it. The CSA 1991 provided a set of remedies; and to impose a duty of care in negligence would be inconsistent with the statutory scheme.

Rowley was essentially a policy decision to stop a flood of claims being brought by aggrieved parents and children.

(viii) Appeals

An appeal against a maintenance calculation can be made to the First-tier Tribunal (s 20). Appeals on matters of law can be taken to the Upper Tribunal (s 24), from whom there is a further right of appeal on a question of law to the Court of Appeal (s 25).

(d)   The Child Support Act 1991 and the role of the courts

The court has jurisdiction to order child maintenance in the following situations: where the Child Maintenance Service has made a maximum maintenance calculation in relation to a payer (i.e. the payer receives weekly gross income of more than £3,000) (s 8(6)); for school fees and fees for advanced education or training for a trade, profession or vocation (s 8(7)); for a disabled child (s 8(8)); for a child who is not a 'qualifying child' under the CSA 1991; when making, varying and enforcing a consent order which embodies child maintenance (s 8(5)); where child maintenance is required from the person who has care of the child (s 8(10)); and where the Child Maintenance Service has no jurisdiction to make a maintenance calculation (for example because the paying parent is not habitually resident in the UK). In *Dickson v Rennie* [2014] EWHC 4306 (Fam) the court confirmed that the court's jurisdiction to 'top up' child maintenance under section 8(6) was available only once the Child Maintenance Service had made a maximum maintenance calculation. In this case, the payee alleged that the payer's income was far greater than that determined by the Child Maintenance Service but the court held that she could not ask the court to determine the payer's true income; and she would instead have to pursue an appeal against the Child Maintenance Service.

The courts do, however, have jurisdiction to make lump sum and property orders for children (see 12.2 and 12.3 below), whether or not an application for child maintenance is made to the Child Maintenance Service.

12.2   Finance and property orders for children from the court

(a)   Introduction

The family courts have jurisdiction to make finance and property orders for children under the following Acts of Parliament: the Domestic Proceedings and Magistrates' Courts Act 1978; the Matrimonial Causes Act 1973 (MCA 1973); the Civil Partnership

Act 2004 (CPA 2004); and the Children Act 1989 (CA 1989). Applications for child maintenance can be heard in the courts only if the Child Maintenance Service does not have jurisdiction to deal with it (see 12.1(d) above). However, as the CSA 1991 is intended to encourage parents to make their own private arrangements, it is possible for parents to apply to court for a consent order containing an agreement about child maintenance, for example as part of resolving their finances after divorce or dissolution proceedings (s 8(5)).

Applications can be made to the court for lump sum orders and property orders to or for the benefit of a child, but, because of the cost of bringing proceedings and the need for sufficient resources against which orders can be made, applications are usually made only where substantial assets are involved (see, for example, *Re C (Financial Provision)* [2007] 2 FLR 13 where capital provision of £2 million was ordered for a child).

(b) Orders for children on divorce and dissolution

Under Part II of the MCA 1973 the divorce court has jurisdiction to make the following orders to or for the benefit of any child of the family: periodical payments orders (maintenance), provided the CSA 1991 does not preclude it; and lump sum orders (s 23). It also has the power to make the following property orders to or for the benefit of a child of the family (s 24): a transfer of property order; a settlement of property order; an order varying an ante-nuptial agreement; a post-nuptial settlement for the benefit of the child; and an order for the sale of property (s 24A). These orders can also be made on the annulment of a marriage or on judicial separation (for more on these orders, see Chapter 7).

These orders can be made for 'a child of the family', that is, one who has been treated by the parties as their child (s 52). This includes the parties' own child, any step-child and a privately fostered child (but not a child in local authority care). An order can be made in relation to: a child under 18; or a child over 18 who is, will be or would be (if an order were made) receiving instruction at an educational establishment or undergoing training for a trade, profession or vocation, or where special circumstances justify an order being made (s 29).

When exercising its discretion, the court must consider all the circumstances of the case, including in particular (s 25(3)): the child's financial needs, income, earning capacity (if any), property and other financial resources; any physical or mental disability of the child; and the manner in which the child is expected to be educated or trained. It must also take into account factors (a)–(d) of the statutory checklist in section 25(2) of the MCA 1973 (see Chapter 7).

Where the court is exercising its powers against a spouse in favour of a child of the family who is not that person's child (such as a step-child) the court must also consider (s 25(4)): whether that spouse assumed any responsibility for child maintenance, and, if so, the extent to which, and the basis upon which, they assumed such responsibility and the length of time for which that party discharged such responsibility; whether in assuming and discharging such responsibility that party did so knowing that the child was not their own; and the liability of any other person to maintain the child.

Similar provisions to those above apply in respect of the dissolution, annulment or separation of a civil partnership (see s 72(1) and Sch 1 to the CPA 2004).

(i) Consent orders

Spouses and civil partners can apply for a consent order in respect of financial arrangements for their children (including child maintenance), which the court has jurisdiction to make under the MCA 1973 and the CPA 2004 (see 7.9). The advantage of a consent order is that, unlike a private arrangement about financial provision for a child, it can be enforced by the court if it is breached.

(c) Orders for children during a marriage or civil partnership

Finance and property orders can be sought from the court to or for the benefit of children during the subsistence of a marriage or civil partnership. However, applications are virtually non-existent as married couples and civil partners are unlikely to take such steps during the subsistence of their relationship, and, in any event, child maintenance can be sought using the various options listed in 12.1(b) above. At one time, however, when divorce was uncommon, these powers were exercised more often.

(i) The Domestic Proceedings and Magistrates' Courts Act 1978

Under the Act, the family courts can make periodical payments orders and lump sum orders for parties to a marriage and children of the family. Lump sums are limited to a maximum sum (s 2(3)). An applicant spouse must prove that the other spouse (the respondent): (a) has failed to provide reasonable maintenance for the applicant; (b) has failed to provide, or to make a proper contribution towards, reasonable maintenance for any child of the family; (c) has behaved in such a way that the applicant cannot reasonably be expected to live with the respondent; or (d) has deserted the applicant (s 1).

The statutory criteria which the court must apply when exercising its discretion are similar to those which must be applied by the divorce court in proceedings for financial relief (see 7.4), but with the additional requirement that the court must consider whether to exercise any of its powers under the CA 1989 (s 8). Similar provisions apply to civil partnerships under section 72(3) and Schedule 6 to the CPA 2004.

(ii) The Matrimonial Causes Act 1973

Under section 27 of the MCA 1973 either spouse can apply to the court for reasonable maintenance (periodical payments and lump sums) on the ground that the other spouse has: (a) failed to provide reasonable maintenance for the applicant; or (b) failed to provide, or to make a proper contribution towards, reasonable maintenance for any child of the family (s 27(1)). Similar provisions also apply to civil partnerships (see s 72(1) and Sch 5 to the CPA 2004).

12.3 Finance and property orders for children under the Children Act 1989

Under section 15 and Schedule 1 to the Children Act 1989 (CA 1989) the family court has jurisdiction to make periodical payments orders, lump sum orders and property orders to or for the benefit of children aged under 18, and for some 'children' aged over 18. The court can make these orders only on an application, unless it is making, varying or discharging a special guardianship order, a child arrangements order regulating the child's living arrangements (para 1(6)) or the child is a ward of court (para 1(7)), when it can make any of these orders of its own motion.

(a) Importance of Schedule 1 for unmarried couples and their children

Schedule 1 is particularly important for unmarried couples and their children because, unlike married couples and civil partners, it is the *only* jurisdiction of the courts available to them if they wish to make applications about property and/or finance for the benefit of their children on family breakdown. However, it is important to remember that the purpose of Schedule 1 is to benefit the child concerned, not the parent caring for them (see 12.3(f) below).

(i) Who is a 'parent' against whom an application can be made for financial provision under Schedule 1?

The people against whom an application can be made under Schedule 1 are confined to: biological parents; people who have become parents by operation of law (such as by adoption or pursuant to the provisions of the Human Fertilisation and Embryology Acts 1990 and 2008); and people otherwise included by paragraph 16 of Schedule 1 (namely a spouse or civil partner who had treated the child as a child of the family). An application under Schedule 1 cannot be made against a person merely by reason of that person being a social or psychological parent of the child. Thus, for example, in *T v B (Parental Responsibility: Financial Provision)* [2010] EWHC 1444 (Fam), Moylan J held that a former lesbian partner who was not the civil partner of a mother whose child was conceived by artificial insemination by an unknown donor was not a 'parent' for the purposes of Schedule 1 even though she was clearly a social and psychological parent of the child and had acquired parental responsibility by virtue of having obtained a shared residence order.

(b) Orders under paragraph 1

On an application by a parent, guardian or special guardian of a child, or by any person who is named in a child arrangements order as a person with whom a child is to live, the court may make any of the following orders against either or both parents of a child (paras 1(1), (2)):

▶ a periodical payments order (maintenance);
▶ a lump sum order, which may include an order to enable expenses to be met in connection with the birth or maintenance of the child which were reasonably incurred before the making of the order (Sch 1, para 5(1));
▶ a settlement of property order; and
▶ a transfer of property order.

These orders can be made in favour of the applicant for the benefit of the child or in favour of the child. Thus, for example, an order may be made requiring a parent to pay regular monthly sums to the parent with day-to-day care of the child, or, in the case of an older child, payments might be made to the child directly.

The powers conferred under paragraph 1 may be exercised at any time (para 1(3)). Periodical payment orders can be varied and discharged (see (c) below). The court can make further periodical payments orders and lump sum orders with respect to a child who has not reached the age of 18, but it cannot make more than one settlement of property order and more than one transfer of property order (para 1(5)). This is so, even though paragraph 1(3) provides that the power to make such orders can be 'exercised at any time' (see *Phillips v Peace* [2004] EWHC 3180 (Fam)).

(c)　Orders under paragraph 2

On the application of a person over 18, the court may make periodical payments orders and lump sum orders in their favour against one or both of their parents. However, unlike orders under paragraph 1, such orders cannot be made against a spouse or civil partner who had treated the person as a child of the family (para 16). These orders can be made on the application of a person aged over 18 who is, will be or (if an order were made) would be receiving instruction at an educational establishment or undergoing training for a trade, profession or vocation (whether or not while in gainful employment). The court can also make an order where special circumstances exist. An application under paragraph 2 cannot be made by any person if, immediately before they reached the age of 16, a periodical payments order was in force with respect to them (para 2(3)). No order can be made under paragraph 2 if the applicant's parents are living with each other in the same household (para 2(4)).

(d)　Variation and discharge of periodical payments

Periodical payments orders made under Schedule 1 can be varied or discharged on the application of any person by or to whom payments were required to be made (paras 1(4) and 2(5)). In exercising these powers, the court must have regard to all the circumstances of the case, including any change in any of the matters to which the court was to have regard when making the order (para 6(1)).

(e)　Agreements about maintenance

Under paragraph 10(3) of Schedule 1 to the CA 1989 the court has jurisdiction to alter the terms of an agreement about maintenance where it appears just to do so having regard to all the circumstances in cases: where there has been a change of circumstances; or where the agreement does not contain proper financial arrangements with respect to the child. In *Morgan v Hill* [2006] EWCA Civ 1602, the Court of Appeal held that it was not necessary to demonstrate that such an agreement was massively inadequate in order to obtain a judicial award greater than the agreed settlement.

(f) The exercise of judicial discretion in Schedule 1 proceedings

Each case depends on its own facts, but, when deciding whether to exercise its powers to make orders under paragraphs 1 and 2, and, if so, in what manner, the court must have regard to all the circumstances, including the following (para 4(1)):

(a) the income, earning capacity, property and other financial resources which the applicant, parents and the person in whose favour the order would be made has, or is likely to have, in the foreseeable future;

(b) the financial needs, obligations and responsibilities which the persons named in (a) have or are likely to have in the foreseeable future;

(c) the financial needs of the child;

(d) the income, earning capacity (if any), property and other financial resources of the child;

(e) any physical or mental disability of the child; and

(f) the manner in which the child is being, or is expected to be, educated or trained.

Where the court is exercising its powers under paragraph 1 against a person who is not the child's mother or father (such as in the case of a step-child), the court must also consider (para 4(2)):

(a) whether that person has assumed responsibility for the child's maintenance and, if so, the extent to which and the basis on which that responsibility was assumed and the length of the period during which he met that responsibility;

(b) whether he did so knowing that the child was not his child;

(c) the liability of any other person to maintain the child.

(g) The approach of the courts

The court adopts the following approach in applications under Schedule 1 to the CA 1989.

(i) The child's welfare

Although paragraph 4(1) does not expressly refer to the child's welfare, and the paramountcy principle in section 1(1) CA 1989 does not apply (s 105(1)), the child's welfare is nonetheless taken into account as part of the court's duty to have regard to all the circumstances; and the child's welfare is 'a constant influence on the discretionary outcome' (*per* Thorpe LJ in *Re P (Child: Financial Provision)* [2003] EWCA Civ 837, approving Hale J in *J v C (Child: Financial Provision)* [1999] 1 FLR 152).

(ii) The child's standard of living

Although paragraph 4 of Schedule 1 makes no mention of the child's standard of living as a factor to be taken into account, the court may take it into account in an appropriate case (see *Re P (Child: Financial Provision)* [2003] EWCA Civ 837, where Thorpe LJ, approving Hale J in *J v C (Child: Financial Provision)* (see above), said that the child was entitled to be brought up in circumstances which bore some sort of relationship to the father's current resources and present standard of living; and *F v G (Child: Financial Provision)* [2004] EWHC 1848 (Fam)).

(iii) The child's entitlement under Schedule 1

The entitlement to financial provision under Schedule 1 arises only during the child's dependency (or until the child has finished full-time education), unless there are special circumstances, for example, if the child has a disability (para 3(2)). For this reason, the court will normally make orders to last during the child's dependency or until the child has finished full-time education (see, for example, *Re P (Child: Financial Provision)* (see above)). This also applies to the provision of a home for the child.

(iv) A home for the child

In respect of the home, the court may make a settlement of property order (a *'Mesher'* type property adjustment order, see 7.7) settling the home on the primary carer for the benefit of the child, so that ownership reverts back to the owner at the end of the child's dependency or full-time education. For example, in *J v C (Child: Financial Provision)* [1999] 1 FLR 152, where the father had won £1.4 million on the National Lottery, Hale J made an order requiring the father to purchase a house for the child to live in with her mother which would be held on trust for the child's benefit throughout her dependency but which would revert back to her father when she reached the age of 21 or finished full-time education, whichever was later. Hale J observed that '[t]here is a long line of authority ... that children are entitled to provision during their dependency and for their education, but they are not entitled to a settlement beyond that, unless there are exceptional circumstances such as a disability, however rich their parents may be'. Thus, for example, in *MT v OT (Financial Provision: Costs)* [2007] EWHC 838 (Fam), where the father was worth £40 million, the court held that, although there is power under Schedule 1, paragraph 1 to order an absolute transfer of property to a child, special circumstances would be required. The extreme wealth of the father was not such a circumstance and so the court ordered that the property would revert to the father once the children had completed their tertiary education.

(v) Financial provision for the benefit of the child

The courts will guard against claims disguised as being for the benefit of a child when they are really for the benefit of the parent who is caring for the child (*per* Thorpe LJ in *Re P (Child: Financial Provision)* (see above), approving Hale J in *J v C (Child: Financial Provision)* (see above)). Nonetheless, the courts have taken a flexible approach in their interpretation of 'for the benefit of the child' and so awards have included: provision for payment of an applicant parent's debts (*Re: M-M (A child)* [2014] EWCA Civ 276); a lump sum to enable the applicant parent to buy a car (*PG v TW (No. 2) (Child: Financial Provision)* [2014] 1 FLR 923); provision for a gardener, domestic help and property repairs (*N v D* [2008] 1 FLR 1629); and a lump sum for home decoration and furniture (*Re P (Child: Financial Provision)* (see above)).

(vi) A broad-brush approach

In *Re P (Child: Financial Provision)* (see above) the Court of Appeal held that a broad-brush assessment should be adopted in claims under Schedule 1, but that the starting point is to decide on the home that the respondent should provide for the child. It also held that a broad common-sense assessment of the amount of periodical payments should be taken, but that, in making that assessment, the judge should recognise the responsibility, and often the sacrifice, of the parent who was the primary, or perhaps the exclusive, carer of the child.

(vii) 'Benefit' can include the provision of legal costs

As the phrase 'benefit for the child' has been given a wide meaning by the courts, an order can include a sum to cover legal costs even though this may also benefit a parent. For example, in *Re S (Child: Financial Provision)* [2004] EWCA Civ 1685, the Court of Appeal held that it could include the cost of the mother travelling to the Sudan to see her child and to pursue legal proceedings there, even though this might be for the benefit of the mother as well as the child. (See also *MT v T* [2006] EWHC 2494 (Fam) and *R v F (Schedule 1: Child Maintenance: Mother's Costs of Legal Proceedings)* [2011] 2 FLR 991, where in both cases lump sums towards legal costs involving the child were ordered.)

(viii) The court has jurisdiction under Schedule 1 after a clean-break order has been made on divorce

The court so held in *MB v KB* [2007] EWHC 789 (Fam) in respect of an application for a lump sum order, but it held that the circumstances had to be exceptional.

(ix) Divorce principles are not relevant

In *Re A (A Child) (Financial Provision: Wealthy Parent)* [2014] EWCA Civ 1577 the applicant appealed the level of child maintenance and capital provision made by the court for the benefit of her son. The respondent was a member of a wealthy ruling family of a Middle Eastern country. The mother claimed that given the extent of the father's wealth (which she alleged he had not properly disclosed), the amount which had been awarded was too low. She also argued that the judge should have ordered periodical payments that were sufficient to ensure that she would be able to maintain a suitable standard of living once her son had reached the end of his dependency. The mother argued that an order made 'for the benefit of the child' could justifiably include a sum to provide for her future needs as this would provide her with financial security and also be emotionally beneficial to the child.

The Court of Appeal rejected all of these arguments. Macur J characterised her case as an attempt to align the principles of sharing and compensation applicable to 'big-money' divorce cases to 'big-money' Schedule 1 cases, despite such principles having no application in a Schedule 1 case. He said that 'Schedule 1 cannot be interpreted as permitting the concept of sharing or compensation for the benefit of the child, nor, by the back door, financial provision for the carer beyond that which is attributable to the care of the child during his minority.' The case demonstrates the differences between provision which may be available on divorce and dissolution and that available under Schedule 1.

The case-law demonstrates that, although the courts have tried to be flexible in their approach, there is a fundamental difference in the purpose and scope of Schedule 1 of CA 1989 when compared to the Matrimonial Causes Act 1973. There is therefore a risk that this may lead to unfairness for unmarried parents as a parent who may have undertaken the main responsibility of raising the parties' child may find themselves in a precarious financial position once the child has reached 18 or finished their education.

12.4 The voice of the child in financial proceedings

In *Morgan v Hill* [2006] EWCA Civ 1602 Thorpe LJ said that in exceptional cases brought under Schedule 1 to the CA 1989 (see above) the court should consider separate representation of the child. In *Re S (Unmarried Parents: Financial Provisions)* [2006] EWCA Civ 479 Thorpe LJ said that the facts in *Re S* provided, in his opinion, 'a neat illustration of the advantages of ensuring separate representation for the child' in some cases brought under Schedule 1. Here the child's father and mother were engaged in an intense and bitter battle and Thorpe LJ said that it was easy to see how, in such circumstances, 'the crux of the case can be lost to view unless there is some advocate there to urge constantly the needs and interests of the child' for whom the award is largely designed.

In practice, however, children are rarely listened to or represented in financial proceedings. That is so even though they may be significantly affected by the decision, for example when the court is considering whether or not the family home should be transferred to a parent to or for the benefit of the child.

Summary

▶ All parents have a duty to maintain their children, and all children have a right to be maintained.

▶ In April 1993, child maintenance disputes were removed, for the most part, from the courts and into a Government agency, the Child Support Agency, with maintenance being assessed according to a mathematical formula. Over the years, the Child Support Agency has been riddled with problems (including, for example, delays, errors in calculation and problems with enforcement), and many amendments to the law have been made. The Government reformed the law to place greater emphasis on parents making their own agreements about maintenance; and has moved statutory child maintenance responsibilities from the Child Support Agency to the Child Maintenance Service.

▶ Parents have several options available with respect to arrangements for child maintenance. If they are in agreement they can make a private 'family-based' arrangement or they can apply to the court for a consent order. If they are unable to agree they can apply to the Child Maintenance Service for a maintenance calculation. In certain limited circumstances, parents can apply to the court for child maintenance orders. They can apply to the family courts for lump sum and property orders as these are not covered by the Child Support Act 1991 (CSA 1991).

▶ If a parent fails to provide maintenance then an application can be made to the Child Maintenance Service, which has the power under the CSA 1991 to calculate, collect and enforce child maintenance. However, charges now apply for use of the service. The maintenance calculation is based on percentages of the paying parent's gross weekly income and the number of qualifying and relevant other children. Deductions are made for shared care. Variations are permitted in certain limited and exceptional circumstances. The Child Maintenance Service is responsible for enforcing payments and can make

Summary cont'd

deduction from earnings orders and deduction orders. It can apply to the court for liability orders and avoidance of disposition orders. Other measures against failure to pay statutory child maintenance include the removal of a driving licence and, in the last resort, imprisonment. Parents cannot apply to enforce statutory child maintenance in the courts as that is a matter for the Child Maintenance Service under the CSA 1991.

▶ Maintenance for children can be sought from the courts in certain cases (for example in school fees cases, where a child is disabled, where the Child Maintenance Service has made a maximum assessment in relation to the payer's income and/or where the Child Maintenance Service does not have jurisdiction). Parents can apply to the court for a consent order incorporating an agreement about child maintenance.

▶ Periodical payments, lump sum and property adjustment orders can be sought for children on divorce, nullity and judicial separation under Part II of the Matrimonial Causes Act 1973 (MCA 1973). The same orders can be sought under section 72(1) and Schedule 5 to the Civil Partnership Act 2004 (CPA 2004) on the dissolution, annulment or separation of a civil partnership.

▶ During marriage, a parent may seek periodical payments (maintenance) and/or a lump sum for a child from the court under the Domestic Proceedings and Magistrates' Courts Act 1978. Civil partners can do the same under section 72(3) and Schedule 6 to the CPA 2004. Periodical payments, lump sums and property adjustment orders for the benefit of children can also be sought during marriage from the court under section 27 of the MCA 1973 (and during a civil partnership under section 72(1) and Schedule 5 to the CPA 2004). In practice, these powers are rarely exercised.

▶ Orders for financial relief (periodical payments, lump sums, settlements and transfers of property) can be sought under section 15 and paragraph 1 of Schedule 1 to the Children Act 1989 (CA 1989) by parents, guardians, special guardians and by any person who is named in a child arrangements order as a person with whom a child is to live. 'Children' aged over 18 can apply under paragraph 2.

▶ In an exceptional case, a child may be separately represented in a financial provision case, but such a practice is extremely rare.

Further reading and references

Bryson *et al.*, 'Child maintenance: how much should the State require fathers to pay when families separate?' [2013] Fam Law 1296.

Tod and Cooke, 'Schedule 1 and the need for reform: *N v D*' [2008] Fam Law 751.

Williams and Blain, 'Voices in the wilderness: hearing children in financial applications' [2008] Fam Law 135.

Websites

Child Maintenance Options: www.cmoptions.org
UK Government: www.gov.uk
Links to relevant websites can also be found at: www.palgravehighered.com/law/familylaw9e

Chapter 13

Child abduction

13.1 Introduction

Child abduction is a distressing consequence of family breakdown. Unfortunately, due to the increasing number of 'international families' and the high incidence of family breakdown, it is also on the increase. Thus, for example, in 2008 the number of global applications made to the central authorities which deal with child abduction under the Hague Convention on International Child Abduction 1980 was 45 per cent higher than in 2003 (see Lowe and Stephens [2011] Fam Law 1216). Figures published in 2013 by the UK's Foreign and Commonwealth Office also showed a 113 per cent increase in the number of new child abduction and custody cases between 2003 and 2013.

The courts in England and Wales have extensive civil and criminal law powers to prevent child abduction and, where it has already taken place, to ensure the swift return of children. There are various international agreements which seek to protect children who have been abducted and to enable parents to secure their return. The most important of these are the Hague Convention 1980 and Brussels II Revised. It is more difficult to secure the return of children who are abducted to countries that are not signatories to these international agreements.

International child abduction cases are different from temporary removal applications by parents wishing to take a child lawfully out of the UK, for example to go on holiday, and should also be distinguished from relocation applications where a parent wishes to take a child lawfully out of the UK in order to move abroad (see 11.7).

13.2 Preventing child abduction

Where there is a risk of child abduction, preventative measures should be taken as soon as possible as it may be difficult to find and return a child to the UK once they have been abducted. In addition to being vigilant, the following preventative measures can be taken.

(a) Police assistance

As child abduction is a criminal offence (see 13.3 below), a parent (or any other person) who believes that a child has been or is about to be abducted can seek police assistance. The police have various powers. They can, for example, arrest any person who is abducting or is suspected of abducting a child. They can also institute a 'port alert' whereby details of the child and the abductor are sent by the Police National Computer to all UK ports and airports in order to prevent the child from leaving the country. An application for a port alert must be *bona fide* and there must be a real and imminent danger of abduction.

(b)   A court order

A court order can be useful where there is a risk of abduction. It provides useful evidence of a genuine risk of abduction, and can be used to prevent the issuing of a passport to a child (see 13.2(c) below). A court order can also be useful if a parent wishes to institute court proceedings and/or seek the assistance of various agencies abroad. Breach of a court order is contempt of court (see, for example, *Re A (Abduction: Contempt)* [2008] EWCA Civ 1138).

(i) Section 8 orders under the Children Act 1989

A useful range of orders is available under section 8 of the Children Act 1989 (CA 1989) (see 10.4). For example, a specific issue order could be sought to decide whether a parent and child should be permitted to leave the UK; or a prohibited steps order could be sought to prevent a child being removed from the UK. A child arrangements order regulating the child's living arrangements (previously known as a residence order) can also be useful, as a child who is subject to such an order cannot be lawfully removed from the UK without the *written* consent of every person with parental responsibility for the child or with the permission of the court (s 13(1)(b)) – except for a period of up to one month by a person named in the child arrangements order as a person with whom the child is to live (s 13(2)). It is also possible for the court to impose a condition on a child arrangements order regulating the child's living arrangements under s 11(7) restricting where the person with whom the child lives is allowed to reside.

The court can make a section 8 order *ex parte* (without the respondent being given notice of the proceedings) where urgent action is needed (see, for example, *Re J (Abduction: Wrongful Removal)* [2000] 1 FLR 78). A section 8 order can be made if a child has already been abducted, but the court may be reluctant to do so if there is likely to be a problem enforcing the order abroad (see *Re D (Child: Removal from Jurisdiction)* [1992] 1 WLR 315).

(ii) Wardship

An alternative to a section 8 order is to have the child made a ward of court (see 8.7). There are two main advantages of wardship over a section 8 order. Firstly, wardship takes effect immediately on the application being made, so that any attempt to abduct the child may be contempt of court. Secondly, as the High Court exercises a supervisory role over the ward, no major step in the child's life (such as taking the child out of the UK) can be taken without the court's consent. However, wardship is used only in exceptional cases, for example where other legal remedies are not available or where the situation is particularly urgent. In *Re S (Wardship)* [2010] EWCA Civ 465, for example, the child was made a ward of court on the application of a local authority which was concerned that the child was at risk of significant harm. The mother had taken the child to Spain to live with the child's father after the local authority unsuccessfully tried to obtain an emergency protection order. As both parents had been complicit in the child's removal to Spain, the case did not come within the jurisdiction of the Hague Convention 1980 (see 13.5 below), and so the court was entitled to invoke its wardship jurisdiction.

(iii) Other powers of the court

The court has power under the inherent jurisdiction (see 8.7) and under statute to order a person to disclose a child's whereabouts (see s 33 Family Law Act 1986 (FLA 1986) and s 24A Child Abduction and Custody Act 1985 (CACA 1985); and *Re H (Abduction: Whereabouts Order to Solicitors)* [2000] 1 FLR 766). The court can also authorise an officer of the court, or a police constable, to take charge of a child and deliver the child to a named person. In addition, the High Court can make the following orders: a location order requiring the 'tipstaff' (the enforcement officer for all orders made in the High Court) to locate the child's whereabouts; a collection order requiring the tipstaff to find the child and deliver the child as directed by the court; or a passport order allowing the tipstaff to seize passports. It can also make an order permitting media publicity about the child; or requiring any person to disclose information about the child to the court; or requesting the disclosure of an address from a Government department or agency.

Under the FLA 1986, the court can also order the surrender of a passport (s 37) and the recovery of a child (s 34). In addition, the High Court can make a declaration under section 8 of the CACA 1985 that the removal of any child from, or his retention outside, the UK was wrongful under Article 3 of the Hague Convention 1980.

(iv) Enforcing a court order in another part of the UK

Under the FLA 1986, a court order relating to a child made in England and Wales can be recognised and enforced in another part of the UK (such as Scotland or Northern Ireland) without the merits of the case being considered afresh. Once the order is registered, the court in the other part of the UK has the same powers of enforcement as if it had made the original order. A parent and any other interested party can object to enforcement on the ground that the original order was made without jurisdiction; or that, because of a change of circumstances, the original order should be varied. The court in the other part of the UK can stay proceedings or dismiss the application (ss 30 and 31), but it is likely to enforce the order.

(c) Passport control

Children are required to have their own passport in order to travel. To prevent abduction, it is possible to contact Her Majesty's Passport Office and object to a child being issued with a passport. However, the Passport Office is unlikely to agree to such a request without a court order as proof of a risk of abduction.

Where there is a risk of abduction, a restriction can be placed on the child's or the suspected abductor's passport. Thus, the court can order a UK passport to be surrendered where an order restricting removal is in force (s 37 FLA 1986; and see *Re A (Return of Passport)* [1997] 2 FLR 137). It can also order the surrender of a non-UK passport under its inherent jurisdiction (see *Re A-K (Foreign Passport: Jurisdiction)* [1997] 2 FLR 569 and 8.7). In proceedings under section 8 of the CA 1989 (see 10.4) an order can be made conditional on a suspected abductor depositing his passport with a solicitor or with the court. The tipstaff can also seize passports (see 13.2(c) above).

(d) Curfews and electronic tagging

In a highly exceptional case the court may make a curfew order supported by electronic tagging. Thus, for example, in *Re A (Family Proceedings: Electronic Tagging)* [2009] EWHC 710 (Fam) the parents agreed that, when the child was with the mother, the mother should on an interim basis be subject to a curfew supported by electronic tagging. The mother had twice abducted the child to her country of origin and the child had been returned pursuant to proceedings under the Hague Convention 1980. Parker J made an interim order giving effect to the parties' agreement, confirming that electronic tagging is available to the court and setting out the procedure for making such an order.

(e) Parents who lack 'parental responsibility' and child abduction

Parents who lack parental responsibility in law (see 9.4), such as some unmarried fathers, may find themselves in a vulnerable position if their child has been, or is at risk of being, abducted. This is because parents without parental responsibility do not automatically have 'custody rights' for the purposes of the Hague Convention 1980 (see 13.5 below). In addition, under domestic law their consent is not normally required for the other parent to take the child out of the UK. In such cases, it is important for the parent concerned about removal to take immediate and urgent legal steps to protect themselves and the child, as otherwise they may find themselves deprived of any effective right of recourse to the Hague Convention 1980. Thus, they should consider obtaining a parental responsibility order under section 4 of the CA 1989 (see 9.4), which can be obtained *ex parte* in an emergency. Another option is to apply for a section 8 order under the CA 1989 (see 13.2(b) above). They should also consider obtaining a declaration under section 8 of the CACA 1985 that they have custody rights for the purposes of the Hague Convention 1980 (which is what the unmarried father did in *A v B (Abduction: Rights of Custody: Declaration of Wrongful Removal)* [2008] EWHC 2524 (Fam) when he discovered that the child's mother, a French national, was about to take their child to France).

The courts have, in some cases, taken a broad view of what constitutes custody rights in respect of an unmarried father for the purpose of making a declaration under section 8 of the CACA 1985 (see *Re W; Re B (Child Abduction: Unmarried Father)* [1999] Fam 1). If, for example, a father has been caring for the child, even though he has no parental responsibility in law, this may be sufficient for him to have custody rights for the purpose of the Hague Convention 1980 (see 13.6 below). But each case depends on its own facts. For example, in *Re C (A Child) (Custody Rights: Unmarried Fathers)* [2002] EWHC 2219 (Fam), Munby J refused to make a declaration under section 8 of the CACA 1985 as there was nothing in the case-law to suggest that an unmarried father without parental responsibility could acquire custody rights within the meaning of the Hague Convention 1980 in circumstances where a mother had remained the primary carer. Thus, the court will not necessarily hold that an unmarried father has custody rights for the purposes of the Hague Convention 1980, even if he has shared care of the child for a considerable length of time (see *Re J (Abduction: Acquiring Custody Rights by Caring for Child)* [2005] 2 FLR 791).

The European Court of Human Rights (ECtHR) held in *B v UK* [2000] 1 FLR 1 that it is not discriminatory (under Article 14 of the European Convention on Human Rights (ECHR)) in conjunction with the right to family life (under Article 8 of the ECHR) for the court to hold that an unmarried father without parental responsibility does not come within the scope of the Hague Convention 1980 on the ground that he has no custody rights. In *B v UK* an unmarried father without parental responsibility, whose child had been removed from the UK without his consent, argued that the UK Government was in breach of Articles 14 and 8 of the ECHR because he was being treated differently from other fathers. His application failed. The ECtHR held that there was an objective and reasonable justification for the different treatment of the father in this case.

Other people who are *de facto* parents, but who do not have parental responsibility, may also find themselves in difficulties. For example, in *Re B (A Child) (Habitual Residence: Inherent Jurisdiction)* [2016] UKSC 4 the applicant was the lesbian partner of the biological mother of the child concerned. The couple had decided to have a child together using donor conception but the applicant was not a legal parent and did not have parental responsibility. When the biological mother removed the child to Pakistan without the applicant's consent, the removal could not be deemed wrongful in law (see further at 13.5(a) below).

13.3 Child abduction – the criminal law

A person who abducts, or attempts to abduct, a child from the UK may commit a criminal offence under the Child Abduction Act 1984 (CAA 1984) or under the common law.

(a) The Child Abduction Act 1984

Persons 'connected with a child' (s 1) and 'other persons' (s 2) can commit a criminal offence under this Act.

(i) Persons 'connected with a child'

Under section 1 it is an offence for a person 'connected with a child' under 16 to take or send the child out of the UK without the 'appropriate consent'. A person 'connected with a child' is (s 1): a parent (including an unmarried father if there are reasonable grounds for believing he is the father); a guardian; a special guardian; any person named in a child arrangements order as a person with whom the child is to live; and any person with custody of the child. 'Appropriate consent' means the consent of each of the following: the mother; the father (if they have parental responsibility); a guardian; a special guardian; any person named in a child arrangements order as a person with whom the child is to live; and any person with custody of the child (s 1(3)(a)).

'Appropriate consent' can include the court's consent granted under Part II of the CA 1989 (ss 1(3)(b), (c)). However, a person named in a child arrangements order as a person with whom the child is to live does not commit a criminal offence if they take the child out of the UK for less than one month, unless this is in breach of another court order (s 1(4)).

It is a defence under the Act if the accused believed that the other person consented to the removal or would have consented had they been aware of all the circumstances (s 1(5)(a)); or the accused was unable to communicate with the other person despite taking reasonable steps to do so (s 1(5)(b)). It is also a defence if the other person unreasonably refused consent to the child being taken out of the UK (s 1(5)(c)), but this does not apply if the person refusing consent is named in a child arrangements order as a person with whom the child is to live (s 1(5A)(a)) or the person taking or sending the child out of the UK did so in breach of a court order (s 1(5A)(b)).

(ii) 'Other persons'

Under section 2 a person who is not 'connected with a child' under section 1 (above) commits the offence of child abduction if, without lawful authority or reasonable excuse, they take or detain a child under the age of 16 so as to remove the child from the lawful control of any person having lawful control of the child; or so as to keep the child out of the lawful control of any person entitled to lawful control (s 2(1)). An unmarried father without parental responsibility falls under section 2, unless he is the child's guardian, special guardian or is named in a child arrangements order as a person with whom the child is to live, or has custody of the child. However, an unmarried father has a defence if he can prove that he is the child's father, or that at the time of the alleged offence he reasonably believed he was the child's father (s 2(3)(a)).

It is also a defence if the accused believed that at the time of the alleged offence the child had reached the age of 16 (s 2(3)(b)). The mental state for an offence under section 2 is an intentional or reckless taking or detention of a child (see *Foster and Another v Director of Public Prosecutions* [2004] EWHC 2955 (Admin)).

The courts have taken a strong line in punishing those convicted of child abduction, and they have been willing to impose prison sentences even where the defendant has been the primary carer of the child for many years (see, for example, *R v Kayani; R v Solliman* [2011] EWCA Crim 2871). In *Kayani; R v Solliman* the Court of Appeal also drew attention to the illogical disparity between prison sentences for offences under the CAA 1984 (where the maximum is seven years) and those for kidnapping (where a life sentence is possible, see below); and invited the Law Commission to address the question of whether cases where children were removed from one parent by the other should be treated as kidnapping offences. In 2014, the Law Commission recommended that the maximum sentence for child abduction be increased to 14 years for the gravest cases (*Kidnapping and Related Offences*, Law Com 355). At the time of writing, a response from the Government is awaited.

(b) The common law offence of kidnapping

A person who abducts a child may commit the common law offence of kidnapping (see, for example, *R v D* [1984] AC 778). Where the child is under 16 and the person removing the child is a person 'connected with' the child under section 1 of the CAA 1984 (see 13.3(a) above), the consent of the Director of Public Prosecutions is needed to bring a prosecution (s 5 CAA 1984). The common law offence of kidnapping is difficult to prove and rarely used, but it may be useful where the child is over 16 as such a child does not come within the scope of the CAA 1984 (see above). In 2014, the Law Commission recommended that the common law offence of kidnapping be clarified and placed on a statutory footing (*Kidnapping and Related Offences*, Law Com 355). This has not yet been taken forward.

13.4   The Hague Convention on International Child Abduction 1980

(a)   Introduction

The UK is a Contracting State to the Hague Convention on the Civil Aspects of International Child Abduction 1980 (Hague Convention 1980) which has been implemented into UK law by Part I of the Child Abduction and Custody Act 1985 (CACA 1985). The text of the Hague Convention 1980 and a list of Contracting States are available on the website of Reunite (a charity specialising in parental child abduction).

Article 1 of the Hague Convention on the Civil Aspects of International Child Abduction 1980

The objects of the present Convention are –

(a) to secure the prompt return of children wrongfully removed to or retained in any Contracting State; and
(b) to ensure that rights of custody and of access under the law of one Contracting State are effectively respected in the other Contracting States.

(i) The policy of the Convention

The Hague Convention 1980 is based on the policy that children should be swiftly returned to their country of habitual residence. It is also based on the principle of 'comity', which is a custom of international law that requires courts to respect the laws of foreign jurisdictions. Thus, the presumption lies in favour of returning a child; and it is also generally assumed that, if a country is a party to the Hague Convention 1980, then the child's case will be dealt with in a welfare-oriented way. Another policy objective of the Convention is to deter abductions. As Baroness Hale has said, the 'message should go out to potential abductors that there are no safe havens among the Contracting States' (see *Re M (Abduction: Zimbabwe)* [2007] UKHL 55).

The objects of the Hague Convention 1980 were described by Baroness Hale and Lord Wilson in the following extract.

▶ *Baroness Hale and Lord Wilson in Re E (Children) (Abduction: Custody Appeal)* **[2011] UKSC 27**

The first object of the Hague Convention is to deter either parent (or indeed anyone else) from taking the law into their own hands and pre-empting the result of any dispute between them about the future upbringing of their children. If an abduction does take place, the next object is to restore the children as soon as possible to their home country, so that any dispute can be determined there …. Factual disputes of this nature are likely to be better able to be resolved in the country where the family had its home.

(ii) How the Convention works

The Hague Convention 1980 is set up to provide a speedy extradition-type remedy whereby Contracting States agree to return abducted children to their country of habitual residence so that the parental custody (or residence) dispute can be dealt with there. In this sense it is a provisional remedy, as Convention proceedings are not concerned with the merits of any custody issue (Article 19). That is a matter for the court in the child's country of habitual residence. In *C v B (Abduction: Grave Risk)* [2005] EWHC 2988 (Fam) Sir Mark Potter P said that it was essential that the court hearing a return application did not usurp the function of the 'home' court by considering broader welfare considerations instead of confining itself to those matters which went to the establishment of the defence being relied upon under Article 13 of the Convention (see 13.8 below). The central question in Convention proceedings is therefore whether the child should be returned to the *court* of their habitual residence, so that the custody issue can be considered there, and not whether the child should be returned to a particular *person*.

As the Hague Convention 1980 is concerned with breaches of custody *rights*, and not custody orders, it is not necessary to have a court order to invoke it. Applications under the Convention are heard by the Family Division of the High Court, which can also make declarations that the removal of any child from, or his retention outside, the UK is wrongful under Article 3 (see 13.2(b) above).

(iii) Central authorities

The Convention works by establishing a network of central authorities which are required to cooperate with each other, and to promote cooperation among the competent authorities in their respective States, in order to secure the prompt return of children and to achieve the other objects of the Convention (Art 7). Central authorities have various duties under the Convention which include: discovering the child's whereabouts; preventing further harm to the child by taking provisional measures; securing the child's voluntary return; exchanging information; and providing information. The central authority for England and Wales is the International Child Abduction and Contact Unit (ICACU) which is based in the Office of the Official Solicitor at the Ministry of Justice. The ICACU is responsible for making administrative arrangements under the Convention in order to secure the return of abducted children and to enforce rights of access. It also provides advice and assistance.

(iv) Speed is of the essence

In abduction cases any delay is contrary to the child's best interests – this is because the longer the situation remains undecided, the more difficult it will be to disturb the status quo. Because of the importance of speed, proceedings under the Convention are summary. Thus, for example, the court will not investigate the parent's relationship or examine the child's welfare. Cases are usually heard and decided on the basis of written evidence (such as a Cafcass report) rather than on the basis of oral evidence. In abduction cases involving the EU (see 13.4(b) below), Article 11(3) of Brussels II Revised provides that a return application under the Convention must be completed within six weeks unless exceptional circumstances make this impossible.

(v) The welfare of the child

The welfare of the child is not paramount in Hague Convention 1980 cases because 'it is presumed under the Convention that the welfare of children who have been abducted is best met by return to their habitual residence' (*per* Butler-Sloss LJ in *Re M (A Minor) (Child Abduction)* [1994] 1 FLR 390). Nevertheless, as Baroness Hale emphasised in *Re M (Abduction: Zimbabwe)* [2007] UKHL 55, the Convention is child-centred, as it is principally directed towards the protection of children, not adults. As Baroness Hale pointed out, the Preamble to the Convention states that the Contracting States are 'firmly convinced that the interests of *children* are of paramount importance in matters relating to the custody of children'. (On the issue of the child's welfare, see also *Neulinger and Shuruk v Switzerland* and *Re E (Children) (Abduction: Custody Appeal)* below.)

(vi) Human rights and the Hague Convention 1980

The European Court of Human Rights (ECtHR) has held that a failure by a national authority (under domestic or international law) to secure the return of an abducted child may amount to a breach of the right to family life under Article 8 of the European Convention on Human Rights (ECHR); and that national authorities must take positive measures to enable parents to be reunited with the child, unless contrary to the child's best interests. Breaches of Article 8 were found, for example, in *Gil and Aui v Spain (Application No. 56673/00)* [2005] 1 FLR 190 and *Maire v Portugal (Application No. 48206/99)* [2004] 2 FLR 653.

In *Neulinger and Shuruk v Switzerland (App No. 41615/07)* [2011] 1 FLR 122, the ECtHR held (by 16 votes to one) that there had been a breach of the mother's and the child's right to family life under Article 8 of the ECHR because a return order had been made even though the mother had raised the Article 13(b) defence under the Hague Convention 1980 that the child would suffer a grave risk of harm if they were ordered to be returned to Israel. The decision caused considerable concern among lawyers and judges in the UK as it seemed contrary to the approach adopted in the UK courts. The approach adopted by the ECtHR in *Neulinger*, which required national courts to base their decisions on the best interests of the child and to conduct an in-depth examination of the facts, seemed diametrically opposed to the approach adopted by the UK courts whereby the priority is to effect the speedy return of a child to their country of habitual residence so the matter can be dealt with there.

The concerns raised by the decision of the ECtHR in *Neulinger* were addressed by the UK Supreme Court in the following case.

▶ *Re E (Children) (Abduction: Custody Appeal)* **[2011] UKSC 27**

After the mother wrongfully removed the two children (aged four and six) from Norway to England, the father applied to the High Court in England and Wales for the summary return of the children to Norway under the Hague Convention 1980. The mother and the children's half-sister opposed the father's application, relying on the Article 13(b) grave risk of harm defence (based on the father's alleged long-term abusive behaviour towards the mother and his approach to the children).

Pauffley J in the High Court concluded that it was overwhelmingly in the children's best interests to return to Norway for their futures to be decided there. The mother's and half-sister's appeal to the Court of Appeal was dismissed, but it granted them permission to appeal to the Supreme Court where they argued, *inter alia*, that the current approach to the Article 13(b) defence, at least in the courts of England and Wales, did not properly respect the requirement that the best interests of the child should be a primary consideration; and they claimed that their appeal was supported by the decision of the ECtHR in *Neulinger* (see above).

The Supreme Court dismissed the appeal. Baroness Hale and Lord Wilson, giving judgment for the Supreme Court, held, *inter alia*, that, although the best interests of the child had not expressly been made a primary consideration in Hague Convention proceedings, there was a general underlying assumption that the best interests of the child would be best served by a prompt return to the child's country of habitual residence (although this assumption was rebuttable in certain circumstances).

(For the Supreme Court's discussion of the Article 13(b) defence, see 13.8(e) below.)

Thus, the Supreme Court concluded that the decision in *Neulinger* did not require the UK courts to adopt a change of approach in cases involving the Convention. It concluded that both the Convention and Brussels II Revised (see further below) had been devised with the best interests of children generally, and of the individual children involved in such proceedings, as a primary consideration. It held that, if the court faithfully applied the provisions of the Convention and Brussels II Revised, then it would also be complying with Article 3(1) of the United Nations Convention on the Rights of the Child. In addition, the decision in *Neulinger* did not require a departure from the normal summary process, provided that the decision made was not arbitrary or mechanical.

In the subsequent case of *X v Latvia (Application No. 27853/09)* [2012] 1 FLR 860, the ECtHR once again stated that the determination of cases involving the Hague Convention 1980 required an in-depth examination of the facts. Nonetheless, in *Re S (A Child) (Abduction: Rights of Custody)* [2012] UKSC 10 Lord Wilson reiterated the point that had been made in *Re E* (above) with respect to *Neulinger* that neither the Convention nor Article 8 of the ECHR required the court to conduct an in-depth examination of the sort described in *Neulinger* and *X v Latvia*, and that for the court to conduct such an examination would be inappropriate.

(vii) Access (contact) rights

Although Article 21 of the Hague Convention 1980 provides that access rights may be secured, it confers no power on the courts to determine matters relating to access, or to recognise or enforce foreign access orders. It merely provides for executive cooperation between central authorities for the recognition and enforcement of such access rights as national laws allow. The International Child Abduction and Contact Unit will provide assistance with finding a solicitor, legal aid and instituting section 8 proceedings under the Children Act 1989 (CA 1989).

If a foreign access order is in force, an application can be made to have it recognised and enforced in the courts in England and Wales under: the European Convention on the Recognition and Enforcement of Decisions Concerning Custody of Children

1980 (see *Re A (Foreign Access Order: Enforcement)* [1996] 1 FLR 561 and 13.10 below); Brussels II Revised if Member States of the EU are involved (see *Re S (Brussels II Revised: Enforcement of Contact Order)* [2008] 2 FLR 1358); or the Hague Convention 1996 (see 13.9 below).

(viii) Breach of a return order

Breach of a return order made under the Hague Convention 1980 can be contempt of court provided there has been deliberate disobedience of the court order applying the criminal standard of proof (beyond reasonable doubt). But each case depends on its own facts (see, for example, *Re A (Abduction: Contempt)* [2008] EWCA Civ 1138).

(b) The Hague Convention 1980 and abductions within the EU – Brussels II Revised

Where a child has been abducted within the EU, it is also necessary to take into account the provisions of Council Regulation (EC) (No. 2201/2003) Concerning Jurisdiction and the Recognition and Enforcement of Judgments in Matrimonial Matters and in Matters of Parental Responsibility (Brussels II Revised), which takes precedence over the Hague Convention 1980 with respect to Member States of the EU (Art 60). Article 11 of the Regulation aims to harmonise the application of the Convention in EU Member States by setting out details of procedure that are binding on the courts. As Schulz (2008) explains, while the Convention contains provisions aimed at 'a quick clarification of the *factual* situation (return of the child)', Brussels II Revised contains provisions aimed at 'a quick clarification of the *legal* situation'; in other words, it enables a final decision about custody to be taken in the court of the State of the child's habitual residence even if the child is not being returned under the Convention (see further below). The central authority in England and Wales for the purposes of Brussels II Revised is the International Child Abduction and Contact Unit.

The following provisions in Brussels II Revised apply in cases involving the Hague Convention 1980 which involve EU Member States:

▶ The court is required in every case to hear the views of the child unless this appears inappropriate having regard to the age or degree of maturity of the child (Art 11(2)).
▶ Proceedings for the return of a child under the Convention must be completed within six weeks unless 'exceptional circumstances make this impossible' (Art 11(3)).
▶ The court may not refuse to return a child on the basis that the defence of grave risk to the child has been made out under Article 13(b) of the Convention (see 13.8 below), if it is established that adequate arrangements have been made to ensure the protection of the child after his or her return (Art 11(4)).
▶ The court cannot refuse to return a child unless the person who requested the return of the child has been given an opportunity to be heard (Art 11(5)).
▶ Brussels II Revised allows a custody decision made in the Member State where the child was habitually resident before the removal to 'trump' a non-return order made in the Member State to which the child has been abducted (Art 11(6)–(8), see below).

(i) Brussels II Revised and non-return orders under the Hague Convention 1980

Brussels II Revised provides additional protection for a parent whose child has been abducted, as Articles 11(6)–(8) allow the court in the Member State where the child was habitually resident before removal to order the child's return even if the court in the country to which the child has been abducted makes a non-return order under the Hague Convention 1980 (provided the non-return order was made on the basis of a successful Article 13 defence, see 13.8 below) (see, for example, *Rinau (Case C-195/08)* [2008] 2 FLR 1495; *Re RC and BC (Child Abduction) (Brussels II Revised: Article 11(7))* [2009] 1 FLR 574; *Re RD (Child Abduction) (Brussels II Revised: Articles 11(7) and 19))* [2009] 1 FLR 586). Thus, Brussels II Revised 'accepts the parallel continuation of return and custody proceedings in two different Member States, regardless of the ultimate outcome of the Hague Convention return proceedings' (Schulz, 2008). In other words, despite a court ordering the non-return of a child in Convention proceedings, the court of habitual residence can revisit the issue and override that decision. Thus, for example, in *Vigreux v Michel* [2006] EWCA Civ 630 the Court of Appeal held that McFarlane J had erred in law in refusing a French mother's application for return of the child to France from England under the Convention when she had already been granted sole parental responsibility for the child by a French court. Thorpe LJ held that the case was one in which the policy of the Convention buttressed by the provisions of Brussels II Revised powerfully outweighed the Article 13 defence.

Where a child has been abducted from England and Wales and the court is exercising its jurisdiction under Articles 11(7) and 11(8), the child's welfare is the court's first consideration and the court can conduct a full welfare inquiry and full hearing. As part of this process the court may decide to order the return of the child or may make other orders, such as that the child should be returned for temporary periods for contact with the 'left-behind' parent. For example, in *M v T (Abduction: Brussels IIR Art 11(7))* [2010] EWHC 1479 (Fam), after the Lithuanian court had refused to return the child to the UK under the Hague Convention 1980, Charles J in Article 11(7) proceedings ordered that the father should still have contact with the child in England or Lithuania but that the mother should be permitted to live permanently with the child in Lithuania (applying *Payne v Payne*, see 11.7). Charles J confirmed that the court's jurisdiction in such a case 'is a welfare jurisdiction and therefore it is a welfare approach that has to be applied' (see also *AF v T and A* [2011] EWHC 1315, where the English court made a contact order under the CA 1989 for the child to have supervised contact with his father following a non-return decision made by the German court under the Convention).

(c) The voice of the child in Hague Convention 1980 cases

As proceedings under the Hague Convention 1980 are summary and speed is of the essence, the usual way in which the voice of the child is heard is by means of a written report compiled either by a Cafcass officer (see 1.7) or by another professional who has interviewed the child. There is no obligation on the judge to hear oral evidence even where an Article 13(b) defence (child's objection to return) is being argued (*per* Sir Mark Potter P in *Re M (Abduction: Child's Objections)* [2007] EWCA Civ 260). In some cases the judge may wish to speak to the child, and this is a practice which, although not common, is more common than it once was. If the judge does meet with the child, there are guidelines the judge must follow and the judge must confine themselves to passively hearing what the child has to say, rather than using the meeting to gather evidence (*Re KP (A Child)* [2014] EWCA Civ 554). In some circumstances the court may order that the child be separately represented (see below).

Although the child's voice may be put before the court, this does not necessarily mean that the child's views will be taken into account. Thus, in *C v B (Abduction: Grave Risk)* [2005] EWHC 2988 (Fam), for example, the views of the nine-year-old child, whose mother did not wish to return to Australia, were put before the court by means of a Cafcass report. However, Sir Mark Potter P held that, while the child was of sufficient maturity to have his views taken into account, those views (anger with his father and concerns about his mother) did not provide a sufficient basis on which to withhold an order of return for him and his sister.

(i) Separate representation of the child in proceedings under the Hague Convention 1980

The court has the power to make a child a party to the proceedings, if it considers it is in the child's best interests to do so (r 16.2 Family Procedure Rules 2010). The test to be applied is whether separate representation will add enough to the court's understanding of the issues arising under the Hague Convention 1980 to justify the intrusion, expense and delay that may result (*per* Baroness Hale in *Re M (Abduction: Zimbabwe)* [2007] UKHL 55).

Although separate representation remains unusual, there has been an increasing trend to permit children to be separately represented. Thus, for example, in *Re C (Abduction: Separate Representation of Children)* [2008] EWHC 517 (Fam) Ryder J directed that all four articulate siblings (aged nine, 11, 13 and 16), who vigorously objected to being returned to France, be joined as parties and that the three younger children be represented by a guardian *ad litem*. Ryder J (applying the test laid down by Baroness Hale in *Re M* above and the approach taken by the Court of Appeal in *Mabon v Mabon* (see 8.6)) held that there would be little additional delay and expense in allowing separate representation; and the younger three children were able to make submissions and defences distinct from those put forward by the mother. However, in *Re H (Abduction)* [2006] EWCA Civ 1247 the Court of Appeal refused permission to allow a girl (aged 15) to be made a party to proceedings under the Hague Convention 1980 as they were summary proceedings where speed was of the essence. Wall LJ said that there were material differences between the question of separate representation for a child in a welfare inquiry under the Children Act 1989 and in summary proceedings under an international convention where the welfare inquiry is to take place elsewhere.

Where a child has a distinctive point of view which needs to be heard separately from that of the parent, the court may decide to grant separate representation, as it did to a 14-year-old boy in *Re L (Abduction: Child's Objections to Return)* [2002] EWHC 1864 (Fam). Similarly, separate representation was granted to the teenage children in *Cambra v Jones* [2013] EWHC 88 (Fam) so that they could fully articulate their case where they were steadfastly opposed to returning to live with their father in Spain.

Separate representation may be appropriate to address a specific issue in the case. In *Re LC (Children) (International Abduction: Child's Objections to Return)* [2014] UKSC 1, the Supreme Court held that the trial judge had been wrong not to make the oldest child a party to the proceedings. The majority held that, while it should not become routine to join children as parties where habitual residence is in issue (as it was in this case), an older child may be able to contribute evidence about their state of mind, not easily given by their parents, which is relevant to determining the issue of habitual residence. Lady Hale and Lord Sumption went further by suggesting that the views of younger children may be equally relevant.

(ii) Are children being heard enough in Hague Convention proceedings?

There has been increasing concern that children are not being heard enough in cases involving the Hague Convention 1980, and that more children should be separately represented. Baroness Hale in *Re D (A Child) (Abduction: Rights of Custody)* [2006] UKHL 51 said that 'whenever it seems likely that the child's views and interests may not be properly presented to the court, and in particular where there are legal arguments which the adult parties are not putting forward, then the child should be separately represented'.

In respect of abductions within the EU, a failure to hear a child may breach Article 11(2) of Brussels II Revised (see 13.4(b) above). This requires courts in Member States, when applying Articles 12 and 13 of the Hague Convention 1980, to ensure that the child 'is given the opportunity to be heard during the proceedings unless this appears inappropriate having regard to his or her age or degree of maturity'. Although Brussels II Revised applies only to EU cases, Baroness Hale in *Re D* (above) held that, as the obligation to hear a child is a principle of universal application and consistent with the UK's obligations under Article 12 of the United Nations Convention on the Rights of the Child (see 8.2), the obligation to hear a child applies not just to EU cases but to all Convention cases. Her Ladyship held that it created a presumption that a child would be heard unless this appeared inappropriate. She warned, however, that listening to a child does not mean that the court should necessarily give effect to those views.

In *Re F (Abduction: Joinder of Child as Party)* [2007] EWCA Civ 393, however, Thorpe LJ said that *Re D* (above) was not to be interpreted as having the effect of lowering the bar with respect to granting party status to the child; and that there remained a need to demonstrate that a case was sufficiently exceptional. Thorpe LJ said that '[h]earing the child is one thing and giving the child party status is quite another'. In *Re F* the Court of Appeal refused leave for the child (aged seven) to be joined in the proceedings, despite the mother's argument that the judge had not observed her obligation to hear the child under Article 11 of Brussels II Revised. The Court of Appeal held that this refusal did not breach the child's human rights under Articles 6 (the right to a fair hearing) and 8 (the right to family life) of the European Convention on Human Rights.

In addition to a slight move towards children being separately represented in proceedings involving the Hague Convention 1980, several cases have drawn attention to the desirability of judges talking to children face to face (see, for example, *De L v H* [2009] EWHC 3074 (Fam); and *Re G (Abduction: Children's Objections)* [2010] EWCA Civ 1232). (For further discussion on the voice of the child see Hale J, 'Listening to children: are we nearly there yet?' [2016] Fam Law 320 and Cobb J, 'Seen but not heard?' [2015] Fam Law 144.)

(d) Construing the Hague Convention 1980

As the Hague Convention 1980 is an international legal instrument, the courts in England and Wales have stressed the importance of it being construed uniformly by courts in Contracting States (see, for example, *per* Lord Browne-Wilkinson in *Re H (Minors) (Abduction: Acquiescence)* [1998] AC 72). To promote uniformity of construction, the Hague Conference has an International Child Abduction Database of leading Convention case-law from Hague Contracting States.

The courts in England and Wales adopt a purposive approach when construing the Hague Convention 1980. In *Re B (A Minor) (Abduction)* [1994] 2 FLR 249 Waite LJ said that the Convention was 'to be construed broadly as an international agreement according to its general tenor and purpose, without attributing to any of its terms a specialist meaning which the word or words in question would have acquired under the domestic law of England'. In *Hunter v Murrow (Abduction: Rights of Custody)* [2005] EWCA Civ 976, the Court of Appeal held that the Convention was a living instrument to be interpreted and applied as necessary to keep pace with social and other trends. It also held that questions involving the construction or interpretation of the Convention were to be answered according to the international jurisprudence of the Contracting States, not simply according to the law of a particular jurisdiction.

In *Re M (Abduction: Zimbabwe)* [2007] UKHL 55 the House of Lords warned that the courts should not add additional words to the Hague Convention 1980 (in that case, an additional test of 'exceptionality' to the circumstances under which a court should refuse to order the return of an abducted child). Baroness Hale, who gave the leading opinion, said that '[t]he Convention itself contains a simple, sensible and carefully thought out balance between various considerations, all aimed at serving the interests of children by deterring and, where appropriate, remedying international child abduction. Further elaboration with additional tests and checklists is not required.' Baroness Hale said that, while the court is entitled to take into account the various policy aspects of the Convention (see 13.4 above), that was 'the furthest one should go in seeking to put a gloss on the terms of the Convention'. This approach to the Convention was reiterated by Baroness Hale and Lord Wilson in *Re E (Children) (Abduction: Custody Appeal)* [2011] UKSC 27 (see 13.4 above) who held that the exceptions to the obligation to return are by their very nature restricted in their scope and do not need any extra interpretation or gloss.

In *Re F (Abduction: Rights of Custody)* [2008] EWHC 272 (Fam) Sir Mark Potter P said that Baroness Hale's express disapproval of the 'exceptionality' test over and above the express requirements of the Hague Convention 1980 applied to all Convention cases, including those brought under Brussels II Revised.

13.5 The Hague Convention 1980 – jurisdiction

To come within the jurisdiction of the Hague Convention 1980, the child must be under 16 and must have been habitually resident in one Contracting State and taken to another. If the child has reached the age of 16 by the time of the hearing, the High

Court can consider the case under its inherent jurisdiction (see 8.7). The Convention does not apply to an unborn child (*Re F (Abduction: Unborn Child)* [2006] EWHC 2199 (Fam)). To come within the scope of the Convention, there must also have been a breach of a right of custody (see 13.6 below).

(a) Habitual residence

Habitual residence is the connecting factor used in the Hague Convention 1980. Thus, the child must have been habitually resident in one Contracting State and moved to another Contracting State. If the child is not, or has ceased to be, habitually resident in a Contracting State, there can be no wrongful removal or retention of the child for the purposes of Article 3(a); and the child will fall outside the scope of the Convention. Whether or not a child is habitually resident in a Contracting State is a question of fact, to be decided by the court.

'Habitual residence' is not defined in the Hague Convention 1980 and its meaning has generated a significant volume of case law, including consideration at the highest judicial level (see, for example, *Re J (A Minor) (Abduction: Custody Rights)* [1990] 2 AC 562, *Re L* [2013] UKSC 75 and *Re LC (Children)* [2014] UKSC 1). Previously, the approach set out in *Re J* was considered the most authoritative but the Supreme Court has expressly disapproved aspects of the approach set out by Lord Brandon in that case. In *A v A* [2013] UKSC 60 and *Re B (A Child) (Habitual Residence: Inherent Jurisdiction)* (see 13.2 above and below) the Supreme Court adopted the European definition of habitual residence, which was set out by Baroness Hale in *A v A* as follows.

> ▶ *Baroness Hale in A v A* **[2013] UKSC 60**
>
> [Habitual residence] must be interpreted as meaning that it corresponds to the place which reflects some degree of integration by the child in a social and family environment. To that end, in particular the duration, regularity, conditions and reasons for the stay on the territory of a Member State and the family's move to that State, the child's nationality, the place and conditions of attendance at school, linguistic knowledge and the family and social relationships of the child in that State must be taken into consideration. It is for the national court to establish the habitual residence of the child, taking account of all the circumstances specific to each individual case.

This approach places more emphasis on the child's perspective and the degree of integration which they have formed with their environment, rather than the intention and purposes of the adults involved. Further guidance on the application of habitual residence was provided by the Supreme Court in *Re B (A Child) (Habitual Residence: Inherent Jurisdiction)* (see 13.2 above and below). Although the case did not fall within the scope of the Hague Convention 1980, because the removal was not wrongful and Pakistan is not a signatory to the Convention, the guidance provided is applicable to cases involving the Convention and Brussels II Revised.

▶ *Re B (A Child) (Habitual Residence: Inherent Jurisdiction)* **[2016] UKSC 4**

The parties lived in England in a same sex relationship which broke down in 2011. During their relationship they had a child together using an unknown sperm donor. After the relationship broke down, the appellant issued proceedings under the Children Act 1989 (CA 1989). However, unbeknownst to her, the respondent had already left the country with the child and taken her to Pakistan. The issue for the court was whether it had jurisdiction to hear the proceedings under the CA 1989 given that this would require the child to have been habitually resident in England when the proceedings commenced. In the alternative, the appellant sought that the court exercise its inherent jurisdiction.

In the High Court, Hogg J dismissed the appellant's application on the ground that by the time proceedings had been issued, the child had lost her habitual residence in England because she had been lawfully removed by her mother with a settled intention of making a new life abroad. The judge also held that the circumstances did not justify the exercise of the court's inherent jurisdiction. The appellant appealed, but her appeal was dismissed by the Court of Appeal. She therefore appealed to the Supreme Court.

By a majority of three to two, the Supreme Court allowed her appeal and held that the child had been habitually resident in England and Wales when the proceedings under the CA 1989 had been issued, shortly after the child left the country. The majority set out the following principles:

▶ Two consequences flowed from the modern international concept of habitual residence. The first was that it was not in a child's interests to be left without a habitual residence. The second was that the domestic interpretation of habitual residence should be consonant with its international interpretation.

▶ The English concept of habitual residence should be governed by the criterion established in European jurisprudence as set out in *A v A*: namely, that there be some degree of integration by the child in a social and family environment. Parental intention (as outlined in *Re J*) is only one relevant factor in assessing the degree of integration.

▶ The modern concept of a child's habitual residence operates in such a way as to make it highly unlikely, albeit conceivable, that a child will be without a habitual residence. The concept operates in the expectation that, when a child gains a new habitual residence, he loses his old one. The concept acts like a see-saw: as the child puts down roots in the new country, the roots he had in the country where he was previously habitually resident will come up.

▶ Identification of habitual residence was a question of fact, but decision-makers should consider the following expectations: (a) the deeper a child's integration in the old state, probably the slower the requisite degree of integration would be in the new state; (b) the greater the amount of adult pre-planning of the move, probably the faster the integration in the new state; (c) the more central figures in the child's life who moved with him, probably the faster the integration in the new state. Conversely, were any of the central figures to have remained behind, probably the less fast the integration in the new state would be.

On the facts of the case, there were several factors indicating that when the appellant issued the proceedings under the CA 1989, only ten days after the child had been removed, the child had not achieved the requisite degree of disengagement from her English environment and that England remained her habitual residence. This meant that the court could make orders under the CA 1989 in relation to the child, including that the mother return her to England.

On the issue of the court's inherent jurisdiction, the court said that, given its conclusion on habitual residence, it was unnecessary to decide whether the inherent jurisdiction could be exercised. The use of the inherent jurisdiction had to be approached with great caution or circumspection, but its exercise was not limited to 'dire and exceptional' cases.

There have been many reported abduction cases involving the issue of habitual residence, from which the following propositions can be extracted.

Habitual residence

Habitual residence may be established even after a short period of residence (see, for example, *Re S (Habitual Residence)* [2009] EWCA Civ 1021 where seven to eight weeks' residence in London was sufficient to establish habitual residence in England and Wales).

A short visit to a country does not necessarily start a period of habitual residence (see, for example, *Re A (Abduction: Habitual Residence)* [1998] 1 FLR 497 where a three-week visit to Greece for something that was akin to a holiday was held to be insufficient to create a new habitual residence).

A child may have no habitual residence at all (see *W and B v H (Child Abduction: Surrogacy)* [2002] 1 FLR 1008). However, this will be highly unlikely (*per* Wilson J in *Re B (A Child) (Habitual Residence: Inherent Jurisdiction)* above).

A child will not necessarily have the same habitual residence as a parent (see *Al Habloor v Fotheringham* [2001] EWCA Civ186 where the High Court refused jurisdiction as the applicant mother's nine-year-old child remained habitually resident in Dubai, even though the mother was habitually resident in England; and *Re LC (Children)* [2014] UKSC 1).

The child's state of mind is a relevant consideration (see Re LC (Children) above where the court held that the child's state of mind was relevant in determining their level of integration into a new environment).

It is not necessary for a person to remain continuously present in a particular country in order for him or her to retain residence there (*per* Millet LJ in *Re M (Abduction: Habitual Residence)* [1996] 1 FLR 887).

Moving to another Contracting State for educational reasons may not constitute a change of habitual residence (see *TPC v JMJ* [2009] EWHC 638 (Fam) where the children were held to be habitually resident in Spain even though they had travelled to Wales with their mother and spent 14 months there, with the father's consent, to improve their English).

(b)   Wrongful removal and retention

To come within the scope of the Hague Convention 1980, there must be wrongful removal from, or wrongful retention in, a Contracting State. Wrongful removal and wrongful retention are mutually exclusive concepts (*Re H; Re S (Minors) (Abduction: Custody Rights)* [1991] 2 FLR 262). Wrongful removal occurs when a child is wrongfully removed from his place of habitual residence in breach of a right of custody. Wrongful retention occurs when, at the end of a period of lawful removal, a parent refuses to return the child. Removal and retention are wrongful only if done in a breach of a right of custody (see below).

(i) A declaration of wrongful removal

Under section 8 of the Child Abduction and Custody Act 1985 (CACA 1985) the High Court, on an application made for the purposes of Article 15 of the Hague Convention 1980 by any person appearing to the court to have an interest in the matter, may make a declaration that the removal of a child from, or his retention outside, the UK is wrongful within the meaning of Article 3 of the Convention. In *Re C (Child Abduction) (Unmarried Father: Rights of Custody)* [2002] EWHC 2219 (Fam) Munby J said that the grant of declaratory relief under Article 15 is always a matter of discretion, but in the normal case where an applicant succeeds in persuading the court that a child has been wrongfully removed, and seeks a declaration to assist his prospects of obtaining substantive relief in the requested State, he can normally expect to have the court's discretion exercised in his favour.

13.6 The Hague Convention 1980 – rights of custody

Article 3 of the Hague Convention on the Civil Aspects of International Child Abduction 1980

The removal or retention of a child is to be considered wrongful where –

(a) it is in breach of rights of custody attributed to a person, an institution or any other body, either jointly or alone, under the law of the State in which the child was habitually resident immediately before the removal or retention; and
(b) at the time of removal or retention those rights were actually exercised, either jointly or alone, or would have been so exercised but for the removal or retention.

The existence of a right of custody is crucial to establishing whether the Hague Convention 1980 applies, as removal or retention is only wrongful if there has been breach of such a right. The rights of custody mentioned in Article 3(a) may arise in particular by operation of law or by reason of a judicial or administrative decision. Article 5(a) provides that, for the purposes of the Convention, rights of custody 'shall include rights relating to the care of the person of the child and, in particular, the right to determine the child's place of residence'.

In *Re P (Abduction: Consent)* [2004] EWCA Civ 971 the Court of Appeal held that the court's task under Article 3 is to establish the custody rights of the parent under the law of the relevant state, and then to consider whether those rights are rights of custody for the purposes of the Hague Convention 1980 (see further below at 13.6(b)).

(a) A purposive construction of custody

In order to give effect to the overriding policy objective of the Hague Convention 1980 that children should be swiftly returned to their country of habitual residence, the courts have adopted a purposive construction of 'rights of custody' and interpreted it broadly to include not just legal custody but also *de facto* (factual) custody. In other words, where a person has no custody rights in law, but is exercising rights of a parental or custodial nature, this may constitute rights of custody under the Convention. In this way, unmarried fathers without legal custody (or without parental responsibility) have been held to have custody rights. A broad view of custody rights was taken by the Court of Appeal in the following case.

> ▶ *Re B (A Minor) (Abduction)* [1994] 2 FLR 249
>
> The parents were cohabitants living in Australia. The mother left Australia and went to England, leaving the child with the father and maternal grandmother. Later, the grandmother took the child to England and failed to return the child to Australia, which was in breach of an agreement made between the mother and father that the child would be returned within six months. The father, who had been an exemplary parent (but who had no legal custody), applied to the English High Court for an immediate return order under Article 12. The judge ordered the child's immediate return to Australia. The mother appealed to the Court of Appeal.
>
> The Court of Appeal, by a majority, dismissed her appeal and held that, as the purposes of the Hague Convention 1980 were, in part, humanitarian, it had to be construed broadly as an international agreement according to its general tenor and purpose, without attributing to any of its terms a specialist meaning which the sort of words in question might have acquired under the domestic law of England. The expression 'rights of custody', in most cases, had to be interpreted to give it the widest sense possible in order to accord with the objective of returning children to their country of habitual residence. Rights of an inchoate nature were sufficient to create rights of custody. The removal and retention of the child were held to be wrongful, and the child was ordered to be returned to Australia.

Re B was distinguished in the case of *Re C (Child Abduction) (Unmarried Father: Rights of Custody)* [2002] EWHC 2219 (Fam). In this case, which concerned an unmarried father, although he shared the role of primary carer with the mother, the court held that, since the mother had at no point relinquished her care responsibility to the father, he had not acquired rights of custody within Articles 3 and 5 of the Hague Convention 1980 and so his application for return of the child was dismissed. The case shows the difficulties which those without parental responsibility may have in establishing custody rights under the Convention. Although it is possible for them to establish custody rights on the basis of inchoate rights, as in *Re B (A Minor) (Abduction)* (see above), such rights will exist only in limited circumstances. In *Re K (A Child) (Northern Ireland)* (2014) UKSC 29 Baroness Hale set out criteria which would need to be satisfied before an applicant can be held to have inchoate rights of custody: they must be undertaking the responsibilities, rights and powers entailed in the primary care of the child; they must not be sharing those responsibilities with the person who has a legal right to determine where the child shall live and how he shall be brought up; that person must have abandoned the child or delegated his primary care to them; there must be some form of legal or official recognition of their position in the country of habitual residence; and there must be every reason to believe that, were they to seek the protection of the courts of that country, the status quo would be preserved for the time being.

(i) The court can possess a right of custody

Removal or retention of a child can be wrongful where it breaches a 'right of custody' possessed by the court. The House of Lords so held in *Re H (Abduction: Rights of Custody)* [2000] 2 AC 291 where it overturned the trial judge's refusal to order that the mother return the child to Ireland (on the basis that the father had no custody rights), as the Irish court possessed custody rights in the child as an 'institution or other body' to which rights of custody could be attributed within the meaning of Article 3. In *A v B (Abduction: Rights of Custody: Declaration of Wrongful Removal)* [2008] EWHC 2524 (Fam) Bodey J confirmed that the courts can have rights of custody and made a declaration under section 8 of the Child Abduction and Custody Act 1985 to that effect. If a child is made a ward of court, the court acquires rights of custody in the child, which enables it to invoke the Hague Convention 1980 if the child is abducted (*Re S (Brussels II Revised: Enforcement of Contact Order)* [2008] 2 FLR 1358). This is particularly useful if the parent concerned about the risk of abduction does not have custody rights.

(b) Seeking a determination about rights of custody

Under Article 15 of the Hague Convention 1980 the court in England and Wales can seek a determination from the authorities of the State of the child's habitual residence as to whether or not removal of the child was a breach of a right of custody under the law of that country. In *Re T (Abduction: Rights of Custody)* [2008] EWHC 809 (Fam) Coleridge J said that it was important that issues such as rights of custody be very clearly settled by the foreign law; and that it would be highly invidious for the English court to trespass into such an area unless it was unavoidable. In *Re T* Coleridge J ordered that there should be a determination by the court in Oregon, USA, as to whether the father had rights of custody (as the mother had argued that he had no such rights).

(i) The status of an Article 15 ruling

The House of Lords held in *Re D (Abduction: Rights of Custody)* [2006] UKHL 51 that an Article 15 ruling from a requesting State is conclusive as to the parties' rights under the law of the requesting State, unless the circumstances are exceptional (for example where a ruling was obtained by fraud or in breach of the rules of natural justice). It held that a foreign court was much better placed than the English court to understand the true meaning and effect of its own laws in Hague Convention terms; and only if its characterisation of the parent's rights was clearly out of line with international understanding of the Convention's terms should the court in the UK decline to follow it.

13.7 The Hague Convention 1980 – return of children

Under the Hague Convention 1980 a person (or an institution or other body) claiming that a child has been removed or retained in breach of a right of custody can apply for assistance in securing the child's return from the central authority in the Contracting State of the child's habitual residence or in any other Contracting State (Art 8). The central authority of the State where the child is present must take all appropriate measures to effect the voluntary return of the child (Art 10). However, if effecting a voluntary return is not possible, then court proceedings will have to be brought.

As the Hague Convention 1980 is based on the presumption that an abducted child should be returned to his country of habitual residence, so that the court there can decide on his or her future, the court hearing a return application must order the child's return if the application is made during the first 12 months after the wrongful removal or retention (Art 12). After that 12-month period, the court must also order the child's return unless the child is 'settled in its new environment' (Art 12) (see below). The duty to return a child is, however, subject to any defence being successfully argued (see below). Because speed is of the essence in abduction cases, judicial and administrative authorities in a Contracting State are required to act expeditiously in return proceedings (Art 11; and see Brussels II Revised at 13.4(b) above).

13.8 The Hague Convention 1980 – defences to a return application

(a) Introduction

In addition to defences based on the court having no jurisdiction to hear the application (for example because the child is not habitually resident in a Contracting State or there is no custody right – see above), the following defences are expressly laid down in the Convention.

Defences under the Hague Convention

▶ The child is now settled in his new environment (Art 12).
▶ Consent (Art 13(a)).
▶ Acquiescence (Art 13(a)).
▶ Grave risk that the child's return will expose the child to physical or psychological harm or otherwise place him in an intolerable situation (Art 13(b)).
▶ The child objects to being returned and has attained an age and degree of maturity at which it is appropriate to take account of his views (Art 13).
▶ Where return of the child would not be permitted by the fundamental principles of the requested State relating to the protection of human rights and fundamental freedoms (Art 20).

In abduction cases involving EU Member States, these defences have to be considered in the light of Brussels II Revised (see 13.4(b) above).

(i) A high threshold for defences

The courts in England and Wales have set a high threshold for defences in order not to frustrate the Convention's primary objective, which is to effect the swift return of abducted children and restore the factual situation which existed before the wrongful removal or retention. Thus, the courts are reluctant to refuse to order the return of abducted children, and constantly emphasise that the underlying aim of the Convention is that the welfare of children is best determined by the court of the child's habitual residence. The alleged abductor therefore has a heavy burden to establish a defence; and, even if a defence is proved, the court nonetheless retains an overriding discretion to order the child's return.

(ii) The overriding discretion of the court

A successful defence based on habitual residence or lack of a custody right will mean that the case does not come within the scope of the Hague Convention 1980, and that will be the end of the matter. In respect of the other defences, a successful defence will not necessarily result in the court refusing to order the child's return. This is because Article 18 of the Convention gives the court an overriding discretion to decide whether or not to order the return of an abducted child.

Before the decision of the House of Lords in *Re M (Abduction: Zimbabwe)* [2007] UKHL 55 (see below), a long line of Court of Appeal authorities had held that, even if a defence was established, the court should order return unless there was something special or exceptional about the case. However, in *Re M* Baroness Hale said it was neither necessary nor desirable to import an additional gloss of 'exceptionality' into the plain wording of the Hague Convention 1980, as the circumstances in which return may be refused were themselves exceptions to the general rule. This was reiterated by Baroness Hale and Lord Wilson, giving judgment in the Supreme Court in *Re E (Children) (Abduction: Custody Appeal)* (see 13.4 above).

(b) The child is now settled in their new environment (Article 12)

Article 12 provides that where an application for return is made more than one year after a child has been wrongfully removed or retained, an order for return must be made, unless it can be shown that the child is settled in their new environment. 'New environment' means the total physical, social, emotional and psychological experience of the child. Each case depends on its own facts (see, for example, *Re H and L (Abduction: Acquiescence)* [2010] EWHC 652 (Fam) where the father's application for a return order was refused as the children were found to be settled in England; and the father had also acquiesced in their removal). However, even if it is proved that the child is settled in his or her new environment, the court has a discretion under Article 18 of the Hague Convention 1980 to order return, as the leading case on Article 12, shows.

▶ *Re M (Abduction: Zimbabwe)* [2007] UKHL 55

Two girls (aged ten and 13), born in Zimbabwe to Zimbabwean parents, lived in Zimbabwe with their father after their parents separated. Four years later their mother wrongfully removed them secretly to the UK where she sought asylum. This was refused, but the mother and the children remained in the UK where the two girls became well settled in their local church and school. The father discovered their whereabouts about six months later but did not seek their return under the Hague Convention 1980 until about two years later.

Despite finding that the two children were settled in the UK and that they objected to return (under Article 12), Wood J ordered their immediate return, applying the principle that only in exceptional cases should the court exercise its overriding discretion to refuse to order an immediate return once a defence was made out. The mother's appeal to the Court of Appeal (where she argued, *inter alia*, that Wood J had fallen into error by applying a test of 'exceptionality' at the discretion stage) was dismissed; and so she appealed to the House of Lords, where the children were joined as parties (having regard to the principles laid down in *Re D (Abduction: Rights of Custody)* [2006] UKHL 51). In addition to the arguments raised before the Court of Appeal, the mother raised the issue of whether the

Court of Appeal had been right in *Cannon v Cannon* [2004] EWCA Civ 1330 to hold that, even if settlement was established under Article 12, the courts retained a discretion under Article 18 to order return.

The House of Lords (with Baroness Hale giving the leading opinion and Lord Rodger dissenting) held that the courts have a discretion to order that a child be returned, even if the child is settled in his or her new environment for the purposes of Article 12. Baroness Hale said that such a construction recognised the flexibility in the concept of settlement, which might arise in a variety of circumstances and to very different degrees; and it acknowledged that late application may be the result of active concealment of where the child has gone. It also left the court with all options open.

Baroness Hale ruled that it was wrong to import any exceptionality into the exercise of discretion under the Hague Convention. She also said that the policy considerations of swift return and comity would carry less weight the longer the abducted child had been in the UK; but that in settlement cases 'the policy of the Convention would not necessarily point towards return'.

Applying the above approach to the facts of the case, the House of Lords allowed the mother's appeal and refused to order that the children be returned to Zimbabwe.

(For a case commentary on *Re M*, see Schuz [2008] CFLQ 64; and see also *Re (O (Children) (Abduction: Settlement)* [2011] EWCA Civ 128 and *F v M and N (Abduction: Acquiescence: Settlement)* [2008] EWHC 1525 (Fam).)

(c) Consent (Article 13(a))

The court can refuse to order return if it can be proved that the applicant for a return order consented to the child's removal or retention. Consent is a question of fact, but it must be clear, unequivocal and informed (*Re P (Abduction: Consent)* [2004] EWCA Civ 971, *Re P-J (Children) (Abduction: Consent)* [2009] EWCA Civ 588). The principles that apply to acquiescence (see below) also apply to consent.

Each case turns on its own facts. Thus, for example, in *M v M (Abduction: Consent)* [2007] EWHC 1404 (Fam) Sumner J refused to order the children's return to Greece as the mother had proved by clear and cogent evidence that the father had consented to her bringing the children to the UK. Similarly, in *K v K (Abduction: Consent)* [2009] EWHC 2721 (Fam) it was found that the father had consented to the mother taking the child from Ireland to visit their maternal grandmother in England, and so his application for the return of the children to Ireland was dismissed. In *A v T (Relocation: Consent)* [2012] EWHC 3882 (Fam) the mother's argument that that father had given unequivocal consent to the children's removal to England was accepted and the court once again exercised its discretion to refuse to order the children's return to Sweden. (See *K v D* [2014] EWHC 3188 (Fam) for an application of the principles in *Re P (Abduction: Consent)* and *Re P-J (Children) (Abduction: Consent)* above.)

(d) Acquiescence (Article 13(a))

The person who removed or retained the child has a defence to a return application if it can be proved that the applicant acquiesced in the removal or retention. A key difference between consent and acquiescence is that consent precedes the removal, whereas acquiescence follows it. The following case, which is the leading case on acquiescence, shows that an attempt to reach a voluntary agreement for a child's return does not necessarily of itself amount to acquiescence.

▶ *Re H (Abduction: Acquiescence)* **[1998] AC 72**

The parents were strict Orthodox Jews, who were married and lived in Israel. The mother took the children to England without the father's consent. The father contacted his local Beth Din (a religious court of law), and it entered its own summons for the children's return, which the mother ignored. The Beth Din later ordered the father to take whatever steps he saw fit, and six months after the children had been removed from Israel he invoked proceedings under the Hague Convention 1980 in the High Court in England. The mother argued that he had acquiesced in the children's removal by failing to make a prompt application. The High Court ordered the children's return, but the Court of Appeal allowed the mother's appeal, holding that the father had acquiesced, applying its earlier decision in *Re A (Minors) (Abduction: Custody Rights)* [1992] Fam 106, where, by a majority, it had applied an objective test to establish acquiescence, and had held that acquiescence could be signified by a single act or communication, even though that act or communication appeared to be at variance with the general course of a parent's conduct. The father appealed to the House of Lords.

The House of Lords held, allowing his appeal and ordering the children's return to Israel, that the objective test of acquiescence laid down by the Court of Appeal in *Re A* was wrong. The correct approach was that adopted by Balcombe LJ who had dissented in *Re A*. Applying this approach, it was clear that the father had not acquiesced in the children's retention in England.

Lord Browne-Wilkinson laid down the following principles on acquiescence:

▶ Whether the wronged parent has acquiesced in the removal or retention of a child depends on his or her actual state of mind. The test is subjective.
▶ The subjective intention of the wronged parent is a question of fact for the trial judge to determine in all the circumstances of the case, the burden of proof being on the abducting parent.
▶ But there is one exception, namely: where the wronged parent's words or actions clearly and unequivocally show and have led the other parent to believe that the wronged parent is not asserting or going to assert his right to the summary return of the child and are inconsistent with such return, justice requires that the wronged parent be held to have acquiesced.

Although each case depends on its own facts, the following approaches to acquiescence have been taken in the case-law.

A custody application made in the child's country of habitual residence is a strong indication that there is no acquiescence (Re F (A Minor) (Child Abduction) [1992] 1 FLR 548).

Making long-term plans for contact may indicate acquiescence (Re S (Abduction: Acquiescence) [1998] 2 FLR 115).

Bringing proceedings for contact in the English courts, even though brought in ignorance of the Hague Convention 1980, may indicate acquiescence (Re B (Abduction: Acquiescence) [1999] 2 FLR 818).

A willingness to be involved in negotiations to sort out what is best for a child and the parties does not necessarily amount to acquiescence (Re I (Abduction: Acquiescence) [1999] 1 FLR 778, R v R [2016] EWHC 1339 (Fam)) as negotiations at the early stage of a difficult broken relationship are to be encouraged (P v P (Abduction: Acquiescence) [1998] 2 FLR 835).

Consenting to full and final residence orders being made in England and Wales may constitute acquiescence (Re D (Abduction: Acquiescence) [1998] 1 FLR 686).

Mere inaction does not necessarily on its own amount to acquiescence (AF v MB-F (Abduction: Rights of Custody) [2008] EWHC 272 (Fam)) including where the delay is due to attempting a reconciliation (Re H (Abduction: Consent: Acquiescence) [2013] EWHC 3857 (Fam)).

It is not necessarily a prerequisite for establishing acquiescence that a parent has correct advice or detailed knowledge of his or her rights under the Hague Convention 1980; what is important is that the applicant knew that they could bring a return application but chose to accept the situation as it was (B-G v B-G [2008] EWHC 688 (Fam)).

(e) Grave risk of harm, or otherwise placing the child in an intolerable situation (Article 13(b))

For this defence to succeed, it must be proved that there is a grave risk that return will expose the child to physical or psychological harm or otherwise place the child in an intolerable situation (Article 13(b)). In the following case, the Supreme Court considered (for the first time) the approach to the interpretation and application of the grave risk of harm defence.

▶ *Re E (Children) (Abduction: Custody Appeal)* [2011] UKSC 27

The case involved an application by the father for his two children (aged four and six) to be returned to Norway. The mother's Article 13(b) defence was that her mental health was so fragile that if she were ordered to return the children there was a grave risk that they would be exposed to psychological harm and/or placed in an intolerable situation by virtue of the impact upon them of the deterioration in her mental health. She argued in relation to Article 13(b) that the requirement laid down by the courts in England and Wales (namely for 'clear and compelling evidence' of a 'grave risk of harm or other intolerability which must be measured as substantial, not trivial and of a severity which is much more than is inherent in the inevitable disruption, uncertainty and anxiety which follows an unwelcome return') was a gloss on the wording of the Hague Convention 1980 and imported a higher than normal standard of proof and a more restrictive meaning than the words of the Convention required.

The Supreme Court held, *inter alia*, with respect to the Article 13(b) defence that:

▶ There was no need for Article 13(b) to be construed narrowly, as the exceptions to the obligation to return are by their very nature restricted in their scope. They do not need any extra interpretation or gloss.

> ▶ In relation to Article 13(b) the burden of proof lies with the 'person, institution or other body' which opposes the child's return. The standard of proof is the ordinary balance of probabilities but the court will be mindful of the limitations involved in the summary nature of the Convention process. It will rarely be appropriate to hear oral evidence of the allegations made under Article 13(b) and thus neither those allegations nor their rebuttal are usually tested in cross-examination.
> ▶ The risk to the child must be 'grave', not just 'real'.

Each case depends on its own facts. The Article 13(b) defence was argued, for example, in the following cases but was not accepted and the children were ordered to be returned: *Re S (Abduction: Intolerable Situation: Beth Din)* [2000] 1 FLR 454 (religious discrimination against women who were Orthodox Jews which would breach the right to family life of the mother and children under Article 8 of the European Convention on Human Rights); *Re S (Abduction: Custody Rights)* [2002] EWCA Civ 908 (terrorism in Israel); *Re W (Abduction: Domestic Violence)* [2004] EWHC 1247 (Fam) (mother subjected to regular abuse, which included violence, threats with a firearm and demeaning sexual practices, but no evidence that the child had suffered distress); and *TB v JB (Abduction: Grave Risk of Harm)* [2001] 2 FLR 515 (alleged physical and sexual violence inflicted on the mother and physical abuse of the children).

For cases where the Article 13(b) grave risk of harm defence was accepted, see, for example: *Re D (Article 13b: Non-Return)* [2006] EWCA Civ 146 (return to Venezuela refused where the mother had been subject to a targeted firearm assault outside her home); and *Re H (Abduction)* [2009] EWHC 1735 (Fam) (return to Spain refused where there was a real risk that the oldest child would attempt suicide if ordered to return).

(i) Allegations of domestic violence

Whether allegations of domestic harm will constitute a grave risk of harm will depend on the circumstances of the case. Return may be ordered even where serious domestic violence is alleged, as the court in England and Wales will presume that the courts in the foreign jurisdiction will be able to provide and implement protective measures. The following case, which went to the Supreme Court and involved allegations of domestic violence, affirmed the approach adopted in the earlier Supreme Court case of *Re E (Children) (Abduction: Custody Appeal)* (see above).

▶ *Re S (Abduction: Art 13 Defence) (Reunite International Child Abduction Centre Intervening)* **[2012] UKSC 10**

The father applied for return of the child (aged two), who had been wrongly removed to the UK from Australia by the mother. The mother raised a defence under Article 13(b) on the basis of alleged abusive behaviour by the father towards her and the potential detriment to her mental health if she was compelled to return. Charles J accepted the mother's Article 13(b) defence and exercised his discretion to refuse to order the child's return. The Court of Appeal allowed the father's appeal and ordered return. The mother appealed to the Supreme Court.

The Supreme Court, allowing her appeal, held, *inter alia*, that the effect of *Re E* (see above) meant that the critical question was what would happen if, with the mother, the child was returned. The Court of Appeal had failed to appreciate that the mother's fears about the father's likely conduct rested on much more than disputed allegations. Equally, it had paid scant regard to the unusually powerful nature of the medical evidence about the mother. Overarchingly, it had failed to recognise that the judgment about the level of risk which was required to be made by Article 13(b) was one which fell to be made by the trial judge and that it should not be overturned unless, whether by reference to the law or to evidence, it had not been open to him to make.

(See also *LS v AS* [2014] EWHC 1626 (Fam) where the defence succeeded due to domestic violence; and *Re F (A Child) (Abduction: Art. 13(b): Psychiatric Assessment)* [2014] EWCA Civ 275 where the principles in *Re S* were applied but the defence failed.)

(ii) The 'grave risk' defence and abductions in the EU

In an abduction involving two Contracting States to the Hague Convention 1980 which are also Member States of the EU, Article 11(4) of Brussels II Revised provides that a court 'cannot refuse to return a child on the basis of the grave risk defence under Article 13(b) if it is established that adequate arrangements have been made to secure the protection of the child after his or her return' (see, for example, *F v M (Abduction: Grave Risk of Harm)* [2008] EWHC 1467 (Fam)).

(f) Child objects to being returned (Article 13)

The court may refuse to order return if it finds that the child objects to being returned *and* the child has attained an age and degree of maturity at which it is appropriate to take account of the child's views. The court has a discretion as to the amount of weight to be given to the child's views, but will bear in mind the policy of the Hague Convention 1980 that abducted children should be returned to their country of habitual residence. The weight to be attached to the child's objections will depend on the age and maturity of the child.

In *AF v MB-F (Abduction: Rights of Custody)* [2008] EWHC 272 (Fam) Sir Mark Potter P, summarising the earlier case-law, including the House of Lords decision in *Re M (A Child) (Abduction: Child's Objections)* [2007] EWCA Civ 260, said that the court must consider the following questions when considering this defence:

▶ Are the objections made out?
▶ Has the child reached an age and degree of maturity at which it is appropriate to take account of his or her views?
▶ Have those views been shaped or coloured by undue influence or pressure directly or indirectly exerted by the abducting parent to an extent which requires such views to be disregarded or discounted?
▶ What weight should be placed on the child's objections in the light of any countervailing factors, and in particular the policy considerations of the Hague

Convention 1980 (namely that deterrence of abductors and the welfare interests of children are generally best served by the making of an order for prompt return; and the need to respect the judicial processes of the requesting State)?

A two-stage approach is adopted in determining whether the exception in Article 13 is made out: a factual stage; and a discretionary stage. At the first stage, the court must be satisfied of the nature of the child's objection along with the child's maturity, strength of emotion and independence of view. If these are satisfied, then the 'gate' is opened to the exercise of judicial discretion. The court will be vigilant to ascertain and assess the reasons for the child not wishing to return; and, although Article 12 requires the child to be returned to the *State* of habitual residence, not to the person requesting the child's return, the court can consider the fact that a child is objecting to returning to a parent rather than to a State.

(i) At what age will a child's objections be taken into account?

Although the original aim of the Hague Convention 1980 was to permit the views of mature adolescents to be taken into account, the trend over the years has been to take into account the views of much younger children. In *Re W (Abduction: Child's Objections)* [2010] EWCA Civ 520, where Black J in the High Court had taken into account the objections of two children aged six and eight and refused to order their return to Ireland, Wilson LJ in the Court of Appeal expressed concern that lowering the age at which a child's objections could be taken into account might gradually erode the policy of the Convention to return children swiftly to their country of habitual residence. However, Wilson LJ drew attention to the safeguard in the expectation set out in *Re R (Child Abduction: Acquiescence)* [1995] 1 FLR 716 that, in the discretionary exercise, the objections of an older child would deserve greater weight than those of a younger child. In *Re G (Abduction: Children's Objections)* [2010] EWCA Civ 1232 the Court of Appeal warned of the dangers of refusing to listen to the objections of articulate adolescent children. In *Re M (Abduction: Child's Objections)* [2007] EWCA Civ 260 the Court of Appeal accepted the objections of the child (an intelligent girl aged eight) and refused to order her return to Serbia.

(ii) Objections are not determinative

The child's objections to return will not determine the matter; their views are one factor to be taken into account by the court at the discretion stage (*Re M and others (Children) (Abduction: Child's Objections)* [2015] EWCA Civ 26). Thus, for example, in *FK v ML* [2016] EWHC 517 (Fam), the court ordered the return of a 13-year-old boy to Ireland, despite his strong objections, due to strong countervailing factors.

(iii) How the child's views are conveyed to the court

The usual way in which the child's objections are put before the court is by way of a report by a Cafcass officer (see 1.7), but in some cases the child may be separately represented. There is also an increasing trend for judges to meet children face to face in appropriate cases (see 13.4(c) above).

13.9 The Hague Convention on Parental Responsibility and Protection of Children 1996

The Hague Convention on Parental Responsibility and Protection of Children 1996 (Hague Convention 1996) came into force in the UK in 2012. It is broader in scope than the Hague Convention on International Child Abduction 1980 (Hague Convention 1980) as it covers a wide range of protection measures for children in international situations, and does not just focus on abduction. For example, it provides for the recognition and enforcement of orders between Contracting States (such as orders for contact and residence), establishes rules of jurisdiction between Contracting States and provides for cooperation between States. It also provides another potential route by which a child who has been abducted can be returned. For example, the Hague Convention 1996 applies to children up to 18 whereas the Hague Convention 1980 applies only to children under 16. The Hague Convention 1996 was useful in the case of *Re J (A Child) (Reunite International Child Abduction Centre and others intervening)* [2015] UKSC 70 where the State (Morocco) had not been recognised as a signatory of the Hague Convention 1980, but was recognised as a signatory of the Hague Convention 1996. Further discussion of the Hague Convention 1996 is beyond the scope of this book, but see Lowe and Nicholls, *The 1996 Hague Convention on the Protection of Children*, 2012, Family Law.

13.10 The European Convention on the Recognition and Enforcement of Decisions Concerning Custody of Children 1980

The European Convention on the Recognition and Enforcement of Decisions Concerning Custody of Children 1980 (the European Convention 1980) was implemented into UK law by Part II of the Child Abduction and Custody Act 1985. The text of the Convention is laid down in Schedule 2 to that Act.

The European Convention 1980 is rarely used in abduction cases because it deals only with the enforcement of custody and access *orders*, whereas the Hague Convention 1980 deals with custody *rights*. The European Convention 1980 has also been largely superseded by the Hague Convention 1980 and Brussels II Revised (see 13.4(b) above), and therefore only a brief outline is provided here. The European Convention 1980 may, however, be useful where the Hague Convention 1980 does not apply (for example to enforce an access order or where the person who has wrongly removed or retained the child has sole custody).

The European Convention 1980 deals with the recognition and enforcement of custody decisions where there has been 'improper removal of a child' (Art 1(d)), by allowing any person who has obtained a custody decision in a Contracting State to apply to a central authority in another Contracting State to have that decision recognised or enforced in that State (Art 4(1)). In no circumstances may the original foreign custody decision be reviewed as to its substance (Article 9(3)).

Decisions on access, and custody decisions dealing with access, can also be recognised and enforced under the Convention subject to the same conditions which apply to custody decisions (Art 11(1)), but the competent authority of the State addressed may fix the conditions for the implementation and exercise of the right of access, taking into account, in particular, undertakings given by the parties on this matter (Art 11(2)). Where there is no decision as to access, or where recognition or enforcement of a custody decision has been refused, the central authority of the State addressed may apply to its own competent authorities for a decision on the right of access if the person claiming a right of access so requests (Art 11(3)).

(a)   Refusal to register an order

The court can refuse to register an order, and thereby fail to recognise and enforce it (see Arts 9 and 10). However, it is unlikely to do so, as the aim of the Convention, like that of the Hague Convention 1980, is to foster international cooperation to effect the return of abducted children.

There are few reported cases on the European Convention 1980 because it is rarely invoked in the courts in England and Wales. It was invoked in *Re L (Abduction: European Convention: Access)* [1999] 2 FLR 1089 (unsuccessfully by grandparents who wished to enforce a French access order) and in *AA v TT (Recognition and Enforcement)* [2014] EWHC 3488 (Fam) (also unsuccessfully by a father who wished to enforce a Turkish custody order). In *Re A (Foreign Access Order: Enforcement)* [1996] 1 FLR 561 a French access order was, however, recognised and enforced by the English courts.

The central authority which deals with the enforcement of orders under the European Convention 1980 in England and Wales is the International Child Abduction and Contact Unit.

13.11 Non-Convention cases

If a child is abducted out of the UK to a country which is not party to any of the Conventions set out above, the 'left-behind' parent is in a precarious position because there is no network of Contracting States which can work together to effect the child's return. A parent will have to endeavour to reach an amicable settlement with the abducting parent; or commence legal proceedings in the country to which the child has been taken, which can be difficult and expensive. Although wardship or the inherent jurisdiction *may* provide a remedy in England and Wales even though the child is not present in the jurisdiction (see 8.7), it may not necessarily do so. Thus, for example, in the case of *Al Habtoor v Fotheringham* [2001] EWCA Civ 186 the Court of Appeal held that there was no jurisdiction to hear the mother's case in wardship because the child was resident in Dubai and was not a British national.

Where a child is brought into the UK from a non-Convention country, a return application can be made to the High Court in wardship proceedings or under the inherent jurisdiction (see 8.7), or in section 8 order proceedings under the Children Act 1989 (CA 1989) (see 10.4). For examples of cases in which the inherent jurisdiction was used, see *Re F (Abduction: Removal Outside Jurisdiction)* [2008] EWCA Civ 842 and *Re U (Abduction: Nigeria)* [2010] EWHC 1179 (Fam).

The High Court has a wide discretion in all of these proceedings, and, unlike proceedings under the Hague Convention 1980, there is no presumption in favour of ordering return. Thus the court can choose to investigate the merits of the case or exercise a 'summary jurisdiction'. In other words, the court can choose to order the child's immediate return without conducting a full investigation of the merits (see further below).

(a)   The governing principles in non-Convention cases

The principles applicable in non-Convention cases were laid down by the House of Lords in the following case, which is the leading case.

▶ *Re J (A Child) (Child Returned Abroad: Convention Rights)* [2005] UKHL 40

The mother took the child to England from Saudi Arabia. The father applied under section 8 of the CA 1989 for a specific issue order for the return of the child to Saudi Arabia, but the trial judge refused the application. The father appealed to the Court of Appeal, which unanimously allowed his appeal. The mother appealed to the House of Lords, which allowed her appeal, and restored the orders made by the trial judge. The House of Lords held that the trial judge and the Court of Appeal had been wrong to leave out of account the absence of a jurisdiction in the home country to enable the mother to bring the child back to England without the father's consent.

Baroness Hale, who gave the leading opinion, laid down the following principles and approaches to be applied in non-Convention cases for the summary return of children:

▶ The child's welfare is paramount and the specialist rules and concepts of the Hague Convention 1980 are not to be applied by analogy in non-Convention cases.
▶ Each case depends on its own facts. In some cases summary return will be in the child's best interests but in others it will not.
▶ In having to make a decision whether or not to order summary return, a judge might find it convenient to start from the proposition that it was likely to be better for a child to return to his home country for any dispute about his future to be decided there. Any case against his doing so had to be made.
▶ It should not be assumed that allowing a child to remain in the UK while his future is decided here inevitably means that he will remain here forever.
▶ An important variable is the degree of connection of the child with each country. This does not involve applying the technical concept of habitual residence, but to ask in a common-sense way with which country the child has the closer connection. In determining this issue of the child's 'home country', the child's nationality, where he has lived for most of his life, first language, race or ethnicity, religion, culture and education are relevant matters. A closely related factor is the length of time that the child has spent in each country. Uprooting a child from one environment and bringing him to a completely unfamiliar one, especially if that has been done clandestinely, may well not be in the child's best interests. But if the child is already familiar with the UK, and had been here for some time without objection, it might be less disruptive for him to remain a little longer while his medium- and longer-term future are decided.
▶ The relevance of the fact that the legal system of the other country is different from that in the UK depends on the facts of each case. It is wrong to say that the future of the child should be decided according to the conception of child welfare which exactly corresponds with that which is current in England and Wales. In a world which values difference, one culture is not inevitably to be preferred to another. For this reason, English law does not start from any *a priori* assumptions about what is best for any individual child. The court must consider the individual child and weigh in the balance the checklist of factors in section 1(3) of the CA 1989 (see 10.3). If there is a genuine issue between the parents as to whether it is in the best interests of the child to live in the UK or elsewhere, it is relevant whether that issue is capable of being tried in the courts

of the country to which he is to be returned. If those courts have no choice but to do what the father wishes, without hearing the mother, then the English courts must ask themselves whether it is in the child's best interests to enable the dispute to be heard. The absence of a 'relocation' jurisdiction in the other country may be a decisive factor, unless it appears that the mother may not be able to make a good case for relocation. There may be cases where the connection of the child and the family with the other country is so strong that any difference between the legal systems in the UK and the other country should carry little weight.

▶ These considerations above must not, however, stand in the way of a swift and unsentimental decision to return the child to his home country, even if that country is very different from the UK. The concept of welfare in the UK is capable of taking cultural and religious factors into account in deciding how a child should be brought up. It also gives great weight to the child's need for a meaningful relationship with both parents.

However, although the child's welfare is the paramount consideration in non-Convention cases, Baroness Hale stated *obiter* in *Re M (Abduction: Zimbabwe)* [2007] UKHL 55 (a case involving the Hague Convention 1980) that in non-Convention cases the court has 'the power to order the immediate return of the child to a foreign jurisdiction without conducting a full investigation of the merits'. Her Ladyship said:

> Thus there is always a choice to be made between summary return and a further investigation. There is also a choice to be made as to the depth into which the judge will go in investigating the merits of the case before making that choice. One size does not fit all. The judge may well find it convenient to start from the proposition that it is likely to be better for a child to return to his home country for any disputes about his future to be decided there. A case against his doing so has to be made. But the weight to be given to that factor and to all the other relevant factors, some of which are canvassed in *Re J* (see above), will vary enormously from case to case.

(For an application of these principles see *S v S* [2014] EWHC 575 (Fam).)

(b) Human rights, Sharia law and abductions

In the following case the mother abducted the child from the Lebanon and, when her application for asylum in England was refused, she claimed that deporting her and her son back to the Lebanon would infringe their human rights. Their claim before the House of Lords was successful, and the House also emphasised the importance of the separate representation of the child. Baroness Hale also considered that the child's human rights were of greater weight than those of his mother.

▶ *EM (Lebanon) v Secretary of State for the Home Department* **[2008] UKHL 64**

The Lebanese mother had obtained a divorce in the Lebanon because of her husband's violence. Under Sharia law, which was applicable in Lebanon, the father (who had seen their son only on the day of his birth) retained custody of the child and would be entitled to physical custody once the child reached the age of seven, with contact with the mother entirely at the father's discretion. When the child reached seven, the authorities sought to enforce the transfer of the child to the father, whereupon the mother went into hiding and fled with the child to England where she sought asylum. Her application was rejected and she appealed, arguing in the House of Lords that deporting her and the child back to Lebanon would infringe their Article 8 right to respect for family life and her Article 14 right to non-discrimination under the European Convention of Human Rights (ECHR). By the time of the hearing, the child was aged 12.

The House of Lords held, allowing the appeal:

▶ The threshold test for determining whether returning a person to a State not bound by the ECHR will involve a breach of their Article 8 right is a stringent one. There must be a flagrant breach of the right, such as will completely deny or nullify it in the destination country. Serious or discriminatory interference with the right protected is insufficient.

▶ In no meaningful sense could occasional supervised visits by the mother to her child at a place other than her home, even if such visits could be ordered, be described as family life. The effect of return would thus be to destroy the family life of the mother and child as it was now lived.

▶ The lower courts had been disadvantaged by the absence of representations on behalf of the child. The hearing before the House of Lords had underscored the importance of ascertaining and communicating to the court the views of a child such as the child in this case. In the great majority of cases, the interests of the child, although calling for separate consideration, are unlikely to differ from those of the applicant parent. If there is a genuine conflict, separate representation may be called for, but advisors should not be astute to detect a conflict where the interests of parent and child are essentially congruent.

BARONESS HALE: The violation of the child's right was of greater weight than that of the mother's. The very essence of his right would be destroyed if he were returned and removed from her, with no justification possible under Article 8(2) since the reasons for its destruction were purely arbitrary and paid no regard to his interests. There had been no family life between the child and his father or paternal family in the Lebanon, and so the circumstances were quite different from the general run of child abduction cases where it is the abduction, rather than the return, that interferes with that family life.

Summary

▶ Child abduction is an increasing problem and a global one. In order to prevent child abduction, the courts in England and Wales have extensive powers. Where child abduction occurs, there are various international agreements to protect children who have been abducted and their parents. The most important of these are the Hague Convention 1980 and Brussels II Revised. However, if children are abducted to countries that are not signatories to such agreements, securing their return is more difficult, and may be impossible.

▶ Where there is a risk of abduction, preventative measures can be taken, such as: seeking police assistance (which can include the implementation of a 'port alert'); making an application for a court order under section 8 of the Children Act 1989 or under the wardship or inherent jurisdiction of the High Court; or seeking the assistance of the Passport Office. Parents without parental responsibility, such as unmarried fathers, are in a vulnerable situation and should consider applying for a court order if there is a risk of their child being abducted. Child abduction is a criminal offence under the Child Abduction Act 1984 and

Summary cont'd

under the common law offence of kidnapping. Under that Act, a child can be lawfully taken out of the UK provided there is no court order prohibiting removal and every person with parental responsibility consents.

▶ The Hague Convention 1980 enables Contracting States to work together to return children who have been wrongfully removed from their country of habitual residence or wrongfully retained in another Contracting State in breach of a right of custody. The Convention has been implemented into UK law by Part I of the Child Abduction and Custody Act 1985. The policy of the Convention is for children to be speedily returned to their country of habitual residence so that the court in that country can decide on the future arrangements for the child. The central authority for England and Wales for the purposes of the Convention is the International Child Abduction and Contact Unit. In Convention cases brought before the UK courts, the welfare of the child is regarded as an important consideration, but not the paramount consideration. This is despite the fact that the European Court of Human Rights has held otherwise. The courts in the UK also take the view that Convention proceedings do not need to be investigated in depth on their merits but are summary proceedings.

▶ Where a child has been abducted within the EU, Brussels II Revised must also be taken into account.

▶ The voice of the child is usually heard in proceedings under the Hague Convention 1980 by means of a Cafcass report, although in some cases the court may allow the child to be separately represented. Judges have also increasingly adopted the practice of meeting the child.

▶ The UK courts adopt a purposive approach to construing the Hague Convention 1980, but the senior judiciary have said that the courts should not add additional words to the provisions of the Convention.

▶ To come within the jurisdiction of the Hague Convention 1980 the child must be under 16 and must have been wrongly removed from a Contracting State to another Contracting State (or wrongfully retained in that Contracting State) in breach of a right of custody. The child must have been habitually resident in a Contracting State. 'Habitual residence' is not defined in the Convention – its meaning must instead be determined by the principles laid down in case-law.

▶ The removal or retention of a child will be considered wrongful where it is in breach of custody rights under the law of the State in which the child was habitually resident immediately before the removal or retention (Art 3). The courts in the UK have adopted a purposive approach to the meaning of 'custody'.

▶ Guidance and assistance about seeking the return of a child can be sought from the central authority in the Contracting State of the child's habitual residence or in any other Contracting State (Art 8).

▶ There are specific 'defences' to return laid down in the Convention, namely that: the child is now settled in his new environment (Art 12); the other parent consented or acquiesced in the removal or retention of the child (Art 13(a)); there is a grave risk that the child's return will expose the child to physical or psychological harm or otherwise place him in an intolerable situation (Art 13(b)); the child objects to being returned and has attained an age and degree of maturity at which it is appropriate to take account of his views (Art 13); or where return of the child would not be permitted by the fundamental principles of the requested State relating to the protection of human rights and fundamental freedoms (Art 20). Even if a defence is established, the court has an overriding discretion to order return (see Art 18), because of the policy objective that abducted children should be speedily returned to their country of habitual residence so that their future can be determined there.

Summary cont'd

▶ The Hague Convention 1996 is broader in scope than the Hague Convention 1980 and provides an additional route in certain child abduction cases. It also provides for the recognition and enforcement of certain orders relating to children between Contracting States.

▶ The European Convention on the Recognition and Enforcement of Decisions Concerning Custody of Children 1980 was implemented into UK law by Part II of the Child Abduction and Custody Act 1985. It is rarely used in abduction cases because it deals with the enforcement of custody and access *orders*, whereas the Hague Convention 1980 deals with custody *rights*. The European Convention 1980 has been largely superseded by the Hague Convention 1980 and by Brussels II Revised.

▶ Where a child is wrongfully brought into England and Wales from a non-Convention country, the court will decide whether the welfare of the child requires it to order the child's return. There is no presumption in favour of return, as there is in cases involving the Hague Convention 1980; but rather the court will exercise its discretion, based on the facts of the case.

Further reading and references

Cobb J, 'Seen but not heard?' [2015] Fam Law 144.

Hale J, 'Listening to children: are we nearly there yet?' [2016] Fam Law 320.

Lamont, 'The EU: protecting children's rights in child abduction' [2008] IFL 110.

Lowe and Stephens, 'Operating the 1980 Hague Abduction Convention: the 2008 statistics' [2011] Fam Law 1216.

Lowe and Nicholls, *The 1996 Hague Convention on the Protection of Children*, 2012, Family Law.

McEleavy, 'Evaluating the views of abducted children: trends in appellate case-law' [2008] CFLQ 230.

Schuz, 'Habitual residence of children under the Hague Child Abduction Convention – theory and practice' [2001] CFLQ 1.

Schuz, 'In search of a settled interpretation of Article 12(2) of the Hague Child Abduction Convention' [2008] CFLQ 64.

Schulz, 'Guidance from Luxembourg: first ECJ judgment clarifying the relationship between the 1980 Hague Convention and Brussels II Revised' [2008] IFL 221.

Websites

Foreign and Commonwealth Office: www.fco.gov.uk/travel

INCADAT (Hague Convention Child Abduction Database): www.incadat.com

Reunite (the International Child Abduction Centre): www.reunite.org

Links to relevant websites can also be found at: www.palgravehighered.com/law/familylaw9e

Chapter 14

Child protection

14.1 The practice of child protection

(a) People involved in child protection

Many people are involved in the task of providing protection and services for children classified as being 'in need'. The emphasis is on a multi-agency and inter-agency approach. Of particular importance are local authority social workers who have a statutory responsibility to work together with other agencies and relevant partners to protect and make provision for children in need. Their responsibilities are laid down in the Children Act 1989 and the Children Act 2004; and they are also in rules of practice, regulations and guidance which local authorities have a statutory obligation to comply with (see *Working Together to Safeguard Children*, 2015). The Children and Family Court Advisory and Support Service (Cafcass) performs a very important function by providing Children's Guardians in public law proceedings, whose role it is to safeguard the welfare of the child in court proceedings involving local authorities. Voluntary agencies, such as the National Society for the Prevention of Cruelty to Children, also provide services to protect and assist children and their families.

(b) The task of child protection – getting the balance right

Social workers engaged in child protection have a difficult task as they must take adequate steps to protect children but at the same time ensure that they are not too intrusive into family life. As social services departments are public authorities for the purposes of the Human Rights Act 1998 (HRA 1998), they must exercise their powers and duties in line with the European Convention on Human Rights (ECHR). Thus, they must respect the rights of children and parents to enjoy a private and family life (Art 8) whilst also ensuring that children do not suffer inhuman and degrading treatment (Art 3). Local authorities can have their acts or omissions challenged both in the courts under the HRA 1998 and in other ways (see further at 14.11 below).

Social workers are sometimes criticised for not intervening enough to protect children; and there is considerable media coverage and concern when children are failed by the child protection system. The Victoria Climbié case, in which an eight-year-old girl died from malnutrition and hypothermia in 2000 after suffering months of torture and neglect despite being known to the authorities, was such a case; and it led to both an inquiry into her death (chaired by Lord Laming) and subsequent reforms of the child protection system by the Children Act 2004 (CA 2004) (see further at 14.2 below). Another case where social workers, and other people working with children, were criticised was that of Baby P who was seen 60 times in eight months by different agencies but who died in 2007 aged 17 months as a result of serious injuries inflicted by his mother, her boyfriend and their lodger. As a result of Baby P's death and the perceived failure of the child protection system, Lord Laming was asked by the Government to prepare a report on how effectively children were being safeguarded following the reforms introduced as a result of the Victoria Climbié Inquiry. Lord Laming's report, *The Protection of Children in England: A Progress Report*, March 2009, HC 330, recommended, *inter alia*, ensuring that child protection work was properly resourced and that changes were made to address inadequacies in the recruitment and training of front-line social workers.

Whilst social workers were criticised for failing to intervene to protect Victoria Climbié and Baby P, they are sometimes criticised for being too interventionist. This was the case in the 'Cleveland affair' in the 1980s when more than 100 children suspected of being the victims of sexual abuse were removed from their homes by social workers on the evidence of two paediatricians without other agencies being consulted. The report of the public inquiry set up to investigate the matter (*Report of the Inquiry into Child Abuse in Cleveland 1987*, Cm 412, 1988) recommended, *inter alia*, better inter-agency cooperation to protect children and better safeguards for parents and children where emergency intervention was needed. The *report* had a considerable impact on the drafting of the Children Act 1989 (CA 1989), in particular in respect of achieving the right balance between family autonomy and state intervention.

The courts must also endeavour to achieve the correct balance between intervention and non-intervention. Thus, as Baroness Hale said in *Re S-B (Children)* [2009] UKSC 17, 'on the one hand, children need to be protected from harm; but on the other hand, both they and their families need to be protected from the injustice and potential damage to their whole futures done by removing children from a parent who is not, in fact, responsible for causing any harm at all'. The courts, like other public authorities, have obligations under the HRA 1998 to comply with the ECHR. Thus, for example, if a court orders a child to be removed from their family without good cause then this could be a breach of Article 8.

Despite the need to respect the right to family life, it is sometimes necessary for children to be placed in the care of a local authority, with the child being looked after, for example, by a relative or a foster-carer. However, taking a child into care is a drastic measure and a step of last resort. Statistics shows that educational attainment is lower for children in care compared to their non-looked-after peers, and they are more likely to be permanently excluded from school (see *Outcomes for Children Looked After by Local Authorities*, 2015, Department for Education). Adults who have been in care are also more likely than the general population to be unemployed, spend time in prison or experience homelessness (see *Finding Their Feet: Equipping Care Leavers to Reach Their Potential*, The Centre for Social Justice, 2015). In order to improve the life chances of children who are taken into care, reforms have been introduced to increase the number of children in care who are placed for adoption (see Chapter 15).

14.2 The Children Act 2004

The Children Act 2004 (CA 2004) was, in part, a response to the tragic death in February 2000 of Victoria Climbié (see 14.1 above). The inquiry into her death found grave errors on the part of social services and criticised social workers and other agencies for failing to intervene (*Laming Report on the Inquiry into the Death of Victoria Climbié*, Cm 5730, 2003). Lord Laming found the legislation, namely the Children Act 1989 (CA 1989), to be fundamentally sound but that there had been gaps in its implementation. There had been poor coordination and a failure to share information, and no one with a strong sense of accountability.

Following the *Laming Report*, reforms were implemented by the CA 2004 to improve the practice of child protection, in particular to provide better integrated services and multi-disciplinary practice. One such reform was the creation of Children's Trusts and Local Safeguarding Children Boards. Local Safeguarding Children Boards are statutory bodies which have a duty to coordinate local arrangements and services to ensure their effectiveness and safeguard children. The parties who must work together to protect children are prescribed by the CA 2004 and include, *inter alia*, local authorities, the National Health Service, the police and Cafcass. Thus, the Act requires local authorities to promote inter-agency cooperation (s 10); and everyone involved in child protection must ensure that their functions are discharged with regard to the need to safeguard and promote the welfare of children (s 11).

14.3 The European Convention on Human Rights and Child Protection

Local authorities and courts must exercise their powers and duties in compliance with the European Convention on Human Rights (ECHR), as they are public authorities under the Human Rights Act 1998 (HRA 1998) (see 1.8). The decisions of the European Court of Human Rights (ECtHR) must be taken into account by the courts (s 2(1)), and are relevant to social work practice. A local authority social services department which is found to be in breach of the ECHR can be ordered to pay damages for breach of a Convention right (s 8).

(a) The right to family life

Article 8 of the ECHR guarantees a right to respect for family life. The aim of Article 8 is to protect individuals against arbitrary action by public authorities. There are also positive obligations inherent in 'respect' for family life. Thus, local authorities must ensure that any interference in family life is lawful, proportionate and necessary, otherwise they risk breaching Article 8. A presumption in favour of keeping children in their families, unless contrary to their best interests, is recognised by the ECtHR. For example, in *Haase v Germany (Application No. 11057/02)* [2004] 2 FLR 39 the ECtHR held that:

- authorities should make a careful assessment of the impact of proposed care measures on parents and children, and of the alternatives to taking children into public care;
- following a removal into care, a stricter scrutiny is called for in respect of any further limitations by the authorities, for example in respect of restrictions on parental rights and access;
- taking a child into care should normally be regarded as a temporary measure to be discontinued as soon as circumstances permit, and any measures of

implementation of temporary care should be consistent with the ultimate aim of reuniting the child with the natural parent; and

▶ taking a newborn baby into care at the moment of its birth is an extremely harsh measure, for which there must be extraordinarily compelling reasons.

In *Hokkanen v Finland* (1995) 19 EHRR 139, the ECtHR held that a 'fair balance has to be struck between the interests of the child in remaining in public care and those of the parent in being reunited with the child', but that in carrying out the balancing exercise 'the best interests of the child ... may override those of the parent'. Public authorities must aim to restore a child to their family as soon as is practicable; and any measure which hinders this, such as prohibiting contact or placing the child a long way away, may violate Article 8 (see, for example, *KA v Finland* [2003] 1 FLR 696).

However, each case depends on its facts. For example, in *Johansen v Norway* (1997) 23 EHRR 33 the ECtHR held that the mother's right to family life had been breached because she had been deprived of her parental and access rights when her daughter had been taken into care and placed with foster-parents with a view to adoption. However, in *Söderbäck v Sweden* [1999] 1 FLR 250 the ECtHR distinguished *Johansen* on its facts and held that the father's right to family life had not been breached when his daughter was made the subject of an adoption order. Although the father in *Söderbäck* had also been deprived of his parental and access rights, the making of an adoption order was not disproportionate in the light of the purpose of the adoption, which was to consolidate and formalise the child's family ties with her step-father, and in the light of the father's limited contact with her.

(b) Newborn babies

Taking a newborn baby into care may violate Article 8 (see *K and T v Finland* (2001) 36 EHRR 255; and *P, C and S v UK* (2002) 35 EHRR 31). However, as each case depends on its facts and the welfare of the child always prevails, the court may hold that such intervention is in the child's best interests. For example, in *Re M (Care Proceedings: Judicial Review)* [2003] EWHC 850 (Admin) the parents sought an injunction to restrain the local authority from commencing emergency protection or care proceedings in respect of their unborn child. Munby J dismissed the application and held that, although the ECtHR had made it clear that removing a child from its mother at or very shortly after birth was a draconian measure requiring exceptional justification, there are cases where the need for such highly intrusive intervention is imperatively demanded in a baby's interests.

In *Re D (Unborn Baby)* [2009] EWHC 446 (Fam) Munby J held that the local authority's proposed course of conduct, namely to conceal its intention to remove the child at birth from the mother and her partner, was lawful despite the mother's right to family life under Article 8. The mother had attempted to kill her other child and, in the highly unusual circumstances of the case, Munby J held that the very exceptional step of not engaging the parents fully and frankly in the pre-birth planning process was entirely justified. Munby J applied the approach adopted in *Venema v Netherlands* (Application No. 35731/97) [2003] 1 FLR 552 (and in *Haase v Germany* (Application No. 11057/02) [2004] 2 FLR 39), where the ECtHR held that it would not be a breach of the Convention to remove a newborn baby provided the public authority had considered all the circumstances of the case and there had been a careful assessment of the impact of the proposed care measure on the parents and child, and that possible alternatives had been considered.

(c)   The right to family life – the principle of proportionality

An important principle applicable to the right to family life is that of proportionality. In other words, local authorities and the courts must ensure that any intervention into family life, by court order or otherwise, is a proportionate response to a legitimate aim, otherwise they risk being in breach of Article 8. For example, it might be a disproportionate response for a local authority to apply to take a child into care before it has exhausted its support obligations, or to remove a child without giving the parent(s) an opportunity to improve their parenting skills.

The following two cases provide examples of the principle of proportionality being applied. In the first case, the local authority's response had been disproportionate in the circumstances, whereas in the second it had not.

▶ *Re C and B (Care Order: Future Harm)* [2001] 1 FLR 611

The Court of Appeal, allowing the appeal, held that full care orders in respect of two children (and permission for the local authority to refuse parental contact) was not a proportionate response in the circumstances. The local authority should have taken time to explore other options. There had been too much speed in the circumstances. Hale LJ, referring to the jurisprudence of the ECtHR on the need for interference to be necessary and proportionate to the legitimate aim, held that, while intervention in the family can be appropriate, cutting off contact and a relationship between a child and his family is justified only by the overriding necessity of the child's best interests.

▶ *Re W (Removal into Care)* [2005] EWCA Civ 642

Care orders were made in respect of five-year-old twins on the basis of a care plan whereby they would remain at home with their parents. As this did not work well, a decision was taken to remove them from their home and the local authority applied to free them for adoption. In response, the parents applied to discharge the care orders and sought an injunction to enable their return under section 8 of the HRA 1998. Their applications failed. The judge held that there had been no breach of Article 8, as the local authority's response was a proportionate and legitimate response to the deterioration of the home situation. The decision was upheld by the Court of Appeal.

The importance of proportionality was highlighted in *Re B (A Child) (Care Proceedings: Appeal)* [2013] UKSC 33 (see further at 15.1), which emphasised the need for judges to actively evaluate proportionality when deciding what, if any, order to make. Lord Kerr explained that 'a decision as to whether a particular outcome is proportionate involves asking oneself, is it really necessary. In order to properly evaluate proportionality a rigorous approach is required by professionals and the courts. In *Re B-S (Children) (Adoption: Leave to Oppose)* [2013] EWCA Civ 1146 (see further at 15.1) the court gave guidance that, when a care order is being made with a view to adoption, the courts must have proper evidence before them addressing all the realistic options for the child and judges must carry out a 'global, holistic and multi-faceted evaluation' which takes into account the pros and cons of each option. Although both *Re B* and *Re B-S* related to children who were being adopted, the emphasis on proportionality, high standards of social work practice and rigorous, holistic, judicial evaluation has impacted the approach in child protection generally. For example, in *Re Y (Children) (Care Proceedings: Proportionality Evaluation)* [2014] EWCA Civ 1553 the Court of Appeal held that the trial judge had erred in making a care order in respect of two children who were to be placed in foster care. This was because she had ruled out the possibility of them staying with their mother based on the negative aspects of that arrangement, instead of conducting a full evaluation and then comparing the realistic options, as she was required to do by the decision in *Re B-S*. (See also *Re W (A Child) (Welfare Evaluation: Functions of Local Authority)* [2013] EWCA Civ 1227 and Bainham and Markham [2014] Fam Law 991.)

(d) Procedural fairness and human rights

Procedural fairness is required at all stages of the child protection process; otherwise a local authority or the court may be in breach of the ECHR. Procedural fairness is required under Article 6 (the right to a fair trial) and Article 8 (the right to family life). A breach of procedural fairness could include, for example, failing to involve parents sufficiently in the decision-making process, failing to conduct appropriate enquiries or failing to give reasons for a decision. Local authorities engaged in child protection may infringe the rights of parents and children under Articles 6 and 8 of the ECHR 'unless overall they conduct themselves with such integrity, transparency and inclusiveness as to satisfy the parents' rights, necessarily to be construed in a wide sense, to a fair hearing and to respect for their private and family life' (*per* Wilson LJ in *Re J (Care: Assessment: Fair Trial)* [2006] EWCA Civ 545).

Procedural fairness was considered in the following cases.

▶ *Re L (Care: Assessment: Fair Trial)* [2002] EWHC 1379 (Fam)

The mother, whose child was the subject of care proceedings, was not permitted to attend a meeting between the local authority, the psychiatrist and the Guardian when concerns were expressed about her parenting. No minutes of the meeting were taken and the mother was not informed of the outcome. Munby J held that the right to procedural fairness under Article 6 of the ECHR was not confined to the judicial process, but to all stages of the process, both in and out of court. His Lordship emphasised certain principles of good social work practice. Social workers must notify parents of material criticisms, and advise them how to remedy their behaviour. All professionals involved should keep clear, accurate and full notes and the local authority should make full and frank disclosure of all key documents at an early stage of proceedings. They should provide reports; and parents should be able to make representations, and have the right to attend meetings held by the professionals involved.

▶ *P, C and S v UK* (2002) 35 EHRR 31

The ECtHR held that the removal of the baby at birth under an emergency protection order breached the parents' right to family life under Article 8 of the ECHR and their right to a fair trial under Article 6 of the ECHR, as they did not have legal representation in the care and freeing for adoption proceedings. The court stressed that emergency measures to remove a child from a situation of danger must be properly justified by the circumstances, and parents must have procedural protection, as part of the right to family life under Article 8, not just under Article 6.

▶ **Re J (Care: Assessment: Fair Trial) [2006] EWCA Civ 545**

The Court of Appeal held that the way in which the local authority had reached its decision and communicated its care plan had fallen short of the proper standard of fairness and transparency expected of a local authority in care proceedings. This was because, *inter alia*, the mother had not been invited to comment on the concerns that were inclining the local authority towards adoption rather than a residential assessment. However, the Court of Appeal held that the local authority's conduct was not sufficiently substantial to constitute an infringement of the mother's rights under Article 6 or Article 8 of the ECHR.

▶ **Northamptonshire County Council v AS, KS, DS [2015] EWHC 199 (Fam)**

A child was placed into foster care when he was 15 days old, under section 20 of the CA 1989. However, the local authority did not issue care proceedings for another nine months, and final orders placing him in the care of his grandparents in Latvia were not made until nearly two years after he was first placed into foster care. The mother and the child (by his Guardian) brought claims under the HRA 1998 for breaches of their right to family life under Article 8 and their right to a fair trial under Article 6 of the ECHR.

The claims succeeded. The court found that the child's Article 6 and Article 8 rights had been breached by the delay in issuing care proceedings, during which time he had no access to representation of his welfare interests; and by the further delays, including the delay in placing him with his extended family. The mother's Article 6 and Article 8 rights were also breached by the delays and mismanagement of the case; and by the local authority's failure to organise contact between her and the child. The court said that such breaches were serious enough in the case of an older child, but were appalling in regard to a 15-day-old baby whose case should be afforded the highest priority.

The ECtHR has held that parents must have access to the information which the local authority relies on for taking measures of protective care (*Venema v The Netherlands (Application No. 35731/97)* [2003] 1 FLR 552). Further, a care order must be capable of convincing an objective observer that it is based on a careful and unprejudiced assessment of all the evidence with the distinct reasons for the care measures being explicitly stated, and with all the case material being available to the parents concerned, even if they have not requested it (*KA v Finland* [2003] 1 FLR 696; and see also *K and T v Finland* (2001) 36 EHRR 255).

(e)   Procedure for human rights claims

A complaint arising under the HRA 1998 before a final care order is made should normally be made in the care proceedings by the court dealing with those proceedings (*per* Sir Mark Potter P in *Westminster City Council v RA, B and S* [2005] EWHC 970 (Fam)).

14.4 The United Nations Convention on the Rights of the Child 1989

The United Nations Convention on the Rights of the Child (UNCRC) (see 8.2) contains various articles which are relevant to child protection. The courts in England and Wales and the European Court of Human Rights (ECtHR) sometimes refer to the UNCRC when making decisions about children and families. Under the UNCRC, States Parties must:

- take all measures to protect children from all forms of abuse while in the care of their parents, guardians and any other person (Art 19);
- ensure the child such protection and care as are necessary for the child's well-being, taking into account the rights and duties of his or her parents or others with parental responsibility, and to this end take all appropriate legislative and administrative measures (Art 3(2)); and
- ensure that a child shall not be separated from his or her parents against their will, except when competent authorities subject to judicial review determine that such separation is necessary for the best interests of the child; and all interested parties must be given an opportunity to participate in the proceedings and make their views known (Art 9(1)).

Other articles are also relevant, for example Article 34 (the right to be protected from sexual exploitation and abuse) and Article 40(4) (the right to care, guidance, supervision, counselling and foster care).

14.5 The Children Act 1989

The Children Act 1989 (CA 1989) (see Chapter 10) is the key Act governing the duties and powers of the courts and of local authorities to take steps to protect children and to provide for children in need. Local authorities have powers and duties: to provide support for children in need under Part III; to seek care and supervision orders under Part IV; and to apply for emergency protection orders and child assessment orders under Part V. Local authorities also have investigative powers and duties (under s 47).

(a) The policy objectives of the Children Act 1989

The practice of child protection under the CA 1989 is based on the following policy objectives.

(i) Keeping children in their families

A major policy objective is that parents, not local authorities, have primary responsibility for children and that children should be kept in their families unless this is contrary to their best interests. Social services and the courts must carry out their functions on the basis of the presumption that intervention in family life is a serious matter and is only justified where it is a legitimate, necessary and proportionate response in the circumstances. The presumption in favour of keeping children in their families is also recognised by the ECtHR (see 14.3 above).

Wall LJ in *Re L and H (Residential Assessment)* [2007] EWCA Civ 213 held that the following words of Lord Templeman in *Re KD (A Minor) (Ward: Termination of Access)* [1988] AC 806 underlie the CA 1989:

> The best person to bring up a child is the natural parent. It matters not whether the parent is wise or foolish, rich or poor, educated or illiterate, provided the child's moral and physical health are not endangered. Public authorities cannot improve on nature. Public authorities exercise a supervisory role and interfere to rescue a child when the parental tie is broken by abuse or separation.

Thus, if the parents have learning or intellectual deficits, that in and of itself is unlikely to result in a child being removed from their care. In *Re L (Children) (Care Proceedings: Significant Harm)* [2006] EWCA Civ 1282 the Court of Appeal held that the courts did not, nor ever should, remove children from their parents on the basis that substitute parents would provide a greater intellectual stimulus. Such social engineering was wholly impermissible. The parental presumption was applied, for example, in *Re D (Care: Natural Parent Presumption)* [1999] 1 FLR 134, where it was held that the child, who was subject to a care order, should be placed with his father rather than his grandmother (even though this would separate him from his siblings). The parental presumption was also applied in the following case.

▶ *Re H (Care Order: Contact)* **[2008] EWCA Civ 1245**

The Court of Appeal allowed an appeal against a care order in respect of a ten-year-old child because not only had the trial judge failed to consider the child's wishes in the light of her age and understanding, but, more importantly, the judge had also erred in failing to perpetuate the fundamental importance of a relationship and life with a parent if at all possible. The child had expressed a strong desire to be reunited with her mother with whom she had a strong relationship. The Court of Appeal ordered that the care order be replaced with a residence order in favour of the mother, but with a supervision order to last for 12 months.

The CA 1989 reinforces the policy of keeping children in their families, where possible, in the following ways:

- ▶ Under section 1(5) the court can make an order (for example a care or supervision order) only if 'it considers that doing so would be better for the child than making no order at all'.
- ▶ Rules and regulations governing social work practice require local authorities to work in partnership with parents to promote and safeguard the welfare of children in order to prevent them being taken into care.
- ▶ Removing a child from his parents is a serious matter, which can only be effected by a court order and only on proof that the child is suffering, or is likely to suffer, significant harm; and only after a thorough investigation and consideration of all the evidence. The only exception where no prior judicial authority is needed is where a police officer can remove a child in certain circumstances (see 14.9(c) below).

The need for a court order before a child can lawfully be removed from a parent was shown in the following case.

> ► *R (G) v Nottingham City Council* [2008] EWHC 152 (Admin)
>
> The local authority had concerns about an 18-year-old pregnant woman who had a history of alcohol and drug abuse and self-harming. Two hours after she gave birth, medical staff removed the child from his mother, acting on instructions from the local authority who intended to initiate care proceedings. However, no court order had been obtained in relation to separating the child from his mother. In judicial review proceedings brought by the mother, Munby J made an order that the child be reunited with his mother, on the ground that removing a child requires prior judicial authorisation. Munby J held that the only time a social worker can intervene without a court order is where it is necessary to protect a child from immediate violence at the hands of a parent or other person.
>
> *Note:* After the child had been returned to the mother, an interim care order was made later that day (which was upheld by the Court of Appeal). The child was placed in foster care with the mother having supervised contact; but, as this proved unsatisfactory, an order for no contact for a limited period was subsequently made.

(ii) Working in partnership with parents

In order to promote the presumption that children should be kept in their families, local authorities are required to work in partnership with parents and to involve them as fully as possible. The guidance, *Working Together to Safeguard Children*, establishes two key policy objectives governing good social work practice: the importance of inter-agency cooperation; and the importance of encouraging partnership and participation with parents. A failure to involve parents and children sufficiently in the process, without good reason, may breach the European Convention on Human Rights (ECHR) (see 14.3 above).

(iii) Inter-agency cooperation

Another policy aim of the CA 1989, and of the Children Act 2004 (CA 2004), is that of inter-agency cooperation, whereby the various agencies (for example social services, local education authorities and health authorities) must consult with each other and be willing to provide help if this is in the best interests of a child. As part of this emphasis on inter-agency cooperation, section 27 of the CA 1989 provides that local authorities, local housing authorities and local health authorities have a right to request help from each other and have a reciprocal duty to provide it, unless this is incompatible with their own statutory obligations. For example, a social services department can ask a local housing department to provide accommodation for a child leaving care. The importance of communication and information sharing about children was emphasised in both the *Cleveland Report* and the *Laming Report on the Victoria Climbié Inquiry* (see 14.1 above).

(b) Local authority powers and duties under the Children Act 1989 – an overview

Local authorities have a wide range of powers and duties under the CA 1989. They have a duty to make such inquiries as are necessary to enable them to decide whether to take any action to safeguard or promote the welfare of the child (s 47). This duty applies if a child is subject to an emergency protection order, police protection or if the local authority has reasonable cause to suspect that a child is suffering, or is likely to suffer, significant harm. In addition, if a question arises with respect to any child's welfare in any family proceedings (such as proceedings in relation to a child arrangements order), and it appears to the court that it may be appropriate for a care or supervision order to be made, it can order that a local authority investigate the child's circumstances (s 37). If access to the child is thwarted, or the local authority has concerns about the child's safety, it can consider applying for an emergency protection order (s 44) or asking the police to intervene (s 46).

If, following initial inquiries, the child is assessed as not being at risk of significant harm, then local authority social services will have to decide whether or not the child and family need support under Part III of the CA 1989 (see 14.6 below). If, however, the child is, or is at risk of, suffering significant harm, then the local authority will have to consider taking steps to protect the child, such as emergency protection measures under Part V of the CA 1989 (see 14.9 below) or care and supervision proceedings under Part IV (see 14.7 below).

14.6 Part III of the Children Act 1989 – support for children in need

(a) Introduction

Under Part III of the Children Act 1989 (CA 1989) local authorities have a duty to provide support for children in need and to promote the upbringing of such children by their families, so far as that is consistent with their duty to the child (s 17(1)). Services may be provided to the child's family, if they are provided with a view to safeguarding or promoting the welfare of the child in need (s 17(3)). 'Family' for this purpose includes not just parents and children, but any person with parental responsibility or any other person with whom the child is living (s 17(10)). Part III duties include the provision of services (ss 17–19) and the provision of accommodation (ss 20, 21). Local authorities have duties to children 'looked after' by them (ss 22, 22A–22G) and must provide advice and assistance (ss 24, 24A); and in some cases secure accommodation (accommodation with the purpose of restricting liberty) (s 25). They must hold case reviews, cooperate with each other and consult with and request help from other authorities within the local area (such as housing and health authorities)), and provide advocacy services (ss 26–30). Schedule 2 to the CA 1989 lists the services which local authorities can provide for children in need and their families.

The provision of support under Part III may remove the need to bring care or supervision proceedings. Help and support for children in their home is the preferred option, with compulsory intervention by court order being the last resort. However, although the CA 1989 lays down a duty to safeguard and promote the welfare of children, the provision of services is a discretionary matter and is dependent on the allocation and availability of resources, which are often limited. For these reasons, it may be difficult to bring a successful legal challenge against a local authority for failing to make provision under Part III of the Act (see, for example, *R (on the application of MM) v Hounslow LBC* [2015] EWHC 3731 (Admin) where an autistic teenager unsuccessfully challenged the local authority's assessment of his needs).

(b) Who is a 'child in need'?

The criteria for when a child is a 'child in need' for the purposes of Part III are laid down in section 17(10).

Section 17(10) of the Children Act 1989

(a) he is unlikely to achieve or maintain, or to have the opportunity of achieving or maintaining, a reasonable standard of health or development without the provision of services by a local authority under [Part III];

(b) his health or development is likely to be significantly impaired, or further impaired, without the provision for him of such services; or

(c) he is disabled.

For the purposes of Part III, 'development' means physical, intellectual, emotional, social or behavioural development; 'health' means physical or mental health; and a child is 'disabled' if he is blind, deaf or dumb or suffers from mental disorder of any kind or is substantially and permanently handicapped by illness, injury or congenital deformity or such other disability as may be prescribed (s 17(11)).

(c) The Part III general duty

The general duty of local authorities to children in need is laid down in section 17(1).

Section 17(1) of the Children Act 1989

It shall be the general duty of every local authority, in addition to the other duties imposed on them by [Part III]:

(a) to safeguard and promote the welfare of children within their area who are in need; and

(b) so far as is consistent with that duty, to promote the upbringing of such children by their families, by providing a range and level of services appropriate to those children's needs.

The scope of the general duty in section 17(1) was considered by the House of Lords in the following case. All three appeals raised the question of whether social services departments were under a duty to provide accommodation for children in need and their families under the CA 1989 when local housing authorities were not able to house or rehouse them.

▶ *R (G) v Barnet London Borough Council; R (W) v Lambeth London Borough Council; R (A) v Lambeth London Borough Council* **[2003] UKHL 57**

In each appeal, a mother argued that section 17(1) required a local authority to assess and meet the needs of a particular individual child in need. As one of the local authorities had adopted a policy of providing accommodation for children in need, but not their parents, the House of Lords had to consider two questions: did section 17(1) create a duty to consider and assess the needs of a particular child; and could a local authority meet a child's needs for accommodation by providing accommodation for the child alone, not for both mother and child, when it would cost no more to provide accommodation for them both?

The House of Lords held, dismissing all three appeals, that section 17(1) sets out duties of a general character which are intended to be for the benefit of all the children in need in the local social services authority's area in general, and not for each and every individual child in need. As a result, a local social services authority was not under a duty to provide accommodation for families so that children could be housed with their families. Although social services could provide accommodation for a child in need and his family, this was not the principal or primary purpose of the legislation. Housing was the function of the local housing authority. An obligation under section 17(1) to provide housing would turn social services departments into housing authorities and thereby subvert the powers and duties of housing authorities under the housing legislation.

(d) Services for children in need

The general duty of local authorities laid down in section 17(1) above is facilitated by the performance of specific duties and powers laid down in Part I of Schedule 2 to the CA 1989 (s 17(2)), which include, for example: the identification and assessment of children in need; advertising available services; keeping a register of and providing services for disabled children; preventing neglect and abuse; providing accommodation for those who are ill-treating or are likely to ill-treat children, in order to reduce the need for criminal or civil proceedings; reintegrating children in need with their families; and promoting contact between a child and their family. The services provided under section 17 may include the provision of accommodation and giving assistance in kind or in cash (s 17(6)). Local authorities also have a duty under section 20 to provide accommodation for children in need (see below); and a duty to provide day care for certain children (s 18).

Before determining what, if any, services to provide for a particular child in need, a local authority must, so far as is reasonably practicable and consistent with the child's welfare, ascertain the child's wishes and feelings regarding the provision of those services, and give due consideration to such wishes and feelings of the child, having regard to the child's age and understanding (s 17(4A)).

(e) Children in need – the provision of accommodation

(i) The duty to provide accommodation under section 20

As part of their general duty to safeguard and promote the welfare of children in their area, local authorities have a specific duty under the CA 1989 to provide accommodation for children in need, in certain circumstances. This duty is set out in s 20(1).

Section 20(1) of the Children Act 1989M

Every local authority shall provide accommodation for any child in need within their area who appears to them to require accommodation as a result of –

(a) there being no person who has parental responsibility for him ...;
(b) his being lost or having been abandoned; or
(c) the person who has been caring for him being prevented (whether or not permanently, and for whatever reason) from providing him with suitable accommodation or care.

Before providing accommodation, the local authority must, so far as is reasonably practicable and consistent with the child's welfare, ascertain the child's wishes and feelings regarding the provision of accommodation; and give due consideration to such wishes and feelings of the child, having regard to the child's age and understanding (s 20(6)). However, the child's wishes are not necessarily determinative (see *Liverpool City Council v Hillingdon London Borough Council and AK* [2009] EWCA Civ 43). The local authority must also draw up a written care plan for the child. A child who is accommodated under section 20 is described as being 'looked after' by the local authority (s 22(1)(b)), whereupon the local authority has certain statutory duties with respect to the child (ss 22–23Z). Children who are in care under a court order are also described as being 'looked after' and are owed duties under the same provisions (s 22(1)(a)).

The ways in which children are to be accommodated are set out in section 22C. Where it is consistent with the child's welfare and reasonably practicable to do so, the child should be accommodated with a parent, someone with parental responsibility or someone named in a child arrangements order as a person with whom the child is to live. Alternatively, the child may be placed with: a relative, friend or other person connected with the child who is also a local authority foster-parent; any other local authority foster-parent; or in a children's home (s 22C(6)). If a child is placed with a friend or relative who is not already a foster-parent then it is possible for them to be approved as such by the local authority.

Accommodation must also be provided for a child in need aged 16 or over if a local authority considers the child's welfare is likely to be seriously prejudiced without it (s 20(3)). Accommodation in a community home can be provided for someone aged 16 to 21 if it will safeguard or promote their welfare (s 20(5)). Thus, for example, in *Re T (Accommodation by Local Authority)* [1995] 1 FLR 159 the court held that the local authority had erred in refusing a 17-year-old girl accommodation as it had failed to consider her future welfare.

A local authority may not provide accommodation for a child in need if a person with parental responsibility objects and is willing and able to provide accommodation or arrange for accommodation to be provided (s 20(7)); and any person with parental responsibility may remove the child from local authority accommodation at any time without giving notice (s 20(8)). However, sections 20(7) and 20(8) do not apply: where a person named in a child arrangements order as a person with whom the child is to live, a special guardian or someone who has care of the child under a court order agrees to the child being accommodated by the local authority (s 20(9)); or where the child is aged 16 or over and agrees to being provided with accommodation (s 20(11)). As the arrangement under section 20 is voluntary, the local authority must comply with the wishes of people with parental responsibility for the child, unless the child is suffering, or is likely to suffer, significant harm, in which case the local authority can apply for a care or supervision order (see 14.7) or an emergency protection order (see 14.10).

There have been concerns voiced about the use of section 20 by local authorities. In *N (Children) (Adoption: Jurisdiction)* [2015] EWCA Civ 1112, Munby P, the President of the Family Division, said that the local authority had misused its statutory powers by placing children with foster-carers under a section 20 placement but not issuing care proceedings for another eight months. The President said that section 20, as a precursor to care proceedings, should be a short-term measure only; and he identified four areas of concern which emerged from the case-law: a failure to obtain informed consent from parents; deficiencies in the drafting of section 20 agreements; section 20 placements continuing for too long (see also *Northamptonshire County Council v AS, KS, DS* [2015] EWHC 199 (Fam)); and a seeming reluctance of local authorities to return a child to their parents immediately upon a withdrawal of parental consent.

(ii) Providing teenage children with accommodation

Local authority social services and local authority housing departments are required to cooperate with each other about the provision of accommodation (ss 27 and 47 CA 1989; and s 213A Housing Act 1996 (HA 1996)). However, the interface between the CA 1989 and the HA 1996 can sometimes cause difficulties, particularly in respect of providing teenage children with accommodation; and it has resulted in challenges by way of judicial review (see further below). The *Homelessness Code of Guidance for Local Authorities* (2006) advises that, once it appears to a local housing department that a 16- or 17-year-old child may be homeless, then it must accommodate the child under section 188 of the HA 1996 pending clarification of whether the local children's services authority owes a duty to provide the child with accommodation under section 20 of the CA 1989. If the criteria in section 20 are met, then the local authority social services department, not the local housing authority, is responsible for accommodating the child.

The House of Lords in *R(M) v Hammersmith and Fulham London Borough Council* [2008] UKHL 14 held that a social services department cannot shirk its responsibility for a child under section 20 of the CA 1989 by passing that responsibility to the local housing authority; and that, if the criteria in section 20 are met (see above), then social services, rather than the housing department, should take responsibility, because the young person would have needs over and above their housing needs that could be better met by social services. *R(M)* was applied in *R(W) v North Lincolnshire Council* [2008] EWHC 2299 (Admin) where a child successfully challenged the local authority's decision that it would not accommodate him under section 20 of the CA 1989 on his release from a young offenders' institution. The judge held, referring to *R(M)*, that he was an eligible child under section 20 as he had been accommodated and supported by the local authority's social services department at various times before he was 16.

The House of Lords in *R (G) v Southwark London Borough Council* [2009] UKHL 26 considered the local authority's duty to provide accommodation under section 20 of the CA 1989 and their power to provide it under section 17(6) (see further below). It held that a local authority's children's services unit cannot purport to have fulfilled its duties to a homeless child merely by referring the case to the local housing authority under Part VII of the HA 1996 (see 4.11). The case dealt with the construction of section 20(1) of the CA 1989 and whether the local authority was entitled to distinguish between 'requiring accommodation' and 'requiring help with accommodation'. Baroness Hale stated that the question for the House of Lords was: if a child aged 16 or 17, who is thrown out of the family home, presents himself to a local children's services authority and asks to be accommodated under section 20 of the CA 1989, is it open to the authority to arrange instead for him to be accommodated by the local housing authority under the homelessness provisions of Part VII of the HA 1996?

▶ *R (G) v Southwark London Borough Council* [2009] UKHL 26

A 17-year-old young man who could genuinely not continue living with his mother applied to the local authority's social services department requesting accommodation under section 20 and an assessment of need under section 17 of the CA 1989. Despite his claim that he should be accommodated under section 20(1)(c) (which would entitle him to the wide range of services available to him as a 'looked-after child' until he was 21 under section 22(1), and would mean that he would thereafter qualify as a 'former relevant child' under section 23C(1)), the local authority said that he did not need accommodation under section 20 but only *'help'* with accommodation' under section 17. The Court of Appeal, by a majority, dismissed his appeal, holding that the distinction made in a local authority *circular* (between a child requiring accommodation under section 20 and one requiring help with accommodation under section 17) was lawful, even though the distinction was not expressly drawn in the CA 1989. The local authority had therefore been entitled to decide in the circumstances that the applicant needed only help with accommodation, and to refer him to the local housing department. He appealed to the House of Lords.

The House of Lords held, allowing his appeal, that he should have been provided with accommodation by his local authority under the CA 1989 and not just provided with accommodation by the homeless persons unit under Part VII of the HA 1996. Parliament had decided the circumstances in which the duty to accommodate arose, and then decided what the duty involved. It was not for the local authority to decide that, because they did not like what the duty to accommodate involved or did not think it was appropriate, that they did not have to accommodate at all. The local authority was not entitled to 'side-step' the duty under section 20(1) of the CA 1989 by giving the accommodation a different label.

It further held that section 27 of the CA 1989 Act empowered a local children's authority to ask other authorities (including any local housing authority) for 'help in the exercise of any of their functions' under Part III; and the requested authority had to provide that help if it was compatible with its own statutory or other duties and did not unduly prejudice the discharge of any of its own functions. A local children's authority could not use section 27 to avoid its responsibilities by 'passing the buck' to another authority; but could ask another authority to use its powers to help the local children's authority discharge theirs (for example a local children's authority could ask a housing authority to make a certain amount of suitable accommodation available for it to use in discharging its responsibility to accommodate children under section 20). The great flexibility provided by section 23(2) of the CA 1989 as to the ways in which accommodation could be provided for children being looked after by a local authority, which included the power to make 'such other arrangements as ... seem appropriate to them', supported the court's construction of section 20(1).

(iii) Is the child under the age of 18?

The duty to provide accommodation is owed to children and young people under the age of 18, except where a child is leaving care (see below). There are many cases where age is disputed, particularly in respect of people arriving in the UK unaccompanied. In *R (A) v Croydon London Borough Council; R (M) v Lambeth London Borough Council* [2009] UKSC 8 (a case which involved two unaccompanied asylum seekers who said they were under the age of 18), the Supreme Court held that, where social workers disputed a person's claim to be under the age of 18 for the purposes of section 20(1) of the CA 1989, the question of age was an objective fact which, in the event of a challenge, was to be determined by the court, not by social workers, as the lower courts had held.

(iv) Providing accommodation for people leaving care

If a child has been looked after by a local authority for a period of more than 13 weeks when they attain the age of 18, then at that date they become a 'former relevant child' (s 23C(1)) in respect of whom the local authority has a range of powers and duties under the leaving care provisions (see ss 23C, 23CZA and 23CA). This may include the provision of accommodation until the age of 21 if the person's welfare requires it (s 23C(4)(c)) and/or accommodation during further or higher education holidays until the age of 25 (s 23C(9) and s 24B(5)(a)).

14.7 Part IV of the Children Act 1989 – care and supervision

(a) Introduction

Voluntary arrangements provided under Part III of the Children Act 1989 (CA 1989) may not work in some cases; or it may come to the notice of a local authority that a child is suffering, or is at risk of suffering, significant harm. In such circumstances a local authority social services department may have to intervene by bringing proceedings for a care or supervision order under Part IV of the Act, or by taking emergency action under Part V (see 14.9 below). The court has jurisdiction to hear an application for a care or supervision order if the child is aged under 17 (s 31(3)) and habitually resident, or present, in England and Wales. (See *Re M (A Minor) (Care Order: Jurisdiction)* [1997] 2 WLR 314 and *Re F (A Child)* [2014] EWCA Civ 789 for the approach to be taken in cases with an international dimension.)

Although the National Society for the Prevention of Cruelty to Children has standing to apply for a care or supervision order (s 31(9)), in practice almost all applications are brought by the local authority who have a statutory responsibility to protect children and a duty to investigate cases where a child is suffering, or is at risk of suffering, significant harm (ss 37 and 47).

(i) Care order or supervision order?

Although the same threshold criteria apply to care and supervision orders (see 14.7(c) below), the orders are different: a care order places the child in the care of a local authority, whereas a supervision order only places the child under the supervision of a local authority social worker, usually while the child remains living at home.

As a care order is a more draconian order than a supervision order (because the child may be removed from their home and possibly placed for adoption), there must be cogent and strong reasons to make a care order rather than a supervision order (*per* Hale J in *Oxfordshire County Council v L (Care or Supervision Order)* [1998] 1 FLR 70). Making a care order where a supervision order would be sufficient to protect a child might also be a breach of human rights (see below).

In *Re T (Care Order)* [2009] EWCA Civ 121 the Court of Appeal said that there were two main reasons for making a care order rather than a supervision order: that the local authority needed the power not only to remove the child instantly but also to plan for long-term placement outside the family without prior judicial sanction; or that it was necessary for the local authority to share parental responsibility with the parents. On the facts, the Court of Appeal held that there were no strong and cogent reasons for making a care order; and that, applying human rights considerations, it was preferable to make a supervision order as this was a sufficient and proportionate response in the circumstances.

As care and supervision proceedings under Part IV of the CA 1989 are 'family proceedings' for the purposes of the CA 1989 (s 8(3)), the court can make a section 8 order (such as a child arrangements order regulating the child's living arrangements) instead of a care or supervision order, either on an application or of its own accord.

The court has no power to compel a local authority to institute care or supervision proceedings. All it can do is make a direction under section 37 of the CA 1989 that the local authority investigate the child's circumstances.

(ii) Human rights and care and supervision orders

A care order must be a proportionate and legitimate response to the circumstances of the case, as otherwise a local authority may be in breach of the European Convention on Human Rights (ECHR). For example, making a care order where a supervision order would be adequate to protect the child might offend the principle of proportionality and be a breach of the right to family life under Article 8.

In *Re W (Children) (Care: Interference With Family Life)* [2005] EWCA Civ 642, Thorpe LJ stated that, whenever a local authority took any step as draconian as the removal of a child, the local authority must have 'due regard to the parents' European Convention rights and the Convention rights of the children' and that removal 'was only lawful if it could be justified on both the heads of legality and proportionality'. In *Re T (Care Order)* (see above), the Court of Appeal reiterated the rule that human rights considerations required the court to make the less draconian supervision order rather than the more draconian care order, unless the child's welfare required a care order to be made; and a care order, rather than a supervision order, was a sufficient and proportionate response to the risk presented to the child.

The European Court of Human Rights (ECtHR) has held as a guiding principle that a care order should be regarded as a temporary measure to be discontinued as soon as circumstances permit, and that any measures implementing temporary care should be consistent with the ultimate aim of reuniting the natural parent and the child (see *Olsson v Sweden (No. 1)* (1988) 11 EHRR 259). However, this principle is subject to the best interests of the child. The ECtHR has also held that, whereas authorities enjoy a wide 'margin of appreciation' in assessing the necessity of taking a child into public care, a stricter scrutiny is required in respect of any further limitations, including restrictions placed on parental rights of access (*K and T v Finland* (2001) 36 EHRR 255; *R v Finland (Application No. 34141/96)* [2006] 2 FLR 923).

(iii) The court cannot dictate how a care order is implemented

If the court makes a care order, it cannot dictate how the local authority should implement it, as to do so would circumscribe the wide discretionary powers entrusted to local authorities by Parliament. However, there are certain controls on local authorities. Thus, for example, a local authority must supply the court with a care plan containing proposals about future arrangements for the child (see 14.7(f) below); and the court must also ensure that the care plan is the best solution for the child and is human rights compliant (see *Hokkanen v Finland* (1995) EHRR 139).

(iv) Reducing delay in care cases

The Government, in response to the Family Justice Review (see 1.2), introduced reforms in an effort to speed up care cases and reduce the delays in the system. The Children and Families Act 2014 (CFA 2014) introduced a statutory 26-week time limit for the completion of care cases. Section 32 of the CA 1989 requires the court to draw up a timetable with a view to disposing of any application made under Part IV of the CA 1989: without delay; and no later than 26 weeks after the application was made. Section 14 of the CFA 2014 also removed the requirement for interim care and supervision orders to be renewed every month by the court. In other words, this means that interim orders can now last until final orders are made.

(v) Government statistics

According to Government statistics, the number of public law applications made by local authorities continues to increase.

> ▶ *Family Court Statistics Quarterly, January–March 2016*, **Ministry of Justice, 2016**
>
> Following the publicity surrounding the Baby P case, the number of children involved in public law applications made by local authorities jumped in 2009 from around 20,000 to almost 26,000 per year, and subsequently increased to nearly 30,000 per year. Figures have remained fairly steady at around 7,000 per quarter, but there has been an increase in the most recent quarters, with 8,287 children involved in public law applications in January to March 2016, an increase of 14 per cent from the equivalent quarter in 2015.

The statistics indicate that the duration of care proceedings is reducing.

> ▶ *Family Court Statistics Quarterly, January–March 2016*, **Ministry of Justice, 2016**
>
> In 2011, the duration of public law cases was almost twice as long as other case types (50 weeks). However, from 2012 the number of weeks to reach a first disposal fell steadily and halved to 27.4 weeks by Q2 2014 (April to June). It has since remained fairly stable, although there has been a further drop of 1.3 weeks over the last year to 26.2 weeks in January to March 2016.

(b) Care and supervision proceedings procedure

Rules of procedure, preparation and case management for care and supervision proceedings are found in Part 12 of the Family Procedure Rules 2010 (FPR 2010) and its related practice directions, which set out the 'Public Law Outline'. Proceedings normally commence in the Family Court but can be transferred to the High Court if, for example, the case is particularly complex. The local authority, the child and any person with parental responsibility for the child are automatically parties to the proceedings, but other people can be joined as parties with leave (permission) of the court. When considering whether to grant leave, the court exercises its powers in the same way as it does in leave applications for a section 8 order (s 10(9)). Thus, for example, in *Re W (Care Proceedings: Leave to Apply)* [2004] EWHC 3342 (Fam) the child's aunt was refused leave to be a party to care proceedings. The court held that it was not necessary to make the aunt a party because she was not putting forward a different point of view from that of the child's grandmother, who was a party in the case. However, even a person who has an automatic right to participate in the proceedings can be excluded from participating in exceptional circumstances. Thus, for example, in *Local Authority v M, F and M and M* [2009] EWHC 3172 (Fam) a married father was excluded from participating in care proceedings because, although he was in prison, he represented a real and substantial risk to the children and their mother.

A parent without parental responsibility (such as some unmarried fathers) has no automatic right to be joined as a party but is entitled to notice of the proceedings; and they are likely to be given leave by the court to participate unless there is good reason to the contrary. A refusal to do so might breach their right to family life under Article 8 of the ECHR (see, for example, *McMichael v UK (Application No. 16424/90)* (1995) 20 EHRR 205 where the ECtHR held that a failure to allow an unmarried father without parental responsibility to participate in a Scottish children's hearing was a breach of Article 8).

(i) The Children's Guardian

In care and supervision proceedings the child will normally be represented by a solicitor and a Children's Guardian (an officer of Cafcass) (see 1.7). The court must appoint a Guardian unless satisfied that it is not necessary to do so to safeguard the child's interests (s 41(1) and r 12.6 FPR 2010). The role of the Guardian is to protect and safeguard the best interests of the child in the proceedings. In *Re S and W (Care Proceedings)* [2007] EWCA Civ 232 Wall LJ said that 'one of the Guardian's functions is fearlessly to protect the children concerned against local authority incompetence and maladministration, as well as poor social work practice'.

The Guardian must be independent of the parties, in order to prevent a conflict of interest arising. In addition to having a general duty to safeguard the child's interests in the manner prescribed by the rules of court (s 41(2)(b)), the Guardian has specific duties which include: ascertaining the child's wishes and whether the child has sufficient understanding, investigating the circumstances; interviewing people involved; inspecting records; and appointing professional assistance. The Guardian has a right to examine local authority records relating to a child, which can be admitted in evidence (s 42), such as minutes of a child protection conference or a report compiled by an area child protection committee (*Re R (Care Proceedings: Disclosure)* [2000] 2 FLR 75). When the investigation has been completed, the Guardian must make a written report advising what should be done in the best interests of the child. The report usually has a considerable influence on the court's decision.

(ii) Children can give oral evidence in care proceedings

In *Re W (Children) (Abuse: Oral Evidence)* [2010] UKSC 12, which concerned the question of whether a 14-year-old girl should give oral evidence in relation to serious sexual abuse, the Supreme Court unanimously held that there was no longer a presumption or even a starting point against children giving evidence in care proceedings. Baroness Hale, giving the leading opinion, held that the existing presumption could not be reconciled with the ECHR, in particular Article 6 (the right to a fair trial) and Article 8 (the right to a family life). The Supreme Court held that the essential test is whether justice can be done to all the parties without questioning the child. (For a discussion of *Re W*, see Hall [2010] CFLQ 499.)

However, although children can now be called to give oral evidence in care proceedings, it is likely to be the exception rather than the rule; and it will depend on a range of factors, including, in particular, the welfare of the child considered in the light of their age and understanding. The principles laid down by the Supreme Court in *Re W* were applied in *Re S (Children)* [2016] EWCA Civ 83, in which a majority of the Court of Appeal upheld the decision of the trial judge not to require a 13-year-old girl to give evidence regarding allegations that she had been sexually abused by her brother. The girl had retracted the allegations but findings were nevertheless made against the brother. The judgments of the majority, and the dissenting judgment of Gloster LJ, demonstrate the difficulties in balancing the interests of the child and the accused in such a case.

(iii) The judge may meet with the child

In the last few years, it has been recognised that it is permissible for judges in family proceedings (including care and supervision proceedings) to meet with children and interview them (see *Guidelines for Judges Meeting Children Who Are Subject to Family Proceedings* [2010] Fam Law 654). In *Re A (Fact-Finding Hearing: Judge Meeting with Child)* [2012] EWCA Civ 185, where five children aged between five and ten made very serious allegations to their foster-parents of sexual abuse by their family and the oldest boy wished to speak to the judge, the Court of Appeal provided guidance to judges on speaking to children in family proceeding to help them to achieve greater confidence in meeting children and in involving them in proceedings.

(c) The 'threshold criteria'

When exercising its powers in care and supervision proceedings, the court must first be satisfied that the threshold criteria are met. These are laid down in section 31(2) of the CA 1989.

Section 31(2) of the Children Act 1989

A court may only make a care order or a supervision order if it is satisfied –

(a) that the child concerned is suffering, or is likely to suffer, significant harm; and
(b) that the harm, or likelihood of harm, is attributable to –
    (i) the care given to the child, or likely to be given to him if the order were not made, not being what it would be reasonable to expect a parent to give him; or
    (ii) the child's being beyond parental control.

'Harm' means ill-treatment or the impairment of health or development including impairment of the child's health or development as a result of seeing or hearing the ill-treatment of another person (s 31(9)). It includes, for example, seeing or hearing domestic violence. 'Health' means physical or mental health, and 'ill-treatment' includes sexual abuse and forms of ill-treatment which are not physical. 'Development' means physical, intellectual, emotional, social or behavioural development. Where the question of whether the harm is significant turns on the child's health or development, the child's health or development must be compared with that which could reasonably be expected of a similar child (s 31(10)).

(i) 'Significant' harm

The word 'significant' is not defined in the CA 1989. Whether harm is 'significant' will depend on the circumstances of the case.

The difference between 'harm' and 'significant harm' was considered in *Re MA (Children) (Care Proceedings: Threshold Criteria)* [2009] EWCA Civ 853, where the Court of Appeal held that, given the underlying philosophy of the CA 1989, the harm must be significant enough to justify the intervention of the State and disturb the autonomy of the parents to bring up their children by themselves in the way they choose. It must be significant enough to enable the court to make a care or supervision order if the welfare of the child so demanded. An evaluative judgment was therefore essential. Wall LJ acknowledged that the line between significant harm and harm was a fine one, and referred to the dictionary definition of 'significant' as 'considerable, noteworthy or important'. The Court of Appeal held that the decision on its facts could have gone either way, but that, where the balance was a fine one, then it was 'a classic case for trusting the judgment of the trial judge' (*per* Hallett LJ). The Court of Appeal, by a majority, therefore upheld the decision of the trial judge not to make a care order. However, the decision in *Re MA* has been strongly criticised (for example by Keating [2011] CFLQ 115 and Hayes, Hayes and Williams [2010] Fam Law 166).

In the earlier case of *Re L (Care: Threshold Criteria)* [2007] 1 FLR 20, Hedley J held, *inter alia*, dismissing the care application, that it was not the provenance of the State to spare children all the consequences of defective parenting; and that significant harm for the purposes of section 31(2) must be something unusual, and more than commonplace human failure or inadequacy. The Supreme Court approved Hedley J's approach to significant harm in *Re B (A Child) (Care Proceedings: Appeal)* [2013] UKSC 33. Baroness Hale explained:

[N]ot all harm which children may suffer as a result of their parents' care falling short of what it is reasonable to expect is significant [for the purposes of justifying intervention]. The dictionary definition, 'considerable, noteworthy or important', is to my mind more helpful .... There would be no point in the threshold if it could be crossed by trivial or unimportant harm.

(ii) Care and the reasonable parent (section 31(2)(b)(i))

Where the court has to consider whether the threshold criteria are satisfied by evaluating parental performance, an objective assessment is required applying the standard of the hypothetical 'reasonable' parent. In *Re K; A Local Authority v N and Others* [2005] EWHC 2956 (Fam), Munby J said that the court 'must always be sensitive to the cultural, social and religious circumstances of the particular child and family, particularly when the parents have recently, or comparatively recently, arrived from a foreign country with different standards and expectations from those in this country'. In this case the 16-year-old girl and her family were Kurdish Muslims from Iraq.

(iii) When must the threshold criteria be satisfied?

The date on which the threshold criteria must be satisfied is when the local authority first intervened; in other words, at the date of the application or, if temporary protective arrangements (such as an emergency protection order) have continuously been in place, the date on which those arrangements were initiated (*Re M (A Minor) (Care Order: Threshold Conditions)* [1994] 2 AC 424). However, in order to establish that the threshold has been crossed at the date of intervention, the local authority can rely upon information acquired after that date; and it can also rely on later events if they are capable of proving the state of affairs at the date of intervention (*Re G (Care Proceedings: Threshold Conditions)* [2001] EWCA Civ 968).

(iv) How the court exercises its powers

If the threshold criteria are met, the court must then decide whether it is in the child's best interests to make a care or supervision order, or a different order, or no order at all. When conducting the second part of the exercise, the court must apply the welfare principle (s 1(1)), the welfare checklist (s 1(3)), the no order principle (s 1(5)) and the no delay principle (s 1(2)) (see 10.3). The court must also consider the human rights implications under the European Convention on Human Rights (ECHR). Article 6 (the right to a fair trial) and Article 8 (the right to family life) are particularly important as these two articles 'affect both the test and the process for intervening in the family lives of children and their parents' (*per* Baroness Hale in *Re S-B (Children)* [2009] UKSC 17).

In *Re B (Children) (Sexual Abuse: Standard of Proof)* [2008] UKHL 35, Baroness Hale said that, although the court has to ask two questions when applying the threshold criteria in section 31(2) ('Has the threshold been crossed?' and 'If so, what will be best for the child?'), care proceedings are not a two-stage process, because threshold issues and welfare issues can be interconnected. Thus, the same factual issues may be relevant to both aspects.

Even if the first stage is satisfied and the threshold criteria are met, the court is under no obligation to make a care or supervision order. Whether it will do so depends on a detailed assessment of the child's welfare in all the circumstances of the case. Thus, for example, in *Re K; A Local Authority v N and Others* [2005] EWHC 2956 (Fam), although the threshold criteria were met, Munby J refused to make a supervision order, applying the no order principle in section 1(5) of the CA 1989. If the court decides to make a child arrangements order regulating the child's living arrangements, instead of a care or supervision order, it must *also* make an interim supervision order, unless it is satisfied that the child's welfare will be satisfactorily safeguarded without it (s 38(3)). The court must also consider the arrangements that the local authority has made, or proposes to make, in respect of contact, and invite the parties to the proceedings to comment on those arrangements (s 34(11)). Expert evidence is important, and the court will also consider the recommendations of the Children's Guardian (see 14.7(b) above).

(d) The standard of proof in care and supervision proceedings

The standard of proof is of considerable importance in care and supervision proceedings. If it is set too high, then there is a danger that a child will suffer, or continue to suffer, significant harm. If it is set too low, then there is a danger that a child will be removed from the care of his parents when they have not suffered, or are not at risk of suffering, significant harm. As Ryder J stated, the problem is 'how to balance the need to protect families from any disproportionate interference by the state with the imperative to protect children against harm' ([2008] Fam Law 30).

In care and supervision proceedings, the ordinary civil standard of proof applies. Thus, the local authority must prove the facts, which it alleges satisfy the threshold criteria, on the balance of probabilities. This means satisfying the court that it is more likely than not that the facts alleged are true. There have been several cases in the House of Lords and the Supreme Court which have considered the standard of proof in care and supervision proceedings and how it should be applied.

(i) The standard of proof in relation to past facts

The leading case is *Re B (Children) (Sexual Abuse: Standard of Proof)* [2008] UKHL 35 (see below), where the House of Lords held that the standard of proof for establishing the threshold criteria based on past facts is the simple balance of probabilities, no more and no less. The court rejected the idea, which had emerged from Lord Nicholls' judgment in *Re H and Others (Minors) (Sexual Abuse: Standard of Proof)* [1996] AC 563 (see below), of a heightened civil standard of proof requiring that 'the more serious the allegation, the more cogent the evidence needed to prove it'.

▶ *Re B (Children) (Sexual Abuse: Standard of Proof)* [2008] UKHL 35

The mother (Mrs B) had two children, aged 16 and 17, by a previous marriage, and two children, aged six and nine, with her current husband (Mr B) from whom she was separated. Allegations of sexual abuse and assault, some of which were certainly false, were made by Mrs B and the elder daughter (R) against the elder son, by the elder daughter against Mr B, and by the elder son against Mrs B. The two younger children were placed with foster-carers and care proceedings were initiated. These proceedings were transferred to the High Court, by which time only the allegations against Mr B remained in issue.

Charles J ruled that he was unable to make a finding as to whether Mr B had abused R. His Lordship said that he could not make a properly founded and reasoned conclusion that it was more likely than not that R was, or was not, sexually abused by Mr B; and that his answer to which of these two possibilities was more likely would be a guess. On the basis, however, that he was unable to conclude that there was no real possibility that Mr B had sexually abused R, he said that he had therefore come to the conclusion that there was a real possibility that he had done so. His Lordship gave leave to appeal to the Court of Appeal, who dismissed the appeal and gave leave to appeal to the House of Lords.

The House of Lords, dismissing the appeal, held the following in respect of the standard of proof in care proceedings:

▶ The standard of proof in finding the facts necessary to establish the threshold criteria under section 31(2) or the welfare considerations in section 1 of the CA 1989 Act is the balance of probabilities.

▶ There is no logical or necessary connection between seriousness and probability. In the context of care proceedings, this point applies with particular force to the identification of the perpetrator. It may be unlikely that any person looking after a baby would take him by the wrist and swing him against the wall, causing multiple fractures and other injuries. But once the evidence is clear that that is indeed what has happened to the child, it ceases to be improbable. Someone looking after the child at the relevant time must have done it. The inherent improbability of the event has no relevance to deciding whether the event actually took place.

BARONESS HALE: I wish to announce loud and clear that the standard of proof in finding the facts necessary to establish the threshold under section 31(2) or the welfare considerations in section 1 of the 1989 Act is the simple balance of probabilities, neither more nor less. Neither the seriousness of the allegation nor the seriousness of the consequences should make any difference to the standard of proof to be applied in determining the facts. The inherent probabilities are simply something to be taken into account, where relevant, in deciding where the truth lies.

LORD HOFFMANN: I think that the time has come to say, once and for all, that there is only one civil standard of proof and that is proof that the fact in issue more probably occurred than not.

(For a case commentary on *Re B* and the standard of proof, see Keating [2009] CFLQ 230.)

(ii) Future risk of harm

In the case of *Re H and Others (Minors) (Sexual Abuse: Standard of Proof)* [1996] AC 563 the issue was whether three children were 'likely to suffer significant harm' in the future based on allegations made by their older sister (who was not the subject of the proceedings) that she had been sexually abused by the mother's partner.

> ▶ *Re H and Others (Minors) (Sexual Abuse: Standard of Proof)* [1996] AC 563
>
> The local authority applied for care orders in respect of three girls (aged 13, eight and two) after the eldest daughter (aged 14) alleged that she had been sexually abused by her mother's partner. The partner was acquitted in criminal proceedings, but the local authority still sought care orders to protect the younger children. The applications for care orders were dismissed at first instance and by the Court of Appeal. This was because the threshold conditions in section 31(2) were not satisfied, as it could not be established to the requisite standard of proof that the 14-year-old daughter's allegations were true and those allegations were the only grounds on which the future prediction of harm had been based. The local authority appealed to the House of Lords.
>
> The House of Lords, by a majority, dismissed the local authority's appeal. The majority held that as it had not been proven, on the balance of probabilities, that sexual abuse of the eldest child had taken place, there was no basis for concluding that there was a likelihood of harm to the other children in the future. Lord Nicholls said that a conclusion that a child is suffering, or is likely to suffer, harm 'must be based on facts, not just suspicion'. However, there would be cases where, although the alleged maltreatment was not proven, the evidence established a combination of profoundly worrying features affecting the care of the child within the family to satisfy the court that the child is likely to suffer harm in the future. However, the court held that this was not such a case.
>
> The House of Lords unanimously rejected a submission that 'likely' in the phrase 'likely to suffer harm' meant probable, holding that 'likely' meant likely in the sense of a real possibility, a possibility that could not sensibly be ignored having regard to the nature and gravity of the feared harm in the particular case.

Some commentators were critical of the decision of the majority in *Re H* because, *inter alia*, it created a complicated standard of proof for allegations of serious abuse. Hemingway and Williams (1997) described the reasoning as flawed, and said that the decision would create a real danger that some children would not be afforded the protection they deserved.

In the case of *Re S-B (Children)* [2009] UKSC 17 (see further below) Baroness Hale said that, when establishing whether the threshold criteria are established, 'the law has drawn a clear distinction between probability as it applies to past facts and probability as it applies to future predictions'. Her Ladyship stated that:

> Past facts must be proved to have happened on the balance of probabilities, that is, that it is more likely than not that they did happen. Predictions about future facts need only be based upon the degree of likelihood that they will happen which is sufficient to justify preventive action. This will depend upon the nature and gravity of the harm: a lesser degree of likelihood that the child will be killed will justify immediate preventive action than the degree of likelihood that the child will not be sent to school.

In other words, the more serious the future harm is, the *less* likely it has to be before State interference can be justified; and, equally, the less serious the future harm is, the *more* likely it has to be before State interference can be justified. This approach was confirmed by the Supreme Court in *Re B (A Child) (Care Proceedings: Appeal)* [2013] UKSC 33.

In *Re S-B (Children)* UKSC [2009] 17 (see further below), Baroness Hale summarised the law established in previous House of Lords decisions in the following three propositions:

1. [I]t is not enough that the court suspects that a child may have suffered significant harm or that there was a real possibility that he did. If the case is based on actual harm, the court must be satisfied on the balance of probabilities that the child was actually harmed.
2. [I]f the case is based on the likelihood of future harm, the court must be satisfied on the balance of probabilities that the facts upon which that prediction was based did actually happen. It is not enough that they may have done so or that there was a real possibility that they did.
3. [H]owever, if the case is based on the likelihood of future harm, the court does not have to be satisfied that such harm is more likely than not to happen. It is enough that there is 'a real possibility, a possibility that cannot sensibly be ignored having regard to the nature and gravity of the feared harm in the particular case' (*per* Lord Nicholls [in *Re H and Others (Minors) (Sexual Abuse: Standard of Proof)* above]).

(e)   Shared care, uncertain perpetrators and the threshold criteria

When proving the threshold criteria in section 31(2) of the Children Act 1989 (CA 1989), what must be proved is that 'the harm, or likelihood of harm, is attributable to … the care given to the child, or likely to be given to him if the order were not made, not being what it would be reasonable to expect a parent to give to him'. The emphasis is on harm, not on identifying the perpetrator, or potential perpetrator, of the alleged harm. In the following case the House of Lords held that uncertainty about the identity of the perpetrator of the alleged harm did not prevent the threshold criteria being proved.

▶ *Lancashire County Council v B* **[2000] 1 FLR 583**

A young baby (A) suffered harm as a result of being shaken, but it was impossible to prove whether A's parents or the child-minder, who also had a child (B), was responsible. The Court of Appeal held that the threshold criteria in section 31(2)(b)(i) (lack of reasonable care) were satisfied in respect of child A, but not in respect of child B (because she had suffered no harm), even though it was unclear whether the parents or the child-minder were responsible for A's injuries. A's parents appealed to the House of Lords, arguing that the harm suffered by their child had to be attributable to their care, and that the continuation of the care proceedings infringed their right to family life under Article 8 of the ECHR.

The House of Lord unanimously dismissed their appeal as the threshold conditions had been met. A majority of the House of Lords said that, under section 31(2)(b)(i), the court had to be satisfied that the harm suffered by the child was attributable to 'the care given to the child', which normally referred to the care given by the parents or other primary carers. However, their Lordships said that different considerations applied in cases of shared care where the child suffers harm but the court is unable to identify which of the carers provided the deficient care. They held that the words 'care given to the child' in section 31(2)(b)(i) embraced the care given by *any* of the carers, and that the threshold conditions could be satisfied where there was no more than a possibility that the parents were responsible for inflicting the injuries. This interpretation, their Lordships said, was necessary to permit the court to intervene to protect a child at risk where the individual responsible for harming the child could not be identified. In other words, the interpretation was necessary to avoid the risk of a child remaining wholly unprotected.

The House of Lords stressed that, in an uncertain perpetrator case, the fact that it had not been proved that the parents had been responsible for the child's injuries could be taken into account at the 'welfare stage' once the threshold conditions had been met. The House of Lords therefore held that there had been no breach of Article 8 of the ECHR as the steps taken by the local authority had been those reasonably necessary to pursue the legitimate aim of protecting the child from injury.

(i) The standard of proof and possible perpetrators

In *Re S-B (Children)* [2009] UKSC 17, which concerned the issue of an uncertain perpetrator in the context of bruising to a four-week-old baby, the Supreme Court, with Baroness Hale giving the leading opinion, held that the test to be applied to the identification of perpetrators was that of the balance of probabilities as laid down in *Re B (Children) (Sexual Abuse: Standard of Proof)* [2008] UKHL 35 (see above). Baroness Hale said the test is 'the balance of probabilities, nothing more and nothing less'. Although her Ladyship in *Re S-B* recognised that it might be difficult for a judge to decide, even on the balance of probabilities, who had caused the harm to the child, there was no obligation to do so, as the threshold criteria were concerned with a finding of harm, not who caused the harm. Baroness Hale agreed with Wall LJ's approach in *Re D (Care Proceedings: Preliminary Hearing)* [2009] EWCA Civ 472 that judges should not strain to identify the perpetrator as a result of the decision in *Re B*. In *Re D*, Wall LJ said that, although the House of Lords in *Re B* had established that the standard of proof to be applied to all findings of fact in care proceedings was the 'simple balance of probabilities' test, that rule did not require a court to come to a conclusion as to which of two people was more likely than not to be the perpetrator in order to satisfy the threshold criteria. Wall LJ said that two parents could, for example, be possible perpetrators.

In *Re S-B*, however, Baroness Hale stated that, even if it was not possible for the judge to identify a perpetrator or perpetrators, it was important for the judge to identify 'the pool of possible perpetrators', as this would sometimes be necessary in order to fulfil the 'attributability' criterion. Her Ladyship said that, if the harm had been caused by someone outside the home or family (such as at school or in hospital or by a stranger), then it was not attributable to parental care unless it would have been reasonable to expect a parent to have prevented it.

(ii) The welfare stage and several possible perpetrators

In *Re O and N; Re B (Minors)* [2003] UKHL 18 the House of Lords unanimously held that in uncertain perpetrator cases, where the judge had found that the child had suffered significant harm at the hands of his parents or carer but was unable to identify which parent or carer had caused the harm, the preferred interpretation of the CA 1989 was that the court should proceed at the welfare stage of care proceedings on the footing that each of the possible perpetrators be treated as such.

In *Re J (Children) (Care Proceedings: Threshold Criteria)* [2013] UKSC 9, the Supreme Court sought to conclusively set out the proper approach that should be taken in unknown perpetrator cases. In this case, the mother's first child had died after suffering injuries caused either by her or the child's father (the court could not say which of the two had caused the injuries as they were covering for each other). The issue was whether the real possibility that the mother had harmed her first child was sufficient to establish that the children in her new family unit (with her new partner) were likely to suffer significant harm and should therefore be removed from her care. The Supreme Court followed the approach set out by Baroness Hale in *Re S-B* (see above), holding that a prediction of future harm had to be based upon findings of actual fact made on the balance of probabilities. Because there was only a 'real possibility' that the mother had harmed her first child, this could not, in itself, be used to justify removal of the children in her new family unit. This is despite the fact that harm had occurred to the first child and had to have been caused by either the mother or the child's father.

The decision in *Re J* has been criticised as leaving children vulnerable to harm, particularly in those cases where it is impossible to establish, on the balance of probabilities, who has perpetrated harm to a child (see, for example, Hayes [2013] Fam Law 1015).

(f)   The local authority's care plan

Where an application for a care order is made in which a final care order might be made, the local authority must, within such time as the court may direct, prepare a 'care plan' for the future care of the child (s 31A(1)). The care plan will include information, for example, about the child's needs, the placement, and the management and support to be provided by the local authority. It will also provide details about contact, as before making a care order the court must consider the arrangements, or proposed arrangements, for contact (s 34(11)).

Reforms introduced by the Children and Families Act 2014 (CFA 2014) to section 31A of the CA 1989 have repealed the prohibition which prevented the court from making a care order without considering the care plan. Instead, under section 31(3A) the court must consider, specifically, the permanence provisions of the plan. This means the provisions of the care plan which set out the long-term plan for the upbringing of the child, such as whether they are to live with a family member, whether they are to be adopted or some other long-term care is intended for them (s 31(3B)). In *Re B-S* [2013] EWCA Civ 1146, Munby P said that when the court is being asked to approve a care plan for adoption, there are two essential requirements: proper evidence from the local authority and guardian analysing all the realistic options; and a global, holistic evaluation by the judge considering the options for the child.

Sufficient detail regarding the permanence provisions will be required in order for the court to properly carry out its duty. In *Re S-W (Children) (Care Proceedings: Case Management Hearing)* [2015] EWCA Civ 27, King LJ gave guidance on the approach to be taken to care plans saying that where a care plan anticipates that a child will live permanently with a family or friend, the identity and sufficient information about that family member or friend must be before the court. Equally, in the case of a long-term foster placement, a description of the placement and of the foster-carers should be provided.

Although the court is not required to consider other aspects of the care plan beyond the contact provisions and permanence provisions, this does not prevent the court from scrutinising other aspects of the plan (*per* King LJ in *Re S-W*). In fact, as King LJ explains:

> [O]ne can imagine any number of situations where a particular child's individual identified needs will mean that the court, whilst not seeking to trespass on the exercise of parental responsibility of the local authority, forms the view that the child's welfare necessitates the court satisfying itself in relation to certain important aspects of the care plan not found within the permanence provisions themselves.

The court can make a final care order even if it is not satisfied about all aspects of the care plan. In *Re K (Care Proceedings: Care Plan)* [2007] EWHC 393 (Fam), Munby J said that only in a rare case would the court's disapproval of a care plan prevent a care order being made when the threshold criteria had been satisfied and a care order was in the best interests of a child; and held that the court should have made a care order even though it was not satisfied about the contact proposed in the plan.

(i) The duty to keep a care plan under review

While the application is pending, the local authority must keep the care plan under review, and revise it or renew it if some change is required (s 31A(2)). It must also do the same once the child is in care (s 26(2)(e)(i)); and, if change is required, it must consider whether an application should be made to discharge the care order (s 26(2) (e)(ii)). A failure to keep a care plan up to date may provide grounds for an appeal, as it did in *Re A (Care Plan)* [2008] EWCA Civ 650 where the trial judge had made a care order on the basis of an outdated care plan.

Once the child is in care, the local authority is not permitted to make significant changes to the care plan or change the child's living arrangements without properly involving the child's parents (and in some cases the child) in the decision-making process and giving the parents a proper opportunity to make their case before a decision is made (see, for example, *Re G (Care: Challenge to Local Authority's Decision)* [2003] EWHC 551 (Fam)).

(ii) Involving parents

A failure to involve a parent in the decision-making process in respect of a care plan, or a change in a care plan, can constitute a breach of a parent's human rights, and may result in a local authority having to pay damages to the wronged parent (see *Re C (Breach of Human Rights: Damages)* [2007] EWCA Civ 2).

(iii) Challenging a care plan

If the local authority fails to comply with its care plan, a parent (and/or the child) can: apply to discharge the care order; make a complaint under the complaints procedure; bring a challenge under the Human Rights Act 1998 (HRA 1998) and/or judicial review; or bring a negligence claim (see 14.11). Independent Reviewing Officers can also provide assistance (see below). In *R (CD) v Isle of Anglesey County Council* [2004] EWHC 1635 (Admin), for example, a 15-year-old successfully challenged a care plan on the ground that it had, *inter alia*, failed to give due consideration to her wishes in respect of the number of nights she should spend with her foster-carers.

(iv) Independent reviewing officers and care plans

Before provisions for the appointment of independent reviewing officers were introduced in the CA 1989 (ss 25A–25B), there was judicial concern that, once a child was in care, a local authority could choose not to implement the proposals in its care plan to the detriment of the child and the court had no power to intervene. The judiciary was concerned that children could drift in care with nobody, including the child, having the right to review the promises made in the care plan. Young children with parents who had no interest in them were in a particularly vulnerable position, even though local authorities were under a duty to conduct regular case reviews.

Concern about care plans was voiced by the House of Lords in *Re S (Care Order: Implementation of Care Plan); Re W (Minors) (Care Order: Adequacy of Care Plan)* [2002] UKHL 10, where in each appeal the local authority had failed to implement the proposed arrangements in the care plan. The House of Lords allowed the appeals, holding that there was a statutory gap in the CA 1989, as a child whose parents were not interested in the matter might be left without an effective remedy to challenge a local authority's failure to implement its proposals in its care plan (as required by Article 6 of the ECHR).

The gap identified by the House of Lords was subsequently filled by new provisions in the CA 1989 requiring local authorities to appoint independent reviewing officers, who have a duty to monitor the performance of local authorities with regard to their functions in relation to looked after children (s 25B). They are responsible for participating in case reviews, for monitoring the local authority's functions in respect of case reviews, and for referring a case to a Cafcass officer where appropriate (s 25B(3)(a)). The Cafcass officer can then, if necessary, seek a court order against the local authority to put right its failings in relation to the care plan, for example by: applying to discharge the care order; applying for contact between the child and another person; or applying for a declaration under the HRA 1998 that the local authority's plans are contrary to the child's human rights. Before bringing court proceedings, the Cafcass officer will attempt to reach a negotiated settlement and will refer the case to mediation if appropriate. By way of example, in *A v Lancashire CC* [2012] EWHC 1689 (Fam) the court made declarations that the local authority and the independent reviewing officer had acted incompatibly with the children's rights under Articles 3, 6 and 8 of the ECHR. Jackson J was critical of the independent reviewing officer in this case for failing to fulfil his task, which was to monitor, persuade, cajole, encourage and criticise his fellow professionals in the interests of the child.

(g)   Effect of a care order – obligations of the local authority

If a care order is made, statutory responsibility for the child passes to the local authority and the court has no power, unless expressly provided by statute, to interfere with the local authority's powers. Thus, for example, the court has no power to impose conditions on a care order in respect of the child's accommodation arrangements; nor to direct how the local authority should look after the child (*Re T (A Minor) (Care Order: Conditions)* [1994] 2 FLR 423; and *Re S and D (Children: Powers of Court)* [1995] 2 FLR 456).

If a care order is made, the child is described as being 'looked after' by the local authority (s 22(1)), whereupon the local authority has various duties and powers in respect of the child. The court no longer monitors the arrangements for the child and has no say in these arrangements unless there is an application before the court. The Guardian's involvement in the case also terminates.

A care order imposes a duty on the local authority to receive and keep the child in its care (s 33(1)), and the local authority has a general duty to safeguard and promote the child's welfare (s 22). A care order discharges any section 8 order, a supervision order and a school attendance order, and it terminates wardship (s 91). A care order remains in force until the child reaches 18, unless brought to an end earlier (s 91(12)).

(i) Care orders and parental responsibility

A care order gives the local authority parental responsibility for the child and the power to determine the extent to which the child's parent(s) or guardian may meet their parental responsibility where it is needed to safeguard and promote the child's welfare (ss 33(3), (4)). The local authority must exercise its parental responsibility in a way which complies with the ECHR, in particular the procedural and substantive requirements of Article 8. Thus, it must inform parents of the decisions it makes, give parents opportunities to be heard and to make representations, and involve them in the decision-making process.

The parental responsibility acquired by a local authority is not, however, absolute, as the child's parents do not lose parental responsibility while a care order is in force; and there is a presumption of reasonable contact between the child in care and their family (see 14.8 below). A parent who has care of the child remains entitled to do what is reasonable in all the circumstances for the purpose of safeguarding and promoting the child's welfare (s 33(5)); and the local authority's powers are subject to any rights, duties, powers and responsibilities in relation to the child and his property which a parent may have under any other enactment (s 33(9)). The local authority is not entitled to take decisions about the child without reference to, or over the heads of, the parents; and it is not entitled to make significant changes to its care plan. Neither is it entitled to make changes to the child's living arrangements without first discussing the matter with the parents, and, in some cases, the child; and it also has no power to give or refuse consent to the child's adoption, or to appoint a guardian, or to change the child's religion (s 33(6)).

(ii) Restrictions imposed by care orders

While a care order is in force no person can change the child's surname or remove the child from the UK without the *written* consent of every person who has parental responsibility for the child, or leave of the court (s 33(7)). However, the local authority can allow the child to be taken out of the UK for up to one month (s 33(8)(a)) and arrange (or assist in arranging) for the child to live outside England and Wales, subject to the court's approval (Sch 2, para 19).

(iii) Placement of the child

The child may be placed with foster-parents, remain with existing short-term foster-carers or be placed with members of the extended family such as a grandparent or other relative. Placing the child can be implemented under the terms of the care order, or under a child arrangements order or special guardianship order. In some cases, the child may be placed for adoption (see Chapter 15). Section 22C lists a hierarchy of people with whom a looked after child should be placed. Parents and people with parental responsibility are at the top, followed by relatives and friends and then unrelated carers. Local authorities must also comply with other requirements regarding placement, such as placing children near their homes, not disrupting their education and keeping siblings together.

(h) Effect of a supervision order

A supervision order, unlike a care order, does *not* give the local authority parental responsibility but instead places the child under the supervision of a designated local authority (s 31(1)(b)). With a supervision order, safeguarding the child's interests remains the primary responsibility of parents. Under a supervision order the local authority, through a social worker, merely assists and befriends the child (s 35(1) (a), (b)); and the operation of any conditions or undertakings depends on parental agreement (*Re B (Supervision Order: Parental Undertaking)* [1996] 1 FLR 676). The supervisor can apply to have the supervision order varied or discharged where the order is not complied with or the supervisor considers the order is no longer necessary (s 35(1)(c)).

Parts I and II of Schedule 3 to the CA 1989 list specific powers in respect of supervision. Thus, for example, the supervisor can give directions that the child live in a certain place, attend at a certain place and participate in certain activities. A supervision order can require a child to have a medical or psychiatric examination, but only with the child's consent if the child has sufficient understanding to make an informed decision, and only if satisfactory arrangements have been, or can be, made for the examination. A supervision order can be made in the first instance for up to one year, but the supervisor can apply to have the order extended up to a maximum of three years (Sch 3, para 6). The court has no power to impose conditions on a supervision order (*Re S (Care or Supervision Order)* [1996] 1 FLR 753).

(i) Interim care and supervision orders

The court has the power to make interim (temporary) care and supervision orders (s 38), the purpose of which is to enable the court to maintain the status quo pending the final hearing, and for it to obtain any information it needs before making a final decision. Although an interim care order is a 'holding' order, once it is made, care of the child passes to the local authority and the manner in which the child is cared for passes out of the court's control. The power to make interim orders can only be exercised where care and supervision proceedings are to be adjourned (such as for inquiries or reports to be made) or where the court makes an order under section 37(1) directing a local authority to investigate the child's circumstances (s 38(1)). An interim order cannot be made unless there are reasonable grounds for believing that the threshold criteria for making a care or supervision order are satisfied (s 38(2)) (see 14.7(c) above).

If the court decides to make a child arrangements order regulating the child's living arrangements in care or supervision proceedings, an interim supervision order must also be made, unless the child's welfare is otherwise satisfactorily safeguarded (s 38(3)). The interim order will have effect for such period as is specified in the order, but will automatically come to an end on the final disposal of the care or supervision proceedings. If the interim order was made to allow the local authority to carry out an investigation under section 37, and no care or supervision order has been applied for, the interim order will expire eight weeks from the date when the order was made or in accordance with any direction made under section 37(4) (s 38(4)).

The court can include in an interim care order a requirement that an alleged abuser should leave the home or be prevented from entering the home and/or an area round the home if it is satisfied that: there is reasonable cause to believe that by doing this the child will cease to suffer, or cease to be likely to suffer, significant harm; and there is a person living in the home who is able and willing to provide reasonable care for the child (s 38A).

An interim care order may provide for removal of the child from its carers. However, in order to justify such a draconian step at an interim stage, the child's safety must require it. In *MG v A Local Authority* [2011] EWCA Civ 745, the Court of Appeal said that the questions which the court must ask itself are: whether the children's safety (using that term to include both psychological and physical elements) requires removal; and whether removal is proportionate in the light of the risks posed by leaving the children where they are. The courts must keep the ECHR in mind when deciding whether or not to make an interim care order (*per* Sir Nicholas Wall P in *Re S (Care Proceedings: Human Rights)* [2010] EWCA Civ 1383).

(j) Directing a medical or psychiatric examination or other assessment of the child

When the court makes an interim care or supervision order it can give such directions (if any) as it considers appropriate with regard to the medical or psychiatric examination or other assessment of the child (s 38(6)). Such a direction may be given only if the court is of the opinion that the examination or other assessment is necessary to assist the court to resolve the proceedings justly (s 38(7A)). In deciding whether to make such a direction, the court must take into account the factors set out in section 38(7B), which were introduced by the Children and Families Act 2014 (CFA 2014).

The aim of a section 38(6) direction is to ensure that all of the evidence is before the court in order to assist it in its decision-making. Thus, as Wall LJ said in *Re L and H (Residential Assessment)* [2007] EWCA Civ 213, before moving children permanently from their families the court must ensure that the case has been fully investigated and that all the relevant evidence necessary for the decision is in place. His Lordship said that Article 6 of the ECHR (the right to a fair hearing) required it and so did the underlying policy of the CA 1989, which was that, wherever possible, children should be brought up by their parents or within their natural families. Wall LJ held that the critical questions for the court are: does this child's welfare warrant an assessment under section 38(6); and, looking at the timetable for the child, is there evidence that the parent or other person will be able to care adequately for the child within that timetable?

A child with sufficient understanding to make an informed decision can refuse to submit to a medical or psychiatric examination or other assessment (s 38(6)); but, as the child's welfare prevails, the court can override a child's refusal, even if the child has the required sufficiency of understanding (see *South Glamorgan County Council v W and B* [1993] 1 FLR 574).

(i) Directing a residential assessment

Under section 38(6) the court may decide that a residential assessment is needed in order to assess the child and/or parents. The court can direct a residential assessment even though the local authority objects, as the purpose of section 38(6) is to enable the court to obtain the information it needs so that it can decide what final order to make (see *Re C (A Minor) (Interim Care Order: Residential Assessment)* [1997] AC 489). However, the court will take into account 'the cost of the proposed assessment and the fact that local authorities' resources are notoriously limited' (*per* Lord Browne-Wilkinson in *Re C* above). For example, in *Local Authority v M (Funding of Residential Assessments)* [2008] EWHC 162 (Fam), Bodey J, having given careful consideration to the local authority's budget, made an order under section 38(6) even though the local authority, although agreeing in principle with the assessment, submitted that it could not afford to pay for it. The cost of any assessment is one of the factors specifically included for consideration by the court in section 38(7B).

The court does not have the power under section 38(6) to give directions for therapeutic treatment. Thus, the House of Lords has held that a section 38(6) assessment does not include an assessment where its main focus is to consider the parents' capacity to respond to therapeutic treatment or to secure therapy for the child or the family (see *Re G (A Child) (Interim Care Order: Residential Assessment)* [2005] UKHL 68).

(k) Discharge and variation of care and supervision orders

A supervision order can be varied or discharged. A care order can *only* be discharged, not varied, as variation would undermine a local authority's responsibility for the child.

(i) Discharge of a care order

An application to discharge a care order can be made by: a person with parental responsibility for the child; the child; or the local authority (s 39(1)). A child does not need leave of the court to apply (*Re A (Care: Discharge Application by Child)* [1995] 1 FLR 599). People without parental responsibility cannot apply for discharge, but can, with the permission of the court, apply for a child arrangements order regulating the child's living arrangements, which if granted will automatically discharge the care order (s 91(1)). Discharge applications are often made by local authorities who have an ongoing responsibility to consider whether to apply for discharge. As an alternative to discharge, the court can substitute the care order with a supervision order, without the need to satisfy the threshold criteria (ss 39(4), (5)).

In some cases, the parents may apply to discharge a care order, for example, where there has been a radical change in the care plan. This was the case in *Re E (A Child) (Care Order: Change of Care Plan)* [2014] EWFC 6, where the child was placed with the parents under a care order but the local authority subsequently sought to remove him from their care. In such a case, the parents should seek an injunction under section 8 of the HRA 1998 preventing removal of the child pending determination of the discharge application.

In a discharge application the court must apply the section 1(1) welfare principle and the other section 1 provisions (see 10.3). There is no need to prove that the threshold criteria no longer apply (*Re S (Discharge of Care Order)* [1995] 2 FLR 639).

(ii) Variation or discharge of a supervision order

A supervision order can be varied or discharged on the application of: a person with parental responsibility for the child; the child; or the person supervising the child (s 39(2)). An order can also be varied on the application of a person with whom the child is living, if the original order imposes a requirement which affects that person (s 39(3)). When exercising its powers, the court must apply the section 1(1) welfare principle and the other section 1 provisions (see 10.3).

(l) Care and supervision orders – appeals

Any party to care or supervision proceedings can appeal against the making of, or refusal to make, a final or interim care or supervision order. The appeal court will not, however, interfere with a discretionary decision made by a lower court unless the judge has erred in law, or is under a misapprehension of fact, or the decision is outside a band of reasonable discretion within which reasonable disagreement is possible. As this is a high threshold, it is sometimes difficult for an appeal to succeed. (See *Re B (A Child) (Care Proceedings: Appeal)* [2013] UKSC 33 for an example of an unsuccessful attempt to appeal a care order, the role of the appellate court and the principles to be applied on an appeal).

14.8 Contact in care

As contact between children and parents is considered to be mutually beneficial, and because children have a right to contact, cogent reasons are required for terminating contact (*per* Balcombe LJ in *Re J (A Minor) (Contact)* [1994] 1 FLR 729). The European Court of Human Rights (ECtHR) has also recognised the importance of a child in care having contact with his or her parents and family. Thus, in *K and T v Finland* (2000) 31 EHRR 18 the ECtHR held that, while there is a wide margin of appreciation in care cases, it nevertheless remains important to scrutinise any restrictions placed by authorities on parental rights of contact. Contact is also important for children in care, because it improves their chances of being rehabilitated with their families. Article 9(3) of the United Nations Convention on the Rights of the Child (UNCRC) recognises that a child who is separated from one or both parents has a right 'to maintain personal relations and direct contact with those parents on a regular basis, except if it is contrary to the child's best interests'.

Section 34 of the Children Act 1989 (CA 1989) makes provision in respect of contact in care. It lays down a duty of contact, and gives the court power to make orders in respect of contact (see below). It also requires the court, before making a care order, to consider the arrangements the local authority has made, or proposes to make, for contact; and it must invite the parties to the proceedings to comment on those arrangements (s 34(11)).

(a) The duty to provide contact

Section 34(1) provides that a local authority must allow a child in care reasonable contact with: parents; a guardian or special guardian; a person with parental responsibility for him under section 4ZA and section 4A of the CA 1989; a person named in a child arrangements order as a person with whom the child was to live; and a person who has care of the child under an order made by the High Court under its inherent jurisdiction. However, a local authority can as a matter of urgency refuse contact for up to seven days without obtaining a court order where it is necessary for the child's welfare (s 34(6)).

(b) Section 34 orders

Under section 34 the court can make two sorts of order: an order in respect of contact; and an order authorising a local authority to refuse contact. These orders can be made on an application, or by the court of its own motion when making a care order, or in any family proceedings in connection with a child in care (s 34(5)). They can be made when a care order is made, or subsequently (s 34(10)). The court can impose conditions on such an order (s 34(7)).

When exercising its powers, the court must apply the section 1(1) welfare principle and the other section 1 provisions in the CA 1989 (see 10.3); and it must also ensure that the order is human rights compliant, in particular with Article 6 (the right to a fair trial) and Article 8 (the right to family life) of the European Convention on Human Rights (ECHR).

As is the case in private law (see 11.5), the courts are aware of the danger of authorising contact where there is a risk of the child witnessing domestic violence. In *Re G (Domestic Violence: Direct Contact)* [2000] 2 FLR 865, where the local authority was given permission to terminate direct contact, it was held that the reluctance of a child to see a parent in a case involving serious domestic violence requires careful consideration by the court.

Orders made under section 34 can be varied or discharged on the application of the local authority, the child or any person named in the order (s 34(9)).

(i) An order in respect of contact

Under section 34(2) the court, on the application of the local authority or the child, can make such order as it considers appropriate in respect of the contact which is to be allowed between the child in care and any named person.

Under section 34(3) the court may also make an order in respect of contact on the application of a person who has a right to reasonable contact under section 34(1) (see above) or a person who has been granted leave to apply. Although grandparents, relatives or friends of a child are not allowed contact with a child in care as of right (unless they fall within section 34(1)), they can apply for leave to apply for an order in respect of contact with a child in care (s 34(3)(b)) (see, for example, *Re M (Care: Contact: Grandmother's Application for Leave)* [1995] 2 FLR 86). Although the test which the court must apply when considering leave applications is laid down in section 10(9), the court is not restricted to considering only those matters set out in section 10(9). In *Re M* the court said that a frivolous or vexatious application, or one where the prospects of success are remote, will be dismissed and that an applicant for leave must prove that there is a serious issue to be tried and a good arguable case. However, in *Re J (A Child) (Leave to Issue Application for Residence Order)* [2002] EWCA Civ 1346 the court warned against substituting the 'test' in *Re M* for the statutory criteria laid down by Parliament in section 10(9) and the need to consider that the order is compliant with the ECHR. Thorpe LJ said:

> [I]t is important that trial judges should recognise the greater appreciation that we have developed of the valuable contribution that grandparents make …. Judges should be careful not to dismiss such a potential contribution without full inquiry. That seems to me to be the minimum essential protection of the Article 6 and Article 8 rights that grandparents enjoy.

(ii) An order authorising a local authority to refuse contact

Under section 34(4) the court can make an order (on the application of the local authority or the child) authorising the local authority to refuse to allow contact between the child and any person entitled to reasonable contact under section 34(1) (see above). If the court refuses to make a section 34(4) order, a further application cannot be made for six months except with leave of the court (s 91(17)). The courts have held that contact is only to be terminated where there is no likelihood of rehabilitation and where post-adoption contact is not considered to be in the child's best interests (see, for example, *Re H (Termination of Contact)* [2005] EWCA Civ 318, where the court refused the local authority's application for an order under s 34(4)).

The court may be unwilling to make an order authorising a local authority to refuse contact between a newborn baby and its mother, particularly when the threshold for a care order has not been established, unless extraordinarily compelling reasons exist. Munby J so held in *Re K (Contact)* [2008] EWHC 540, even though, on the facts, a section 34(4) order was granted because the child's safety imperatively demanded that the court make the order. The contact between the mother and child had been poor, and during one contact session the parents had been involved in a fight and the mother had thrown the baby to the contact supervisor.

14.9 Part V of the Children Act 1989 – emergency protection

Part V of the Children Act 1989 (CA 1989) provides the legal framework for dealing with children who need protection in an emergency by making provision for, *inter alia*, child assessment orders and emergency protection orders. Part V orders are subject to certain safeguards so as to prevent unjustifiable intrusion into family life. For example, they are of short duration and are open to challenge. In some cases, emergency action will be followed by an application for a care or supervision order (see 14.7).

Under Part V a local authority also has various investigative duties when it is informed that a child who lives, or is found, in its area is the subject of an emergency protection order or is in police protection, or if the local authority has reasonable cause to suspect that such child is suffering, or is likely to suffer, significant harm (see s 47(1)). Once a local authority has obtained a Part V order, inquiries must be made to decide what action should be taken to safeguard or promote the child's welfare (s 47(2)).

As Part V proceedings are not 'family proceedings' for the purposes of the CA 1989 (s 8(4)), the court cannot make any section 8 order in the proceedings. When considering whether to make a Part V order the child's welfare is the court's paramount consideration (s 1(1)) and the other section 1 principles apply (see 10.3), except for the section 1(3) welfare checklist, as conducting the section 1(3) exercise is lengthy and would defeat the purpose of a Part V application which is for immediate short-term emergency protection.

The following are available for emergency protection of a child under Part V: a child assessment order (s 43); an emergency protection order (s 44); and police protection (s 46). In practice, however, local authorities often prefer to make agreements with parents that a child be accommodated with the local authority instead of applying for an emergency protection order or requesting police protection (see Masson [2005] CFLQ 75.). In this way, they comply with one of the policy objectives of the CA 1989, which is that local authorities should work in partnership with parents.

(a) Child assessment orders

Under section 43 the court can make a child assessment order, which is an order enabling a medical or psychiatric assessment of the child to take place in order to establish whether or not the child is suffering, or is likely to suffer, significant harm. A child assessment order allows a local authority to intervene to protect a child where the circumstances are not sufficiently urgent or serious to justify other intervention. With such an order the child can remain at home, and so it is less severe than an emergency protection order. In practice, however, child assessment orders are not commonly made.

(i) Grounds

The court can make a child assessment order on the application of a local authority (or the National Society for the Prevention of Cruelty to Children) if it is satisfied that: the applicant has reasonable cause to suspect that the child is suffering, or is likely to suffer, significant harm; and an assessment of the state of the child's health or development, or of the way in which he has been treated, is required to enable the applicant to determine whether or not the child is suffering, or is likely to suffer, significant harm; and it is unlikely that such an assessment will be made, or be satisfactory, in the absence of an order under this section (s 43(1)).

The court can treat the application as one for an emergency protection order (s 43(3)). It cannot make a child assessment order if the grounds for an emergency protection order exist; and it considers an emergency protection order, rather than a child assessment order, ought to be made (s 43(4)). The child assessment order must specify when the assessment is to begin (which must not last longer than seven days) (s 43(5)). The effect of the order is to require any person in a position to do so to produce the child to the person named in the order and to comply with any directions in the order (s 43(6)). The order authorises the person carrying out the assessment, or part of it, to do so in accordance with the terms of the order (s 43(7)). A child of sufficient understanding to make an informed decision may refuse to submit to a medical or psychiatric examination, or other assessment, regardless of any term in the order authorising assessment (s 43(8)), but the court can override the child's refusal if this is in their best interests (see *South Glamorgan County Council v W and B* above).

A child can be kept away from home for the assessment, but only if this is necessary for the purposes of the assessment, and only in accordance with directions and for the period(s) of time specified in the order (s 43(9)). The order must contain directions about contact (s 43(10)). Before the application is heard, the local authority must take reasonably practicable steps to ensure that notice of the application is given to: the child's parents; any person with parental responsibility for the child; any person caring for the child; any person named in a child arrangements order as a person with whom the child is to spend time or otherwise have contact; any person who is allowed to have contact with the child by virtue of an order under section 34; and the child (s 43(11)). This notice requirement is to ensure that, where possible, the hearing takes place between the parties in order to prevent unjustifiable intervention. A child assessment order can be varied and/or discharged (s 43(12)). The court is required to appoint a Cafcass officer for the child unless it is satisfied that it is not necessary to do so in order to safeguard the child's interests (ss 41(1), (2)).

(b) Emergency protection orders

Under section 44 of the CA 1989 the court can make an emergency protection order, which is an order providing an immediate but temporary remedy in a genuine emergency. In an emergency, an application can be made *ex parte* (without notice), although, where possible, proceedings must be heard *inter partes* (with notice).

(i) Applicants

Section 44 provides that 'any person' may apply for an emergency protection order, but in practice it is local authority social services departments who do so.

(ii) The grounds for making an emergency protection order

The applicant must prove that there is reasonable cause to believe that the child is likely to suffer harm if: he is not removed to accommodation provided by or on behalf of the applicant; or he does not remain in the place in which he is being accommodated (s 44(1)(a)). The court can also make an emergency protection order on the application of a local authority if enquiries in respect of the child are being made under section 47(1)(b) and those enquiries are being frustrated by access to the child being unreasonably refused to a person authorised to seek access; and the applicant has reasonable cause to believe that access to the child is required as a matter of urgency (ss 44(1)(b), (c)). Local authorities must keep parents informed about what is happening at the hearing, and they have a continuing duty to keep the case under review.

(iii) The approach of the courts

The courts adopt the following approach when considering whether or not to make an emergency protection order:

▶ As an emergency protection order is a severe and extremely harsh measure requiring exceptional justification and extraordinarily compelling reasons, the court will not make the order unless it is necessary and proportionate and no other less radical form of order will promote the child's welfare (see *P, C and S v UK* (2002) 35 EHRR 31 which involved the removal of a newborn baby).

- Separation of the child will be contemplated only if immediate separation is essential to secure the child's safety. Imminent danger must be established (see *Re M (Care Proceedings: Judicial Review)* [2003] EWHC 850 (Admin)).
- An emergency protection order should not be made for any longer than is absolutely necessary to protect a child.
- The evidence in support of an emergency protection order must be full, detailed, precise and compelling.
- Save in wholly exceptional cases, parents must be given adequate prior notice of the date, time and place of the application for an emergency protection order, and the evidence relied on.
- An *ex parte* (without notice) application will normally be considered appropriate only if the case involves a genuine emergency, great urgency or some other compelling reason to believe that the child's welfare will be compromised if the parents are alerted in advance (but even then some kind of informal notice to the parents may well be possible). As a result of their obligations under the Human Rights Act 1998 (HRA 1998), the courts must ensure that making an *ex parte* emergency protection order does not breach the European Convention on Human Rights (ECHR), for example Article 6 (the right to a fair trial) and Article 8 (the right to family life), and in particular the principle of proportionality under Article 8.
- A Children's Guardian (an officer of Cafcass) (see 1.7) must be appointed immediately upon the issue of proceedings for an emergency protection order.

The rules above were set out and applied by Munby J in the following case, where he described an emergency protection order summarily removing a child from his parents as a 'terrible and drastic remedy'.

> ▶ *X Council v B (Emergency Protection Orders)* [2004] EWHC 2015 (Fam)
>
> Three children were taken into foster care under *ex parte* emergency protection orders. Munby J held that, while child assessment orders, and possibly even very short-term emergency protection orders, had been appropriate to enable medical tests and examinations to take place, it was not clear that there had been any justification for removing the children into foster care. His Lordship said that the local authority had failed to address itself adequately to the requirements of sections 44(5) or (10) of the CA 1989; and it was not clear that it had exercised the exceptional diligence called for by Article 8 of the ECHR. The distress suffered by the children and parents due to their separation had been exacerbated by the unacceptably limited amount of contact permitted, and by the interventionist manner in which contact had been supervised. Munby J said that the Court of Appeal had repeatedly emphasised that any intervention under Parts V (and IV) of the CA 1989 should be proportionate to the legitimate aim of protecting the welfare and interests of the child. As Hale LJ had said in *Re O (Supervision Order)* [2001] EWCA Civ 16, 'proportionality ... is the key'.

In *Re X (Emergency Protection Order)* [2006] EWHC 510 (Fam), McFarlane J, approving the factors referred to by Munby J above, emphasised that emergency protection orders should be made only in a genuine emergency and only for the purpose of providing immediate short-term protection; and that lack of information or a need for assessment could not on their own justify the making of an emergency protection order.

(iv) Duration of an emergency protection order

An order can be made in the first instance to last for up to eight days, but can be extended for up to a further seven days on application if the court has reasonable cause to believe that the child is likely to suffer significant harm if the order is not extended (s 45).

(v) Effect of an emergency protection order

While an emergency protection order is in force it operates as a direction to any person who is in a position to do so to comply with any request to produce the child to the applicant (s 44(4)(a)). It authorises the child's removal to accommodation provided by or on behalf of the applicant and the child being kept there; or it prevents the child's removal from any hospital, or other place, in which the child was being accommodated immediately before the order was made (s 44(4)(b)). It is a criminal offence intentionally to obstruct a person authorised to remove the child or to prevent the removal of the child (s 44(15)). An emergency protection order gives the applicant limited parental responsibility (ss 44(4)(c), 44(5)(b)).

While an emergency protection order is in force, the local authority cannot remove the child from his home or retain him in a place for longer than is necessary to safeguard his welfare, and must return the child or allow him to be returned when safe to do so (s 44(10)). The child can be returned to the care of the person from whom he was removed or, if that is not reasonably practicable, then to a parent, a person with parental responsibility or to such other person as the applicant with the agreement of the court considers appropriate, although while the order is in force the applicant can exercise his powers with respect to the child where it is necessary to do so (ss 44(11), (12)). Local authorities must make arrangements (subject to directions in the order as to contact and medical assessment or examination) to allow the child reasonable contact with the following persons and any person acting on their behalf: parents; any other person with parental responsibility for the child; any person with whom the child was living immediately before the order was made; any person named in a child arrangements order as a person with whom the child is to spend time or otherwise have contact; any person who is allowed to have contact with the child by virtue of an order under section 34; and any person acting on behalf of any of those persons (s 44(13)).

(vi) Imposing directions on an emergency protection order

When an emergency protection order is made, or while it is in force, the court can give directions and impose conditions as to contact and/or may give directions with respect to the medical or psychiatric examination or other assessment of the child, which can include a condition that no examination or assessment be carried out unless the court directs (ss 44(6), (8) and (9)). Where a direction as to medical or psychiatric examination or assessment is made, a child of sufficient understanding to make an informed decision may refuse the examination or assessment (s 44(6)). Directions in an order can be varied at any time (s 44(9)(b)).

(vii) Challenging an emergency protection order

There is no right of appeal against making, or refusing to make, an emergency protection order. However, an application for discharge can be heard 72 hours or more after the order was made (ss 45(9), (10)) on the application of: the child; their parent; any person who has parental responsibility for the child; or any person with whom the child was living immediately before the order was made (s 45(8)). An emergency protection order can be challenged under the HRA 1998, and judicial review proceedings may provide a useful way of challenging an order. In *X Council v B (Emergency Protection Orders)* (see above), Munby J held that, while an application for judicial review is not normally an appropriate remedy for challenging an emergency protection order, it is not necessarily precluded in an appropriate case in order to correct an error or injustice. His Lordship said that, as the effect of an emergency protection order was to remove a child from a parent for up to 15 days without a statutory right of appeal, judicial review might provide a mechanism for review of an unreasonable decision by the court.

(viii) An exclusion requirement

The court can include in an emergency protection order a requirement that an alleged abuser should leave the home or be prevented from entering the home and/or an area round the home if it is satisfied that: there is reasonable cause to believe that by doing this the child will cease to suffer, or cease to be likely to suffer, significant harm; and there is a person living in the home who is able and willing to provide reasonable care for the child (s 44A).

(c) Police protection

Under section 46 of the CA 1989 the police have various powers in emergency cases involving children. Thus, any constable who has reasonable cause to believe that a child would otherwise be likely to suffer significant harm can remove the child to suitable accommodation or take reasonable steps to prevent the child's removal (s 46(1)). This power lasts for up to 72 hours, during which time the police must ensure that inquiries are conducted by a designated officer and that the child is accommodated by the local authority (ss 43(3)(e), (f)). The police must inform the local authority, the parents and the child of any steps it proposes to take. While the child is in police protection, the police do not have parental responsibility for the child but must do what is reasonable to safeguard or promote the child's welfare. While the child is accommodated under section 46, the parents cannot remove the child, but they are permitted to have contact.

According to research by Masson ([2005] CFLQ 75) police protection is widely used. Masson ([2010] Fam Law 1088) is, however, critical of the trend in practice for local authorities to seek the exercise of police powers (due in part to resource limitations) rather than to apply for an emergency protection order. In her view, the police are likely to be reluctant to use their resources to support children's services which will be 'catastrophic for some children and families'.

14.10 Local authorities' duties towards 'looked-after' children

Local authorities have duties under the Children Act 1989 (CA 1989) towards children 'looked after' by them, whether accommodated under a voluntary arrangement or under a care order (s 22(1)). A local authority must safeguard and promote the child's welfare and make such use of services available for children cared for by their own parents as appears reasonable in the case of the particular child (s 22(3)). Before making a decision about a child being looked after, or proposed to be looked after, the local authority must ascertain the wishes and feelings of the child, his parents, any person with parental responsibility and any other relevant person (s 22(4)). It must also consider their wishes in respect of the child's religion, racial origin and cultural and linguistic background (s 22(5)). It must advise, assist and befriend the child with a view to promoting his welfare when he ceases to be looked after by it (s 24(1)). A local authority must encourage rehabilitation by allowing the child to live with his family, unless contrary to his welfare, and ensure that the accommodation provided is near the child's home, and that brothers and sisters remain together (s 22C). A local authority's general duties to a child are facilitated by more specific duties, such as the inspection of foster-parents' and children's homes. Local authorities also have a duty to promote contact (Sch 2, para 15) (see 14.8 above).

(a) Children leaving care

Sections 23A–24D of the CA 1989 and Schedule 2 (see paras 19A–19C) impose certain duties on local authorities with respect to children who leave care. Each local authority is required to provide a comprehensive after-care service to ease the passage of looked after children into adulthood. It has a duty to advise, assist and befriend the child with a view to promoting his welfare when it ceases to look after the child (para 19A). It must keep in touch with a care leaver and prepare 'needs assessments' and formulate 'pathway plans' in respect of education, training, careers and financial support until the person leaving care reaches the age of 21 (para 19B). It must appoint a personal adviser to keep in touch with the person leaving care (para 19C). A local authority is also required to provide financial support, including the cost of education and training up to the age of 25.

If a local authority fails to comply with these statutory requirements, a challenge can be made in judicial review proceedings. In *R (J) v Caerphilly County Borough Council* [2005] EWHC 586 (Admin), Munby J held that a local authority has a duty to carry out its statutory obligations even if the person leaving care is uncooperative and unwilling to engage, or refuses to engage, with the local authority. In *R (Berhe and Others) v Hillingdon London Borough Council* [2003] EWHC 2075 (Admin), Sullivan J held that asylum-seeking minors who had been looked after by a local authority were entitled, on reaching adulthood, to benefit from the provisions of the CA 1989, as amended by the Children (Leaving Care) Act 2000. In *R (G) v Nottingham City Council and Nottingham University Hospitals NHS Trust* [2008] EWHC 400 (Admin), an 18-year-old mother successfully challenged the pathway plan prepared for her by the local authority under sections 23A–23C and Schedule 2. Munby J held that there had been a serious failure by the local authority to comply with its statutory duties.

14.11 Challenging local authority decisions about children

Parents, relatives, children, foster-parents and others may sometimes be dissatisfied with action taken, or not taken, by a local authority. In such cases it may be possible to resolve a grievance informally; and if this is not possible, the following procedures can be invoked.

(a) Using the Children Act 1989

One way of challenging a local authority is to appeal against an order (where this is possible) or apply to have it varied or discharged. Another option is to make a complaint to the Secretary of State who has the power to declare a local authority to be in default, if it fails without reasonable cause to comply with a duty under the Children Act 1989 (CA 1989), and who can require compliance within a specified period (s 84).

(b) The complaints procedure

The CA 1989 requires local authorities to establish a complaints procedure (s 26). Complaints can be made in respect of the duties and powers of local authorities under Parts III, IV and V of the Act. Those eligible to make a complaint are set out in sections 26(3)–26(3C).

(c) Advocacy services for children

A child making a complaint can make use of an independent advocacy service (s 26A). Local authorities must make arrangements to provide assistance (such as advocacy services and representation) for children and young persons who make, or intend to make, complaints under the CA 1989 procedures (s 26A(1)). This duty applies to the standard complaints procedure (s 26) and to the procedure for young people leaving care (s 24D). The assistance which local authorities must put in place include representation (s 26A(2)). Local authorities can choose whether to provide the assistance themselves or use the services of an advocacy service provider.

(d) A challenge under the Human Rights Act 1998

As local authorities are public authorities for the purposes of section 6 of the Human Rights Act 1998 (HRA 1998), they must act in a way which is compatible with the European Convention on Human Rights (ECHR). Any person who is a victim of an unlawful act (or proposed act) of a local authority may bring an application either by way of a free-standing application against a local authority or by relying on a Convention right in any legal proceedings (s 7). Damages can be awarded for a breach of a Convention right (s 8). Human rights challenges can be made in proceedings under Parts III, IV and V of the CA 1989 or in judicial review proceedings (see below).

Human rights claims against local authorities are usually brought on the basis of a breach of Article 6 (the right to a fair trial) and/or Article 8 (the right to family life) of the ECHR, as the following cases show.

▶ *Re G (Care: Challenge to Local Authority's Decision)* **[2003] EWHC 551 (Fam)**

The parents applied for discharge of care orders and an injunction under section 7 of the HRA 1998 to prevent their children's removal into care, as the local authority had delayed in making a decision about the children, and had kept no minutes or written records of meetings and decisions made. Munby J held that the local authority was in breach of the right to family life under Article 8.

▶ *Re M (Care: Challenging Decisions by Local Authority)* **[2001] 2 FLR 1300**

The child in care's parents had a long history of alcohol and drug abuse. At a planning meeting, to which the parents and their solicitors were not invited, the local authority finally ruled out any prospect of the child living with the father. Each parent commenced separate free-standing applications under section 7 of the HRA 1998 arguing that they were victims of an unlawful act of the public authority, and that the placement should be set aside. Holman J held that the local authority had acted unlawfully under section 6 of the HRA 1998 in respect of the way in which it had conducted the planning meeting, which was contrary to the parents' right to respect for their family life under Article 8. As the local authority had failed sufficiently to involve the parents at critical moments, Holman J quashed the decision made at the planning meeting.

▶ *Re C (Breach of Human Rights: Damages)* **[2007] EWCA Civ 2**

The trial judge made a declaration under the HRA 1998 that there had been a significant breach of the mother's human rights caused by the local authority's decision to abandon the care plan without giving the mother an opportunity to participate in the decision-making process; but did not make an order for damages.

▶ *Re P (Care Proceedings: Kinship Placement: Appeal)* **[2014] EWCA Civ 888**

The appellant parents, who were Polish, appealed against care and placement orders in respect of their daughter on the basis that the local authority had failed to properly investigate the child being placed with her grandparents in Poland, who had indicated that they could care for the child. During the proceedings the judge expressed a final view against placing the child with her grandparents in Poland, which meant that the grandparents had taken no further steps to put themselves forward as carers.

The Court of Appeal held that the care and placement orders should be set aside as the care proceedings had been conducted inappropriately. The local authority had a positive obligation under Article 8 to consider ways of retaining the child within her family, but had failed to take the necessary steps. The judge was also under a duty under Article 8 and his observations gave insufficient weight to the Convention jurisprudence.

(e) Judicial review

Judicial review is an administrative law remedy which may be made against a public law decision by an aggrieved person, including a child. An application is made in the Administrative Court. The court can grant the following remedies: a 'mandatory order' (directing the respondent to take a particular course of action); a 'prohibitory order' (prohibiting the respondent from taking a particular course of action); or a 'quashing order' (quashing the decision of the respondent). It can order damages in conjunction with one of these orders. The Administrative Court can also issue declarations and injunctions.

Strict rules govern judicial review applications. Thus, permission must be obtained from the court for the case to proceed to a full application on its merits, which will only be granted if the court considers that the applicant has sufficient interest in the matter and an arguable case. Permission to apply must be sought promptly and no later than three months from the date on which the grounds for the application arose. The grounds on which judicial review may be granted are: illegality; procedural impropriety (procedural unfairness); and unreasonableness. As the nature of judicial review is discretionary, the court may refuse a remedy even if a ground is proved.

As local authorities are public authorities for the purposes of the HRA 1998, and judicial review is a means of challenging the action or inaction of public bodies, challenges by way of judicial review are often based on, or supported by, human rights arguments, as the following case shows.

▶ *R on the Applications of L and Others v Manchester City Council; R on the Application of R and Another v Manchester City Council* **[2001] EWHC 707 (Admin)**

The children successfully applied for judicial review of the local authority's policy whereby it paid substantially lower fostering payments to short-term foster-parents who were friends or relatives of children. Munby J held that the local authority's policy was irrational, and that it also breached Article 8 of the ECHR (the right to family life) as it was neither a necessary nor proportionate response under Article 8(2). The local authority had a positive obligation when exercising its duties under Part III of the CA 1989 to secure respect for family life under Article 8. The policy was also held to be discriminatory under Article 14 of the ECHR, as the reference in Article 14 to 'other status' included family status.

Where a local authority has wide discretion in a particular matter (as it has under the CA 1989) it is difficult to succeed in an action for judicial review; and, where there is another procedure for challenging a local authority, the court may not grant judicial review before that procedure has been pursued. Judicial review is therefore a remedy of last resort, and may be refused where there is another equally effective and convenient remedy (such as bringing a complaint under section 26 of the CA 1989, see *R (On the Application of Appiatse and Another) v Enfield Borough Council* [2008] EWHC 1886 (Admin)).

A considerable disadvantage of judicial review is that, if a 'quashing order' is granted, the local authority's obligation is merely to reconsider its original decision. Provided that the reconsidered decision is not illegal, procedurally improper or irrational, it can come to the same conclusion as it did the first time. The drawbacks of the court's powers in judicial review proceedings were referred to in *Re T (Judicial Review: Local Authority Decisions Concerning Child in Need)* [2003] EWHC 2515 (Admin) in which Wall J held that, while the court was in a position to direct the local authority to reconsider the question of the services it should provide under Part III of the CA 1989 for the child in question, it could not direct the local authority in respect of what to decide or direct that it make any special provision for the child.

There are many reported cases involving applications for judicial review in the context of local authorities' powers under the CA 1989, for example for: failing to allow a solicitor to attend a child protection conference and failing to supply the applicant with the minutes (*R v Cornwall County Council ex parte LH* [2000] 1 FLR 236); failing to obtain parental permission to move a child from residential care to foster care (*R v Tameside Metropolitan Borough Council ex parte J* [2000] 1 FLR 942); and refusing to carry out assessments of children in need (*R (On the Application of S) v Wandsworth, Hammersmith and Lambeth London Borough Council* [2002] 1 FLR 469). Placing a child on the child protection register can be challenged by judicial review (see *R v Harrow London Borough Council ex parte D* [1990] Fam 133), but the courts have held that the complaints procedure under section 26 of the CA 1989, rather than judicial review proceedings, should be followed (*R v Hampshire County Council ex parte H* [1999] 2 FLR 359; and *A and S v Enfield London Borough Council* [2008] EWHC 1886 (Admin)).

(f) Local Government Ombudsman

A complaint can be made to the Local Government Ombudsman, who has a duty to investigate complaints of maladministration by local authorities. This is a lengthy and limited remedy.

(g) An application to the Children's Commissioner

A complaint can be made to the Children's Commissioner.

(h) An application to the European Court of Human Rights

A parent, child or other aggrieved party who has exhausted all domestic remedies can apply to the European Court of Human Rights (ECtHR) in Strasbourg, alleging that the UK is in breach of the ECHR (see, for example, *Z and Others v UK* [2001] 2 FLR 603; and *RK and AK v UK* [2009] 1 FLR 274).

(i) An action in negligence

Social workers and other persons working in the child protection system are not immune from liability in negligence, although the courts are aware of the difficult task social workers have and that local authorities have limited resources. At one time claims were struck out on the ground that there was no duty of care for policy reasons, but there has been a change of attitude, due largely to the enactment of the HRA 1998 and decisions in the ECtHR. As a result, the courts in England and Wales are now much more likely to allow a case to proceed to trial. Whether a local authority has been negligent will depend on whether it has breached its duty of care and whether the damage caused was reasonably foreseeable in the circumstances, judged by an objective standard. Damages can be awarded. The following cases are examples of claims brought in negligence. The case immediately below involved a series of related appeals involving negligence claims against local authorities in which the UK courts took a restrictive approach, but where the ECtHR subsequently allowed the victims' claims.

> ▶ *X (Minors) v Bedfordshire County Council and Related Appeals* [1995] 2 AC 633
>
> In the first appeal negligence claims were brought by five children against Bedfordshire County Council for failing to take steps to protect them from the years of neglect they had suffered, even though the defendant had been informed on several occasions that they were suffering harm. In the second appeal, the child and the mother sued the local authority (Newham London Borough Council) because the child had been mistakenly taken into care (for about one year) after a child psychologist employed by the local authority had wrongly identified the mother's cohabitant as having abused the child. The House of Lords held in respect of both appeals that the defendant local authorities owed the claimants no duty of care in negligence, and so the cases were struck out as disclosing no cause of action.
>
> *Note:* Four of the children in the 'Bedfordshire case' subsequently took their case to the ECtHR in Strasbourg (see *Z and Others v UK* [2001] 2 FLR 603), which held that there had been a breach of Article 3 (as the children had suffered inhuman and degrading treatment) and Article 13 (because they had not had an effective remedy). The child and the mother in the 'Newham case' also took their case to the ECtHR (see *TP and KM v UK* [2001] 2 FLR 545), which also held that there had been breaches of Articles 3 and 13.

For a case with similar facts to that of *X v Bedfordshire* (above), but which shows how the approach to negligence claims against local authorities has changed (largely as a result of the impact of human rights), see *ABB, BBB, CBB and DBB v Milton Keynes Council* [2011] EWHC 2745 (QB). The defendant local authority, which had failed to protect four children who had suffered appalling sexual abuse for many years at the hands of their father, was held to be vicariously liable in negligence and ordered to pay damages.

> ▶ *A v Essex County Council* [2003] EWCA Civ 1848
>
> The parents were successful in claiming damages in negligence (including damages for psychiatric injury) against the defendant local authority for failing to give them sufficient information about a boy who had been placed with them for adoption and who subsequently attacked them and their own child.
>
> ▶ *D v East Berkshire Community NHS Trust; MAK v Dewsbury Healthcare NHS Trust; RK v Oldham NHS Trust* [2005] UKHL 23
>
> The parents in the three appeals claimed that the medical professionals had negligently misdiagnosed child abuse of their children, when in fact the children had genuine health problems; and that this had disrupted their family life and caused them psychiatric injury. The House of Lords held by a majority (Lord Bingham dissenting) that the defendants owed no duty of care in negligence to the parents on grounds of public policy because doctors must be free to act in the best interests of children generally.
>
> *Note:* The parents in the *RK* case successfully took their case to the ECtHR (see *RK and AK v UK* (2008) 48 EHRR 707), which awarded them substantial damages as there had been a breach of Article 13 (the right to an effective remedy). This was because the parents had an arguable complaint concerning interference with their family life but had not had any redress for obtaining compensation for the damage they had suffered.

Summary

▶ A wide range of different people are involved in child protection and providing services for children in need. A multi-agency and inter-agency approach is adopted. Of particular importance are local authority social workers. Local authorities have duties and powers under the Children Act 1989 (CA 1989) to safeguard and promote the welfare of children.

▶ Local authority social workers engaged in child protection have a difficult task as they must ensure that children are protected, but they must also ensure that they do not intervene too much into family life.

▶ The Children Act 2004 (CA 2004), which was enacted in response to the failures of social services in the Victoria Climbié case, made structural changes to the way in which the various agencies operate to protect children. Key developments included the creation of Children's Trusts and Local Safeguarding Children's Boards.

▶ Local authorities are public authorities under the Human Rights Act 1998 (HRA 1998) and must therefore ensure that they exercise their powers and duties in line with the European Convention on Human Rights (ECHR). Of particular importance is the right to family life (Art 8) which requires that any intervention in family life must be lawful, necessary and proportionate. Procedural fairness is also important in order to ensure compliance with Article 6 (the right to a fair trial).

▶ The United Nations Convention on the Rights of the Child (UNCRC) contains various articles which are relevant to child protection, such as Article 19 which requires States Parties to take all measures to protect children from all forms of abuse while in the care of their parents, guardians and other persons.

▶ The CA 1989 is the key Act governing the duties and powers of the courts and of local authorities to take steps to protect children and to provide for children in need. Local authorities have a wide range of powers under the Act, which include a duty to make inquiries (s 47) and to investigate a case if so ordered by the court (s 37). They have powers and duties under Part III to provide support for children in need. They can apply for care and supervision orders under Part IV; and can take emergency measures under Part V.

▶ Under Part III of the CA 1989 local authorities have a duty to provide a range of services for children in need and for disabled children, including the provision of day care and accommodation. As part of the general duty to safeguard and promote the welfare of children (see s 17(1)), a local authority has a duty to provide accommodation for children in need (s 20). However, the accommodation provisions of the Act cannot be used to 'by-pass' the housing and homelessness legislation (see 4.11).

▶ Under Part IV of the CA 1989 local authorities can apply for care and supervision orders, which may be granted by the court if the 'threshold criteria' in section 31(2) are satisfied, and the court considers the child's welfare requires such an order to be made. In assessing welfare, the court must apply the welfare principle (s 1(1)), the no delay principle (s 1(2)), the welfare checklist (s 1(3)) and the no order presumption (s 1(5)). Children can give evidence in care proceedings, but the usual way in which the voice of the child is conveyed to the court is by a Children's Guardian (an officer of Cafcass) who works in tandem with the child's solicitor.

▶ The standard of proof in care and supervision proceedings is the balance of probabilities. Cases where there is more than one possible perpetrator of significant harm are difficult, but the House of Lords and the Supreme Court have held that uncertainty about the perpetrator of the alleged harm does not necessarily prevent the threshold criteria being proved.

Summary cont'd

▶ In care proceedings in which a final care order might be made the local authority must prepare a care plan about the future care of the child (s 31A(1)). The plan must be kept under review (s 31A(2)).

▶ A care order gives the local authority parental responsibility for the child, but a parent does not lose parental responsibility. A supervision order places the child under the supervision of a designated local authority officer or a probation officer.

▶ The court has the power to make interim care and supervision orders (s 38).

▶ The court can direct a medical or psychiatric examination or other assessment of the child (s 38(6)), the aim of which is to put all the evidence before the court to help it reach its decision. A child with sufficient understanding to make an informed decision can refuse to submit to the medical or psychiatric examination or other assessment; but the court can override the refusal if it is in the child's best interests.

▶ A supervision order can be varied or discharged, but a care order can only be discharged, not varied (s 39).

▶ A local authority has a duty to allow a child in care to have reasonable contact with parents, guardians, persons with parental responsibility, a person named in a child arrangements order as a person with whom the child was to live, and a person who has care of the child under an order made by the High Court under its inherent jurisdiction (s 34(1)). However, contact can be terminated for up to seven days as a matter of urgency (s 34(6)). Under section 34 the court can make orders in respect of contact and orders authorising a local authority to refuse contact.

▶ Under Part V of the CA 1989 the following are available for emergency protection of a child: a child assessment order (s 43); an emergency protection order (s 44); and police protection (s 46). The grounds for making an emergency protection order are that there is reasonable cause to believe that the child is likely to suffer harm if: they are not removed to accommodation provided by or on behalf of the applicant; or they do not remain in the place in which they are being accommodated (s 44(1)(a)). The court can also make an emergency protection order on the application of a local authority if: inquiries in respect of the child are being made under section 47(1)(b) and those inquiries are being frustrated by access to the child being unreasonably refused to a person authorised to seek access; and the applicant has reasonable cause to believe that access to the child is required as a matter of urgency (ss 44(1)(b) and (c)). As an emergency protection order is regarded as a severe order, such an order must be lawful, necessary and proportionate.

▶ Local authorities have certain duties to children 'looked after' by them whether under a voluntary arrangement or a court order. They also have duties under the CA 1989 to children leaving care.

▶ There are various ways in which to bring a challenge against a local authority, namely by: applying to discharge or vary an order made under the CA 1989; using the statutory complaints procedure under section 26 of the CA 1989; using the advocacy services (in the case of a child); bringing a challenge under the HRA 1998; bringing judicial review proceedings; making a complaint to the Local Government Ombudsman; and bringing a claim in negligence.

Further reading and references

Balley-Harris and Harris, 'Local authorities and child protection – the mosaic of accountability' [2002] CFLQ 117.

Bainham, 'Interim care orders: is the bar set too low?' [2011] Fam Law 374.

Bainham and Markham, 'Living with Re B-S: Re S and its implications for parents, local authorities and the courts' [2014] Fam Law 991.

Driscoll and Hollingsworth, 'Accommodating children in need: R (M) v Hammersmith and Fulham London Borough Council' [2008] CFLQ 522.

Hall, 'What price the logic of proof of evidence?' [2000] Fam Law 423.

Hall, 'The misfortune of being straightforward? The impact of Re W on children giving evidence in care proceedings' [2010] CFLQ 499.

Harwin and Owen, 'The implementation of care plans, and its relationship to children's welfare' [2003] CFLQ 71.

Hayes, 'Child protection – from principles and policies to practices' [1998] CFLQ 119.

Hayes, 'Farewell to the cogent evidence test: Re B' [2008] Fam Law 859.

Hayes, Hayes and Williams, '"Shocking" abuse followed by a "staggering" ruling: Re MA (Care Threshold)' [2010] Fam Law 166.

Hayes, 'The Supreme Court's failure to protect vulnerable children: Re J (Children)' [2013] Fam Law 1015.

Hemingway and Williams, 'Re M and R: Re H and R' [1997] Fam Law 740.

Howe, 'Removal of children at interim hearings: is the test now set too high?' [2009] Fam Law 320.

Keating, 'Suspicions, sitting on the fence and standards of proof' [2009] CFLQ 230.

Keating, 'Re MA: the significance of harm' [2011] CFLQ 115.

Masson, 'Emergency protection, good practice and human rights' [2004] Fam Law 882.

Masson, 'Emergency intervention to protect children: using and avoiding legal controls' [2005] CFLQ 75.

Masson, 'Reforming care proceedings – time for a review' [2007] CFLQ 411.

Masson, 'Emergency protection: the impact of court control' [2010] Fam Law 1088.

Masson et al., Protecting Powers: Emergency Intervention for Children's Protection, 2007, John Wiley & Sons.

Perry, 'Lancashire County Council v B: section 31 – threshold or barrier?' [2000] CFLQ 301.

Ryder, The Honourable Mr Justice, 'The risk fallacy: a tale of two thresholds' [2008] Fam Law 30.

Websites

Ministry of Justice: www.justice.gov.uk
NSPCC (National Society for the Prevention of Cruelty to Children): www.nspcc.org.uk

Links to relevant websites can also be found at: www.palgravehighered.com/law/familylaw9e

Chapter 15

Adoption and special guardianship

This chapter deals with adoption and special guardianship. Adoption terminates the parental responsibility of a child's birth parents and gives parental responsibility to the adoptive parent or parents. As such, it is a draconian step and the courts therefore apply a rigorous approach to adoption applications. Adoption law and procedure is closely related to the law and procedure governing child protection (see Chapter 14). This is because most children who are adopted, and those who are looking for adoptive families, have been in local authority care.

Special guardianship is a status which was created specifically as a less extreme alternative to adoption, but one that would still provide children with security. Although special guardianship is not part of the adoption legislation, it is dealt with in this chapter as it may provide a more suitable alternative to adoption in some circumstances.

15.1 Adoption – introduction

Adoption of a child is effected by an adoption order which extinguishes the parental responsibility of the child's birth parents and that of other people, and vests it in the adopters. Adoption involves the complete legal transfer of parental responsibility and makes the child a full legal member of the new family.

The making of an adoption order is the final stage of the adoption process. In many cases, this stage will be preceded by a placement stage (see 15.6 below). When a child is 'placed' for adoption it means that they are formally left in the care of the prospective adopters for a period of time before the final adoption order is made, usually by an adoption agency. Placement can take place with the consent of the birth parents or pursuant to a placement order.

The law of adoption is set out in the Adoption and Children Act 2002 (ACA 2002). Adoption procedure and practice are governed by the Family Procedure Rules 2010 (FPR 2010), *Practice Directions* and various regulations.

(a) Adoption and human rights

As adoption agencies and courts are public authorities for the purposes of the Human Rights Act 1998 (HRA 1998) they must exercise their powers and duties in accordance with the European Convention on Human Rights (ECHR) (see 1.8). Thus, they must ensure that adoption does not breach the right to family life of the child and their natural parents under Article 8 of the ECHR. Any interference in family life must be legitimate, necessary and proportionate (Art 8(2)). Cases decided by the European Court of Human Rights (ECtHR) must also be taken into account by the courts and public bodies responsible for adoption in England and Wales. For example, in the following case the ECtHR emphasised the importance of children and biological parents having a right to the mutual enjoyment of each other's company.

> ▶ *Johansen v Norway* **(1997) 23 EHRR 33**
>
> The child, who was in care, had been placed in a foster home with a view to her adoption, and the mother had been deprived of contact. The ECtHR held that: 'the mutual enjoyment by parent and child of each other's company constitutes a fundamental element of family life and domestic measures hindering such enjoyment amount to an interference with the right protected by art. 8'. The ECtHR held that there had been a breach of the ECHR, as the far-reaching measures taken were inconsistent with the aim of reuniting the mother and child and should only have been taken in exceptional circumstances where they could be justified in the best interests of the child.

However, each case depends on its facts. For example, in *Söderbäck v Sweden* [1999] 1 FLR 250, an adoption order was held not to breach Article 8 in the circumstances of the case.

In *Keegan v Ireland* (1994) 18 EHRR 342, the ECtHR held that placing a child for adoption shortly after birth, without the natural father's knowledge or consent, may breach Article 8. However, in a similar case, *Eski v Austria (Application No. 21949/03)* [2007] 1 FLR 1650, the father's Article 8 rights were held not to be breached, as the domestic court had carefully examined the case and given reasons; and the assessment of the interests of the child and the father's limited relationship with her lay within the 'margin of appreciation' (see 1.8) of the domestic court, which justified a proportionate interference with the father's rights.

A refusal to allow a person to adopt a child on the ground of their sexuality may breach the ECHR. In *EB v France (Application No. 43546/02)* [2008] 1 FLR 850, the ECtHR held that the refusal of the French authorities to allow a lesbian woman in a stable and long-term relationship to adopt a child, on the basis, *inter alia*, of there being no paternal role model for the child, breached Article 14 (the right to enjoy Convention rights without discrimination) taken in conjunction with Article 8. The ECtHR held that the case differed in a number of respects from *Fretté v France (Application No 36515/97)* [2003] 2 FLR 9 where a single homosexual man was refused permission to adopt a child on the basis, *inter alia*, that there was no common ground among Contracting States as to the merits of permitting adoption by homosexuals and therefore the State had a margin of appreciation as to how it approached the issue.

(b) The importance of proportionality in adoption

Like the ECtHR, the courts in England and Wales have recognised the seriousness of making an order which severs a child's ties with its birth family and the need to consider proportionality in such cases. The following cases set out important principles which are relevant to the law and practice of adoption and child protection (see Chapter 14).

▶ *Re B (A Child) (Care Proceedings: Appeal)* [2013] UKSC 33

The child was placed in foster care at birth due to concerns about the parents who had psychological, personality and anger management issues. The parents maintained contact with the child, which was positive. The judge at first instance made a final care order and approved a care plan for the child to be adopted. The mother appealed unsuccessfully to the Court of Appeal and subsequently to the Supreme Court.

The Supreme Court, by a majority of four to one, dismissed the mother's appeal. On the facts, the majority held (Baroness Hale dissenting) that the trial judge had not been wrong to make a care order with a view to the child's adoption. He had been entitled to conclude that the threshold criteria had been satisfied (on the basis of likely future harm) and that an order for adoption was the only viable option for the child's future. Although the mother's appeal failed, the Supreme Court highlighted the draconian nature of non-consensual adoption.

LORD NEUBERGER: A care order in a case such as this is a very extreme thing, a last resort, as it would be very likely to result in Amelia being adopted against the wishes of both her parents … it is clear that a judge cannot properly decide that a care order should be made in such circumstances, unless the order is proportionate, bearing in mind the requirements of Art 8. It seems to me to be inherent in s1(1) that a care order should be a last resort, because the interests of a child would self-evidently require her relationship with her natural parents to be maintained unless no other course was possible in her interests.

The high threshold to be crossed before a court should make an adoption order against the natural parents' wishes is also clear from the United Nations Convention on the Rights of the Child 1989.

BARONESS HALE: We all agree that an order compulsorily severing the ties between a child and her parents can only be made if 'justified by an overriding requirement pertaining to the child's best interests'. In other words, the test is one of necessity. Nothing else will do.

▶ *Re B-S (Children) (Adoption: Leave to Oppose)* [2013] EWCA Civ 1146

The mother's two children had been removed from her care by the local authority, made the subject of care and placement orders and placed with prospective adopters. The mother applied under section 47(5) of the ACA 2002 for leave to oppose the adoption on the basis of her change of circumstances. Parker J refused her application and made the adoption orders. She appealed to the Court of Appeal.

The Court of Appeal unanimously dismissed the mother's appeal. Munby P, who gave judgment on behalf of the court, set out guidance about the proper approach to be taken in adoption cases in the light of *Re B* (above).

SIR JAMES MUNBY P: First … although the child's interests in an adoption case are paramount, the court must never lose sight of the fact that those interests include being brought up by the natural family, ideally by the natural parents, or at least one of them, unless the overriding requirements of the child's welfare make that not possible.

Second … as required by section 1(3)(g) of the 1989 Act and section 1(6) of the 2002 Act, the court 'must' consider all the options before coming to a decision. As Baroness Hale of Richmond JSC said at para 198 it is 'necessary to explore and attempt alternative solutions'. What are these options? That will depend on the circumstances of the particular cases. They range, in principle, from the making of no order at one end of the spectrum to the making of an adoption order at the other. In between, there may be orders providing for the return of the child to the parent's care with the support of a family assistance order or subject to a supervision order or a care order; or the child may be placed with relatives under a residence order or a special guardianship order or in a foster placement under a care order; or the child may be placed with someone else, again under a residence order or a special guardianship order or in a foster placement under a care order. This is not an exhaustive list of the possibilities; wardship for example is another, as are placements in specialist residential or healthcare settings. Yet it can be seen that the possible list of options is long ....

Third ... the court's assessment of the parents' ability to discharge their responsibilities towards the child must take into account the assistance and support which the authorities would offer ....

[Munby P then went on to highlight two things which the court agreed were essential when the court is being asked to approve a care plan for adoption or when it is being asked to make a non-consensual placement order or adoption order:]

Adoption – essentials: (i) proper evidence

First, there must be proper evidence both from the local authority and from the guardian. The evidence must address all the options which are realistically possible and must contain an analysis of the arguments for and against each option ....

Adoption – essentials: (ii) adequately reasoned judgments

The second thing that is essential, and again we emphasise that word, is an adequately reasoned judgment by the judge .... The judicial task is to evaluate all the options, undertaking a global, holistic and ... multi-faceted evaluation of the child's welfare which takes into account all the negatives and the positives, all the pros and cons, of each option.

(c) The role of the Children and Family Court Advisory and Support Service in adoptions

The court will appoint a Reporting Officer from the Children and Family Court Advisory and Support Service (Cafcass) (see 1.7). Their role is to is to ensure that the parent or guardian of the child are fully aware of the implications of adoption and their consent to placement for adoption is given unconditionally and with a full understanding of the nature and effect of their consent. They are also responsible for witnessing pre-court consent to adoption and reporting back to the adoption agency prior to the court application for an adoption order. If consent is not forthcoming, or special circumstances exist, the court will appoint a Children's Guardian (also an officer of Cafcass). The case will then be investigated in more depth.

(d) Adoption procedure

Rules of court and practice directions govern the procedure for adoption (see Part 14 of the FPR 2010 and its related practice directions).

(e) The problem of delay

Due to concerns about delays in the adoption process, particularly with respect to children who are adopted after entering care, the Government published *An Action Plan for Adoption: Tackling Delay* (Department for Education, 2011) setting out a range of proposals aimed at, *inter alia*, speeding up the adoption process for children. Subsequently, the Children and Families Act 2014 (CFA 2014) included provisions designed to reduce delays, for example by providing for 'fostering for adoption' and removing the emphasis on a child's racial, cultural and religious background in the matching process (see 15.3 below). However, the Government remains concerned about the length of time it takes for children to be adopted and further reforms are planned (see *Adoption: A Vision for Change*, Department for Education, 2016).

(f) Agency and non-agency adoptions

Agency adoptions are those where the adoption is arranged by an adoption agency and these adoptions involve children who are in the care of a local authority. Adoption agencies may be local authority adoption services or voluntary adoption organisations (see the Consortium of Voluntary Adoption Agencies). Local authorities have statutory responsibilities under the ACA 2002 for making arrangements for adoption and placing children for adoption, which they can discharge through their own adoption services or by using voluntary adoption organisations (ss 2–16). Local authorities are required to maintain adoption and adoption support services, which they must advertise, including counselling, advice and information about adoption (ss 3 and 2(6)). Some adoption agencies specialise in arranging intercountry adoptions which involve adopting children from overseas who may have been abandoned, orphaned or removed from their birth parents.

Non-agency adoptions, on the other hand, are adoptions which have not been arranged by the local authority or a voluntary adoption agency. They usually involve children who are not in the care of a local authority, for example children who are being adopted by a step-parent or a member of their wider family (such as a grandparent) and also some children who are adopted from overseas. People who wish to adopt a child who is not placed for adoption with them by an adoption agency must give notice to their local authority so that they can investigate the situation (see 15.5 below).

(g) Illegal arrangements, placements and transactions

The arrangement of adoptions is tightly regulated in order to protect the welfare of children and to prevent exploitation of children and their birth parents. Thus, it is a criminal offence for a person or body other than an adoption agency to make arrangements for adoption and for unauthorised people to prepare adoption reports (ss 92–94). It is also unlawful for people to advertise for adoption (ss 123, 124). Certain payments made in connection with adoption are prohibited (s 95), although the court may retrospectively authorise them. There are also prohibitions on bringing overseas children into the UK for the purpose of adoption (s 83).

(h) 'In family' adoptions

These involve an adoption by a relative, step-parent or civil partner. Such adoptions can have drawbacks, as they affect the child's legal and social relationship with the other birth parent and the birth parent's family. At one time step-parents would often seek to adopt a step-child in order to acquire parental responsibility, but they had to make a joint application for an adoption order with the child's natural parent (which meant, rather bizarrely, that the natural parent was adopting their own child). However, the ACA 2002 now permits a step-parent to make a sole application for adoption; and step-parents have other ways of ways of obtaining parental responsibility, such as by means of a parental responsibility agreement or order (see 9.4 and 9.5), a special guardianship order (see 15.4 below), or a child arrangements order regulating the child's living arrangements (see 10.5).

(i) Alternatives to adoption

As adoption is a radical step, in that it terminates the birth parents' parental responsibility and gives it to the adopters, it may be in the child's best interests for parental responsibility to be acquired by the child's carer(s) or prospective carer(s) in one of the following ways instead: a parental responsibility agreement or order (see 9.5); a special guardianship order (see 15.14); or a child arrangements order regulating the child's living arrangements (see 10.5). However, the disadvantage of these alternatives is that they lack the certainty and finality of an adoption, which may cause insecurity for the child and the child's carer(s).

15.2 Adoption trends and the development of the law

(a) Adoption trends

At one time adoption was much more common than it is today. For example, in 1971 there were 21,495 adoptions. However, during the 1970s the number of adoptions declined rapidly, and it continued to decline steadily in the decades that followed. Currently only about 6,000 children are adopted in England and Wales each year (see below).

The decline in adoptions has been due in part to fewer babies being available for adoption as a result of improved contraception, the legalisation of abortion, and the fact that single mothers are no longer stigmatised and put under pressure to give up their babies. Children available for adoption today are usually older, most of whom are in local authority care.

Family Court Statistics Quarterly, October–December 2015,
and *Family Court Tables*, Ministry of Justice, 2016

▶ Between January and December 2015, there were 6,191 adoption orders made.
▶ During October to December 2015, there were 1,473 adoption orders issued, down 11 per cent for the equivalent quarter in the previous year.
▶ In 69 per cent of these, the adopters were a male/female couple, while in 15 per cent the adopter was a sole applicant. In a further 8 per cent of adoption orders, the adopter was a step-parent and in 8 per cent the adopters were a same sex couple
▶ 61 per cent of adoption orders made between October and December 2015 were in relation to children aged between one and four years old.

The Government's aim is to try to increase the number of children who are adopted from care. The number of children adopted from care has increased since 2011, but with some fluctuations.

Children Looked After in England Including Adoption: 2014 to 2015, Department for Education, 2015

There were 5,330 looked after children adopted during the year ending 31 March 2015. The number of looked after children placed for adoption at 31 March, which rose from 2011 to 2014, has decreased by 15 per cent in 2015 to 3,320. This is consistent with the decrease in the number of looked after children with a placement order in place at 31 March which has dropped by 24 per cent from 2014. The National Adoption Leadership Board has linked decreases in placement orders to the impact of two relevant court judgments, known as *Re B* and *Re B-S* (see 15.1 above).

(b)   The development of the law

When the Labour Government came into power in 1997, it announced that it was committed to improving adoption (see para 1.5, *Supporting Families*, Home Office, 1998). It also considered that, because of major failings in the care system, adoption could provide a better alternative for children in care. The 'Waterhouse Report' (*Lost in Care – Report of the Tribunal of Inquiry into the Abuse of Children in Care in the Former County Council Areas of Gwynedd and Clwyd*, 2000) identified 'drift' in care as one of the major failings of the child protection system. Tony Blair, the then Prime Minister, reacted to the Waterhouse Report by announcing that he would personally lead a thorough review of adoption policy in order to ensure that the Government was making the best use of adoption as an option to meet the needs of children looked after by local authorities (see *Prime Minister's Review: Adoption*, Performance and Innovation Unit of the Cabinet Office, 2000). The subsequent White Paper (*Adoption: A New Approach*, 2000, Cm 5017) set out the Government's plans to promote greater use of adoption, improve the performance of the adoption service and put children at the centre of the adoption process. These developments led to the enactment of the Adoption and Children Act 2002 (ACA 2002), which came fully into force on 30 December 2005.

The ACA 2002 replaced the Adoption Act 1976 and modernised the legal framework for adoption in England and Wales. It made the following important changes to adoption law.

Changes to adoption law made by the Adoption and Children Act 2002

The ACA 2002:

▶ aligned adoption law with the Children Act 1989 (CA 1989) by making the child's welfare the paramount consideration in all decisions relating to adoption;
▶ introduced a new welfare-based ground for dispensing with parental consent;
▶ abolished freeing for adoption orders and introduced new measures for placement for adoption (by parental consent or placement order);

- overhauled eligibility to apply for adoption by enabling single people, married couples, civil partners, and, for the first time, unmarried couples (opposite sex and same sex) to apply, and introduced new provisions to enable step-parents to make sole applications for adoption;
- placed a duty on local authorities to maintain an Adoption Service, including new arrangements for the provision of adoption support services;
- established an independent reviewing mechanism to enable prospective adopters who had been turned down for adoption to be entitled to an independent review;
- established an Adoption and Children Act Register to suggest matches between children waiting to be adopted and approved prospective adopters;
- introduced new measures for tackling delay in the process (courts are required to draw up timetables to prevent delay, and to consider a 'no delay' principle akin to that in the CA 1989); and
- introduced special guardianship to provide permanence for children who could not return to their birth families, but for whom adoption was not the most suitable option.

A major aim of the ACA 2002 is to encourage the wider use of adoption for children in care. With a view to encouraging more adoptions of children in care, and to make them succeed, the Act places a duty on local authorities to provide comprehensive support services. To prevent delay in matching children with adoptive families, the Adoption and Children Act Register suggests matches between children waiting to be adopted and approved prospective adopters (ss 125–131).

Changes to the ACA 2002 were made by the Children and Families Act 2014 (CFA 2014) following a further Government drive to increase adoption from care. The changes included: new requirements in relation to 'fostering for adoption'; provisions for post-adoption contact; a refocus of the court's scrutiny in relation to care plans; new rules in relation to the appointment of experts; and removal of the need to specifically consider a child's religious, racial, cultural and linguistic background in adoption cases (the latter only applies in England).

15.3 The welfare principles applicable to adoption

Section 1 of the Adoption and Children Act 2002 (ACA 2002) lays down the welfare principles which must be applied by courts and adoption agencies when coming to a decision relating to the adoption of a child (s 1(1)). They are similar to the welfare principles in the Children Act 1989 (CA 1989) (see 10.3).

(a) The welfare principle (section 1(2))

The welfare principle is as follows.

Section 1(2) of the Adoption and Children Act 2002

The paramount consideration of the court or adoption agency must be the child's welfare, throughout his life.

Unlike the CA 1989, the welfare principle in adoption requires an analysis of the child's welfare through childhood into adulthood and for the rest of the child's life. It therefore emphasises that adoption is something with lifelong implications. The welfare principle also applies to the issue of dispensing with consent (see 15.8 below).

(b) The no delay principle (section 1(3))

The no delay principle is as follows.

Section 1(3) of the Adoption and Children Act 2002

The court or adoption agency must at all times bear in mind that, in general, any delay in coming to the decision is likely to prejudice the child's welfare.

Despite this provision, delays in adoption are still a matter of concern.

(c) The welfare checklist (section 1(4))

Section 1(4) contains a list of factors which creates a framework for the exercise of judicial discretion in the application of the welfare principle in section 1(2) above.

Section 1(4) of the Adoption and Children Act 2002

[A] court or adoption agency must have regard to the following matters (among others)—

(a) the child's ascertainable wishes and feelings regarding the decision (considered in the light of the child's age and understanding);
(b) the child's particular needs;
(c) the likely effect on the child (throughout his life) of having ceased to be a member of the original family and become an adopted person;
(d) the child's age, sex, background and any of the child's characteristics which the court or agency considers relevant;
(e) any harm (within the meaning of the Children Act 1989) which the child has suffered or is at risk of suffering;
(f) the relationship which the child has with relatives, and with any other person in relation to whom the court or agency considers the relationship to be relevant, including –
   (i) the likelihood of any such relationship continuing and the value to the child of its doing so;
   (ii) the ability and willingness of any of the child's relatives, or of any such person, to provide the child with a secure environment in which the child can develop, and otherwise to meet the child's needs;
   (iii) the wishes and feelings of any of the child's relatives, or of any such person, regarding the child.

'Relationships' in section 1(4) are not confined to legal relationships (s 1(8)(a)), and 'relatives' includes, *inter alia*, the child's mother and father (s 1(8)(b)). 'Harm' in section 1(4)(e) includes seeing or hearing the ill-treatment of another (such as witnessing domestic violence). As sections 1(2) and 1(4)(c) require courts and adoption agencies to consider the child 'throughout his life', inheritance and succession interests may be relevant considerations.

(d) The child's religious, racial, cultural and linguistic background (section 1(5))

This provision was repealed by the Children and Families Act 2014 (CFA 2014) in relation to England, although it still applies in Wales. It was repealed in England in order to achieve the Government's aim of increasing the number of adoptions, which it said were being delayed in order to achieve a perfect or near ethnic match between adoptive parents and the adoptive child (see *An Action Plan for Adoption: Tackling Delay*, Department for Education, 2011). However, despite the amendment, in *Re N (Children) (Adoption: Jurisdiction)* [2015] EWCA Civ 1112, which concerned the proposed adoption of two Hungarian children who were living in England, Munby P emphasised the need for the court and professionals to give careful consideration to 'those parts of the checklist which focus attention, explicitly or implicitly, on the child's national, cultural, linguistic, ethnic and religious background'. Therefore, these factors will still be taken into account under sections 1(2) and 1(4), particularly under section 1(4)(d).

(e) Duty to consider other powers and the no order principle (section 1(6))

The duty to consider other powers and the no order principle is as follows.

Section 1(6) of the Adoption and Children Act 2002

The court or adoption agency must always consider the whole range of powers available to it in the child's case (whether under this Act or the Children Act 1989); and the court must not make any order under this Act unless it considers that making the order would be better for the child than not doing so.

As with the no order principle in section 1(3) of the CA 1989, the aim of section 1(5) of the ACA 2002 is to discourage courts from making unnecessary orders and to ensure that orders are made only if they will positively improve the child's welfare.

15.4 Eligibility for adoption

(a) Who can be adopted?

The child must be under 18 on the date of the adoption application (s 49(4)), but an adoption order can be made if the child reaches 18 before the conclusion of adoption proceedings (s 49(5)). An adoption order cannot be made if the child is aged 19 or over, or if they are married (ss 47(8), (9)).

(b) Who can adopt?

Couples and single people can apply to adopt a child, provided they satisfy certain domicile and age limit requirements (ss 49–51):

- ▶ *Couples (section 50)* Married couples, civil partners, and cohabitants (opposite sex and same sex who are living as partners in an enduring family relationship) can apply (s 144(4)). Each applicant must be at least 21 (s 50(1)), unless one of the couple is the child's mother or father, in which case they only need to be 18 (s 50(2)).
- ▶ *Sole applicants (section 51)* Applications can be made by a sole applicant who is at least 21 years old and is not married or a civil partner (s 51(1)). An application may also be made by a person who has attained the age of 21 years and is the partner of a parent of the person to be adopted (s 51(2)) – in other words, a step-parent or a civil partner of the child's parent can apply. In addition, an application can be made by one person who has attained the age of 21 years and is married or a civil partner if: the court is satisfied that the other spouse cannot be found; *or* the couple are separated permanently and are living apart; *or* the other spouse is incapacitated due to physical or mental ill-health (s 51(3)).

In rare circumstances, a natural parent may wish to become the sole adoptive parent of their own child, to the exclusion of the other parent (see, for example, *Re B (A Minor) (Adoption: Natural Parent)* [2001] UKHL 70). However, a mother or father can only apply to adopt their own child if the court is satisfied that: the other natural parent is dead or cannot be found; *or* by virtue of section 28 of the Human Fertilisation and Embryology Act 1990 or sections 34–47 of the Human Fertilisation and Embryology Act 2008, there is no other parent; *or* there is some other reason justifying the child being adopted by the applicant alone (s 51(4)).

(c) Foster-parent applicants

A local authority foster-parent can apply to adopt a foster-child provided the child has had their home with the applicant at all times during the period of one year preceding the application (s 42(4)); or if the court grants leave (permission) for the application to be made (s 42(6)). The legal principles relevant to a leave application are the same as those for applications for leave to apply for revocation of a placement order under section 24(2) of the ACA 2002 (see 15.6 below). (See, for example, *Re A; Coventry County Council v CC and A* [2007] EWCA Civ 1383, where a foster-mother was granted leave to apply for an adoption order.)

(d) Domicile requirements

At least one of the couple (in the case of an application under section 50) or the applicant (in the case of an application under section 51) must be domiciled in part of the British Islands; or both of the couple (in the case of an application under section 50) or the applicant (in the case of an application under section 51) must have been habitually resident in a part of the British Islands for a period of not less than one year ending with the date of the application (s 49).

(e)   Baby adoptions

Special provisions apply to the adoption of babies who are less than six weeks old. Thus, although such a baby may be placed for adoption without the need for formal consent under section 19 (see 15.8 below) or a placement order (s 18(1)), any consent by the birth mother to placement for adoption or adoption is ineffective if given within six weeks of the child's birth (ss 52(3) and 47(4)). This time limit is to allow the mother to recover from the child's birth and to be sure that adoption is what she really wishes.

15.5   Preliminaries to making a placement order or an adoption order

Before a placement order or an adoption order can be made, various procedures must be complied with as required by the Adoption and Children Act 2002 (ACA 2002), the Family Procedure Rules 2010 (FPR 2010) and the adoption regulations. Failure to comply with the requirements may result in an order being set aside. Thus, for example, in *Re B (Placement Order)* [2008] EWCA Civ 835, a placement order was set aside as the local authority adoption agency had failed to provide the Agency Adoption Panel with the required experts' reports and had seriously misrepresented the views of one expert.

(a)   Probationary residence requirements for adoption

In an agency adoption, or where the child is placed for adoption pursuant to an order of the High Court, or where the applicant is a parent of the child, the child must have had his home with the applicant(s) at all times for a 10-week period preceding the application (s 42(2)).

In a non-agency adoption, the residence requirements are as follows: if the applicant is the step-parent or civil partner of the child's parent – a continuous period of at least six months preceding the application (s 42(3)); and if the applicants are local authority foster-parents – a continuous period of at least one year preceding the application (s 42(4)), except where the court grants leave to apply (s 42(6)). In any other case (for example an application by a relative such as a grandparent), the child must have had their home with the applicant(s) for a cumulative period of at least three years (which need not be continuous) during the five-year period preceding the application (s 42(5)), except where the court grants leave to apply (s 42(6)).

(b)   Agency adoptions –- duty to provide a report (section 43)

The adoption agency must submit to the court a report dealing with the suitability of the applicants and any relevant section 1 welfare issues in respect of the child (s 43(a)); and must assist the court in any manner the court directs (s 43(b)).

(c)   Non-agency adoptions – notice of intention to adopt (section 44)

The prospective adopter(s) must give notice to the appropriate local authority of their intention to apply for an adoption order (ss 44(1), (2)). This must be given not more than two years, or less than three months, before the date on which the application for the adoption order is made (s 44(3)). On receipt of notification, the local authority must arrange for the matter to be investigated (s 44(5)); and it must submit a report to the court, in particular in respect of the suitability of the proposed adopters and any other matters relevant to the welfare issues under section 1 of the ACA 2002 in relation to the application (s 44(6)).

(d) Suitability for adopting and the independent reviewing mechanism

Under the adoption regulations, an adoption agency is required to take into account various matters for determining the suitability of the prospective adopter(s), and for reporting as to their suitability. If an adoption agency decides that a person is unsuitable to become an adoptive parent, that person (or both people in the case of a couple adoption) can challenge the refusal by applying for an independent review under the independent reviewing mechanism.

In *Hofstetter and Hofstetter v Brent London Borough Council* [2009] EWHC 3282 (Admin), Charles J emphasised that the independent reviewing mechanism was not intended to be an appeal process, but was part of a process that provided a second opinion from an independent panel of people with relevant skill and experience. Charles J stated that, although a decision as to the suitability of applicants as adopters is for the adoption agency, the decision of an independent reviewing mechanism panel is an important matter; and a decision by an adoption agency to ignore it might result in a successful judicial review challenge. Thus, for example, in *R (AT, TT and S) v Newham London Borough Council* [2008] EWHC 2640 (Admin), the parents successfully challenged the local authority's decision to overturn the unanimous decision of the independent reviewing mechanism panel that they were suitable people to adopt a child. Bennett J granted their application on the ground of procedural unfairness, quashed the local authority's decision and ordered that the matter as to their suitability be considered afresh. Bennett J also held that the welfare principle in section 1(2) of the ACA 2002 does not apply to cases of suitability to adopt.

15.6 Placement for adoption

Sections 18–29 of the Adoption and Children Act 2002 (ACA 2002) contain provisions on placement for adoption. The aim of placement for adoption is to enable consent to adoption to be resolved at the placement stage; and a parent or guardian cannot subsequently be granted leave (permission) to oppose the making of an adoption order unless the court is satisfied that there has been a change in circumstances after the placement order was made (s 47(7)).

An adoption agency may place a child with prospective adopters or leave the child where they have already been placed, provided the child is at least six weeks old and either the parents have consented to the child being so placed or a placement order has been made (s 18(1) and see 15.8 below). The adoption agency must be satisfied that the child ought to be placed for adoption with the prospective adopters (s 18(2)). Once a child is placed, or is authorised to be placed, for adoption by a local authority, the child is described as being 'looked after' by the local authority (s 18(3)) for the purposes of the Children Act 1989 (CA 1989), whereupon it has certain obligations to the child (see 14.10).

(a) Placement by consent of the parents (section 19)

An adoption agency can place a child for adoption (except a baby aged under six weeks), provided it is satisfied that each parent or guardian has consented to the child being placed for adoption and that such consent has not been withdrawn (s 19(1)). 'Consent' must be given unconditionally and with full understanding of what is involved (s 52(5)). A parent who consents to a child being placed for adoption may at the same time, or subsequently, give advance consent to the making of a future adoption order (s 20(1)).

Advance consent to adoption can be withdrawn at any time (s 20(3)). However, if the consent is not withdrawn before the adoption application is made, and the birth parents do not wish the child to be adopted, they will have to apply to oppose the final adoption order, which requires leave of the court (see 15.9 below).

(b) Placement by placement order (section 21)

A child can be placed for adoption by way of a placement order, which is an order 'authorising a local authority to place a child for adoption with any prospective adopters who may be chosen by the authority' (s 21(1)).

(i) Preconditions

A placement order can only be made if: the child is subject to a care order; or the court is satisfied that the threshold conditions for making a care order are met (see 14.7); or the child has no parent or guardian (s 21(2)). The court must be satisfied that: each parent or guardian has consented to the child being placed for adoption with any prospective adopters who may be chosen by the local authority and that that consent has not been withdrawn; *or* that their consent should be dispensed with (s 21(3) and see 15.8 below).

(ii) A duty or a discretion to apply

A local authority has a duty to apply for a placement order in some circumstances, and a discretion to apply in others.

A duty to apply   A local authority *must* apply for a placement order if: the child has been placed for adoption by them or is being provided with accommodation by them; no adoption agency is authorised to place the child for adoption; the child has no parent or guardian; or the authority considers the threshold criteria for a care order are met (see 14.7); *and* the authority is satisfied that the child ought to be placed for adoption (s 22(1)). A local authority *must* also apply for a placement order if it is satisfied that the child ought to be placed for adoption *and*: an application has been made (and has not been disposed of) on which a care order might be made in respect of a child; or the child is subject to a care order and the appropriate local authority is not authorised to place the child for adoption (s 22(2)).

A discretion to apply A local authority *may* apply for a placement order if: the child is subject to a care order; *and* the local authority is authorised to place the child for adoption by parental consent (s 22(3)).

There is no duty or discretion to apply for a placement order if: there is notice of an intention to adopt (unless four months have passed since notification without an application having been made, or the application has been withdrawn or refused); or an application for an adoption order has been made but has not been disposed of (s 22(5)).

If a local authority is under a duty to apply for a placement order, or has made an application but it has not been disposed of, the child is described as being 'looked after by the authority' (s 22(4)).

(iii) Making a placement order – the exercise of discretion

When considering whether to make a placement order, the court must apply the welfare principle and the other principles in section 1 of the ACA 2002 (see 15.3 above). Before making the order, the court must consider what arrangements for contact the adoption agency has made, or proposes to make, for the child, and must invite the parties to comment on those arrangements (s 27(4)). The court may also make an order as to contact (s 27(5)). However, the court cannot make a placement order unless efforts have been made to notify the child's parent(s) or guardian(s) with parental responsibility about the application (ss 141(3), (4)).

The court will not make a placement order merely on the basis that the long-term aim is for adoption, although the possibility of substantial difficulty and delay in finding a suitable adoptive placement, or even an ultimate failure to do so, does not prevent the court from making a placement order (see *Re S-H (A Child) (Placement Order)* [2008] EWCA Civ 493, where Wilson LJ said that the 'necessary foundation for a placement order is that, broadly speaking, the child is presently in a condition to be adopted and is ready to be adopted.')

In *Re H (Care and Placement Order: Application of Principles)* [2012] EWCA Civ 743, where the mother's appeal against both care and placement orders was allowed, the Court of Appeal held that placement orders do not follow automatically or consequentially from the making of care orders. It held that they are orders of the greatest significance and that, if they require parental consent to be overridden, albeit on welfare grounds, they must be preceded by preparations and processes that duly respect the rights of the parents in Article 6 of the European Convention on Human Rights (the right to a fair hearing). Here, on the facts, it was held that there had been no opportunity for the mother to prepare and present arguments to resist the application, which was decided far too prematurely.

(iv) Duration of the order

A placement order remains in force until revoked; or an adoption order is made; or the child marries or becomes a civil partner; or the child reaches the age of 18 (s 21(4)).

(v) Representation of the child

A child is party to placement order proceedings; and the court has a duty to appoint a Children's Guardian to safeguard the child's interests, unless it is not necessary to do so (under section 41 of the Children Act 1989 (CA 1989)). Separate representation for the child may be appropriate in some circumstances.

(vi) Revocation of a placement order (section 24)

Any person can apply to revoke a placement order (s 24(1)). However, unless that person is the child or the local authority, they can only apply for revocation if leave (permission) to apply has been granted by the court *and* the child has not already been placed for adoption by the local authority (s 24(2)). In simple terms, this means that once the child has been placed, the parent's ability to apply to revoke the placement ends; and if they want to oppose the process, they will need to do so at a later date, for example, when the application for an adoption order is made.

Leave to revoke a placement order can only be granted if there has been a change of circumstances since the placement order was made (s 24(3)). When considering whether to grant leave, the welfare of the child is not the court's *paramount* consideration (as section 1 of the ACA 2002 does not apply), but it is a *relevant* consideration. The court's approach to leave applications is similar to the approach to leave applications for section 8 orders under the CA 1989. Thus, the applicant must have a real prospect of securing revocation of the placement order; and the court must take account of the delay that granting leave might cause. In *Re A; Coventry CC v CC and A* [2007] EWCA Civ 1383, Wilson LJ provided guidance as to the approach to an application for leave to apply for revocation of a placement order; and held that, on the establishment of a change of circumstances, a discretion to grant leave arose in which the welfare of the child and the prospect of success should both be weighed.

Even where there has been a change of circumstances, the court has discretion as to whether to grant leave to apply for revocation. Thus, for example, in *M v Warwickshire County Council* [2007] EWCA Civ 1084, the mother applied for leave to apply for revocation of placement orders on the basis of a change of circumstances (that she had, *inter alia*, abstained from drugs, reduced her alcohol consumption and attended an HIV clinic), but her application for leave was refused by the Court of Appeal.

In *Re S-H (A Child) (Placement Order)* [2008] EWCA Civ 493, the Court of Appeal held that it would occasionally be appropriate to grant leave even though there was no real prospect that a court would find it to be in the interests of the child to return to live with the parents. Here the Court of Appeal held that it was in the child's interests to grant leave to revoke the placement order, in order to give the court an opportunity to examine the apparent change in the child's suitability for adoption.

In *Re T (Children) (Placement Order: Revocation)* [2014] EWCA Civ 1369, the Court of Appeal approved the application of the approach set out in *Re B-S* (see 15.1 above), which related to leave to oppose an adoption order, to the father's application for leave to revoke a placement order (see 15.9 below). The father successfully appealed against the lower court's refusal of leave.

A child is not 'placed' until they begin to live with the proposed adopters or, if they were already living with them in their capacity as foster-carers, when the adoption agency formally allows the child to continue living with them in their fresh capacity as prospective adopters (*Coventry City Council v O* [2011] EWCA Civ 729). In *Re F (Placement Order)* [2008] EWCA Civ 439, the Court of Appeal by a majority

Restrictions on removing the child pending a placement order (sections 30 and 34)

A child who is being accommodated pending a placement order being made cannot be removed from that accommodation except with leave of the court or the local authority (s 30(2)). Where a placement order has been made, only the local authority can remove the child (s 34(1)). Thus, once the placement order has been made, parents have no automatic right to have their children returned to them.

Placements

adoption agency may place a baby who is less than six weeks old for adoption the voluntary agreement of the parent or guardian, whereupon the baby becomes ed after' child of the local authority. However, the placement provisions do y. Thus, the adoption agency has no power to determine to what extent the responsibility of any parent, or of the prospective adopters, can be restricted tion 25(4) of the ACA 2002.

ng for an adoption order

otion order (section 46)

der is an order made by the court on an application under section 50 or on and Children Act 2002 (ACA 2002) giving parental responsibility he adopter(s) (s 46(1)). It extinguishes the parental responsibility ents, and any other person with parental responsibility; and it r made under the Children Act 1989 (CA 1989) (s 46(2)). However, parent adoption, an adoption order does not affect the parental es of the person who is the adopted child's natural parent (s 46(3) r extinguishes any duty to pay child maintenance (whether by er), except where the maintenance duty arises under a trust or ment which expressly provides that the maintenance duty is 46(4)). An adoption order may be made even if the child to dopted child (s 46(5)).

g an adoption order (section 47)

n adoption order it must be satisfied that one of the t:

h parent or guardian consents to the making of the advance consent (s 20) and does not oppose the or the court is satisfied that the consent of each spensed with (s 47(2)).

hild has been placed for adoption by an adoption oters, either with the consent of each parent or of the mother was given when the child was placement order, and no parent or guardian order (s 47(4)).

(Thorpe LJ dissenting) refused to grant leave for an ap
placement order (as the child had already been placed for
the applicant for leave, who was the child's father, had
proceedings for care and placement orders as he had
heart attack. The father's arguments based on huma
Appeal held that section 24 of the ACA 2002 was al

(vii) Effect of a placement order (section 25)

A placement order gives parental responsib
and to the prospective adopters while the
responsibility of any parent or guardian
until such time as a final adoption or
power to determine the extent to w'
or guardian, or of the prospective
power to remove the child from I'
failing), whether or not any par

Once placement for adopti
sections 8 or 34 of the CA 1'
prevent an application fo
Act (see 15.10 below).

While a placement

▶ No one may ca·
from the UK
the child's '
guardian'

▶ Any ca·
sectio
(s ?
c'

(vii)

(ix) Baby p

An a
with t
a 'look
not app
parental
under sec

15.7 Applyi

(a) The ado

An adoption or
51 of the Adopti
for the child to
of the child's par
terminates any ord
in the case of a step
responsibility or duti
(b)). An adoption ord
agreement or court ord
by the terms of an agre
not to be extinguished (
be adopted is already an

(b) Conditions for mak

Before the court can make a
following two conditions is me

1. The 'consent condition' – ea
adoption order or has given
making of the adoption order
parent or guardian should be d

2. The 'placement condition' – the
agency with the prospective ado
guardian (and where the consent
at least six weeks old); or under a
opposes the making of the adoption

g·
order.
applying u.

Section 47 is subject to the provisions on parental consent in section 52 (see 15.8 below).

(c) How the court exercises its power

The court must take into account the welfare principle and the other principles in section 1 of the ACA 2002. Before making an adoption order, the court must consider whether there should be arrangements for allowing any person to have contact with the child; and for that purpose the court must consider any existing or proposed arrangements and obtain any views of the parties to the proceedings (s 46(6)).

(d) Restrictions on making a further application for an adoption order (section 48)

Where a previous application for an adoption order has been refused by any court, a second application for an adoption order by the same applicant(s) in relation to the same child may not be heard unless it appears to the court that there is a change in circumstances, or any other reason, which makes it proper to hear the application (s 48(1)).

(e) The status of the adopted child (section 67)

An adopted person is treated in law as if they were born as the child of the adopter(s) (s 67(1)). An adopted person is the legitimate child of the adopter(s) and, if the child is adopted by a couple or one of a couple under a step-parent or civil partner adoption, the child is treated as the child of that relationship (s 67(2)).

15.8 Consent to placement for adoption and adoption

The issue of consent is very important in placement for adoption and adoption. Section 52(5) of the Adoption and Children Act 2002 (ACA 2002) provides that 'consent' means 'consent given unconditionally and with full understanding of what is involved; but a person may consent to adoption without knowing the identity of the persons in whose favour the order will be made'.

(a) Whose consent is required?

The consent of each parent or guardian of the child (including a special guardian) is required before an adoption agency may place a child for adoption (s 19(1)) or the court can make an adoption order (s 47(2)). As 'parent' for the purposes of consent means a parent with parental responsibility (s 52(6)), the consent of an unmarried father (or any other parent) without parental responsibility is not required. However, where an unmarried mother consents to adoption under section 19 (placement by parental consent), a father who subsequently acquires parental responsibility is to be treated as having at that time given consent in accordance with section 52 of the Act on the same terms as the mother (ss 52(9), (10)). Where a father acquires parental responsibility after an application for an adoption order has been made, he can, with leave of the court, oppose the adoption order on the basis that there has been a change of circumstances. Although the consent of the child's relatives is not needed, the court can take their wishes into account under the welfare checklist (s 1(4) and see 15.3 above).

(b) Mother's consent within six weeks of birth (section 52)

In respect of an adoption order, any consent given by a mother is ineffective if given less than six weeks after the child's birth (s 52(3)). However, in respect of a placement order, a mother's consent may be given at any time after the child's birth.

In *A Local Authority v GC and Others* [2008] EWHC 2555 (Fam), the parents had signed the consent to placement for adoption (under section 19) and to the making of a future adoption order (under section 20) when their child was only four weeks old. Despite the error, Eleanor King J held that the adoption was lawful on the basis that the parents' consent could be dispensed with so that the six-week requirement did not need to be satisfied.

(c) Formalities (section 52)

Consent to placement for adoption and to the making of an adoption order (including advance consent) must be given in the prescribed form (s 52(7)). Cafcass officers are responsible for witnessing consent, and for reporting to the court on matters relating to the child (s 102).

(d) Withdrawal of consent (section 52)

Once an application for an adoption order has been made, any consent given with respect to the placement for adoption or to the making of a future adoption order can no longer be withdrawn (s 52(4)). Parents who wish to oppose the adoption order after the cut-off point must obtain leave to do so (see 15.9 above).

(e) Advance consent (section 20)

A parent or guardian who consents to the child being placed for adoption by an adoption agency (under section 19) may at the same time, or at any subsequent time, consent to the making of a future adoption order (s 20(1)). Advance consent can be withdrawn (s 20(3)), but any withdrawal is ineffective if made after an application for an adoption order has been made (s 52(4)). A parent who gives advance consent can at the same time, or subsequently, give notice to the adoption agency stating that they do not wish to be informed of any application for an adoption order (s 20(4)). If a parent gives advance consent and chooses not to be notified of the application for the adoption order, placement and adoption can proceed without that parent being involved in any way. However, parents are given some protection as they have a right to be notified of the date and place of the adoption application (s 140(3)), whereupon they can apply for leave to oppose the making of the adoption order, which the court can grant if there has been a change of circumstances since consent was given (s 47(7)). Advance consent is subject to the provisions governing dispensing with consent (see below).

(f) Parents without parental responsibility – consent to and involvement in adoption

Although there is no requirement in the ACA 2002 for parents without parental responsibility, such as some unmarried fathers, to give their consent to placement for adoption or to adoption, the courts have been increasingly willing to involve them in the adoption process, particularly with the coming into force of the Human Rights Act 1998 (HRA 1998) and the risk of breaching a parent's rights under Article 8 (the right to family life) and Article 6 (the right to a fair hearing) of the European Convention on Human Rights (ECHR). In *Re R (Adoption: Father's Involvement)* [2001] 1 FLR 302, Thorpe LJ commented on the shift towards unmarried fathers without parental responsibility being accorded greater involvement in adoption proceedings, and held that the unmarried father might have been justified in raising a complaint under Article 6 of the ECHR if he had not been given notice of the adoption proceedings.

In most cases an unmarried father will be notified about the adoption. In fact, in *Re H; Re G (Adoption: Consultation of Unmarried Fathers)* [2001] 1 FLR 646, Butler-Sloss P held that, as a matter of good practice, judges would be expected to give directions so that unmarried fathers were informed of adoption proceedings, unless good reasons to the contrary existed (for example where there was no family life between the father and the child). In *Re C (Adoption: Disclosure to Father)* [2005] EWHC 3385 (Fam), Hedley J, referring to Butler-Sloss P in *Re H: Re G*, directed that the father without parental responsibility who was serving a prison sentence be informed about the adoption proceedings despite the mother's wishes to the contrary. Hedley J said that where family life was established, as it had been here as they had parented other children together, then there had to be 'very compelling reasons indeed' why a parent should be shut out from notice of the existence of the child or proposals for the future of the child.

Despite the shift towards recognising the importance of unmarried fathers and their involvement in bringing up their child, and the recognition of the importance of the child having a right to know their identity and origins, the court may in the exercise of its discretion decide that it is not in the best interests of the child for the father to be informed about pending adoption proceedings. That is what the Court of Appeal did in the following case.

> ▶ *Re C (A Child) (Adoption: Duty of Local Authority)* [2007] Civ 1206
>
> The child had been born as a result of a 'one-night stand' and the 19-year-old mother did not wish her parents or the child's father to know about the birth. The trial judge directed the local authority to disclose the existence and identity of the child to the extended maternal family and, if he could be identified, the father and any extended paternal family. The mother appealed.

> The Court of Appeal allowed the appeal and gave directions pre-empting the Guardian from taking further steps to identify the father. Arden LJ, applying sections 1(4)(c) and (f) of the welfare checklist in the ACA 2002, held that there is no duty of an absolute kind for inquiries to be made about the child's father when a decision needs to be made about the long-term care of a child. Such a duty only arises if it is in the child's best interests. There was no breach of the father's right to family life under Article 8 of the ECHR, as he had had no family life with the child. Neither was it a violation of the ECHR to deprive him of the possibility of obtaining a right to family life. The child's grandparents did have a right to family life under Article 8, but they would be able to obtain the information by making their own application under the Children Act 1989 (CA 1989).

(For a commentary on *Re C*, see Sloan [2009] CFLQ 87, who criticises the Court of Appeal for using 'an unnecessarily narrow conception of welfare' and for giving 'undue weight to the interests of the child's mother.')

(g) Grounds for dispensing with consent

Section 52(1) of the ACA 2002 lays down two grounds on which the court can dispense with the consent of a parent or guardian to the child's adoption or placement for adoption:

▶ that a parent or guardian cannot be found or is incapable of giving consent (s 52(1)(a)); or
▶ that the welfare of the child requires the consent to be dispensed with (s 52(1)(b)).

The paramountcy of the child's welfare (s 1(2)) and the section 1(4) welfare checklist (see 15.3 above) apply to dispensing with consent.

Although the ECHR is relevant to the question of consent, particularly Article 8 (the right to family life), the Court of Appeal has held that the test for dispensing with consent in section 52(1)(b) does not, for this reason, demand an enhanced test beyond the welfare test set out in section 1(2); but that cogent justification must exist before consent can be dispensed with and adoption must be a proportionate and legitimate response (see *per* Wall LJ in *Re P (Placement Orders: Parental Consent)* [2008] EWCA Civ 535). In *Re Q (Adoption)* [2011] EWCA Civ 1610 Munby LJ reiterated this point and said that the word 'requires' in section 52(1)(b) accurately captured the essence of the Strasbourg jurisprudence on necessity. (See also *Re B (A Child) (Care Proceedings: Appeal)* [2013] UKSC 33 at 15.1 above.)

15.9 Challenging an adoption order

There are various ways in which an adoption order can be challenged.

(a) Opposing the making of an adoption order

If a parent or guardian wishes to oppose the making of an adoption order, then leave of the court is required under section 47(3) or section 47(5) of the Adoption and Children Act 2002 (ACA 2002). However, the court cannot grant leave unless it is satisfied that there has been a change in circumstances since the consent of the parent or guardian was given or the placement order was made (s 47(7)).

The courts have held that the right to oppose the making of an adoption order after care and placement orders is likely to be very limited. For example, in *Re W (Adoption Order: Set Aside and Leave to Oppose)* [2010] EWCA Civ 1535, Thorpe LJ said that leave would be granted only in 'exceptionally rare circumstances'. However, in *Re B-S (Children)* [2013] EWCA Civ 1146 (see 15.1 above), Munby P, President of the Family Division, said that the use of such phrases as 'exceptionally rare circumstances' should cease as they are apt to mislead, with potentially serious adverse consequences. Munby P instead approved the two-stage approach set out by Wall LJ in *Re P (Adoption: Leave Provisions)* [2007] EWCA Civ 616 which requires the court to ask itself two questions: has there been a change of circumstances of a nature or degree sufficient to warrant the exercise of judicial discretion; and, if so, should leave to oppose the making of an adoption order be granted, taking into account the parents' prospects of success if they were given leave and the impact on the child's welfare either way? Munby P said that judges had to consider carefully whether the child's welfare really required the refusal of leave, bearing in mind that adoption was a last resort. He also urged judges to bear in mind the words of Wall LJ in *Re P (Adoption: Leave Provisions)* (para 32, see above), that 'the test should not be set too high because ... parents ... should not be discouraged either from bettering themselves or from seeking to prevent the adoption of their child by the imposition of a test which is unachievable.' (For a commentary on the impact of *Re B (A Child) (Care Proceedings: Appeal)* [2013] UKSC 33 and *Re B-S* (see 15.1 above) and the law and policy relating to contested adoptions see Doughty [2015] CFLQ 331.)

(b) Appealing an adoption order

An appeal against an adoption order can be brought on the ground, for example, that the trial judge was wrong or that there was a procedural irregularity and/or a breach of human rights. Appeals on the basis of procedural irregularity or unfairness are sometimes brought (see, for example, *Re T (Adoption)* [2012] EWCA Civ 191).

(c) Setting aside an adoption order

Once an adoption order has been lawfully and properly made, it is only in highly exceptional circumstances that the court will permit the order to be set aside. The principles to be applied are set out in *Re B (Adoption Order: Jurisdiction to Set Aside)* [1995] Fam 239 and *Webster v Norfolk County Council and the Children (By Their Children's Guardian)* [2009] EWCA Civ 59. In *Webster* the parents failed in their application to set aside adoption orders on the ground that three of their children had been taken into care and adopted on the basis of a wrong diagnosis of non-accidental injury. The court said that it would only be in highly exceptional and very particular circumstances that the court would permit an adoption order to be set aside. Thus, for example, in *PK v Mr and Mrs K* [2015] EWHC 2316 (Fam), the court exercised its inherent jurisdiction to revoke an adoption order on the application of a 14-year-old girl who had been adopted and then suffered significant abuse at the hands of her adoptive family.

15.10 Contact

Applications for contact at the placement for adoption stage are governed by sections 26 and 27 of the Adoption and Children Act 2002 (ACA 2002). Post-adoption contact is governed by sections 51A and 51B of the ACA 2002, which were introduced by the Children and Families Act 2014 (CFA 2014). Prior to the reforms, a post-adoption contact order could only be made under section 8 of the Children Act 1989 (CA 1989). With the introduction of sections 51A and 51B of the ACA 2002, the court now has a specific power to make an order for post-adoption contact when the court is making an adoption order or when an adoption order has been made.

(a) Contact and placement for adoption (sections 26 and 27)

Sections 26 and 27 of the ACA 2002 contain provisions with respect to contact in the context of placement for adoption. Once the adoption agency is authorised to place a child for adoption, it must consider what arrangements it should make for allowing any person to have contact with the child. The court will also have to consider contact between, *inter alia*, the child and their parents and relatives when it conducts the welfare exercise (s 1(4), see 15.3 above).

(i) Children Act 1989 contact orders not effective and applications barred (section 26)

Where an adoption agency is authorised to place a child for adoption (whether by consent or under a placement order), any provision for contact under section 8 or section 34 of the CA 1989 ceases to have effect (ss 26(1)). While an adoption agency is authorised to place a child for adoption, or the child is placed for adoption, an application for contact cannot be made under the CA 1989 (s 26(2)).

(ii) A section 26 contact order

Where an adoption agency is authorised to place a child for adoption (by parental consent or placement order), or the child is placed for adoption, the court can make a contact order under section 26 of the ACA 2002 requiring the person with whom the child lives, or is to live, to allow the child to visit or stay with the person named in the order, or for the person named in the order and the child otherwise to have contact with each other (s 26(2)). The following people can apply for a section 26 contact order: the child; the adoption agency; parents, guardians or relatives; any person in whose favour provision for contact had been made under a court order which ceased to be effective by virtue of the child being placed for adoption; any person named in a child arrangements order as a person with whom the child was to live, which was in force immediately before the placement, at a time when the child was less than six weeks old; any person who had care of the child under an order made by the High Court under its inherent jurisdiction; and any other person who has obtained leave of the court (s 26(3)). The court can make a section 26 contact order of its own initiative when making a placement order (s 26(4)).

The welfare principle in section 1(4) and the other section 1 principles apply to the exercise of the court's discretion (see 15.3 above). The order may provide for contact on any conditions that the court considers appropriate (s 27(5)). The contact order is only effective while the adoption agency is authorised to place the child for adoption, or the child is placed for adoption, but it may be varied or revoked by the court on the application of the child, the adoption agency or the person named in the order (s 27(1)). The court may authorise the adoption agency to refuse to allow contact, if necessary to safeguard or promote the child's welfare, provided refusal is decided as a matter of urgency and does not last for more than seven days (s 27(2)).

(b) Post-adoption contact

Before making an adoption order, the court must consider whether any arrangements should be made for allowing any person contact with the child, and must consider any existing or proposed arrangements and obtain the views of the parties to the proceedings (s 46(6)).

The provisions relating to post-adoption contact are contained in sections 51A and 51B of the ACA 2002. Where the child concerned was placed by an adoption agency, the court may, on the making of the adoption order, or at any time afterwards, make an order for contact between the child and the people named in the order (ss 51A(1) and (2)). The people who may be named in the order are: any person who would be related to the child by blood (including half-blood), marriage or civil partnership; any former guardian of the child; any person who had parental responsibility for the child immediately before the making of the adoption order; any person who was entitled to make an application for an order under section 26 in respect of the child by virtue of subsection (3)(c), (d) or (e) of that section; and any person with whom the child has lived for a period of at least one year (s 51A(3)). The court can also make an order prohibiting someone named in section 51A(3) from having contact with the child (s 51A(2)). However, only the adopter and the child have the automatic right to apply for such an order; any other person, such as a birth parent or relative, who wishes to apply for contact must first obtain leave of the court (51A(4)). This reflects the finality of the adoption process.

When the court is deciding whether to grant leave, it must consider: any risk there might be of the proposed application disrupting the child's life to such an extent that he or she would be harmed by it; the applicant's connection with the child; and any representations made to the court by the child, or a person who has applied for the adoption order or in whose favour the adoption order is or has been made (s 51A(5)). Where section 51A applies, no section 8 order under the CA 1989 in relation to the provision of contact may be made between the child and any person who may be named in an order for post-adoption contact (51A(8)).

(i) The approach of the courts

The courts have traditionally been very reluctant to impose post-adoption contact on unwilling adopters, as the cases of *Re R (Adoption: Contact)* [2005] EWCA Civ 1128, *Oxfordshire County Council v X, Y and J* [2010] EWCA Civ 581 and *Re T (A Child)* [2010] EWCA Civ 1527 below demonstrate. Although post-adoption contact may help children resolve feelings of separation and loss, and give them a sense of their biological and social origins, the concern is that it may be disruptive to the child and may deter potential adopters from coming forward to adopt children. Although the court has specific powers to order post-adoption contact under sections 51A and

51B of the ACA 2002, Bainham ([2015] Fam Law 1356) criticises such legislative measures as being 'theoretical' and notes how 'pride of place is given to the negative consideration of the risk of disruption to the child and consequential harm. There is no express acknowledgment of the positive benefits which the child might enjoy through ongoing contact with the birth family.'

Although contact following adoption has become more common, the imposition on prospective adopters of orders for contact with which they are not in agreement is extremely unusual (*per* Wall LJ in *Re R (Adoption: Contact)* [2005] EWCA Civ 1128 where the half-sister's application for leave to apply for a contact order under section 10(9) of the CA 1989 was dismissed). Wall LJ's words were cited with approval by the Court of Appeal in *Oxfordshire County Council v X, Y and J* [2010] EWCA Civ 581 where the court refused to order that the natural parents should receive an annual photograph of their former child. (For a commentary on this case, see Hughes and Sloan [2011] CFLQ 393). Wall LJ's words were also referred to in *Re T (A Child)* [2010] EWCA Civ 1527, where a grandmother's application for a contact order (after she had been granted leave to apply) was dismissed because of, *inter alia*, the fact that the proceedings were having a highly adverse effect on the adoptive parents and therefore on the child. In *Seddon v Oldham Metropolitan Borough Council* [2015] EWHC 2609 (Fam), the court reiterated that adoption ended the family life between a parent and child under Article 8 of the ECHR and that section 51A did not in itself create or maintain any Article 8 rights of the birth mother in relation to the child.

A greater willingness to order post-adoption contact can, however, be seen in the case of *MF v Brent LBC* [2013] EWHC 1838 (Fam), where the court made an order for unsupervised contact every six or seven weeks to allow the adopted child to maintain a relationship with his maternal grandmother and sister, which the court held was necessary to safeguard the child's long-term welfare. Ryder J commented that courts should be more willing to consider whether making a contact order might give reassurance to the child by maintaining an enduring relationship that is important for their welfare throughout their lives.

15.11 Adoption by step-parents, partners, relatives and foster-carers

(a) Step-parent and civil partner adoptions

A step-parent can apply to adopt a step-child and a civil partner can apply to adopt a child of a civil partner, although there are other ways of acquiring parental responsibility for the child (see 15.1 above). Step-parents and civil partners who wish to adopt must satisfy certain residence and notice requirements. Thus, the child must have had their home with the applicant at all times during the six months preceding the application (s 42(3)). Also, as this type of adoption is a non-agency adoption, the step-parent or civil partner must have given notice of their intention to adopt to the local authority not more than two years, or less than three months, before applying for the order (ss 44(2), (3)). This enables the local authority to investigate and submit a report to the court in respect of the applicant's suitability for adoption and any section 1 welfare issues (ss 44(5), (6)). The consent requirement must also have been satisfied (s 47(2)). (For an application of the principles to be applied in a step-parent adoption see *Re P (A Child) (Adoption: Step-parent's Application)* [2014] EWCA Civ 1174.)

(b)   Adoption by relatives

A relative of a child can apply to adopt the child, provided the child has had their home with the relative for not less than three years, which need not be continuous, during the five years ending with the application (s 42(5)) or the court grants leave to apply (s 42(6)). The relative must have notified the local authority of their intention to adopt not more than two years, or less than three months, before applying for the order (s 44(3)). The relative must be suitable for adoption (s 45), and the consent condition must be complied with (s 47(2)).

Although adoption by a relative may be in a child's best interests where the child's parents are dead, or where a relative has been caring for a child and the parents are no longer involved, it may be better for a relative to obtain parental responsibility by means of a special guardianship order (see 15.14 below) or a child arrangements order regulating the child's living arrangements (see 10.5) so as not to sever the child's links with other members of their birth family.

(c)   Adoption by local authority foster-carers

Foster-carers can adopt a foster child in their care, but the rules differ depending on whether the case is an agency adoption or a non-agency adoption. As an alternative to adoption, foster-parents can acquire parental responsibility by obtaining a child arrangements order regulating the child's living arrangements (see 10.5) or a special guardianship order (see 15.14 below).

(i) Agency adoption cases

An agency adoption case is one where the local authority decides to place a child with a foster-carer or to convert a foster placement into an adoption placement. A foster carer can seek local authority approval to become a prospective adopter of a foster-child. If approval is given, the child lives with the foster-carer as the prospective adopter, provided any parent or guardian has consented to adoption under section 19 of the ACA 2002 or a placement order has been made. Once the child is placed with the foster-carer(s) as prospective adopter(s), only the local authority may remove the child (ss 30, 34). Preliminary requirements must be satisfied before an adoption order can be made. Thus, the child must have had their home with the foster-carer(s) at all times during the ten weeks preceding the adoption application (s 42(2)); and an investigation and report as to their suitability must have been made and satisfied (s 43).

(ii) Non-agency adoption cases

A non-agency adoption case is one where the local authority has not placed the child with the foster-carer for adoption and has refused to give its approval when it was sought; but where the foster-carer still wishes to apply for adoption. The child must have had his home with the foster-carer for a continuous period of not less than one year, although the court can give leave to waive this requirement (ss 42(4), (6)). The foster-carer must give notice to the local authority of his or her intention to adopt not more than two years, or less than three months, before the date on which the application is made (s 44). The consent condition in section 47(2) must also be satisfied.

15.12 Adopted people – access to information

Adopted people, on reaching adulthood, can investigate their origins and seek to make contact with their birth family.

(a) Access to birth certificates

An adopted adult can obtain a copy of his or her original birth certificate, but the Registrar General has a discretion to refuse to provide a copy. Thus, for example, in *R v Registrar-General ex parte Smith* [1991] 2 QB 393, the Registrar General's refusal to supply a copy to an adopted person who was serving a life sentence for murder was held to be lawful. Local authorities are required to provide a counselling service for adopted adults before they decide to obtain information about their birth records.

(b) The Adopted Children Register and the Adoption Contact Register

(i) The Adopted Children Register

The Registrar General has a duty under the Adoption and Children Act 2002 (ACA 2002) to maintain this Register (s 77) and an index of the Register (s 78). The Register is not open to public inspection or search, but any person may search the index of the Register and have a certified copy of any entry in the Register (s 78(2)) and thereby trace the original birth registration of an adopted child. Where the adopted person is under 18, a person is not entitled to a certified copy of an entry in the Register unless the applicant has provided the Registrar General with certain prescribed particulars.

The courts have no power to restrict the information placed in the Register, but the High Court may under its inherent jurisdiction prohibit the Registrar General from providing details of the adoption to any applicant while the child is under 18 (see, for example, *Re W (Adoption Details: Disclosure)* [1998] 2 FLR 625). The court can also authorise the Registrar General to disclose information, as it did, for example, in *Re H (Adoption: Disclosure of Information)* [1995] 1 FLR 236, where it authorised the Registrar General to provide information so that a 53-year-old adopted person with a treatable genetic disease could trace her brother so that he could be screened and treated if necessary.

(ii) The Adoption Contact Register

The Registrar General has a duty under the ACA 2002 to maintain this Register (ss 80 and 81), which enables adopted people to register their interest in contacting birth relatives (in Part I); and for relatives searching for an adopted person to register their interest in being contacted (in Part II). If there is a match, the Registrar General gives the adopted person the relative's name and address, but no information is provided to the relative. The decision to initiate contact is left to the adopted person.

The Registrar General has a duty to make traceable the connections between the register of live births and any corresponding entry in the Adoption Contact Register, and to disclose that information, or any other information which might enable an adopted person to obtain a certified copy of their birth record (s 79). The Registrar General is under a duty to give the connecting birth-record information to an adoption agency in respect of a person whose birth record is kept by the Registrar General. In *FL v Registrar General* [2010] EWHC 3520 (Fam), a daughter in her late sixties applied to the court for it to authorise the Registrar General to provide her with information so that she could find out more about her father's birth family, but her application was refused as the court is only permitted to give such authority in exceptional circumstances (s 79(4)).

Adopted people or birth relatives of people who have been adopted may also request the help of an intermediary service to help them to find and get in contact with their relatives.

(c) Disclosure of information

Sections 56–65 of the ACA 2002 and accompanying regulations lay down provisions governing the disclosure to adopted persons of information held by adoption agencies in connection with adoption, and for access to birth records. These provisions also cover the release of adoption agency information to birth relatives and other persons. Under these provisions, adoption agencies act as a single point of access to identifying information (including information necessary to access birth records), as they are the bodies best placed to provide support and counselling for the sensitive task of disclosure.

15.13 Intercountry adoption

An intercountry adoption is an adoption of a child who is habitually resident in one country by an individual or couple who are habitually resident in another. The law is primarily found in the Adoption and Children Act 2002 (ACA 2002), accompanying regulations (including the Adoptions with a Foreign Element Regulations 2005, SI 2005/392) and the Hague Convention on Protection of Children and Cooperation in Respect of Intercountry Adoption 1993 (Hague Convention 1993). The law is complex and only a brief outline is given here, but further information is available, for example from the International Adoption Centre.

(a) Taking a child out of the UK for an adoption abroad

Sections 83–91 of the ACA 2002 govern adoptions with a foreign element. It is unlawful to take a child out of the UK for the purposes of an adoption overseas unless the prospective adopters have been granted parental responsibility for the child under section 84 of the ACA 2002, which the court has power to do if it is satisfied that: the applicant(s) intend to adopt the child under the law of a country outside the UK; they do not meet the requirements for domicile or habitual residence in England and Wales which have to be met in order for an adoption order to be made; and they have had the child living with them during the preceding ten weeks (s 84(4)). The order confers parental responsibility on the applicant(s) and extinguishes that of any other person (for example, that of any parent and the local authority where a care order is in force). In *Re G (Adoption: Placement Outside Jurisdiction)* [2008] EWCA Civ 105, Sir Mark Potter P held that section 84(4) did not require the physical presence of each adopter during the ten-week period in order to satisfy the proposition that the child's home was with the adopters throughout that period. Thus, for example, in *Re G (Surrogacy: Foreign Domicile)* [2007] EWHC 2814 (Fam), an order was made under section 84 to facilitate the adoption of a child in Turkey in a case involving an English surrogacy arrangement.

(b) The Hague Convention on Protection of Children and Co-operation in Respect of Intercountry Adoption 1993

Intercountry adoptions present challenges because, although adoption may give children from abroad a quality of life they did not have in their country of origin, there is a danger that such adoptions may exploit the needs of children by being too adult-centred. Intercountry adoptions may fail to take account of the importance of children remaining in touch with their cultural roots and birth family, and they may have been arranged privately without the checks and safeguards which exist for adoptions under domestic law.

In response to concerns about intercountry adoption, there have been an increasing numbers of safeguards put in place under international and domestic law, including, in particular, the Hague Convention 1993, to which the UK is a signatory. (The Permanent Bureau at the Hague has information on the Convention, a list of Contracting States and a guide entitled *The Implementation and Operation of the 1993 Hague Intercountry Adoption Convention: A Guide to Good Practice*.)

The Hague Convention 1993 provides a framework for the regulation of intercountry adoption by setting out minimum standards for the control and regulation of the flow of children between the signatory States. The effect of the Convention is that any person in England and Wales who wishes to adopt a child from overseas must undergo the same procedures as they would if adopting a child under domestic law. Under the provisions of the Convention, there are restrictions on intercountry adoption and stringent penalties, including imprisonment, for those who fail to comply with the requirements. Any person who is habitually resident in England and Wales who wishes to adopt a child from abroad is required to be assessed and approved to be eligible and suitable to adopt.

The number of contracting parties to the Hague Convention 1993 has grown over the years – as at September 2016, there were 98 Contracting States. Article 1 of the Convention states that the objects of the Convention are:

a) to establish safeguards to ensure that intercountry adoptions take place in the best interests of the child and with respect for his or her fundamental rights as recognised in international law;

b) to establish a system of co-operation amongst Contracting States to ensure that those safeguards are respected and thereby prevent the abduction, the sale of or traffic in children;

c) to secure the recognition in Contracting States of adoptions made in accordance with the Convention.

The underlying rationale of the Hague Convention 1993 is for Contracting States to work together to ensure that adoption is in the best interests of the child, and only after possibilities for placement of the child within the State of origin have been given due consideration (Art 4(b)). The aim is for children to stay within their own communities where possible. Where this is not possible, the Convention makes provisions to regulate the adoption process. It does so by requiring central authorities to be established whose function it is to work together to protect children during the adoption process and to monitor the operation of the Convention. Central authorities are responsible, *inter alia*, for: exchanging information about the child; ensuring that the child is adoptable; that the relevant consents have been given after appropriate counselling and that they have not been induced by payment or compensation; and that the prospective adopters are eligible and suitable to adopt the child. The Convention also provides for the automatic recognition in all Contracting States of adoptions certified by the central authority concerned as having been made in accordance with the Convention.

(c) Non-Convention adoptions

There will be cases which fall outside the Hague Convention 1993. For example, in some cases people living in England and Wales may wish to adopt a child from a country that is not a signatory to the Convention. Certain overseas adoptions, which are not Convention adoptions, are capable of recognition in England and Wales provided they are listed in the Adoption (Recognition of Overseas Adoptions) Order 2013/1801. In other cases, where the foreign adoption order is not recognised, it will be necessary for the parents to apply to adopt the child in England and Wales, even if they have already adopted the child overseas. As part of this process, the local authority will need to investigate and complete a report on the suitability of the adopters to ensure that the welfare of the child is protected.

15.14 Special guardianship

Sections 14A–14F of the Children Act 1989 (CA 1989), which were inserted into the Act by the Adoption and Children Act 2002 (ACA 2002), make provision for special guardianship. Special guardianship was introduced with the aim of giving children for whom adoption is not suitable the security and permanence of a legal family placement.

A special guardianship order gives the applicant parental responsibility for the child without taking parental responsibility away from the birth parents. They were designed in part to provide a framework of permanency for 'children being cared for on a permanent basis by members of their wider birth family' (*Adoption: A New Approach*, Cm 5017, 2000). They are also intended to fill the gap between child arrangements orders regulating a child's living arrangements and long-term fostering at one end of the spectrum and adoption at the other. The aim is to provide a long-term care option similar to adoption, but without the legal break with the birth family and the finality associated with the making of an adoption order. Special guardianship may be appropriate, for example where it is not in a child's best interests to have their legal relationship with their birth family severed by adoption, or where the child is an older child in foster care who does not wish to be adopted, or where there are cultural and religious difficulties with adoption. However, research on special guardianship by Hall ([2008] Fam Law 148) found that, whilst special guardianship was being used by 'kinship carers', it was not proving to be very popular with foster-carers.

(a) Special guardianship distinguished from adoption

The following table shows the main differences between special guardianship and adoption.

	SPECIAL GUARDIANSHIP	ADOPTION
Status of the child	The child lives with/is cared for by the special guardian but remains the child of the birthparent(s).	The child is the child of the adopter(s). The adopters are the child's parents.
Parental responsibility	Vests in the special guardian, but is retained by the birthparent(s).	Vests in the adopters.
Restrictions on the exercise of parental responsibility	Parental responsibility can be exercised by the special guardian to the exclusion of all other people, but they will need the agreement of everyone with parental responsibility (or otherwise the court) to: take the child out of the UK for more than three months; change the child's surname; consent to the child's adoption; and consent to the child having serious medical treatment.	There are no restrictions on the exercise of the parental responsibility of the adopters.
Duration of the order	A special guardianship order ceases automatically on the child reaching 18, if not revoked earlier by the court.	An adoption order is permanent.
Revocation or discharge of the order	Birth parent(s) can apply to revoke or discharge the special guardianship order, but leave of the court is needed, which it can grant only if there has been a significant change of circumstances. The court can discharge a special guardianship order of its own motion in any family proceedings.	An adoption order cannot be revoked (except in a wholly exceptional case, such as where there has been a serious procedural impropriety).
Maintenance of the child	Birth parent(s) continue to have a maintenance obligation to the child.	Any maintenance obligation owed by the child's birth parent is extinguished on adoption, unless there is any such obligation in a trust deed.
Death of the child	The special guardian must notify the child's parent(s) who have parental responsibility.	The adopters need not notify the birthparents of the child's death.
Intestacy (death without making a will)	The child has no right to inherit from a special guardian who dies intestate.	The child has a right to inherit from the adopters on the adopters' intestacy.

(b) Applying for a special guardianship order

(i) Applicants (section 14A(5))

The following people are entitled to apply for a special guardianship order:

- a guardian of the child;
- a person who is named in a child arrangements order as a person with whom the child is to live;
- any person with whom the child has lived for a period of at least three years out of the previous five years;
- a person who has the consent of each of the people who are named in a child arrangements order as a person with whom the child is to live;
- a person who has the consent of the local authority if the child is in care;
- any person who has the consent of each of those with parental responsibility for the child;
- a local authority foster-parent with whom the child has lived for a period of at least one year immediately preceding the application; and
- a relative with whom the child has lived for a period of at least one year immediately preceding the application.

The applicant must be at least 18 years old and must not be a parent of the child (s 14A(2)). A joint application can be made (ss 14A(1), (3)). Other people can apply for a special guardianship order with leave of the court (s 14A(3)). When considering whether to grant leave, the court applies the same factors as those which apply to leave applications for section 8 orders (s 14A(12)) (see 10.9). A child can apply for a special guardianship order with leave of the court, which it can grant if the child has sufficient understanding to make the proposed application (s 14A(12), s 10(8)). The court can also make a special guardianship order of its own motion in any family proceedings (see 10.9), which includes adoption proceedings (s 14A(6)).

(ii) Local authority duty to provide a report (section 14A)

At least three months before an application is made, written notice of an intention to apply for a special guardianship order must be given to the relevant local authority (s 14A(7)), so that they can properly investigate the matter. The three-month notice period is not required if sections 29(5) and (6) of the ACA 2002 apply, which provide for the making of special guardianship orders where a placement order is already in force in relation to the child. On receipt of the notice, the local authority has a duty to investigate the matter and prepare a report for the court about the suitability of the applicant(s) for special guardianship, and any other relevant or prescribed matters (s 14A(8), (9)). The court cannot make the special guardianship order until it has received this report dealing with the matters referred to in section 14A(8) (s 14A(11)).

(iii) Making a special guardianship order – the exercise of discretion

When considering whether to make a special guardianship order, the court must apply the welfare principle and the other principles in section 1 of the CA (see 10.3). Also, before making an order, it must consider: whether a child arrangements order containing a contact provision should be made with respect to the child; whether to vary or discharge any existing section 8 order; whether any enforcement order relating to a child arrangements order should be revoked; and whether any existing activity direction should be discharged (s 14B(1)). On making the order, the court may also grant leave for the child to be known by a new surname and/or to leave the UK generally or for a specified purpose (s 14B(2)). To reduce delay, the court must draw up a timetable and give directions to ensure that the timetable is adhered to (s 14E).

A special guardianship order is appropriate only if, in the particular circumstances of the case, it is best fitted to meet the needs of the child concerned (see *Re S (Adoption Order or Special Guardianship Order)* [2007] EWCA Civ 54). Each case therefore depends on its own facts. The court will sometimes have to decide whether it is in the child's best interests to make a special guardianship order or an adoption order (see further below).

(iv) Effects of a special guardianship order

The effects of a special guardianship order are as follows:

- ▶ *Parental responsibility* The special guardian acquires parental responsibility for the child, which (subject to any other order in force with respect to the child) can be exercised to the exclusion of any other person(s) with parental responsibility (s 14C), apart from any other special guardian. This power to exercise parental responsibility to the exclusion of other people with parental responsibility is the most significant effect of a special guardianship order, and one which distinguishes it from a child arrangements order regulating the child's living arrangements. However, certain restrictions apply to parental responsibility acquired under a special guardianship order. Thus, while a special guardianship order is in force, no one may change the child's surname or remove the child from the UK for more than three months without the *written* consent of every person with parental responsibility for the child or with leave of the court (ss 14C(3), (4)); but these restrictions do not apply where a placement order is in force (s 29(7)(b) ACA 2002). A special guardian must take reasonable steps to inform each parent of the child with parental responsibility, and each guardian of the child, should the child die (s 14C(5)).
- ▶ *A right to support services* Special guardians have a right to local authority support services, including financial support, similar to those available to adopters. They can also bring a challenge by judicial review. Thus, for example, *B v Lewisham London Borough Council* [2008] EWHC 738 (Admin), a special guardian (the maternal grandmother) and the child were successful in bringing an application to have Lewisham's allowance scheme for special guardians quashed as being unlawful.
- ▶ *Effect on other orders* The making of a special guardianship order discharges any existing care order or related order for contact under the Children Act 1989 (s 91(5A)). However, it does not prevent a care order or a child arrangements order regulating the child's living arrangements being made whilst the special guardianship order is in force (s 10(7A)), whereupon an application will have to be made to have the special guardianship order varied or discharged (see below).

(v) Where a placement order is in force (section 14A)

A special guardianship order cannot be made while a placement for adoption order is in force (s 14A(13)) unless: an application has been made for a final adoption order, and the person applying for the special guardianship order has obtained leave under section 29(5) of the ACA 2002; or, in the case of a guardian of the child, they have obtained leave under section 47(5) of the ACA 2002. Written notice of an intention to apply for a special guardianship order must be given to the local authority which is looking after the child or in whose area the applicant is ordinarily resident (s 14A(7) CA 1989; s 29(6) ACA 2002).

(vi) Variation and discharge

A special guardianship order can be varied or discharged by the court of its own motion in any family proceedings in which a question arises with respect to the child's welfare (s 14D(2)) or on an application made by: the special guardian; a parent or guardian with leave of the court; the child with leave of the court; any person who is named in a child arrangements order as a person with whom the child is to live; a local authority designated in a care order with respect to the child; and any person with leave of the court who has, or immediately before the making of the special guardianship order had, parental responsibility for the child (ss 14D(1), (3)). The court can grant leave to applicants other than the child if there has been a significant change in circumstances since the order was made (s 14(D)(5)).

(vii) The principles applicable to a leave application to discharge a special guardianship order

The issue of leave was considered in the following case where it was held by the Court of Appeal that a leave application to apply to discharge a special guardianship order should be determined in the same way as a leave application to discharge a placement order under the ACA 2002 (see 15.6 above).

▶ *Re G (Special Guardianship Order)* [2010] EWCA 300

The mother applied for leave to apply for the discharge of a special guardianship order under section 14D(5) which had been made in respect of her child (now aged four) with the maternal grandmother as special guardian. The mother applied for discharge as the circumstances had changed, in that she was no longer causing concern for the local authority as she had successfully parented a second child on her own for more than two years. The application for leave failed at first instance as the circumstances were found not to be 'significant' for the purposes of section 14D(5); and the judge considered, applying section 10(9)(c) of the CA 1989, that there would be a risk of disruption to the child's life if the application were to succeed. The mother appealed.

The Court of Appeal allowed the appeal. It held, *inter alia*, that, until the emergence of more robust jurisprudence in relation to the proper approach to the determination of applications for leave to apply for the discharge of special guardianship orders, the approach should be that commended in *M v Warwickshire County Council* [2007] EWCA Civ 1084, namely that the principles which apply to leave applications to discharge a placement order should apply to leave applications to discharge a special guardianship order.

(c) Special guardianship or adoption?

Whether a child's best interests are better promoted by making an adoption order or a special guardianship order will depend on the facts of the particular case.

The following case is the leading case on the principles to be applied when the court is considering whether to make an adoption order or a special guardianship order.

▶ *Re S (Adoption Order or Special Guardianship Order)* [2007] EWCA Civ 54

The child (aged six and in care of the local authority) was placed with a foster-mother but the child's mother had regular contact, and the father had contact. The foster-mother applied to adopt the child but the judge concluded that adoption was not the best way of securing the child's welfare and made a special guardianship order of her own motion. The foster-mother appealed to the Court of Appeal.

The Court of Appeal, dismissing her appeal, held, *inter alia*, that:

▶ The key question which the court must ask itself when deciding whether to make a special guardianship order or an adoption order is which order would better serve the welfare of the child, applying the welfare checklists in the CA 1989 and ACA 2002.

▶ Because of the importance of such cases to the parties and children concerned, judges must give full reasons and explain their decisions with care.

▶ Provided the judge has carefully examined the facts, made appropriate findings and applied the welfare checklists, it is unlikely that the court would be able to interfere with the exercise of judicial discretion, particularly in a finely balanced case.

▶ The risk of prejudice caused by delay is likely to be of less pivotal importance in this type of case; and in many cases it might be appropriate to pause and give time for reflection, particularly in cases where the order is being made of the court's own motion.

▶ The court must be satisfied that the order it decides to make is a proportionate response to the problem, having regard to the right to family life in Article 8 of the European Convention on Human Rights (ECHR). Special guardianship involves a less fundamental interference with existing legal relationships than adoption, and in some cases the fact that the welfare objective could be achieved with less disruption of existing family relationships could properly be regarded as tipping the balance. However, in most cases Article 8 of the ECHR is unlikely to add anything to the considerations contained in the welfare checklists.

▶ Special guardianship does not provide the same permanency as adoption (as the child's parents can apply for a residence order without leave and other section 8 orders with leave, and the leave threshold is set relatively low), although a court can make a section 91(14) order under the CA 1989 to prevent further applications to the court by the child's parents. The fact that special guardianship cannot give the same permanency as adoption might tip the scales in favour of adoption.

▶ When applying its own motion powers to make a special guardianship order the court can take into account the fact that the person concerned does not wish to be the child's special guardian. But if, applying the welfare checklist under the CA 1989 (including the potential consequences to the child of the refuser implementing the threat to refuse to be appointed a special guardian), the court came to the view that a special guardianship order would best serve the welfare interests of the child, then that is the order the court should make.

(i) Intra-familial cases – special guardianship or adoption?

Whether special guardianship instead of adoption will be the preferred option in an intra-family adoption will depend on the facts of the case, applying the principle that the welfare of the child is the court's paramount consideration. While special guardianship may be better than adoption in an intra-familial case (for example in the case of an applicant grandparent or relative) because it has the benefit of not skewing family relationships, adoption may be better in other situations because of the security it provides for the child. In *Re AJ (Adoption Order or Special Guardianship Order)* [2007] EWCA Civ 55 (see below), the Court of Appeal stressed that special guardianship orders had not necessarily replaced adoption orders in cases where a child had been permanently placed within the wider family. Thus, for example, adoption may be better than special guardianship where the relationship between the applicant family member and the child's birth parent is difficult (see *Re EN (A Child) (Special Guardianship Order)* [2007] EWCA Civ 264 and *Re M-J (Adoption Order or Special Guardianship Order)* [2007] EWCA Civ 56 below).

The following cases provide examples of where the court had to decide whether to make a special guardianship or an adoption order. They show how decisions about whether to make an adoption order or a special guardianship order are very fact-specific.

▶ *S v B and Newport City Council; Re K* [2007] FLR 1116

Hedley J made a special guardianship order in favour of the grandparents with whom the child (aged six) had been living under a care order since he was six months old. He did so, despite the grandparents' preference for an adoption order, because adoption would skew the family relationships. Hedley J also made an order under section 91(14) of the CA 1989 prohibiting any further applications to the court by the child's parents and an order under section 14B(2)(a) giving leave for the child to be known by the grandparents' surname. Hedley J said that the case was 'one of those cases for which special guardianship was specifically designed' as it permitted familial carers, who were not the parents, 'to have all the practical authority and standing of parents, whilst leaving intact real and readily comprehensible relationships with the family'.

▶ *Re AJ (Adoption Order or Special Guardianship Order)* [2007] EWCA Civ55

The Court of Appeal upheld the adoption order in favour of the child's aunt and uncle, on the basis that the child had been living with the aunt and uncle since the age of six months, and because adoption, unlike a special guardianship order, provided the assurance that the security of that placement would not be disturbed. The child's father had made aggressive telephone calls to the aunt, and she was concerned that the parents were unpredictable and would litigate issues concerning the child's care. The Court of Appeal agreed with the judge that an adoption order would in the circumstances of the case not unduly distort the family dynamics.

▶ *Re M-J (Adoption Order or Special Guardianship Order)* [2007] EWCA Civ56

The child, who was subject to a care order, had been removed from his parents and looked after by his aunt since he was six months old (because of the mother's alcohol and drug dependency). The aunt applied to adopt the child but this was opposed by the child's mother. The judge considered that, although many of the child's needs could be met by a special guardianship order combined with a section 91(14) of the CA 1989 order restricting the child's mother from making further applications to the court, those orders did not provide total security. He found that no lesser order than adoption would meet the child's welfare; and that an adoption order was a proportionate order to make in the circumstances. The mother's appeal, on the basis that a special guardianship order was more appropriate in a family placement, was dismissed by the Court of Appeal, which held that there was no rule that a special guardianship order was to be preferred to adoption in family placement unless there were cogent reasons to the contrary.

> ▶ *Re EN (A Child) (Special Guardianship Order)* [2007] EWCA Civ 264
>
> The paternal grandmother, who had cared for her grandson (aged three) for most of his life, was refused a special guardianship order because of her fraught relationship with the child's mother. Despite the inevitable loss of the child's primary attachment to the grandmother and the potential for long-term attachment difficulties, the child psychiatrist recommended that child be removed from his grandmother because the 'deep rift' between the mother and grandmother would be a cause of ongoing emotional distress for the child. The child was placed with prospective adopters.

(See also *DF (Children) (Placement Order or Special Guardianship Order)* [2013] EWHC 2607 (Fam) for an application of these principles.)

Summary

- ▶ Adoption is effected by an adoption order which severs the legal link between the birthparents and the child and creates a new legal link between the adopter(s) and the child. The law on adoption is laid down in the Adoption and Children Act 2002 (ACA 2002). Adoption procedure and practice are governed by the Family Procedure Rules 2010 and related practice directions, and various regulations. Human rights are also relevant, particularly the principle of proportionality.

- ▶ Cafcass officers play an important role in the adoption process.

- ▶ The Government has taken steps to reduce delays in the adoption process.

- ▶ Agency adoptions are adoptions involving local authority adoption services or voluntary adoption organisations which have various obligations under the ACA 2002. Non-agency adoptions usually involve children who are not in care and who are being adopted, for example, by a step-parent, relative or foster-parent. Applicants in non-agency cases must give notice to a local authority of their wish to adopt.

- ▶ It is a criminal offence for a person or body other than an adoption agency to, *inter alia*, advertise, make arrangements for, or provide payments or rewards in connection with adoption.

- ▶ As adoption is a drastic step, it may be better to consider other ways of acquiring parental responsibility for a child, namely by way of a special guardianship order, a child arrangements order regulating the child's living arrangements, or a parental responsibility agreement or order.

- ▶ The number of adoptions has declined over the years due in part to fewer babies being available for adoption.

- ▶ At one time step-parent adoption was common as adoption enabled a step-parent to acquire parental responsibility for a step-child, but changes to the law now enable a step-parent to acquire parental responsibility in other ways.

- ▶ After discussions of reform of adoption law, the ACA 2002 was enacted and made radical changes to adoption law. A major aim of the ACA 2002 is to encourage the wider use of adoption for children in care. It also made other changes, in particular by introducing placement for adoption to replace freeing for adoption; and it made changes to the Children Act 1989 (CA 1989) to create a new status of special guardianship.

Summary cont'd

▶ Section 1 of the ACA 2002 lays down the welfare principles which must be applied by a court or adoption agency when a decision is being made relating to the adoption of a child. The welfare principle requires an analysis of the child's welfare through childhood into adulthood and for the rest of the child's life (s 1(2)). Courts and adoption agencies must apply the welfare checklist in section 1(4). They must also consider the range of other powers available to them under the ACA 2002 and the CA 1989 (s 1(6)), as well as the no delay (s 1(3)) and the no order principles (s 1(6)).

▶ A child under the age of 18 who is not, or has not been, married can be adopted (s 49). Joint and sole applications for adoption can be made (see ss 50 and 51). Married couples can make a joint application, and so can cohabitants. A step-parent can make a sole application for adoption; and so can a civil partner in respect of the child of his or her civil partner. A local authority foster-parent can also apply to adopt a foster-child.

▶ Various preliminary procedures must be complied with before an adoption order or placement order can be made (such as residence requirements, reports and consent being given). These requirements are strict, and any failure to comply may result in an order being set aside.

▶ Sections 18–29 of the ACA 2002 govern placement for adoption. A child can be placed for adoption with the consent of the birthparents (s 19) or by way of a placement order (s 21). The court can only make a placement order if: the child is subject to a care order; or the court is satisfied that the threshold conditions for making a care order are met; or the child has no parent or guardian. When considering whether to make a placement order, the court must apply the welfare test, the welfare checklist and the other section 1 principles. The court also has a duty to consider what arrangements for contact have been, or should be, made for the child. A placement order gives parental responsibility to the local authority or the prospective adopters while the child is with them, although it does not extinguish the parents' parental responsibility. A placement order remains in force until revoked; or an adoption order is made; or the child marries or becomes a civil partner; or the child reaches the age of 18.

▶ An adoption order (s 46) transfers parental responsibility from the birthparents to the adopter(s). The welfare test, the welfare checklist and the other section 1 principles set out in the ACA 2002 must be applied by the court. An adopted child is treated in law as they were born as the child of the adopter(s). One of two conditions must be satisfied that the parents or guardians have consented to the adoption or their consent has been dispensed with; *or* the child has been placed for adoption (s 47).

▶ Consent to adoption must be given, but can be dispensed with under section 52 of the ACA 2002 if: the parent or guardian cannot be found or is incapable of giving consent; or the welfare of the child requires consent to be dispensed with. There are restrictions about a mother giving consent where her baby is less than six weeks old. Parents and guardians can give advance consent (s 20). Although the consent of unmarried fathers without parental responsibility is not required to adoption or to placement for adoption, the courts have been increasingly willing to involve them in the adoption process.

▶ An adoption order can be challenged by: opposing the order (s 47); appealing against it; or applying to have it set aside. However, once an adoption order is made it is difficult to challenge it.

▶ The ACA 2002 makes provision for contact in the context of placement for adoption. In the context of placement for adoption, a contact order can be made under section 26 of the ACA 2002. The welfare test, the welfare checklist and the other section 1 principles apply to the exercise of the court's discretion. If contact is sought post adoption, an application can be made under section 51A of the ACA 2002. However, applicants other than the child and the

Summary cont'd

adopter require leave of the court to apply. The courts have traditionally shown themselves to be unwilling to make post-adoption contact orders where this is opposed by the adopter(s).

▶ A step-parent, civil partner, relative or foster-carer can apply for an adoption order. Certain residence and notice requirements must be complied with, and notice must be given to the local authority. There are, however, alternative ways in which such persons can acquire parental responsibility. These include: a parental responsibility agreement or a parental responsibility order; a child arrangements order regulating the child's living arrangements; or a special guardianship order.

▶ An adopted child on reaching the age of 18 can obtain a copy of his or her original birth certificate. The Registrar General has a duty to maintain the Adopted Children Register (s 77), an index of the Register (s 78), and the Adoption Contact Register (ss 80 and 81). Sections 56–65 of the ACA 2002 lay down provisions governing the disclosure of information held by adoption agencies in connection with adoption and access to birth records.

▶ Various provisions are in place which govern intercountry adoption, including, in particular, the Hague Convention on Protection of Children and Co-operation in Respect of Intercountry Adoption 1993.

▶ The ACA 2002 inserted sections 14A–14G into the CA 1989 which make provision for special guardianship, which was introduced to give children for whom adoption is not suitable the security and permanence of a legal family placement. A special guardianship order gives a special guardian legal responsibility for the child without taking responsibility away from the birth parents. The governing principle is that the welfare of the child is the court's paramount consideration. If the court is considering whether to make a special guardianship order or an adoption order, it must apply the welfare checklists in section 1 of the CA 1989 and section 1 of the ACA 2002, but each case depends on its own facts.

Further reading and references

Bainham, 'Swimming against the tide: challenging contact arrangements in the public law' [2015] Fam Law 1356.

Choudhry, 'The Adoption and Children Act 2002, the welfare principle and the Human Rights Act 1998 – a missed opportunity' [2003] CFLQ 119.

Cullen, 'Adoption – a (fairly) new approach' [2005] CFLQ 475.

Curry, 'EB v France: a missed opportunity?' [2009] CFLQ 365.

Doughty, 'Myths and misunderstanding in adoption law and policy' [2015] CFLQ 331.

Hall, 'Special guardianship and permanency planning: unforeseen consequences and missed opportunities' [2008] CFLQ 359.

Hall, 'Special guardianship: a missed opportunity: findings from research' [2008] Fam Law 148.

Hayes, 'Giving due consideration to ethnicity in adoption placements – a principled approach?' [2003] CFLQ 255.

Hitchings and Sagar, 'The Adoption and Children Act 2002: a level playing field for same-sex adopters?' [2007] CFLQ 60.

Hughes and Sloan, 'Post-adoption photographs: welfare, rights and judicial reasoning' [2011] CFLQ 393.

Quinton and Selwyn, 'Adoption: research, policy and practice' [2006] CFLQ 459.

Further reading and references cont'd

Ray, 'Placement for adoption or legal limbo?' [2012] Fam Law 979.

Sloan, '*Re C (A Child) (Adoption: Duty of Local Authority)* – welfare and the rights of the birth family in "fast track" adoption cases' [2009] CFLQ 87.

Sloan, 'Conflicting rights: English adoption law and the implementation of the UN Convention on the Rights of the Child' [2013] CFLQ 40.

Smith and Logan, 'Adoptive parenthood as a "legal fiction" – its consequences for direct post-adoption contact' [2002] CFLQ 281.

Thoburn, 'The risks and rewards of adoption for children in the public care' [2003] CFLQ 391.

Webb, 'Leave to oppose an adoption: unhelpful legislation' [2012] Fam Law 1119.

Websites

Adoption UK: www.adoptionuk.org

CoramBaaf Adoption & Fostering Academy: www.corambaaf.org.uk

Consortium of Voluntary Adoption Agencies: www.cvaa.org.uk

First 4 Adoption: www.first4adoption.org.uk

Hague Conference on Private International Law: www.hcch.net

International Adoption Centre (IAC): www.iacentre.org.uk

Links to relevant websites can also be found at: www.palgravehighered.com/law/familylaw9e

Index